Emperor Iyasu II, left, with his mother Empress Mentewwab, right, from an
early 18th century Ethiopic manuscript of the Acts of St George in the British
Library (Orient 715).

PRUTKY'S
TRAVELS IN ETHIOPIA
AND
OTHER COUNTRIES

Translated and edited by
J. H. ARROWSMITH-BROWN

and annotated by
RICHARD PANKHURST

THE HAKLUYT SOCIETY
LONDON
1991

ISBN 0 904180 30 1
ISSN 0072 9396

Typeset by J W Arrowsmith Ltd
Printed in Great Britain at
the University Press, Cambridge

Published by the Hakluyt Society
c/o The Map Library
British Library, Great Russell Street
London WC1B 3DG

CONTENTS

Preface   xi
Introduction   xiii
Maps   xix
Prutky's original title page   xxv
Preface by Prutky's Amanuensis   xxvii
 1. The journey to Abyssinia or Ethiopia   1
 2. The city of Suez   5
 3. Mt Sinai through the Red Sea   8
 4. Arrival at the city of Gidda   18
 5. The city of Gidda   22
 6. Various facts about Gidda, and the costume of   31
     its inhabitants
 7. The city of Mecca and the caravans   35
 8. Further points of interest about the Mahometan   40
     temple
 9. Journey to Medina to Mahomet's tomb   46
10. Further details of this area, and of the cures for   52
     illness
11. The journey towards Abyssinia   59
12. Messaua island, and the Emperor's letter   66
13. Departure from the island to Abyssinia   75
14. Syre the capital of the third kingdom   83
15. Arrival at the royal city of Gondar   92
16. The origins of Abyssinia   103
17. Succession of the kings of Abyssinia   111
18. Derivation of the imperial title Johannes   116
     Presbyter, or Prester John

19.	The modern state of Abyssinia	122
20.	The extent of the Emperor's power today	138
21.	The soldiery and wars of the Ethiopians	147
22.	The Emperor's costume, retinue and palace	153
23.	Method of giving audience, the Queen's costume, etc.	158
24.	The Emperor's dining establishment, and customs at table	164
25.	The quarters, and the burial, of sons of the royal blood, and the childhood of the Emperor Jasu	170
26.	The disposition of the Abyssinians	176
27.	Their common languages	181
28.	The weather and climate of Ethiopia	185
29.	Crops and fruits	192
30.	Fish and birds	198
31.	Animals	204
32.	Minerals and money	211
33.	True description of the source of the Nile	215
34.	Faith and religion of the Ethiopians	222
35.	Extreme unction, holy orders and matrimony	235
36.	The ten commandments	240
37.	The errors of the Abyssinians from times past, in which they still abide	247
38.	Festivals and the worship of the Saints	256
39.	Fasts	264
40.	Religious life and morals	267
41.	Manners and customs	276
42.	Their food, drink, and other practices	283
43.	Worms, and the cure for them	289
44.	The swarming locusts of Abyssinia	293
45.	Other beasts	298
46.	Healing the sick	302
47.	The persecution of the missionaries	306
48.	The Emperor's letter of expulsion written in the Ethiopian language	320
49.	Return from Abyssinia	324
50.	Mount Malmo, and the area beyond	329
51.	Arrival at the city of Syre, and other places	337
52.	The cities of Serai and Dobarua	343

CONTENTS

53. Return from the city of Gondar to the island of   351
    Messaua
54. Departure from the island of Messaua   358
55. The city of Mocha   363
56. Details worth noting of this city   372
57. Other happenings in Mocha   379
58. Our departure for India   385
59. Our arrival in India   396
60. Indian clothing, and some of their customs   407
61. Indian fruits   411
62. Heathen customs and burial ceremonies   415
63. Departure from India for Europe   421
64. The island of Bourbon   426
65. Ascension Island   431
66. Daily log of our voyage through the Indian   438
    Ocean
67. The port of L'Orient in France   444
68. Other cities on our journey through France   450
69. The cities of Tolosa, Beziers, Agde and Cette   454
70. The city of Telonius, or Tolonius, or Toulon   459
71. Short report on the position of the mission to   462
    Ethiopia as presented to the Sacred
    Congregation
72. How for the future a mission could be   470
    maintained in Ethiopia
73. Departure from Rome for Germany   473
74. Arrival in Vienna in Austria   476
75. Departure from Vienna through Italy for   479
    Leghorn
76. Departure from Leghorn for a second journey   482
    to Egypt
77. Fresh departure from Cairo for Rome   486
78. The Archipelago and some of its islands   491
79. Malta or Melita and other small islands   495
80. Arrival at the city and harbour of Leghorn   499
81. Third arrival at the Holy City of Rome   501
82. Third return from the Holy City to the Egyptian   503
    mission, and the acceptance in its stead of the
    office of chaplain to the army of the Grand
    Duke of Tuscany

Appendix I.   The mission to Russia and its outcome: 506
          also the expulsion from Russia and the death of
          the author of this book of travels
Appendix II.   Letter of invitation to the missionaries to   519
          visit the Empire of Ethiopia
Bibliography   523
Index   533

ILLUSTRATION

Emperor Iyasu II with his mother
     Empress Mentewwab   Frontispiece

MAPS

Fig. 1. Part of the East African Grid   xix
Fig. 2. Area around Asmara   xx
Fig. 3. Area around Gondar   xxi
Fig. 4. Area around Maqalé   xxii

PREFACE

This work, volume 174, Second Series of the Hakluyt Society publications, is the translation of Part II of the Latin manuscript of Remedius Prutky, a Franciscan stationed in Egypt, who in 1751 led a mission to Ethiopia in response to a letter of invitation from the reigning Emperor Iyasu II. His account of his travels is in two parts, part I describing Egypt, Sinai and the Holy Land, and culminating in the Letter of invitation from the Emperor to the Franciscans, while in part II he describes his travels in Arabia, Ethiopia, India and Europe. Only the second part has been translated, together with the last chapter of part I, which appears here as Appendix II. Prutky's manuscript, duly lodged by him in Prague, passed eventually into the possession of Prague University Library. News of its existence reached the then Librarian of the Institute of Ethiopian Studies in Addis Ababa, Professor S. Chojnacki, who obtained a microfilm copy of it through the good offices of the late Semitist Professor K. Petraček. On its arrival in Addis Ababa Professor Richard Pankhurst, who was then Director of the Institute, was impressed with Prutky as a valuable but little known source for Ethiopian history, and soon afterwards produced an article in collaboration with a colleague, Dr Tony Pearson, on the Czech missionary's account of traditional medicine which was published by the *Ethiopian Medical Journal* in 1972. On moving to Britain a few years later Pankhurst also mentioned the existence of the microfilm to Mrs Felicity Dracopoli, an English woman in Italy who was working on a biography of James Bruce and was much interested in Prutky as a traveller who had visited Ethiopia immediately prior to the period she was studying. She accordingly procured a second copy of the microfilm from Addis Ababa through the assistance of the

Institute's present Librarian, Ato Degife Gabre Tsadik, and later passed it to Pankhurst. The latter, then Librarian of the Royal Asiatic Society, was more convinced than ever of the need of a Prutky translation, and raised the matter with his friend the late architectural historian Ruth Plant, whose *magnum opus, Architecture of the Tigré,* London 1985, was in production with J. W. Arrowsmith Ltd the Bristol printers.

This connection led to an introduction to the translator Henry Arrowsmith-Brown, whose version of chapters 1–54, that is the journey from Cairo to Ethiopia and then to Mocha, was annotated by Richard Pankhurst, who also edited chapters 71–72, Prutky's report to the Sacred Congregation, and Appendix II, the letter of invitation from the Emperor to the Franciscans. When it was found that Prutky's journeys extended to India and Europe, Professor Charles Beckingham very kindly agreed to annotate chapters 55–65, Mocha to France, while the translator undertook the remaining chapters, though he gratefully acknowledges some valuable notes contributed by Charles Beckingham to these and to the earlier chapters.

TRANSLATOR'S ACKNOWLEDGEMENTS

I am chiefly indebted to my colleagues in this work, Professor Richard Pankhurst and Professor Charles Beckingham; to Richard who initiated the project and involved me in it, and to Charles who rescued it when it was found that Prutky's travels went beyond the confines of Ethiopia. I am most grateful to the Hakluyt Society for agreeing to publish it and to Charles and to Dr Greville Freeman-Grenville for their great editorial help. I would also acknowledge and express my sincere thanks for the help of Dom Philip Jebb, OSB, of Downside, who corrected my wording of many ecclesiastical expressions, to Mr Mark Grant of the University of St Andrews who translated *bricocoli* and other plant names for me, to Father Cormac Nagle, OFM, Definitor General of the Curia Generalizia dei Frati Minori and Father Maurice Carmody, who kindly extracted for me a quantity of detail about Prutky and his colleagues from the Propaganda Fide archives, to Mrs Ellen Carter who helped me with the typing, to my daughter who introduced me to Prutky, and especially to my wife, who as well as patience and encouragement has in many places supplied a more correct expression than I could find.

INTRODUCTION

Remedius Prutky, whose baptismal name was Václav, was born in 1717 in the small Bohemian town of Kopidlno. He says of himself that he attended the famous medical school of the University of Prague, where he graduated as doctor of medicine, and in 1735 at the age of eighteen he entered the Reformed Order of the Friars Minor, or Franciscans, being assigned to the province of Bohemia. In 1749 he spent ten months in Rome at San Pietro Montorio, the missionary college of his order.

In May 1750 Prutky and a fellow-collegian were posted to Cairo to the mission to Egypt of the Reformati, which, including the new arrivals, numbered fourteen missionaries under their Prefect James Ržimarž or Kzimar of Kromeriz in Moravia, called by Prutky James of Kromeriz; they reached Cairo in July. There is extant a report by the Prefect, dated 29 December 1750, on the conduct of each missionary, of which the important ones for Prutky's travels are:

> Paul of Agnona, aged forty-one and with twelve years' experience as a missionary, who for three years had been Superior at Girga in Upper Egypt, Girga lying on the Nile between Asyût and Qena. In 1751 he succeeded Fr James as Prefect of the mission.
>
> Martin Lang, of Bohemia like Prutky, aged thirty-three and with one-and-a-half years' experience as a missionary, of which one year had been spent at Girga. He had already learned so much Arabic under Fr Antony that he was able to hear confessions in that language.
>
> Antony of Aleppo, aged forty and with six years' experience as a missionary, an expert in Arabic and a teacher of the younger missionaries. He was by birth a Greek from Aleppo and a Melchite Christian, who entered his novitiate in the Order in 1742.

Of Prutky the Prefect reports only that he applied himself enthusiastically to the study of Arabic.

By May 1751 Prutky had been sent to Girga to join Frs Paul and Martin. In the interval the course of his duties or talks with his colleagues gave him sufficient information to compile the first book of his travels, a sort of tourist's guide of Egypt, Sinai and the Holy Land, though the last-named he specifically tells us he was unable to visit personally. On May 31 the three missionaries in their lonely outpost suffered 'the persecution of Girga', when on the visit of the governor they were thrown into prison on trumped-up charges and formally sentenced to death by impalement. Displaying remarkable firmness and refusing to ransom themselves they were on June 2 released with an apology, and resumed their normal life of preaching the Roman Catholic faith to the Copts, administering the sacraments and attending to the sick.

Meanwhile on May 24 there had arrived at the mission headquarters in Cairo from the Emperor of Ethiopia Iyasu II the letter of invitation which is printed as Appendix II. In response to this, on July 8 Frs Remedius Prutky and Martin Lang received orders from the Prefect to proceed to Cairo preparatory to undertaking the mission to Ethiopia, but when they arrived in Cairo on July 30 Fr Martin's health was so bad that it was unlikely that he could fulfil the task assigned to him. In this emergency there arrived from Jerusalem the Arabic expert Fr Antony of Aleppo, who was ordered to join the missionary expedition, and, Fr Martin making an unexpected recovery, the three of them set off from Cairo on August 21, as Prutky describes in chapter 1. Though Prutky does not mention it, they were accompanied by one Michael, the Emperor's envoy from Ethiopia, who had brought the letter of invitation. On August 24, just after his departure, Prutky was formally nominated vice-prefect (i.e. superior) of the mission to Ethiopia by his Prefect James Řzimarž.

Travelling by way of Suez and the Red Sea the missionaries reached the port of Massawa on November 30. There they waited, like many travellers before and after them, for permission from the Ethiopian Emperor to enter his domains. A letter from Emperor Iyasu II, and another from his treasurer, duly arrived, and Prutky and his party set forth for the interior on 22 February

1752; they reached Gondar, the then Ethiopian capital, on March 19, eighteen years before their more famous contemporary James Bruce. On the following day they were received by the Emperor at his palace by the Qaha river. They were kindly welcomed by the monarch, to whom they presented a letter from their superior James Ržimarž (Jakub Riman). Iyasu spoke to them warmly, and ordered them to be installed in his palace, where they resided for the next nineteen days before moving to other quarters assigned to them. They were frequently visited by the Monarch who discussed many religious and other matters with them, and also enquired about the political situation in Europe. Prutky and his companions also conversed with the redoubtable Regent, Empress Mentewwab, who, they believed, was favourably inclined to their cause. During this time Prutky collected and recorded much data about the country, its religion, politics, history, habits and customs, flora and fauna, climate and topography, and visited the source of the Blue Nile. He also recorded a considerable number of Amharic words which were later embodied in his *Vocabularium linguae Gallicae, Arabicae et Abyssinicae* which remains to this day unpublished.

The three missionaries, largely because of their knowledge of medicine, won popular sympathy at Gondar, but their presence was soon opposed by the Ethiopian clergy who had not forgotten the conflict with the Jesuits more than a century earlier. Prutky and Lang were therefore ordered on December 12 to leave the country, and set forth from Gondar on December 26, but Antony of Aleppo was kept behind, on Iyasu's orders, to translate the Pentateuch into Arabic. Antony was detained in Ethiopia for a further nine months, and returned to Cairo in June 1754, shortly before Prutky and Lang arrived in Rome.

On leaving Gondar Prutky and Lang spent a month at the nearby Muslim town before joining a Massawa-bound caravan on January 26. Arriving in Massawa on April 6 the missionaries sailed for Mocha on April 29 and arrived there on June 2. Here they decided that shortage of funds made it impracticable to return by way of Suez, and prevailed on a French trading ship to convey them to Pondicherry, whence on October 19 Governor Dupleix arranged for their passage to L'Orient in Brittany. From there they journeyed by the Canal du Midi to Marseilles and then to Rome in July 1754.

From Rome Prutky set off almost immediately for a visit to his home in Bohemia, and, after calling at the Imperial Court in Vienna and paying his respect to Maria Theresa and her consort Grand Duke Francis of Tuscany, Holy Roman Emperor, departed again for Cairo by way of Leghorn and Alexandria. In Cairo when he arrived in July 1755 he resumed his missionary work, but after just a year was sent again to Rome on business connected with the mission, leaving Cairo in July and eventually reaching the Holy City in November 1756. Here he wrote two official reports dated December 15 (his journey) and January 3 (affairs in Ethiopia) of which he reproduces the substance in chapters 71 and 72, and which have formed the basis for earlier historians' accounts of his mission.

He was now in March 1757 destined again for Egypt, but being delayed in Leghorn accepted from Grand Duke Francis, with the permission of the Sacred Congregation, the post of chaplain to the Florentine army, and was almost at once engaged in the rigours of the Seven Years War; on its conclusion in 1763 he returned to Tuscany where he served for a further two years, until the death of Grand Duke Francis in 1765 put an end not only to his employment but to his hopes that the Grand Duke would publish his Itinerarium.

Applying again for employment to the Sacred Congregation he was in December 1765 appointed prefect of the mission to Russia, a post of some delicacy since the Catholics of St Petersburg had a tradition of opposing the prefect chosen for them by Rome. In April 1769 a complicated intrigue secured his expulsion from Russia by Catherine the Great, and, after journeying to Rome to give an account of his stewardship, he died in Florence on 9 February 1770.

All proper and place names have been transliterated exactly as Prutky wrote them; in the manuscript all are underlined, however often they appear, but in the text they are italicized only on their first appearance, and are thereafter printed in roman. Clearly Prutky wrote down the spoken rather than the written name, as English speakers will perceive from chapter 62, where Fort St David is written by Prutky as Forsendevi.

Prutky gives to all clerics the honorific P for Pater (occasionally RP for Reverendus Pater) and PP if there are more than one. At the Society's request I have written this as Fr or Frs, but the reader must not suppose this to mean Frater or Friar.

Fig. 1.   Index map showing area covered by figs. 2, 3 and 4 in East Africa

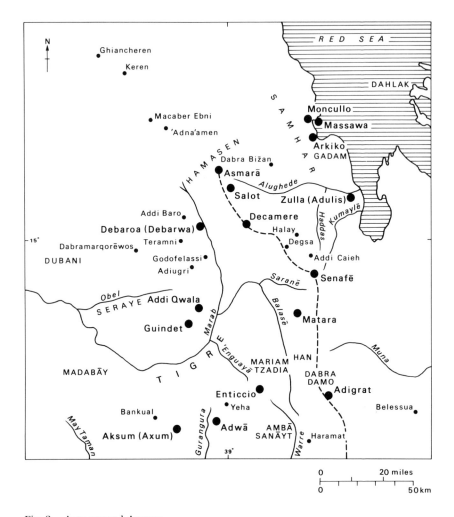

Fig. 2. Area around Asmara

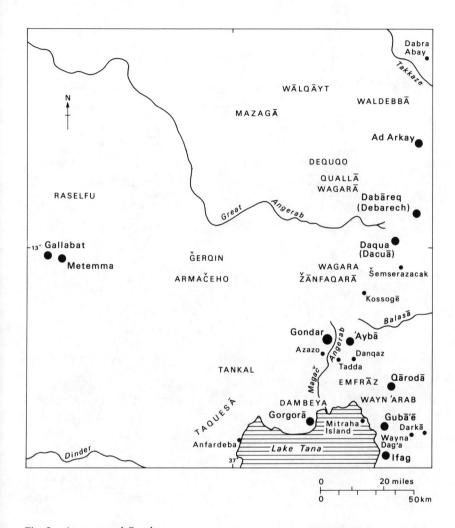

Fig. 3. Area around Gondar

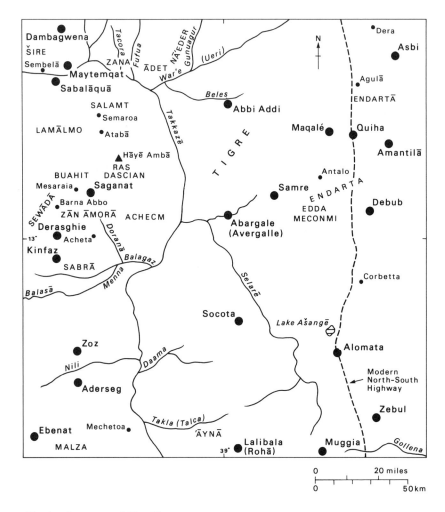

Fig. 4. Area around Maqalé

THE REVEREND FATHER REMEDIUS PRUTKY

of the Reformed Order of the Friars Minor of St Francis, Province of Bohemia, and Graduate Doctor of Medicine of the College of St Wenceslaus: who for many years was apostolic missionary in Egypt, Abyssinia or Ethiopia, and other adjacent countries, and finally in Russia.

HIS TRAVELS

in which are faithfully and authentically described all the empires, kingdoms and provinces, their larger cities and towns with their antiquities, rarities and matters of interest: their mountains and valleys, seas and rivers, ports and promontories, Scyllas and Charybdises, rocks and crags, birds and beasts, fishes and wild animals: the mines of gold, silver and base metal, the various minerals, the gems and precious stones: the trees and fruits, grain and roots, spices and drugs whether to eat or to drink: also the peoples and nations, their religion and rites, customs and habits, life and intercourse, the vices and virtues of either sex etc. Everything here related the Missionary saw with his own eyes, heard with his own ears, experienced in his own person and presence, during a nine year journey; then in his own hand he wrote it down and divided it into two parts, with sixteen illustrations added.[1]

---

[1] Only the second part of the Travels has been translated, though as Appendix II there appears here the 'Letter of invitation from the Emperor to the missionaries,' which comprises the last chapter of the first part. Of the sixteen illustrations, only two refer to part II, and these have been omitted, as being of minor interest and at the same time unsuitable for reproduction.

For the handwriting, see note 6 to chapter 82.

R.P. Remedii Prutky,

Ord. Mior. S.P. Francisci Reform. Provinciæ
Bohemiæ S. Wenceslai P. et ch. Alumni, per plures
annos Egypti, Abyssiniæ, seu Æthiopiæ, aliarumq. Regio-
num adjacentium; deinde etiam Magnæ Russiæ Missio-
narii Apostolici

ITINERARIUM

In quo

Omnia Imperia, Regna, et Provinciæ, earumq. prin-
cipaliores civitates, et Oppida cum suis antiquitatibus,
raritatibus, et memorabilibus, Montes, et Valles, Maria,
et flumina, Portus, et Promontoria, Scylla, et Charybdis,
Scopuli, et Vortices, Volatilia, et quadrupedia, Pisces,
et feræ; auri-argenti-metalli fodina, ac diversa mi-
neralia; gemmæ, et lapides pretiosi, Arbores et fructus,
herbæ et radices, aromata, et medicamenta, esculenta
et potulenta; Item Populi et Nationes, earumque
Religio, et Ritus, mores et consuetudines, Victus, et con-
versatio, vitia, et virtutes utriusq. Sexus &c. &c.
fideliter, et genuine describuntur.

Quæ omnia memoratus Pr. Missionarius p. oculis vidit,
auribus audivit, nec an personali præsentia per novon-
nalem peregrinationem expertus est; deinde vero
propria manu conscripsit,
et in duas Partes
divisit.

Cum adjunctis Sedecim Tabulis.

PREFACE BY PRUTKY'S AMANUENSIS

The Itinerary here set before us was completed by its author in September 1765, in the city of Florence, where at the time he was serving as army chaplain to the forces of Grand Duke Francis I[1] of Tuscany and Holy Roman Emperor, ever august: to whom he was in hopes to dedicate this work, and to live out his days under his munificent patronage. The Grand Duke's early death, which occurred suddenly on 18 August of that year, put an end to these hopes, which however were revived in the person of his glorious and merciful son and successor Grand Duke Peter Leopold[2] of Tuscany. But alas these hopes also came equally to nothing: once peace was made with the King of Borussia[3] the Florentine army was reduced by demobilization, and along with it its chaplain, the author of these Travels, who was thereupon appointed by the Sacred Congregation for the Propagation of the Faith to be Prefect of the St Petersburg mission in Russia.

As he passed through Moravia to take up his duties, he desired to send this work to the press at his own expense, and despatched it to the Provincial censors with a deposit of one hundred gold pieces; they however had no heart for the enterprise, partly because of the roughness of the style and faults of grammar and syntax, and partly from the labour involved in corrections. The author therefore asked to have this his manuscript sent back to him in St Petersburg, together with the money deposited for its

---

[1] The consort of Maria Theresa, Grand Duke of Tuscany as Francis II from 1737, Holy Roman Emperor as Francis I from 1745. He died on 18 August 1765.

[2] Grand Duke of Tuscany as Leopold I, 1765–90, Holy Roman Emperor as Leopold II, 1790–92.

[3] See note 2, chapter 82.

printing, and this was duly done. Returning from the St Petersburg mission through Bohemia to Rome, he gave an account of his stewardship there, and then was wishful to return to his mother province, but yielded to fate in Florence on 9 February 1770, at the hospice of the Reformed Order there. His religious equipment, together with his manuscripts and this Itinerary (except for the first three chapters, which are missing) was despatched to Prague. That his labour might not be in vain and his manuscript scattered, it was collected into this volume. The illustrations engraved are preserved in the library at Prague and, in one copy, are appended to the end of this work. No outsider is permitted to read it, until certain items have been deleted.

CHAPTER 1

JOURNEY TOWARDS
THE KINGDOM OF ETHIOPIA

We had at length provided ourselves with everything necessary
for a visit to so remote a country. Relying on our favourable
letter of invitation[1], and discreetly, with little or no warning to
the Coptic Patriarch or to the other Europeans, we set out from
Cairo, God being with us, on 21 August 1751. We had hired six
camels to carry our gear, at a price of 270 medins[2] each, and
they were in such condition that, though any of them was supposed to carry a 600 pound weight, one man sitting on each was
the most they could bear. At this happy time of departure we
experienced an extraordinary sense of internal relief and gladness, thinking ourselves truly fortunate that we had escaped the
persecutions of Egypt without martyrdom, yet hoping that this
glory lay before us in the future and that the Almighty would
crown us with his abounding grace. We knew well that the vast
kingdom of Ethiopia was for many years to be a rough and stormy
sea for those preaching the holy Gospel, but we firmly trusted
to divine help and grace that the little boat of the Roman Catholic
faith would sail forward with favourable winds, and spreading
its sails would ship a cargo of thousands of souls saved from
damnation. So we set out with a light heart on a journey that we
knew would be punishing, directing our steps over those deserts
once crossed by the Children of Israel. As part of a large[3] caravan

[1] Printed as Appendix II.
[2] Medin, a European name for the Ottoman para, a silver coin used in Egypt
and Turkey. Forty para were equivalent to one piastre or qirsch, a silver coin of
about twenty-three grams.
[3] Large caravans on this route were not unusual. William Daniel, undertaking
the same journey half a century earlier in 1700, travelled with a caravan of 12,000
camels. W. Foster, *The Red Sea and adjacent countries at the close of the seventeenth
century* (London, 1949), p. 63.

we crossed a plain, beautiful but empty, exposed to the sun's heat but bearing neither flowers nor grass, trees nor crops, water nor bread; as Genesis i. 2, says *the earth was without form, and void.*

Journeying to the east, in three hours we came to a place called by the Arabs *Bercke,*[4] where we halted by a lake which marks the point to which the inundation of the Nile annually extends; the whole caravan collected together under tents, and, forming a line of camps, in the form of a city, retired to rest. On the next day the drums sounded, all bestirred themselves in loading the camels and mounting them, and awaited the order of the Commander: the signal given, it was wonderful to see with what speed so many thousands of animals were loaded, and then prepared, for the journey. Within a quarter of an hour, on asses, on horses, a few on dromedaries, but most on camels, they marched away in perfect order. With his troops going before him and surrounded by his slaves and soldiers, the chief of the caravan, called *Bassa Elcafle,*[5] encouraged and urged forward the laggards at the rear, lest they be ambushed and robbed, or killed, by the Arabs,[6] so that each strove to outstrip the other, always without causing confusion, and steadily until sunset pursued the agreed day's march. At the Mahometans' hour of prayer we prudently halted, dismounted, and said prayers at the time called *Amagreb,*[7] when we took a little food. Then after half an hour the drums once more gave the signal, and we proceeded on our road through the desert, mounted on our camels and supplied with water from a zemzemla,[8] which is nothing but a bag made of tough leather stitched together and slung over the camel to hang down on either side; the heat of the sun raises it almost to boiling point, but when the body is sweating so one drinks it greedily. The camels are infested with great quantities of lice,[9] of two sorts, a smaller and a greater, dark in colour like a hazel nut, against

---

[4] Arabic *birkah*, a pool, here referring to Birkat al-Ḥajj, the Pilgrimage Pool, which is marked on Niebuhr's map of Lower Egypt, Tab. x, as Birket el Hadj. (C. Niebuhr, *Voyage en Arabie*, facing p. 71.)

[5] Arabic *Bāshā al-qāfilah*, "the Pasha of the caravan".

[6] Lord Valentia, half a century later, reported that the robbers in this area were 'not supposed to exceed in number five hundred'. George, Viscount Valentia, *Voyages and travels to India, Ceylon, the Red Sea, Abyssinia and Egypt* (London, 1809), iii. 362.

[7] Arabic *al-maghrib*, the time immediately after sunset.

[8] Arabic *zamzamiyyah.*

[9] A reference no doubt to jigger-fleas.

2

which careful watch must be kept, for when full of blood their feet and head are indistinguishable; they withdraw into the shade to avoid sunlight, and lie in wait for human flesh, and if by mischance they reach a human body they can in no way be removed by rubbing off. The smaller sort so penetrate the flesh that one can scarcely see them to pick them off, and only when they are swollen with blood can they be removed, with considerable pain, so when mounted on camelback a careful watch must be kept lest they penetrate the skin.

Camels are the only transport animals suited to such desert travelling, and indeed possess outstanding advantages, for, though by their nature they are delicate beasts, they march on with their loads for the whole length of the journey without food or drink, as long as their burden is within their strength. But if they are loaded beyond this, the first sign they give is to look behind them, then to wail and as it were whistle through their teeth and shake their heads: if their load is not lightened they continue for a certain distance, and then fall down all at once with their load and, failing to stand up again, perish. So throughout the desert there is nothing but the bones of camels, or a few stones placed here and there as direction posts for travellers. The richer Mahometans, to avoid these fatigues, are carried comfortably on litters borne by two camels, like the sedan chairs of our own magnates; or those who can afford the expenditure on water and food use horses, mules and asses: the rich women use two closed in seats called *musne*,[10] which are strapped to a camel and in which, comfortably seated and gossiping together, they enjoy an easy journey.

We poor missionaries on the other hand, without tents or other conveniences of travel, laboriously followed the caravan, toiling in the indescribable heat, sweat pouring from our whole body, and suffering an extreme of thirst: for water being short is drunk moderately in the camel-train, so that at the midday halt for refreshment one's whole nature is so worn down by the continual

---

[10] These two types of transport accommodation were later described by Valentia. The first, a five-foot long box called a takterouane (*takhtirawān*), was 'slung between two camels by large shafts', and was 'very uncomfortable'. The second, known as mohaffa (*miḥaffah*), was 'a kind of little couch', two of which were 'slung sideways on the opposite sides of a camel, with an awning spread between to keep off the sun'. Valentia, *op. cit.*, iii. 361.

burning of the sun that it appears to be ill. For to the camel rider, because of the wretched pace they keep, the body is continually shaken, the spine, the neck and all the limbs seem to be being broken: the hurt and pain is unexampled, and the travellers suffer an indescribable torment. At halting places we were content with a little warm water and biscuit bread, and had but little sleep, partly through over-tiredness, partly through bodily pain from the wretched camel-pace, partly from the hordes of robbers who infest this desert. All were in fear and on the alert, all collected well together lest we suffer loss of our property or even of life itself. For none of the pilgrims to Mecca or Medina dares to take this desert road without a caravan on his pilgrimage to the false prophet Mahomet, for else he would surely lose all his goods and his very life. A similar caravan of at least a hundred thousand and often of more is accustomed to make the pilgrimage, well armed, and yet every year thefts are committed by robbers stealing in secret: what would happen if two or three were to presume to undertake the journey? We three missionaries were as it were private persons in company with an excitable host of Mahometans, and could not appear much among them; but at every desert halt we stayed quietly in our own place, barely daring to raise our head, lest any of their holy men might accuse us of being desirous of looking at their women. But despite the hardships of the desert which the children of Israel had crossed, on the first day of September we reached the city of Suez, small in size, scantily fortified, with gates of some antiquity, the houses built of stone for the most part, comfortable enough after the Eastern manner. It is three hours distant from the Red Sea, and those who are to sail from it have to transport their goods to it by land.

CHAPTER 2

THE CITY OF SUEZ

Suez should rather be called a town, and is inhabited mostly by Turks, by a few Coptic Christians and fewer Orthodox Greek merchants. There is a dire shortage of food here, everything having to be transported from Cairo at great inconvenience; meat is rarely on sale; the water of the sea not being drinkable, and there being no springs, streams or aqueducts, they carry in drinking water from a site seven hours distant through the desert in leather skins by camel-back, and for one small skin of two pints they charge eight medins, which is about ten Roman bajocs.[1] If this water were good and perfectly sweet it would be welcome to the traveller, but although it smells, is full of mud, dirty, reddish-brown, brackish, wormy and rotten, it is in great demand. All the pilgrims here, who are to sail from the port, try to get hold of the first ships available, which carry corn, rice and other food to Gidda, together with many hundred pilgrims, who are fanatics for their own sect, hate Christians as they hate dogs, regard them as unworthy at this holy season of theirs to come on board ship with them, and blame solely on the Christians all the storms and mischances of the sea. So we three missionaries found no small difficulty in boarding the first ships, and then discovered that, because we were three Franks, as they term Europeans, we must either put down a hundred gold pieces for a wretched cramped berth, or be left in Suez. Seeing that this excessive sum of gold was beyond our means, and that it was impossible to pay out so much money for the first ship and still make the long voyage to Abyssinia and pay for our food thereon,

---

[1] The baioccho, a bronze coin issued by the Papal States. One hundred baiocchi were equal to a scudo.

we tried hard to negotiate a lower price for the voyage, using as mediator an Orthodox Greek merchant to whom we had been kindly recommended by our Catholic Greek friends in Cairo. Through his faithful service we agreed a lower price of sixty-three Turkish gold pieces called *mahbubs*,[2] about ninety-four Roman scudi,[3] and paid them over immediately to the ship's captain, being eager to leave quickly because the Coptic heretics were beginning to murmur against us and we were afraid that if we stayed longer in Suez we should be brought before the Coptic Patriarch in Cairo, and easily stopped from proceeding on our way. But the Turkish authorities helped us, and on September 10, after imploring divine help and after many trials and tribulations, we succeeded in getting all our baggage carried to the sea-port, where it had to be loaded onto a small lighter while we boarded a larger ship.

Yet again were we imposed upon by the pilot, to whom for a quarter of an hour's passage we had to pay five scudi: at our first entry on to the ship the crowd of Mahometans gazed at us like dogs or devils, and hurled blasphemies at us. We took up our quarters, a tiny hole in the bottom part of the ship, wretched, stinking, hardly one cubit high, through which the other passengers descended to relieve their bodily necessities. Here we sat on board as in a prison for three days awaiting a favourable wind, for ever being bothered and disturbed in our fine quarters, and surrounded by the stink of those relieving themselves: the more that every night-time through the self-same hole the anchor was let down into the sea and every morning hauled up from it, causing no small noise and disturbance, and drenching our quarters with water from the anchor-ropes. Each of these troubles we bore with cheerfulness, provided that we could stand upright, sit comfortably, and stretch out our bodies to permit the due circulation of the blood; but the first and second of these were lacking to us, as though we were sitting in prison, or if we lay down it was at the cost of a severe cramping of our limbs.

But with God's help we began our voyage on September 13, and came next day to a wider part of the sea called *Bercke*

---

[2] A gold coin called Zeri Mahbub (*zar-i maḥbūb*), struck during Ottoman times in both Turkey and Egypt, weighing about 2·6 grams, and worth twenty-five piastres.
[3] Scudo, a silver coin issued by the Papal States, of about the same value as a silver dollar, i.e. 26·5 grams.

Elpharaun,[4] or Pharaoh's pool, a stretch of sea about thirty Italian miles wide bounded to the south by lofty mountains through which penetrates what is almost a valley; here Pharaoh pursuing the children of Israel perished with so many thousands of men, though the Jews are believed to have crossed it: Exodus xiv. 27. On the other side to the north are some lower rocks where there is an abundant spring of water, like a hot bath, in which by drinking and bathing many are restored to health: but there are also many poisonous insects to be found there, as well as fish, snakes and scorpions. In this area the Red Sea is wider and more dangerous than in other parts, but the ships' captains, being always sure of a favourable wind, are in the habit of keeping to this part of the sea; in it are commonly encountered terrible waves, foaming and leaping, and unless a really good wind is blowing the pilots refuse to sail into it, calling it 'the place of Pharaoh', and the sailors fear it as they would a whirlpool. Over this we sailed for two days in great danger, the ship rolling and pitching in the waves despite its considerable size and Indian construction; nor were the sailors without fear, especially as we had the recent news that a few hours previously a ship had been sunk with four hundred men on board and only twenty-eight saved; but by the Almighty's aid we came safely through the pool of Pharaoh.

Then in a few hours we saw near the coast an island called *Hassane*,[5] inhabited by Arabs; from the barrenness of the soil it produced nothing, and wretchedly do they sustain a poor livelihood on nothing but fish, which they dry and make into a sort of bread. Towards evening we put in to a neighbouring place called *Koba*,[6] for all ships sail on the same course lest by departing from the correct one they may be lost among the rocks as in a labyrinth and unable to get through, if they have strayed from the accustomed course. So for putting in they keep to defined places, which are situated so as to give the convenience of a port; and if they cannot reach them by nightfall, either they return to last night's resting place, or to another nearby, however favourable the wind, and remain in port overnight.

---

[4] Arabic *Birkah Fir'aun*. This site was visited by a number of seventeenth and early nineteenth century visitors, among them J. Pitts (Foster, *op. cit.* p. 19), C. Niebuhr, *Description de l'Arabie* (Amsterdam, 1774), pp. 354–60, and M. Parkyns, *Life in Abyssinia* (London, 1853), i. 49.
[5] Not identified.
[6] Not identified.

CHAPTER 3

MOUNT SINAI
THROUGH THE RED SEA

Some of the dangers of the Red Sea behind us, we thankfully put in on September 17 near our longed-for Mount Sinai,[1] where Moses received the tablets of the commandments of God[2] and where *all the people saw the thunderings and the lightnings, and the sound of the trumpet, and the mountain smoking.* Exodus xx. 18. We did not disembark, because at that time it was not permitted bodily to touch the bones of St Catherine V & M[3] which the Angels had placed there, but spiritually we gave her heartfelt reverence.[4] A wonderful mountain! Its lofty summit seems to be split like two of Moses's tablets, and it is situated close to the Red Sea, from which the mountain can be reached in two hours if you climb the right path. We missionaries were forbidden to set foot off the ship on to land, although most of the Mahometans disembarked for the shore in small craft to collect a supply of water, while we had to be patient in our stinking hole. The mountain is called by the Arabs *Gebl Ettur,*[5] or Mount Sinai, or

---

[1] Sinai is the site of a Greek Orthodox monastery dedicated to St. Catherine which had been visited half a century earlier by William Daniel and Charles Poncet. The latter, who was drawn up by a pulley and cords, states that the monastery was 'solidly built, with good and strong cords'. Foster, *op. cit.* pp. 81, 161–2. See also *The travels of Monsieur de Thevenot into the Levant* (London, 1687), i, 167–70.

[2] This was the prevailing view as recorded for example by Daniel who was shown a cave 'where Moses lived during the forty days that he was upon the mount'. Foster *op. cit.*, p. 81.

[3] St Catherine of Alexandria, Virgin and Martyr, is believed to be buried in the famous monastery named after her on Mt. Sinai, to which angels had transported her body.

[4] Views of the monastery are reproduced in C. Niebuhr, *Voyage en Arabie* (Utrecht, 1776) i, plates xlvii and xlv.

[5] *Jabal al-Ṭūr.*

8

commonly the High Mountain, and can easily be reached overland from Suez within four days, in a journey of fifty-six hours,
though it is more comfortable to allow five days. Elsewhere I
have sketched out the overland road to Sinai, and now, approaching by sea en route for Abyssinia, I found several noteworthy
things, such as a village under the mountain not far off, inhabited
with complete freedom by Christian Greeks, Copts, and even
Arabs, some way from the Red Sea but nearer to Mt Sinai: it is
about two days' journey away among the foothills, which here
follow one after the other in almost a straight line. The Turks,
elsewhere proud and overbearing, can do no harm to the
aforesaid inhabitants, who are protected by the Arabs; the Christians have built two small houses out of shingle from the sea, of
unusual construction and wonderful to see, veined, spotted, and
marbled; exhibiting such beautiful variety that certainly would
be rated very highly in the provinces of Christendom. But houses
like this are easily built, because all the inhabitants turn out to
help, receive a little bread or vegetable for their labour, and
extend this mutual charity to each other. Because there is sweet
water here all the ships put in to take in sufficient stores for
sailing onward: there are first-rate pears here, different sorts of
apples, grapes, dates and almonds, brought down by the Arabs
from the mountains where likewise there are abundant streams
of sweet water which they use to irrigate trees, plants and other
fruits, for no rain reaches this far. Here is the site of the ancient
Greek monastery of St Basil, once the seat of the senior bishop
of Mt Sinai, but now through the continual encroachments of
the Arabs occupied by only two or three monks to irrigate the
fruit trees, who live extremely sparely, refraining even from fish
in fast time and ordinarily living on vegetables seasoned with a
little rancid oil. At that time one of the three monks seemed
almost dead; he had been hung up by his hands between two
trees by the Arabs, whom he had been trying to drive from the
orchard where they were picking the fruit: no one dared to free
him until on the third day the Arabs were graciously pleased to
take him down half-dead; so that it is but rare for someone to
stay there of his own choice.

At the foot of the mountain where the garden lies there is
towards the wall a spring of hot water called by the Greeks the
Bath of Moses: here took place that miracle when Moses, at God's

command, led the people who complained of thirst *Behold I will stand before thee there on the rock of Horeb, and thou shalt smite the rock, and there shall come water out of it that the people may drink.* Exodus xvii. 6. Around the outflow is a precinct three or four paces square where the water wells out, slightly warm: and toward the mountain is a rock in which are five holes distinct from each other as though laid down by the palm of the hand, full to the middle with water. The monks say that Moses fixed his five fingers there when he drew out the water, but, because the holes are spaced a long way from each other, the story seems unlikely, because Moses would have had to have hands of an extraordinary size; I would rather believe that the miracle happened in another higher rock where one can see the mark of the hand. All the Christians who cross this place are bound to pay a fixed tribute to the Arabs, a florin[6] or sometimes a real[7] per person. The reason is that, many ships being wrecked in the Red Sea, those who escape death are at once despoiled by the Arabs and left naked, except for those who pay tribute and show a receipt for tribute paid: these are defended, even if they are loaded with gold or precious stones, and are led off safely to Mt Sinai; all the others, even Turks, who refuse to pay, are stripped and robbed of everything. So ships as they leave the port are regularly accompanied by the Arabs, so that, if they are wrecked in that narrow stretch of sea, they can be despoiled: from Suez up to the head of Mt Sinai the sea is of about the same breadth, in places barely fifteen Italian miles wide: but to the sailors it is often unlucky.

The sea is called Red not only in common talk but even in Holy Scripture, not because the sea is of a red colour, or as some writers would have it because the shores are red, but because the Red Sea is otherwise called the sea of Edom, after the country Edom, and in the Hebrew tongue this sounds like Red; for this reason the Greeks call it Red. This same name Red is derived from the coral, which reddens the trees and rocks which reflect

---

[6] Florin, or ducat, an Italian gold coin of Florentine origin, containing about 3·5 grams of gold. Venetian gold coins of this denomination were also issued, and were known as sequins, from their Venetian name zecchino.

[7] Real, a Spanish gold coin weighing about 3·5 grams. The term was also popularly used for the eight-real pice, or 'piece of eight', as well as for the Spanish pataca, or dollar.

the shining sun; or from the abundance of red fish-scales or red sea-shells; for all these reasons the common name for it is the Red Sea.[8] Otherwise it is like other seas, more difficult only in the navigational sense, and more dangerous partly from the ignorance of the Mahometan ship-masters or ships' navigators: in each ship there are two called *Roban*,[9] who make out that they have experience because they have often made this voyage: one of them is in charge of the helm, the other oversees the navigational chart, and they offer advice to the captain of the ship. They are in fact pilots, and parallel to them there are two captains, one of them the commander of the ship, the other in charge of the sails.

Each such ship brings its owner a freightage, net of expenses, of 50 purses, that is 16,700 reals; for a purse is worth 25,000 medins, and, the medin standing at 75 to the real, one purse is worth 334 reals. The captains of the ships, being greedy, load their ships with their own goods beside the freight; and so excessively that at every strong gust of wind they take fright and are afraid of sinking; for the same cause they often drop anchor during the day, and travel only by day and never by night, lest they be lost together with the crew. They voyage from Suez to Gidda only with the tramontane[10] or north wind, which blows every year at the same season, from the end of August through September and October to the middle of November, during which time they are continually transporting cargoes; but in the months of February, March and April the sirocco which ordinarily prevails takes them conveniently to Suez back from Gidda. They bring with them different products of the sea, coral both red and white with its tendrils, pearl shell partly with mother

---

[8] Prutky's contemporary, James Bruce, who agreed that the Red Sea was 'in colour nothing different from the Indian or any other ocean', believed that the sea owed its name to the existence of coral which spread 'every where over the bottom of the Red Sea, perfectly in imitation of plants on land.' J. Bruce, *Travels to discover the source of the Nile* (Edinburgh, 1790), i, 287.

[9] Arabic *Rubbān*, pilot.

[10] Almost a century later Lieutenant Wellsted noted that north-westerly winds prevailed in the northern portion of the Red Sea, but attained their 'greatest strength' in June, July and August, when they extended beyond the straits of Bab el Mandeb. Southerly winds on the other hand prevailed in the southern stretch of the Sea, particularly in October, November and December when they 'not infrequently' blew vessels all the way to Suez. J. R. Wellsted, *Travels in Arabia* (London, 1838), ii, 300–2.

of pearl and keeping its colour, partly of varying colour, figured shells, vessels which can be adapted for sacred use as the pyx, wonderful stones with different engravings on them, fossilized plants and fungi, and pietra dura with beautiful patterns of great elegance. It was on account of these rarities that Necos king of Egypt, as Herodotus writes in his second book, tried to dig a canal from the river Nile (where 120,000 men died in the attempt), to open a sea-link with the Red Sea; after abandoning this he sent some Phoenicians down the Red Sea and through the southern ocean, who at length returned to Egypt past Cadiz.[11]

As I noted in my diary of our journey, on September 21 we weighed anchor and continued our journey from Mt Sinai. A number of rocks surrounded us to our great danger, and a pilot stayed continually on deck to steer us through the narrow passage, which was hard for a ship to negotiate, its course at times being a bare three feet from the rocks. Great as was our anxiety among such numbers of coral rocks and reefs, lest we strike on them and founder, yet we made an almost miraculous passage without loss, though a considerable strain was imposed upon the crew. Thus far along the shore the Arabs had kept as close to us as guardian angels, hemming us round with a view to robbery, for they well know how to swim under water.

At the head of these mountains, on the sea-shore, there is visible a Turkish mosque dedicated to one Santoni,[12] who is regarded as a holy man by the Mahometans and particularly reverenced by sailors. That they may escape the perils of the sea and be saved from the rocks they build model ships complete with sails and rudder, and put out into deep water within view of the mosque; there they celebrate a festival, shouting and rejoicing, partly in gratitude for having journeyed safely so far, and partly in prayer for a safe journey onward. Then they carry their model in procession round the ship, and from every traveller the sailors in chorus request an offering, half of which they keep themselves and half offer to the demon; then loading the model with corn, money and various offerings they set it afloat in the sea, and swear that it is carried by the hands of angels to the bones of the demon Santoni – although every eye can see that it

[11] Herodotus ii. 158, and iv. 42.
[12] A generic term for a Muslim holy man, often credited with miraculous powers.

sinks under the waves of the sea. Nevertheless they firmly believe that the ship is carried by the angels to the mosque, and hung up there as a perpetual memorial.

That same night we dropped anchor in a place called by the Arabs *Elkadi Elhai*,[13] that is, The Living Judge. On the morning of 27th, the wind being favourable, we put in to *Gembua*,[14] or Place of Fountains, where not far off on the other side of the sea appears the city of *Jembo* or *Lembo*, which has an excellent harbour, where however sailors rarely put in unless compelled by storm to do so: for there live the nobles of Mecca, and practise all sorts of tyrannies and exactions, laying claim to half of all cargoes; even if a ship fails to use the port, yet for display's sake they salute it with cannon shot. This harbour has two noticeable rocks, and is furnished with a strong and handsome fort with four towers in a square, though with not many guns; next to it is the aforesaid city of *Lembo* at latitude 25° and longitude 62° 30′: distant from Suez 100 French leagues. Most of its houses are covered with straw, the heat of the sun being unbearable, and they grow enormous dates there in great quantity, longer than one's finger and in flavour and sweetness exceeding all others.

Next morning there was a thick fog, that we had never seen in Egypt, and this caused the Mahometans to rejoice as at an omen for a prosperous voyage given by the prophet Mahomet. At this time a poor young foreigner died, jet-black in complexion, and, to the shame of many Christians, the Mahometans exercised the greatest charity towards him, washing and anointing his corpse, wrapping it in a white cloth, reading a funeral service to the whole ship's company, and buring him at sea by tying a large empty amphora to his feet. By his death our number was by no means diminished, but rather increased, when two poor women gave birth – whereupon they were taken from their poor quarters into better ones, a feast was made for them, shouts and cries of joy were raised, as is the Egyptian custom, on the day of the birth and on the eighth day after, and suitable food was provided for

---

[13] Arabic *al-Qāḍī al-ḥayy.*
[14] Gembua, Jembo and Lembo all represent Yanbuʻ, which means 'spring'. The town is divided into two by an inlet. It is the port of Medina, and was, as Poncet had earlier noted, 'a pretty considerable town', defended by a castle. Foster, *op. cit.* pp. 67, 76, 161, 179–80. Niebuhr, who reproduces an engraving of the settlement, states that it was surrounded by a wall. Niebuhr, *Voyage*, i, 213 and plate liii.

them. At that time I noticed in myself, in my colleagues and in many other people a complete change, both physically, and in the atmosphere and the extraordinary heat; all we three missionaries were ill, short of air, scarce able to breathe, and sensible of a peculiar smell, from which and from many other symptoms I correctly deduced that in the neighbourhood of Lembo we had crossed the tropic of Cancer. As we sailed on we endured the indescribable heat of the climate, having to revive us only stinking water full of worms like snakes two fingers in length – and but little of that: indeed we seemed near to death.

On October 1 we came to a place called *Rabeck*[15] near a small mountain and dropped anchor among the rocks. The land held sacred by the Mahometans begins here, a small village at 23° 30' latitude and 63° longitude, fifteen leagues from Lembo, not far from a mountain of the same name *Rabeck*. As soon as they drew near the mountain the Mahometans began to prepare themselves for their ceremonies, and these pilgrims had come for the first time to do honour to the false prophet; so, with the dawn, all refrained from selling anything or from entering into a business contract, took off their clothes, completely washed their whole body and scraped themselves with their hands, and covered themselves with a white robe in two parts, the lower to cover the waist and legs, the upper over the shoulder like a cloak. Their heads are bare, and their feet naked, and any great men or nobles who are present can be seen to slash their footwear with knives so that through the many holes their bare feet may be seen: so, lightly clad, by day in the heat and by night in the cold, they persist in this way until they visit the mountain of sacrifice in Mecca. Each of them carries a piece of wood like a shard with which to scrape themselves. However, if anyone from ill-health, poverty, or modesty, refuses to remain so clothed, he is obliged to sacrific a lamb on the mountain of sacrifice, where two poor men, or even three, offer one lamb between them: if even this is beyond their means, they fast for three days as they do in Ramadan.

A number of criminals in similar garb can be seen in the stocks, at the bidding of the instructors or masters of the law, who teach the customary ceremonies and prayers. Everyone at once embarks

[15] *Rābigh.* Bruce, who refers to this place as Rabac, described it as a 'small port' and states that its water-supply was 'not bad'. Bruce, *op. cit.*, i, 262.

on board ship two and two in due order, and one priest, mounting aloft, preaches of the happiness of the Mahometan people,
of their future joys and of the abundance of women in the
Mahometan paradise, of the consolations of the faithful and other
filthiness – and at the end of each paragraph the congregation
replies *Amen*. At the end of this ceremony all disembark into
small boats and make for the aforesaid mountain of Rabeck,
following, they claim, the commandment of Mahomet. Every
pilgrim picks up three stones to throw into the pit in the middle
of the mountain, for a perpetual memorial, as laid down in the
Alkoran[16] which the angel delivered; in this they rely on their
false doctrine, of which they even tried to persuade us missionaries, who knew better. For it is well-known that it was Sergius
the excommunicated who wrote the Alkoran, and that he plotted
with Mahomet, who called the whole people together to show
them a miracle, and had in advance secretly located Sergius in
a pit in the middle of the mountain. Then Mahomet preached
in a sermon that it had been revealed to him by God that He was
sending a revelation to him by an angel's hand, from the pit in
the mountain, and that for the future the whole people must
accept this law as true, and delivered by a true prophet: at this
moment Sergius lifting the book on high brought about the
prophecy's fulfilment, to the cheers and applause of the populace.
Then Mahomet, pretending that he had received a new revelation
from God, declared that the whole congregation present should
throw stones into the pit: so the whole crowd covered with a pile
of stones the evil Sergius, who thus met the just deserts of his
blasphemous crime. Mahomet was afraid that in the course of
time some dispute might arise because of the title Prophet, and
in this devious way he ensured that the honour of Prophet was
reserved to him alone, notwithstanding that he was stupid, dolt-
ish, ignorant of everything, a herdsman of pigs and camels. And
yet to this very day the Mahometans continue to throw their
stones, being deceived by their elders with false doctrine.

Meantime each pilgrim is continually scraping and thereby
sanctifying himself, though care is taken not to let the blood flow;
to this end he holds in his hand the aforementioned wooden
shard, and is freely permitted to help his neighbour's necessity.
Fervently and continuously, to show their devotional zeal, they

[16] The Koran, *al-Qur'ān*.

repeat a prayer made up partly of Arabic and partly of Turkish words of whose meaning they are ignorant: *lebeck, lebeck, Allah, hom ellebeck, lebe, lebe ja schiricke lebei, elhamdt, a uamedel mond.*[17] Some were saying *Molck ja schiricke lebei.* Several told me that this prayer was not made to the glory of Mahomet but to the house of Abraham the Patriarch, just as though they had come simply to Abraham's house.

In these ceremonies three days passed, when the Arabs brought us fish called in Arabic *schoromback,*[18] grown in a shell like oysters and like them producing pearls. The flesh was very tough, as difficult to cook as snails, and to us to whom they were offered a treat such as we never knew to have eaten before; for many days now we had eaten nothing but biscuit-bread and stinking water full of worms. The Arabs told us that they found in these shells pearls of great value, and I myself, finding a small one, realized that these shells were well worth the gathering. Often they cling to the rocks and stones, and the Arab boys and youths seek them out and tear them from the rocks, and sell a great quantity for a small price.

At last the Mahometans had completed their foolishness, so irksome to us, and we sailed from here, full of longing to make a landfall; for there was little food left, meat we had never tasted, and we had made do with a little biscuit-bread and a little rice, while the stinking water, which by a cloth filter we cleared of worms, we used up to the last drop from the insupportable heat

[17] These words represent the invocation known as the *talbiyah,* of which the usual version is:
   Labbaykḍ, labbaykḍ, Allāhumma, labbaykḍ.
   Lā sharīka laka, labbaykḍ.
   Imna 'lḥamda, wa' n-ni'mata laka, wa' lmulk.
   Lā sharîka laka, labbaykḍ.
   It may be translated:
   Here I am at Thy service! O Allah! here am I
   No partner hast Thou, here am I:
   The praise and the grace are Thine, and the dominion –
   No partner hast Thou, here am I!
   None of the words is Turkish.
[18] This represents Ar. *surumbāq* (R. Dozy, *Supplément aux dictionnaires arabes,* 1881, p. 650). Forskål (*Descriptiones animalium,* ed. C. Niebuhr, 1775, p. xxxiii) describes it under no. 77 in his list of shell-fish from the Red Sea coasts, and calls it *Strombus gallus.* Mrs Solene Morris of the Natural History Museum informs us that it is now known as *Strombus tricornis,* but that Prutky's description is not compatible with a stromb, which is mobile. She considers that, in spite of the name, he probably referred to an oyster or a giant clam.

16

and thirst, and drank as though it were manna from heaven. We had to remain always in our aforementioned stinking tiny wretched hole, and rarely showed our heads to the Turks for the various injuries they threatened us. The more eagerly did we look forward to the end of our imprisonment, while the pilgrims, urged on by the ship's captain, maintained their raging spite against us, and we had to endure a prison-like existence with patience, for fear of injury, despite the fact that our various discomforts had brought on several bodily ailments and even a dose of fever: after twelve days of chastisement at the hand of the Blessed Lord, we yearned for land as soon as possible. Meanwhile there were still various rocks to be passed, which beset us sorely, near a place called by the Turks *Fatme*,[19] where we almost died from the sun's heat: on the next day we rounded safely a prominent neck of the land, or cape projecting out into the sea like an arm, and from afar off the port of Gidda[20] appeared. Still we had to sail through a labyrinth of rocks and shoals, and scarcely ever had we been so anxious, partly because of the rocks on each side of us, and partly because of the lack of sufficient depth of water; here and there the ship had to turn quickly to pick out the narrow passage, for the port of Gidda is extremely difficult and full of danger, and therefore safe from enemies. For this reason almost all the Indian ships, at one day's distance from the harbour, shoot off their guns; at which signal the harbour-master sends to the incoming vessel a pilot boat with a pilot, which safely guides it through the rocks to the harbour, and points out the one sure passage through the labyrinth to the port of Gidda. Praise God, on the festal day of the angelic saint our Seraphic patriarch Francis, we reached it, to our great consolation, in the fourth hour of the afternoon, and weighed anchor. Next day we decided to hire a small boat to take our belongings, and had to pay seven florins for a trip of barely one Italian mile from the land, but at last we landed on the soil of the city of Gidda.

---

[19] Fatme (Fāṭimah). 'A rocky bank, on which lie some islets and numerous reefs, borders the coast from a position about three miles northward of Ras Khurma to a position about ten miles southward of Ras Hatiba.' (*Red Sea and Gulf of Aden pilot*, 1955, p. 297).

[20] Jeddah, according to Bruce, *op. cit.*, i, 265, was 'very extensive', and consisted of 'numberless shoals, small islands, and sunken rocks, with channels, however, between them, and deep water'. A plan of the port is reproduced in Niebuhr, *Voyage*, i, 223.

CHAPTER 4

ARRIVAL AT GIDDA

It is necessary on landing to go through the customs, where we had deposited the mission's luggage in six boxes. We saw many thousand Mahometan pilgrims, and could hardly get through the crowd, who blasphemed and spat at us as though we were dogs, so that it was difficult if not impossible to make our way to have our belongings examined, and, if we had not been protected by the recommendation of our Catholic Greek merchant friends in Cairo and of a Mahometan nobleman, we should have suffered even greater trials and tribulations. But truly God is wonderful and merciful, and never fails his servants! Together with our boxes full of medicines, books, and ecclesiastical vestments we slipped successfully through, and were let in without delay and examined: though the customs officials raged against us and demanded to know why they had to let Christian dogs through before Mahometans, and we had to put up with insult upon insult. But the aforesaid nobleman, to whom we had been recommended, had sent his senior servant to the quayside to assist us; and through his effective protection we were treated to a considerate examination, to the wonder of the bystanders, and were excused all excise duties apart from the usual one for servants of five thalers.[1] But the sweat was pouring from our bodies, from fear of how we might be treated, from the heat of the sun, and from the weight of two hundred silver scudi which we were carrying on our persons; for, to avoid having to pay a tax of ten per cent, each of us was obliged to carry two hundred scudi. But

[1] Thaler (or in English Dollar), the original German name for large silver coins first minted in Bohemia. The Maria Theresa or Levant dollar circulated widely in the Near East during the eighteenth and and nineteenth centuries. See G. S. P. Freeman-Grenville 'The late Francesco Carbone's collection of thalers from Yemen,' *Numismatic chronicle*, 1977.

our thanks to God were said with a sincere heart, Who deigned to guard and preserve us so triumphantly from among the Mahometan wolves. We were then led to the house assigned to us, with all our belongings, where we stayed for a while resting and reviving our tired bodies.

The Vizier had been told of our arrival, and suddenly on the next day summoned me to his palace, wherein I entered to find a full concourse of nobles. I paid my respects to him as he sat on his divan, although no Christian was permitted to appear there, and to everyone's surprise he ordered me to sit near him. Then, refreshed by a good cup of coffee, I was asked what goal was I seeking here in the heart of the Turkish dominions. Following the customs of the Orient I replied that I was following my star into these regions, and that I had come hither to cure diseases, to cut or open veins, to use scalpels or cupping-glasses, and to provide other services of this kind to his people. Hearing this the Vizier held out his hand to me and 'Master' he said 'please feel my pulse'. Satisfying him in this I was kindly allowed free access to him on audience days, and was able without hesitation to enter the houses of other citizens, where later I gave various medical treatment to the women, and by blood-letting cured two favourite wives from a diurnal fever in quite a short time; in the days to come I was letting blood, curing diseases, restoring many to health, so that, thanks be to God, I established myself as a miracle-worker in the eyes of the Mahometans, and among a race of barbarians acquired a name for goodness. Many times was I asked by various nobles of Gidda to make their city my permanent resting place, and they promised me a great sum of money in return, as this is a city of rich merchants. But our wants were to be satisfied not with gold or with silver, but with souls redeemed by Christ's precious blood, and we pretended that we were going on to the next city, because if the Vizier had learned that our destination was Abyssinia he would have denied the means of departure, or would have exacted for his permission such an exorbitant sum of money that our resources would not have sufficed for us to continue our planned journey. For this reason I kept pressing my good noble friend to solicit the Vizier for our departure, because already the rumour was being spread by the heretic Greeks, ever hostile to Roman priests, that we were only pretending to be Frankish doctors, but that the goal of our journey was Abyssinia. Fearful lest the Mahometans be warned by their malice and detain us, we made diligent enquires for a ship to take us further on our way; besides which, we had already spent eighteen days in this city, we were paying a good price for food, water and meat, every day for a small room we paid a florin and each week in addition a Roman scudo for a wretched hovel, though we were trying to avoid any great expense: for bread we paid a florin a day, and our hunger was but partly appeased hereby, because, as always at inns, the grain had been ground very fine by our standards and sold at one medin a loaf, so that a European stomach scarcely noticed twenty or thirty. So we ate but little, lest later in our journey we might be deprived of other necessities. The poorer natives eat a bread made from Arabian corn called *durra*,[2] being unable to pay for the expensive bread. The merchants on the other hand, whose riches are a thousand-fold, live very well, and reward highly enough a small service done to them, as I know from my own experience: for the help of a simple purgative or sudorific medicine they were paying seven Spanish patacas[3] or cross-stamped thalers, for cutting a vein three, and similarly for other quite small medical services. I found one merchant of nearly eighty years of age, a very wealthy man, suffering for some years past with the white flux, who showered me with many favours and promised me many more if I could restore him to his former state of health; the nature of his disease needed purgation, and, for a simple purgative which had a good effect, he sent me next day twenty patacas in an embroidered purse. Later by the application of a few medicines he was cured, by God's grace, of his white flux; deeply grateful, he heaped kindnesses upon us during our whole time in Gidda, and so alleviated our distress that not only did we maintain intact the money handed to us by the Sacred Congregation, but were even enabled to meet all our expenses and carry away with us a small addition to it. Indeed if through Almighty God we had not been so assisted through our medical remedies, not only would we have spent the whole of the Sacred Congregation's money by

---

[2] Colloquial pronunciation of *dhura*, originally millet, later used for maize also.

[3] The Spanish pataca, a popular name for the eight-real piece, or 'piece of eight.' Prutky doubtless refers to them as 'cross-stamped' because the cross was a prominent design on mid-eighteenth century eight-real pieces. Bruce, *op. cit.*, i, 323, equates 'patacas' with 'imperial dollars.'

the middle of our journey, but should have had to endure a terrible shortage of drink and food. Indeed it was due to the Grace of God that even the enemies of our holy faith comforted us with good food, sweet water, and the finest fruits of the earth, and for each one in turn we rendered thanks to the Supreme Lord of the Heavens.

The city of Gidda is noteworthy for many curiosities, and as I have applied what care I could to their collection, I set them out that they may be better known in future.

CHAPTER 5

THE CITY OF GIDDA

The city of Gidda is by sea about forty French leagues from the village of Rabey, at latitude 22° longitude 64° 30', on the shore of the Red Sea. On each side it has a fort[1] armed with a few cannon: the one towards the north is occupied by the Bassa,[2] while the southern one, which projects into the sea, being without guns contains no important officer but is guarded solely by some janissaries. The distance from one side to the other is half an Italian mile, and the road runs in a circle from the sea out on the eastern side and back to the sea again. The whole city is surrounded by a simple wall,[3] of which the circuit totals one and a half Italian miles, well enough made of stone, intermixed towards the sea with many small houses covered with straw. There are just three town gates,[4] one by each fort, and one facing east, better built after the European fashion: this is called the Mecca gate, as it leads thither, which they dignify by the name of Holy gate, or gate of the Prophet, since it leads to the district made holy by his burial. This gate alone is guarded by Janissaries, disciplined soldiers, and is occupied by several officers who perform their duties communally. No Christian dares to cross, being thought unworthy even to approach, and if, even in ignorance, he approaches the portal of this gate, he is forcibly compelled

[1] The Jeddah battery, according to Niebuhr, *Voyage*, i, 223, was 'entirely ruined' and the cannons in front of the Pasha's house fired only ceremonial salutes.

[2] i.e. Pasha.

[3] The wall, Niebuhr, *op. cit.*, i, 233, says, was so badly ruined that people could in several places enter or leave the town freely.

[4] Niebuhr, *op. cit.*, i, 233, refers to these three gates as the Bâb es scherîf, the Bâb el sjedîd and the Bâb Mékke, i.e. the Bāb al-Sharīf, 'the Sharif's gate' or the 'noble gate', the Bāb al-jadīd, the 'new gate', and the Bāb Makkah, the 'Mecca gate'.

22

either to turn Turk or to be burnt alive. So the Christian merchants are afraid even to approach the nearby streets, lest they
come to harm. The other two gates are free of access, and walking
here is permitted. During my stay in Gidda it happened that I
was called out to a sick Janissary, and had an unusual opportunity
to see the gate; but because of the outcry of the Mahometans the
sick man was transferred to another house out of reverence for
the sanctity of the holy gate, and I had to cure him there. But
on another occasion, when my noble Turkish friend took me as
a special favour outside the city walls, I was able to see it. The
Mahometans claim that this is the sepulchre of our first mother
Eve,[5] and that it is from her that the city takes its name, Gidda
in Arabic meaning the same as Grandmother, and they claim
that by an ancient tradition she was buried here. The area outside
the Mecca gate is held in greatest reverence by the Mahometan
population, and I was led through at great speed lest I be seen
by the crowd, but I saw a building resembling a chapel, which is
in the form of a square, with a great window protected by an
iron grille, a cupola on top, and without doors, the Mahometans
contenting themselves with looking through the window. They
claim that Eve's body rests within, and that it was so enormous
that the whole chapel is built on her navel: at a stone's throw
from the seaport, it was later joined to the Holy Way that leads
to Mecca and is on the left hand side.

While the city is of adequate construction, the merchants'
houses are especially well built in stone[6] which is broken up and
dragged out of the Red Sea. Every day for six hours the tide
flows and ebbs, receding from the city by two and as much as
three Italian miles; they break up the stone and keep working
even while the sea is flowing again, when you can see them
swimming like fishes. So unusual are these stones, and so marked
the singularities appearing in them, that in Europe they would
fetch a high price. Streaks and designs, flowers and figures are

[5] This tradition had earlier been noted by Joseph Pitts. Foster *op. cit.*, p. 34. A
sepulchre associated with Eve lay immediately south of the port. Niebuhr, *op.
cit.*, i, 223 and plate lvi. See also R. Burton, *Personal narrative of a pilgrimage to
Al-Madinah and Meccah* (London, 1893), ii, 273. In Arabic Eve is *Hawā*, which
is like Latin *Ava* grandmother, which is *Jaddah* in Arabic).
[6] The city, according to Niebuhr, *op. cit.*, i, 224, had several 'fine buildings'
constructed of coral, particularly near the coast.

arrayed in wonderful order, and the stone is durable: it is chiselled into blocks for building, and those which are pure white are found to be the best. The cost of the materials for the parts of the houses can easily be reckoned from the cost of stone, since being without sun-dried or kiln-baked bricks they build entirely in stone: a block two feet long costs a real, a mason is paid a florin a day, other labourers, and the stone cutters, half a florin. They mix clean sand with earth instead of lime, add a little lime, and build their houses of stone, putting wood between the walls and binding the walls together with beams, which if they have to be used cost a real each. Timber being scarce here, they mostly use beams made from date-palms, and the cost of a modest-sized house is from eighty to one hundred purses. However, because houses like this are built with many rooms or cubicles, they bring in high rents for their owners, who easily collect a thousand gold pieces a year. Many of the houses by the sea are wretchedly made, either wholly of straw or else with pieces of wood or of stone interspersed in the straw, like our peasants in Europe, and the doors similarly are of straw; some are made of mud covered with straw, with the wall protected outside by thorns and briars, and wretched do they look. The houses built of stone are not covered by roofs, for the sake of cooling them after sunset; and so that the women may not be seen they build the outer walls to a greater height. They have no windows of glass, which is expensive, and in their place set beautiful iron grilles decorated with figures, though it is not the town natives who practise this skill, but the foreigners, either Indian or Christian.

Permanent residence in this city is granted to no Christian, Jew, or idolater, because it is a land sacred for Mahometans. But because this is the chief commercial port on the Red Sea, they are allowed to stay for a moderate length of time. Of the Mahometan inhabitants none are of noble birth, but are raised to prominence solely by their riches, and are each of them slaves or sons of slaves, who, continually intermixing, comprise the city's inhabitants. Every year a great number of black slaves are brought in, part from Ethiopia, part from Sennar,[7] or other nearby kingdoms, to the number ordinarily of 1,200 and sometimes as

---

[7] Sennar in what is now central Sudan. For a contemporary description of the country and its government see Bruce *op. cit.*, iv, 429–99.

much as 1,500; ordinarily the price of one slave is one hundred florins, but a handsome boy or beautiful girl sells at eighty or sometimes one hundred gold pieces, and the Abyssinian women are the dearest as they are more beautiful than all the others.

Like beasts the slaves for sale are herded into the market-place for all to see, though before this at their first arrival the *gellabi*,[8] that is the slave masters, have presented their slaves to the Bassa or Governor who chooses ten for himself out of every hundred. The rest are exposed naked in the market-place like cattle, a pitiful sight, with one or other covering his private parts with a piece of cloth. The Abyssinians, especially the women, are stationed apart from the others, human creatures of all sorts, mothers with babies at the breast, young men and old, boys and girls, all are set up for examination and put through their paces like mules or horses. The buyers examine their faces, hands, feet, teeth, and other limbs, strike them on the chest, and practise various acts of beastliness upon them. Their lamentations are bitter, especially when mothers and children are separated, when the mother is bought up by one master and the child by another and they know that they will never, or but seldom, see each other again. The cries and tears excite the compassion of the onlookers.

Such a mixture of races and breeding of children arises from this, that when the masters die there is no legitimate heir, and the whole estate falls to the slaves. The citizens of Gidda are part white, part black, and part mixed. The inheritance laws are such that, when the head of the family dies, the inheritance goes in equal portions not only to the children of the four legitimate wives, but to the sons and daughters of the slaves, with the condition that males get twice as much as females. So the nobility prides itself on nothing but its wealth, because the individuals have enriched themselves by nothing save their commercial practices. They trade by sailing through the Red Sea, and many are enriched by the number of slaves which they buy at a low price and then in course of time sell at a greater; others abuse their slaves until they are sated and resell them at the first opportunity, while yet others behave like our noble merchant friend, in whose house we lived, who bought a fourteen year old Abyssinian slave girl for two hundred gold pieces, and abused her out of all

[8] Arabic *jallāb*.

proportion like a bull never leaving her alone, so that within the space of eight days she died in misery.

Every year the Indians[9] come here with their goods, and when the cargoes are sold they usually sell off also the ships themselves, which are well made and belly-shaped to adapt to navigation among rocks, the Red Sea being without any large headland. They fetch eighty or ninety purses. To ensure that government is kept on the right lines and under political control, a new Bassa is appointed each year by the Sultan in Constantinople, unless by special favour he be permitted to remain longer: he stations himself in the fort next to the sea at the northern end of the city, together with his staff. The fort is surrounded by a very old wall of no defensive value, with many lean-to hovels beside it, and before its gate twelve cannon of different weights. When the Bassa goes in or out they fire off three or four, a signal which is also meant to give the alarm of any unexpected attack. Inside the fort is a prison for one hundred criminals, and the city houses another hundred.

The Bassa's staff consists of the *Kiechia*[10] and some minor officers, and in Turkish fashion all the rest are slaves, called Mamelukes, smartly dressed. To do him honour he maintains three or four trumpeters, six or eight oboists that the Germans call *Schalamai*,[11] four or five big drums and one small one in the Mahometan fashion; twice every day they play, once in the evening at sunset, and once two hours after nightfall, when the Bassa says his prayers, that is *Fasser* and *Aaschia*.[12] The *Kiechia* is the Bassa's lieutenant accountable to him in full like a prime minister. The second is the *Tendi*, as it might be secretary, the *Chasnades*[13] is the treasurer who has charge of the valuables and of the money, the *Sardar* is the captain of the slaves, who come under his control, and the *Saragg* is in charge of the stables, who when the Bassa

---

[9] Bruce, who saw nine ships from India at the port, some worth as much as £200,000, records that Indian brokers played an important commercial role. Bruce, *op. cit.*, i, 277–8.

[10] Turkish *Kāhyā*. This official was *inter alia* in charge of customs. Niebuhr, *op. cit.*, i, 218–20, 223, 225.

[11] German Schalmei, ('shawm').

[12] *Fajr*, the dawn prayer, '*Ishā*', the evening prayer. Burton, *op. cit.*, i, 233.

[13] Arabic *khaznadār*, treasurer, *sirdār*, commanding general, *sarrāj*, saddler. Turkish *bayrakdār*, properly standard-bearer, *shi'āljī*, properly torchbearer. *Tendi* may represent *tezkeneji*.

rides abroad keeps his hand continuously on the Bassa's horse. The soldiers who go before him holding axes are called *Nejackter*, and the *Schaali* is the executioner. All the rest are slaves and Mamelukes. The city is under the Bassa's sole governance, and the revenue or customs tax he shares with the Scherif,[14] or nobleman resident in Mecca.

As it rains barely twice or sometimes three times a year they endure a great shortage of water, which is of a black, red or green colour according to the colour of the worms breeding in it, is stinking to drink, but is sold at a considerable price when the worms have been cleaned out by a cloth filter. The great men, that is the richer men, keep cisterns for their own use, and sometimes supply water to their closer friends, cooking it with liquorice to make its rottenness more palatable. As the dearer sorts of wine are sold with us, so here they grudgingly sell half a sextarius[15] for two para,[16] or a German groschen,[17] and if no rain has fallen in the year then even at one florin it is difficult to buy water.

Few crops are grown here from the drought, and they import garden produce from near Mocha in Arabia Felix, along with herbs, fruit and other food. Only in their so-called winter, when it rains a little but is never cold, do they bring in, from a place called *Taif*,[18] vegetables such as white and yellow turnips, okra like cucumbers but sweeter and bigger, and with spiky bark, aubergines like half melons, radishes of which only the leaves are eaten, Indian beans, parsley, lettuce and leeks; Arabian fruits, pears, peaches, plums, very good grapes but very dear, raisins twice as large as in Europe, so that each weighs as much as three of ours, that is, three drams: from these I made a strong Eucharistic wine, wine being very rare indeed. A pound of grapes was

[14] Arabic *Sharīf*, the descendant of the Prophet who was governor of Mecca. It was normal Ottoman practice to appoint governors for very short terms of office.

[15] A Roman liquid measure containing a sixth part of a modius.

[16] The para was an Ottoman coin of silver or bronze circulating in Egypt, Turkey, etc., forty of which were the equivalent of a piastre, a silver coin of about twenty-three grams.

[17] Groschen, the name for small silver coins used throughout Germany, Poland, etc. In some parts of Germany the groschen represented twelve pfennigs.

[18] Taif (Ṭā'if), a village in the mountains south-east of Mecca, and the summer residence of some of the latter city's prominent citizens. Burton, *op. cit.*, i, 393, ii, 148; C. M. Doughty, *Travels in Arabia Deserta* (London, 1924), ii, 478–80, 672; H. St J. B. Philby *The heart of Arabia* (London, 1922), i, 185–203.

fetching two medins, and was on sale in Gidda for fully five months, from the end of July until Christmas. Lemons are also to be had, otherwise called Persian apples, oranges, sweet and bitter, figs both ordinary and Indian, and the fig of Adam, called by the Arabs *mus*,[19] excellent of taste, yellow and green in colour, long like cucumbers, with a smooth rind or skin without seeds inside, of a musky scent, soft and sweet, delicious to taste having an exquisite flavour of pears – we ate it with great relish, its flavour being superior to almost all fruits. Its plant is low, six feet broad, with leaves a foot wide, producing thirty or forty figs at a time, so that one person can hardly carry a branch. I found them in India even better, bigger and longer, and they have an unusual method of propagation, because before the old plant dies a new shoot springs from the root, since they do not live for long. Also in Gidda I ate very good pomegranates, extremely large, blood red and of beautiful flavour: the inhabitants call them the apple of the Prophet. A few almond trees grow and a few citrons.

Corn of whatever sort is not grown, and is imported from Egypt at great expense. From India comes a variety very popular with the inhabitants called *Ketzeri*,[20] rather like pounded lentils, with this distinction that the outside is black and the inside yellow: the Arabs cook it with half the quantity of rice, and much enjoy it, as do the Indians. Meat is on sale in plenty, good goat's flesh, beef, and lamb, and often buffalo and camel, which is indistinguishable from beef, are brought in by the neighbouring Arabs. The lambs you would call dogs but that their bleating betrays them, so like dogs are they with long ears hanging down, wool hard like the hair of dogs or goats, and with long tails as in Egypt. Fowls are hard to come by, except for a few hens, one being priced ordinarily at ten para or medins, with an egg selling for a medin, occasionally for half a medin. There are a few pigeons, and doves both domestic and wild, with another variety called by the Arabs *Gatta*,[21] very similar to the pheasant and of excellent

[19] Arabic *mauz* or banana. It was called the fig of Adam because of the belief that it was the forbidden fruit of the Garden of Eden.

[20] Possibly *kedgeree*, a mess of rice and pulses. H. Yule and A. C. Burnell, *Hobson-Jobson*, (London, 1903), p. 476.

[21] Arabic *ghaṭā, ghaṭāṭ*, sand-grouse. Mr Richard Porter informs us that the reference can only be to the Chestnut-bellied Sandgrouse, *Pterocles exustus*, as no other is found in that area. The Arabic name is an imitation of the bird's call.

flavour, which are found in plenty in the open plain in flocks with the doves; in addition great numbers of sparrows are to be seen with a few other species of birds and some birds of prey.

At one time before the coming of the Mahometans the city was inhabited by idolaters who like Indians worshipped the cow, and, in memory of this, the inhabitants tell the story that, the crows being accustomed to perch on the cows' backs, the people out of ancient respect would not suffer this, and by invoking the black art banished all the crows from the city, and that to this day not a crow is to be seen, although in Mecca,[22] a day's journey off, they are to be found in their thousands. They also say that the scorpions to be found here, though poisonous, do no damage to human beings, they declare that they have a miraculous sort of wood that leaves no ash when it is burned, and they claim that the inhabitants do not suffer loss by theft. These miracles, or marvels, are easily credible to the ignorant, but by no means so to the informed pilgrim: my own poor wits refute the argument that there are no crows in Gidda by the reflection that in Gidda there are neither water nor trees and that the crows cannot live there, whereas Mecca being provided with wells of water has crows in plenty. Whether scorpions, despite being poisonous, do humans no harm, I have not learned by personal experience and cannot affirm or deny. The third marvel is certainly noteworthy as the same thing happened in Cairo, but there the lack of ash was due not to witchcraft but to the sort of wood burnt. As for the freedom from theft, a great deal of merchandise, almost all of it, is left open and exposed in the public street by day and night, and one never hears of losses, though the place is full of thieves; but then the criminal is impaled without mercy on the spot where he is caught. In Mecca there are said to be even more thieves, and property is at risk even when shut up and locked away in the house; our merchant friend at this very time was robbed of a slave out of his own house.

Because they leave out in the street corn, rice, flour and so on, there is an enormous number of mice, and great quantities of

---

[22] Pitts had earlier reported that there were at Mecca 'thousands of blue pigeons, which none will affright or abuse, much less kill them'. Foster, *op. cit.*, p. 29. Pilgrims, according to Burton, *op. cit.*, ii, 174, considered it a duty to provide these birds with 'a plentiful meal'.

dormice,[23] which the Turks do not kill or capture, so that they become household pets and can almost be caught by hand. There is also a different species, called by the inhabitants musk rats,[24] which are markedly different from the ordinary ones, for they are neither so large as the dormouse nor so small as the common mouse, but midway between them, almost like a mole; their colour is like ashes, but light tending to white through their whole body, they have feet webbed with skin like a mole, a tail shorter than a dormouse's but fatter, and their hair though thick is very short so that they almost look naked. The body is thick as a piglet's, the head shaped like a mole's, and the eyes are tiny, like the eye of a needle, which is the reason why they are half-blind by day but have acute night-vision: the mouth is long, pig-like and pointed, and has at the end as it were two little globules, while the many teeth are like human teeth of which the four front ones of the upper jaw are bent backwards: this animal is regarded by the natives as dangerous because if it chances to bite anyone the wound is hard to cure. There are other matters of interest which I append in a separate chapter.

[23] Dr David L. Harrison informs us that this must be *Eliomys melanurus*, which is still found in the Hijaz, though it is now 'quite rare'.

[24] Dr Harrison informs us that this is the Indian House Shrew, *Suncus murinus*, which 'is still a common species in Jeddah'. He characterizes Prutky's description as 'really very good' and notes that they 'would indeed be seen quite frequently as they are active in the daytime'.

CHAPTER 6

VARIOUS FACTS ABOUT GIDDA,
AND THE COSTUME
OF THE INHABITANTS

Gidda lying next to the Red Sea is abundantly supplied with fish of all imaginable species, colours and shapes, such as is beyond man's intellect to understand or his pen to describe, save only His whose word created all things. Fish white as snow or dullish white, black, black and white, red and white, wholly red, green, of all the colours that nature can show, all are here; though very many are dark or bright red, or green or beautifully striped; and as the most high God created the animals of the earth in very diverse kinds, so in the waters He multiplied the number of fishes, to describe whose kinds in detail would need several large volumes. I saw a very unusual sort of fish[1] which instead of scales had long pointed bristles not unlike a pig's or a hedgehog's, black in colour and four feet long, very good to eat. Often in calm sea I have seen sea-dogs approach the ship, a most curious species, in various shapes never seen before. Because this country borders the Red Sea, the principal food is fish, since in many areas they are without any other form of nourishment, and although some

---

[1] Dr P. H. Greenwood, FRS, of the Natural History Museum informs us that this was certainly a member of the family Diodontidae, the so-called Porcupine or Puffer fishes, 'whose scales are modified into long spine-like objects, loosely embedded in the skin. When the fish is alarmed or threatened in any way it either gulps air or water, and in so doing blows its body up into a substantial sphere. The loose scales then stand erect.' Dr Greenwood suspects that Prutky's fish belonged to the genus *Chilomycterus* but is not able to assign it to a species on the evidence available. He can find no record of a *Chilomycterus* reaching 4 ft in length and also notes that the flesh of Diodontids is considered tasteless and watery.

species are said to be injurious to health, they are eaten freely just the same.

The people here are different from the Cairenes or others dressed after the Arabic fashion, in that that part of the sash which elsewhere is twisted into a turban is here left hanging on the left side. The clothing of the rich is magnificent especially in summer time, when they put on the thinnest of shifts made of Indian cloth, with long sleeves as European noblewomen wear bracelets, and they let the shift hang down outside slippers made of the same material. On this they put an expensive caftan or long dress reaching to the ground, very tight round the breasts at the top, worked with tiny knots, and gird themselves with a silken sash ornamented with beautiful flowers and various designs; then on top of this they put another dress, also constricted round the breast but somewhat shorter, coloured white or red or blue. In the two months of November and December, when it is a little cooler, they put on three or four caftans of silk, and on top of these an oblong dress made of English or Dutch cloth, again constricted at the breast, and generally red in colour. All orientals go barefoot, but these wear sandals of red or yellow leather very finely made. The ordinary and poor men, apart from foot bandages if they have them, wear solely a simple shift, tightly belted in; but the Arabs for the most part walk naked, with but one garment a few spans in size to cover their nakedness. On the left side, reaching almost halfway to their feet, they wear a long knife, and they let their hair grow long in the Turkish fashion and sometimes curl it. This it is the custom of the women to do, and to wear on their head a three-horned coif of wool; most of them wear on their bare arm a bracelet made of iron, the richer ones one of silver – and on their ankles also. They wear sandals instead of slippers. The women of greater standing like their men wear slippers, or small socks halfway up the calf, and above the heel an anklet of silver or gold; the ordinary women wear anklets of silver alloy, at least one finger thick, like a fetter, to make a noise when they walk; to obtain something of magnificence they put on long and wide ribbons of coloured stuff hanging to their heels, and if they have just a short trip to make they lift their skirts so that these fine ribbons can be visible. They wear a big shift as the men do, made of part-silk and hanging to their shoes, and an expensive caftan: the face is always covered with a costly veil which stretches from the forehead to the ground, as with our nuns, and over the faces, stretching to the waists, they wear another veil, pierced with holes just so that they can see. As part of their attire they display their ears adorned with five or six holes and laden with gems, precious stones, or rings of gold and silver. If they are of the Mahometan as opposed to the Christian faith, their splendour is completed by a gold or silver nose-ring in their perforated noses. The poor put on rings of glass or of iron instead of gold or silver. The forehead and even the neck is filled with golden pendants, and in addition, almost like a golden fleece, they wear gold pendants from the neck to the bust. I saw them with fruit, like little apples on a cord, strung around their neck as a further adornment.[2] Because the women are extremely fond of this fruit, a method of cultivation is practised, so that they can enjoy them throughout the year, whereby the tree is caused to bear three or four times a year: when the tree has borne its first crop, they uncover the roots and take all the earth away, whereupon in a day or so the leaves shrivel on the tree, and fall: then they again cover the roots with earth, water the tree, the tree puts out buds and then green leaves, and then, blossoming shortly after, it bears its second crop. By doing this three or four times a year they satisfy their appetite for apples, but trees treated like this do not last for long.

Although the women guard their faces so solicitously, that they be not seen, yet they pay little attention to the other parts of the body, especially the poor: for it often happens, when they leave the house to wash their shifts and ribbons, that, having no others save those they are wearing, they stay at the river washing as naked as God made them, with only their faces covered, and sit their while their washing dries in the sun; just as snakes care nothing for their tail, but guard their head and face and pay too little heed to the rest of the body.

When first their city took over the territory holy to Mahomet the natives gained several prerogatives, and none more beneficial than that the route via Gidda gives the most convenient access to the Prophet's tomb: the pilgrims throng in to Gidda, the alternative, reached either by the Red Sea or by an inconvenient

---

[2] Engravings of the costumes of Jeddah are reproduced in Niebuhr, *Voyage*, i, plates lvi and lvii.

little route by the sea shore, being a place called *Confede*,[3] an area to the south looking out over the furthest stretches of the empire of the Grand Sultan. From Gidda the pilgrims go on to Mecca, and ordinarily take fourteen hours on the journey, starting in the third hour of the afternoon, walking all through the night, and reaching Mecca at sunrise; through all that length of journey there is neither village nor habitation, only here and there Arabs living in tents, for the most part thieves and notable bandits whose aim is to despoil, often to murder, the pilgrims. Just as we Christians fare in the Holy Places of Palestine, so it goes on here with the Mahometans. The direct road to the east leads along the plain through the mountains where the Arabs live, and it is easy for them to kidnap the pilgrims, who because of the mountains cannot be freed.

---

[3] Qunfudhah. Bruce, who refers to the port as Konfodah, describes it as a 'small village, consisting of about two hundred miserable houses, built of green wood, and covered with mats made of the doom- or palm-tree.' Bruce, *op. cit.*, i, 297.

CHAPTER 7

THE CITY OF MECCA
AND THE CARAVANS

The Turkish city of Mecca is holy, is surrounded like Gidda with
a simple wall,[1] and is a little larger than that city: it is situated in
Arabia Deserta, near to Arabia Felix. Here dwells the *Scherif* or
Noble of the city, and governs it independently and absolutely,
although he is appointed thither by the Grand Sultan. It is to
him that the city looks, and for its defence he maintains about
nine hundred janissaries at his own charges, and, as my
Mahometan friends told me, the city is better built, of stone of
better shape and greater regularity, than is Gidda which I lately
described. And although several Christian writers boast that they
have personally visited Mecca, this is hard to accept as truth, since
this city, being regarded as holy by the Mahometans, may not be
entered by any Christian on pain of death, since they are thought
unworthy, and but dogs.[9] The mother city and birthplace of the
false prophet, and the goal of their pilgrimages, is held by his
followers in every imaginable honour.

Every year come six caravans, the first from Schami,[3] that is
Damascus, of twelve thousand people; the second from Cairo of
as many thousands or sometimes more; the third from Magreb[4]

---

[1] Mecca had long ceased to be a walled city.

[2] Prutky is misinformed. The Italian Lodovico di Varthema and the Englishman
Joseph Pitts had published eye-witness descriptions of Mecca in 1510 and 1704
respectively, the former having been a soldier in the escort of the pilgrim caravan,
and the latter a slave who had been forcibly converted to Islam. There had been
other European visitors to Mecca, the Venetian Dragon Zeno and the Portuguese
Pero da Covilhǎ in the fifteenth century, and the unknown author of a description
of the pilgrimage included by Hakluyt in the second edition of his *Principal
navigations.*

[3] Arabic *Shām*, Syria or Damascus. Burton, *op. cit.*, i, 69, states that the gate
through which the Damascus caravans came was called the Bāb al-Shāmī, or
'Syrian Gate'.

[4] *Maghrib*, i.e. N.W. Africa.

of about five thousand, smaller than the others but very warlike, because while the other caravans are always robbed by the Arabs in every pilgrimage, this one, from a warlike people, drives off the Arabs and chases them away; the fourth, the Baghdad, is from Babylonia, Persia, Armenia and suchlike places, and is two thousand strong; the fifth from the Yemen in Arabia Felix is two thousand; the sixth from Bassera[5] in India and the region bordering on Muscat is three thousand; Agami[6] provides four thousand.[7] The myth is that every year at least seventy-seven thousand must visit the *Beit Alla*,[8] as they call the temple and house of God, and that in default of this number the angels descend from Heaven to make up the deficiency. By the same token they affirm that seventy-seven winds, all birds, and every species of winged creature, must visit the temple once a year, and that all the Prophets of God of old used to visit it, especially Noah, at the time of the Flood, when the world was covered with water, who came with his ark to this site in Mecca where now stands the temple of God; and that removing his clothing, as I earlier recounted about the Mahometan pilgrims, he clothed himself in one single white garment called a *harram*,[9] and did what *Tavaf*[10] did, that is went seven times round the city in his *harram* in the Mahometan fashion, an observance that the modern pilgrims carefully repeat.

This Beit Alla is the principal mosque of the Mahometan world, the goal of all the pilgrimages from all the provinces of this sect: as their fable tells it, God at the creation of the world made a little spittle in the place where now is the Beit Alla, and by divine command that was transformed into earth, from which the angels later made the temple; and that God told them that it was his

[5] Basra is, of course, in Iraq, not India.

[6] Arabic '*Ajam*, non-Arabs especially Persians.

[7] Burckhardt in the early nineteenth century estimated that Mecca was visited annually by over 120,000 pilgrims, while Wellsted believed that 2,000 arrived from India, 1,800 from the Malay coast, 4,000 from the Persian Gulf, 20,000 from Turkey, Asia Minor, the interior of Africa, Suez and Kosair, 3,000 from Hodeida, Mocha and the South Arabian ports, and 2,000 from 'ports on the Abyssinian side, Suwākin, Dahlak, etc.' Wellsted, *op. cit.*, ii, 269–70.

[8] *Bayt Allāh*, 'the House of God,' the mosque incorporating the Ka'bah. This building has been described by many travellers, among them Joseph Pitts (Foster, *op. cit.*, pp. 24–31), and, at considerable length, Burton, *op. cit.*, ii, 294–326.

[9] Arabic *iḥrām*, the prescribed clothing assumed by all pilgrims when they enter the sacred territory. Pilgrims, according to Burton, *op. cit.*, ii, 139, wore 'nothing but two new cotton cloths, each six feet long by three and a half broad, white with narrow red stripes and fringes'.

[10] Arabic *ṭawāf*, the circumambulation of the Ka'bah.

will to create the race of mankind in that very place, that mankind might adore his divine Majesty; at the time of the Flood the angels carried the temple up to Heaven, leaving fourteen figures made of horn called *kiab* – from which the name *Kiabe* is given to the pilgrimage to Mecca.

They also maintain that when the Patriarch Abraham came here, God ordered him to rebuild the temple in the same place and to the same design as the first temple which the angels had taken up to Heaven, and that it stood so exactly perpendicular that if the old temple chanced to fall it would fall exactly onto the old foundations. While Abraham was rebuilding the temple, a stone beneath his feet moved of its own accord and raised itself upwards as the needs of construction demanded, like a working platform, so that to this day it is called the Stone of Abraham, is held in the greatest awe, is covered always with a cloth worked in green, gold and silver, and has on top of it a round roof made of lead. Anyone wishing to see this stone or to kiss it must pay ten reals and a fine garment for the privilege, and, a cavity being visible on the stone, which is said to have been worn into it as an everlasting sign by Abraham's feet when he was standing during the construction, the cavity is filled with water which is drunk with great reverence.

With the lapse of time and during the course of various wars the temple, the Beit Alla, was again destroyed, but again rebuilt, and idols were installed there, and worshipped until the coming of Mahomet. He earlier had for many years worshipped at Jerusalem, the story goes, until an angel appeared and ordered him to leave Jerusalem and betake himself to Mecca, telling him that from henceforth only in Mecca was the house of God to be found, and that only there should God be worshipped; though up to this time this house of God had been unknown to the whole world. Such is the Mahometan myth of the origin of Mecca, and such is the reason why at least once in his lifetime each Mahometan is bound to visit the Beit Alla and there worship God; and wherever Mahometans are, when they pray, they always turn their faces to this holy place, for only thus are prayers granted.

Finally through various accidents to the fabric the temple of God was again destroyed, and again rebuilt by the Sultan Murat,[11] whose descendants rule today as his successors, through the intercession, say the devout, of his friend Mahomet the beloved

[11] Sultan Murad IV, 1623–1640.

of God. The temple is built in the form of a square with no roof, as I am told, and with a cloister provided for walking; when the rains come the water runs off in a golden channel, and everyone considers themselves indeed fortunate, as they are enabled to wash themselves, and they declare a jubilee and a general remission of sins. Within the temple is written up in large letters *Sultan Murat Chan built this.* The one gateway is eight feet high, to be climbed by seven steps, the whole made out of silver gilt, key, bolt and all; the temple walls are of white marble, are inscribed with Arabic characters, and are wholly covered with black tapestries beautifully interwoven with gold, and embroidered so that the ends of the threads bear in gold letters the words *Alla, u Mahometh* (God and Mahomet), as I have more minutely described in part 1. With great pomp the tapestries are escorted to Mecca, and are changed every year; the beneficiaries are the old Eunuchs, the guardians of the temple, who cut the old tapestries into tiny pieces and sell them at a high price as especially holy relics; however, that part of the tapestry which covers the gate belongs to the *Scherif*, and, when the day of the pilgrimage called *Hagg*[12] falls on a Friday, it is called *Hagg Gebir*,[13] a great day, as it were a Jubilee or holy year, and then that part which covers the gate belongs to the Sultan in Constantinople. The Mahometans declare that those who visit Mecca on a great day like this derive as much spiritual benefit as they would from seven successive years of pilgrimage.

Outside the temple some black stones, beautifully worked, greatly adorn the mosque, which however the Turks dare not always enter at will, but only on fixed days and months. To understand this you must know that the Arabs divide the year into twelve lunar months: 1 *Aaschur*, 2 *Sofar*, 3 *Rabiaa Elauol*, 4 *Rabbiaa Eltani*, 5 *Gemad Elauel*, 6 *Gemad Elarhek*, 7 *Ragaab*, 8 *Schabuan*, 9 *Ramadan*, 10 *Schaual*, 11 *Gade*, 12 *Elhagg*.[14] So in

[12] Arabic *ḥajj*, or pilgrimage to Mecca.
[13] Arabic *ḥajj kabīr*, or 'great pilgrimage'. This occurred (Burton, *op. cit.*, ii, 281, notes) when the 'day of Arafat' happened to fall, auspiciously, on a Friday.
[14] The names of the Muslim months are: 1. Muharram 2. Safar. 3. Rabī'al-awwal 4. Rabī'al-thānī 5. Jumādā al-ūlá 6. Jumādā al-ukhrā 7. Rajab 8. Sha'bān 9. Ramaḍān 10. Shawwāl 11. Dhū al-qa'dah 12. Dhū al-ḥijjah. Prutky's Aaschur represents 'Āshūrā, which is not the name of the month but of the commemoration of the death of the Prophet's grandson Husain at the battle of Karbālā, A.D. 680. For further information on the calendar, see G. S. P. Freeman-Grenville, *Muslim and Christian calendars*, 2nd edition, Oxford, 1977.

the month of *Aaschur* the temple may be entered on the tenth day, in the month of *Rabiaa Eltani* on the twelfth when they solemnly celebrate the birthday of Mahomet. In the seventh month *Ragaab* it is the twenty-seventh day, and in the eighth month *Schabuan* the fifteenth. In the ninth month *Ramadan* it is open twice, on the first and last day of ceremony when they celebrate the end of the fast, for they observe a fast for the whole of this month. In the month of *Gade* the day of opening is the twelfth, but in the month of Hagg the temple may be entered only by the two princes of Cairo and of Damascus, who have with their own hands brought their two precious tapestries to be hung in the temple.

For the whole time of the pilgrimage it is strictly forbidden to gamble for money or to play cards on pain of death, and all other contracts or mutual pledges of whatever sort are said to be *haram*,[15] that is unlawful and punished by excommunication; an example to all Christians, who, worshipping the true God, ought to keep truly holy the days of festival, and to refrain from so many unlawful silly jokes and chatter.

It should be noted that while the temple is open on definite days, except during Hagg, on the day following it is open solely for women, for either sex is strictly enjoined to enter separately, only the men on one day and only the women on the next. In other places women are refused entrance to the mosques as being impure, so that they believe that they are shut out from the Kingdom of Heaven, and will linger outside Heaven's Gate in a special place of their own; but as a special favour, and by a dispensation granted by four doctors of the law, they are permitted to enter this temple. For this reason all the noblewomen of Gidda journey to Mecca for the specified occasions and stay there for two or three days, doing honour to the false prophet Mahomet.

[15] Arabic *haram*, whatever is prohibited under religious law.

CHAPTER 8

FURTHER POINTS OF INTEREST
ABOUT THE MAHOMETAN TEMPLE

This temple of God, as the Mahometans believe it, is set in a precinct surrounded by an arcade, whose columns are war cannon, two and two making up one column, their muzzles filled with iron and each supporting the other; the Mahometans say that these cannon were captured in victories over the Christians. In the four corners of the arcade stand four pulpits, into each of which mounts a doctor of the law and preaches therefrom.[1] The doctors are divided into four different sects, and preach four different sermons, each praising up his own sect; but the sect of the Grand Sultan is reckoned the chief, as being descended lineally from Mahomet, and all the others are subordinate.

In the month of Hagg there is a great celebration of the tenth day, called the Day of Sacrifice; thus on the eighth day the pilgrims come to Mecca with a leader or teacher who instructs them in the accustomed prayers and ceremonies to be observed in Tavaf, that is the walking round or visitation which the inhabitants frequently repeat and solemnize in their pig-like manner. Then on the ninth day of this month one and all hasten off, some on camels and some on asses, to a mountain twelve hours to the east of Mecca called *Gebel Elauraffat*,[2] the Mount of Recognition, otherwise Mount of Sacrifice. Those learned in the Alcoran relate

---

[1] The four doctors represent the four schools of law. See J. Schacht. *Introduction to Islamic law*, Oxford, 1982.

[2] Arabic Jabal 'Arafāt. This place of pilgrimage was said to have been visited, according to Pitts, by 'no less than seventy thousand souls every year', though he doubted if they could actually amount to that number. Foster, *op. cit.*, pp. 34–35. Pilgrims leave Mecca on the eighth day of the month and pray on the mountain of Arafat early the following morning. Burton, *op. cit.*, ii, 289–90. See also Eldon Rutter, *The holy cities of Arabia* (London, 1928), i, 158–9 and map opposite p. 154.

that it was here that Abraham made to sacrifice Isaac; the reason
for the name Recognition is that according to their lewd myth
they lewdly fabricate that Adam after the expulsion from Paradise
here for the first time had carnal knowledge of Eve in the
matrimonial bond; and that to this day the bottom of the rock
retains his footprints, which are several paces apart from each
other because Adam's feet were as long as columns, and he was
of enormous stature to match.

The mountain is of no great size or height, but middling, with
a large flat space at the foot, where the pilgrims individually try
to climb: but if from old age or infirmity any is unable, he stays
at the foot of the mountain, along with those for whom there is
no room on the mountain because of the crowd. Notwithstanding
this, everyone who makes the due sacrifice is approved by the
doctors of the law as though they had made the climb. For crowds
of individuals hurry out on the ninth day of this month to find
a place on the mountain wherein to sleep and prelude their
sacrifice with filthiness and the iniquities of the flesh. On the next
day, the tenth of the month and the seventh of the week, is the
Festival of Sacrifices, and everyone slaughters a male lamb: if
anyone is kept by poverty from paying for one, four or five club
together for a sacrifice: if even that is beyond their means, they
have to fast for the preceding three days. When in the course of
sacrifice they strike the lamb with the knife, they utter up these
words *Alla hu ackbar*[3] (God is Most Great), adding that this
oblation is for the remission of their sins. The lamb having been
slaughtered, the flesh is given over to the poor, and because they
cannot eat up so large a quantity, most of it goes rotten. The
story behind *Alla hu ackbar* is this: before Mahomet's coming the
local inhabitants worshipped idols, and with all their fellows used
to worship on this mountain their god called *Ackbar*, which in
Arabic means Most Great: to this god they made offerings of
incense and other barbarous blood sacrifices. The Turkish belief
is that on this mountain Mahomet preached to the inhabitants
the tenets of his sect, that they must worship one God and obey
the Alcoran; but when they showed themselves unwilling to
relinquish their god Ackbar, to conciliate them he permitted

[3] The Arabic incantation *Allāhu Akbar!* 'God is most great!' The comparative
major in Latin means both *very(most) great* and *greater*, giving more force to the
pun at the end of the paragraph.

them to worship the true God, and to serve their idol Ackbar at the same time. So in their sacrifices the Turks pronounce words that sound and mean *Alla u Ackbar*, or 'Let us sacrifice to God and also to our idol Ackbar;' and because it is in the Alcoran the Mahometans observe this to the letter. Many years later when this practice had spread throughout Arabia and outside this particular sect, the Mahometans realised that it was a gross error to render honour not only to the true God but also to the idol *Ackbar* as well, and to the letter *u* added the letter *h*, the letters *hu* together meaning 'is' in Arabic; in this way they kept to Mahomet's precept. By this piece of clever sophistry, Alla hu Ackbar, God is most great, avoids all taint of idolatry, meaning that God is greater than any idol.

When the sacrifice is finished the Scherif, or another senior official, begins in a loud voice to declaim the usual Turkish prayer with great devotion, the congregation repeat it after him with tears, and the ceremony is over. An express is at once sent to the Sultan in Constantinople, notifying him that the debt of sacrifice has been paid with due devotion. When evening has come everyone comes down the mountain and goes on elsewhere, to a smaller mountain called *Gebel Giamrat*[4] or Mount of Stones, although literally it should be taken as Mount of Sparks. There the individuals pick up stones, called *giamrat*, and throw them on to the Mount of Sacrifice, not knowing the reason for this but everyone following his own judgement. But, as I mentioned earlier, the Mahometans on Mount Sinai throw stones as a memorial of the receipt of the Alcoran, and in their ignorance these do the same here also. Mahomet being quite unlettered was incapable of producing a book like the Alcoran, but as I said previously it was mainly composed by a Nestorian monk called Sergius, and by another person called Aali; the Arabs give to Sergius the honourable title of *Abu Becker*.[5] To establish the divine origin of the Alcoran, as I mentioned in Chapter 3, Mahomet had previously hidden Sergius in a water tank, or in a pit in the middle of the mountain, with the written book of the law; then to persuade the people that it truly was of God, he held up in

[4] Jabal Jamrah, the mountain of the pebbles, where the pilgrims throw stones, the lapidation of Satan.
[5] Abu-Bekr, 'Father of the Virgin', (572–635), was in fact Muhammad's father-in-law and became the first Caliph. Sergius the Nestorian remains unidentified.

his hand another book of blank pages and addressed them; 'Look carefully, here I have a book, totally unwritten, which I am about to put into this tank, and you are about to see written upon it the whole of the law which I have previously declared to you.' Persuading them with various conjuring tricks that he was speaking to God, he at length cried out: 'If it be the will of God, let writing appear on this book which I have put into the tank, and let it be shown again to the people that they may see it.' To the general audience Sergius replied out of the tank, and tying the written book to the same rope to which the blank one had been tied, he deceived the people with a pretended miracle. Mahomet then made out that it had been divinely revealed to him that everyone must collect three stones and throw them into the tank, as an everlasting memorial of the divine grace; so Sergius was stoned to death and reaped his just reward. The annual stone-throwing of such crowds of pilgrims has raised in this place quite a little hill.

On the next day, the eleventh of the month, all betake themselves to the nearby village of *Mina*[6] where they wash, cut their hair, trim their nails, resume the clothes that they had previously taken off, and return to Mecca, where they remain for two more days: then on the third day they are free to sell and to buy what is needful for them. They go to a place opposite the temple of God called *Zemzem*,[7] where there is a well of water; the Mahometans claim that when Abraham cast his handmaid Hagar out from his household together with their son Ishmael (Genesis xvi and xxi), it was in this place that the water failed her and she spoke the sacred text *Let me not see the death of the child,* and sat herself down a good bowshot off. Whereupon the angel appeared to her and showed her the well of water. Hagar seeing the water ran rejoicing to the place where she had left the child, and returning to the well revived both of them. For this reason all Mahometans alike, small and large, young men and old, are bound to walk three times round this well, and those who through

---

[6] Minā, later known as Munā, was three miles N.E. of Mecca. Burton, *op. cit.,* ii, 180, described it as 'a place of considerable security,' and says that during the pilgrimage period it became 'a 'World's Fair' of Moslem merchants'. See also Foster, *op. cit.,* pp. 36–37.

[7] Zamzam, the holy well of the Mosque of the Prophet. Foster, *op. cit.* pp. 33–4, 38–9, Burton, *op. cit.,* i, 331, 338, ii, 162–4.

infirmity are not strong enough must at least lift their feet and make as though they were walking. So ignorant are they of the Scripture, and so uneducated, so credulous of the lies and machinations of their false prophet.

They treat the well with the utmost devotion, washing face, hands and feet in it, and drinking it, so that they may take it away with them all over the world. But when all this is done, they are permitted to stay no longer than the fourteenth of the month, and anyone kept later than this by business transactions must pay a large sum to the Scherif for permission to delay; their licence may be extended until the eighteenth of the month, but on this day all without exception must take their departure. It is indeed a sight to see so many thousand pilgrims, laden with goods, quickly packing their belongings and eagerly preparing for departure; so they return through the desert to Medina.

One further point to note is that, when the pilgrims having resumed their clothing are returning to Mecca from Mount Giamrat, that is the day on which the princes of Cairo and Damascus, who have brought the new tapestries, hang them in the temple. The old ones are taken down, cut into small pieces, and taken off into the farthest corners of the world as precious relics. The Scherif is each year obliged to send a gift to the Sultan at Constantinople, and, if the Day of Sacrifice falls on a Friday, he also has to send him a piece of the tapestry. But it is easy for him to deceive the Sultan and avoid this obligation: he purposely changes the first day of the month, and counts from the first day on which the moon becomes visible there; thus they pretend that they have seen the moon one day earlier or later, the Scherif is freed from his obligation to send gifts, and the Feast of Sacrifice instead of on the tenth is held on the eleventh day.

The Mahometans maintain that within Mount *Aarafat* there is another rock formation or hole in the rocks, and that, when the fallen angels were cast down from Heaven into the Abyss, they fell into this cleft in the rocks, which is called to this day *Bellad Elablis*[8] Land of Devils.

At this time of sacrifice the women, at other times kept strictly within doors, enjoy complete freedom as though at a time of carnival. They play games and practical jokes, they walk abroad

---

[8] Arabic *Bilād Iblīs*, the land of Iblis.

for these five days in their best clothes, they wander the streets visiting houses large and small, and they regard themselves as being made new, or restored, by this year, and as if they were outside themselves; when they meet notables they dare to strike them in joke, they chatter with fun, beat drums, dance in the streets, sing songs, and visit and feast each other. Then on the night of the tenth all collect together and in one crowd of drummers, handclappers, singers, they roam the streets for hours: for these five days they court every sort of meeting with men, which at other times is forbidden them, and live as they please. The holiday over they each return to their old homes as though to a prison, looking forward with great eagerness to the next Year of Sacrifice. This privilege, outside Gidda, is extended to no woman in the whole Turkish empire.

In this days of jubilee the whole city could easily be looted, and by the weakest of enemies, because apart from the women there are scarcely twenty military men left, the rest being either invalids or old men.

CHAPTER 9

JOURNEY TO MEDINA
TO MAHOMET'S TOMB

With the ceremonies completed, the pilgrims leave Mecca and make their way to Medina to the north, and are so plagued by midges and flies on the way that they can scarcely advance without perpetually defending themselves from the attacks as it were of swarms of bees. There are three alternative practicable routes to Mecca (*sic*), one by sea *via* Gidda, another by land, for those travelling towards Jemen, while the third route leads to Medina over the desert, taking eight days, and this is the one usually chosen by individuals.

The city of Medina was of old called *Trebat*,[1] and even now many Mahometans are called Trebati. It was once the seat of a Greek bishopric, and is of a good size and well built, with houses like those in Mecca. The governor, appointed by the Grand Sultan, is always a *Tavass*[2] or eunuch, and the choice goes to one who has long shown himself the faithful guardian of the imperial harem. The young boys are castrated in their fifth or sixth year; not simply the testicles after the Christian fashion, but the whole of the genitalia are cut off, and thus, the wound being difficult to cure, most of them die; so those who are cured fetch a good price. To such eunuchs is entrusted the governorship and rule, and having proved themselves faithful in guarding the Sultan's wives, so in other spheres will they be faithful: in Medina is an enormous treasure to guard, given by the chiefs of the

---

[1] Trebat represents Yathrib, a pre-Islamic name for the city. Muslim personal names are not derived from it, and it was not the seat of a Greek or any other bishop.
[2] The principal of the great mosque at Medina was traditionally a eunuch, in Arabic ṭawāshī. For the castration of eunuchs, see N. M. Penzer. *The harem*, 1936.

Mahometan sects, and because the eunuchs can hope for no children, their desires turn towards the acquisition of treasure: such is the Sultan's political guile.

There are a thousand janissaries stationed in Medina to guard the body of Mahomet who is buried in the mosque there. So many writers have declared that his body is held in an iron coffin which hangs in the air held up by four pillars of adamant, but this is confirmed neither by oral tradition nor by the written works of the Mahometans. I have been told by many acquaintances, by eminent Turkish friends, by natives of substance, and indeed by a Venetian spy and explorer called Nicolao, that the corpse is buried, with the head covered, in the middle of the floor of the mosque, and sealed by a sepulchral stone a foot high. This area near the stone is held in great reverence, and to avoid the defilement of human feet it is always kept closed, and covered by a black cere-cloth, ornamented with gold and silver, which is the gift of the last-appointed sultan of Constantinople: he has the obligation of preserving it for the whole of his life, and with his death his successor provides a fresh one. The burial place is fenced off by a grille of gilded iron about two feet high, with hanging lamps at intervals, and the only permitted entrants are the sacristan, the senior Scherif or holy man, to trim and repair the lamps, and the two princes before mentioned. Apart from these no one, neither from devotion nor, even less, curiosity, may lift the cere-cloth or view the place of the stone. The story is that some years ago a general decay was noticed under the cloth, and that, wishing to remove it, the authorities sent in an unfortunate young man for this purpose, who on completion of his task was struck dead, they say because he had seen the tomb of the prophet.[3] The pilgrims enter the mosque, touch and kiss the grille in all devoutness, and greet Mahomet each in his own manner, calling him friend of God, holy Prophet, lovable, God's most loved creation; their tears and sighs put to shame the Christians' colder demonstrations of reverence.

The natives of Medina claim that being situated among mountains their city is cold in winter; as neither snow falls nor water freezes, it cannot even be called chilly by Italian standards. It is

[3] This tradition had earlier been mentioned by both Pitts and Daniel, neither of whom however paid it any credence. Foster, *op. cit.*, pp. 47, 77.

only to the natives that this seems so, being so used to excessive heat that at a light breath of cold wind they shiver throughout the veins of their body and almost freeze to the marrow of their bones. But their doors and windows being ever open they are exposed to every breath of draught, as I have learned by my own experience.

Near Mecca, three days' journey from Gidda, is a village to the east called Taif, inhabited by Arabs, where in winter the climate is quite cold and in the height of summer tempered from the heat. Here in the hot weather come most of the inhabitants of Gidda from that city to this, because the heat at Gidda is enough to take away the appetite for eating, while at Mecca or Taif they eat with good appetite, and the more because the figs and fruit are better there; the mountains nourish streams of water which irrigate the land, and the various fruit and produce are carried thence to Gidda and the neighbourhood.

At Gidda for at least five months the heat is so excessive that neither pen nor tongue can describe it, and only experience can bring comprehension of it; around noon for six or seven hours it is so hot that neither man, beast nor bird can be seen in the open, and the natives of the city go about the streets stark naked with just their cloth leg-bands, or a shift, or a loin-cloth to cover their private parts. Inside, the houses are like furnaces, while outside, exposed to the heat of the sun, they are like burning coals, and all nature droops. One remarkable thing I noticed, the opposite to Cairo, where it is the south wind that brings the great heat similar to that at Gidda, while the north wind, which generally gets up in the evening after sunset, brings coolness and relief; the south wind by contrast brings the heat with it, prevents sleep at night like a flame bursting forth from a lit stove, suffocates, lowers vitality, causes constitutions to fail – so that most of the inhabitants sleep on the verandah, or, in extremity, out of doors. In Gidda and Mecca, on the other hand, and in neighbouring parts, it is the south winds which bring the cool temperate air, and what revives the people of Cairo brings tribulations to the people of Gidda: the cause that produces these effects may be a quirk of nature or some natural property of the terrain.

It is true to say that between Cairo, the Mediterranean and the Ocean there lie the three Arabias; Arabia Petrosa or Rocky starts this side of the river Jordan in Palestine, and extends to the shores of the Adriatic Sea (*sic*) and down to the Red Sea, to the Egyptian boundary at Suez; it includes Mount Sinai, and all that territory where the children of Israel wandered in the Arabian desert for forty years after the crossing of the Red Sea, as the holy text says in Exodus xvi. 35 *The children of Israel did eat manna forty years, until they came to a land inhabited.* There is nothing in that desert but high mountains, rocks and crags, and nothing grows there but a few medicinal herbs and, where water is found among the mountains, some fruit and vegetables. Next to this is Arabia Deserta, an enormous plain, empty and bare, containing a few sandy mountains, rough but not very high; it has a few inhabitants towards the Nile and extends to the shores of the Red Sea, from Lembo to Gezan and almost to the mountains near Mt *Tombol*,[4] where the Grand Sultan's empire bounds the kingdom of Jemen: it contains Gidda, Mecca, Medina, etc. Next to this is Arabia Felix, in which lies the kingdom of Jemen. I call it Felix not because all felicity is to be found there, but because it has more produce than the other two Arabias: much coffee, which is exported to all parts of the world, peaches, lemons, pears, and many other sorts of fruit, of remarkable flavour because there is little or no cold weather. The natives give the name winter to the month of February, when the south wind blows and makes the climate cool for twenty or at most thirty days – whereupon the intense heat returns. In these few days the temperature drops as low as in the month of May or June in Germany. The south winds last only to the end of June, and the ships sail from Suez with the north wind to Gidda, and return thence with the south wind. This can be seen each year; but if this rule is neglected the voyage takes eighty or ninety days, and many a time they put out from one port four or five times, and have to return; not only is navigation impeded, but ships are often wrecked and cast away.

In this area rain generally falls in the months of December and January, more in some years, less in others, always preceded by a storm of six hours duration, which generally happens four or five times a year. Without wells or streams all the inhabitants are careful to collect this rainwater for use throughout the year.

---

[4] Qadimbal islet, Bruce's Kotumbal, off the Arabian coast about 85 kms. S. of Hali, *Red Sea and Gulf of Aden pilot* (London, 1955) p. 340.

The rich build themselves cisterns outside the town called *saharig*;[5] a hole is dug in the earth and lined throughout with squared stone which is ground together and covered with a seal of lime and oiled flax or tow; the base is then pounded for eight days with twigs or rods, care being taken not to crack the stones lest the water leak out through the crack and the cistern run dry: so carefully are the stones joined together and sealed with oil that they appear glued into one single piece of stone. The cistern is kept filled with water for a whole year, with the proviso that for the first year the water is not good, but tastes foul to drink, with the taste of the stone, the lime, the oil and the salt from the stone chippings; but in years following the water is good, sweet and clear to drink. The poor having no cisterns drink the water that collects during the rains in ponds or ditches; at the beginning of February this is good enough, but later in the year, when it has been exposed to the sun's great heat, their drinking water is stinking and full of worms. Indeed in the other ten months the water turns all sorts of colours, green, red, white or black, dependent on the colour of the worms therein: they are present in such quantity that in one measure of water, when the worms are strained off it, they make up one eighth part of the whole, of different shapes and sizes. The worst months for the populace are October and November, when the water, because of its content of worms, can scarcely be drunk without injury to heath, and the Bassa sets penalties on the drinking of stagnant water: all are compelled to buy cistern-stored water at a high price, which is very profitable for those who have a greater or more ample supply. But when the rains tend rather to fail, then there is a great shortage, and one German pint sells for two florins; the poor die of thirst in no small numbers, despite the great charity with which the Mahometans treat them, the Alcoran requiring provision to be made for ten out of every hundred poor.

Seldom in this city does one encounter a merchant who is not rich,[6] and not only the natives but foreign men of ability attain

----

[5] Arabic *ṣahārīj.*

[6] Bruce, who states that a 'great and sudden influx of wealth from the India trade' took place once a year, claims that 'very little advantage' however accrued to the port. The customs revenue, he claims, was 'immediately sent to a needy sovereign, and a hungry set of relations, dependents and ministers at Mecca', while the gold was returned to the ships 'in bags and boxes.' *Op. cit.*, i, 279.

to great wealth by continual trading with India, Egypt, and various European countries. Currency is to be seen in such quantity as can be matched scarcely anywhere else,[7] Austrian imperial reals, Venetian gold pieces, Spanish patacas, occasional florins, a few half and quarter florins: in very short supply is Turkish small change, medins or para as they are called: for one real the rate of exchange is scarcely seventy-five para, though in other parts of the Turkish empire it is at least eighty. So many thousands of people make their livelihood simply in money changing, and get rich from it. Whereas among the Mahometans the Venetian gold piece passes for currency, and in Cairo has a value of two reals and five medins, yet in Gidda, Mocha and the neighbourhood it is exchanged only for two reals; so that Europeans travelling to these parts must carry not gold pieces but Imperial reals, but must conceal them on the person and not carry them in the purse, lest they pay to the customs the ten per cent tax.

[7] Jeddah, because of its position in international trade, made use of many kinds of currency. Niebuhr, *Voyage*, i, 227, mentions the circulation of money from Venice, Cairo, Constantinople and Germany.

CHAPTER 10

FURTHER DETAILS OF THIS AREA,
AND OF THE CURES FOR ILLNESS

I mentioned earlier that in Gidda thieves were seldom or never to be found, because those arrested are rigorously punished: for the first and the second offence they are mildly reprimanded, but on the third occasion they are executed without any formal process of trial. In Cairo or elsewhere in the Turkish empire there is no such hesitation, but at the first offence the guilty party is executed by decapitation, or, as a mark of favour, the hands or feet are amputated and the stumps plunged into boiling oil to stop the flow of blood; or, more arbitrarily, the knife is plunged into the offender's neck, and he dies a barbarous death. Justice being so strict, although the goods of many thousands of arrivals are spread out over a wide area for the customs' examination, none of them is lost and they are kept in perfect condition. Furthermore the honesty of the Turks is praiseworthy, whether in weights or in measures: they reckon a hundredweight at one hundred and twenty pounds, a pound at twelve ounces, and an ounce at twelve drams. For anyone seeking to have his boxes of goods transported to his lodging, there are at hand a number of what are called *Hamalin*,[1] who to the admiration of the onlookers carry a weight of four hundred and even five hundred pounds, which elsewhere two or three men would hardly be able to lift; but they string a rope or belt around the load, put it on their back, bind the belt carefully round the forehead, and step freely forward, now up now down, as though their load were but light: such strength have they acquired from the continued exercise of their labour, exceeding that of any European.

---

[1] Arabic *ḥammāl*, porter, colloquial plural *ḥammālīn*.

I said earlier that there are quantities of flies and midges, though no fleas even in the hottest weather: the mosquitoes are everywhere and particularly virulent at night when they disturb one's sleep, though in January and February, which are a little cooler, they disappear, and in their place come clouds of fleas which are worse than the mosquitoes. The Arabs make large bags out of finely-woven material, and they and their wives remove their clothing and get into these bags; then they tie them with a string about the head, and sleep soundly well protected from the mosquitoes and fleas alike: this is the custom throughout the whole kingdom of Jemen.

We missionaries on our way to Ethiopia reached Gidda at a time of unbearable heat, and spent three weeks there, when we suffered in no small degree from flies, midges, and mosquitoes.[2] Since I was the only skilled surgeon, my colleagues enjoyed a measure of rest, but I was busy with nothing but treating diseases: visiting the sick, preparing and administering medicine, treating bruises and wounds, cutting veins and letting blood: I had hardly a free minute from sunrise to sunset, and this seemed the more difficult for me in that my two colleagues knew nothing of medicine and I had to do all the work by myself alone: I asked for no fee in return, and worked solely for the love of the Only God, unless a patient made me an unsolicited present. This surprised the Mahometans considerably, who were in ignorance of our true profession, much more of our design of gaining souls for God. I was intent to persuade the natives to favour our onward journey, and we all three prayed to the Most High God, for the sake of the souls we were to gain, to deign to bless my medical labours and to give them a successful outcome. God at all times works miracles through unworthy hands, and whatever remedies I applied even in the most extreme cases brought a cure: the sufferers from accidents and wounds, even the most ulcerated, were successfully healed, as I recounted in Chapter 4. The result was that the sick came in to me from Mecca, *Hodide*[3] and the neighbourhood, and thanks be to the Most High they almost all went away in better health: whereupon even more came in with

---

[2] The Jeddah area was described by Bruce, *op. cit.*, i, 279, as 'the most unwholesome part of Arabia'.

[3] The port of Ḥudaydeh, some seventy miles south of Luhaiya. Niebuhr, *Description*, p. 199.

their troubles, and several poor men who stank of putrefaction were cured of discharging ulcers. I must mention two Arabs, whose feet were rotted and eaten away to the bones and sinews and crawled with worms, at the stench and horror of which I was sick when I saw it; I applied the appropriate remedies, and a few days later dawned the hope of a cure, and healthy flesh started to form. A poor native of Jerusalem, a worker in copper or brass, who suffered from a cancer in the bone of the foot, was cured in seven days to the general amazement, and departed in good health. When another was brought to me, a paralytic who was gangrened throughout his whole body, my every sense abhorred the sight of him. But compassion overcame my reluctance, and I applied first some corrosives and smeared him with Egyptian ointment: the patient then suffered a relapse, from his very poor internal condition, and I feared that he was about to die, all the more that I knew the temper of the Mahometans, and that I should not have escaped death myself, as they would have held me responsible for the death of another. But thanks to God's mercy, within a few days he was better and began to be cured of his gangrene; whereupon the whole population brought me expensive articles of food and unsolicited presents of money, and I gained unasked more food than I had eaten while remaining with my colleagues. God is truly merciful, who deigns to entrust the virtue of healing to the hands of the feeble, and we praise the Holy Providence of His pitying Godhead. We were everywhere believed to be in all the world the most renowned wise men, doctors and surgeons, the populace not knowing that the divine Doctor works through the feeble hands of his servants. Just then the favourite wife of the chief commander was unexpectedly struck down with a lethal illness, and was in great agony, and for two days unable to speak. When they called me in to attend her I was much concerned that, if I brought too effective a relief to such a dangerous condition, we might suffer further delay on our already protracted journey, and that I might lose all the advantage that I had built up by previous cures. But by the further assistance of the divine Doctor, Who knows the real desires of our hearts and minds, I eased the patient with a mild sudorific after previously administering some drops of strengthening cordial: she grew visibly better, and in a short time was restored to her former good health, to the general admiration.

Those who linger in these parts are much to be pitied. If disease attacks them there is neither doctor nor medicine, and they die wretchedly, save those who by the chance of good luck are restored to health, and give thanks to God. Worse than this, the dead have to suffer the loss of their goods as well as of their life, for the local judges, just and unjust alike, seize a tenth part, called *beitelmal*,[4] of all goods and chattels, though there is no law to support them. The unjust judges moreover, with real inequity, share out among themselves not the tenth part but the bulk of the inheritance of orphans, so that not seldom the children of the richest parents find themselves in beggary, and are debarred from any recourse. It is important for foreigners to watch carefully over their own health, lest with death come loss of possessions. In the long period of great heat and bodily perspiration it is easy to catch cold in the evening air and be laid low with a sudden fever; a careless failure to consult a doctor immediately, and one's life is in danger. As with the visiting caravans, so with the individual who neglects the climate, alike they lose their life and their goods, and bring no small profit to the local Bassa.

The Bassa with pomp and ceremony goes out to meet the two arriving princes of the caravans of Cairo and Damascus, and the order of march is as follows: First a horseman riding before the Bassa, carrying a white or red standard, followed by two other finely dressed officers accompanied by a crowd of slaves on foot. Second, four fine horses covered with tiger skins, one led behind the other. Third, two so-called Nejacter with silver axes, with one hundred Janissaries behind them. Fourth, many noble Turks on foot, richly dressed in the Constantinopolitan manner with lofty turbans and gold and silver sashes set with precious stones; behind these the two major officers the Kiechia and the Vizier of the Bassa. Fifth, the junior officers. Sixth, the Bassa himself on horseback, richly apparelled in the greatest splendour and magnificence, with around him four Mamelukes or slaves equally splendid; there is also present one called the Saragg, who marches

---

[4] Arabic *bayt al-māl*, the Treasury.

close to the Bassa and keeps his hand on the Bassa's horse. Seventh, a further hundred marching Janissaries, his own body-guard, the previous hundred being the garrison which the city has to maintain. Lastly, the musicians, mounted on camels, four small drums and four large, trumpets blown in the Turkish manner, and some fifes. An innumerable crowd followed shout-ing and applauding to dignify the ceremony; though, when we saw it, nothing could better restore our spirits than our immediate departure over the Red Sea.

Our Mahometan friends were much grieved by our departure, so contrary to their wishes, the less welcome because unexpected, and tried all ways to detain us within the city. The principal citizens guaranteed us, beside an annual stipend, an abundance of goods, and generous free accommodation, and those who had been cured gave surety for even more. Their promises were empty and afforded us little or no temptation, for we were fired with the desire not of money but of converting souls, and we had long despised the perishable riches of this world. Seeing that none of their promises were proving effective, they prepared for us a further snare, and the rich offered their own beautiful daughters in marriage to us, both black and white, and sought to entice us with the desires of the flesh. By the help of the Most High I overcame these tricks of the Devil, and told one of my closer friends that already before leaving Egypt I had contracted myself to marry the most fair, beautiful, and graceful girl with whom it was impossible for me to break faith, for two reasons: first, that the Egyptian was of such elegance and beauty, and was the first to receive my vows, and that save always for the Holy Virgin her like was not to be found, and that she was my dearly loved betrothed whom it was wrong to desert. The second reason was equally inhibiting, that Christians are not allowed to have two wives at the same time. This reply amazed the Mahometans, who know not this mystery, and seeing that they were losing their labour in persuading us they sorrowfully complained: 'What a pity it is that you are not Turks, or you could drive out of Mecca all its medical profession, where our ignorant doctors almost hand their patients over to the undertaker, and cure them out of life into death. Even though they possess the genuine balm of Mecca, which easily cures all the ills there are, they know not how to apply it, and lose their labour thereby.'

The balm of Mecca[5] is known throughout the whole world, and is otherwise called white Indian, or Egyptian, balm, its origin being in the region around the city of Mecca. In ancient times it was found also in some parts of Egypt, but, due to the passage of time and the slothfulness of the Arabs, the trees are everywhere cut down, and it is now only gathered near Mecca from the few remaining trees, whose leaves are not unlike those of the lemon tree; it is tapped from the trees, in the same way that in the Tyrol they tap the turpentine called Venetian turpentine. The Arabs carefully collect this effluxion, and take it to sell in Mecca and then in Gidda, where one pound is sold for two florins: then in India and in Cairo and district it is sold at a higher price, and in Europe at the highest of all: yet it is often adulterated with a mixture of other oil, and those who do not know the genuine article are easily deceived. It is a thick fluid that goes hard in winter, light yellow in colour, pleasant to smell, sticking to the fingers if touched, if tasted filling the mouth with its odour but leaving a bitter taste behind. To test its genuineness, if three of four drops are put into a glass of water, they float and spread over the surface like a spider's web, and the whole can be collected with a piece of wood, leaving the water scented, but bitter. However, if anything is mixed with it, not only does it not float, it does not spread over the surface of the water. When the balm is some years old it remains hard and can only be liquefied by heat, and if it is wanted to anoint a sore, it is necessary to add yeast, or in default of this some olive oil: but after this the proof that I mentioned no longer functions, and it cannot be wholly collected from the water.

The uses of this balm are many and wonderful, and its effects are beneficial in all cases and circumstances of gangrene, where it is similar to Peruvian balm: indeed modern medical practice in the East, after wide experimentation, declares it to be better than Peruvian balm, as there are cases where the Peruvian, as with other particular kinds of balm, is injurious and does positive harm, though with the balm of Mecca this is unknown. With a little theriac added it is an excellent antidote against poison, while

[5] Bruce, *op. cit.*, v, opposite pp. 16–17, reproduces two engravings of this plant, which was, as Niebuhr, *Voyage*, i, 224, indicates, a major export. See also Bruce, *op. cit.*, i, pp. 374–5, and H. F. M. Prescott, *Once to Sinai*, 1957, pp. 115–23, for the garden of balm at Matariya, Cairo, with illustration.

in cases of wounding or internal bruising or other conditions almost uncurable by other means, balm of Mecca alone, if the wounds be previously washed in wine and well cleaned out, will effect a cure. With a recent sword-cut, if the part-severed limb be washed free of blood and wiped with balm, and well bandaged, nothing more is needed until the wound is cured. Taken internally in less than one or two drops it is a great promoter of heat, and gently draws out an ulcer and disperses any extraneous matter. Administered on occasion to cases of hectic fever or of consumption, it brings a good measure of relief, and to many other diseases it may be applied with excellent results: for missionaries it is an all-purpose remedy. The Arabs and Mahometans apply it as a cosmetic for their women, spreading it on dog skin and putting it against the face for a whole month without removing it, when they say that they are as it were re-born and rejuvenated by the balm. In different cases of sickness and debility it produces good results, as I have learned by my own experience.

Meanwhile we were more and more anxious to continue our journey and to reach the goal of our obedience; before the departure of the pilgrims for Medina I gained audience of the Kiechia who was well disposed to me for different cures I had effected; I humbly begged him for licence to depart, pretending that we wanted to continue to another neighbouring island. I obtained from him a kindly-worded permission in writing, though he warned me to be careful where I sailed, because after the pilgrims' departure no other ship would put to sea until the caravan returned. He added to our gratitude by not only allowing us freedom from all further tribute, but even relieving us of customs duty; with no more than three Roman scudi to be paid to the servants, we safely loaded on board all the mission's belongings, and, with hearts of gladness to be freed from such wretchedness, we sailed onwards, our sails by God's grace filled with a favourable wind, on the day before the departure of the Mecca caravan, around noon on 23 October 1751.

CHAPTER 11

OUR JOURNEY
ONWARDS TOWARDS ABYSSINIA

Thus far protected by divine providence, we had even softened the hearts of the barbarians, and as well as unaccustomed marks of favour from the Vizier I had obtained another written recommendation, as we sailed towards the island of Arabia Felix, that we should be well received by the local commander. This piece of good fortune buoyed me up for but a brief time, since on the first day of our voyage the Most Merciful God deigned to inflict on me yet another illness: my temperature fluctuated, my head ached, my whole body was wracked with discomfort, for three days I took nothing but a little medicine, and murmured to myself Physician, heal thyself. After those days of rest on land the sea had its natural contrary effect, and much upset my stomach; the first time that I embarked upon it, the effect of the waves was to disturb me to continual nausea; it seemed that I should vomit up my entrails, my head ached with confusion, all the veins in my body were a-tremble, I thought that I should die from the motion. However, it pleased Thrice-blessed God to restore me to my previous state of health after nine days, though I had fared badly enough through lack of the necessities of such a condition, and of suitable diet.

Then we were sailing by the mountain called *Gebel Tombol*, inhabited, believe the Arabs, by the spirits called *Gennet*[1] or underground demons: those who pass that way show them all honour, and construct or complete the construction of a model ship, which they set sail in the sea laden with fruit, bread and

[1] Arabic *jinn*.

goods; sweet water too, rice, bread and butter, they throw into the sea, with two Mahometan choir-leaders singing as it were litanies, and the whole ship's company following them and repeating *Al alatundo*:[2] they are beseeching the spirits of the other world to give them a favourable wind and safe arrival at their port of call, and in their honour many sacrifices are offered and prayers said. As they thus raised their voices, the favourable wind dropped at that very moment, leaving them becalmed and befooled, much to our inward amusement, though outwardly we dared not even mutter to ourselves in case we were thrown overboard, every ill-fortune being commonly blamed on Christians. A little later the ship unfortunately struck on a rock or reef with such force that we were near to ruin, our courage failed us, and we were afraid of shipwreck; had we not by the providence of the only God, not of demons, escaped into safety, the ship would have broken up into a thousand pieces and we should have perished. For a long time we sailed onwards in bewilderment, not knowing what harm we had suffered, but then cast anchor. Once again there broke out the superstitious prayers in honour of those spirits; then a different misfortune troubled us, a quarrel between them as to the cause of their disaster, some cursing us Franks, others disputing this but putting the blame on some wretched women whom they were taking with them as paramours; the majority turned against the women, and together with some boys kept as catamites they put them all out on the sea-shore, telling them to wash away their sins in the sea so that thus cleansed they and the boys could return to the ship and the voyage continue.

We soon passed an island called *Gebel Firan*,[3] a place of danger because of an adjacent rock called *Ras Elfaras*,[4] commonly Horse's Head: there are concealed reefs here and there under the water, making the passage very difficult for the shipmaster, the more so that it looks out on all sides on to little islets, and the helmsman who has no knowledge of it is almost in a labyrinth and is at a loss where to steer. Only by God's guidance did we advance by minute degrees like moles, with one sail set, until we fortunately

---

[2] This ceremony and incantation we have been unable to identify.

[3] Bruce, *op. cit.*, i, 305, who terms this island Jibbel Foran (i.e. *Jabal Fīrān*), or Mountain of Mice, describes it as rocky, with some trees at its southern extremity.

[4] Arabic *Rās al faras*, or horse's head.

quitted the labyrinth and reached a place called *Gezan*,[5] a sort of village pleasantly situated at the foot of a mountain; on the southern side is a view of the mountain with a range of foothills and crags. All the houses are made of straw, with straw roofs, the sea-port is quite convenient, and there are innumerable crabs to be found there and different sorts of edible birds, making up the general food on which this very poor population lives; so wretched, poverty-stricken, starving, without bread of any kind, and tortured by the unbearable heat. More than sixty wretches disembarked from our ship hoping to satisfy their wants and appetites for food and water and seeking the comforts of land, but the inhabitants in their poverty were unable to meet our wants, apart from some fish and some roots that grow there; they go barefoot without shoes, are all affected, nay burned up, by the baking hot sand, and can hardly stand for the blisters on their feet; the heat there could truly be called hellish, men are unnaturally enfeebled and nature seems to fail.

The ship's company returned on board with lamentations, and on the eleventh day of our voyage, around the middle of the night when the ship's captain was asleep and the crew off their guard and in part asleep also, a strong and sudden storm came up and would have had us shipwrecked and foundered, had not we three missionaries been awake and raised a noisy alarm to furl the sails with all speed: without doubt otherwise we should have plunged to the depth of the sea. But God's providence again sustained us and, with sails reefed, we won fearfully through to safety, for which we praised God's goodness. At last on November 2, after so many hopes and fears, we put in to the harbour, to our great comfort, of the island called *Elluhaja*,[6] or as others prefer *Ellochia*, the meaning of which is *little beard*.

We had with us letters of recommendation not only from the Vizier but also from our Mahometan friend and benefactor the nobleman of Gidda, got through the customs safely at but a

---

[5] Qīzān, pronounced Jīzām. This village, which Bruce refers to as Djezan, was built, he says, with straw and mud. The settlement had once been 'a very considerable place for trade', but as a result of the growth of commerce in coffee, had been replaced in importance by Luhaiya and Hodeida. Bruce, *op. cit.* i, 305.

[6] Luḥayyah, according to Bruce, *op. cit.*, i, 306, was 'built upon the south-west side of a peninsula, surrounded every where but on the east by sea'. A plan and drawings of the town are published in Niebuhr, *Voyage*, i, plates lx and lxi.

small fee, and gained audience of the ruler of the island: our reception by him was friendly, he lodged us in one of his houses, and we rested for ten days, away from the disturbance of the high seas and safe from intrusion by Arabs, until we could embark in another ship and continue towards the island of Messaua; refreshed on both counts we rebuilt our strength to resume our voyage.

This island is but small, lying at the foot of a mountain with a good harbour to the south, and is visited only by Turkish vessels, as no commerce is permitted there with Europeans; there are many rocks there below the surface of the Red Sea, and navigation for large ships is impossible, or only to be undertaken at great risk. The people live mostly on fish, of which the best of the different sorts can be bought, fresh caught, three times a day, in the morning, at midday, and in the evening. Lodged in the Governor's house we paid an advantageous price for our room, and received every kindness from the natives, partly because of the respect in which the Governor held us, and partly because of the free medical attention that we gave to their illnesses: letting blood and treating different sorts of weaknesses, we gained the affection of the people, and on every hand God's help to us was manifested.

On sale in the island, at a low price, are beautiful murrhines, commonly called Chinese or Indian porcelain; different sorts of green vegetable and fruit are to be bought cheaply, though the climate and the heat make cultivation difficult, and the people are very poor: they are Mahometan or idolatrous, they go for the most part naked, with a small piece of woven cloth or of leather to hide their private parts, they are of black complexion, and they are fanatics for their own sect. Although that period was a time of fast by the holy rules of our seraphic order, we fortified ourselves with excellent fish and with rather better water, not quite so fetid. We bought five or six pounds of fish for three medins or three Roman bajocs, and gave thanks to the Divine Majesty for this clear sign that we were to build up our strength, having tasted nothing for six months but biscuit-bread and fetid water. We were also refreshed by that delightful-tasting fruit called by the Arabs *mus*, one finger long and shaped like the European cucumber; they are good indeed, sweet, fragrant and possessed of a four-fold distinct flavour, with as it were a taste of every other fruit, nor did I find any *mus* so good as these in any other part of the East: even when eaten in large quantities they do no harm but rather are beneficial. Being near to Arabia Felix the island is stocked with different aromatic herbs from that country together with expensive Mocha coffee,[7] which does not come from India as I had long heard many Europeans say, or from the Grand Sultan's empire, but only from Arabia Felix, and indeed from some of the hills near this island of Elluhaja, as I saw for myself; then it is shipped through the Red Sea to Gidda, Cairo and Alexandria, and then across the Mediterranean to Constantinople: from Constantinople it goes to Vienna in Austria and to other parts of Europe. Some Europeans maintain that coffee originates in Constantinople, but with little reason, because coffee needs a warm climate and a hot summer, whereas in Constantinople the winter and the cold are severe and of some duration, with no small amount of snow; coffee reaches Persia by way of India. The Arabs of Elluhaja drink it in great quantity, eight cups of coffee without sugar being sold for one medin, that is, half a German groschen. If this countryside were but inhabited by true Christians, its produce would increase a hundred-fold, but the Arab race, stupid, lazy, engrossed in fleshly pursuits, doing little to till the soil, enjoy the fruits of it just the same, and, wicked and intent on nothing but idleness, they spend their time drinking, eating, lazing and idling: despite their poverty their pride is greater than Lucifer's, and above all they hate Christians. Yet this is not surprising, the influence of the stars and their nearness to the sun breeds arrogance in them, they despise the rest of the world, and deem nobody their equal.

A ship was ready to sail for Messaua, we had received a fresh letter of recommendation from the Governor, the wind was fair, and on November 14 we weighed anchor and set sail. Our ship was a hulk, cobbled together of spars and ropes after the Arab fashion and small of size, and we had no expectation of a prosperous voyage in her: but we commended ourselves to the Divine Navigator, prayed of Him for a happy end to our journey, and

[7] The importance of Mocha coffee had been noted half a century earlier by John Ovington, who stated that it was 'the only commodity of repute' available at the port where there was 'no scarcity of it at all'. Foster, *op. cit.*, p. 176. Coffee, according to Niebuhr, was also the principal article of trade at Luyaiha, and was shipped, he confirms, to both Egypt and Turkey. Niebuhr, *op. cit.*, i, 243–4.

after a few hours reached a bay of the Red Sea where the sea was of the roughest and the danger great, at least for the wretched vessels of the Turks and Arabs, with a strong current that set towards Mocha, the East Indies, Messaua, and other places. But woe to those who are compelled to sail with ignorant Arabs! Scarcely had we entered the bay than our ship was buffeted by huge waves, only one mast stayed upright, we were filling with water, and we put out our anchors. For three days we waited for a more moderate wind, but our hopes were in vain, and a new storm arose with a new swelling of the waves, until we weighed our anchors to avoid losing them, and wildly, driven all ways at the mercy of the angry waves of the surging sea, with the hull leaking, we were in peril of our lives for six hours of a pitch-black night, exposed to the chances of the waves and thinking that we were food for the fishes. But our merciful God hearing the sincere lamentations of our hearts and our many prayers, Who has set a bound to the Ocean, stilled the waves, and joyfully on the next day we beheld the land, the port of the island of Messaua, which we reached on the feast of the holy apostle St Andrew, with a feeling of relief the greater that our voyage had been so unfortunate.

Now we were assailed by another misfortune: for the third time we submitted to the tyranny of the customs-house, where not only were our boxes examined to the bottom, and all our goods thrown out on the ground and inspected one by one, but our church vestments and sacred vessels were taken up in sacrilegious hands and held out to the mockery of the onlookers. Pictures and statues of the Virgin and of St Athanasius, that we had brought as gifts to the Emperor of Abyssinia, were jeered at by jacks-in-office who peered into every detail of all our goods. In view of the crowd of onlookers, in this place noted for its robbers, we were close to suffering the loss of everything. But we were protected and carefully aided by the presence of three Christian Greeks, and got through without loss, though we had been exposed for about two hours in the heat of the sun to the fury of the Infidel. We were led to the principal house of the island where we chose a room at a cost of one Roman scudo a week. We were well pleased with our quarters, because the house was well built of stone and proof against prying eyes, so that we were secure from the depredations of the Arab thieves; we had the privacy after a few days to offer to the Almighty, at the second hour of the night, the holy sacrifice of the Mass: our previous dwellings, being built of straw, had given us insufficient privacy for our ministry. But for the location of Messaua, please read the next chapter.

CHAPTER 12

THE ISLAND OF MESSAUA

The island[1] is the last port on the Red Sea towards Abyssinia, and is inhabited only by Mahometans, apart from occasional Greek Orthodox traders or other orientals who call with trade goods and stay for a short time.[2] No Christian is permitted to take up permanent residence there,[3] because the island being small, barely one Italian mile in length and breadth, is scarcely large enough for its inhabitants; such houses as there are are wretched, built mostly of straw or sticks,[4] and the natives are extremely poor, apart from four or five who have grown rich by trade. The more difficult and wretched it is therefore for all foreigners to buy food, and at a high price, since all the necessaries of life are imported from Ethiopia, Gidda, Egypt and other places, Messaua producing nothing of value. We three missionaries, despite such a shortage of victuals, praised God's manifest providence that we were in all kindliness supplied with food by the enemies of the Catholic faith and of the cross of Christ, and

[1] Massawa, locally known as Metewwa, was, according to Bruce, *op. cit.*, iii, 1, 'a small island immediately on the Abyssinian shore', with 'an excellent harbour, and water deep enough for ships of any size to put in to the very edge of the island'.

[2] The only foreigners at Massawa mentioned by Bruce, *op. cit.*, iii, 55, were Banians, who, he says, were 'once the principal merchants' at the port, but were in his day 'reduced to six'. They were 'silver-smiths, that make ear-rings and other ornaments for the women in the continent', as well as 'assayers of gold', but made 'but a poor livelihood'.

[3] A century and a half earlier Almeida had noted that Christian traders were allowed to visit Massawa, but that Muslims were 'better received and more welcome there'. C. F. Beckingham and G. W. B. Huntingford, *Some records of Ethiopia 1593–1646* (London, 1954), p. 55.

[4] The houses of Massawa, according to Bruce, *op. cit.*, iii, 52, were 'in general built of poles and bent grass', though there were also 'about twenty' of stone. 'Six or eight' were of two storeys, though the second floor seldom consisted of more than one room, 'and that one generally not a large one'.

sustained by the charity of the Gentiles and Mahometans; for, having been named as doctors on our first arrival, we drew towards us many ailing people, suffering from a variety of complaints,[5] and we did not fail, as elsewhere, to perform works of charity on their behalf, prescribing medicines, letting blood, and salving wounds and blows, all of which by God's grace had a happy outcome, although we were detained there for seventy days. I treated a variety of ailments, a detailed list of which would be tedious to relate, and the fortunate outcome of each of them secured to us the affection of the inhabitants, so that we gained of the Governor perfect liberty of residence, though in other circumstances he would have felt aggrieved at having to extend to Christians such freedom of behaviour.

Often was I invited to dinner by many of the chief inhabitants, who as though they were our closest friends would send to our quarters meat, bread, honey, even whole sheep; even more, one of the richer Mahometans, whom I had restored to health, supplied me in recognition, together with my colleagues, with three loaves of wheaten bread every day for two months, although in these parts it is dear and very scarce, and the whole nation, for want of wheat, eats a tasteless bread made out of a grain called *tam*.[6] The great paucity of victuals and the poverty of the island is burdensome to foreigners, but I for my medical skill gained unrestricted permission to shoot on the foreshore of the Red Sea, which daily ebbs to a distance of at least half an Italian mile. There I bagged so many birds of different kinds[7] that our daily wants were plentifully supplied, because a great number of birds fly there for the worms and the small fishes; their variety was a delight to the eyes, and their plumage was beautiful.

We further refreshed ourselves with rice cooked in camel's milk, a great restorer of our strength, and each day large amounts

---

[5] Bruce, *op. cit.*, iii, 33, describes Massawa as 'very unwholesome'. For an account of diseases prevalent at the port see iii, 33–49.

[6] Arabic *ṭaʿām*, or grain. R. B. Serjeant, 'The cultivation of cereals in mediaeval Yemen', *Arabian studies* (1974), i, 34.

[7] The abundance of other wild life had been noted early in the sixteenth century by the Portuguese who declared that the mainland opposite Massawa was occupied by 'many gazelles and other kinds of game, and so many hares that the men kill them on foot'. H. Thomas, *The Discovery of Abyssinia by the Portuguese in 1520* (London, 1938), p. 89. For maps of the area see R. Pankhurst, 'Some notes on the historical and economic geography of the Mesewa area (1520–1885)', *Journal of Ethiopian studies* (1975), xiii, No 1, pp. 89–116.

of asparagus were sent in to us in baskets, which we bought at a
cheap price and ate in great quantity, well cooked in boiling
butter and seasoned with powdered mace; when this caused us
some digestive problems, I was at a loss as to the reason, but
happening by chance to be called by the Governor to a town
called *Arckicko*[8] in another part of the Red Sea to treat one of
his wives, I had scarcely transferred myself across the strait to
the other part of the island when I found a wide plain beside
the shore. Wandering here among the marshes, set with shrubs
which were full of red and white flowers giving forth a delicious
scent, I was unable to determine the species of the trees, but,
noticing at last some different leaves, like protruding buds with
the flowers not yet open, identical with the asparagus which we
had so often eaten on the island, I realised in wonderment that
it was not asparagus, but the beautiful flowers of the aloe[9] that
we had eaten, and that it was no wonder that they had upset our
stomachs; I avoided them in the future and presumed not to eat
them. Indeed had not their natural hardness caused us to cook
them for longer than usual, so that in the boiling they had lost
their poison, we should without doubt have suffered a real injury
to our health. But guided and protected by our most blessed God
we took no harm from them and other dangers to our constitutions; though as we lingered in Messaua for a long time enough
we were exposed to every sort of illness.

We wanted nothing more than to reach the end of so long
drawn out a journey, and to look on royal Gondar, but since no
Christian is allowed[10] without the Emperor's[11] express permission

---

[8] Arkiko, or as it is locally known Hergigo, consisted, according to Bruce, *op.
cit.*, iii, 63, of 'about four hundred houses', a few of which were 'built of clay,
the rest of coarse grass like reeds'. There was 'water enough for large ships' close
to the port, but the bay, 'being open to the N.E.', made it 'uneasy riding in
blowing weather'.

[9] The shoots of the aloes were later reported by W. P. E. S. Rüppell, *Reise in
Abyssinien* (Frankfurt, 1838–40), i, 197, to be eaten in great quantities by the
Banian or Indian traders of Massawa, who, as vegetarians, found them a par-
ticularly convenient food.

[10] The principle that a foreigner could not enter the country without the
sovereign's permission was well-established and long-enduring. Over a century
later it caused Hormuzd Rassam, Queen Victoria's envoy to Emperor
Tewodros II, to assert that 'it was against the usages of the country for anyone
to visit the Sovereign without his accorded permission'. H. Rassam, *Narrative of
the British mission to Theodore, King of Abyssinia* (London, 1869), i, 41.

[11] The reigning Emperor was Iyasu II, also known as Adyam Sagad II, who
had succeeded his father Bakaffa in 1730.

68

to enter another part of his domain, we three missionaries were anxiously awaiting its arrival; and all the more that some of the inhabitants were beginning to form false opinions about us, that we were spying out the provinces or were evil-intentioned robbers. Had we not been protected by the Emperor's letter of invitation, we should have not only been mulcted on our first arrival by unjust customs charges, but also burdened by various exactions from the *Najeb*,[12] the governor of Arckicko. This Najeb, performing the duties of governor for both the Turkish and the Ethiopian emperors simultaneously, dared not act against us, although, urged on by the ill-disposed of the citizens, he claimed that a charge of at least fifty scudi[13] was payable for entry to Ethiopia:[14] pointing to our poverty, and to the fact that we carried no merchandise, we made it plain that we were being asked to pay the impossible. Furthermore, another official, the *Kaimackan*,[15] appointed each year to the customs by the Bassa of Gidda to collect the duty on merchandise, looked for a present from us in the form a a wayleave; he likewise got nothing.

Meanwhile our excessively long stay enabled us to observe a number of foolish customs, of which the chief was their method of burying the dead. Crowds of women gather at the dead man's house to bewail him, a large jar of mead having previously been placed in the middle of the bed; they then begin in Egyptian fashion to weep and to sing sorrowful dirges leading to even more bitter lamentations, they dance, clap their hands, strike themselves in the face, tear with their nails their features, breast, forehead and temples till the blood flows down, wounding themselves beyond reason. When they have bewailed enough, they seize the mead jar and drink deeply, strengthening themselves for further lamentation; some of their behaviour is obscene, they leap, wail, prostrate themselves on the ground, then, all theatrical

[12] Arabic *Nā'ib*, literally 'deputy'. This title was held by the governor of the port of Arkiko, who was usually a chief from the mainland. W. Munzinger, *Ostafrikänische Studien* (Schaffhausen, 1864), pp. 162–3; J. S. Trimingham, *Islam in Ethiopia* (London, 1852), p. 98.

[13] The principal coins in circulation at the port, according to Bruce, *op. cit.*, iii, 53, were Venetian sequins and Austrian patacas, i.e. thalers or dollars.

[14] The Nā'ib was later to make similarly extortionate demands on Bruce, who states, *op. cit.*, iii, 58, that the chief attempted to extract 1,000 patacas, or dollars, from him.

[15] Arabic *Qā'im-maqām*, literally 'deputy', a word widely used in the Ottoman empire. This title was given, as Prutky notes, to the Turkish governors of Massawa, who were then appointed by the rulers of Jeddah. Rüppell, *op. cit.*, i, 189.

behaviour put aside, their tears pour forth in abundance, not so much from heartfeld grief as from the plentiful quantity of mead that they have drunk. When one jar is empty another is brought, and they keep this up until the close of the day. At night-fall they kindle a large fire and move thither the deceased's body, wailing the while, and in the fire they burn effigies of demons, so that that which is being burned in Hell they burn also on earth. The burnt effigy is taken to the place of burial with songs and dances on the way as on a feast day, while the corpse is quickly washed and the head and body shaved of hair. The dead man's virtues are proclaimed in public, and his worldly sins enumerated, and after every sentence the people shout and wail and show their sympathy; at last they bury him and pile stones over the corpse.[16] Everyone is paid for the mourning functions they have performed in Venetian glass beads called *borrziko*,[17] which the women wear on the neck and hands as an ornament; with these in place of money can be purchased items of food or dress at the rate of 4,000 beads to one scudo, and much time is wasted in counting them; one must be careful too in exchanging them, because they are nowhere current save in the island of Messaua and the district round about.

After many days' delay we sent two messengers with letters to the Emperor, humbly begging his permission to enter his realm, but when forty days passed without an answer a new outburst against us blew up; their hatred of us was due partly to envy, partly to a grudge not so much against our faith as that we had been freed of custom duty. It was firmly believed that our aim in entering Ethiopia was to make money, that we were about to escape with the protection of powerful ministers, that we were held in esteem by the Emperor, that we were about to make an enormous fortune. For all these causes were we envied by a

---

[16] A not dissimilar account of mourning procedure at Massawa is given by Bruce, *op. cit.*, iii, 49–50.

[17] Amharic *Berčeqo*, or 'glass'. Bruce, *op. cit.*, iii, 53, who confirms that 'glass beads, called Contaria, of all kinds and colours, perfect and broken', passed for 'small money' at Massawa, gives the following table of the 'relative value of money' at the port:

1 Venetian sequin,	$2\frac{1}{4}$ Patacas
1 Pataca or Imperial dollar,	28 Harf
1 Harf	4 Diwani
1 Diwani, or para,	10 Kibeer
1 Kibeer	3 Borjooke, or grains.

people who knew not that it was souls alone that were valuable to us. They took counsel together, and decided, if the Emperor's reply did not come soon, some that we should be robbed, some that we should be expelled with ignominy, some that we should be thrown into the sea, some that other punishments should be inflicted upon us. Under the pretence of friendship the *Najeb* or governor visited us, in order to perceive the details of our household and get to know the extent of our imaginary wealth. Our hearts at this time were indeed full of fear, for when he came with all his retinue we did not know whether he might not perhaps have already formed the wicked resolve to kill us; so we welcomed him with respect and submission, and refreshed him and his followers with sweetmeats that we had brought from Cairo: indeed at that time I played in fear and trembling the instrument of David, trusting fervently in the Lord, '*When the evil spirit from God was upon Saul, David took a harp, and the evil spirit departed from him.*' 1. Samuel xvi. 23. So it was by God's grace, and the wicked plan towards us departed from the Najeb: merciful God had heard our groans and our sighs and softened the heart of the governor, who told us that he was expecting in another eight days the reply that we had so long desired, and departed with goodwill towards us. That night we again besought divine help, and through His intervention there arrived next day two imperial officials bearing letters full of affection towards us, and letters likewise from the imperial treasurer called in Ethiopian *Nagadras*.[18] The meaning of the letters is set out below.

The Emperor's letter, written in Arabic,[19] reads thus in Latin translation.

'*Praise to the One God*
From the presence of the Emperor of Emperors, acknowledged by the Christian and Turkish emperors as the successor to the Lord of the world, his gerent both for things secular and for things sacred, established ruler over the business of created creatures, through whom God administers justice to man and rules human

---

[18] Amharic *Nagadras*, i.e. *ras*, or head, of the *nagadi*, or merchants. The term was given, as Nathaniel Pearce noted in the early nineteenth century, to officials responsible for the collection of taxes on trade. N. Pearce, *Life and adventures* (London, 1831), ii, 11–12.

[19] Because of the prevalence of Arabic throughout the Middle East it was not unusual for Ethiopian rulers to use this language in their letters. R. Pankhurst, 'Letter writing and the use of royal and imperial seals in Ethiopia prior to the twentieth century', *Journal of Ethiopian studies* (1973), xi, No. 1, pp. 179–80.

affairs aright, and brings light to lands and to provinces. He is strong in counsel, of perfect prudence, he is a benefactor of mankind in that he has left a memorial, which was proclaimed in all lands, promoting justice, goodness, and benefits. He is established in his empire from ancient times, the successor of his fathers, of his grandfathers, and of his great-grandfathers. He is a fount of liberty, of benefits, of goodness, he is our lord the supreme Emperor and honourable King ruling in happiness, he is a hill whose magnificence bears witness throughout all creatures both particularly and communally. He has so many titles that they outnumber the very stars themselves, and the multitude and the density of the clouds. The manners and behaviour innate to him are such that their tender restraint can be likened scarcely to anything else under the shining sun, and in respect of them all others become feeble. He is so high lifted up that all the kings wished to imitate him but none were able to attain to him, for they found him more noble than all the princes of Christendom. He is moreover greater than all the kings of the Christian faith, and is more excellent from the time when first he was bathed in the waters of baptism: he is the defender of the law of his church and the dealer of justice between the souls of the Turks and the Christians. His conscience is pure, he is rooted in his faith and church, and established in the Christian nation in Gondar, which is guarded and protected by the emperor Jasu Odiam Saghed,[20] son of the emperor Backaffa Masich Saghed.[21] May his days be multiplied, may justice be done, and may the nights of his prosperity be renewed, through the excellence of Jesus Christ and of His Mother, amen. To you three doctors the Emperor sends greetings, praying to find you well and in health, and telling you, so that you may remain in safety, to come quickly to us with my slaves, and nothing will happen but what will please you and exalt your hearts with happiness and content, and you will have at our court honour, justice and safety.'

This letter, which we had awaited with such longing, we read through with wonder and gladness of heart, though we found in it nothing except simply the lengthy imperial title, wonderful to read and by European royal standards extraordinary, after which the whole content of the letter was set out in a few lines. The sealed letter had been enclosed in a bag,[22] and sealed

---

[20] Iyasu II, or Adyam Sagad, who reigned from 1730 to 1755.

[21] Emperor Bakaffa, also known as Masih Sagad, ruled from 1721 to 1730.

[22] Such pouches had earlier been reported by Alvarez who states that letters sent from Emperor Lebna Dengel to the King of Portugal were placed in 'little bags of brocade'. C. F. Beckingham and G. W. B. Huntingford, *The Prester John of the Indies* (Cambridge, 1961), ii, 377.

moreover as I had noticed with the prince's seal.[23] Spanish wax is not used in Ethiopia: they burn incense, smother the seal with its smoke, heat it until the whole seal is blacked, and press it onto the paper; thus they express it properly as though in Spanish wax. Other Ethiopians send all their letters unsealed, and it is only the Emperor who folds his into a long document, places it in a bag made of some precious material, fastens it again, seals it with ordinary wax, and attaches a note outside bearing the name of the person to whom it is to be sent. Every document in the name of the Emperor is perforce transacted by his treasurer, for the Emperor is ignorant of writing[24] and it is not the custom for kings or emperors in Ethiopia to sign their letters or decrees: they confirm them with their seal, and think it dishonourable to learn to write, because the task of writing is for simple men and slaves, and not for emperors and kings. If a written communication has to be made to another party, however private and however secret it may be, it has to be entrusted to a secretary, a practice often detrimental to security, for if a matter is to be confided even to one's best friend, there is nothing for it but to make use of a scribe, or, even worse, to communicate it orally through the mouth of a messenger: whence serious harm is often caused. His two messengers handed over the Emperor's letter to us, together with one from the royal Treasurer, Lord George Draco[25] of Nios,[26] an Orthodox Greek, the style and tenor of

---

[23] This seal, like other Ethiopian seals of this period, was in Arabic. R. Pankhurst, 'Ethiopian royal seals of the seventeenth and eighteenth centuries', G. Goldenberg, *Ethiopian studies. Proceedings of the Sixth International Conference, Tel-Aviv, 14–17 April 1980* (Rotterdam, 1986), 406–15.

[24] Learning to read and write was not an essential part of the traditional upbringing of the Ethiopian nobility as described by Mahtama Sellase Walda Masqal, 'Portrait retrospectif d'un gentilhomme éthiopien', *Proceedings of the third international conference of Ethiopian studies* (Addis Ababa, 1970), iii, 60–8.

[25] The name does not appear in Ethiopian sources, but a *Gebt*, or foreigner of the Orthodox faith, called Ani (possibly the same individual?) had been appointed chief of the treasury in the previous year. I. Guidi, *Annales regum Iyasu II et Iyo'as* (Paris, 1912), p. 154. A number of Greeks, as Bruce noted, held 'considerable posts' at Gondar. They included Petros, who acted as treasurer to Emperor Iyoas, and three who had served the latter's father Iyasu II. They were Anthulé, the treasurer and master of the king's wardrobe; Abba Christophoros who was both a priest and a physician; and Sebastanos, an elderly cook. Petros's brother was Janni, the customs chief at Adwa, and Anthulé was the latter's son-in-law. Bruce, *op. cit.*, iii, 187, 210–11, 225, 231, 435, 490, 545, iv, 95, 201, 208, 210, 251.

[26] Nios, or Ios, a small Greek island south-east of Athens. See chapter 78.

which was as set out in the following:

The letter of Lord George Draco of Nios, Treasurer.

'*Honour to the One God*
To the friends, colleagues, noblemen of honour, the three fortunate doctors who have come from Cairo, we declare to you everything that is good and fair, and we tell you to have no more fear, we thank our Blessed Lord for your arrival in good health, because you have been preserved from the dangers of the sea and the dangers and hindrances of men. Everything that you have desired has come in complete and perfect form to the ears of the Emperor, who consents to all, and sends two ministers for you, with slaves. Do not delay, do not fail to come quickly, and may our Lord God prevent you from long delay. Farewell, I remain ever your friend.

George Draco of Nios Royal Treasurer'
The Palace at Gondar
4 February 1752.

When the imperial ministers were still one day's distance from Messaua with our letters, the news was suddenly brought to the Governor or Najeb, who changed his whole attitude towards us, sent us that evening four sheep and wheaten bread, and besought us to forget all his ill-treatment of us and to tell the Emperor nothing of what had happened. Despite our harsh treatment we were so desirous of the Emperor's reply that, when we saw the ministers with the two letters that I mentioned, we were so elated that we remembered nothing of the injuries that he had inflicted on us, and made our preparations for departure.

CHAPTER 13

DEPARTURE FROM THE ISLAND OF
MESSAUA TO ABYSSINIA

For over eighty days we waited miserably in the island of Messaua, paying high prices for our daily food, and, to expedite the day of our departure and entry into Abyssinia, we despatched to Gondar two express messengers in our eagerness to be off. In case one alone might come to harm, two messengers are always sent, so that if one falls sick or is devoured by beasts at least the other will get through.[1] Such was the advice of the inhabitants, in accordance with which we contracted with our two men that they should reach Gondar within twelve days and return with a reply within another twelve, for which we would pay each of them four drams[2] of gold. We gave them a little Ethiopian pepper and the usual daily allowance of bread, and sent them off. We could reasonably hope that according to contract they would return within not more than thirty days, but when these were up, and in a further forty days no messenger had appeared, we became extremely concerned and disturbed, because we knew no reason for the delay but suspected either that both had been devoured by lions or by tigers,[3] or that perhaps the Emperor was refusing to permit us into his kingdom, and that we should be sent back to Cairo, contrary to our design. To our private fears

---

[1] The Ethiopian practice of making duplicate letters had earlier been noted by Alvarez, who, unlike Prutky, does not however explain the reason behind it. Beckingham and Huntingford, *Prester John*, ii, 377.

[2] *Dram*, or *drachma*. At Gondar this unit was equal, Bruce notes, to forty grains Troy, or one tenth of a *waqet*, or ounce. Bruce, *op. cit.*, 3rd edition (London, 1813), vii, 78.

[3] There being no tigers in Ethiopia the reference is perhaps to leopards, or possibly striped hyaenas.

was added the harassment of the Najeb, who took us for spies and put us in peril of our life.

We sighed and prayed continually to God, Who deigned to help us in our troubles and, when least we hoped for it, took pity on our misery and sent to us the two imperial ministers, forty slaves, and sixteen baggage mules. These reached us after a wait of about seventy days, and brought the letters I have already described. Relying on their favourable tone we accepted without further delay our dismissal by the Najeb on receipt of the Emperor's order, and once again took our belongings to the customs, where we were more kindly treated than on our first arrival and our baggage was opened more as a matter of form. We rendered thanks to God that we had been freed from the tyrannies of the Mahometans, and, rejoicing in the Lord, on 22 February 1752 we crossed the last port on the Red Sea, opposite Messaua on the other side, called the shore of *Gerar*,[4] and stationed ourselves there. We collected what we needed for the journey and awaited the gathering of the caravan; for four days we lived in the open until the royal ministers arrived with their slaves, with mules to carry our baggage and others, well caparisoned, for our own use.[5] On February 25, after noon, we climbed and descended through the woods of the wild Ethiopian mountains, always accompanied by the ministers, and in the afternoon reached a place among the mountains and forests where water was to be found; here we spent the night in the open, in the centre of a fire which had been lit in a circle round us, well satisfied with bread and water, having passed a few small habitations. On the third day of our journey, through forests and wooded mountains which were rough and hard for travellers to cross, we reached a place called *Kinda*[6] where, in the custom of the country, all the inhabitants met together to welcome the imperial ministers, and after discussion presented us with a fat

[4] Gerar, the name of the peninsula north-west of the island of Massawa, R. Pankhurst, *History of Ethiopian towns* (Wiesbaden-Stuttgart, 1982–1985), i, 80, 233.

[5] Prutky in travelling inland took a somewhat more southerly route than Bruce was to follow, for the latter had been advised, *op. cit.* iii, 65–6, to avoid Debarwa because of its control by the Nā'ib. Most of the places mentioned in the next few paragraphs therefore do not figure in the Scotsman's narrative, and cannot in all cases be located.

[6] Ginda'e, on the edge of the northern Ethiopian highlands twenty-five miles from the coast. Pankhurst, *History of Ethiopian towns*, ii, 116.

ox. I supposed that it would be impossible that very night to eat an animal of that size, but I knew not the ways of the Ethiopians. I saw a little later, to my great surprise, that the ox was slaughtered according to the Jewish rite,[7] and was eaten almost at once by the ministers and their retinue while it was still raw and still warm.[8] This way and that they cut the raw meat with their long *schotel*[9] or knives, and swallowed it whole with great appetite; being raw it is impossible to chew it, and their practice is to swallow it down in gobbets so that the blood runs down their chin; in one hour's time there was little left of the ox. At this I was curious to see what they would do with the intestines, and whether they would wash them, or at least cleanse them properly. But lo with what wonderment did I behold them shake out on a stone the reeking excrement within, plunge the entrails for a moment in a bright fire, and then like dogs eat them all up greedily.[10] What, pray, dear reader, would you think of this barbarous race if you saw it as I? Certainly you would say that not even the dogs of Europe would devour intestines complete with their filth, or that less than forty men would in two or three hours consume an ox of this size. But to Ethiopians it was no great quantity, and in addition to the meat they were well able to consume as well their daily portion of bread: for any traveller who would not die of hunger on the way must carry with him flour for himself and his accompanying slaves, the local population being able to provide little or no sustenance, and there being no inns on the road to put up at, in the European fashion. In the whole of Abyssinia there are but three towns of any size, *Dobarua, Serai and Syre,* in which money can buy you the necessities

[7] Bruce, *op. cit.,* iv, 487, states that the Ethiopians 'satisfied the Mosaical law' by pouring six or seven drops of blood upon the ground. For a modern discussion on the slaughter and bleeding of animals in Ethiopia according to Pentateuchal requirements see E. Ullendorff, *Ethiopia and the Bible* (London, 1968), pp. 102–3.

[8] The practice of eating raw meat had been described by several earlier writers, including Alvarez, Almeida, and Lobo. Beckingham and Huntingford, *Prester John,* i, 190, 224; *idem, Some records,* p. 63; D. M. Lockhart, *The Itinerario of Jerónimo Lobo* (London, 1984), pp. 170–1.

[9] Amharic *šotal,* a curved sword or dagger. A. D'Abbadie, *Dictionnaire de la langue amariñña* (Paris, 1881), p. 226.

[10] The eating of entrails was mentioned by several other writers, notably Alvarez, Almeida and Lobo, and, much later, Mansfield Parkyns. Beckingham and Huntingford, *Prester John,* i, 234; *idem, Some records,* p. 63; Lockhart, *op. cit.,* p. 171; Parkyns, *op. cit.,* i, 376–7.

of life and supply the travellers' convenience. Each principal is expected to supply his slaves daily at midday with one small helping of what is called *durcko*,[11] made from teff[12] flour, and for supper another; and for want of teff they make do with maize flour. Besides this, at least three times a week must be added a little butter and a little of what is called *schiro*,[13] made from another sort of flour, a dish of thick soup in which to dip their bread: without this the slaves will do nothing right, and in their resentment will cause losses and make a great deal of trouble. Since schiro is not to be found in Messaua, but only in the kingdom of Ethiopia, at the beginning of the journey our escort had to content themselves with butter until, further into the kingdom, they could be provided with schiro, with which the Ethiopians are so enamoured that they would give their lives for it.

Of the necessities for a journey I shall speak further in later chapters. On the fifth day we got so far as to reach the village of *Malhovitz*,[14] where our slaves refreshed themselves with raw flesh; nearby was the church of the Blessed Virgin, and a little further on another village called *Asmera*,[15] near to which likewise was another church, built by Europeans, Lusitanian missionaries of the Society of Jesus. This was still well fitted with columns, arches, and windows, exceeding the capacity of the Ethiopians, and had been built of stone about one hundred and thirty years previously by Portuguese living in Ethiopia; it showed not the least sign of ruin.[16]

On February 27 we came to a town called *Tadazecka*[17] where was established an imperial official, a minister entitled

[11] Amharic *dergo*, a ration of provisions traditionally provided in Ethiopia for the ruler's guests or visitors. I. Guidi, *Vocabolario amarico-italiano* (Rome, 1901), p. 661.

[12] Amharic *teff*, or finger millet, variously known as *Eragrostis abyssinica, Eragrostis teff* and *Poa abyssinica*. Bruce, *op. cit.*, v, 76–80; Pankhurst, *An Introduction to the economic history*, p. 200.

[13] Amharic *šero*, a vegetable stew made from chick-peas, lentils, peas etc. Guidi, *Vocabolario*, p. 209.

[14] An unidentified locality.

[15] Asmara, a settlement dating back to mediaeval times. Pankhurst, *History of Ethiopian towns*, i, 73–4.

[16] The construction of this church is described by the early seventeenth century Portuguese missionary Emmanuel Barradas. C. Beccari, *Rerum Aethiopicarum scriptores occidentales* (Rome, 1905–17), iv, 87–8, 208–9, 268–70.

[17] Sa'azzaga, a village in Hamasen, ten miles west of Asmara. The oral history of this politically important settlement was recorded by Kolmodin, *Traditions de Tsazzega et Hazzega* (Rome-Upsal, 1912–15).

Dadaczmacz,[18] who governed the entire country roundabout including Dobarua[19] and its vicinity: this was once an important city, but is now scarcely as large as a village, and is the ordinary residence of the Minister.[20] This minister, before we had seen him, we had thought to find begirt with splendour and magnificance, as befitted a prince and governor of a whole province, but alas, on entering his chamber full of straw we found him among beasts, mules, slaves, and maidservants, sitting naked on his bed with but a white sheet to cover him. There we paid our respects to him, totally without furniture or chairs, worse housed than in the poor hovels of our peasants. When we rendered homage to him he received us in a humane enough way, bade us be seated near his bed on the dirty floor, and conversed in a friendly fashion. When we handed over to him our letter of recommendation from the Emperor, he showed himself even kinder to us, offered us whatever meat we wanted, and displayed good feeling towards us. Because it was Lent we thanked him but refused the meat, making do with a few lentils and an Ethiopian wine called *tacz*,[21] made of honey and herbs. He was distressed that he could not provide us with better fare, but in those parts fish is scarce and expensive, indeed very scarce at whatever price, the inhabitants being without fish pools among the mountains and forests, and there being no rivers large enough to breed eatable fish. Though nothing could be provided for us, our body guard and slaves were the more lavishly feasted on raw flesh. One especial favour this Governor did to us; the mules sent

[18] Amharic *Dajazmač*, literally 'commander of the (King's) gate', an Ethiopian military and court title second only to that of *Ras*. G. Massaja, *Lectiones grammaticales pro missionariis qui addiscere volunt linguam amaricam* (Paris, 1867), p. 255.

[19] On the old town of Debarwa, twenty-one miles S.S.W. of Asmara, and its decline, see Pankhurst, *History of Ethiopian towns*, i, 65–72.

[20] The Minister would seem to have been the *Bahr Nagaš*, or ruler of the sea (province), a functionary to whom Prutky later refers in chapter 47. The position of *Bahr Nagaš*, though by this time of but modest importance, had once been one of the most prestigious in the realm. In the early sixteenth century, according to Alvarez, he 'wore a crown of gold', and was 'the lord of many lords, and of many lands and peoples'. Bruce later stated that the office had once been 'one of the most lucrative' in the empire. Beckingham and Huntingford, *Prester John*, i, 114, 116; Bruce, *op. cit.*, iii, 250. On this functionary see also Beckingham and Huntingford, *Some records*, pp. 72, 182, and Foster, *op. cit.*, pp. 146–7, 149, 151, 183; Valentia, *op. cit.*, iii, 6, 10–18.

[21] Amharic *taj*, or mead, the principal drink of the Ethiopian aristocracy. Its traditional method of preparation was described by Almeida. Beckingham and Huntingford, *Some records*, pp. 64–5.

to us by the Emperor had now foundered, because of the terrible mountain roads, and were unable to carry further the chests containing our gear, so he assigned to us porters to carry them to Dobarua: in this way we were quicker to reach on March 1 a town called *Addobaru*,[22] one night further on our journey. Meanwhile the governor from Tadazecka, who had been following us, appointed further porters to take us to the next official.

Here we left one minister with half the slaves to see to the carriage of our baggage, while we went ahead with the other minister and the other half of the slaves, and ordered the others to follow later, so that, in accordance with the orders of the Emperor's letter, we could reach his presence the sooner. Travelling light and fast, and with nothing further to delay us, we left Dobarua on March 2, crossed a plain full of stones that tried our feet, and reached the town of *Addomongolo*[23] where lived another official Dadczmacz: he received us respectfully, in a better dwelling than his predecessor's, and lodged us comfortably, giving our servants a bellyful of beef but only bread and water to us, there being nothing else edible to hand. Next day we thankfully descended, in good time, from the hills; but there were few plains thereabouts, and only after climbing up and down steep mountains did we reach on March 4 the city of Serai,[24] whose inhabitants, more barbarous and less obedient to their Emperor, took our arrival in bad part. Their governor for long refused to receive us, despite the mandate from Gondar and the expostulations and threats of the minister, and persisted stubbornly until, quite late at night, he assigned us as lodging a place covered with branches and leaves, and offered us neither bread nor other food,

[22] Addi Baro, apparently the place referred to by Alvarez as Barra, five miles N.W. of Debarwa. Beckingham and Huntingford, *Prester John*, ii, 575.

[23] Possibly Addi Mongonti, a village N.W. of Addi Wegri where a local chief, Dajazmač Gabra Krestos (d. 1713), established a market, or alternatively Mount Monguda north of Debarwa. Kolmodin, *op. cit.*, ii, 55, 65, 165, 223, 237 and map.

[24] Saray, Sarayé or Sarawé. This was the name of a district north of the Marab river. Though loosely mentioned with settlements in the early sixteenth century by two of Alessandro Zorzi's informants, and later indicated on Ludolf's map, no town or village of this name was mentioned by any other traveller. The place Prutky visited was presumably in the district of Saraye, but probably had another name. The principal town in the area was referred to by Alvarez as Barra, and was perhaps Addi Baro. O. G. S. Crawford, *Ethiopian itineraries circa* 1400–1525 (Cambridge, 1958), pp. 144–5, 154–5; Beckingham and Huntingford, *Prester John*, i, 98, ii, 389, 577.

though he provided a little sustenance for our servants; when we left in the early morning we were indeed astonished to have found an official so disobedient to his Emperor.

Serai is a well-provided and large town, undefended by walls, and open, without gates, surrounded by the ancient stonework of the famous old city and unable to withstand any hostile assault. From here for seven hours on end we were crossing mountains, to the very great fatigue of men and beasts, and the name of this whole neighbourhood and adjacent parts is *Kaher*.[25] Despite our extreme weariness we hastened onwards without further rest, across more mountains and hills with very little flat land, and through woods and scrub with one or two huts on the tops of the hills. On March 7 we reached a small place called *Marab*,[26] situated on a huge rocky mountain; when I reached its midpoint, the royal minister and all his slaves shouted from above that I must get off my mule and go on foot; not knowing the reason I refused to dismount until halfway to the top, when I enquired the cause why I was being told to walk on foot. 'Lord,' I was told, 'here everyone on horseback is excommunicated, and from reverence for its sanctity one must walk over this ground,' because this is the dwelling of the religous monks of the Abbey of St. Anthony.[27] Not wanting to give way to their stupid superstition I stayed seated on my mule so as not to seem to hear them or to care about their excommunication; but when their cries and anger grew greater against me, I submitted to their commands, being at the top of the mountain, and dismounted from the mule. And how holy a place did I find these monks to inhabit? All of them keep two or three concubines, or at least one, and live in a continuous state of sin, putting some away or taking others entirely as they pleased, with a thousand sins of the flesh and other wickedness, entirely contrary to true religion: but I shall write more fully later of the life and morals of the Abyssinians. They are by the same token disobedient to their Emperor, for

---

[25] It has not been possible to identify this district.

[26] This village also has not been located.

[27] Alvarez, over a century earlier, had noted that the Ethiopians showed 'great reverence' to churches, so that 'no man riding on a mule passes before a church, even though he is going in a great hurry, without dismounting, until he has passed the church and churchyard a good way'. This dismounting, in the case of the more important religious establishments, took place 'further off'. Beckingham and Huntingford, *Prester John*, i, 120–1, 254.

when we showed them our mandate that they should supply us with provisions, they refused to supply us anything to eat, though they enjoy the produce of the whole territory roundabout. Next morning therefore they sent us quickly on our way, and once again we crossed nothing but mountains, passing near by to a very lofty one, part of a range of mountains and hills by the name of *Thabor*.[28] Here on a hilltop we saw more than forty apes, as big as bears and tall with it, who rushed down the mountains towards us with loud cries; we were considerably alarmed, not knowing what the outcome would be, but they did not attack us, and apart from their shouting they did us no harm. On March 8 we were again climbing a steep mountain for four hours at a stretch, and then down by the river *Merev*,[29] where we refreshed ourselves in its sweet water and rested for two hours. Moving onward we were to spend the night at the village of *Sammama*,[30] but the villagers refused to supply either bread or water or firewood, thinking us to be Egyptians[31] and complaining that all Egyptians despoiled them and ate their food without payment. So when day came we set out starving on our way on empty stomachs, and by night reached the third kingdom, the city of *Syre*, for a more detailed description of which I open a new chapter.

[28] Possibly a reference to the Tabor or Madebay Tabor mountains which are however immediately south of the Marab river. Kolmodin, *op. cit.* ii, 247, 250.

[29] The Marab river which Bruce, *op. cit.*, iii, 115, described as the boundary between Tegré and the country of the Bahr Nagaš. This river ran over a 'bed of soil', and was 'large, deep and smooth', but 'upon rain falling' was 'more dangerous to pass than any river in Abyssinia', on account of the frequent holes in its bottom.

[30] Probably the village indicated as Semana, twenty-six miles west of Aksum, in the Consociazione turistica italiana map of 1938.

[31] By Egyptians the local people probably meant Ottoman Turks who had been in occupation of Massawa since 1557, and were from time to time in conflict with the inhabitants of the hinterland. Bruce, *op. cit.*, ii, 456–7, iii, 4–6, 119.

CHAPTER 14

THE CITY OF SYRE, CAPITAL
OF THE THIRD KINGDOM

Having now crossed two of the kingdoms of Abyssinia we were
no little exhausted, our strength impaired by a diet of water and
poor bread; but when we saw the third kingdom our spirits rose,
despite our observations of the different usages and customs of
this barbarous people. It was night-time when we reached Syre
the capital city, which without walls or gates lies open to anyone,
and is a poor place of low and wretched houses.[1] We gazed on
the residence of the imperial minister who was the governor, a
stone-built house of adequate construction: the riches he had
amassed had made him a wealthy man, whose self-conceit refused
over many years to appear in Gondar before the Emperor, for
whom he cared little and obeyed less, but exalted himself in his
riches. He refused to grant us audience, or bread, or any vegetable, so that we remained fasting, and from our extreme exhaustion resembled whited sepulchres. Later in the night he sent to
our slaves an ox and the wine called tacz: we, rejected, made of
each trouble an offering to God. Our strength was impaired partly
by the fatigue of the rough road we had travelled, and partly
from the rigorous fast we had observed, which deserved the name
rather of hunger or starvation; in default of any other resource
I took with me an Ethiopian Turk who knew Arabic, and went
around the houses humbly seeking to purchase food for cash –
and none was to be found. At last I entered the house of a widow

[1] Siré, at this time apparently the principal settlement in Tegré, was described
by J. Bruce, *op. cit.*, iii, 151, as larger than Aksum. The houses of Siré, he says,
were made of clay and had conical thatched houses, and the settlement was
'famous' for its coarse cotton cloths which circulated instead of money throughout
Tegré.

and showed how my colleagues and I were without food, trusting
solely in God's providence and humbly begging alms in His name;
when lo! what I had been unable to buy for money I received
here for the love of God, in one gift both oil, and lentils, and
flour for bread-making. How I blessed the mercy of God and
marvelled at the ways of His clemency, Who by the charity of an
infidel widow and a Turkish intermediary had bestowed upon
me His abiding grace, so that, in a state of severe want, and even
of danger to life, we were a little strengthened. Meanwhile the
imperial ministers, who knew how to lay their hands everywhere
on good bread and beef for themselves and their slaves, cared
for us not a whit, while they stuffed their own bellies.

On March 11, with nothing to hold us back, we arrived at the
village of *Dambabokuna*,[2] surrounded by pretty woodland, and,
journeying on all day through a plain, reached on March 12 a
lofty and almost impassable mountain, at whose foot flows the
river *Teckezi*,[3] bigger than all the other rivers of Ethiopia. At
flood time it is impossible to cross, and so fast-flowing that often
those rash Ethiopians who attempt it each year perish wretchedly
with the loss of their goods; in the absence of a bridge they cross
by wading, and the rush and depth of water in midstream throws
them violently to the bottom and drowns not a few: fifty or sixty
people are overwhelmed in a moment of time. But the Ethiopians
are heedless of the lessons of the dangers that others have run,
and try the crossing buoyed upon leather bags filled with straw.
Equally of these many lose their lives, for they are so lazy and
slothful that they build no bridge, though timber is abundant,
nor do they permit one to be built by foreigners, given their own
ignorance, and they care nothing that with every returning year
of flood so many souls perish in these waters.[4] A further danger
lurks in the river from the savage and predatory animals which
come out of it stealthily in the evening to attack the unwary, and
which even devour human beings; from two sorts of animal
especially do the Abyssians suffer attack, one the *Kumari*,[5] a

[2] Dambagwena, a village on the mountain of the same name some twelve miles
N of the Takkazé river.
[3] The importance of the Takkazé was also noticed by Bruce, *op. cit.*, iii, 156,
who described it as 'next to the Nile the largest river in Upper Abyssinia'.
[4] On traditional Ethiopian methods of crossing rivers see R. Pankhurst, *Introduction to the economic history of Ethiopia* (London, 1961), pp. 273–4.
[5] Amharic *gumaré*, or hippopotamus. Guidi, *Vocabolario*, p. 715.

hippopotamus bigger than our horse, and the other the *Azo*, or crocodile.[6] Of these the traveller sees such a quantity, if he is overtaken by night on the banks of a river, that he often suffers loss thereby, while lions, tigers and the many robbers of the countryside are liable to attack him: unless the greatest care is taken to maintain a watch, many perish. The river that we found, thanks to God, was neither so deep nor so swift-flowing, as the rains had not then started, and we crossed successfully without hindrance, after which we climbed a most troublesome mountain, of great height and of such steepness as to cause us injury unless we paid attention to our footholds; *Hayda* is its name,[7] and that of the surrounding countryside. Worn out with our climb we could go no further, and spent the night on its slopes; then on March 13 in the early morning we went forward, and, wearied and imperilled by the steepness of the mountains, we descended between the peaks of other mountains to the river *Buja*,[8] beside which we again took a night's rest from our fatigue. We slept in the open, after our usual ration of bread and water, in the midst of a circle of fire which we kept alight throughout the night against the wild beasts, lions, tigers, bears,[9] wolves etc; half the caravan kept watch and with shouts and cries drove off the beasts as they approached the fire, while the other half slept, within the circle of fire, carefully protected from the jaws of the lions: in such manner, in daily peril from robbers and wild beasts, must one fare across the Empire of Abyssinia; and yet although those on guard maintain a great volume of noise, still the roars of the starving lions, tigers, bears, wolves and other animals are so frightening that sleepers and guards alike are terrified.

The sun had scarcely risen on March 14 when, through hills and thorns, we reached another stream called *Enzu*,[10] and crossed it, a manoeuvre which we repeated four and forty times, with

---

[6] Amharic *azzo*, or crocodile. Guidi, *Vocabolario*, p. 484.

[7] Hayda, three miles south of the Takkazé river. Bruce, *op. cit.*, iii, 176, whose journey here followed that of Prutky, referred to this place as Hauza, and states that its mountains were of 'many uncommon forms' and had 'a very romantic appearance'.

[8] The Buya, a tributary of the Takkazé river.

[9] There are of course no tiger, bears, or wolves in Ethiopia.

[10] The Enzu, another tributary of the Takkazé, situated some 12 miles north of Amba Ras. Bruce, *op. cit.*, iii, 179, who refers to this river as the Anzo, says its bed was 'full of large, smooth stones,' and its sides were 'composed of hard rock'.

always more land before us over which we picked our circuitous way. We then climbed three huge mountains, and after noon in weariness came to rest beside the road at the spring of the same river: for the whole day we had been walking over the tops of mountains, bodily rest was an absolute necessity, and it was impossible to cross all those hills in this one day. We were compelled to halt below the mountains by a well in a place called *Derokavia*,[11] in Latin *area*, when new troubles came upon us: although we wanted to rest in order to press forward the faster next day, we were unable to do so because we were suddenly surrounded by a band of robbers: we were in fear of our lives, lest we be massacred for no reason, but our guide the imperial minister informed them that we were poor men without trading goods, and persuaded them to desist from their intention. The robbers, under a pretence of friendship, were for advising us to stay the night there without fear, doubtless so that they could rob us during the night of the few necessaries we carried with us, and even, in case of our resistance, murder or heap other punishments upon us. They were rebels against the Emperor, and in the minister's presence pretended friendship to him, promising to call up other rebels and in our company go before the Emperor to make peace with him. But well did the minister discern their deceit, and when the rebels had gone we refreshed ourselves with a drink of water and again hastened up the mountains, until towards nightfall we reached the village of *Debbebahar*.[12]

From the harshness of the mountain road five mules had now foundered, and for the next four days we had to complete the whole march on foot. Despite the fatigue the mountains caused us, no respite was in sight, and we suffered such pain in our feet and legs, and such weariness in our body, that never before in

[11] This name, which cannot exactly be identified, seems to contain the Amharic word *daraq*, i.e. 'dry'. Guidi *Vocabolario*, p. 657. Hence Prutky's use of the Latin word *area*, a level or dry piece of land. The location of the place cannot be established, but like the other places on this route, must have been on the main trade route to Gondar.

[12] Debbeb Bahr, a caravan halt on the Gondar road, later mentioned in the chronicle of Emperor Iyasu I who stopped there on several occasions. I. Guidi, *Annales Iohannis I, Iyasu I et Bakaffa* (Roma, 1903), pp. 160, 179, 195. The place which appears on the map of 'Lamalmon' in Lejean's atlas would appear to mean the 'sea' (*bahr*) of the *deb*, literally 'bear', but by extension a wild animal. Guidi, *Vocabolario*, pp. 309, 668; Lejean, *Voyage en Abyssinie* (Paris, 1872), Atlas.

our whole life had we experienced such misery, and we judged it better to die a hundred deaths in Ethiopia than to resume our journey yet again. But despite our extreme tiredness we feared to fall into the ambush of the robbers, and pressed on fast to the aforementioned village. Here we spent a whole day in rest and recruited our exhausted energies; bread alas was unobtainable, but at last after many prayers we acquired from the houses some schombera,[13] a sort of seed that is suitable for animal food and can be fed to humans in extreme need. It is like peas, but bitter, and without delay we pounded it with stones, and of half of it, roughly ground, we made unleavened bread, while the other half we boiled with a little salt to make a thick soup; to tell the truth, the dogs of Europe would hardly touch it, but in our exhausted state it tasted better than the most delicate confectionery.

With our strength a little restored we set out before dawn on March 17, because we were to climb Mt *Malmo*,[14] the highest mountain in all Ethiopia, and wished not to be overcome by the sun's rays; for two hours we hastened towards it, and then took almost five hours in climbing it, to our great distress: there was only one path going up or down, dug deep into the rocky terrain, and hardly wide enough for one animal or two men walking close together. Although it was cut into living rock, yet the feet of many travellers had brought quantities of dust which impeded us whether climbing or descending. This enormous mountain, the biggest in all Ethiopia, affords a beautiful prospect from its summit of the wonderful parts of this extensive empire, mountains, hills, forests and valleys. Every traveller who reaches the top is forced to take breath for a long time, in admiration of its natural strength. Accessible on no side, it forms as it were the outwork of the imperial seat of Gondar, and even the bravest

[13] Amharic *šembera*, or chick-pea. Guidi, *Vocabolario*, p. 206.

[14] Lamalmo was a huge mountain which all travellers between Massawa and Gondar had to pass. Almeida observed that it was necessary to climb 'as if in a spiral, along a path often so narrow' that it was 'very frightening', for there were 'such precipices that if you once stumbled and fell, there would be nowhere you could stop'. Many donkeys in fact fell and were 'dashed to pieces over the precipices'. Beckingham and Huntingford, *Some records* p. 40. Bruce, who also travelled by this route, states, *op. cit.*, iii, 179, 184, that the 'high conical top' of Lamalmo would be 'reckoned to be the highest hill in Abyssinia', and that the air on the summit was 'pleasant and temperate'.

enemy could be overwhelmed by nothing but stones hurled down from it, if the Ethiopians knew anything of warfare. But the Ethiopian nation, though stalwart, strong, and fierce to look upon, is by nature timorous, ignorant, unskilled in war, lacking in weapons, and apt to flee, so that it can be conquered by even a weak and unwarlike enemy. To speak the truth I judge that one can scarce find in the whole universe a mountain similar to this, and that not even in the mountains of other parts of the world can one find anything like these Ethiopian mountains. The Ethiopians themselves, who know the paths, often suffer falls, with their animals, break their necks, and die in misery. Generally they take better precautions and descend the mountains on foot, because these precipices induce terror and vertigo in their beholders, and it is often necessary to crawl on hands and feet, no secure foothold being practicable. In a word, to tell how punishing, tiring, dangerous, disastrous, full of misery is this road, is beyond the powers of my poor pen, and I would say that a quick death is not so bitter as is this road to the traveller: this will not easily be believed by the reader until he has tried it for himself. For my part I declare openly, that if it were not for my sacred obedience, and the prize of the redemption of souls through Christ's blood, I would humbly beg to be excused, for whatever reward in this world's goods, from taking this road a second time.

When we had sufficiently rested ourselves on the top of the mountain, and recruited our strength a little, we resumed our journey through the level ground we had longed for, and at midday climbed a little hill where stood a church in the sacred name of Jesus. Its situation was beautiful, in the midst of fields full of crops, part ripe, part in flower, part in leaf, and others just planted; I gazed on them with wonder. About evening we reached the village of *Daver*,[15] in a delightful plain, where the fields laughed in their ripe corn. Being now so near to royal Gondar we were hoping that at least on this night we might get something for supper, but it was at a late hour of the night that we stayed ourselves with some lentils, on which lightly cooked with a little salt we fed with great appetite; for water we had to possess ourselves in patience, and not until the middle of the night, after many prayers and humiliations, did we get hold of any; it was our sole consolation amid our many distresses, known

[15] Evidently a village immediately south of Lamalmo.

only to God. Indeed had not a colleague and I gone begging round the houses, when we could no longer bear the tortures of thirst, we should scarce have had any. So many were the discomforts we endured in this journey that to relate the whole length of them would be tedious, and we offered them individually as sacrifice to Him from Whom they came. Following our friends' advice we were so far fortunate as to bring with us a little corn, to furnish supplies in case the petty village officials denied us, and thus it happened that when apart from the first two officials we obtained nothing despite the imperial letters of recommendation, we fed ourselves on the corn we had brought with us. In the time of Lent, which by Orientals is kept up most strictly until sunset, we dared not eat meat, lest our journey arouse against us the anger of this barbarous people, and for the whole of this very punishing journey we had so far been frugally feeding ourselves on lightly cooked lentils and schombera boiled with salt. We were without bread except for a few days, when we comforted ourselves with unleavened bread made from the corn we had brought with us pounded with stones; when this was gone we ate nothing more to fill our stomachs than schombera flour, which we mixed with water, without any leaven, and spread on an iron plate to make unleavened bread half cooked, or rather half raw, which we ate as though it were delicate pastry.[16] But what was enough to sustain nature was not enough to satisfy it, and often in default of corn to grind we ate just this bitter tasteless roughly-bruised grain, mixed with water and sprinkled with salt, in the form of thickish porridge, although with an appetite as great as though we were eating the finest food sumptuously prepared. For fear of want later in the journey we exercised frugality from day to day, ever praising God Who had deigned to endow us with courage and firmness in adversity to resist the hardships which we bore so willingly in his name, and Who kept us always healthy and always safe, though in the whole of our life we had never eaten such wretched food.

These troubles behind us we reached on March 18 a village called *Mailecko*,[17] after crossing some small hills in a westerly

---

[16] Prutky is here describing Ethiopian pancake-like bread, which, Lobo noted, was 'as large as the wide brims of a cleric's hat of the very largest kind and as thin as the same brims'. Lockhart, *op. cit.*, p. 170.

[17] This name is apparently preserved in the Makalako river, a tributary of the Takkazé N.E. of Gondar.

direction. Here we passed a wretched night, and in the morning set out after dawn, a new delay being caused by a shortage of mules to carry our modest baggage; after much entreaty we obtained some asses and mules for our assistance, and went rejoicing onwards, for we were drawing near to the palace of Gondar and earnestly desired to reach the end of our tiring journey, which we had difficulty in pursuing, what with sore feet, hunger and weakness.

Behold! thanks to God's mercy, when we had no thought of refreshment, and were still two miles from Gondar, we saw coming from afar a band of men hastening towards us with three mules decorated with precious ornaments of gold and silver and covered with saddle-cloths. On reaching us they dismounted from their mules, bowed to the earth and kissed it in the accustomed form, in the name of his Imperial Majesty saluted us on behalf of the lord court-treasurer Gregory Draco of Nios, and presented us with a fine lunch of fish, good bread, grapes, beautiful peaches, and some aqua vitae.[18] At sight of them we duly praised God's heavenly providence, and the mercy He showed to His unworthy servants, and our spirits were uplifted that we who had been starving and weak were so kindly raised up, saved, made strong and filled with food. We sat ourselves down on the green grass, Ethiopian tentage was spread over us to keep off the sun's rays, and we ate our repast, all woes forgotten. From here on we were in greater safety and in good heart, no longer in the midst of mountains and forests or within the protection of the guard-fires; the joys of paradise were upon us. Triumphantly, and to the joy of the crowd, we mounted the three mules prepared for us, and crossed two lofty mountains, called with the neighbourhood *Ockara*,[19] to reach a small river flowing below called *Ankareb.*[20]

From there, on Sunday March 19 the day of the Passion of our Lord Jesus Christ,[21] at about six o'clock in the evening, we

[18] Gondar, as the early nineteenth century British visitor William Coffin notes, was well supplied with fish as well as such fruit as peaches and grapes. Pearce, *op. cit.*, i, 236–7.

[19] The district of Wagara, between Gondar and the Samén mountains. Bruce, *op. cit.*, iii, 195–6, 258.

[20] The river Angerab, situated immediately east of Gondar.

[21] Dr Freeman-Grenville informs us that, until 1969, this was the name given to the fifth Sunday in Lent; which fits exactly with an independent calculation of the date of Easter for 1752 as April 2.

reached the environs of the royal city of Gondar, which is situated on the slope of a high mountain. No longer were we in fear of the beasts of the forest, the tigers, lions, wolves, bears, elephants, hippopotami, wild boars and many other wild and predatory animals harmful to travellers, nor of the robbers and thieves by the wayside: in a place of safety, in a beautiful green valley set with trees, we dismounted and sat ourselves down, and again refreshed ourselves with grapes and peaches, while we sent to the royal Treasurer the news of our safe arrival, eagerly awaiting his reply as to whither finally we should direct our steps.

After a short delay for a reply, we climbed uphill through the city, mounted on our caparisoned mules among a big crowd of onlookers, guarded by royal soldiers armed with lances and shields, and were led to the house of the royal Treasurer. After hardly an hour's wait, other servants sent by the Emperor and soldiers armed with swords and lances conducted us to the imperial palace, his majesty at that time residing in another palace; he was staying with his court at a place called *Kaha* about one hour from Gondar, for a change of residence and a holiday.[22] Many of the old writers assert that the royal city was once *Axum,* as does Alvarez in *Ethiopian Journey,* Chapters 37–42, and also Tellez in book 22: indeed in olden days the Ethiopians were called *Axumites* after the name of that city. Today however, taught by my own experience, I call Gondar the royal city. It lies on 13° north parallel of latitude, about 66 degrees longitude, in the province of *Amhara,*[23] and is distant from the island of Messaua fourteen days by express messenger, or by caravan forty or even fifty days, journeying from the east towards the west. If anyone were to come from Egypt by the valley of the Nile, the cataracts, and Sennar, then just from Sennar to Ethiopia would take ten days, or with a caravan twenty-five days.

A better account of the individual changes and chances of our first arrival will be given in the next chapter.

---

[22] Bruce, *op. cit.,* ii, 618–19, also refers to the 'King's palace' by the Qaha river. On this building see R. Pankhurst, *History of Ethiopian towns,* i, 124, 157.

[23] Amhara was described by Bruce, *op. cit.,* iii, 253, as the province south of Tegré, and separated from it by the Bašelo river.

CHAPTER 15

ARRIVAL AT THE
ROYAL CITY OF GONDAR

Completely exhausted by our misfortunes and dangers by land and sea, and by the onslaughts of men, robbers and wild beasts, we appeared as men reborn when at about the eighth hour of the night we were respectfully ushered in to the imperial palace at Gondar.[1] There shortly appeared the royal Treasurer and two important ministers, one his brother Lord Joanne Draco of Nios, and the other of equal rank to him; they were the Bogiarands[2] of all Gondar and the judges of the Mahometan[3] population. They came up to us with every mark of affection, welcomed and embraced us, and commiserated with us over the hardships we had suffered. We were cheered by the good supper served to us by the Emperor's command, and they stayed with us until midnight celebrating our arrival and showing every affection towards us. The hour of sleep approaching, they showed us to three separate comfortable beds in the palace, and then withdrew.

After a night's rest, in the morning of the next day March 20 we were saluted by the royal Treasurer with the usual greetings and informed that it was the Emperor's gracious will that we should be taken as quickly as possible to his abode at Kaha and presented to him. Obeying him at once, we mounted caparisoned

---

[1] Gondar was shortly afterwards described by Bruce, op. cit., iii, 380. He says it was 'situated upon a hill of considerable height, the top of it nearly plain'. The settlement consisted of 'about ten thousand families in times of peace', and the houses were 'chiefly of clay, the roofs thatched in the form of cones.' For a plan of the city at this time see also op. cit., iv, pp. between 138 and 139, and, for engravings, R. Pankhurst and L. Ingrams, *Ethiopia engraved* (London, 1988), pp. 40–4.

[2] Amharic *Bajerond*, the term for a treasurer. Guidi, *Vocabolario*, p. 349.

[3] Gondar, like most cities in Christian Ethiopia, had a sizeable Muslim population, whose commercial importance was later noted by Bruce, op. cit., iii, 198, 381.

mules, as three days previously, and in the same style as the Treasurer hastened to our first audience, accompanied by a crowd of people and guarded by fifty slaves bearing lances.

The residence at Kaha lies between two mountains, with a stream of clear water flowing beside it and set about with a variety of tall trees, a pleasant and pretty location where it is always summer. A wall three fathoms high surrounds it, and within the circuit of the wall are at least ten houses, each set with its own wall, so that one cannot pass from one house to another without opening the doors, which are always kept closed. No one can know in which of these pavilions the Emperor is to be found, nor is it permitted for anyone to enter without previous notice and the announcement of the visitor's name.

When we reached Kaha the slaves were prompt to announce us, and after a short time we were called into audience together with the Lord Treasurer. Removing the shoes from off our feet at the palace gate we entered with reverence, and in Ethiopian fashion prostrated ourselves before the presence of the Emperor, who was seated on a couch spread with gold cloth instead of a throne. Having kissed the ground, we raised ourselves somewhat and bowed in the Emperor's direction. He bade us be seated on the ground, and after a little while, in accordance with their custom, I began to speak in a reverential tone, in company with the Treasurer; at that time the Treasurer interpreted for me sentence by sentence, as I had not yet learned much Ethiopian: 'We have come with all speed, being unable to disobey the command of your Imperial Majesty contained in your letter summoning us from Cairo, and ordered thereto, on our obedience, by our Superior Father James, Head of the mission in Egypt, Apostolic Vicar of Upper Egypt. We have been despatched in haste, with orders to obey all Your Majesty's commands which are not contrary to God or the true Catholic faith as preached in words and example by our Master Christ, and by the holy apostles Peter and Paul: each command of yours we will execute. Only we humbly beg, that you suffer us for a little while until we better understand the language of Ethiopia; until then we will exert all the powers that God has given us to the service of the Empire, and beseech only your Majesty for favour, protection and assistance, to those who will ever remain your obedient servants.' To this this Emperor graciously replied: 'From a full heart I embrace you three doctors and rejoice in your safe arrival, as I expressed at greater length in the letters I sent you, and, as long as I live and rule this kingdom, I promise you all favour and assistance. I was much grieved by the death of the late doctor, but derive the greater consolation from the presence of you three, because from childhood up I longed to see Europeans.'

We then discussed other topics in an atmosphere of cordiality, the form of holy Scripture, and the old and new testaments, which we declared we had brought with us in their whole true and incorrupt state, and then proceeded to subsequent questions: 1. Where are the tablets of Moses?[4] 2. Sheba, queen and ruler of the kingdom of Abyssinia.[5] 3. In what language will Christ judge the world? 4. What language did Christ speak, and what was the first language? We answered these questions as best we could, and the Emperor was much encouraged and replied: 'As your arrival has greatly pleased me, so am I mightily satisfied with your answers.' Our discussion lasted for about two hours, when her Excellency the Queen Mother[6] came to visit the Emperor, and we were bidden retire meanwhile to another room. On her departure we were granted a second audience, and were asked: 1. The customs and life in the kingdoms of Europe. 2. The route we had taken to his kingdom, whether we had been well lodged by his ministers, and whether we were pleased to be in his dominions. 3. European music, other liberal arts, and engineering. We gave adequate answers, whereupon he rose from his seat and said 'To show my goodwill towards you I give you my own habitation as your permanent abode,' and retired elsewhere, but next door to us. We were greatly struck with this mark of favour and even more encouraged, and again gave thanks to

[4] This question was obviously inspired by the old Ethiopian tradition, embodied in the *Kebra Nagast*, or 'Glory of Kings', that the Ark of the Covenant had been purloined by Menilek, son of Solomon and the Queen of Sheba, and taken to Aksum. E. A. Wallis Budge, *The Queen of Sheba and her only son Menyelek* (London, 1922), pp. 68–84.

[5] This question, like the preceding, had its origin in the old tradition that the Queen of Sheba was an Ethiopian. On this legend see Wallis Budge, *op. cit.*, passim, and Ullendorff, *Ethiopia and the Bible*, pp. 131–45.

[6] Empress Mentewwab (c. 1706–1773) was the *de facto* ruler of Ethiopia during the reign of her son Iyasu II (reigned 1730–1755) and part of that of her grandson Iyo'as (reigned 1755–1769). The consort, and later widow, of Emperor Bakaffa (died 1730), she was also known by her Christian name Walatta Giyorgis and her royal name Berhan Mogasa.

him and kissed the ground: to the Lord Treasurer we gave thanks likewise for the help and assistance he had afforded us, and when he returned to Gondar we accompanied him to the threshold of our quarters.

From this time of audience onwards we were confined within the imperial residence, and were permitted to see or converse with no one save the imperial servants who brought us our daily food and drink, and the young men of the Court. From all else we were shut away, for all the pavilions in the residence are enclosed with walls and their gates shut, which may not be opened without the Emperor's permission. It is the custom throughout Ethiopia to keep the houses locked up at all times behind guard-walls, partly from the wild beasts that day and night lurk to attack, partly from the inconvenience of human intrusion. Whoever of his friends wishes to visit the master of a house must first knock on the door and introduce himself. If the porter replies that the master is at home, but the master is not pleased to receive the person introduced, then the porter returns the reply that the master is out, and not within doors: this often happens even to lords and ministers of great importance, and they depart in embarrassment. This happens so frequently because they are so importunate in their visits, with always some boon to ask for, or because they want something to eat or drink, and their visits are indeed lengthy. The doors are also kept shut against the attacks of crowds of aggressive, poor, and idle good-for-nothings, of which the kingdom contains plenty. Indeed at night, when the robbers, wolves, lions, tigers, and other wild beasts cause countless losses and devour human beings, it is but right to protect the houses with gates, thick hedges, and walls even higher than they are. But it is ridiculous for servants to tell visitors that their master is at home, and then when the name is announced to say that he is not.

We three missionaries, in the seclusion that was the custom of the country, knew not what would become of us. Would we remain for ever in the company of only the Emperor, or would it be only for a short time; would our solitude be without end? For as long as it lasted we could hope for no reward in the shape of conversions, as we were not doing deeds of charity among the populace or engaging them in friendly discussions, and could not reach the goal of our vocation, the saving of souls. Though our immediate prospects were serious, expediency demanded that we be content.

On the following day at our new abode and dwelling place, on March 21, the Emperor himself honoured us with his presence. Saluting him with the greatest respect I handed him the letter from our superior Father James of Kromeriz, Apostolic Prefect of Egypt, which had been well translated into Ethiopian and which he looked on with some pleasure saying, 'We had supposed that this letter was from the Pope.' To this I replied that it had not been possible, in the course of our sudden and unexpected departure from Cairo, for a letter to come to us from Rome, and that for that reason Father James of Kromeriz, acting as apostolic vicar for the supreme pontiff, his lordship Pope Benedict XIV, had given notice to Rome before despatching us to Ethiopia, and that I doubted not that the Roman Curia would not delay to transmit an apostolic brief to His Majesty. I had brought also other letters, to her Excellency the Queen Mother and to the deputy emperor his brother, but these the Emperor out of hand forbade me to deliver, lest at this stage it be known that we three missionaries were in holy orders, as he feared that this might have a bad effect and prejudice our position. After we had cleared up a number of problems he withdrew to his own pavilion.

On March 22 we were again honoured by the Imperial presence, and for five continuous hours he developed arguments on nothing other than the faith which ensures salvation, with the words 'Do not hide what you hold in your hearts, but tell it to me freely.' At this I took courage, and thinking it a good opening replied that, while on the subject of the faith that leads to salvation and of the vicar of Christ I could not but tell the truth, the cause of our coming to Ethiopia was simply this, that we might preach the truth of the doctrine of the gospel to all in Ethiopia. I did not judge it prudent, at this first beginning, to preach through an interpreter the faith that leads to salvation, lest it fail in its effect, and I feared that when such a favourable chance had been offered I might destroy at the very beginning the whole bulk of the edifice of the spirit, and bring to ruin its wonderful mechanism. Little by little I sowed the seeds of a discourse about holy scripture, affirmed that it was only the Catholic faith that led to salvation, praised what was consonant with it and condemned what it disallowed, never contradicted the opposite point of view, and drop by successive drop instilled a taste of the milk of our holy Mother Church. The Emperor heard me attentively, and gave his complete approval to the true doctrine, saying: 'Dear doctors, there are resident in my kingdom many evilly-disposed and wicked men who use the diabolic art to do men harm: into my heart they have struck terror, and it was for this cause that I summoned you to my kingdom, that you might protect my person from all such wickedness.' Who at that point could doubt that the Holy Faith would make gains, and reap a harvest a hundred-fold? But when he asked us a little later whether we carried with us remedies which could counter such spells, we were unable at that time to remove his superstitions by argument, still less to apply medicines to that sort of disease, and perceived from his previous words that he looked on us as *Magrebini*,[7] a certain Mahometan sect that worships idols and deludes the populace with the deceits of the devil. We had to answer cautiously that being endowed only with natural reason we could only advance arguments that dealt with nature and things contrary to the light of nature: but to make it clear to him that we were taking notice of his errors, and to destroy the credibility of the superstitious charms which hung from all parts of his body, from hands, feet, and thighs, and in whose validity he placed the utmost faith, I replied guardedly that on this day it was right to have no concealments from His Majesty, but that I would pronounce to him an infallible truth, that the real servants of Christ could take harm from no trick of the Devil, and that if His Majesty were to put away from him and heartily abjure every charm that he wore upon his body, and professed himself faithful to Christ alone, then I promised that by virtue of the holy Catholic faith he would be freed from all present evils and from future evils to come: I should thus be applying a truly spiritual medicine. When he heard this the Emperor took in good part my reference to the charms that he wore, but the purity of the holy scriptures seemed to be here and there contaminated by doubts as to their meaning, and by various false promises taken from the Alcoran.

Since as yet I did not understand the Abyssinian language sufficiently well to refute doctrinal fallacies, I could not bring

[7] Presumably North African Arabs from the Magreb whose presence in Ethiopia had been mentioned over two hundred years earlier by Alvarez. Beckingham and Huntingford, *Prester John*, I, 187, 252.

our discussion to the desired conclusion, nor in such a short time did I find his disposition properly ready as yet to accept our holy faith and abjure his own. He was strongly that way disposed, but at this stage was so entangled in the snares of the devil, confused by the darkness of heresy, and trapped by his sins, that he lacked the strength all of a sudden to gaze on the rays of Heaven and the brightness of God's love, or to smell the sweet odour of supernatural faith. As we continued for some hours our discussion on the faith that leads to salvation, the Emperor said to us: 'If you agree, I will have summoned a Turk, my Arabic Secretary, who well understands the Ethiopian language, and will better explain your arguments' – no doubt in accordance with a pre-arranged suggestion. The secretary came, and questioned us face to face on the different mysteries of our holy faith otherwise unknown to the Mahometans, such as the incarnation, the two-fold nature of Christ, the ten commandments, and the customs of our religion, about each of which he asked us questions in Arabic. Our detailed explanations he transmitted to the Emperor and greatly admired them. Seeing the handbook of our Seraphic rule and opening it at the fifth chapter, he expounded it in its entirety in Ethiopian, and especially that relating to obedience, holy poverty, and perpetual chastity. In wonder he repeated 'Alla Alla, God God: indeed these three Christian doctors are far removed from Ethiopian Christians: they have a better knowledge of God, they know how to distinguish good from evil, and from a foundation of reason they can approve good and avoid evil. In truth' he repeated to us 'you are blessed: the Ethiopians live a Christian life altogether dissimilar, and the commands of the decalogue, which you proclaim in common with all Christians, they fail to observe, and practise the complete contrary, while of the way of life followed by you of the faith called Catholic, they fulfil few or none of the teachings.' In these and similar terms he extolled our faith leading to salvation, and praised it to the Emperor. God is in truth wonderful, Who inspires even the enemies of His sacred name to proclaim the truth, that the Catholic faith is to be admired and worthy of the highest praise. On this day we were granted a signal token of the Emperor's esteem, which he marked by sending for us four horses notable for their beauty, size, and colour, so that by horse-exercise we could refresh our spirits after such long hours of discussion: he then withdrew to his own palace.

Who after that could doubt that we had an excellent hope of effecting his conversion, and all the more that on March 23 he again visited us and prolonged his talk for at least two hours, posing us new questions, such as how far we differed from the Copts in matters of faith? I replied that they are far removed from Roman Catholics, and confirmed my arguments with reasons, which he followed admiringly, about divorce and the breaking of the marriage bond for trivial reasons, second baptism, the circumcision of both sexes, the single nature of Christ, and other common errors of the Coptic heresy. The Emperor's heart was in no small way stirred by these replies of mine, and he was given cause to think better of them, because he was of the same Coptic rite and heresy, or at least in name so professed himself. Despite this he heard us with an eager spirit, and we watched his disposition in surprise, realizing that we were but poor men of religion and unworthy of the honour of his presence. Again on 24 and 26 he showed us even greater favour and revealed to us the genealogy that hung from his neck, written in Greek, Arabic, and Abyssinian, and tracing his descent from the time of King Solomon: his boast was that the emperors of Ethiopia were of the seed of Solomon,[8] the legend being that the Queen of Sheba, who brought countless treasures from Ethiopia to his court, conceived and bore a son by him, from whom they trace their line. From then onward, since the principle is established and the Abyssinian emperors still take concubines, every son born to them is accepted in the genealogy as a legitimate successor to Solomon in the collateral line: the distinction is not therefore of much value. The Emperor told us, as he showed us his gold-encrusted genealogy, that we could reckon up in the European way by how many generations he was descended from Solomon, but because on that occasion there was not time enough to count, and no such favourable chance happened again, I was unable to reckon up each step of his lineage, although I would gladly have done so: my attempt was imperfect as I shall show in the sequel.

As we discussed with him various matters of faith, the Emperor with all the force of his personality urged the Turkish interpreter to embrace Christianity. He further asked us how many years have passed since the creation of the world, and when we had

---

[8] A genealogy of this kind, running from Adam to the Biblical King Solomon and thence to the Gondarine monarchs, was included in Iyasu II's chronicle. Guidi, *Annales regum Iyāsu II et Iyo'as*, pp. 3–8.

elucidated this and other matters we were greatly encouraged, and were hoping even more for the conversion of the Emperor, so obliging and so inclined to us did he show himself, and so unlikely did the contrary appear. If the duties of government kept him from honouring us with his own presence, he sent us daily at least one of his young men in accordance with our ability to converse. At length on March 28 we were summoned to his palace, bade sit on the ground in Oriental fashion, and interrogated afresh. First, what was the difference between the Roman, the Armenian, the Syrian, the Greek, and the Coptic faiths? which, not to be tedious in writing it all down, I answered as I should. Second, whom did the Catholics most affect, the Turks or the Jews? I replied that we love all our neighbours, even idolaters, but the Jews more than the Turks because of the old law which once was true and given by God; the Turkish sect by contrast was perverse, lustful, and stupid, and had been devised by a wanton and impudent man. Nonetheless this was strange, because the Turks affect the Christians more than they do the Jews, who, wherever and whenever they can, deceive Christians and lead them astray, a treatment we rarely receive at the hands of the Turks. The Emperor considered this carefully, and replied that in times past there had been many Catholics in his kingdom, but that they had been murdered in the many wars and rebellions that then arose: was this, he said, known in Europe? I replied that it was fully recorded in our history books, together with the last unjust death by stoning of our three reverend brothers:[9] we also knew that in the year of our Lord 1624 the greater part of Ethiopia had returned to their obedience to the Roman pontiff in the reign of the Emperor *Celtan Cequed*.[10] 'But alas', I groaned, 'in but a short time they shook off the easy yoke of Christ and

[9] Three Capuchin missionaries, Liberato de Wies, of Austria, Michael Pie de Zerba, of Padua, and Samuel de Beano, entered Ethiopia without permission during the reign of Emperor Dawit III (1716–1721). On interrogation at an ecclesiastical council they were condemned as heretics, and were stoned to death, together with a child who had accompanied them. E. A. Wallis Budge, *A history of Ethiopia* (London, 1928), II, 440–1. They were buried at Gondar near the church of Abbo. Bruce, *op. cit.*, ii, 581, recalls that he had 'often, both on purpose, and by accident, passed' by the place, 'where three large, and one small pile of stones, cover the bodies of these unfortunate sufferers.' See also Bruce, *op. cit.*, iii, 286–7.

[10] Emperor Susenyos, or Seltan Sagad, who reigned from 1607 to 1632 and attempted to convert the country to the Roman Catholic faith.

fell back into their original darkness of error, where they linger to the present day.' To this the Emperor replied in a kindly tone and countenance 'If it be the will of God, I am about to despatch one of you with friendly letters to the supreme pontiff, so that we may resume our previous good relations' . The conversation then turning to Father James of Kromeriz the vicar general, he remarked 'That Father James is indeed more obedient to me than my own kingdom and people, in that he complied so promptly with the letters I sent, and despatched you to my kingdom: I admire the readiness of his goodwill to me.' Lastly, because the Abyssinians have many dealings with the Jews, he asked questions also concerning the Talmud, and whether we agreed with that same. Pure myths and fictitious stories, by no means supported by holy scripture, I replied at once, whereupon the Emperor, his various questions asked and answered, replied 'I confess that your words convince me and I cannot disagree. Pray for me, and return to the peace of your apartments.'

From then on each day we were in conversation with no one except the Emperor within the walls of his palace, and knew not what the future held for us, until on March 30 when her Excellency the Queen Mother came to greet the Emperor and we too were admitted in audience. Our humble greetings to her were kindly received, and we were assured that the longer we stayed in the kingdom of Abyssinia the more we should enjoy the imperial grace and favour. Listening daily to such comfortable words as these, who could have doubts of an abundant harvest after such an excellent seed time, or thoughts of hesitation? As the sheaves ripened into harvest the barns of the heavenly treasury seemed assured of an abundant inflow of corn, and when on the eighteenth day we preached the word of God at length in the royal palace, we were buoyed up by an excellent hope of future benefit. On April 8 the Emperor betook himself to his palace at Gondar and wished to leave us behind in Kaha, his ordinary residence, but since this seclusion inhibited the performance of our apostolic function, and in such a secluded place we could not present ourselves to the populace, we made our humble prayers to him and were admitted to Gondar. That part of the royal palace once the abode of the emperor's father was made over to us for our future dwelling, and we entered therein: the favours and munificence of the Emperor were heaped upon us, and we were well provided with sustenance, bread, salt, butter, honey, meat, wood and the other necessaries of life. We besought God's Majesty on behalf of so merciful and kindly an Emperor, that the rays of the true faith might shine upon him, and that he be gathered into the one fold of Jesus Christ, now in the twenty-third year of his reign, and in the year of salvation 1752:[11] that he be granted illumination in ruling and governing to do those things that be right, that he walk in God's ways, and that at the last, the good deeds of Faith being heaped upon him, he come to triumph and with the King of Kings in heaven possess the reward of His unimaginable munificence. In the event these prayers were hard to bring to fruition, given the depravity of Ethiopian customs, life, and faith, and that sacred text can well be believed *This people honours me with its lips, but its heart is far from me.* The Ethiopians are depraved in morals, life, and faith, and believe that eternal life will consist simply of pleasure, as in the later pages I shall to some extent bring to light, and at some length. More immediately however I have thought it advantageous to describe other matters of the greatest importance for travellers to this enormous kingdom.

---

[11] Iyasu, who, according to his chronicle, was born two years and one month after the accession of his father Emperor Bakaffa in May 1721, succeeded the latter in September 1730. Guidi, *Annales regum Iyasu et Iyoa's*, pp. 22, 27–8.

CHAPTER 16

THE ORIGINS OF ABYSSINIA

Many writers have discussed the problem of the unknown origins
of Abyssinia, as of the beginning of many other nations, since
any race may from its origin draw glory and honour; it is therefore
quite understandable that it is the general view of the Ethiopians
that they are descended from Ham, son of Noah, from whom
they count a succession of one hundred and sixty-two kings as
far as king *Facilides* or *Basilides*.[1] Strabo's usual name for all who
dwell to the south and east of the Red Sea is Ethiopians or
Abyssians: holy scripture's name for all black peoples is *Cushite*,
which the Greek and Latin fathers have rendered *Ethiopian*, as
in Numbers xii *Miriam and Aaron spake against Moses because of
the Ethiopian woman whom he had married,* and Moses their brother
took their criticism in bad part, as he had taken to wife Zipporah,
whose brother was Ruel the Midianite. From this it seems that
the name Ethiopian was given to all black inhabitants alike of the
eastern and of the western part, that is that part of Asia and
Africa that today is truly called *Ethiopia.* Those who live across
the Red Sea are called *Homeritae,*[2] for the reason that the prince
of this race and founder of the royal line was called *Homer;* while
the same prince, who was the fifth king of the kingdom of Jemen,
gave his name to the Jemenites also. Now these same Arabs or
Homeritae also bear the name of *Sabaeans,*[3] and that name comes
from *Saba,* the principal metropolitan city of Arabia; reference

---

[1] Emperor Fasiladas (or Basilides), also known as Seltan Sagad II and Alam
Sagad, was the son, as Prutky says, of Emperor Susenyos, and reigned from 1632
to 1667.

[2] The Himyarites, who were referred to in the *Periplus of the Erythraean Sea*
and other early writings as the Homeritae or Homerites, were Semitic inhabitants
of southern Arabia. The term Himyarites often includes the Sabaeans.

[3] The Sabaeans were the first Arabians to develop an important civilization.

to this is made by Philosturgius[4] in his *History of the Church* Books 2, 3, 4 and 6, when he says that the nation which used to be called Sabaean from its metropolis Saba is now called Homeritan. The Ethiopians who dwell in Africa, to the west of the Red Sea, are properly called Axumites from their principal city Axum which was once a famous metropolis. That the Ethiopians according to ancient authors place their origin in Arabia Felix should not be a matter of dispute, for the sea strait is narrow and easy to cross by ship. Thus Procopius of Caesarea Book 1 page 32 'From the territory of the Homeritae come the Ethiopians, whose kingdom is in Axumis, and the sea which lies in between can be crossed with a favourable wind in three days and nights': elsewhere he says that 'the Axumites are Ethiopians'. This is as much as to say that the people originally Homeritae crossed the Red Sea, or Sea of Edom, and thereafter were first called Axumites, but now Abyssinians or Ethiopians. The reason for the connection is: firstly *worship*: the Homeritae worship idols, the sun, the moon[5] and demons, and before their conversion the Axumites did the same, when they worshipped a snake,[6] besought oracles from it, and made sacrifices to it alone, as the history of the Ethiopians relates. Secondly *rites*: they practice circumcision and keep up the custom to this day, though others hold that it was introduced by the Queen of Sheba.[7] Thirdly, *bodily characteristics*: the shape of their body and face, and their hair, points to an origin in Asia, because the swollen lips, snub nose, and curly hair of the other black Africans are not found among them. Fourthly, the *authority of Scalier* who writes *de Emend. Temp* 2, 7 *in Compend. Ethiop. P.* 80. 'The Abyssinians are not indigenous, but came in from Arabia', and later, 'without doubt they are Arabian by origin'.

At what date did they change their abode, and cross to Ethiopia? This is a difficult question. Eusebius of Caesarea says that it occurred at the same time as the Jewish captivity in Egypt, about

---

[4] Philosturgius, *Historia Ecclesiastica*.

[5] The religion of the South Arabians comprised a planetary astral system in which the moon-god took precedence over the sun-god. This belief spread into Ethiopia with the result that some of the early Aksumite coins and obelisks bore the effigy of the sun and moon. Budge, *History of Ethiopia*, i, 149.

[6] On ancient snake worship see Budge, *History of Ethiopia*, i, 143–4.

[7] For modern accounts of the Queen of Sheba legend in both Ethiopia and Arabia see H. St. John Philby, *The Queen of Sheba* (London, 1981) and J. B. Pritchard (ed.), *Solomon and Sheba* (London, 1974).

the year 2345 of Creation of the World. On the other hand Syncellus book 4 chapter 1 puts their arrival later, at the time of Judges, when *Amenophis,* or according to others *Amessius,* ruled in Egypt, Creation of the World 2422. This proves that the nation of Ethiopia is of great antiquity, and it prides itself that its emperors are the true descendants of King Solomon, tracing their descent from the Queen of Sheba, by whose intervention it came about that the whole of Ethiopia came to the knowledge of the True God and of the law of Moses: When the Queen of Sheba heard of the fame of Solomon she came to Jerusalem in the name of the Lord to prove him with hard questions and herself to experience his wisdom. 1 Kings x. 1–10: satisfied on each particular she broke out into praise of him. *Blessed be the Lord thy God which hath set thee on His throne: v. 9. And King Solomon gave unto the Queen of Sheba all her desire whatsoever she asked, much more than she had brought to him. So she turned and went to her own country, she and her servants,* and she brought with her the worship of that same God: but of what territory she was the ruler, Holy Scripture does not say.

Origen, followed by Torniello[8] in his *Annals* Vol 2 year 3043, reckons that the queen was descended from the sons of Abraham by Keturah[9] whose son Tesca or Jesau begat Sheba, and that from her are descended the Sabaeans, the inhabitants of Arabia from whom descended the Queen of Sheba: on this refer to Godinho *de Rebus Abyssiniorum* Bk 1 chap. 18. The name Sabaei was long applied by the Greeks and Romans to that Arabian people, and Holy Scripture Genesis x. 7 names them: *the Sons of Cush: Seba, and Havilah, and Sabtah, and Raamah, and Sabtechah; and the sons of Raamah; Sheba, and Dedan.* Saba was identified by the Greeks with Arabia Felix. Virgil *Georgics* i.57 says 'India sends ivory, the gentle Sabaei their incense'. Thus both in Ethiopian and in Hebrew she is called Queen of Sheba, and it is beyond doubt that she came from Arabia Felix, and took her name from her ancestors the Sabaeans, or from Saba the capital city of Arabia Felix, which we believe exercised authority over Ethiopia on the other side of the Sea of Edom, Abyssinia having been first occupied by the Sabaeans some five hundred years before. This

[8] A. Torniello, *Annales sacri et profani* (Frankfurt, 1616), ii, 29–30.
[9] Cethura. Torniello, *op. cit.,* ii, 30.

is confirmed by Job Ludolph[10] N18 fol. 237, where he says: It is true to say that the kings of Arabia Felix (whom he confirms as the ancestors of the Queen of Sheba) have from the first exercised dominion over both sides of the Red Sea, including that side adjacent to Ethiopia, and have retained under their rule for some length of time their colonies in Abyssinia; this theory is thought probable by other writers, such as Godinho,[11] Vincent Le Blanc,[12] and Josephus.[13] One can reasonably conjecture from this that the light of the Old Law was brought into her country by the Queen of Sheba, though not equally throughout all the provinces. I say nothing here of the eunuch Ebed-melech, who persuaded King Zedekiah to release the prophet Jeremiah from the dungeon of Malchaiah the son of Hammelech before he died of hunger (Jeremiah xxxviii. 9) into which he had been cast at the instance of the princes of the court, who said *we beseech thee let this man be put to death (v. 4)*.

That the Law of the Gospel was introduced there in later years is more firmly established by Acts viii. 27: *and behold on the road a man of Ethiopia, a eunuch of great authority under Candace queen of the Ethiopians, who had the charge of all her treasure, and had come to Jerusalem for to worship, was returning, and sitting in his chariot read Esaias the prophet. Then the Spirit said unto Philip, Go near, and join thyself to the chariot. And Philip ran thither to him, and heard him read the prophet Esaias, and said, Understandest thou what thou readest? And he said, How can I, except some man should guide me? And he desired Philip that he would come up and sit with him. The place of the scripture which he read was this, He was led as a sheep to the slaughter etc.*, a text to be explained as applying to Jesus Christ. *And as they went on their way they came unto a certain water: and the eunuch said, See, here is water; what doth hinder me to be baptized? And Philip said, If thou believest with all thine heart, thou mayest. And he answered and said, I believe etc. and he baptized him.* After the baptism, *the Spirit of the Lord caught away Philip, that the eunuch saw him no more: and he went on his way rejoicing.* As soon as he

[10] H. Ludolf, *Ad suam historiam Aethiopicam antehac editam commentarius* (Frankfurt, 1691), p. 231.

[11] N. Godinho, *De Abassinorum rebus deque Aethiopiae patriarchis Joanne Nonio Barreto et Andrea Oviedo*, libri tres (Lyons, 1615), pp. 37–49.

[12] Vincent Le Blanc, *The world surveyed; or the famous voyages and travailes of V. Le Blanc, or White* (London, 1660), quoted in *Commentarius*, p. 231.

[13] Flavius Josephus, *The antiquities of the Jews*, Book i, Chapter 6.

reached Ethiopia, according to common tradition, confirmed by Iraenaeus, Eusebius, Cyril of Jerusalem, Nicephorus and St Jerome, quoted by Baronius in *Annals* Vol II year 36 fol. 253, this eunuch preached the Christian faith; as some authorities have it, following Godinho *de rebus Abyssiniorum* bk 1 C 18, Baronius *loc. cit. Re-evangelization of Ethiopia,* and Jeronimo Lobo[14] in *Itinerary* vol 1 lines 3–39, he also baptized Queen Candace,[15] a name which was generic for all queens, her own name being Judith; and this is confirmed by Fr Alphonsus Sandoval Vol I.

The only question to settle is, of which Ethiopia were these queens the rulers, for they could have ruled both Arabia Felix and the other part of Ethiopia across the Red Sea, the island of Messaua, *Suaquen*[16] and places nearer the coast. It is clear that in the interior of Ethiopia which St Matthew the Apostle won for Christ there was another king. Anyone who wanted to maintain that one king ruled the whole of Ethiopia would have to deny the authorities of Rodriguez cited above and of Alphonsus that it was the eunuch who brought baptism to the queen of Ethiopia, for it is certainly an article of faith that the queen was baptized by St Matthew the Apostle. This is apparent in the abridged readings about the Apostle, and is confirmed by Simeon Metaphrastis in the two treatises he completed on the life of the Apostle, and also by St Antoninus Archbishop of Florence, by Joachim, by Berinius, and by another author called Abdia of Babylon; it is in conformity with the Roman Breviary revised by Pope Pius V. This contains under the heading St Matthew, subsection St Alphonsus, folio 666: After the resurrection, St Matthew, before proceeding to the province assigned to him for preaching, stayed first in Judaea to write in Hebrew for the sake of those of the circumcision who believed the gospel of Jesus: later he departed for Ethiopia and came to a city called *Nadauer* where he encountered two sorcerers, one called *Zarve* the other *Arfarat,* who by their magic arts had deprived most of the inhabitants of the use of their limbs and of their wordly goods. At the coming of the Apostle, the sick, the blind, the lame etc. were restored to health, and of whatever other evil they were

[14] J. Lobo, *Voyage historique d'Abyssinie* (Paris and La Haye, 1728).
[15] On Queen Candace see Ullendorff, *Ethiopia and the Bible,* pp. 9–11.
[16] Suakin (Sawākin), a port 280 miles north of Massawa in what is now Sudan.

afflicted, they were cured by the laying on of his hands. The eunuch baptized by St Philip had been appointed to that city, says St Luke, to be in charge of the treasury, and he received St Matthew into his house; thus it came about that many were converted to Jesus Christ, the eunuch inviting them to his house to hear the Apostle's teaching. When this became known to the sorcerers, by their evil arts they sent two serpents, which of old the Ethiopians had worshipped as gods, to devour the Apostle. But the holy servant of God drove them back with the sign of the Cross, and compelled them to return as tame as lambs to the desert. Seeing this miracle the Ethiopians begged to be freed from the sorcerers whom they were forced to worship, and, provided that they duly believed in Jesus Christ, the mystery of the incarnation, etc., they were set free in the Faith. Meanwhile it became known that the king's daughter was sick, and the two sorcerers were summoned to cure her: but alas in vain, she died in their presence. St Matthew was led in by the eunuch, and, speaking to her, brought her back to life; to the great wonderment of the king, Egippus, who sent out to the different parts of Ethiopia to call the population to witness a god in human form who brought the dead back to life. This miracle is referred to by St Isidore in his breviary, who also recounts many others, including that of the two serpents driven back by St Matthew. Him the Ethiopians made to honour as a god, but he vigorously forbade them, saying that he was but the servant of God, and that they should worship Him by whose power the miracles were performed, even Jesus Christ. Then a Christian temple was built, the king, queen, daughter, courtiers, and a great number of the people were baptized, and the faith of Jesus Christ was preached.

The Apostle remained in Ethiopia for twenty-three years, and under the influence of his preaching the King's only daughter Iphigeneia took the vow of virginity, with many of her friends; on the death of her father King Egippus his brother Hirtacus succeeded to the throne, and sought Iphigeneia in marriage. Recognizing that it was due to the Apostle's preaching that she was dedicated to God, he asked him to dispose of her hand in marriage to him. Meanwhile the Apostle had been strengthening her in her resolve, and washed her head together with the heads of her friends, by which sacrament, together with the uttering of the three-fold vow of chastity, poverty, and obedience, he

108

confirmed them as true Daughters of Religion, the first such in the history of the church of God, it is believed. When he learnt of this, Hirtacus was mad with rage and confirmed in his wicked intentions. He gave orders that St Matthew should be killed as he said mass before the altar, and the monastery burned down with Iphigeneia and her friends inside it; but God's holy apostle appeared on high and extinguished the flames, while God struck down the tyrant with a loathsome leprosy, and shortly afterwards removed him from this world, to be succeeded by Iphigeneia's brother, the legitimate son of King Egippus.

It remains in obscurity what sort of progress the Ethiopians made in their practice of Christianity during the course of time, what with the early date, the changes and chances of Oriental affairs, and the slothfulness of humanity. The Ethiopians themselves make no mention of any progress in Christian morality in such of their own annals as I read in Gondar the capital in 1753 (sic). They pass over in silence all preceding events, and plunge straight into the account of a monk sent to them by St Athanasius Patriarch of Alexandria; nor do they even give him his proper name, but call him *Abba Salam* the father of their salvation, attributing to him their true salvation; more than two hundred and fifty years are supposed to have passed since the death of St Matthew, and yet not until then do they reckon that they received the faith that leads to salvation. In our own chronicles I find in the fourth century a saint Frumentius,[17] whom I believe to be[18] the same as him whom the Abyssinians call Abba Salam:[19] he is denoted as having been consecrated bishop by St Athanasius[20] Patriarch of Alexandria, and sent to Ethiopia to fill the office of Patriarch there. Thereafter he took part in the canonical Council of Nicaea, held in the year 330,[21] at which this saint was present

---

[17] Frumentius's conversion of the Axumite state took place c. 330. Budge, *History of Ethiopia*, i, 147.

[18] Prutky's belief is now generally accepted, for, as Ullendorff observes, Frumentius is called by the Ethiopians 'Abba Salama'. E. Ullendorff, *The Ethiopians* (Oxford, 1973), p. 96.

[19] Abba Salama, literally 'Father of Peace' (not 'Salvation'). His identification as Frumentius had already been made by both Pero Paez *Historia da Etiopia* (Oporto, 1945), i, 56, ii, 168, and J. Ludolf, *New history of Ethiopia* (London, 1684), p. 252.

[20] Athanasius, Patriarch of Alexandria from 328 to 373.

[21] The Council of Nicaea was in fact held in 325.

together with his superior Alexander,[22] Patriarch of Alexandria; here it was laid down by canon 36, to be found among the Arabian canons, entitled Creation of the Patriarch of Ethiopia, and his Powers: It is unlawful for the Ethiopians to create or choose a patriarch except he be dependent on Alexandria, but if there be one among them who performs the duties of a Patriarch, he must be entitled Catholicus. He shall have no right to appoint archbishops, as a patriarch usually does, since he does not possess the authority or rank of Patriarch. If a council chance to be held in Greece, and he attends, the Prelate of Ethiopia shall occupy the seventh place, after the Prelate of Seleucia; he has the power of consecrating bishops, but it will not be lawful for him to appoint an archbishop.[23] Whoever disobeys this the Synod will punish with excommunication.

I plan to write elsewhere on the business of the synods, on the progress of the Faith, on prelates, and on changes in spiritual affairs, but I now turn to setting out as best I can a list of the emperors of Abyssinia.

---

[22] Alexander, Patriarch of Alexandria from 312 to 328.

[23] This, according to Bruce, *op. cit.*, i, 534, had resulted from a thirteenth century 'treaty' between Emperor Yekuno Amlak of Šawa, and Na'akweto La'ab, the last of the Zagwé rulers, the fourth article of which 'provided that no native Abyssinian could thereafter be chosen Abuna, and this even though he was ordained at, and sent from, Cairo'. The practice was prescribed by a supposed canon of the Council of Nicaea. The term Catholicus was not in fact used in Ethiopia, and Abuns did not attend councils in Greece or anywhere else outside the country.

For a modern view of the origin of the Ethiopian people, the subject of Prutky's speculations in this chapter, see R. Schneider 'Les débuts de l'histoire éthiopienne', *Documents pour servir à l'histoire de la civilization éthiopienne*, (1973), vii. pp. 47–54, and other articles in that issue. See also Sergew Hable Sellassie, *Ancient and medieval Ethiopian history to 1270* (Addis Ababa, 1972).

CHAPTER 17

THE SUCCESSION OF
THE KINGS OF ETHIOPIA

As I recounted in the last chapter, the king of Abyssinia at the time of the Apostle Matthew was Egippus, whose dead daughter St. Matthew restored to life, when he won for Christ the king, the queen, and the whole province. Egippus was succeeded by his brother Hirtacus the tyrant, whose reign was short, God afflicting him with leprosy and shortly removing him from this earth; his successor was the holy Iphigeneia's brother whose name and reign are unknown to the Abyssinians. In the course of time disasters afflicted the country, wars brought ruin and persecution, apostolic missionaries were martyred for the Catholic Faith, and, even at the moment when they were most confident that the Lord's vineyard was firmly planted, they were overwhelmed by the tempest of the heathen and denied their hope of continued evangelism. In these circumstances no succession of kings could be traced, although I, overwhelmed by a like storm, have prepared some sort of list of the kings of the country, which I set down as far as the year 1753.

330   Elesbar,[1] or Caleb the holy. Others would put his reign later, in 521, but the Ethiopians are quite ignorant of the history of the intervening years; through laziness, ignorance, and a growing lack of knowledge due to the absence

---

[1] Ella Asbeha, also known as Kaléb, is generally thought to have reigned from 514 to 542. One of the greatest rulers of the Aksumite kingdom, he undertook an expedition to South Arabia in 525. Budge, *History of Ethiopia*, i, 261–2. S. C. Munro-Hay gives the most up-to-date account and dating of the early Aksumite rulers, for example in "Aksumite chronology: some reconsiderations" *VIII international conference of Ethiopian studies, Addis Ababa Nov. 1984*, publ. in *Jahrbuch für Numismatik- und Geldgeschichte XXXIV* 1984, pp. 107–28.

111

of learning, they maintain no sort of annals and walk in utter darkness: only on the arrival, centuries later, of European missionaries and traders did they develop any interest in their history. Though no more than names, there have been recorded the following rulers of Ethiopia:

1440 Constantius Zara Jacub,[2] who attached himself to the Church of Rome at the Council of Florence.

1500 Baeda Mariami,[3] who had two wives,[4] the first of whom bore him a son Hahau, while the second, Helena Sallo Vangela, had no issue.

1510 Hahau,[5] who had two sons, Naodi and David. The elder Naodi was passed over, and David was chosen king, at about nine years of age, his mother Helena acting as regent meanwhile.[6]

1520 David,[7] who had three sons by the year 1523, Claudius, Jacobus, and Mennas; Claudius[8] succeeded to the throne after the death of David.

1541 Claudius called Aznaf Saghed. Together with his son Naodi,[9] aged eighteen years, he was killed in battle without other issue, and the kingdom devolved anew upon the youngest son of David.

[2] Zar'a Ya'qob, also known as Qʷastantinos, or Constantine, and one of the greatest of mediaeval Ethiopian rulers, reigned from 1434 to 1468.

[3] Ba'eda Maryam I, also known as Cyriacus, was the son of Emperor Zar'a Ya'qob, and reigned from 1468 to 1478.

[4] Prutky is here confused. Ba'eda Maryam had two main wives: Romna, also known as Eléni, i.e. Helena, who bore him Eskender, or Alexander, also known as Qʷastantinos, (reigned from 1478 to 1494), and Qalyupa, the mother of Na'od, also known as 'Anbasa Basar, who was emperor from 1494 to 1508. Sabla Wangél was the wife not of Ba'eda Maryam but of the latter's grandson Lebna Dengel. J. Perruchon, *Les chroniques de Zará Yâ'eqôb et de Ba'eda Maryam* (Paris, 1893), pp. 155–6.

[5] By Hahau the author presumably means Na'od, or 'Anbasa Seyon, who was referred to by Alvarez variously as Nahu and Nahum. Beckingham and Huntingford, *Prester John*, i, 241, 256–7, ii, 356, 375, 495.

[6] This paragraph is confused. Na'od (also known as Anbasa Bazar) was not the son of Ba'eda Maryam, but of 'Amda Seyon, and actually ruled from 1494 to 1508. Dawit was in fact the son of Na'od.

[7] Dawit II, also known as Lebna Dengel and Wanag Sagad I, reigned from 1508 to 1540.

[8] Galawdéwos, or Claudius, also known as Asnaf Sagad I, reigned from 1540 to 1559.

[9] The chronicle of Galawdéwos makes no mention of his having any son called Na'od.

1559 Mennas[10] the brother of Claudius, called Adam Saghed. He had a son Sereza Denghel, and on his defeat and death in battle his son succeeded him.

1563 Sereza Denghel[11] called Malack Saghed, who had a son Jacobus who succeeded him.

1596 Jacobus,[12] aged seven years, called like his father Malack Saghed. Then in the year 1603 his people[13] rebelled and deposed him.

1603 Aznaf Saghed or Zadenghel, cousin of Jacobus. He was killed in battle after a short reign, whereon the throne was once more ascended by

1604 Jacobus.[14] After various adventures he was wretchedly put to death by Susneus in 1607, for ambition's sake, it is believed.

1607 Susneus,[15] called Malack Saghed, who in course of time took the name Sultan Saghed. The great-grandson of King David, he had a son Basilides, who succeeded his father after a reign of twenty-five years.

1632 Basilides, on September 16. Called like his father Sultan Saghed, he had a son Joannes and ruled tyrannically for thirty-two years. He was a persistent enemy to the Catholics, and expelled the Fathers of the Society from the kingdom.

1664 Joannes[16] called Af-Saghed. He had a son Jasu or Jasock. He too, before his death, not only expelled from the kingdom all Catholics, but forced all the descendants of the Portuguese to migrate to Sennar.

[10] Minas, also known as Wanag Sagad II, and brother, as Prutky says, of Emperor Galawdéwos, reigned from 1559 to 1563.

[11] Sarsa Dengel, also known as Malak Sagad, was the son, as Prutky correctly states, of Minas, and reigned from 1563 to 1597.

[12] Ya'qob, also known as Malak Sagad II, was, as Prutky notes, the son of Sarsa Dengel, and reigned from 1597 to 1603. He was deposed in the latter year, but was restored in 1604, and killed, as suggested by the author in a later paragraph, in 1607.

[13] Za-Dengel, also known as Asnaf Sagad II, was the son of Sarsa Dengel's brother, and reigned for two years, 1603-4.

[14] Ya'qob, already mentioned by Prutky two paragraphs earlier.

[15] Susenyos, also known as Malak Sagad III and Seltan Sagad I, was the grandson of Ya'qob, and, as Prutky states, was the great-grandson of Dawit II. He reigned from 1607 until 1632.

[16] Yohannes I, also known as Alaf Sagad, was the son of Fasiladas, and reigned from 1667 to 1682.

1680   Jasu[17] called Adam Saghed. He had a son called Tecklehaimanut, and after a reign of twenty-five years he yielded the throne to his son, who in a conspiracy with his mother cruelly murdered his father Jasu in 1706.

1705   Tecklehaimanut.[18] He by God's justice was murdered by his supporters early in his reign.

1708   Theophilus,[19] brother of Jasu. After only two years of rule, he died a natural death.

1711   Justus[20] succeeded to the throne, called Zei Saghed, that is Sun in Splendour. The son of Jasu's sister, he was duly elected by the nobles at the time when he was in command of the army. He showed great favour to the European catholics, but incurred the hatred of various people and was killed by poison.

1716   David,[21] on February 16. The son of king Jasu, he was eighteen years of age. He had a son Hennes, and inflicted the crown of martyrdom on our three venerable Fathers, Liberatus, Michaelus Pius, and Samuel; after five years of rule he died a natural death in September 1721.

1721   Backaffa[22] Masich Saghed, the elder brother of David. Aged twenty-six years, he had a son Jasu, and welcomed and favoured Father Franciscus of Rivarolo, missionary for the Propagation of the Faith, of the Reformed Order of St. Francis; he reigned for ten years.

[17] Iyasu I, also known as Adyam Sagad, was the son, as Prutky says, of Yohannes I, and reigned from 1682 to 1706, in which year, as stated above, he was murdered.
[18] Takla Haymanot, also known as Abrak Sagad, Le'ul Sagad, and Gerum Sagad, was the son, as noted by Prutky, of Iyasu I. He reigned from 1706 to 1708.
[19] Téwoflos or Theofilus, also known as Asrar Sagad, was the brother, as Prutky says, of Iyasu I, and reigned from 1708 to 1711.
[20] Yostos, or Justus, also known as Tahay Sagad, is generally held to have come from outside the Solomonic line. He reigned from 1711 to 1716. The Ethiopian chronicle of this time states that Yostos 'died of disease', but Bruce says that whether the king's end was due to a 'violent or natural death' is not known. R. Basset, 'Études sur l'histoire d'Éthiopie', *Journal Asiatique* (1881), xviii, 335–6; Bruce, *op. cit.*, iii, 575–6.
[21] Dawit, or David, III, also known as Adbar Sagad I, was the son, as Prutky says, of Iyasu I, and reigned from 1716 to 1721.
[22] Bakaffa, also known as Asma Giyorgis, Adbar Sagad II and Masih Sagad, was the son as Prutky notes of Iyasu I, and reigned from 1721 to 1730.

1731 Jasu[23] called Odiam Saghad. The son of Backaffa Masich Saghed, his age at the beginning of his reign was eight or nine years, and his mother the queen acted as regent until he reached years of discretion. It was in his reign that I the author arrived with the two missionaries my colleagues in 1751.

Everything that occurred I have noted down in different chapters with an account of the character, way of life, and faith, in Ethiopia. King Jasu by that time had two sons, future rulers of the kingdom. I had often heard in Europe of the name *Prester John*, and also read about him in books, and I enquired about its origin, and whether by chance the title still persisted in the imperial line.

Everyone denied knowledge of it, but as I spent some time there I told the Emperor himself that he was entitled in Europe Prester John, and begged him to pronounce upon it. He was astonished, and told me that the kings of Abyssinia had never been accustomed to call themselves by this name.[24] I therefore deduce some other origin for this name, which today is wrongly applied to the emperors of Ethiopia.

[23] Iyasu II, also known as Berhan Sagad and Adyam Sagad II, was the son as Prutky says of Bakaffa, and reigned from 1730 to 1755.

[24] This would appear the first recorded statement by an Ethiopian monarch that he and his forebears were unaware of the legends concerning Prester John which had circulated for so long in Europe – and are discussed in the following chapter.

For much of the history thus briefly covered in this chapter see Taddesse Tamrat, *Church and State in Ethiopia 1270–1527* (Oxford, 1972) and Budge, *History of Ethiopia*, and on the Ethiopian chronicles of the time, on which Prutky (unlike Bruce) does not seem to have been familiar, see Basset, 'Etudes sur l'histoire d'Ethiopie', F. Béguinot, *La Cronaca abbreviata d'Abissinia* (Rome, 1901), J. McCann, 'The Ethiopian chronicles; an African documentary tradition', *North East African Studies*, (1979), i, pp. 47–61, and, more generally, G. W. B. Huntingford, *The historical geography of Ethiopia* (Oxford, 1989).

CHAPTER 18

DERIVATION OF THE IMPERIAL
TITLE PRESTER JOHN, AND
THE GOODS THAT SHOULD
ACCOMPANY THE TRAVELLER

In personal conversation with the inhabitants, and indeed with
the Emperor himself, I was told that the title Prester John,
contrary to European opinion, is never applied to the Emperor
of Abyssinia; I therefore consulted books and manuscripts, *Asia*,
the treatise of Dom Joannes Barros,[1] Christian adviser to the
King of Portugal, and accounts of eastern conquests by land and
sea, and found the country called *Zanquebar*,[2] which borders on
one of the main rivers of Africa the *Niger*.[3] This river starts in
Nigritia and after flowing for 800 leagues enters the sea through
various mouths in West Africa, at the end of which lies the Cape
of Good Hope discovered by the Portuguese; Ptolemy calls it
Raptus,[4] and, whereas its course lies otherwise than to the south,
its furthest springs are in the territory of the ruler of Abyssinia,
in the mountains of *Graro*, where it bears the name of *Obin*. The

[1] *The treatise of Dom Joannes Barros*, the *Asia* of the celebrated Portuguese
historian João de Barros. He was not entitled to the prefix Dom.
[2] *Zanquebar*. Zanzibar, but Barros, in the passage on which Prutky relies here
(*Asia*, dec. I, liv.ii, cap.4) applies the name to the coast between Quelimane and
Cape Corrientes, far to the south of Zanzibar.
[3] *Niger*. The Niger was confused with almost all important African rivers; it
was often thought to originate in central Africa, to flow north through Lake
Chad, and then to reach the Atlantic as the mouths of the Senegal and the
Gambia. What Barros calls the Obi is the Zambezi.
[4] *Rhapta* was a river and a port in East Africa. Its location is a matter of dispute,
but the port was probably near Ras Kimbiji, about 50 km. S.E. of Dar es Salaam.
L. P. Kirwan 'A pre-Islamic settlement from al-Yaman on the Tanzanian coast',
L'Arabie préislamique et son environnement historique et culturel. Actes du Colloque
de Strasbourg 24–27 juin 1987, Université des sciences humaines de Strasbourg,
Travaux du centre de recherche sur le Proche-Orient et la Grèce antique, 10.

116

old Portuguese writer calls the country of Abyssinia by another name, *Aian*,[5] that is, the territory of the sources and springs of the Nile, called by the Arabs the eye of *Aain*. Now, because the dwellers near those springs are all black, the first Portuguese and Spanish conquerors of the Indies gave to the kingdom of Abyssinia the name *Prete*,[6] which sounds the same in their language as *black*. This then is the origin of the name Preteiani: the peoples of Abyssinia who dwelt by the sources of the Nile being black, the name *Preteiani* was given by the Spanish and Portuguese to the black inhabitants of that area; then by bad translation from Portuguese to French the name Presbyter Joannes[7] was coined.

This however is a title which the Emperor of Abyssinia has never borne and never wishes to hear, especially when you consider that he is not a priest, but a layman who has been advanced to the imperial title, and that the glory which surrounds him is owed to himself alone for the constant revolts which he has had to subdue. Though the realm itself is of the richest and most extensive, he cannot enforce his taxes from such widely dispersed provinces, each governor follows his own judgement far removed from the imperial palace, and the emperor collects but little of the annual revenue. Of any other source of income he is without knowledge, and although the veins of the land abound in ores of all sorts, gold, silver, iron, etc. in great quantity, yet for want of suitable managers, which he lacks, the richest emperor of olden times is now become poor, and the most splendid is now become wretched. Neither iron, nor precious metal, nor metal such as copper, lead, tin, mercury, have they the wit to find, in a land that flows with milk and honey; much the less can they mine silver or gold, beyond what they find on the surface of the earth. The Abyssinians are lazy, ignorant, idle, over-bearing, they labour long at nothing, they go naked and gorge themselves on raw flesh, and they aspire to nothing further:

[5] *Aian.* Barros applies this name to the country between Quelimane and Cape Guardafui. *A'yan* is a plural of the Arabic *'ayn* meaning 'eye' or 'spring, source'.

[6] *Preto*, Portuguese for 'black'.

[7] Prutky's account of the origin of the legend of Prester John is entirely fanciful. For the history of this mythical figure see V. Slessarev, *Prester John, the letter and the legend* (Minneapolis, 1959); C. F. Beckingham, '*The achievements of Prester John*' (1968); *idem*, 'The quest for Prester John", *Bulletin of the John Rylands University Library* (1980), lxii, 291–310.

with all their laziness they hold gold itself in little or no esteem, despite its plentifulness, as I shall describe later.

The would-be traveller to Ethiopia will have great difficulties to overcome, to minimize which it will be ncessary to take with him a number of articles. White sashes or cummerbands of Indian cloth for turbans, interwoven with gold,[8] saleable at three gold ounces: fabrics of all degrees of fineness, moreens, cassimirs, farandines, shalloons, which are useful as a special gift to the upper classes, who affect the Turkish style of dress; red, blue, violet, and yellow cloth, but red above all appeals to the Abyssinian taste. Knives, spoons, needles, mirrors, different sorts of trade goods, as well as muslin, otherwise called *baft*,[9] which is popular with Abyssinians for the dress of noblemen. Material interwoven with precious metal, such as silver and gold,[10] can only be worn by the Emperor, and occasionally, by his permission, by his ministers, who are often rewarded for a piece of faithful service by the gift of a precious garment. Before all things the Emperor[11] welcomes cannon and munitions of war, as these are seldom to be found in his kingdom, much less fabricated by the Abyssinians. Perfumes of all kinds for their concubines, such as oil of cinnamon from India, oil of cloves, sandalwood, musk with which they anoint themselves, are very highly valued. They are pleased also with seeds of garden vegetables or of flowers of all sorts, quite lacking in Abyssinia, and they also like scented water, as rose-, marjoram-, Hungary-, lavender-water etc. Sugar is very popular among them as they can seldom obtain it, except occasionally from Mocha or the East Indies: nutmeg, all sorts of spices especially pepper, which they eat in quantity with their raw meat

[8] Half a century earlier the French consul in Cairo, Charles de Maillet, had drawn up a not dissimilar list of articles suitable for taking into Ethiopia. This list is given in C. Beccari, *op. cit.*, xiv, 178–81, and summarized in Pankhurst, *Introduction to the economic history of Ethiopia*, pp. 352–3.

[9] From Persian *bāfta* 'woven', a name given to a variety of textiles.

[10] The restriction on the wearing of gold by the general public is recorded by several early nineteenth century travellers to Šawa, including C. Johnson, *Travels in southern Abyssinia* (London, 1844), ii, 337, and W. C. Harris, *The highlands of Aethiopia* (London, 1844), iii, 33. See also Pankhurst, 'Status, division of labour and employment in nineteenth and early twentieth century Ethiopia', *University College of Addis Ababa Ethnological Bulletin* (1961), ii, No. 1, pp. 7–57.

[11] Iyasu was here voicing a preoccupation which he shared with countless earlier and later rulers of the country. R. Pankhurst, 'Misoneism and innovation in Ethiopian history' *Ethiopia observer* (1963), viii, 287–320.

and for a pound of it pay a dram of gold, which in value is worth one European gold piece. Of especial value to the traveller will be fine Bombay cloth embroidered in part-silk with a pattern of flowers, blue for monks and gold for nobles. Silver or gold thread, with stronger thread to ornament their leggings – all these individual items arouse great wonderment in this race of barbarians, especially when they see fringes of gold or silver; whatever they admire of gold, they pay for liberally without haggling over the price. Little knots made up in the Arabian style from fine white and red threads of part-silk, thread indeed of all sorts, cotton cloth of Bengal or Surat in India they value above all others. Table knives (though they do not eat with them but use nothing but their fingers), forks, razors, hammers, forceps, axes, saws, tools of all sorts, tin-plate for lanterns, finished lanterns, surgical instruments, lancets, medicaments, none of which can be found in Ethiopia, they are glad to buy for unbelievable sums of money. As I recounted in Egypt, both men and women use kohl for eye make-up, as a cosmetic.

Stirrups for their mules they are unable to fabricate, having neither smiths[12] nor iron; writing paper, or gilded paper, is entirely lacking, and they write everything on parchment; millwrights would be welcome, with the skill to prepare grindstones and make flour, for they have no mills; and wooden trays, and other household utensils, for there is nothing like this to be found in the country. Missionaries should take care to bring with them holy pictures both black and coloured, crucifixes, figures of the Virgin, of the Apostles, and of the Holy Fathers of the East,[13] camp beds made of iron, such as are used when campaigning, which can be folded up, and from the corners of which canvas can be stretched to give protection from the rain. Glass too will be useful on the journey, and bottles, for what in Europe sells for one crossed thaler, that the Italians call a quarantano, sells

---

[12] Both statements are incorrect. The existence of blacksmiths in Ethiopia had been noted by both Alvarez and Almeida, as well as by Ludolf's informant Abba Gorgoreyos, and Prutky himself later tells of the smelting of iron. Beckingham and Huntingford, *Prester John*, i, 149; idem, *Some records*; Ludolf, *New history*, p. 390.

[13] On the effect on Ethiopian art of such pictures see S. Chojnacki, *Major themes in Ethiopian painting*, (Wiesbaden, 1983), p. 32, who argues that the copying of foreign models was 'by no means mechanical', and permitted 'ample space for new stylistic, and even iconographic interpretations'.

here for a dram of gold. A skilled craftsman in any trade or art will enjoy unimaginable esteem, profit, and glory. Jars and stills with which to distill aqua vitae and different sorts of spirit and medicine; glass coloured with pictures, so popular with our peasants, they find attractive, as also Venetian glass and small and large Venetian beads,[14] of different colours, from which they make rosaries. They also like all sorts of objects made of glass, figurines, earrings of stone covered with silver or gold, or of metal, and diamonds for cutting glass.

Although they have plenty of olive trees[15] growing with their fruit, they are avid for imported olive oil and know not how to press their own; cotton, which grows a-plenty on bushes throughout the country, they value not at all, yet admire it from abroad. The traveller must further realise that it is necessary not to rely on boxes for transport, as they are almost impossible to carry over the terrific mountains, and that provision must be made of waterproof cloth, into which each item can be packed, as the merchants do into bundles and bales, and covered with a further protection to keep out the torrential rain. Leather sacks, also called *kerbe*,[16] must be included in the baggage, both large and small, to carry flour, and other stronger ones to carry water, and to fetch it from the streams; leather ropes or strong straps called *maczina*,[17] with which to strap up the goods; everything has to be strapped firmly on to mules and carried over lofty mountains, so that a further necessity is leather bags filled with straw, like horsecloths, with which to cover the mules and asses,

---

[14] Bruce, who took beads with him for purposes of exchange, observed that they were 'a dangerous speculation', for their popularity depended upon fashion, 'and the fancies of a brown, or black beauty, there, gives the *ton* as decisively as does the example of the fairest in England. To our great disappointment', he adds, 'the person employed to buy our beads at Jidda had not received the last list of fashions from this country; so he had bought us a quantity beautifully flowered with red and green, and as big as a large pea; also some large oval green and yellow ones; whereas the *ton* now among the beauties of Tigre were small sky-coloured blue beads, about the size of small lead shot, or seed pearls; blue bugles, and common white bugles, were then in demand, and large yellow glass, flat in the sides . . . . All our beads were rejected by six or seven dozen of the shrillest tongues I ever heard'. Bruce, *op. cit.*, iii, 107–8.

[15] The fruit of the Ethiopian wild olive, the *wayra* (*Olea africana*) is virtually inedible, and cannot be used for the production of olive oil.

[16] Perhaps *qarbat*, the Amharic for a leather bag. Guidi, *Vocabolario* p. 261.

[17] Amharic *mačanna*, or leather thongs used to tie loads on beasts of burden. Guidi, *Vocabolario*, p. 850.

lest their loads gall them on the long punishing mountainous trail, and all the goods and necessaries be abandoned at the roadside. Take care in addition not to tie up the merchandise or necessaries into large bundles, or the mules on so taxing and long a journey through the mountains will be unable to bear them, and, once their backs are galled, they are of no further use. Every item of gear must be tied up into two equal bales, strapped strongly down so that it takes at least three men to lift, and the load placed on the mule, who is used to such a weight and will easily carry it right to the palace at Gondar. Each traveller moreover should provide himself with good leggings, or with what are commonly called half-boots, to preserve the feet from damage from thorns and brambles as he passes through the woods, or from the countless thistles. Everyone is forced to guard his eyes, lest one be scratched out, and hands, faces, and feet stream with blood like a man scratched by a cat, while one's clothes fare even worse because while guarding one's eyes the caravan continues on its way, and one can guard nothing else. When out of the wood, as though after a battle, everyone is torn and bleeding and makes a sorry spectacle in the open plain, while others point in grief to their torn skin, and only gradually do the lamentations grow silent.

Europeans who enter Ethiopia will find this advice extremely profitable. Now particular attention should be paid to the next chapter.

CHAPTER 19

THE MODERN STATE OF ETHIOPIA

I here intend to set out the facts necessary to a better understanding of the state of Ethiopia, otherwise called Abyssinia or, vulgarly, *Habesch*. Of the various areas to which the ancient geographers gave the name of Ethiopia, the main ones seem to be those lying further to the east, the same sources applying the name Ethiopia to the part lying south of Egypt. Many say that India gets her name for the same reason, that in olden times various peoples from the regions washed by the Indus migrated in crowds and fixed their abode elsewhere. This area of Africa acquired many different names, both in holy scripture and among the sacred writers, but it is not part of my purpose to mention them. Some writers have wanted to call the whole area Ethiopia or Abyssinia, and to give the name Abyssinians to the Ethiopians both to the west and east and in the parts between, who were unknown to the ancient geographers: this too is a falsehood. What is certain is that the name Abyssinia can be applied neither to middle nor to western Ethiopia which borders on the interior of Libya, nor to that part which contains the land of Zanzibar, nor finally to that which borders the kingdoms of Congo, Angola, the rest of Guinea, or the neighbouring provinces, and to which the ancients did not attribute the name of Abyssinia. Abyssinia relates only to that part which lies below Egypt, and includes only those Ethiopians who inhabit the eastern regions of Africa; furthermore, not all those peoples who live in Ethiopia thus defined can truly be called Abyssinian, but only those who are subject to that emperor commonly called Prester John, as I have found noted by some writers.

It is generally agreed that the Ethiopia which we are discussing is defined by the following limits: on the east by the strait of the

Red Sea, which starts almost as a narrows, and stretches northward from the tenth to the nineteenth degree of latitude as far
as the island and maritime city of the same name which modern
geographers call Suaquen and ancient ones *Aspis*. On the west it
is defined by lofty ranges of mountains, which fall down in long
sweeps to the streams of the Nile, and its extent is closed by two
lines on each side, one of which runs from Suaquen in a straight
line northwards to that island, which was once called *Meroe*;[1] the
other, starting from the west of the Nile, goes eastward and then
extends on a curving course as far as the kingdom of *Avia*,[2] the
most southerly of all those regions. From here it goes eastward
again and borders on *Adel*,[3] the kingdom of the Saracens[4] whose
capital is *Ara*,[5] and which extends over nine degrees of latitude
from the equator northward. The whole region with the four
sides which enclose it contains about six hundred and seventy
leagues, though others reckon it at seven or even eight hundred:
but the figure I have given is that approved by the more skilled
geographers.

As for the name Abyssinia, I have made many enquiries and
know that it is agreed that this was not its ancient name. Some
of the later writers, who realise that the name is corrupt, derive
it from a royal city, called *Ptolemais Auxume*, one of whose citizens
is said to be that eunuch of Queen Candace who appears in the
Acts of the Apostles; others hold that the word Abyssinia or
Abassia comes from *Abatos*, with a considerable change of letters,
and maintain that *Abatos* means a part of the world abounding
in gold, silver, gems, and precious stones, remarkable for the
nobility and excellence of its inhabitants, magnificent in its buildings, and flowing with an abundance of all good things. Such at
least is the region they mean, which we call Abyssinia or Abassia.
Another theory has it that Abassia or Abyssinia is the same in
Arabic, Turkish, and Ethiopian, and denotes a people that is
free, enslaved to no foreign prince, subject to no other power,

---

[1] The region of Meroe in Sudan was considered as an island, Bruce, *op. cit.*,
iv, 539, explains, because it was bordered by four rivers: the Marab, the Takkazé,
the Atbara and the Blue Nile.
[2] Probably Hadya is meant.
[3] Adal, the Muslim-inhabited lowland region between Zayla and the Ethiopian
highlands.
[4] Saracens, i.e. Muslims.
[5] Ara, probably the old Muslim city of Harar, in eastern Ethiopia.

and under the sway of no tyrannical ruler; if I wished to refute this, it is not worth the trouble. I believe, as Strabo says, that the name comes from the Egyptians, who gave the name Abases to inhabited parts which are separated from the rest by deserts and wastes, as indeed are the parts in which Abyssinia lies – as Strabo confirms.[6] However, as to when the name began to be applied to the native inhabitants, I know not, nor can I find any authority whose writings contain any plausible theory.

Joannes Gabriel,[7] one of the early Portuguese to settle in Abyssinia, and the commander of the Portuguese legion, a distinguished soldier, man of honour and responsibility, and renowned for his upright life, recounted the tradition that Abyssinia comprised in ancient law twenty-six realms divided into fourteen regions, and that it was bounded by a line which runs from the north eastwards through the nearby shores of the Red Sea towards the Ocean, and then bending rather to the west, reaches the borders of the kingdom of *Melindi*;[8] after which it veers from east to north and ends at Cairo. Westwards from the island of Suaquen there are eight separate realms one after the other. The first of these is called *Tigré*[9] or *Tigris*, of considerable length and breadth, and contains seventeen provinces of a good size, each ruled by a chieftain who administers public affairs equally in war as in peace. In this realm the maritime area is in Turkish

[6] Prutky was misinformed. It is now generally agreed that the term Abyssinia is derived from Habašat, the name of a tribe thought to have migrated across the Red Sea from Yaman to Ethiopia. It is, however, popularly held by many Ethiopians that the word is connected with *habaša*, the Arabic word for 'to collect a mixture of things', and the name Abyssinia is for this reason widely said by them to have a derogatory connotation. D'Abbadie, *Dictionnaire*, p. 9; Budge, *History of Ethiopia*, i, 120–1, 130.

[7] João Gabriel the leader of the Portuguese community in Ethiopia. Beccari, *op. cit.*, ix, 327, 383, 436, 438, xiii, 321, 402, 433.

[8] Malindi on the Kenya coast.

[9] Tegré, the principal province of northern Ethiopia. Ludolf, *New History*, pp. 16–17. Bruce, emphasising the province's then political importance, wrote: 'What in special manner makes the riches of Tigre is that it lies nearest the market, which is Arabia; and all the merchandize destined to cross the Red Sea must pass through this province, so that the governor has the choice of all commodities wherewith to make his market. The strongest male, the most beautiful female slaves, the purest gold, the largest teeth of ivory, all must pass through his hand. Fire-arms moreover, which for many years have decided who is the most powerful in Abyssinia, all these come from Arabia, and not one can be purchased without his knowledge to whom it goes, and after his having had the first refusal of it'. Bruce, *op. cit.*, iii, 251–2.

hands, the next area inland is held by the Saracens, while the interior is inhabited by Ethiopians and Christians together, who live in misery and poverty, are black in colour and misshapen in body, and live their lives on no rational principle, with morals to match. Tigré gives way to *Dancali*,[10] or so the next realm is called, which on the east is washed by the waves of the Red Sea, and then stretches westward in a short and infertile tract of land; the inhabitants are Moors by race and Mahometans by religion, who act as customs officers for the Emperor of Abyssinia. Next comes *Angote*,[11] another realm whose eastern edge marches with Tigré, on the side further from the sea, the fourth realm is called *Boa*, the fifth *Amhara*,[12] the sixth *Leca*;[13] these four are inhabited only by Christians. The seventh is very extensive, containing seventeen provinces, inhabited partly by Christians and partly by pagans, and called *Abagamedri*.[14] After this comes *Dambea*[15] which consists only of two provinces and is inhabited by Christians and pagans living side by side.

On the other side of Dancali towards the narrows of the Red Sea, and along the sea-shore, there stretches *Aucaguerle*[16] which is watered by the river *Gari*,[17] and is inhabited by Moors who

[10] Dankali, or Afar, the lowlands east of the Ethiopian plateau.

[11] Angot, a small province north-east of Amhara, Ludolf, *op. cit.*, p. 14; Bruce, *op. cit.*, iii, 253. Prutky here and throughout much of this chapter seems to have based himself on Nicolao Godinho's *De Abassinorum rebus* (Lyons, 1615). This work referred to Boa as the 'fourth kingdom' of the realm, but Ludolf in the *Commentarius* to his History (Frankfurt, 1691) expressed himself unable to identify the place. The name Bua was conceivably an error for Bur, a province between Akala Guzay and the Red Sea. Beckingham and Huntingford, *Some Records*, 231; Ludolf, *New History*, p. 17.

[12] Amhara, a province in north-west Ethiopia, referred to by Prutky in chapter 13. Bruce, *op. cit.*, iii, 255, who describes the province as a 'very mountainous country, full of nobility', estimated that it measured 120 miles from East to West and 40 from North to South, and says that its inhabitants were 'reckoned the handsomest in Abyssinia, as well as the bravest'.

[13] Leca was apparently Godinho's mistake for Holeca, i.e. Walaqa, a region north of the Abay river. Beckingham and Huntingford, *Some records*, p. 241; Ludolf, *op. cit.*, pp. 13, 18; idem, *Commentarius* p. 86.

[14] Abagamedri, Bégamder. Beckingham and Huntingford, *Prester John*, ii, 459.

[15] Dambeya, a province immediately north of Lake Tana. Beckingham and Huntingford, *Prester John*, ii, 578; Ludolf, *New history*, pp. 15, 19. Bruce, *op. cit.*, iii, 258, who describes it as the 'granary of Abyssinia', says that it was a 'a low province', 'all sown with wheat' and supplied grain to the Emperor's household.

[16] Aucaguerle or Awsa Gurrale, the modern Awsa, east of Tegré. Beckingham and Huntingford, *Some records*, p. 229.

[17] Gari, a river which has not been identified.

have never submitted to the Emperor of Abyssinia. The next realm is *Adel*, twelve degrees of latitude north of the Equator, of which the principal city, called of old *Avalites*[18] and now *Zeila*,[19] is remarkable, at least in this part of the world, as a centre of trade; the whole realm is inhabited by Moors who are bitter enemies to the Emperor and who, on the testimony of the fathers of the Society, have always from olden times waged war against him. It was this realm which produced *Gragna*[20] the Mahometan ruler, who subdued by force of arms nearly the whole of Abyssinia, and was then defeated by the Portuguese in many battles and finally captured, whereupon his head was struck from his body, and he paid the just penalty of his wicked deeds.

After this comes *Dahali*,[21] which stretches towards Mombasa[22] as far as the Equator, inhabited partly by Christians and partly by Saracens, and paying tribute to Abyssinia, and then *Oecie*,[23] which fronts towards the interior, is subject to Abyssinia, and is inhabited by Mahometans and pagans in equal numbers; other authorities call it *Ved*,[24] and our last Holy Martyrs make mention of it, as they crossed through it from Messaua on their way to royal Gondar. The next realms are *Arium*,[25] *Fatagar*,[26] and *Zingerum*,[27] the first two of which are Christian, and the last pagan. Zingerum, or *Gengero*[28] as it is called by Holy Martyr Father

[18] Avalites, probably Assab possibly Zeila (Zayla').

[19] Zayla', a port on the north coast of Somalia. Pankhurst, *Ethiopian Towns*, i, 305–9.

[20] Ahmād Ibn Ibrāhīm al-Ghāzī (1506–1543), the early sixteenth century Muslim ruler of Eastern Ethiopia, nick-named in Amharic Grañ, or the 'left handed'. Trimingham, *op. cit.*, pp. 84–90. He was not captured but killed in battle.

[21] This locality, which had earlier had been mentioned by Godinho, was unknown to Ludolf, as the latter states in his *Commentarius*, p. 86.

[22] Mombasa, a port on the Kenya coast.

[23] This locality, which the Jesuit travellers referred to as Aoage, was identified by Ludolf as Waj, but from the context seems more likely to have been Wag, the area north of Lasta. Ludolf, *Commentarius*, p. 86; Beckingham and Huntingford, *Some records*, p. 228.

[24] Ved, probably Wed, also referred to by Portuguese writers as Ogge, a district south of Lake Zway. Beckingham and Huntingford, *Some records*, pp. 240–1; Ludolf, *New history*, p. 18.

[25] This name, earlier used by Godinho, was in the opinion of Ludolf a contraction of Davvaro, i.e. Dawaro, the Muslim state in which Harar was situated. Ludolf, *Commentarius*, p. 86; Beckingham and Huntingford, *Some records*, p. 234.

[26] Fatagar, a region between Waj and Bali, north of the Webi Šabelli river. Ludolf, *New history*, pp. 15, 18.

[27] Zingerum = Janjero. Zinj country was never part of Ethiopia.

[28] Janjero, a state in the south-west. Bruce, *op. cit.*, ii, 320.

Liberatus, is no longer subject to Abyssinia but to *Galla*,[29] because of its repeated insurrections. The sixteenth realm, called *Rosanagum*[30] is inhabited by Christians, but has never been subject to Abyssinian authority: on the eastern side of this realm march others to the north. *Roxa*[31] is the seventeenth, inhabited by pagans, and *Goma*[32] is the name of its next neighbour, with a mixed population of pagans and Christians, and obedient to the Emperor. Contiguous with *Monomotapa*[33] is *Ennaria*[34] or *Neria*, a very large realm inhabited by Christians and pagans, and three times larger than the realm of *Bagemdra* or *Bagameder*; Ennaria is fertile, and abounds in gold, musk, ivory, and other precious goods that the Africans neglect.

The next realm is *Zethe*,[35] inhabited by pagans, and subject to the Emperor, and after this *Conche*,[36] *Mahaola*,[37] *Goroma*,[38] the first two not large, and inhabited only by pagans, but the third of considerable extent and containing twenty provinces of Christians and pagans. To a great extent it is bordered by the Nile,

[29] Galla or Oramo, the Cushite people of southern Ethiopia, described by Bruce, *op. cit.*, i, 402–3, ii, 216–37.

[30] This name and description was borrowed from Godinho who also used the form Rozanegus. Ludolf, unable to identify the locality, was sceptical about its existence, and asked why, if its inhabitants had never been subject to Abyssinian rule, did Godinho include the area as part of the empire. Ludolf, *Commentarius*, p. 87.

[31] This locality is also unidentified, though Ludolf, *Commentarius*, pp. 86–7, thought the name was conceivably a mistake for Boxa, i.e. Boša in Enarya. Beckingham and Huntingford, *Some records*, p. 231.

[32] Gomma, a region in the south-west. Beckingham and Huntingford, *Some records*, p. 80.

[33] Monomotapa, supposedly a powerful kingdom on the Zambesi. Lockhart, *op. cit.*, p. 162; E. van Donzel, *Foreign relations of Ethiopia. Documents relating to the journeys of Kodja Murād* (Istanbul, 1979), pp. 72, 215.

[34] Enarya, a kingdom in the south-West, which Ludolf, *New history*, p. 15, had earlier described as 'inhabited by Christians and gentiles'. Bruce considered it 'the southernmost province of the Abyssinian empire', and 'abundantly supplied with gold'. Bruce, *op. cit.*, ii, 312–3, iii, 260.

[35] Zet or Set, north of the Gibé river. Beckingham and Huntingford, *Some records*, p. 56; Ludolf, *New history*, pp. 16, 18; idem, *Commentarius*, p. 87.

[36] Conch or Konta, south of the Gojab river. Beckingham and Huntingford, *Some records*, p. 232; Ludolf, *New history*, p. 15; idem, *Commentarius* p. 87.

[37] Mahaola, an unidentified locality earlier mentioned by Godinho. Ludolf, *Commentarius*, p. 87, observed that it was impossible even to guess where it could be located.

[38] This name had earlier been used by Godinho, but was a mistake, according to Ludolf, *Commentarius*, p. 87, for Gojjam, almost encircled by the Nile.

of which it is almost an island, it is scarcely ever untouched by war, as different enemies beset it on all sides with hostile armies, and it is so plentifully supplied with food as to support several armies at the same time; the fertility of the soil is the reason why when going to war the Ethiopians do not usually carry food with them in the army, but, when they have used up what each has brought with him, they turn to what they can loot from somewhere else, pass through the land like locusts,[39] and devour everything. The soil's fertility is such that at the same time as the harvest is being reaped, the seed is sown in the land, the reapers going in front and the sowers following behind: no other cultivation is necessary.

On the other side of the Nile, towards Egypt, lie the three last kingdoms, *Damote*,[40] *Sua*,[41] *Fasculum*.[42] Sua in the local dialect is called Heart of the Emperor, because in times past it was his principal seat. Fascul or Fasculum is the start of the road to the city of Cairo, is inhabited by Mahometans of the Moorish race, and is the location of that road down which every year, in times past, a great crowd of pilgrims came in Lent from the realm of Dambea, and set off in their thousands for Jerusalem, for religion's sake.

In antiquity different writers gave different names to those realms and provinces, names which are now unknown as new names have been given them; but the ancient realms of Abyssinia extended to six hundred and seventy-two leagues, and in circumference was undoubtedly much larger than in the present century. Most things yield to the march of time, and even stones are changed and hollowed out by drops of water; so the empire of Abyssinia, once so powerful, has been torn asunder by hostile

---

[39] The comparison between soldiers and locusts had earlier been drawn by Almeida, who observed that whereas the latter destroyed what was in the field, the former ravaged also what had been gathered into the houses. Beckingham and Huntingford, *Some records*, p. 46.

[40] Damot, a province immediately north of the Blue Nile. Beckingham and Huntingford, *Prester John*, ii, 578; *idem, Some records*, pp. 232–3; Ludolf, *New history*, p. 15. Bruce, *op. cit.*, iii, 257, states that it extended 40 miles from North to South and 20 from East to West.

[41] Šawa, the southern part of traditional Ethiopia. Beckingham and Huntingford, *Some records*, p. 243; Bruce, *op. cit.*, iii, 255–6; Ludolf, *New history*, pp. 16, 19; idem. *Commentarius*, p. 87.

[42] Fascul or Fasculum, Fazughli on the Blue Nile in the Sudan, 45 miles S.E. of Roseires.

Mahometan neighbours, emptied of its native Ethiopians sometimes by pagans, sometimes by idolators, and utterly corrupted
in morals. What it was to its contemporaries in the flower of its
magnificence is abundantly clear in holy scriptures; embracing
all the southern part of the interior of Ethiopia, its enormous
riches are proved by the Queen of Sheba, who brought to
Solomon wonderful treasures of gold, precious stones, myrrh,
and other spices. *She gave the king a hundred and twenty talents of
gold, and of spices very great store, and precious stones: there came no
more such abundance of spices as these which the Queen of Sheba gave
to king Solomon*: I Kings x. 10. Later the ravages of time, of revolts
and of wars, the ignorance, lack of skill, and idleness of the
inhabitants, and also the inactivity of the emperors, have diminished the empire, which is beset on all sides by enemies, pagan,
idolatrous and Mahometan, and which has to face, as well as the
Saracens, Turks and Gallas, the people of Nigritia,[43] which by
right is subject to Abyssinia but which threw off its yoke, and
overran its province by force of arms; the Emperor begged the
help of the king of Portugal, but when his enemies had been
driven off he had still lost not a few of the provinces that he had
anciently governed, yet to this day rejoices in the imperial title
of his predecessors: Jasu Odiam Saghed,[44] son of the Emperor
Backaffa Masich Saghed.

There follow here the names of the provinces which he has
retained under his authority and rule, together with his officials,
each with the proper title of their office.

Provinces
  1. Hanesim:[45] under an official, Bahr Nagasch.
  2. Serai:[46] under an official, Bale Gama.[47]

---

[43] Nigritia, possibly a reference to the black populations on the western borders
of Ethiopia.

[44] Iyasu II, or Adyam Sagad II, son of Emperor Bakaffa or Masih Sagad.

[45] Hamasén, the most northerly highland province of Ethiopia situated towards
the Red Sea. Beckingham and Huntingford, *Prester John of the Indies*, ii, 450;
Ludolf, *New history*, p. 17.

[46] Sarayé, also known as Sarawé, a highland district on the northern side of
the Marab river, traditionally under the rule of the Bahr Nagaš. Beckingham
and Huntingford, *Prester John*, ii, 513; idem, *Some records*, p. 243; Ludolf, *New
history*, p. 17.

[47] Ba'ala? significance unidentified.

3. Syre:[48] under an official, Nagarit.[49]
4. Adaua:[50] under an official, Dadaczmacz.
5. Enderta:[51] under an official, Dadaczmacz.
6. Laesta:[52] here lives the Emperor in the city of Gondar and the official is Bittode.[53]
7. Belasa:[54] under an official, Belatin Keta.[55]
8. Begember:[56] under an official, Dadaczmacz.
9. Ambasel:[57] under an official, Janserac.[58]
10. Godgiam:[59] under an official, Dadczmacz.
11. Damut: under an official, Dadaczmacz.
12. Amhara: under an official, Dadaczmacz.

[48] Siré, a province of Tegré west of Aksum between the Marab and Takkazé rivers, said by Bruce to be 'about 25 miles broad, and not much more in length'. Beckingham and Huntingford, *Prester John*, ii, 577; idem, *Some records*, p. 243; Ludolf, *New history*, p. 17; Bruce, *op. cit.*, iii, 152, 252.

[49] Amharic *nagarit*, literally a drum. This instrument was carried in procession in front of certain provincial rulers, and therefore served by extension to refer to the governor or governorate. Guidi, *Vocabolario*, pp. 397–8.

[50] Adwa, the district around the town of that name, described by Bruce, *op. cit.*, iii, 119.

[51] Endarta, a province of Tegré, north-east of Maqalé. Beckingham and Huntingford, *Some records*, p. 227; Ludolf, *New history*, p. 17.

[52] Presumably a confused reference to Lasta, actually to the east of Bagémder, described by Bruce, *op. cit.*, iii, 253, as 'mountainous province ... often in rebellion' whose inhabitants were 'esteemed the best soldiers in Abyssinia, men of great strength and stature, but cruel and uncivilized'.

[53] Amharic *Bítwaddad*, an important court official, often equated with High Chamberlain. Guidi, *Vocabolario*, pp. 339–40.

[54] Belessa, a district in Bagémder described by Bruce, *op. cit.*, iii, 383, as a 'wild, uncultivated territory ... famous for no production but that of honey'.

[55] Amharic *Blattén géta*, literally 'master of the pages', i.e. Grand Chamberlain. Guidi, *Vocabolario*, p. 315.

[56] Bagémder, a province in the north-west between Lasta and the Sudan border, said by Bruce, *op. cit.*, iii, 253, to 'constitute the strength of Abyssinia in horsemen'. See also Beckingham and Huntingford, *Some records*, p. 230; Ludolf, *New history*, p. 14.

[57] Amba Sel, a district 20 miles north of the modern town of Dassé. Beckingham and Huntingford, *Some records*, p. 227.

[58] Jan Serar, a chief of certain districts, notably Ambasel. G. W. B. Huntingford, *The land charters of northern Ethiopia* (Addis Ababa, 1965), pp. 40, 109, Guidi, *Annales regum Iyasu II et Iyoa's*, pp. 51, 150, 155, 214.

[59] Gojjam, the province within the great curve of the Blue Nile south of Lake Tana. Bruce, *op. cit.*, iii, 256, states that it measured about 80 miles by 40, and was 'a very flat country and all in pasture' with 'few mountains' and 'full of great herds of cattle'. See also Beckingham and Huntingford, *Prester John*, ii, 580; idem, *Some records*, p. 237; Ludolf, *New history*, pp. 16, 19.

13. Enebesi:[60] under an official, Eschalaga.[61]
14. Ebegniat:[62] under an official, Dadaczmacz.
15. Agau:[63] under an official, Dadaczmacz.
16. Korhara:[64] under an official, Dadaczmacz.
17. Gananuara:[65] under an official, Dadaczmacz.
18. Beltzagadi:[66] under an official, Dadaczmacz.
19. Uelkait:[67] under an official, Dadaczmacz.
20. Senin:[68] under an official, Dadaczmacz.
21. Dambea: under an official, Kantiba.[69]
22. Thilckim:[70] under an official, Habertu.

Of the areas denoted in modern times by these names, some are large and truly deserving of the name of kingdom, that is, Serai, Syre, Adaua, Laesta, Godgiam, Amhara, while the rest should rather be called principalities, or marquisates; furthermore, when in Messaua or in Mocha I asked the inhabitants from these parts whence they came, they usually answered 'From the kingdom of Habesch': we can assume therefore today that the kingdom of Ethiopia, or Habesch, or Abyssinia, being the same territory, extends beyond the Red Sea towards the north from the sixth degree of latitude to the twentieth, and from the forty-seventh degree thirty minutes of longitude to the sixty-sixth, and is about two hundred and eighty leagues from south to north,

[60] Ennebese, a district between Mota and the Blue Nile, considered separate from Gojjam. Beckingham and Huntingford, *Some records*, p. 240.
[61] Amharic *Šalaqa*, literally commander of 1,000 (men), a minor military title. Guidi, *Vocabolario*, p. 203.
[62] Ebenat, a district near the Takkazé river. Beckingham and Huntingford, *Some records*, p. 30.
[63] Agaw, or Agawmeder, a province formerly occupied by the Agaw people between Wag and Samén. Buckingham and Huntingford, *Prester John*, ii, 569; Bruce, *op. cit.*, iii, 257.
[64] Korhara, possibly Addi Qorqora.
[65] Possibly Gamarcansa, an area in Gojjam mentioned by Lobo. Lockhart, *op. cit.*, pp. 234–5.
[66] Beltzagadi, possibly Sagadé.
[67] Walqayt, a province north-west of Samén and north of Gondar. Beckingham and Huntingford, *Some records*, p. 238; Ludolf, *New history*, pp. 18–19.
[68] Samén, the high mountains north-east of Lake Tana. Ludolf, *New history*, pp. 16–19; Bruce, *op. cit.*, iii, 252.
[69] Amharic *Kantiba*, a title given to the rulers of Dambeya, Hamasén and several other locations. Guidi, *Vocabolario*, p. 542; Beckingham and Huntingford, *Some records*, p. 72.
[70] Thilckim, an unidentified locality.

and three hundred and sixty leagues from east to west. Robbe[71] places Ethiopia between the twentieth degree of latitude north and the fourteenth degree south of the equator, and between the fortieth and seventy-fourth degrees of longitude. This enormous territory is unknown to Europeans, and each writer describes it in his own way, he being the further from the truth who further extends the horizons of the country. Thus Job Ludolf[72] in his *Historia Aethiopica* cites Nicolao Godinho Bk. 1, c. 4, who says: 'The kingdom of Abyssinia by ancient custom contains twenty-six kingdoms divided into fourteen regions'. Father Jeronimo Lobo in his history says that Ethiopia of old extended from the Red Sea to the Congo, and from the borders of Egypt to the Indian Ocean.

Coming to Abyssinia through the Red Sea, the first kingdom entered is Tigré, which is very large and used to comprise thirty-four provinces, though it is now reduced to seventeen, and extends from the island of Messaua on the Red Sea as far as Mount *Semen* for three hundred Italian miles, and is almost as much in width. According to many accounts, it was this kingdom which was the first, before any other in Ethiopia, to receive at the hands of the eunuch of Queen Candace the Romano-apostolic faith that leads to salvation. Its next neighbour is the kingdom of Dancali, small, infertile, narrow and sparsely populated, and together with its Mahometan inhabitants subject to the rule of a chieftain. Here by the shore of the Red Sea, and opposite the territory of the city of Mocha, lies at the entrance to Ethiopia the Ethiopian port of *Babel-Mandel*,[73] where the Red Sea joins the Ocean; it is a beautiful port, large and safe from storms, a natural harbour, whose other name is *Beilul* or *Beilal*.[74] But as the Ethiopians are idle, lazy, and negligent, and conduct no trade with other nations, it is completely deserted, in the occupation

[71] Jacques Robbe, *Méthode pour apprendre facilement la géographie* (Paris, 1685), ii, 200.

[72] Ludolf, *New history*, p. 17, had previously listed twenty-seven prefectures in Tegré.

[73] Bāb al-Mandab, straits at the southern end of the Gulf of Aden. Ludolf, *New history*, p. 11; Bruce, *op. cit.*, iii, 311, 314–5; Valentia, *op. cit.*, ii, 13–15.

[74] Baylūl, the principal Afar port on the Red Sea coast. E. J. van Donzel. *A Yemenite embassy to Ethiopia 1647–1649* (Stuttgart, 1986), p. 30 *et passim*; Valentia, *op. cit.*, ii, 20–1; Pankhurst, *Introduction to the economic history of Ethiopia*, pp. 332–3. It is not in the Strait of Bāb al-Mandab but about 50 km. N of Assab.

of a few Arabs who have no fortifications, and ships do not nowadays call there. Once when the Portuguese sailed to Ethiopia, General Alfonso Mendez[75] reached this port on his way to the interior; the emperor of Abyssinia in the year 1715 besought Leopold the Holy Roman Emperor[76] for the help of some troops to occupy and hold more surely this port of Beilul, and urged him strongly to do so.

The old accounts of Abyssinia give names to the kingdoms that are different from the above-mentioned ones, but since in modern times they are not known by the old names, I have taken trouble to denote them by the names that are now used: their ancient glory and splendour has fallen into ruin, and they fear an even more lamentable future. The one kingdom of all that is the most flourishing and richest, the kingdom of Schanckalle,[77] has rebelled against the lordship of Abyssinia and obeys it not, though it abounds in stores of gold, musk, and other precious things. So sunk is it into barbarism that the female babies that are born are exposed beside the public roads and left as prey to the wild beasts; lost to all natural affection they adopt this wicked practice, avoid the many inconveniences of bringing up girl children, and find it easier to despoil the neighbouring kingdoms, by fraud or by force, of their best-looking women to secure wives: only boy babies do they rear themselves.[78] This is the custom observed by the superstitious Chinese in the kingdom of *Hsi-an*, where if the first child is found to be a girl it is a terrible augury of evil of all sorts, and they ensure that all such first-born births take place outside the home in the fields or woods; wherefore the missionary fathers have by the rite of baptism preserved many souls if not from temporal death yet certainly from death eternal.

In times past the capital city of Suaquen and the islands of

[75] Alfonso Mendez, the Jesuit Patriarch of Ethiopia. C. F. Rey, *The romance of the Portuguese in Abyssinia*, (London, 1929), *passim*. Presumably Prutky calls him General as being Father General.

[76] The Holy Roman Emperor at this time was in fact Charles VI who reigned from 1711 to 1740.

[77] Šanqella, a general term for the black Nilotic people inhabiting the country to the west of Gondar and other areas towards the Sudan frontier. They were described in detail by Bruce, *op. cit.*, ii, 546–68, iv, 327–8, who refers to them as Shangalla. See also *idem* (3rd edition), vii, 105.

[78] This statement, which would appear dubious, is not corroborated by Bruce.

Dahlack[79] and Messaua belonged to the kingdom of Tigré, but
were conquered by the Turks and are today ruled by the Governor or Beglerbey. Towards the west of this is to be found the
people called *Balvus*,[80] who are shut off by mountains from this
part of the sea, and who are subject to the Emperor of Ethiopia,
partly Mahometan and partly pagan. Yet another grief to the
Empire is the loss of the kingdom of *Sennar*,[81] which is subject
to a Mahometan chieftain, and which stretches toward the Nile
in the fourteenth north degree of latitude between Egypt and
middle Ethiopia; it is sometimes called the kingdom of *Nubia*,[82]
and Pliny calls it *Tampsis*. This, together with the kingdom of
Fungi[83] and several other provinces, was in a series of unjust
wars removed from the authority of the Emperor by a number
of rebellious petty chieftains, and little by little the empire was
diminished. The kingdom of *Galla*, which was rightly subject to
the emperor's sway, and one of his best kingdoms, violently freed
itself from his obedience due to his inexperience in war and in
wielding arms, the sloth of his rule, and his ignorance of useful
knowledge, and despite many warlike attempts he has been
unable up to the present time to compel them to resume their
obedience. The father of the present reigning Emperor Jasu
tried repeatedly to overcome and subdue this rebellious people,
but was ever foiled in his purpose, and equally his son the reigning
Emperor Jasu, who every year marches against them with a huge
military force, has never overcome their resolute resistance,
ignorant as he is of the art of war.

So with great loss of life was Ethiopia deprived of two of her
kingdoms, which were full of gold, ivory, and valuable musk such
as can be found nowhere else in the whole universe. In Galla are
to be found great numbers of cats[84] that produce an excellent
musk, which is much sought after by Orientals and customarily

[79] The Dahlak islands, off the port of Massawa and north of the Bur peninsula.
Bruce, op. cit., i, 348–64; Valentia, *op. cit.*, ii, 32–44.
[80] The Balaw, former inhabitants of the Agordat region of N. Ethiopia.
[81] On the kingdom of Sennar in what is now Sudan see *inter alia* Bruce, *op.
cit.*, iv, 455–99. It was never subject to Ethiopia.
[82] Nubia, a region in the central Sudan. Bruce, *op. cit.*, iv, 419–28.
[83] On the history of this state see O. G. S. Crawford, *The Fung kingdom of
Sennar*, (Gloucester, 1951).
[84] The reference is to the civet cat, the extraction of musk from which was also
described in Poncet (Foster, *op. cit.*, pp. 136–7) and Bruce *op. cit.*, iv, 296.

sold by the Ethiopians at a great price. They are larger than ordinary cats, about as big as a middle-sized dog, but catlike in shape, with a long muzzle like a wolf's, long teeth, in body and tail like other cats, dark in colour; between their legs under the anus they have a hole partly covered with skin, in which the musk forms and is extracted thus: the cat is shut up in a small narrow iron cage so that he cannot move sideways, and then he is teased, provoked and angered almost to frenzy, which makes him sweat: if at that time he manages to bite, the wound is fatal, and he is therefore at this point seized by the tail, or by a leg away from the musk-hole so that he cannot move. Then with a spatula or spoon the sweat, dull white in colour, is removed from the musk-hole near the anus between the legs. This is the musk, very highly valued, to be found in such quality nowhere else in the world, like butter to look at: twice daily it is collected thus. The Abyssinian merchants keep great numbers of cats, which they feed on meat and gruel, in order to collect the musk. Newly gathered it is dull white in colour and of an unpleasant smell, almost like very strong-smelling excrement; indeed, if ever it loses its sweet musk-like scent it has to be stored away in the latrines to regain from the human excrement its original sweet smell, whereupon, although its virtue seem exhausted with age, if it be exposed to the air it regains its dark chestnut colour and its virtue returns to it. To prove it, place one drop on live coals, and, if it be totally consumed and leave nothing behind, it is good and genuine; but if any wetness or liquid be left on the coal, that is a sign that something has been added and that the musk is not pure.

The traders need to keep it for a long time, and generally shut it inside cowhorns and seal it with skin, thus preventing transpiration by keeping it from contact with the air, lest its virtue evaporate. Thus preserved the musk is exported in quantity by both Christian and Mahometan[85] Ethiopians to Messaua, Dahlack, Mocha, Gidda, Cairo and other parts of Arabia, Egypt and India, an ounce of musk generally selling for three patacas or six German florins; if however the true musk reaches Europe, it fetches a much higher price. When in the persecution I was

[85] Trade for centuries had been largely in Muslim hands. Pankhurst, *Introduction to the economic history of Ethiopia*, pp. 284–6.

expelled from Ethiopia with my colleague, I wanted to make a special present to his august majesty Francis I of two or three ounces, and carefully enclosed it in a silver pyx. But when I reached Vienna in Austria and thought to present him with an unexpected and unsolicited gift, I examined the pyx and found that the musk had all disappeared and evaporated away; then I realised how true it was that only in a cowhorn can it be preserved, in the Ethiopian manner; and I grieved for my valuable musk that had vanished. The Ethiopians themselves have but small taste for the scent of musk, and frequently exchange it with the caravans for another object of trivial value, as their wives rarely make use of it, whether Christian or Mahometan. Conveyed to the capital Gondar or to a town one day's journey from Gondar commonly called *Entfaras*,[86] it fetches a price of half a dram of gold, say two florins, for an ounce, and as it goes further afield its price ever increases, so that in Messaua it rises to three drams, where the Arab women, who are Mahometan, are accustomed to anoint themselves with it and use it in quantity.

In the same way gold[87] is to be found in great quantity in the hills during the rainy season, when it is washed from the bowels of the mountains in stones of considerable size, and is visible in the rivers and torrents. The passing caravans gather it freely and take it to Gondar and the neighbourhood, where it is valued at little or nothing because it has not been refined, and is black in colour; the Abyssinians give it away freely in exchange for a trifle, a lump of salt, a piece of cloth, or a wretched piece of stuff for a loin-cloth. When the stones have been crushed, and smelted in

---

[86] Emfraz in the mountains overlooking the north-eastern shore of Lake Tana, was situated, according to Bruce, *op. cit.*, iii, 386, 'on a steep hill' the 'way up to it' being 'almost perpendicular like the ascent of a ladder'. The houses were 'all placed above the middle of the hill, fronting the west, in number about 300', and above them were 'gardens, or rather fields, full of trees and bushes, without any sort of order, up to the very top'. The town 'commanded a view of the whole lake, and part of the country on the other side'. See also Ludolf, *New history*, pp. 18–19, and Pankhurst, *History of Ethiopian towns*, i, 94–100.

[87] The amount of gold in the country had also impressed earlier travellers. Alvarez believed that 'most' came from the province of Damot, though there was 'much' of 'inferior' quality in Gojjam. Almeida stated that there was 'much gold' in the south-west, especially towards Enarya, though some had also been mined for a time in Tambén. Poncet reported that after the rains the torrents became swollen, and carried pieces of gold with them which the peasants then picked up. Beckingham and Huntingford, *Prester John*, ii, 455, 457, 459; *idem, Some records*, pp. 42–3; Foster, *op. cit.*, p. 127.

the fire like lead, they produce sometimes as much as five or ten ounces of excellent gold, which the inhabitants exchange at the pleasure of the purchaser for coloured glass beads, with which the women adorn their hands, feet, and necks, or for a piece of any sort of metal, like lead or iron, or for some similar object of no value.

These are the two most flourishing kingdoms, and the present Emperor is the third to suffer under their loss. He has to content himself with the other twenty-two, but always he remembers in his heart that Solomon ruled from Dan to Beersheba.

CHAPTER 20

THE EXTENT OF THE
EMPEROR'S POWER TODAY

That this prince once wielded enormous power is a tradition denied by none of the writers on Ethiopian affairs, and indeed its likelihood is confirmed by the consideration that he held under his sway all the many kingdoms and provinces that I have just enumerated. One must however agree that the greater part of that power has now departed, and that day by day the Abyssinian Empire is sinking further and further into decay, arousing the reasonable fear that in the course of a few years it will totally collapse in ruin and misery. The sea coast is beset by the harsh rule of the Saracens, who mostly either pay tribute to the Sultan of Turkey by agreement, or are subjected directly to his rule; the continental territory is inhabited by many who are partly pagan and partly Mahometan, who abjure the Emperor's obedience along with his religion, acknowledge as their overlord either the Turkish monarchy or no one, and live under their own laws and mastership. Where the Abyssinian Emperor once wielded supreme power, his forces now are so diminished, his wealth reduced, and his strength impaired, that he can scarcely make good his imperial title, and, alike against the enemies on his frontiers and his own subjects, who throughout his empire are conspiring against his person, he is forced to implore the help of foreign princes.

In the days of his prosperity he demonstrated his majesty by separating himself, so it is said, from all human intercourse, as though he were divine, nor did he permit himself to be seen by anyone save with great difficulty and after many formalities.

Mahon,[1] along with Tigrius and Barnagassus,[2] were kings of some renown, but were only with difficulty enabled to obtain the privilege of speaking with him, and when they came within his presence their marks of obeisance were such that you would have believed them to be slaves rather than princes. When any subject in the whole empire, whatever his worth and importance, heard that the Emperor's messenger was approaching him, he immediately removed the clothes from the upper part of his body, left his house, and at the messenger's first words bowed down his head and touched the earth with his hand. The ambassadors of kings were forbidden to approach him, and transacted their business through the imperial ministers, and only on their point of departure did they reach to kiss his feet, in token of their respect for him; yet not even then were they held worthy to see the Emperor's face, which he kept covered with a blue veil whenever he appeared in public. Only thrice in the year did he permit his people to see him without his veil, once at Christmas, and again at Epiphany when Christ was adored by the Magi: the third time was at the keeping of the feast of the Assumption of the Virgin Mother of God, when he took food on a golden single-legged table with no cloth on it. They say that while he was eating, following an old custom, he held before his eyes a glass jar full of ashes, the sight of which was a memorial to the eater of his last day, so that he could take warning and, amid his feasting, regulate his conduct aright: similar acts are reported of other princes, lest the honours paid them puff them up, or their pleasures dissipate their vigour. The pomp, the magnificence,

---

[1] Tegramahon, or *Tegré makʷannen*, was the title given to the governor of Tegré. Foreign writers, by extension, often applied the name to the province or in some instances to the district of Hawzén which was customarily assigned to that official for his upkeep. Beckingham and Huntingford, *Prester John*, ii, 585; idem, *Some records*, p. 94; Ludolf, *New history*, p. 233.

[2] The foreign practice of referring to the kingdoms of Barnagassus and Tigremahon was discussed by Ludolf and Abba Gorgoreyos. The former explains that when he asked about these terms the latter, 'after a short hesitation . . . understood them to be compound words, in which the Titles of the *Vice-Roys* were conjoined with the Names of the Regions over which they were made Governors'. *Barnagassus* was thus a way of writing *Bahr-Nagash*, a compound word of *Bahr* which signifies the Sea, and *Nagash*, a Governour, 'as much as to say a Commander or Admiral of the Sea', while Tigremahon meant 'Judge or President of Tigre'. Ludolf, *New history*, p. 20.

the crowd of ministers, and the other splendours of the imperial court, are described by the historians in terms more glowing than I believe, who have seen them, but, if they are really true, then in this empire, as in so much also, can be seen the inconstancy of human affairs, and how nothing in mortal life exists which should be held in high esteem. Of this magnificence not one vestige can be seen today, and He alone must be looked to and sought out, Who is Himself always the same and Whose years fail not.

I will add here, since the place is appropriate, that the Emperor of Abyssinia, the ruler of twenty-two kingdoms, could be proclaimed as wealthy, magnificent and splendid enough, if he but knew how to rule and govern his subjects; gold and precious stones could be found in quantity, if the Ethiopians had but the skill to prospect for minerals and to work in the bowels of the earth; on all sides the mountains are full of gold and silver ore, and mines are abundant. Three kingdoms especially are valuable to the emperor, Saba,[3] Zambra,[4] Cafate,[5] in which lie concealed enormous riches of gold and silver: and, aside from these, the extensive realms of Ethiopia ensure that their Emperor should truly be proclaimed a most powerful monarch, certainly potentially: not however in fact and practice, since he lacks the prudence necessary to act, to govern, and to prospect, and the skill to order matters aright. Yet he lacks not the resources of many millions of men, or of precious metals in the bowels of the earth, such as no other empire can show. Indeed in times of old it is quite apparent that the Emperor's worth could be reckoned in countless millions of ounces of gold,[6] and not without reason, for even today the whole world proclaims this to be a land flowing

[3] Saba or Sabaim, a locality west of Aksum, and the place where the Queen of Sheba was said to have lived. Beckingham and Huntingford, *Prester John*, i, 164, ii, 496.

[4] Zambra, the name given by Urreta to an apparently mythical Ethiopian town, probably designated the country of the Cafates. Beccari, *op. cit.*, i, 378, ii, 201.

[5] Gafat, a country in southern Gojjam between the districts of Wambarma and Wamet. Beckingham and Huntingford, *Some records*, pp. 235–6; Ludolf, *op. cit.*, p. 16.

[6] Typical of such exaggerations is the observation of Bermudes who claimed that the Prester John 'could spend a million [cruzados] of gold and more, for his riches are innumerable'. R. S. Whiteway, *The Portuguese expedition to Abyssinia in 1541–1543* (London, 1902), p. 136.

with milk and honey, and full to overflowing of gold, silver, metals, emeralds, jaspers, sapphires shading from red to black, topazes glittering with gold, rubies red as fire: so speak the ancient writers, whose books are full of the praises of Ethiopia. Yet in truth, just as all that glitters is not gold, so not all the praise of history, nor all the encomia of ancient emperors, can today in Abyssinia support the present Emperor:[7] times change and we with them, and the things of this world and their marvels. There was a time when Ethiopia had been prosperous, and Catholic: now she is wretched and heretical, pagan, idolatrous, Mahometan, Judaist. Once she was worthy of every praise, now she is worthy of none, for of the Ethiopians of today, *Eyes have they but they see not, they have ears and hear not* Psalms cxv. 5, 6. Not the past, still less the present, have they the wit to examine or comprehend, they are a people thoroughly lazy, stupid, barbarous, ignorant, justly to be described as blind to all the arts and sciences of this busy century, yet with it overweeningly arrogant. What profits it for the Emperor to be powerful potentially, but not in fact, to possess territories and kingdoms but not to see the fruits of them, to be hailed as Emperor but to lord it over very little, for the mountains and rivers to teem with gold and silver, and to know not how to find them? To want, but to obtain nothing, to be hungry, but not to eat, is uselessness.

To this day the Emperor proclaims that he is the one true ruler and plenary lord of this his enormous territory, that he possesses it of his own right, and permits of no participation in his rule as do the princes, counts, and barons of Europe: as complete master and sole emperor he possesses the provinces as his own for free disposal. Every year in the month of June or July he summons the individual chiefs throughout the whole empire and makes appointments to office and ministry, allocating the provinces by merit to what minister he wishes, confirming in office many, deposing others, punishing some and rewarding others. Many

---

[7] The Armenian jeweller T'ovmačean, describing the treasury at Gondar in the mid-1760s, observed: 'Do not imagine that the treasures of the Abyssinian King are as great as ours, for they do not have immeasurable quantities of gold and silver'. Nersessian and Pankhurst, 'The visit to Ethiopia of Yohannes T'ovmačean, an Armenian jeweller, in 1764–66'. *Journal of Ethiopian studies* (1982) xv, 85.

are deprived and others promoted, so that a minister who last year was of the most powerful and wealthiest, finds himself next year the weakest and poorest, his province entrusted to the administration of another by its absolute master the Emperor, and all its crops, cattle, and resources in the possession of his successor.[8]

The outgoing minister, who is empowered to retain nothing in his possession, is rendered a poor man unless he has already provided himself with a secret store, and the common advice given to ministers is to put wealth aside through the hands of friends, and by fraud to anticipate future poverty by hiding something away. The disobedience of a minister, and his refusal to appear at court, is passed over in silence lest he join himself to the forces of rebellion, and he is shortly confirmed in office lest his revolt injure the state, until such time as he appears of his own will, even if he committed enormities against the Emperor: but then every crime of his life is held against him. It is clear from this that in Ethiopia there exists no flourishing aristocracy, as in Europe, and that only by performance of duty to the Emperor's pleasure can the worth of the different ministers be judged, who, living ever in fear, are rendered more faithful in the performance of their duties, lest they be deposed from their power and their wealth and plunged into weakness and poverty. Thus it happens that the Emperor of Ethiopia retains many ministers disposed about the Empire, and fosters many within his own court, though he is not accustomed to enter into council with them, but issues decrees according to what pleases and attracts him, and rules at his own personal discretion. I would here note that those who in proximity to the imperial court are

---

[8] Earlier travellers had taken a similar view. Alvarez, describing the position of officials in the sixteenth century, remarked, 'The Prester John deposes them and appoints them whenever he pleases, with or without cause'. (Beckingham and Huntingford, *Prester John*, i, 173). Almeida (*idem, Some records*, pp. 88–9) a century later observed 'what makes this King great is that he is lord *in solitum* of all lands that are in his kingdoms, so that he can take and give them when and to whom he sees fit. Private persons, great and small, have nothing except by the King's gift and all that they own is by favour and *ad tempus*. It is so usual for the Emperor to exchange, alter and take away the lands each man holds every two or three years, sometimes every year and even many times in the course of a year, that it causes no surprise.'

obedient, dutiful, and prompt to obey his desires, when they are further from it become disobedient, recalcitrant, and rebellious, and that the further they live from the palace at Gondar the more recalcitrant a temper do they show; they know quite well that as soon as they submit they will get off scot-free without penalty, and without paying tribute.

Judges are chosen and posted to the towns and cities, and their appointment confirmed by the Prince's authority, but there is no course of legal studies, their judgements are made at their own discretion with no knowledge of law or justice, they render to the Emperor no account of their judgements, if they find the accused guilty he suffers, if they find in his favour he gets off free of any punishment: their intelligence is low, their knowledge of law is deficient, they generally make their judgements on face value or under the influence of bribery, and if their judgements are merciful they know well that the Emperor will not upset them, while there is no limit set to their sentences whatever prejudice they display. Of justice therefore there is little or none, as they have neither magistrates nor doctors of the law, nor lawyers.

On the different provinces and on the officials appointed to them, there is imposed an annual tribute of gold for the coming year, to be paid to the Emperor; to preserve the more distant provinces from rebellion, the burden imposed on them is less, a hundred or two hundred ounces of gold, while the nearer ones are expected to pay a total of four or five hundred ounces: the annual tribute thus scarcely reaches twelve thousand ounces, or in European money ninety-six thousand gold pieces.[9] This is the extent of the total wealth of this most powerful and richest emperor, so proclaimed throughout the whole world, and unless I myself in my own experience had learned it personally from the royal Treasurer, who received into his own hand the receipts from all subjects, I should never have given it credence: furthermore, not even this amount can be counted on every year, for most of the Ethiopians are thieves, cheats and double dealers,

---

[9] This picture is confirmed by T'ovmačean, who stated that the Gondar treasury in the mid-1760s contained no more than 3,000 to 4,000 *waqét*, or ounces, of gold. Nersessian and Pankhurst, *op. cit.* p. 85.

producing a variety of excuses, avoiding the quota assigned to them, refusing to appear when summoned, or openly declaring themselves rebels for a time and refusing to pay their tribute, small though it is. If ever they return to their allegiance they are absolved from the tribute they owe, because the Emperor is ever afraid to punish rebellion, and makes himself a pauper thereby. And yet if the provinces were governed in the way they should be, if the subjects maintained their allegiance and the transgressors were punished, a large treasury could be built up and Abyssinia be again what she was of old, a monarchy of preeminent magnificence. When I kept company in true friendship with the royal Treasurer, who has to provide for all the Emperor's needs, to pay their imperial salaries to the ministers, officials, and servants, and to meet all expenses as they arise, he told me that it was hard for him out of such a small revenue to meet the obligations of his office, and that from shortage of money it was often only with difficulty that he could obey the commands of the Emperor.[10] In the sixth year, during my own stay in Ethiopia, the crops were devoured by locusts,[11] little or no tribute was brought in, and ministers and subjects excused their nonpayment on grounds of incapacity; yet in other years, when the crops are excellent, the story is put about that the imperial income amounts to twenty-four thousand ounces of gold, and, standing the argument on its head, the Emperor ensures his people's fidelity by exacting too little tribute, not a fiftieth part of what it justly could be.

The Emperor Jasu was seven years old when he came to the throne on his father's death; his mother the Queen administering the state meanwhile until his majority.[12] All the revenues she

---

[10] The critical financial situation of the Gondarine monarchy is confirmed by the royal chronicale which states that when Iyasu II died in 1755 his mother, Empress Mentewwab, ordered gold to be brought from the treasury to pay for the funeral commemorations, but no more than 80, or, in another verion, 20 dinars could be found, for Iyasu and 'wasted his riches'. Guidi, *Annales Regum Iyāsu et Iyo'as*, p. 182.

[11] Two serious plagues of locusts were mentioned in Iyasu II's chronicle, in 1747 and 1748. Guidi, *op. cit.*, pp. 150, 154.

[12] Prutky's statement is confirmed by Iyasu's chronicle, which indicates that the monarch was born around June 1723, and acceded to the throne in September 1730. Guidi, *op. cit.*, pp. 22, 27–8.

kept for herself, reserving nothing for her young son, and, on his taking charge, she kept to herself and was up to now enjoying possession of at least half the kingdom, while a great part of the provinces was in the possession of the Coptic Archbishop,[13] the representative of the Patriarch of Alexandria, and many other members of the royal family possessed territory divided amongst themselves, for which they paid no tribute: necessary revenue was lost thus, and the imperial treasury is sadly diminished. If, as I said, the practice of European rulers were followed, if there were a just distribution of revenue, a just payment of tribute, and an equitable administration, it is certain that, as in antiquity, the Emperor would be richer than other kings and more magnificent than other Emperors. As it is he is hemmed about with so many enemies, idolators, pagans, Turks and heathen, so beset by continual rebellion within the Empire, that to avoid greater tribulations and overpowering evils he allows many provinces to go free of tribute, and contents himself with the imperial name without the substance; he lives more by the charity of his vassals than on just tribute justly exacted, and dares not exert his imperial authority against most of his subjects.

As well as money he receives a yearly tribute of animals, four thousand oxen and as many sheep, besides a variety of fowls: of the different sorts of grain growing in the empire six thousand giaras[14] (giara is a measure roughly equal to a quarter of a European modius): six thousand giaras of honey to make the drink tacz, for water is drunk only by the poor. He also receives for the clothing of his servants and slaves twelve thousand pieces of cotton cloth,[15] and there are certain other small items of tribute

---

[13] The wealth of the *Abun*, or Coptic archbishop, was noted by many subsequent travellers, among them Charles Dufton who a century later observed that the country's religious community, 'consisting, under the Abuna, of innumerable priests and debteras, numbering a quarter of the population, had, through previous royal grants and private legacies, obtained the possession of one-third of the realm'. C. Dufton, *Narrative of a journey through Abyssinia* (London, 1867), p. 140. The concept of 'one-third' should not, however, be taken literally.

[14] Probably a reference to the $q^w era'e$, an Ethiopian unit of variable capacity. D'Abbadie, *Dictionnaire*, p. 271.

[15] Cattle, grain and cloth constituted the traditional tribute in kind. For a collation of seventeenth and eighteenth century estimates of such taxes, see R. Pankhurst, 'Ethiopian taxation prior to the time of Menilek', *Northeast African Studies* (1984), v, No. 3, pp. 59–81.

145

– but I shall hardly stir the reader to admiration of so small a tribute for so vast an empire. We must note that when the Emperor goes to war against another king or his Turkish neighbours, the whole kingdom is obliged to march with him, and the armies, whether led by the Emperor or entrusted to another general to lead against the enemy, are fed at the expense of the cities, and the same cities pay the wages alike of the soldiers who go to battle and of those to whom the emperor's person is entrusted. Seeing then that the emperor pays out nothing on his own account for anything save the maintenance of his court and family, whatever money in cash and in kind is received from the tributary peoples could amount to a considerable sum; the ministers too, who hold the provinces divided among themselves, act as captains and colonels, while their servants form the body of troops. Thus if the tribute of the subjects were set down accurately, Abyssinia could still truly take pride in her wealth. To understand this better, turn now to the next chapter.

CHAPTER 21

THE SOLDIERY AND
WARS OF THE ETHIOPIANS

In time of peace the ministers of the provinces are provided
with servants according to the pressure of their needs, and in
wartime these become soldiers, so that at times in the larger
provinces, such as Tigré, Syre and Serai, as many as two thousand
servants are supported, while elsewhere the number reduces to
one thousand, or in a smaller province five hundred, and so in
proportion elsewhere. When war breaks out they all march out
in companies under the command of their minister, each man
being fed and supplied by his colonel or captain with food, arms,
and ammunition, with none of which the emperor is concerned:
it was with this in mind that all the provinces were allocated to
ministers, whose servants, the governors told me, marched to the
number of more than three hundred thousand infantry or more
usually two hundred thousand cavalry.[1] But marching without
order, training, or military discipline, with shields, lances, swords
and at the most ten thousand muskets,[2] advancing confusedly
like cattle who know not the handling of their weapons nor the

[1] Bruce, *op. cit.*, iii, 308–9, was of the opinion that 'great exaggerations' had
been used in speaking of the military strength of the Ethiopian armed forces.
'The largest army that ever was in the field', according to his informants, was
that assembled in his day for the battle of 'Serbraxos', i.e. Sarbakusa, when the
rebel army numbered about 50,000, a figure which later increased to 'above
60,000 men, cowards and brave, old and young, veteran soldiers and blackguards'.
He therefore did not imagine that any king of Abyssinia 'ever commanded 40,000
effective men at any time, or upon any cause whatever, exclusive of his household
troops'.
[2] Bruce, *op. cit.*, ii, 681, iv, 63, 116, later estimated the number of fire-arms in
the country variously at 7,000 and 10,000, and stated that the soldiers of Tegré
had 'six times the number that the rest of Abyssinia could furnish.'

art of war, keeping no kind of battle order and without artillery,[3] they go into battle relying solely on their battle cries and on the harsh music of their long trumpets or fifes.[4] Before them goes the Emperor, whose custom it is to lead them into attack, and if he sees himself endangered or wounded in the first onslaught he is the first to turn his back on the foe, throws his own forces into confusion, and often loses the battle from his own fault, having taken no previous counsel of his ministers: so he is ruined, is often unfortunate enough to lose his life, and the empire progressively loses territory: yet all the border tribes, under chieftains much weaker than himself, he could outface and reduce to complete subjection through his superiority in numbers. This failure is more due to the military incompetence of his people, who are ignorant of the handling of arms, defend themselves only with lances and swords, and, once they have thrown two or three lances against the enemy and failed to repulse him, run away empty handed and cause confusion among such of their own troops as are still resisting. The provincial governors are provided with at least three hundred muskets, but are little able to use them, some being out of order, some enormously long, and some so heavy as to be impossible to carry; when they shoot they miss their target, and are better at hand-to-hand fighting with lances, swords, and shields: indeed in time of peace, wherever the Ethiopians go, they walk abroad with always three of four lances and a good sword. The Ethiopians cannot hope for the victory of their cause as long as they are unable to use gunpowder to despatch their shot any distance, and their musket balls will not travel more than fifteen or twenty paces; indeed they have no leaden bullets, and use iron ones which they buy at great expense from the Mahometans or Arabs, so that to tell the truth if but a thousand European soldiers invaded Ethiopia and joined battle with their forces for one day, they would defeat them all and see the exhaustion of the whole of the Emperor's munitions of war. The manpower, valour, and total war-making capacity of Ethiopia is thus revealed, and the soldiers' courage is reduced by the knowledge as they go into battle that no

[3] On the weapons of the Ethiopians in this period see Pankhurst, *Introduction to the economic history of Ethiopia*, pp. 164–5.

[4] On Ethiopian trumpets and other wind instruments see M. Powne, *Ethiopian music* (London, 1968), pp. 25–39.

148

provision has been made to supply them with victuals: the Emperor takes no care for this, his ministers but little, while the colonels of the columns concern themselves with it only for a short time, and whereas in time of peace they are responsible for providing food for the people of the province allotted to them, yet in war they make provision for no more than two months: if the war goes on longer, the soldiers like flies or locusts devour everything as they pass through.[5] Oh the wretchedness then to be seen in a body of five hundred thousand troops: tongue cannot tell of it nor pen describe. Crossing mountains, hills and deserts, finding nothing in the inhabited areas, they carry in their hands or on pack animals their whole means of sustaining life, and sometimes their provision is for scarcely fourteen days. The officials, colonels, and captains, whose duty it is, who in peacetime fill their own pockets, employ the same principle in the stress of war, think nothing of the common good, and bring down no inconsiderable harm and loss on the head of the Emperor and the Empire. With a sufficiency of food they would easily be strong enough to conquer their enemies, and defeating them would win back their old possessions, but for lack of basic necessities their aims are thwarted. Lack of food brings on the extremes of hunger, returning officials told me, many die, many turn back half way, and many more plunder the inhabitants into poverty and ruin, seizing their cattle, devouring their crops, and inflicting on the wretched inhabitants enormities of loot and rapine. Meanwhile the Emperor is besought by his fleeing subjects for protection, for justice, and for the restitution of their stolen goods, and however sincerely he wishes to act righteously he can in no way help them. He sees with grief that all those ills have come about from his own fault and deficiency, and that every outrage and indiscipline of the soldiery springs from his own culpable negligence, for by now the troops are like ravaging lions, are aflame with the madness of anger, care little for the authority of the Emperor and less for that of the officials, and, when led out to war without the necessities of life, are reasonably acting according to the desires of their nature. Every excess is tolerated, each man

---

[5] Almeida, taking a similar view, had observed over a century earlier that the soldiers were 'always going about the whole country, eating, plundering and looting everything'. Beckingham and Huntingford, *Some records*, p. 46.

is permitted every liberty, order is departed, and everlasting misery is the rule in Ethiopia.

During times of war, when the whole population is at arms in the military camps, it is easy enough for enemies to invade all the Ethiopian provinces, towns, and cities, for they do not follow the European practice of setting military guards, and every position lies open, without walls or fortifications, only the wolves, lions, and tigers are left to keep watch, while the fearful populace keep within their homes, where often enough the wild beasts devour them. The women, old men, young boys, and cripples remain behind in the provinces and are exempt from military service; and yet plenty of women go to the battlefield, carrying on their backs different supplies for their menfolk the soldiers, and when war breaks out up to fifty thousand women are involved.[6] There is a dearth of all supplies, confusion reigns among the war-makers causing ever more disorder and trouble, the soldiers are idle and mutinous, and God himself is provoked to anger. The Emperor when he goes to war has carried before him a piece of the wood of the holy cross of our Lord Jesus Christ, together with a golden crown: some years ago, carrying war to Sennar,[7] he lost the crown, since when he has been grieving in his heart for his lost crown, and his mind turns ever to making war on Sennar, partly because the soil is fertile, partly because there is more gold there than in the rest of the country, and partly because of the imperial crown, which he lost there about eighteen years ago, and seeks to recover. He grieves for his own carelessness: in his invasion of Sennar he put his enemies to flight, returned in victory, and gave free rein to his soldiers to eat cattle, drink tacz, sleep off their drunkenness, keep no watch, and indulge in the insolence of victory; when he was again attacked by the Mahometans, when least he expected it, most of his men were killed, captured, or put to flight, and he lost the

[6] Almeida had declared that 'the camp followers and the baggage train amount to many more than the soldiery' and that there were usually 'more women than men in the camp'. Beckingham and Huntingford, *Some records*, p. 78.

[7] Iyasu's disastrous campaign against Sennar took place in March and April 1744. No mention of the loss of a crown is made either in the royal chronicle of the time (Guidi, *Annales regum Iyasu II et Iyo'as*, pp. 124–126) or by Bruce, *op. cit.*, ii, 640. Both sources state on the other hand that the enemy captured the *Kwer'ata re'esu*, or picture of Christ with the Crown of Thorns, and other relics, notably a piece of the True Cross.

imperial crown. Seeing his cause lost, the Emperor with his own hand slew the guardian of the crown, who was still drunk, and sadly retraced his steps homeward without the crown. Even today he is wracked with sorrow at its loss, and grieves for his crown, and not without cause: for if rebellion and disobedience broke out elsewhere in his domains and the rebels made an issue of the loss, he could easily lose his Empire. Officials have told me that it was made of antique gold, and contained five designs, a relic of some centuries old, and that it was set with precious stones and gems as big as a pigeon's egg: they added the fable that this was the crown once brought by an angel to the kings of Israel. This grieves the Emperor even more, and he declares that he can never know happiness until he has recovered it by force of arms: but this is impossible, because the Turks would never leave the gold in its present state, but will either have melted it down, or, as many believe, will have sent it as a present to the sultan at Constantinople from the king of Sennar as a trophy of his memorable victory over the Ethiopians: from Constantinople it is irrecoverable.

A war in Ethiopia never exceeds two months in duration, and, when this period of time has elapsed, even if they are in occupation of the enemy's territory, the soldiers care nothing for acquiring territory or provinces, but content themselves with putting their enemies to death and returning to their own homes with such booty as they have secured. Seeing that the Emperor often despatches his army against the nearer neighbours of the Empire, the custom among them is to cut off the private parts of the slain enemy,[8] and as a sign of courage and loyalty carry them all back to the Emperor: one by one in solemn ceremony, in red bundles carried on their heads, they deposit before the imperial palace the genitals that they have cut off. With the whole court looking on a day of grave solemnity is observed: one by one each trophy is removed from the bundle, and the soldiers in its presence perform different dances and gestures and make threatening bodily movements for a long time: they leap in the air with their weapons, demonstrate their trophies with hands held high, perform gymnastic feats like acrobats, look to the emperor for applause and reward, and in similar manner perform over again

[8] The emasculation of the enemy in battle is described *inter alia* by Bruce, *op. cit.*, iv, 125, 131, 176–8.

their feats of military prowess. As the trophies lie on the ground they approach near to them, make as if to catch sight of them in terror, take a sudden leap backwards, and finally depart in a long outburst of jubilation, and a fanfare of trumpets and shouting.

Just as the Ethiopians attack Sennar every year, so too they harry Schanckalle and Galla with particular bitterness: their inhabitants are regarded as rebels and in great numbers are slain, or captured and enslaved, old men and youths, men and women. By the same token the said rebels retort on the Ethiopians, and lose no chance of slaughtering, capturing, and reducing them to slavery, and from either side arise to heaven the mourning and lamentation of parents, kindred, and children.

Rewards and preferment are used to encourage the soldiers, and these are no other than the eating of raw oxen and the drinking of tacz,[9] and the presentation of long leggings of cloth of about a cubit's width called *surri*,[10] of red or blue Indian cloth for the common soldiers, while for officials a more elaborate gift is made of tunics of valuable material along with the surri, the tunic being girt with a long knife like a Turkish small sword. So clad, they are applauded as in a triumph by a large crowd, trumpets, drums, and various pipes strike up, they display them-selves to the inhabitants, with a baldachin held over the heads of the officials, and they bask in the applause of the whole people; when they have worn this presentation clothing for some time, they take it back to the Treasurer when torn and ask for an equivalent present instead – as though the Minister would be grateful for their dirty rags. Meanwhile they joyfully celebrate their triumph; many cattle are slaughtered throughout the city, they eat, drink, and are merry, and the crowds gather to watch and to show to the officers and soldiers the gratitude and recogni-tion due to their faithful service, so that in the future they may fight gloriously for their country.

---

[9] Raw meat and *taj*, i.e. mead, were two privileges reserved for the aristocracy, and thus constituted status symbols. Alvarez in the early sixteenth century noted that 'nobody from the common people may kill a cow (even though it is his own) without leave from the lord of the country'. Beckingham and Huntingford, *Prester John*, ii, 515. The restriction on the drinking of taj was later noted by several nineteenth century writers, including Johnston, *op. cit.*, ii, 170–1, and Harris, *op. cit.*, iii, 9.

[10] *Surri*, the Amharic for trousers, Guidi, *Vocabolario*, p. 155.

CHAPTER 22

THE EMPEROR'S COSTUME, RETINUE, AND PALACE

The ancient authorities have different accounts of the costume of the Emperor of Ethiopia, describing how rich is his adornment of gold, gems, and countless jewels, and how the Emperor seldom shows himself to his people, who can view the splendour and magnificence of his majesty on at most two or three occasions a year. These and other tales I leave to the ancient authors, but affirm that in modern times, at the date of my residence in Abyssinia, nothing like this was to be seen, no beauty, no splendour, no precious stones or other magnificence. The Emperor wraps himself in a white cloth as a cloak, the dress of his subjects, wears long white leggings called *Surri*, a longer shift, in Arab style, of fine Indian cloth with large sleeves at least half an ell wide, and is girt with a collar or girdle of gold five fingers wide; on his left side he is armed with a hanging knife called *schotel*,[1] his head is always bare, and he goes barefoot within the palace but at times wears sandals. His hair he keeps curled, and makes it serve as a cap and outer covering of his head, dressing it in different ways to enhance its elegance, and on feast days anointing it liberally with mutton fat or fresh butter,[2] which when struck by the rays of the sun gives the appearance of morning dew on meadow grass; furthermore, to avoid ruffling the tresses and curls on his head, he does not use a pillow for his head when he goes to bed, but places it on a crescent-shaped piece of wood

---

[1] Amharic *šotal*, a curved sword already mentioned by Prutky in chapter 13.

[2] Almeida states that the Ethiopians had many styles of dressing their hair, and often soaked it in unrefined butter, which in his opinion produced 'an odd perfume'. Beckingham and Huntingford, *Some records*, p. 61.

about a span high and covered with silk, and goes to sleep on his face: alternatively he fixes in the ground a framework a foot high, puts his neck between its two sides, and goes to sleep with his head thus suspended, in order not to ruffle the arrangement of his coiffure.[3] For all of my time in Ethiopia this was the costume I saw on the Emperor, except in the cooler season of June, July and August when he clothed himself in Arab style, but without the turban and sandals: indeed, if presented by his ministers with sandals for his feet, he wore them two or three times and then discarded them, returning to his original habit. Such was his costume, rather than the costly and magnificent apparel depicted by other writers.

I was still more surprised to see him walk barefoot in the palace on a pavement made simply of pebbles brought from the river, a decoration with which he embellishes all his dwellings, and one which is an obvious cause of difficulty and discomfort to those not accustomed to it; but the Emperor, who is well used to it, has no difficulty in walking barefoot around the whole palace. This however should rather be styled a simple house, yet not one house but a number of pavilions[4] surrounded by the same wall, like the dwellings of the Carthusians: but in Abyssinia this is the royal palace. The pavilions are small and entirely detached from each other, constructed without elegance, without dignity, almost without craftmanship; they are generally round in shape, and covered with mud and straw. The imperial residence at Kaha, not far from Gondar, consists of at least ten such pavilions near to each other, the Emperor occupying one for a short time and then another, sleeping in one, drinking and eating in another, giving audience to his people in a third: at his pleasure he passes from one to another during the time he spends there, visible to

[3] Almeida noted that the Ethiopians made use of a bolster 'like a small wooden fork on which they rest, not the head, which is in mid-air, but the neck'. Beckingham and Huntingford, *Some records*, p. 58. Mansfield Parkyns, *op. cit.*, i, 539, later described these head-rests as 'about seven or eight inches high', with the part on which the head rests 'crescent-shaped'. He comments, 'This form of pillow is very necessary to people who, from the custom of having their hair fancifully tressed and arranged and plastered with butter, could not lay their heads on an ordinary one, as they would saturate it with grease, besides seriously damaging their coiffure'.

[4] Bruce, *op. cit.*, iii, 380, describing these pavilions, recalls that 'a succession of kings' had built a number of apartments beside the earlier castle of Fasiladas. They were made 'of clay only, in the manner and fashion of their country'.

no one save to the youths his courtiers, since a good high wall[5] surrounds the Residence and protects him from casual intruders. Each pavilion contains only one room and a small cell, without courtyard or other ornament, the walls are bare and unadorned, the bare earth is simply covered with a Turkish carpet, there are neither chairs nor tables, but in each pavilion there is a single couch spread with a silver-embroidered cloth and two embroidered cushions, where the Emperor takes his seat when he enters. Generally the buildings are circular, and are strongly thatched with straw against the torrential rains, as by this means the water, even over so many months, cannot penetrate the thatch; they are few in number, oblong in shape and not very large, like the cottages of European peasants: they are made of unmortared stone and daubed with mud within and without. Lime is scarce and expensive, as they do not know how to work it, and no one save the Emperor presumes to use mortar in building a house, or even whitewash; if its use were permitted, the humble cell of a hermit would cost an ounce of gold to whitewash, so what would be the cost of a whole house? They submit without argument to this decree, and have no wish to use whitewash, much less mortar.[6] Only occasionally does the Emperor himself require the use of mortar in house building, but the nobles have the interiors of their bedchambers whitewashed, though not in the Emperor's style: they cover the walls with white cloth roughly smeared with lime by hand, for the most part inefficiently: they know not how to handle whitewash, and waste their material. Glass being unknown in Ethiopia their houses are without glazed windows, and in their place they construct four or five big doors, of timber roughly hewn with the axe as a beam would be, and put in place in the crudest possible manner without hinges. Seeing that either part cannot be fitted to the other for the roughness of the workmanship, the door is closed in two separate parts, and shut on the outside with a chain, like the door of a horse's stable: when they want to let light into the room, they open all the doors. Certainly

[5] This *makkababya*, or encircling wall, seems to have been already in existence in the late seventeenth century, Pankhurst, *History of Ethiopian towns*, i, 134. Bruce, *op. cit.*, iii, 380, described it as 'substantial stone wall thirty feet high, with battlements upon the outer wall, and a parapet roof between the outer and the inner, by which you can go along the whole and look into the street'.

[6] This restriction on the use of mortar was not mentioned by any other observer.

an inhabitant of Europe, at first sight of this house, would marvel to call it a palace, yet the interior is decorated to the height of the walls in glowing red colours in a wonderful though crude taste, as a richer European bourgeois might adorn his dwelling, though with less sophistication and symmetry.

While most of the imperial pavilions are but mud-daubed within, they are all surrounded by a wall at least two fathoms high instead of fortifications, and each pavilion is separated from the next with one small communicating door manned by a porter, who acts as sentry to ensure that the Emperor is protected against any chance of hostile attack; an intruder who gained access to one pavilion would find himself separated by a wall from the next, and the third, and the fourth, and his chance of reaching the Emperor would be remote: the walls and the porters perform the function of military sentries, which he does not maintain apart from some personal slaves who are armed with swords and lances, which they retain beside them whether they eat, drink, or sleep. Other military protection is not available, because the troops all owe their loyalty to the provincial governors, who maintain them in arms, and only serve the Emperor in foreign wars. Since however the Ethiopian people are often disaffected, the governors of the three provinces nearer to the palace of Gondar, who in their military capacity are able to command the help of at least four thousand men, ensure the Emperor's security in any emergency,[7] while, more immediately, the three imperial ministers in Gondar the capital, white-skinned eastern Greeks by nationality, command a force of at least two thousand fighting men, and would fight fiercely to defeat an enemy, seeing that the Emperor trusts more in their loyalty than in that of his own subjects. Following ancient custom, the Emperor is for ever shut away behind walls, and is seldom to be seen in public, save when he rides from Gondar to Kaha or back again.[8] Then a large crowd

[7] The Emperor's household troops, according to Bruce, op. cit., iii, 310–11, consisted of about 8,000 infantry, 2,000 of whom carried fire-arms. These soldiers were divided into four companies, 'each under an officer called Shalaka, which answers to our colonel'. There were in addition four regiments, which seldom amounted to 1,600 men, depending directly on the monarch. Their officers were 'all foreigners' and had 'charge of the royal person while in the field'.

[8] Bruce, op. cit., iii, 282, similarly wrote that 'the king of Abyssinia never is seen to walk, nor to set his foot upon the ground, out of his palace', and elsewhere, iii, 278, states: 'the kings of Abyssinia were seldom seen by their subjects'.

gazes at him from afar, surrounded by officials and guarded by servants and slaves, who permit no one to approach him and who drive off with blows whoever meet him in the highroad and do not withdraw.[9] Any who beyond expectation draw near to the Emperor on horseback are unable to gaze upon his features, because he is veiled up to the eyes in a white cloak, and only the flash of his eyes is visible. Generally he is preceded by two hundred muskets, and at least a thousand lances surround him: while long trumpets such as shepherds use, and four smaller pipes, like flutes which maintain one note, commonly called *flautrover*, pay respect to the Emperor as he rides on his way, with all his officials greater or less accompanying him, and servants beating hand-drums until he reaches the palace entrance; then everyone returns to his own home.[10]

To the visitor to Abyssinia it is a wonderful sight to see for the first time both the dwellings of the Emperor and, even more, those of the ministers and great lords, all of them circular in construction, and all thatched with straw the better to withstand the tremendous rainfall.

[9] The Emperor, according to Bruce, *op. cit.*, iii, 265, had 'an officer called Serach Massery, with a long whip', which he cracked 'making a noise, worse than twenty French postillions.'

[10] In a not dissimilar passage Poncet describes Iyasu I, half a century earlier, walking in procession 'with his trumpets, kettle-drums, flutes, hauteboys, and other instruments going before him', with his musketeers and archers in the rear. Foster, *op. cit.*, p. 117.

CHAPTER 23

METHOD OF GIVING AUDIENCE,
THE QUEEN'S COSTUME AND
CERTAIN OTHER MATTERS

When the Emperor has been ceremoniously conducted to the palace, often lingering in the doorway with his closer advisers, the company demonstrate their horsemanship in Turkish fashion: each courtier follows the Emperor in a circle on horseback and rides for a long time, performing various tricks of equitation, exercising their weapons, charging each other until exhausted; in the midst of these feats, which are performed with enthusiasm, quite unexpectedly the Emperor withdraws from their midst into the palace, leaving them all outside: no one knows into which pavilion he has gone, so many does he maintain, each provided with doors and doorkeeper, and his exact whereabouts is unknown, whether he is in this pavilion or that. Whoever desires audience has to wait many hours before the first door, and, when it is opened, he has to experience further delays at the second, at the third, at the fourth: often days pass before he makes his way through the sixth door, where dwells the Emperor. Here each piece of business is transacted through wretched youths, whom alone, as I shall say elsewhere, he employs about him, and when access has been granted the Emperor is to be seen reclining on an ornate couch with a large cushion and coverlet, or outside the pavilion sitting on a rug on the green grass. Eight or ten youths are with him and he has a great sword set beside him, unsheathed, and a lance and shield: so he spends all his time in the company of boys, talking continually with them, asking silly questions, amusing himself with horses while his servants sit beside him, occasionally calling on one of them to play the fool – so he spends his valuable time in silly chatter. Trusting none

of his principal officials, ever suspicious lest they be plotting evil against him, he contents himself with the company only of boys, through whose mediation all the affairs of the kingdom are conducted orally, nothing being reduced to writing.

Whoever of the principal ministers desires audience must wait outside the last door until one of the young courtiers comes out, admits him, and answers his question as to whether he will obtain audience. When this is at last favourable, he removes the cloth which covers him and wraps it round his hips, and barefoot and bowing approaches the imperial presence; then with the greatest reverence he prostrates himself on the ground at least thirty paces from the Emperor, a closer approach being forbidden to Ethiopians on account of the distrust in which he holds them lest they be plotting in their hearts against him. So at a distance they kiss the earth and explain their petition, and after every word of their request, and of the reply with which the Emperor honours them, they bend and kiss the ground for the whole time that the reply is being given; indeed for anyone who talks for a long time with the Emperor, the fatigue is considerable just of the prostration and osculation. The audience concluded, the subject retires backward, again prostrates himself and kisses the ground before the threshold of the gate, and returns homeward.

We missionaries were in oriental dress when we approached the imperial presence, removed just our sandals from our feet before the door, retaining our *terlick*[1] or light leather slippers, and, kissing the ground only at the entrance to the apartment, were granted audience beside the Emperor's couch. He then bade us be seated on the ground, and declared that he harboured no evil suspicions against us; 'Franks are good men, just and God-fearing, and I avoid them not nor do I fear them. But my own people' he repeated 'are evil, treacherous, ever harming their neighbour, to be handled carefully, and to be feared'. Seldom therefore does he admit any Ethiopian to his presence, and as soon as his visitor reaches the first door he has to divest himself of his cloth from off his body, to present himself barefoot and bareheaded, and to do honour to the very walls and stones, as being in the imperial presence. We Europeans by contrast retained our white cloaks, bared just our right arms to do honour

---

[1] Turkish *terlik*, a slipper.

159

to the Emperor alone, and, save for the first time at the entrance, we refrained from kissing the ground, except occasionally for some exceptional benefit, promised or received.

At times, when more pressing business is afoot, the more reliable ministers are summoned together before the last door to receive the Emperor's replies, and especially when the people are making an outcry in the hills and are gathered together too close to the palace, shouting endlessly for their Emperor with the words *Jan Hui Jan Hui*,[2] that is, Your Majesty, continually repeated. This is the custom that obtains among this people in all case of need, of calling upon their emperor, because they have neither parliament, nor law-court, nor minister of justice; in case of oppression they have no recourse save to appeal to the Emperor for help and to cry interminably Jan hui: until he sends one of his servants to ask what their demand is. Outcries like this are heard almost every day, a second beginning when the first ceases, monks crying out Jan hui equally with the laity, and they are indeed distracting since it is impossible to satisfy so many people. Often even nightfall puts no end to the horrible clamour, which is kept up continually though transferred from one place to another, and, unless force be used, they do not cease.[3] And true it is that force must be tempered with discretion, lest they take offence and fall into rebellion, and however much the Emperor hates the daily and nightly noise, he has not the power to repress or quieten it.

In addition to this, it is the custom for all those who for their own evil doing are sufferers from syphilis to outlaw themselves and gather in the hills shouting Jan hui: they demand help, that is food and drink, during the time of their cure; until then they do no work, but waste their time washing themselves in the mountain streams for as long as their disease lasts: their petition in such circumstances is seldom or never denied, and they are

---

[2] Amharic *Jan hoy*, an expression used when addressing an Ethiopian monarch; Guidi, *Vocabolario*, p. 637. See also Bruce, *op. cit.*, iii, 274; Guèbrè Sellassié, *Chronique du règne de Ménélik II, roi des rois d'Ethiopie* (Paris, 1930–1) ii, 734; C. H. Walker, *The Abyssinian at home* (London, 1933), pp. 137, 162.

[3] Bruce, *op. cit.*, iii, 273, notes that it was the 'constant practice in Abyssinia to beset the King's doors and windows within his hearing, and there, from early morning to night, to cry for justice as loud as possible, in a distressed and complaining tone, and in all the different languages they are master of'. For early nineteenth century accounts of this long-enduring custom see Pearce, *op. cit.*, i, 339, and Johnston, *op. cit.*, ii, 141.

sent to the royal treasury for a donation of bread and wine, for the whole period of their cure. If ever a decree is promulgated which fails to please the people, thousands of men surround the palace in the hills and call unceasingly Jan hui, until the decree is revoked: all this more in accordance with the popular wish than with the execution of the imperial will, but the protesters are the very servants of the provincial governors, the soldiers in time of war, the defenders of the kingdom, and if these turn rebel, who else will aid the Emperor? No one. Against this gathering in the hills how will the Emperor, with eight or ten unarmed youths decked out neck, ears, feet, and hands with golden bangles, and with about one hundred slaves armed with lances and shields, defend himself against so many thousands? Shut up within the palace he grants individual petitions as best he can, while the wretched crown of Ethiopia causes its wearer more trouble and anxiety than joy, and ever disturbs his peace of mind. So fear possesses him, and within four walls, like a private citizen, he lives with his young courtiers, with neither conversation nor intercourse with the outside world, nor with any pastime worthy of his position: splendid hunts could be organized, for elephant, tiger, lion, ape, and many other sorts of game, but he fails to interest himself in this.[4] No spark of prudence is to be found in him, or of good judgment, and when he has converse only with boys, and imparts to them secrets which should be revealed only to his principal advisers, how can state affairs remain confidential if the boys know not how to be discreet? How desirable is prudence, how disastrous its lack. By their lack of discretion the whole government is indecisive, composed of youths who have not reached the age of reason. In the old days it was the splendour, magnificence, and enormous power of the Ethiopian emperors that withdrew them from the gaze of mortals, now it is the fear of suffering injury that keeps them in hiding and out of common sight.

The same observances are maintained by the Emperor's mother[5] the queen regent, who lives with a number of young

[4] Court life, if we can believe Prutky, was at this time somewhat staid, but Iyasu in his youth had undertaken several notable hunting expeditions. Guidi, *Annales regum Iyasu II et Iyo'as*, p. 92; Bruce, *op. cit.*, ii, 630–1.

[5] The Emperor's mother, Empress Mentewwab, was a great stateswoman. Bruce, *op. cit.*, iv, 242, relates that when she returned to Gondar in his day, after a largely self-imposed exile, it was 'impossible to conceive the enthusiasm with which the sight of the old queen inspired all sorts of people'.

girls[6] apart from general intercourse, but as subject as the
Emperor her son to the outcries of her subjects; indeed the same
scene is enacted before the houses of the principal ministers,
especially when they are due to be confirmed in office, and crowds
of women gather before their houses, dancing, singing, clapping
their hands and gesturing, until they receive the present of an
ox. The better to humour them the Queen appears before them,
dressed in the same white cloak as the Emperor, the sleeves of
her shift worked into narrow and complicated pleats, her shift
reaching to her knees outside wide and valuable leggings, her
stockings carefully arranged with tongued shoes of red or yellow
leather: her hair she wears curled, and variously plaited together
and anointed in the same way that I have described in the last
chapter. She wears a golden girdle, and over all her other clothing
a white cloak which covers her head and hangs to the ground:
her face is covered, only her eyes being visible,[7] and each time
she leaves the palace she mounts a richly-caparisoned mule, as
there are no wheeled vehicles: no small company of ministers
and servants precede her, in the same array as the Emperor's
with weapons, lances, shields, trumpets, and drums, but in front
of all these men run at least a hundred serving women, in
laughter, cackle, and disorder. As well as these she likewise
maintains within the palace a number of young girls, to whom
she entrusts the handling and execution of business and the
giving and receiving of answers: the seeker of an audience is
admitted by young girls, who always attend the Queen, clothed
like the Emperor's courtiers, and who always come before the
royal presence and stand afar from the Queen, to keep harm
from reaching her. When I myself was admitted to audience I
found her standing behind a small grille as in a European nun-
nery, and she spoke very kindly to me and did me many favours
and benefits. While she keeps the palace, she is attended day and
night by a monk who is of her own kindred, to whom in affection

[6] Mentewwab's palace, according to Bruce, op. cit., iv, 272, was situated at
Q^{w}esq^w am, in the hills north-west of Gondar. The inner court was 'reserved for
the queen's own apartments', and her unmarried attendants.

[7] Miguel de Castanhoso, describing Empress Sabla Wangél's dress two centuries
earlier, stated that 'she was all covered to the ground with silk, with a large
flowing cloak' and was 'clothed in a very thin white Indian cloth and a burnoose
of black satin, with flowers and fringes of fine gold . . . and so muffled in a very
fine cloth that only her eyes could be seen'. Whiteway, op. cit., p. 18.

she denies nothing, and whose mediation ensures the securing of a petition. If she gives a public audience, she sits, as the Emperor does, on a couch with an embroidered covering, with cushions beneath her, and, covered to the eyes with a white cloak, she replies to the petitions, while the young scantily-clad attendants stand around the couch. Indeed the splendour and magnificence of antiquity is missing in the modern kingdom of Ethiopia, alike in apparel as in entertainment, as I shall briefly describe.

CHAPTER 24

THE EMPEROR'S DINING ESTABLISHMENT, AND CUSTOMS AT TABLE

Just as the Emperor seldom appears to his subjects, so seldom or never is he seen by them at table, nor indeed the Queen Mother, as they think it demeaning that their vassals, who are unworthy of the honour, should view them there: partly too they are swayed by the common superstition that men or devils by breathing upon their food could do them harm, and they always eat and drink in private, with only their small retinues of youthful courtiers. A low table is set ready scarce two hands high off the ground; round loaves of unleavened bread like cakes are piled in heaps one upon another instead of plates, in the midst of the piles of bread is set raw meat, and in the centre of the table a dish of curds and another of *teps*,[1] or meat which has been grilled in the fire and slightly charred. If it happens that the Emperor and his mother are dining together, one end of the table is put by the Queen's couch and one by the Emperor's, and they are fed by their attendants,[2] touching nothing with their own hands; they eat hurriedly, finish in a short time, and separate each to their own quarters. When they do not eat together, each has a small table prepared, and when the meal is over no one is permitted to enter their presence for at least an hour. In short the Emperor's meal consists of a sauce, like thick soup, into which is dipped their soft bread mixed with curds, and of which the attendants make pieces of two or three ounces weight and place in the mouth of the Emperor and his mother; on five or six of these pieces or dumplings, and on raw meat cut into pieces which

---

[1] Amharic *tebs*, or roasted meat. Guidi, *Vocabolario*, p. 817.
[2] Bruce, *op. cit.*, iii, 303, describing this practice, observed, 'No man in Abyssinia, of any fashion whatever, feeds himself, or touches his own meat'.

they swallow whole, they make their meal, and no side dish, or sweet course in European style, appears on their table.

On Sundays, when the Emperor's dinner has been cleared away, a public feast is set out for the ministers: the table is spread close to the Emperor's couch, on which he sits shrouded up to the eyes in his usual white cloak, his youths around him, and his sword, lance, and shield displayed. The ministers are admitted to the presence of the imperial family, take their seats on the ground around the table, and one after the other, the lesser after those held in greater esteem, they fall to voraciously and gobble up the choice portions of meat wrapped in bread; at these feasts, as I shall describe in another chapter on Ethiopian food, there is present a slave girl, naked to the waist, who places in the midst of the table three large dishes on which she piles loaves of bread: from this she tears off pieces of five or six ounces weight and places them in the mouths of the ministers in the order of their importance, until each have devoured six pieces or rolls. At this point from one of the bread piles she breaks up the loaves, which are soft and intricately kneaded, cuts up small pieces of meat and wraps them in the bread, and with her hand places one in the mouths of each of the guests, who sit around in the same order of importance. Five or six such good portions are enough to satisfy them, and they devour it with their mouths full until they seem to be suffocating, while, in a manner truly appetising, from the hands and fingers of the slave-girl fall drops of blood and fat, and from the mouths of the feasters all sorts of filth drip from mouth to chin, as mouthful follows mouthful, at least three pounds in weight of food, and their hunger is partly appeased. Meanwhile pieces of raw meat of ten or twelve pounds weight have been put on the table among the bread; unsheathing their knives called schotel two and two and lifting them on high, they snatch up the meat and vigorously carve it up as they will, so that if for example twenty people were sitting at table the joints of meat would be set among the bread in ten places, one joint being sometimes of thirty pounds' weight: from which they hack off gobbets and, sometimes each for himself and sometimes one feeding the other, swallow down at least two pounds each,[3] being unable to chew it with their teeth because it is raw. They start to

---

[3] Bruce, op. cit., iii, 304, states that the Ethiopians justified these practices with the proverb, 'Beggars and thieves only eat small pieces, or without making a noise'.

sigh heavily, to puff, to belch, and to indicate that they have eaten to satiety. Arising from the table, they sit on the ground, with their backs to the wall, and wipe off on the walls their blood-stained hands and mouths, as though in a shambles. A draught of tacz is their next pleasure, of which they drink glass after glass of a pint each, until intoxication often ensues:[4] nor are they ashamed to disgrace the Emperor's presence with drunken behaviour. He meanwhile lies on a cushion on his couch, veiled as usual to the chin, watching in silence this genteel behaviour, and exposed to all manner of smell. At the greater feasts of the year, as a mark of especial favour to his subjects, he sits with his face unveiled, but with his usual weapons beside him nevertheless, as though he were brooding over the consumption of the economy of his country.

When this feasting of the ministers is over, another table is spread, rather further from the imperial couch, at which the junior officials take their seat, and when they have finished their meal, which they eat in the same way as their seniors, they arise and stand behind the senior officials, receiving but one cup of drink. At the third sitting the same table feeds the favourite slaves, among whom are some formidable old women, and as soon as they sit to the table the slaves unsheathe their swords, as the imperial bodyguard, and raise them aloft: this strikes fear to the eyes of the beholder lest their greed in cleaving and eating the meat cause them to do harm each to the other. However, this way and that they carve the raw flesh, and devour it with such a noise of chewing and swallowing as pigs, God save the mark, would make at the trough. Meanwhile the same half-naked slave-girl stands in the midst and performs her duty of filling mouths from what remains of the bread, sauce, and curds; she carefully gives preference to those she regards as her friends, and I once gazed in amazement at three of four open mouths, all ready to eat, each anxious to eat before the others, a sight which to a European excited disgust and no small degree of amusement. When they see their stomachs distended, they arise, wipe on the walls their bloody hands and mouths, and rub their

---

[4] Bruce, *op. cit.*, iii, 393, states, 'The Abyssinians say, you must plant first and then water; nobody, therefore, drinks till they have finished eating'. On this custom see also Lobo (Lockhart, *op. cit.*, p. 171), and Bruce, *op. cit.*, iii, 304.

faces this way and that against them: behaviour that barbarians would call disgraceful. These too in the same way dispose themselves in a third rank behind their seniors, receive the draught they have been awaiting, and replacing their swords in their sheathes withdraw from the imperial chamber.[5] To the fourth sitting, to eat up the remains, come the Emperor's youthful companions and favourites, for whom is brought on a lightly-cooked dish of vegetables, and who gobble up the remains of the raw meat at great speed and swallow it down, returning without delay to the side of the imperial couch, their usual station, though some proceed outdoors if no draught of drink be offered them: the young courtiers drink a sort of beer[6] called *busa*,[7] made from water and barley, while the other young slaves make do with water. At last to the fifth sitting come a crowd of naked young slaves, five or six years of age, who finish up everything left on the table and take the bread away with them: the noise of their lamentations is tremendous, especially when an older slave with a long stick strikes the noisy ones on the head, when their cries become louder: but each of these annoyances is tolerated by the Emperor in patience and silence. The table is removed, and two slaves clear up from the floor-covering the piles of food, fragments, and crumbs; the imperial chamber is made as nauseating as a shambles.

When the room has been cleaned, a curious sound of music is heard outside the door, and the shouts of those desiring admittance to entertain the Emperor and his ministers. On admission they begin to play with no further tuning up, a noise like the caterwauling of a hundred cats: two play an instrument like a one-stringed cittern,[8] which they pluck continuously with plectrum, finger, or some such, and assail the ear therewith, one has

[5] T'ovmačean (Nersessian and Pankhurst, *op. cit.*, pp. 86–7) and Bruce *op. cit.*, iii, 301–5, 393–4, both also describe eighteenth century banquets, but Prutky would appear to be the first foreign observer to notice the practice, reported by later observers, of having a succession of different classes or categories of diners. On this custom see W. Plowden, *Travels in Abyssinia and the Galla country* (London, 1868), p. 212; Pankhurst, *Economic history of Ethiopia 1800–1935* (Addis Ababa, 1968), pp. 703–5.

[6] Beer, in Amharic *talla*, unlike the aristocratic drink *taj*, or mead, was mainly drunk by the general public, as reported for example by Bruce, *op. cit.*, iii, 548, iv, 392.

[7] Beer, referred to by Bruce, *op. cit.*, iii, 548 and iv, 392 as 'bouza'.

[8] The *masanqo*, or one-string fiddle. Powne, *op. cit.*, pp. 39–43.

167

another six-stringed instrument[9] like a harp of David,[10] which maintains a low melody and which he plucks, all six strings at once, with a piece of ivory to maintain the bass, while two others play on separate one-stringed instruments to make a noise like a cat. All together produce an effect which to a European ear sounds like the cry of bears or cats, especially when to this musical accompaniment they burst into song in fulsome praises of the Emperor. In the midst of this harmony it is the custom for one or two foolish dancing-girls to perform their acts, falling over like bears, tumbling like acrobats, kissing the earth in the Emperor's honour, and continuously repeating *Jaz*,[11] or *Hate Jemut*,[12] that is, May Jasu, or the Emperor, die, adding various words in the Emperor's praise: by this phrase they do not mean that they wish for the Emperor's death, but this is their only way to express that, if my prayer be not genuine may he die, or, just as surely as I do not wish death to the Emperor, so surely is my prayer genuine and sincere.[13] In the same way, servants who are being questioned to establish the truth of an affair reply, in face of their master's questioning, *Uld-Elut-Jemut* (giving the master's name), May my master die, *Uld-Elut*, unless what I say is true: servants give credence to no statement unless it has been preceded by the oath, May my master die.

These and other trifling performances completed, and the Emperor's appetite for music, and the performers' for tacz, duly satisfied, they all depart, together with the officials, for their own homes, and leave in peace the Emperor and his mother. I could not wonder enough how the Emperor could for such a long period of time endure the wretchedness of these inanities, could sit through to the end of five feasts, could support such noise, undescribable stench, intolerable smell of human bodies, and musical discord which lasted at least four hours: throughout all he sat silent and unmoved, propped up on his cushion, and,

[9] The six-stringed instrument is the *krar*, which has a shallow circular bowl. Powne, *op. cit.*, pp. 43–53.

[10] The instrument usually associated with the harp of David is the *bagana* which is likened to the harp of David but actually has ten strings. Powne, *op. cit.*, pp. 53–8.

[11] Prutky's abbreviation for Jasu, i.e. Emperor Iyasu.

[12] *Iyasu* or *Ate yemut*.

[13] The custom of swearing by the death of the king, saying for example *Menilek yemut*, i.e. 'May Menilek die if . . . ,' was long established. See for example Walker, *op. cit.*, pp. 25, 35, 41, 102, 146, 154, 175, 198.

however vexatious this ceremony might be, yet, because it has been the custom since ancient times, it is observed in Gondar every Sunday – though not in his residence in Kaha where he is as it were a private person.

I myself when acting as doctor to the Emperor, along with the imperial treasurer and the other minister the imperial judge, by birth Greeks[14] from the Archipelago, was by virtue of my position compelled to put in an appearance every Sunday: however, to avoid having to sit at the distinguished official table, I used to appear later at the third table. One day it happened that I arrived too early, and was bidden to seat myself at table, whereupon the slave-girl immediately tried to honour me by offering to place in my mouth a particularly choice morsel: I refused, and withdrew towards the Emperor's couch, and, had not the slave-girl been instructed to refrain from such an office, my stomach would have been seriously upset. I was more careful in future, and the Greek ministers and I used to appear towards the end, but long indeed did the delay seem before the end of the belches and smells of that indescribable meal. The Emperor marked us out from the rest and showed us a distinct sign of his favour, in that when we had made our obeisance to him he signed to us to sit on the ground, refreshed us with a drink of tacz, and, to mark us out from his own subjects, he tendered to us smaller glasses, of European size. These we drank throughout the rest of the feast, but the noise was disagreeable, and the cloak that I was wearing, of fine cloth, was torn in the tumult. The crowd of people behaved as in a European tavern: offensive gestures, quarrels, noisy separations, coarse laughter, beastlike belches, we longed for the end of this lavish entertainment, and a detailed description of the glory and splendour of the imperial feasts is beyond the power of my poor pen. My personal presence made it no more tolerable.

A further description will follow when I talk of Ethiopian food and table manners.

---

[14] There were, as noted in previous chapters, several Greeks in the Emperor's service.

CHAPTER 25

THE QUARTERS AND THE BURIAL
OF THE SONS OF THE ROYAL
BLOOD, AND THE CHILDHOOD
OF THE EMPEROR JASU

I wrote earlier of the imperial authority and importance in modern times, so far from agreement with the accounts of the ancient writers, and that now there exists but the shadow of the Abyssinian emperor and only the name persists. It is difficult to liken him to any European prince, because he is raised to the imperial dignity not by right of succession but by open election, the nobles voting either for the son of the deceased emperor, or for another descendant in the direct, or the collateral, line.[1] This in the past was the cause of grave disagreements, one party inclining to the emperor's son, another to some other descendant, so that every election was marked by bloodshed; to prevent this the custom was introduced in the present century that all the sons of the reigning Emperor at six or seven years of age should be removed from their father's palace to a mountain by the Nile called *Ohni*.[2] High and precipitous, this is inaccessible both climbing and descending save by a system of ladders and ropes, by which the royal sons were hauled to the mountain top and down again. The summit is in the form of a beautiful and broad plain,

---

[1] Bruce, *op. cit.*, iii, 262, in his account of succession, observes that 'the crown in Abyssinia' was 'hereditary' within the family supposed to be descended from Solomon and the Queen of Sheba, but was 'nevertheless elective in this line', for there was 'no law of the land, nor custom, which gives the eldest son an exclusive title to succeed to his father'.

[2] Mount Wahni, a steep *amba*, or flat-topped mountain, south-east of Gondar, used as a place of detention for members of the royal family. See *inter alia* Bruce, *op. cit.*, ii, 429–31, iii, 307–8, and for a modern account T. Pakenham, *The mountains of Rasselas* (London, 1959).

like a small island, precipitous on the one side and on the other guarded by the stream of the Nile, so that anyone who has once reached the summit can never return unless released by the treachery of one of the guards. Once recaptured his life is forfeit, unless by special favour of the ruling Emperor he is mutilated of a limb, nose, ear, hand, or foot, which would render him incapable of assuming the imperial dignity. The Ethiopian people are barbarous, ever ready to rebel, prompt to every act of evil, and anyone who escaped from the mountain would have no difficulty in raising a revolt against the ruler; to prevent such evils the Emperor's sons were strictly guarded, and any leaving the mountain without the Emperor's permission savagely punished.

Harsh indeed is the imprisonment of all the descendants of the royal blood, and though each is allowed what he will in the matter of say concubines, they lead a wretched life, with nothing to do but collect the food allowed to them for their sustenance.[3] Since so many royal descendants are to be found in one place, the new generation continually increases, all by law eligible to be chosen for the imperial throne, their number generally in excess of three hundred and not easily disposed of. The collateral line ever continues, and, following the death of the Emperor, one of them, at the election of the nobles, is removed from the mountain and crowned as the new Emperor. Mount Ohni lies next to the beautiful province of *Belasa*,[4] to which is assigned the duty of providing for the princes, and from this province come the necessary food and clothing which are drawn up the mountain by ladder: no subject is permitted to climb, and by day and night the imperial guards are under arms, well able to prevent any ascent of the mountain. So the unfortunate sons of the emperors are never permitted to leave the mountain, and for all their life are deprived of any further solace or human converse, their only company each other and their concubines, on whom they beget descendants, which by now have reached such a number that, when one is withdrawn to ascend the throne, there is no fear

---

[3] Bruce, *op. cit.*, iii, 308, states that the allowance set aside for the royal prisoners of Mt Wahni consisted of 750 cloths and 3,000 ounces of gold, but this revenue had been 'so grossly misapplied in his day that some of the detainees were said to have died of cold and hunger'.

[4] Belessa, a district south-east of Gondar referred to in chapter 19.

with so many pretenders that the imperial line may fail. Although the greater number are illegitimate, as the sons of concubines, yet the Ethiopians have the singular custom of regarding them as legitimate heirs, and boast that they trace their royal line continuously from Solomon: indeed as I have earlier written the present Emperor Jasu wears his genealogy on his person wrapped in a golden locket, of which he showed me the writing in Greek, Chaldean, and Arabic, and which he guards as a priceless treasure. Wretched indeed is the condition in Ethiopia of the sons of the Emperors, spiritually deprived for their whole life long. Like prisoners they pass their time in misery, without arms, lances, swords or other weapons of war, lest in disgust or boredom, and valuing their life at nothing, they do each other to death. For all their life all solace is denied them.

From this legalized imprisonment the present Emperor Jasu was rescued by the sagacity of the Queen his mother, with the help of some foremost nobles of the empire, her good friends. When Jasu was a boy of three years of age, she secretly conveyed him to the province of Syre, where at that time the Dadaczmacz or Governor was of the royal blood and the queen's party, and pretended to the populace that her young son had been taken to Mt Ohni.[5] He was secretly brought up in the province of Syre until he had reached his tenth year, when his father the Emperor met his end, but the Queen Mother, who now rules jointly with her son, by a further ruse concealed the death for a whole year,[6] making out in public that the Emperor was suffering from a serious illness which prevented him from appearing before his people at the appointed times; her foresight succeeded in effecting the deception, whereupon with feminine cunning she brought

[5] This part of Prutky's account is at variance with Iyasu's chronicle. The latter confirms that the prince was never confined to Wahni, but suggests that he spent much of his youth quite openly in his parents' company. It is further claimed that Bakaffa, realizing that his end was near, had himself given orders that Iyasu should succeed him. On the Emperor's death his courtiers are said to have at once gone to find the young prince in his mother's quarters, and announced that he was to succeed to the throne. The courtiers, we are told, all agreed in Bakaffa's choice of his successor 'because it was the will of God'. Guidi, *Annales regum Iyasu et Iyo'as*, pp. 27–9.

[6] The concealment of a monarch's death seems to have been a well-established practice in Ethiopia, and was practised as late as the time of Emperor Menilek II in 1913. P. Mérab, *Impressions d'Ethiopie* (Paris, 1922), ii, 240–7; H. G. Marcus, *The life and times of Menelik II, Ethiopia 1844–1913* (Oxford, 1975), p. 261.

the young prince secretly to royal Gondar, and prudently guarded him within the palace, which had been built in the past by the Portuguese and was well fortified. Here she laid in a good store of weapons to resist her people, and had her son elected as the new Emperor, thanks to the terms of friendship which she fostered with the principal nobles: she then revealed that the old Emperor was dead, and proclaimed to the public that by legitimate succession the crown had passed to her young son Jasu. When indeed this unheard-of state of affairs became known, the people insisted on a free election and called on one of those in Mt Ohni to leave the mountain and be elected Emperor, and then crowned in the palace. Each of these steps was opposed by the resolution of the Queen, who declared that the youthful Jasu was now the established Emperor, elected by a majority of the nobles, and that the next step was to crown him. The Ethiopians refused to yield up the right of which they had been deprived, and from all sides crowds of hostile rebels appeared, who surrounded the palace, attempted to force an entrance, and cut off the supply of food and water.[7] The palace's construction was of immense ingenuity and strength, of squared stone and cement, and in default of artillery they could force neither the wall nor the gates: the palace is the most magnificent building in the whole Empire, the best suited to the protection of the Emperors, and even though it is now in Ethiopian fashion split up, within its walls, into nine separate habitations, yet it remains difficult to storm however great the besieging force.[8] For eight days the boy and his mother endured a dearth of food and especially water, and the Queen Mother and her party were at their wits end, on

[7] A major rebellion is known to have taken place in 1732, only two years after Iyasu's accession. This insurrection, which is described in the chronicle of this time (Guidi, *Annales regum Iyasu et Iy'oas*, pp. 54–80) was led, according to Bruce, *op. cit.*, ii, 618, by several of the 'principal men' of Gondar who were 'possessed of great riches and dependencies throughout the whole kingdom'.

[8] The palace was later described by Bruce, *op. cit.*, iii, 380, as 'a square building flanked with square towers'. Formerly 'a structure of considerable consequence' it was by then largely in ruins, 'having been burnt several times, but there was still ample lodging in the two lowest floors of it, the audience chamber being 'above one hundred and twenty feet long'. The palace compound also contained several 'small apartments, or houses of one storey', which had been built 'in different parts of the area, or square, according to the fancy of the prince then reigning'. These houses, though 'composed of the frail materials of the country, wood and clay, thatched with straw', were all 'magnificently lined, or furnished'. Bruce, *op. cit.*, ii, 622–3.

173

the point of yielding to the superior strength of the rebellious faction, and desperately planning their escape, when quite unexpectedly there appeared from the province of Godgiam another of their party, with a force of thirty thousand soldiers. Uncertain whose party he was assisting, the people little expected his attack on the youthful Jasu's enemies, whom he overbore, put to flight, and raised the siege of the young now-reigning Emperor, who received a cup of water at the hands of his liberator, as his first act of homage. The Queen Mother's party now united to advance the young man to the throne, to exact from the whole people their necessary agreement, and to assist in the coronation and proclamation of the new Emperor. If this help had failed to arrive in time, young Jasu would certainly have been killed, or savagely mutilated and exiled to Mt Ohni, to join the others in their life of misery.

As Jasu grew to years of discretion he planned a better future for his own sons, and advanced to important posts the greater number of the princes who were related by ties of blood or friendship to himself or his mother;[9] he placed in them the greatest trust, promoted, supported, and favoured them, and discerned that, on his own death, the same action might be taken on behalf of his two surviving sons as had been taken on his own. He no longer despatched them to be imprisoned on Mt Ohni, but advanced them as possessing an hereditary right to the throne, which in future should go no longer by election but by succession, since he judged it absurd that the sons of the Emperor should spend all their lives in prison, and wanted nothing more than to rule his empire as do the princes of Europe. For the future the prison of Mt Ohni was to be abolished.

Only the dead departed from Mt Ohni: as soon as a prisoner died his corpse was fast sealed in a coffin and carried down the mountain by ladder to the river Nile, in whose water the corpse was thoroughly washed and the hair removed from head and

[9] Bruce, *op. cit.*, iii, 609, states, on the other hand, that this appointment of relatives was carried out on the initiative of Empress Mentewwab whose 'first care' on assuming power was 'to call her brothers to court'. As for the royal children the Scotsman observes that 'Iyasu had been married very young to a lady of noble family in Amhara, by whom he had two sons, Adigo and Aylo'. Their mother's later attempts to share in the government so hurt Mentewwab that 'she prevailed on the king to banish both the mother and sons to the mountain of Wechne' i.e. Wahni.

body. It was returned to the coffin, with the ceremonies elsewhere described, and taken away to a place near the Nile called *Matraka*,[10] where in the imperial church, the burial place of all his ancestors, he was honourably interred.

The better to understand the present and future state of Ethiopia it is necessary to gain some realization of its character.

[10] The island of Mitraha, site of the mausoleum of Emperor Iyasu I. R. E. Cheeseman, *Lake Tana and the Blue Nile* (London, 1936), pp. 189–93.

CHAPTER 26

THE ABYSSINIAN DISPOSITION

I had studied carefully the previous accounts of Abyssinian affairs given by the Fathers of the Society in the years 1607 and 1608, when they began to be active in Ethiopia and to reap no small harvest of souls, having at that time built a seminary in a place they named Fremona:[1] writing for European eyes they thus referred to it: 'The boys are of that golden Abyssinian disposition, and preserve the ancient piety of their fathers and an inclination even today to all sorts of virtue.' In one of the letters, chapter x, p. 38 we read: 'According to the experience of the Fathers so far in Ethiopia, many fewer sins are there committed than in other parts of the world, even in Europe where our holy faith has remained pure.' On p. 39 after heaping praise on the Abyssinians he concludes: 'The Abyssinians possess all the virtues to make them the most excellent Christian state in the world, if they could but return to the true light of the pure faith, and the Fathers find that this truth is borne out in the persons of such of their flock as are Catholic, of whom they declare that they are generally of the purest of heart.' Similar witness is borne by the Patriarch Alfonso Mendez, in an account printed in Rome in 1620, and again by a book entitled *Lettere annue d'Etiopia, Malabar, Brasil e Goa dall'anno 1620 fin'al 1624* printed also in Rome[2] and dedicated to Father Mutio Vitelleschi, general of the whole Society. This was a well-phrased eulogy full of exceptional praise of Ethiopian virtue, and after the expulsion of the Fathers of the

[1] Fremona, which was established by the Jesuits, and called after Frumentius who had brought Christianity to Ethiopia as a state religion, was situated at May Gwagwa, ten miles east of Aksum. It was the principal Jesuit settlement in Tegré, and site of a church built by Pero Paez. Rey, *op. cit.*, pp. 217, 220, 240; Beckingham and Huntingford, *Some records*, p. 235.

[2] In 1627.

Society the holy missionaries of the Minor Reformed Order wished to experience it, and, in due obedience to the Sacred Congregation for the Propagation of the Faith, they joyously took up the task of cultivating this outstandingly fruitful vineyard.

Already by the year 1715, when they were established in Ethiopia, they had by their own experience learned that the truth was the opposite to this, and Father Michael Pius of Zerba,[3] later the venerable martyr of Ethiopia, wrote as follows: 'The Ethiopian inhabitants of the district are lazy and negligent above all men, and would rather die of hunger than do work, and it is certain that in the whole world there is no nation like to this one, which abounds in nothing but evil. They are thievish, murderous, envious, given to wine, drunkards, lascivious, shameless, and all of them ungrateful and treacherous, responding to kindness by ever worse behaviour: they acknowledge upon themselves no constraint of gratitude, but persecute their benefactors and hold them in especial hatred.' Later on he writes: 'Such is the policy of the nobles, and the law of nature seems to be foreign to their hearts. All foreigners are regarded among them as slaves, servants, and bondmen, and are called by the name *Baria*[4] which in English means slave. If ever it happens that rich foreign merchants come here with trade goods, they return empty-handed in poverty, stripped of all they possess. Indeed to leave the country is a great difficulty, for the return from Ethiopia is far from easy, no one being permitted to leave the country without the Emperor's seal and authority, which few Emperors grant, and to few travellers. The Emperor Jasu used to deny exit from the country to all and sundry, thus causing unheard-of cruelty, so that the Ethiopians successively rob all foreigners, and then refuse to let them go.[5] They are so envious that, though themselves totally naked and unadorned, yet, if they see anyone wearing a good cloak or shift, they put themselves about to take it from him and assume it themselves, a cruel robbery which they practice through right and wrong.' At the end he adds 'Of the

---

[3] Michael Pius of Zerba, as noted in chapter 15 footnote 9, was one of three Capuchins stoned to death at Gondar during the reign of Emperor Dawit III. Budge, *History of Ethiopia*, ii, 441.

[4] Amharic *bareya*, or slave. Guidi, *Vocabolario*, pp. 327–8.

[5] Bruce, *op. cit.*, iv, 89, goes so far as to assert that the Ethiopians had an 'ancient and general rule', namely, 'Never to allow a stranger to return home.'

many Ethiopian tales told by the authorities, either they have not seen them themselves, or they are idly concerned to give circulation to the lies of others.'

So far the aforesaid venerable martyr. For my part, who lived in Ethiopia with my two missionary colleagues in 1752, I would confirm the truth of his account, and am bound to add as follows: the Ethiopians are of various complexions, swarthy, or pale, or olive-skinned, or black shading to red, or, in Schanckalle and neighbouring provinces, jet-black; their swarthiness varying according to their proximity to the Equator, as they live in different degrees of latitude: their blackness is not due to differences of race, but comes from their proximity to the Equator and should be ascribed to this. All of them are well made, of great height, strong, active, most barbarous and fierce, their hair naturally short and curly, or curiously plaited up like women, or simply shaven from their heads, going barefoot and bareheaded. They are insatiable eaters, of uncultivated manners, arrogant, puffed-up, lazy, work-shy, ingrates, vagabonds, revengeful, without crafts, trades, or tradesmen, pitiless in requiting injury, superstitious, lustful in the extreme, all of them like thieves, cruel and bestial. Many of them, lords and simple alike, cast their sons from out their house, others sell them in slavery as children to the Mahometans for a mere pittance,[6] being in terror lest they be killed by their offspring: indeed this is often the case, and when the sons grow to be men they murder their parents to be able the sooner to enjoy their estate. That this happens so often is due to the flood of strangers who come in to the different provinces and become inhabitants of the empire, some of whom are native born, some naturalized strangers, and some slaves who have been captured in warfare. The native born are the best in disposition, gentler and more civilized, more handsome of feature and form, of more elegant gait, not so black, of finer features

[6] Bruce, *op. cit.*, iii, 91, believed that 'about five hundred' slaves were exported annually via the port of Massawa. Three hundred were Pagans who had been sold at the market at Gondar; the remainder kidnapped Christian children. He elsewhere asserts, *op. cit.*, ii, 314, that many slaves were taken from Enarya, and sold by Muslim merchants at Gondar. 'At Constantinople, India, or Cairo,' he adds, 'the women are more esteemed as slaves than those of any other part of the world, and the men are reackoned faithful, active, and intelligent. Both sexes are remarkable for a cheerful, kind disposition, and, if properly treated, soon attach themselves to their masters'.

than the other blacks, their eyes larger, and in all personal particulars more polished than the other two classes: the nose and lips shaped more in the European style, and less mis-shapen than in the case of the other Africans called *Caffer*:[7] these, whether from Asia, or America, or from the coast of Malabar, from Mozambique, Dongola etc., have upturned and snub noses and lips that are disproportionately large.

It is because the Ethiopians are so handsome that as slaves they fetch a higher price among the Mahometans than the natives of other races, and the Mahometan Arabs on the borders of Ethiopia prey on them incessantly; by night they lie in wait, by day they chase them on horseback, in the fields they snatch up the little boys and girls, in the sheep pastures the grown youths and women, whom they tie over their saddles and seek safety in flight. The poor wretches are then taken by the *gelabi*[8] or middle-men to Upper Egypt, Gidda, Mocha and other parts of the world, and are put up for sale in the market place like animals, according to their age and physique fetching fifty to one hundred gold pieces a head. In Gidda I had seen an Abyssinian girl sold for a thousand florins, though in poor health, and I had been called in by her owner to cure her: she knew no Arabic, but when she saw me she broke into lamentations and in Ethiopian called me *Abbati*[9] Father, giving the sign of the cross and so indicating that she wished not to be sold to the Turks but for me to purchase her. At that time I was unable to understand what she wanted, as I was still ignorant of her language, but I recognised that she was a Christian, and when I visited her a few days later I found her nigh to death: in a whisper she groaned out the words *Ezgetnam Mariam*,[10] calling on the Virgin Mary, and I thereupon gave her a conditional absolution, and she breathed her last.

The native Ethiopians are more highly regarded than the other blacks because, at least in appearance, they live better lives, and up to the present time preserve at least some spark of the Christian faith, and, although ringed on all sides by heathens, pagans, idolaters, and Mahometans, they ever pride themselves on the

---

[7] Cafres, the name applied by the Portuguese to pagan negroes from Arabic *Kāfir*, 'unbeliever'. Beckingham and Huntingford, *Some records*, p. 9.

[8] Arabic *jallāb*, 'slave merchant.'

[9] *Abbaté*.

[10] *Egze'etena Maryam*.

name of Christian, as though it were an especial distinction. The black Ethiopians who fall victims to leprosy[11] become whiter, but the white colour, or rather brown, is liker to that of the dead than of the living, their skin looking dry and burnt out. In the vanity of their hearts they anoint themselves almost daily, especially the women, with mutton fat, or oil, or some other unguent, and rub and massage the skin until they shine like mirrors as they stand in the rays of the sun; so the proper texture is restored to their dry skin, the proper blackness returns, and this is reckoned the height of beauty. The women perfume themselves with different sweetsmelling, and indeed fetid herbs, and the more they smell, or stink, of them, the more acceptable they are to their husbands.

The Ethiopians of the second and third classes are much rougher, more stupid, and more barbarous, are bereft of manners, are of varying degrees of blackness, but all rejoice in the qualities I have listed above. The women so much exceed their menfolk in these vices, are so vicious, bold, immodest, wanton, lost to all sense of shame, that I could say as much more about them as I have already written, but their disposition is so perverse that I have no wish to bore the reader with a list of their vices, nor to offend the ears of modesty.

[11] Some Ethiopian manuscript illustrations of lepers depict them as white or with white patches. R. Pankhurst, 'The history of leprosy in Ethiopia to 1935,' *Medical history* (1984), xxviii, 61.

CHAPTER 27

THE COMMON
LANGUAGE OF ETHIOPIA

Of the various languages spoken in Ethiopia none is more widely-used, aristocratic, or highly regarded than Amharic,[1] called from the province of Amhara, which is spoken by the upper classes, nobles, monks, and more important people, and used in all official writings and decrees and even for Holy Scripture, just as with us in Europe Latin is pre-eminent over the languages of the individual countries. Mariano Vittorius[2] writes about this flowery and ornate manner of speech in his *Principles of the Ethiopian Language* printed in Rome in 1552, but the language now in use is less polished in its letter forms than that used in Holy Scripture, official decrees, poetic works, and oratory. As well as Amharic another common language is Tigraean,[3] whose origin is in the province of Tigré, and is entirely different from Amharic with hardly a word in common. In the neighbouring provinces dialects are spoken which differ in whole or in part from these two; many of the old writers used to maintain that Amharic contained two hundred and fifty-five letters,[4] but now there are far fewer. The

---

[1] The author seems to have been unaware of the distinction between Amharic, the vernacular of Amhara province, and Ge'ez, the classical language used in both ecclesiastical and official writings. On these languages see E. Ullendorff, *The Semitic languages of Ethiopia. A comparative phonology* (London, 1955).

[2] Mariano Vittorius (1518–1572) was the author of the first Ge'ez grammar *Chaldeae seu Aethiopicae linguae institutiones*, published in Rome in 1552.

[3] Tegreñña, a Semitic language spoken in northern Ethiopia. Prutky would seem to exaggerate the difference between this language and Amharic. See Ullendorff, *op. cit.*

[4] The figure of 255 was not so far from the truth as Prutky imagined. Amharic has 33 basic consonants, each of which exists in seven vowel forms, making a total of 231 characters. To this number may be added four diphthongs, each of which exists in five vowel forms, thus making an overall total of 251 characters.

language is wrongly called Chaldean, since it is widely believed to be a true descendant of Hebrew, from the fact that the harder passages of Holy Scripture, which are difficult to translate from Hebrew, can with the help of Ethiopian Amharic be very easily explained. The Ethiopians, who engage in the study neither of grammar nor of the humanities, still less of philosophy or theology, are totally unlearned in every branch of knowledge, and are satisfied some with just being able to read and write, others, who have ambitions of church preferment, with getting by heart some sacred verses, or the psalms of David, and think that this is sufficient in the matter of learning.

The only reason why the Emperor retains in some measure his people's loyalty is that he keeps them in idleness and ignorance: he lavishes temporal advantages upon them, and presents them with territory, farmland, and possessions, since he by absolute right is lord of all the provinces of the kingdom, and the outright owner of the total of all resources, which are his to give or to take away from whomsoever and whensoever he wishes. No subject can call anything his very own, unless granted to him by favour of the Emperor, and even the highest in the land possess whatever they have by the Emperor's assent; tomorrow they may be reduced from riches to poverty, or vice-versa, and as I have described elsewhere the greatest minister may become the least. Frequently and customarily it happens in Ethiopia that whatever one possesses is handed over, changed and taken away, and twice in the year, in the months of July and August,[5] governors are deposed and others promoted to their place, the possessions of one are given to another, and rarely is anyone permitted to enjoy his possessions until the day of his death. Often it happens that one man ploughs, a second sows and a third reaps, whence it is rare for anyone to give proper attention to his own, far less to plant a tree or to cultivate or clear the land, since he knows that only occasionally will he reap the benefits he

---

[5] The appointment and dismissal of officials in the early nineteenth century often took place at the festival of Masqal when taxes were usually handed to the sovereign. It was at that time, according to Pearce, that 'those the governor is pleased with he promotes; and those who have not given him satisfaction he displaces, and puts others in their stead'. Pearce, *op. cit.*, ii, 278. See also Parkyns, *op. cit.*, ii, 230; Harris, *op. cit.*, ii, 74.

proposed to himself.[6] On the death of any minister whose crops are still unreaped or profits not collected, all is snatched away together with his possessions into the imperial treasury, and his family are left in misery and poverty.

This tyrannical procedure is of considerable advantage to the Emperor, since all are dependant on his favour, and many in fear of losing power, others in the hope of gaining it, are willing to give him faithful service not only in time of peace but also in time of war. The Ethiopians celebrate with great solemnities the feast of the Exaltation of the Holy Cross, when many of his subjects make donations[7] to the Emperor, by which they hope to obtain richer territories the more or the less they influence his affection. The Emperor's other method of retaining his people's obedience is his policy of only occasionally showing himself in public, as I have already explained. In these and similar ways the subjects, not only to gain advantages for themselves but also to retain the Emperor's favour, find it convenient to speak Amharic which is the Emperor's language, and in which and no other he gives audience: unless they spoke the same language they would get but little, and only this language is heard in the imperial court. It is therefore called the royal, or imperial, language.

The Ethiopians claim that the Abyssinian script is their own invention, and that they were learned in its intricacies much earlier than the Arabs were: they use the argument that, since the Hebrew of Holy Scripture can in many passages be easily explained with the help of Amharic, therefore Hebrew is clearly derived from an Ethiopian origin. Since the Ethiopians have commercial dealings only with the Mahometans,[8] and a few Greek

---

[6] Prutky is here echoing Almeida who had observed, 'Often one man ploughs the soil, another sows it and another reaps. Hence it arises that there is no one who takes good care of the lands he enjoys; there is not even anyone to plant a tree because he knows that he who plants it very rarely gathers its fruit'. Beckingham and Huntingford *Some records*, p. 89. For other contemporary accounts of land tenure see Pankhurst, *State and land in Ethiopian history* (Addis Ababa, 1967), *passim* and *idem, Introduction to the economic history of Ethiopia*, pp. 119–32, 179–94.

[7] Confirmation that taxes were usually paid at Masqal is provided by early nineteenth century observers, notably Pearce, *op. cit.*, i, 139–40, ii, 277–8; Parkyns, *op. cit.*, ii, 84–5; and Harris, *op. cit.*, ii, 74–87.

[8] On Greek and Arab merchants in this period see Pankhurst, *Introduction to the economic history of Ethiopia*, pp. 289–306, and P. G. Fouyas, 'James Bruce of Kinnaird and the Greeks in Ethiopia', *Abba Salama* (1971), ii, pp. 161–78.

heretics, many in the Abyssinian empire speak Arabic, as well as Greek on occasion. The province of Godgiam,[9] which transacts much business with Amhara, is fluent in that language as well as in its own.

---

[9] Amharic was in fact the principal language of Gojjam, though Agaw, a Cushite language, was also spoken. See M. L. Bender, J. D. Bowen, R. L. Cooper and C. A. Ferguson, *Language in Ethiopia* (London, 1976), pp. 40–2.

CHAPTER 28

THE WEATHER AND
CLIMATE OF ETHIOPIA

As I begin to describe the climate of the empire and to give my
readers a true account of it, my personal experience will perhaps
be found to contradict earlier accounts, seeing that most previous
writers, who have never seen the country or travelled in it, but
have relied on the accounts of earlier geographers and on
assumptions drawn from its latitude, maintain that in Abyssinia
the heat is insupportable, since it lies in the ninth degree north
of the equator. For myself, before the Sacred Congregation had
sent me, on my holy obedience, to this immense land, I had read
the books of other writers and was alarmed at what I reckoned
its intolerable heat; and my revulsion from it was the stronger
in that the heat of Egypt had afflicted me with a stroke, and in
the twenty-fourth degree of latitude, about one hundred leagues
south from Grand Cairo towards the cataracts, it seemed impossible for me to tolerate the intense heat, which caused me to sweat
copiously almost to the point of fainting. What then of Abyssinia,
thought I, in the ninth degree of latitude? For Europeans, I
reasoned, it would be uninhabitable. However, when in the course
of time I reached that country, I found that the contrary was the
case.

As soon as I entered the outer confines of Abyssinia, on
February 25, I immediately felt a change in the climate from that
of Messaua island, where the heat was intense, though we had
but to pass the Red Sea port called Gerar,[1] which faces Messaua
from the Ethiopian side, a half hour's journey: here the temperature still seemed hot, but the nights were cool, as in Ethiopia

---

[1] The promontory of Gerar, facing the then island port of Massawa, mentioned
in chapter 13.

they always are especially in the months of February, March and April. As from this date we progressed farther into the interior, I found the temperature agreeable, though at night-time very cold because of the winds and the height of the mountains, like mid-April in my native Germany. A fur wrap would have been welcome, and we three missionaries, clothed in light garments after the Arabian fashion, suffered uncomfortably from the cold, being scarce able to sleep during some nights, though worn out by the day's march: we slept on the ground in the open air, with no tent above us and only a light rug beneath, and we were drenched with the dew that fell in the middle of the night and at dawn. Of snow, or of ice, there was no sign, but after sunset and before dawn thick clouds blew up and threatened rain, which chilled the traveller considerably, but when the sun was up the temperature rose. I had thought at the time that the months of May, June, July and August up to mid September would be a season of continuous intense heat, but divine Providence so disposed that those months, sometimes including the end of April, were a season of copious rainfall, which reduced the daytime temperature. Generally the rain fell every night, beginning in the afternoon, and so heavily that the water seemed to be coming down in buckets, but at sunrise it ceased and the sun's warmth so dried the earth that by noon all traces of the rain had disappeared and a pleasant refreshing breeze sprang up, though sometimes not until two o'clock, and the climate was most pleasant. Then, quite unexpectedly, a great flash of lightning, a roll of thunder in the heavens whose reverberations were everywhere, and the day of judgement seemed upon us, with a continuous noise in the sky as of roaring lions, so that we thought that the heavens were falling: and this is the Abyssinian winter, no day without rain.[2] Foreigners and strangers are struck with some fear by this commotion, but the natives ignore it, and I at every moment pictured ruin and unimaginable horror, but, as time passed, I like the Ethiopians realised that the arrow that can be seen cannot harm.

In these months, in royal Gondar and elsewhere where the water cannot drain away, the mud is such that no one except

---

[2] Ludolf had earlier quoted his Ethiopian friend and informant Abba Gorgoreyos as observing, 'There is no making War in Ethiopia in Winter time; neither does the Enemy attack us, nor we them; by reason of the great falls of Rain and the Inundations of the Rivers'. Ludolf, *New history*, p. 217.

servants can walk abroad, and people of any standing visit each other not on foot but on muleback; this is also true when they transact any necessary marketing, for the roads are impassable on foot for the flooding of the rainwater, the muddy water not draining away but forming great lakes. However, outside Gondar in the towns and villages situated in the hills, the rainwater drains away and walking is unimpeded, the rays of the sun drying the ground and removing all traces of the rain.

The whole of Abyssinia is mountainous, and the torrents of rain do no harm to the crops of corn, and, more surprisingly, even in the rainy season the corn ripens and is gathered into the barns, because at sunrise every day the rains cease, the sun shines until midday, and the crops ripen in the fields and are harvested to perfection. The Abyssinian climate is most temperate all the year through, and was to me extremely recuperative, more so than that of other countries, and though I lived for some months in the Asian Indies and for some weeks in American Martinique, and was born in Europe, yet I never found a climate that was better, healthier, or more suited to the human physique than that of Ethiopia, on the one hand never too cold, on the other hand not failing to induce a healthy sweat. The temperature is exactly suited to the human disposition, and only in the five months I have mentioned do the inhabitants find the nights to be too cold, the seven others being warmer; indeed this is not surprising, because the heat arising from its location, which the writers who have not lived in Ethiopia describe, and which ought to be excessive, is tempered by the continual rain, or at other times by pleasant breezes, which reduce the heat and make the climate not only not unpleasant, but positively delightful.

In the incessant rain all the rivers, streams and torrents flow extremely high, and for five months continuously make the roads impassable for travellers, so that in that season neither caravans, nor the usual traders, nor the very inhabitants themselves nor their animals are found outside, but stay always within doors or in caves. There is not a bridge throughout the Empire,[3] river crossings are impossible, the torrents flow too fast and the rivers

[3] Ludolf, op. cit., p. 217, had written that the Ethiopian did not 'Know how to make Bridges', but several such structures were in existence, on which see Pankhurst, Introduction to the economic history of Ethiopia, pp. 274–6. River-crossings nevertheless presented many difficulties, also described in Pankhurst, op. cit., pp. 273–4.

too deep for crossing to be practicable without obvious danger to life, and the caravans that set out too early often fall a victim to the wild beasts of the forests and rivers, with the loss of all their goods and to the detriment of their owners.

The climate being so healthy, the inhabitants never complain of any infectious disease or pest-borne plague and, apart from deliberate homicide, die a natural death, whether of old age or accidentally. Their illnesses are few and very seldom serious, apart from the damage and heating of the blood caused by the excessive amount of pepper[4] they sprinkle on their food or raw meat, by the amount of ginger they eat, by over-indulgence in mead, and by a venereal disease[5] which some of them catch from the women, and from which they perish from inability to wash themselves in the watercourses due to the continual rain.

In the first days of the rainy season the waters flow through the mountains in the streams and rivers until their junction with the Nile, and then when its windings are finished they pour over the cataracts into Egypt: it is easy to determine how far it is from Ethiopia to Egypt from the length of the flow of water, which begins to collect at the beginning of May, while in Egypt the flooding of the Nile can be observed about the twelfth day of June. The Nile slowly rises, until on the tenth or twelfth of August it spreads over the land, irrigating the fields in abundance so that the corn grows strongly. Just as in Abyssinia the month of September sees a decrease in the rainfall, so in Egypt the Nile begins to fall, and thus divine Providence has mercifully disposed that the rains shall not only be of benefit to Abyssinia, but also of paramount necessity to Egypt, where without the flooding of the Nile the whole country would perish of hunger and thirst, for the aridity of the land makes it impossible to find water elsewhere, and rain never falls, except by a miracle once every five or six years, when for a moment there may occur a few drops. The Ethiopians say that it would not be difficult to divert

[4] Dr Mérab, the first twentieth century pharmacist in Addis Ababa, similarly argued that the Ethiopians, because of their considerable consumption of *barbaré*, or red pepper, suffered from gastritis and other complaints of the stomach. P. Mérab, *Médecins et médecine en Ethiopie* (Paris, 1912), pp. 97–8.

[5] On the high incidence of venereal disease, which seems to have been mentioned by Bruce, *op. cit.*, iii, 38, see Pankhurst, *Economic history of Ethiopia*, pp. 627–8.

the course of the river[6] and render Egypt infertile: I fear that this is easier to say than to do, like other projects which appear beforehand to be easy but which human industry has never been able to effect.

We see that Abyssinia is fortunate in its temperate climate and abundance of rain, the like of which can scarcely be found elsewhere in the world, favourable alike to man, to beast, and to agriculture. Notably in the province of Gondar[7] did I rejoice in its temperateness, where, as in early spring in Germany, the cold of the nights was more to be feared than the heat of the day. The inhabitants wear the same clothes in summer as in winter, in fact a white cotton cloth, and reckon that the months of winter comprise May to September, and those of summer October to April, during which time there is no rain, but the sun shines, and bunches of grapes and other fruits are eaten ripe off the tree from January until the end of April. The crops can be harvested almost every month, as often as they wish and are inclined to the labour of it, for the fruits of the earth are there for the gathering. The rains in Abyssinia certainly bring some degree of chill with them, and the human body needs defence there more against cold than against heat, particularly at night, since by day the heat of the sun opens the pores of the skin, which at night are the more vulnerable to the cold, the effect being enhanced by the cold's persistence. This is entirely contrary to the beliefs of the ancient writers who maintain that the torrid zone is uninhabitable from the excessive heat which they imagine there. So Aristotle Bk ii. chap. 5. and so Virgil *Georgics* i. 233 'Five zones comprise the heavens; whereof one is ever glowing with the flashing sun, ever scorched by his rays.' So too Pliny Bk i. chap. 5 discourses on the torrid zone being uninhabitable 'The middle part of the earth' he says 'where the sun's track is burnt out and consumed in flames, is more usually scorched with heat,' as though the scorching heat made it uninhabitable. The answer to this should be in the words of Fr Tellez[8] who in his

[6] On the question of diverting the course of the Blue Nile see Bruce, *op. cit.*, i, 529–31, iii, 712–5, and Pankhurst, *Introduction to the economic history of Ethiopia*, pp. 269–91. Ludolf, *op. cit.*, pp. 40–4, was perhaps rightly sceptical about the then ability of the Ethiopians to divert the course of the river.

[7] Presumably the region around the city of Gondar north of Lake Tana.

[8] B. Tellez, *Historia geral de Ethiopia a alta* (Coimbra, 1660).

characteristically excellent but cautious way confounded in advance the commentary of certain astronomers who believed that they had arrived at the truth about the ten celestial spheres. 'It is not unreasonable that men should be mistaken in the movement of the heavens, where they cannot fly, when they make so many mistakes in the affairs of the earth, which they daily tread with their feet: they are wrong to believe that men in the torrid zone are not simply sun-tanned but quite scorched, despite the fact that in that zone dwell men innumerable, some of whom enjoy the same temperate conditions as the Europeans of the localities of Spain and Lombardy.' That this is entirely true my own experience bears out, since I have twice dwelt near to the equator, in the torrid zone: furthermore in America, the mountains of Peru, which are in the torrid zone, are perpetually covered in snow, and because of the great and continuing cold it is impossible for the Peruvians to cross to the province of Chile, whose inhabitants live beyond those mountains: the greater or lesser intensity of the sun's heat does not depend solely on the degrees of latitude from the torrid zone but on the overall effect of climate and locality. Here is an example from experience: Mocha lies on the thirteenth degree of latitude, the same as that of royal Gondar: in Mocha the heat I felt was as the heat of the nether regions, while in Gondar the climate was most temperate.[9] Before my time the same experience is recorded by D. Job Ludolph: *Commentarius* Bk II chap. 5 fol. 97 'Abyssinia, lying in the torrid zone, is subject to intense heat, but enjoys a mild climate similar to Portugal's, and to that of regions where cold is the enemy rather than heat: the terrific heat of the dog days in Portugal is barely noticeable.' This is confirmed by Tellez in his *Itinerary* II chap. lxix. p. 479 'Ethiopia is cold, like Aleppo and Damascus.' On the other hand the area near to the Red Sea, like Sennar, is hotter: in his account Patriarch Alfonso Mendez, describing his journey in Ethiopia, quoted by Tellez Bk iv. chap. xxxviii. p. 404, says of crossing the province of *Dongola*[10] in May

---

[9] Differences of temperature were due to differences in altitude. This was well known to the Ethiopians who, as Almeida shows, distinguished four main categories of land: *déga*, or highlands, *wayna* (or grape) *déga*, or lands of medium elevation, *qolla*, or lowlands, and *baraha*, or deserts. Beckingham and Huntingford, *Some records*, pp. 20–1.

[10] Prutky has confused Dongola, which is in Sudan and which Mendez never visited, with the Dankali country which he traversed on his journey from Baylul to Ethiopia.

and June: 'In Dongola journeying must be done by night, the heat of the sun being such that men and beasts are almost transfixed by it, and boot soles charred as though by hot coals.' Dongola lies on the other side of the Red Sea from Mocha, where in 1705 the father of our mission, under Fr Prefect Benedictus of Theano, in the attempt to enter Abyssinia through Sennar, suffered such heat at about eleven a.m. that the skin was burned off the paws of the dog they had with them. The clear deduction from these facts is that heat does not depend on the degree of latitude, but on climate, on the lie of the land, and on the surrounding mountains.

As for summer and winter in Abyssinia, this has been well described, before my own time, by Fr Emmanuel D'Almeyda: 'On the western shore of the Red Sea, from Messaua to Dongola, the winter lasts for the months of December and January: this holds true for a distance of only ten or twelve leagues inland, where there is very little cold and a modest amount of rain. This is also true of Mocha itself and the adjacent territory, on the other side of the Red Sea. However, further into the interior of Abyssinia, in the mountains of the monastery of *Bizen*[11] this side of Dobarua,[12] winter lasts not just for these months, but begins in the month of May or June and lasts until the middle and sometimes the end of September, during which time the rainfall is intense.'[13] In the same way in India the winter starts in June and lasts until September, especially on the coast of *Dacan*[14] and *Malabar*. In the dominions of the Great Mogul it remains remarkably cold in the months of December, January and February, like April weather in Europe. The natives of Abyssinia however, as I mentioned elsewhere, give the name of winter to their rainy season, and of summer to the rest of the year, which they consider to be all the same season.

[11] The famous monastery of Dabra Bizan which had been described by several earlier travellers. Thomas, *op. cit.*, pp. 75–81; Alvarez (Beckingham and Hunting-ford, *Prester John*, i, 68–73); Lobo (Lockhart, *Itinerario*, pp. 88–9); and Foster, *op. cit.*, pp. 152–4.

[12] Debarwa, the then capital of the *Bahr Nagaš*, a settlement mentioned in chapter 13.

[13] This passage is a paraphrase, not an exact quotation, of what Almeida wrote. See Beckingham and Huntingford, *Some records*, p. 21.

[14] The Deccan.

CHAPTER 29

CROPS AND FRUITS

If Egypt is called the granary of the world, Abyssinia has an equal right to that title, as it grows fine crops of corn and fruit and abounds in food of all sorts, provided only that the idle populace are willing to work: I marvelled to see four sowings in the year and four crops come to fruition, while of the corn-fields some are filled with ripe corn, some with green ears, some are standing in young corn, while in others the young shoots are just showing.[1] The soil yields a variety of grain, of which the most extensively grown, and prized by the Ethiopians above any other for their daily bread, is the grain called teff,[2] which is both white and black, and small like poppy-seed, the common people eating the black and the nobility and officials the white. There is an abundance of excellent wheat, of rye, barley, rice, millet, panic-grass, runner-beans, vetch, lentils, and great quantities of another vegetable unknown in Europe; oats are not widely grown, but Ethiopia is full of the grain known in Europe as maize. *Tam*[3] is an Egyptian variety of wheat, the name being Turkish, and is of a white and a red variety; the grains are equal in size to pine seeds, and the plant grows till the stalk is as high as a man on horseback. This grain supplies the bread eaten by the majority in this area, and, if fresh-ground and still warm, it is extremely palatable, but once cold it becomes bitter, and to a European scarcely eatable. Millet in the same way grows taller than the height of a man, and is pleasant to eat, and they are very fond of a grain called *maschilla*,[4]

---

[1] This is an exaggeration. Even the best lands, as Henry Salt later noted, gave no more than 'two crops annually'. Valentia, *op. cit.*, iii, 232.

[2] *Eragrostis tef*, described, and illustrated, by Bruce, *op. cit.*, v, 76–80.

[3] *Ta'am*, from Arabic *ta'ām*, 'food' mentioned in chapter 12.

[4] Amharic *mašella*, or greater millet, *Sorghum vulgare*. Guidi, *Vocabolario*, p. 77.

which is generally parched before eating. *Scharua*[5] is a species of corn which travellers grind into flour and eat as bread while still warm: the daily ration, or *Golbit*, of servants and slaves is a measure of the yellow flour obtained from this Scharua, which they much prefer to wheat; wheat is only eaten parched in the grain, and whenever they grind it into flour and make wheaten bread, however small the amount, they complain that it is tasteless and injurious to the stomach, and regard it as fit only for feeding to their animals, their bulls and cows.

The land of Abyssinia is mostly full of caverns, and gaping holes are frequently encountered: in the midst of a cultivated plain the mountains on all sides rise precipitously to an extraordinary height and in war-time form the fortresses of the people. Excellent flax grows everywhere, but it is of no value to the inhabitants who make no use of the seeds to produce oil for fuel or of the stalks to produce thread for garment making, but who simply use it as animal litter.[6] With these and other natural advantages Abyssinia could be described as one of the richest of nations, but the people are lazy, idle and without thought for the future, each for the most part tilling only so much land as will satisfy his own needs, so that their livelihood is but a bare one. Their inactivity is ingratitude for the gifts of God: when one crop has been reaped, without further preparation or fertilizing a little soil is turned over, another sort of seed sown, and they reap the crop without further difficulty.

Although in some localities Ethiopia is not only not abundant but actually deprived of those advantages which are necessary to human life and cultivation, yet where the land is watered by rivers the soil is most fertile; for example in Tigré where there are many streams, and in Godgiam which is bounded by the Nile, the land is kind and able to bear two or three crops a year. In years when there is no rainfall from the months of October to March and sometimes until April, the traveller would imagine that no crops would grow, but in fact, during the rainy season,

[5] Amharic *Šaro*, a dish of peas, lentils, chick-peas, etc., flavoured with salt, pepper and spices. Guidi, *Vocabolario*, p. 209.
[6] Flax, as Alvarez and Almeida had both noted, was not used for clothing. Almeida states that its seeds were, however, made into linseed oil out of which people made a 'thin pap' to moisten their bread. Beckingham and Huntingford, *Prester John*, ii, 513; idem, *Some records*, p. 46.

the crops are abundant, and in areas that by some means are kept watered throughout the year, or where irrigation ditches have been led down the hills to the field, wonderful crops are gathered. I myself saw a level area where a splendid harvest was growing, where the dew fell abundantly from sunset to dawn and watered the land sufficiently to render it fruitful.

In many areas sown crops grow abundantly, and the earth produces cabbage, garlic, onion and every European vegetable, as well as many others unknown in Europe. Of trees there is no great variety, and their fruit is of poor quality and little value compared with the eulogies of ancient authorities; nowadays there are but few to be seen as destruction has come upon them partly through the passage of time, and partly through the idleness and ignorance of the natives: only the peach grows larger, finer, and better flavoured than any in Europe, and is eaten ripe from February until April inclusive. Fine bunches of grapes[7] are presented to the Emperor in January, their season lasting into April; twice as large as our grapes, they are not found all over the Empire, but only in one district two days' journey from Gondar, and since they grow as nature dictates, without hoeing, or cultivation, or the pruning of unwanted leaves, the shoots grow into great branches which bear no fruit: however, if the vine were grown through the whole empire, the harvest would be great. Some years previously the vine was little to be seen, but now there are a few vine-dressers at work, enough at least to supply the needs of missionaries for their daily mass. The grapes are not permitted to ripen properly, with the result that the wine is likely to turn to vinegar, or to be of great strength, so that it must be drunk sparingly: when I was in the service of the Emperor I had wine in abundance, brought to me by the people in thanks for my cures, and also presented to me by the Emperor: the Abyssinians set no store by wine, and prefer their mead.

---

[7] Grapes were little known in Ethiopia except in the Gondar area where, according to Bruce, op. cit., iii, 253, 284, 335, 394, 'excellent strong wine' was produced in the 'two small governments' of 'Dreeda and Karoota'. This wine was also mentioned by the late eighteenth century Ethiopian cleric Abu Rumi, sometimes known as Abraham or Abram. W. Jones, 'A conversation with Abram, an Abyssinian, concerning the city of Gwender and the sources of the Nile', Asiatick researches (1788), i, 384.

There are figs[8] available in April and May, but few in number and small in size because they like the vines are neither planted nor transplanted nor tended, so that they grow ever smaller and hang wild on the trees without cultivation; many other species of tree abound, covered in variegated and beautiful blossom with a most delicious scent, but scarcely one can be seen in a garden receiving industrious cultivation. I never saw the cypress elsewhere so thick or so tall; at one time there were no olive trees, but they now reach a great size, as big as oak trees, with a most plentiful crop of olives, but very small ones. Lemon and citrus trees, of the apple family, grow naturally, without any attempt at cultivation, and there are great numbers of plane trees, cedars, ebony, *holy wood*,[9] and many other valuable timber trees: I must not omit the apple, of which the fruit is excellent, the pear,[10] the punic apple otherwise called pomegranate, the orange, the almond, sugar cane, and similar plants among them the date palm and what is known as the Indian fig, which in all ages has been indeed remarkable for beauty, fruitfulness, use, and popularity. In certain areas the coffee bushes have grown into entire woods, which produce a large crop sold very cheaply,[11] and the Abyssinian coffee is the first and best, being much superior to that of Mocha, to which district coffee was first introduced from Abyssinia, since when it was planted in the hills there and now grows in profusion. Originally however it came from Ethiopia, from whose beans coffee cannot be infused until they have been previously soaked in spring water: they then produce coffee much stronger than that of Mocha, but if the soaking is neglected it is bitter to drink owing to excess of oil in the bean.

Garden vegetables are little in evidence, cabbages, small white radishes called in Abyssinian *komen*,[12] like our pot herbs, a few

---

[8] The reference is presumably to the fruit of the Ethiopian wild fig *šola* or *warka*, *Ficus Vasta*, known in Tegreñña as *dahro*. H. F. Mooney, *A glossary of Ethiopian plant names* (Dublin, 1963), p. 56; Guidi, *Vocabolario*, pp. 202, 567.

[9] Latin *lignum sanctum*, unidentified.

[10] Prutky's account of fruit is at this point defective, for, as Ludolf *New history*, p. 50, rightly observed of the Ethiopians, 'Apples and pears ... they have none'.

[11] This would appear to be the first detailed account of Ethiopian coffee which grew profusely in many parts of Ethiopia, notably on the promontory of Zegé by Lake Tana, with which Prutky was familiar. Cheesman, *op. cit.*, p. 146.

[12] Amharic *gomman*, or cabbage. Guidi, *Vocabolario*, p. 718.

lettuces, and some other greens; but the pomegranates are large and very plentiful, though acidic and far from sweet, and the fruits of the citron grow in the woods past counting, small in size like a hen's egg, full of juice and with a tender skin, which every passer-by may pluck as he pleases. The lemons, as I mentioned previously, are large and plentiful but lacking in juice. As well as these there are in the woods a variety of fruits which the Ethiopians do not eat and of which they know neither their names nor yet their properties; except for one particular one, similar to the European cherry, which is sweet enough to eat but sticks to the lips like glue and is tasteless on the tongue: the passing caravans refresh themselves with it. I saw yet another fruit whose outer and inner shell, and the taste of the kernel within, were like our Italian nut only sweeter, and I tasted yet another, small and of triangular shape, which with its kernel was good to eat and resembled the walnut: but the Ethiopians not eating them were ignorant alike of their name and their properties. As I journeyed through the forests I saw many other pleasing sights, wonderful varieties of flowering trees full of scent and varieties of colour, like an earthly paradise, but yet the Abyssinian populace knows it not and reckons it of no worth. Heedless of the results of their actions they use the timber solely to feed the fires, with which at nights the caravans protect themselves from the beasts of the forest. Yet the timber of these trees is hard and of a beautiful colour with veins of different hues and markings; the black terebinth, a rare species, useful for many purposes, the holy wood used in other countries for medicinal purposes, of a delightful fragrance, and valued by the Mahometans for use with their pipe tobacco – these are unknown to the Ethiopians who account them as nothing, save when they notice their beautiful scent.

For the varieties of beautiful flowers, of delightful fragrance, which were certainly endowed with their remarkable property by the merciful Creator Himself, they care nothing, and never reflect how *wonderful He is in His holiness, and Holy in all His works* Who has deigned to arrange all things for our good and use. The laziness of man slowly turns even the golden age to iron, and so it is with the empire of Ethiopia, which is so fertile, and where the fruits of the earth and the crops of corn are there for as often as it pleases the natives to sow or to reap, and where

196

it is possible to reap the harvest from one field and, sowing seed in the next, reap there a second crop, if the natives but possessed the proper spirit of diligence. Ever the more did I marvel and praise the providence of the almighty Creator when I saw the land of Abyssinia, almost wholly mountainous, rocky, full of thorns, yet throughout all parts a flat area of agricultural land and the mountains covered with soil, so that beautiful crops were springing up on all sides. From times of old the Ethiopians have neglected all garden flowers and all improvements in fruit cultivation, with the result that little garden produce is to be found beyond what I have listed, and that itself owes its existence to the kindness of the soil rather than to any work or application on the part of the husbandmen. Ginger grows profusely in one district only towards the province of Godgiam, without cultivation, and is free for the gathering: the passing caravans carry it away with them in green form and use it for their daily cooking; the remainder they chew as a refreshment on the march.

CHAPTER 30

FISH AND BIRDS

As Ethiopia lacks almost nothing which is necessary, useful, or delightful to human existence, so too do the rivers and torrents teem with different sorts of fish, to say nothing of the variety of species in the Nile, but the natives make no efforts to catch them and find no pleasure in fishing, being ignorant of the usual methods and without the usual equipment such as hooks, nets, and other gear. They make use only of the flowers and fruit of a certain tree, so bitter that it causes vomiting in humans; the fruit is in the form of tiny seeds like peas, of which the fish eat avidly and are easily caught.[1] The seeds scarcely touch and float upon the water, before such a shoal of fish collects to eat them that they can easily be caught in the hand. Many species of fish are to be found, the list of which would be long to set down, so that I shall confine my account to the electric ray, which is found in the rivers and lakes, and which is so well known as the subject of the thoughts and arguments of the philosophers. The experience of many establishes that the peculiarity of this fish is that if he is held in a man's hand and there remains motionless nothing happens: but if he stirs a little, his motion is so painful to the holder that arteries, knuckles, nerves, joints, all the limbs of the body feel such a shock of pain as to numb all feeling; when the fish is let go all pain and numbness vanishes. The superstitious natives believe that this creature possesses the power to cast out devils from the human body, as though the evil spirits were sensible of the tortures which afflicted the body they inhabit. It is said with certainty, though I myself have never witnessed it,

---

[1] Alvarez had observed that 'some little' fish, 'but not much' was 'caught for the great lords'. Beckingham and Huntingford, *Prester John*, i, 390. On the practice of stupefying fish, with the sap of the $q^w olq^w ol$, *Euphorbia candelabrum* and other poisons, see Pearce, *op. cit.*, ii, 40–1, and Parkyns, *op. cit.*, i, 137.

that if a live electric ray be introduced among a number of dead fish, and bestir itself among them, the fishes which it touches are so affected by an internal spasm, of unknown origin, that they give the appearance of being alive. The researchers and investigators into natural science would do well to examine the source of this motive power which the electric ray can impart to dead fishes. Great quantities of it are to be found in the Nile, on the confines of the province of Godgiam, where there is a marsh without bottom containing many perennial springs of bubbling water, where the Nile has its source, as I shall later relate.

An especial delicacy, widely eaten, is a fish called swordfish, four feet in length, which is also found off the coast of Italy, and which carries on its forehead a device like a sword set about with teeth, with which it seems to transfix and drive off other enemy fish. Many other varieties, of different shapes, colours, and sorts, inhabit the rivers, torrents, and lakes, but the Ethiopians do not like them, rarely eat them, and reckon them of no value. If ever they chance to dine off a fish, they first remove all the skin, wash the fish four or five times in lemon juice, lightly boil it, and then eat it without other seasoning. Only seldom are fish brought in to the towns, but are always conveyed by the fishermen by night to a mountain a mile from Gondar, in the fear that, if they display them in the public market at a price that exceeds the unrealistic expectations of the buyers, their wares will be forcibly seized, according to custom, and they themselves deprived alike of their price and of their fish. The buyers also show equal caution, and in the early morning cross Mt *Abbo*[2] and the Mahometan settlement,[3] and the other mountains, and venture to approach, a few at a time, the mountain where the fish are on sale; their fear is that the vendors may take fright when they see a great crowd of people, and flee away with their fish before they are robbed of it. As long as few buyers appear they stand their ground, but sell to them at a low price that favours the buyers, generally ten pounds of fish for one piece of salt. Servants carrying fish to market are often liable to be robbed, so that they journey in

[2] Abbo, the name of a church and parish of Gondar. It lay on the eastern side of the town as indicated in a plan published by Bruce, *op. cit.*, iv, op. pp. 138–9.

[3] Bruce, who also resided in the Muslim settlement, stated that it comprised 3,000 houses, 'some of them spacious and good'. There were in addition, he says, 'about a thousand houses' occupied by Muslims on the opposite side of the Qaha river. Bruce, *op. cit.*, iii, 198, 381, and iv plate op. pp. 138–9.

companies of five or six together for self-defence, as necessity demands. Both buyers and sellers are afraid of violence, and go out to the mountains stealthily by night, revealing themselves there in the morning. I saw in Abyssinia many remarkable kinds of fish, and dearly wished to record the names of each, but the idle and ignorant inhabitants cared nothing for them and were ignorant of their names, so that I could not accomplish my desire.

The country is full of all sorts of domestic and wild birds, like those of Europe, but as the natives rarely or never eat poultry, hens, ducks, geese, guinea-fowl or pigeons, which can be seen in all the farmsteads and ponds, they often revert to the wild state, being neglected by the husbandmen. To avoid the huntsman, the birds betake themselves to the woods, which are full of duck, geese, partridge, water fowl, peacock, pheasant, that beautiful creature commonly called the parakeet, turtle-dove, wood-pigeon, all nesting in the forests; along with many other species unknown to Europe, birds large and small, black, white, red, blue, variegated, their colour a delight to the eye and their song thrilling to the ear: I looked on them and marvelled, as also on finches that were entirely black, or distinguished by red streaks in their wings. I pass over here such birds as that eagle called by the Ethiopians *Erkum*,[4] which is large, black, long-legged and very swift of flight: as also the bird called *Schumello*,[5] which is held in especial regard; similar to the peacock it has a large body and elegant wings, is remarkable for its glorious colours, and is found nowhere but in Abyssinia, though the nobility of Europe would pay highly to possess it. The *Sockon*,[6] a white ostrich beautifully pied with black feathers, is everywhere a common sight: twice as big as an eagle, long-legged, with a long neck and a tiny head like a goose, it has a foot instead of a claw, which is split like the hoof of an ass, and, being of great strength, it can easily kill a man with a blow of its foot; its speed is such that it can outrun a galloping horse, as it uses its wings to counteract the effect of its own weight. Its egg is round and dark, the shell hard and thick, the size of a human head: it is good to eat, but when my colleagues and I ate one, despite its excellence we could not finish it in one meal. The nightingale is white in colour, with a tail two hands long which it spreads out in flight to resemble

[4] Amharic *erkum*, or *Buceros abyssinicus*. Guidi, *Vocabolario*, pp. 436–7.
[5] Amharic *šemala*, or *Ciconia Abdimii*, a species of stork. Guidi, *Vocabolario*, p. 205.
[6] Amharic *sag^wen*, or ostrich. Guidi, *Vocabolario*, p. 193.

a sheet of paper. The partridge is very numerous, and is bigger and better to eat than those of Europe, while the sparrow as in Europe flies in flocks, in each of which there are generally one or two birds of different shape and distinguished by red wings, a beautiful sight: these appear to act as the king or leader of the flock. The wild fowl is ashen in colour, speckled all over with round white dots, and is exported in great numbers to Mocha, Arabia Petrosa and neighbouring parts, and can even be bought in Cairo at a reasonable price.

The *Pipi* is a remarkable bird especial to Africa which is claimed by the Ethiopians to act as their pointer to game and guide to the huntsman, and to possess almost supernatural powers: its other name is *Fonton*. It is about the size of a lark, and as soon as it sees in the forest a gazelle, or snake, or a bee's nest, or a wild beast, or anything either useful or harmful, it flies around the huntsman and everywhere pursues him, urging him by cry and by song to approach the prey. As soon as the Ethiopians recognise him they follow his flight, with the words *Fenton Kere*: as they follow him the Fonton advances and cries out in front of the huntsman, until he finds the prey.[7] The bees make their nests

[7] Prutky's account of these birds would seem to be based on Ludolf, *Historia*, chapter 12. The latter, however, provides several interesting additional details, for it states: 'there is a little Bird, by those of *Tygra* call'd from the Noise which it makes *Pipi*, which, strange to tell, will lead the Hunters to the Places where the Wild Beasts lye hid, never leaving their Note of *Pipi*, till the Hunters follow them, and kill the discover'd Prey. *Gregory* related to me, *That as he was walking with one of his acquaintance, an Inhabitant of Tygro; this Bird cry'd Pipi over their heads; thereupon, understanding the meaning of it from his Friend, he resolv'd to try the Truth of the Story. The Bird conducted them to a Shady Tree, about the boughs of which, a Monstrous huge Snake had Curl'd herself; at the sight whereof, he and his friend made more hast back again, then they did in coming to satisfie their Curiosity.* And indeed, it is not safe to follow this Bird, unless a man be provided with all his Hunting Instruments: nevertheless, the Bird has her own ends in her double diligence too, for she is sure to have her share of the Slaughtered Carcase too. Nor is this Bird to be found only in *Habessinia*, but also in *Guiny*... where they give it the Name of *Fonton*, being about the bigness of a Larke, where it is reported to betray not only wild Beasts, but also Serpents and Bees.' *New history*, p. 64.

The above story of a bird that assists hunters seems to have had its origin in the existence of the bee-guide (of the species Indicator) which helped people to trace bee-hives – but not animals and snakes as Ludolf and Prutky claimed. The existence of a bird that assisted in the finding of wild bees' nests had been reported by Lobo (Lockhart, *op. cit.*, p. 169), but this was ridiculed by Bruce, *op. cit.*, v, 178–82, who argued that he had not heard 'a single person' in Ethiopia suggest that this, 'or any other bird', behaved in this way, and that since the country abounded in bee-hives the services of such a bird were not needed. The Scotsman's argument was, however, disproved by later evidence. Mansfield Parkyns, *op. cit.*, i, 282, for example learnt of a 'little brown-looking bird' which was 'a sure guide to persons in search of wild honey'.

in trees, in the ground, in underground caves, and in rocks, and fill them with honey to overflowing, but are so careful to close up the entrance that the nests would be hard to find,[8] if it were not for the little bird flying around and leading the way to the right part of the wilderness; as a signal that the prey has been reached the bird changes its note, and the Ethiopians search diligently and easily find the honey, of which they always leave a portion for the bird. As so much of the honey is underground it is black in colour, and I could truly call Ethiopia a land flowing in honey, butter and milk, were the populace not so idle. The nests of bees are nowhere in greater number, nor better supplied with honey and wax, of which the reason is the quality and excellence of the wild flowers.

Another bird of Ethiopia is called *Satan's Horse*,[9] as big as a stork, with a majestic style of walking; with outspread feathers it runs very swiftly, and if pursued escapes by flying even more swiftly. I have heard tell from the Ethiopians of an enormous bird[10] that dwells in the mountains, and preys on goats and cattle; called the *Candor*, its size varies in the different provinces. A missionary called Fr James relates that he saw a huge bird of which one wing, and one leg, was twenty-four hands[11] in length and three in width: the quill from root to tip was five hands, as thick as a medium-sized arm, and so hard that the barbs, which were equally arranged to support each other, could hardly be torn apart by force; the wing, which was black in colour, was so broad that several people could shelter beneath it from rain or sun. Though I am reluctant to believe what I am told, I have not only seen a bird's leg of six pounds' weight, but have climbed the high mountains and have seen from afar a bird with a huge frame: after consideration, I do not know if it could be pronoun-

[8] These underground bees' nests are described by Pearce, *op. cit.*, i, 303–4.

[9] Amharic *Saytan faras*. This bird had earlier been mentioned by Lobo. Lockhart, *op. cit.*, p. 168.

[10] The largest Ethiopian bird, according to Bruce, *op. cit.*, v, 155, was the golden eagle. One which he shot was 8 ft. 4 ins. from wing to wing, 4 ft. 7 ins. from tail to beak, and weighed 22 pounds.

[11] This account is apparently based on Ludolf who refers in his *Historia* to large birds called Condar, a word which is translated in the English edition as 'winged Horses'. A footnote quotes the Jesuit Bolivar as asserting that 'he saw one of the smaller Feathers of that Bird, twenty Spans long, and three broad: and the Quill it self being three Spans long, and as thick as an ordinary Mans Arme'. Ludolf, *New history*, p. 65.

ced to be of such weight and size, and my fear was such that I dared not approach closer, but it is probable that this was the bird I there observed, in external appearance similar to an ox, but with the face of an eagle. Their habitat always is the highest mountains and clefts, and their acute vision enables them to spot the oxen, cows and other animals as they graze, whereupon they swoop rapidly downwards, grab with their talons the ox or cow, and in full flight remove it to the mountain top, where they devour it eagerly. The natives of the area, who are anxious to protect their flocks from loss and to capture the bird, take an animal and tie it firmly to a tree: the bird swoops and fixes its talons in the body, but is unable to fly away with its prey and has difficulty in detaching its talons; even if it succeeds, it falls to the ground, from which in default of a wind its weight prevents it from rising, much less from flying: the natives rush up and kill it with terrible blows from lances or clubs. They keep for themselves nothing but the feathers, the flesh being left to the birds and beasts. There is an account of a similar bird in America, in the province of Peru, though not so large, say the sailors: myself I have not seen it and cannot confirm it – nor wish to do so.

More wonderful was the sight of birds of a variety of species, but of wonderful beauty, all building their nests in the one tree; the nests are not built for concealment, as in Europe, but can be seen hanging together openly from the branches, thirty or forty at a time. They rear their young quite without fear, or nest-robbing by the natives, and there is such variety of species, such difference of song, and such diversity of plumage, as can hardly be matched elsewhere in the world. The very Ethiopians have not names to distinguish the one from the other.

CHAPTER 31

ANIMALS

Ethiopia breeds all the animals found in Europe, but to a higher standard of excellence, and their horses are of such distinction, speed, and beauty that no other country can equal them.[1] However, through lack of iron shoes the horses find the mountains difficult to climb and are the less used, for that reason, for everyday tasks: however handsome the horses they fetch a low price, or are given in exchange for a mule or an ass. Of the living creatures of the earth there is all the abundance and all the variety that nature can furnish as food for the table or spectacle for the multitude. Mules are found to be best for all mountain work and are large in size: they are highly valued, and even senior ministers and nobles mount themselves on mule-back for their surefootedness over the mountains, in this way securing their safety among the precipices, and in the confidence that an accident will seldom or never overtake them. The domestic ass also is a great boon to the inhabitants both in trade and for internal transport.

The *Zecora*,[2] or wild ass, is a most handsome and remarkable creature, striking in colour and delicate in physique, the first sight of which strikes the beholder with astonishment at its beauty. The zecora is no larger than the domestic ass, its head is oblong, its ears long like asses' ears, its body not unlike an ass's in shape, but its colour is altogether different and unusual, such as no painter's art could equal: its back is marked by a straight line of

---

[1] Ludolf, *New history*, p. 53, had rightly observed that the horses of the Ethiopians were 'courageous and strong', but were used only in battle, so that mules were used both on long journeys and for the transportation of supplies.

[2] Or zebra. This animal, which had been described with similar admiration by both Almeida and Tellez, was said by Ludolf 'for beauty to exceed . . . all the Four-footed Creatures in the World'. Beckingham and Huntingford, *Some records*, p. 52; Ludolf, *New history*, p. 56.

glossy black, and the whole of the rest of the body by other lines
of black and white mixed, a finger in width, terminating at the
belly: the head is similarly striped, the ears black, white, and
yellow, the legs marked also but with round not vertical stripes,
in fact ring-shaped. Faced with such admirable order and proportion the stranger marvels at what an unusual creature he has
met, and at the beauty and variety of nature's handiwork. The
same unusual beauty and the same strangeness of colouring mark
the camel, whose neck is long, and like the dromedary's thinner
than in the desert camel: its whole form is naturally beautiful.

The rhinoceros, though not found in Europe, is known to
travellers, and is commonly called *Abadam*: the name rhinoceros
is Greek in origin, taken into Latin, and is derived from the horn
which he bears on his nose: the horn is four feet long and tapers
to a point, which turns a little upwards at its extremity. The beast
is of the colour of boxwood, and its bodily frame as large as that
of three oxen together. The horn is short for the size of the body,
the eye is tiny, the ear small, sharp, and standing straight upright
like the ear of a horse. The head is huge, the tail hairless and
short, the whole body covered with scales whose surface is so
hard as to be impenetrable by weapon or musket ball. When
about to fight the elephant, his natural enemy,[3] he sharpens his
horn on a stone, seeking to rip up with it his enemy's belly, his
softest part. He is naturally a beast of the forest, untameable,
ferocious, arrogant, and there is no art by which to capture him,
once he is grown. He is found in the province of Godgiam at the
foot of the Mountains of the Moon, by the source of the Nile,
and nowhere else; there he is hunted and killed by the use of
an ape for a bait, the body being laid out on the ground to entice
and deceive the beast. The horn is sought after as an antidote to
poison,[4] and is believed to be more effective if the beast be killed
at a particular time. In the same province of Godgiam dwells the
Monoceros,[5] which is rarely visible, and which lives in the inaccessible parts of the Mountains of the Moon, whence it occasionally

[3] Lobo had earlier asserted that the rhinoceros was the only animal which
elephants feared. Lockhart, *op. cit.*, p. 166.
[4] Bruce, *op. cit.*, v, 92, on the other hand reports that cups made from rhinoceros
horn were 'sold to ignorant people as containing antidotes against poisons'.
[5] Lobo had earlier claimed that the 'fabulous unicorn' had been seen in the
kingdoms of Agaw. Lockhart, *op. cit.*, p. 166.

descends to the plains to change its horn, as stags do: it is by finding these horns that the country people know that the beast inhabits the mountain. This beast is like none other commonly depicted, its body almost equal to an elephant's, its feet likewise, in colour and hide it recalls the buffalo, in head the wild boar, and in habits the pig as it delights in muddy places; the horn in the middle of its forehead is black, hard, and pointed,[6] and the tongue is so rough as to rasp what it licks.

The elephant is found in plenty, much larger than the Asian elephant, and lives in the open in the high places in the forest, whence morning and evening it descends from the hills to drink in the rivers and forests. One follows behind another in great numbers, causing damage to the crops and pasture, and those who climb into the hills must beware of them, lest they do them an injury or kill them; their long ears hang down behind their eyes going uphill, so that they quickly notice a man and chase him, but going downhill their ears fall over their eyes so that they can see little, and then they are innocuous. To kill an elephant confers a great honour upon an Ethiopian and is a signal mark of courage: one method is to dig a deep pit and cover it with branches and leaves, then, engaging the attention of the elephant in the forest, to retreat towards the pit: in blind pursuit the beast falls into the pit, is prevented by its weight from climbing out, and is thereupon transfixed by the lances of a crowd of men, who rush up and kill it in a hail of blows. The tusks are removed and sold at no great price in Arabia Felix and Arabia Petrosa: they are of enormous size, such that it takes three or four men to carry one quite a short distance. There is another easier way to take an elephant: two mounted men, armed with lances and swords, rouse the elephant to fury and take it in turns to retreat before him: the elephant charges in pursuit of his tormentors, whereupon one horseman leaps from his horse and conceals himself in a tree or large thicket, while the elephant, not noticing the one enemy in hiding, pursues the other horseman. The man in concealment skilfully directs his weapon into

---

[6] Ludolf, *op. cit.*, p. 59, states that John Gabriel in Damot had caught a glimpse of 'a Beast with a fair Horn in the Fore-head, five Palmes long, and of a whitish Colour, about the bigness and shape of a middle-siz'd Horse, of a Bay Colour, with a Black Main and Tayl, but short and thin'. He adds that the Portuguese had seen 'several such *Unicorns* feed in the Woods' of Gojjam.

the beast's rear hamstrings, or his arteries, and the wound soon causes the elephant to stop, unable to charge. The man then breaks from his tree, cuts the other hamstrings, and as the beast lies helpless the pair beset him with renewed ardour and slaughter him with their lances:[7] sometimes the flesh is eaten, at other times it is left where it lies and only the tusks removed, which fetch a price anywhere. The ivory of Abyssinia is of two kinds, the white and the yellow: if the tusks are not immediately removed from the body of a slaughtered elephant but are allowed to remain for a few days in the putrefying corpse, they turn a yellow colour, but if they are removed immediately they remain white.

Frequently great lords take sport in capturing elephants alive: a stockade is built in the forest with three gates, into which is introduced a domesticated female, who has been well treated: each day the female is freely permitted through the gates into the forest, whence she returns daily for her food, and when she comes on heat male elephants follow her into the stockade. The elephant tamer, who is watching at the gate, admits the female, with the male, through the first and second gates, which are closed behind them. The elephants are then left for a day or two without food, until the tamer throws in some food from afar, or sugar cane, or some fruit, talking to them meanwhile as though they were beings endowed with reason 'What unfortunate creatures you are, kept here without food or attendance, you who are the king of the animals.' This continues for several days, the tamer approaching ever closer, until at last he gets quite close and feeds them by hand. So little by little they become tame, and can be mounted and ridden, their taming and training making them as manageable as horses.[8] Of their intelligence and sharpness of wit I judge it superfluous to write, seeing that many years ago Cicero in *De natura deorum* has declared that their intellect approaches the human. I saw in India various activities of these creatures, who carried on their backs pieces of cannon, loads of iron, and enormous weights: a single servant sat on the beast's

[7] Bruce, who reports that this method of hunting was practised by the 'Agageer' people on the borders of the Sudan, describes the way they cut the elephant's tendons in some detail. Bruce, *op. cit.*, iv, 298–9, v, 94. For a later account see S. W. Baker, *The Nile tributaries of Abyssinia* (London, 1867), pp. 171–4.

[8] Elephants do not appear to have been tamed in Ethiopia, at least in this period, and Prutky must therefore be assumed to be here describing a custom he had learnt of in India.

back and guided him with a long pointed bar of iron, with which he touched him lightly under the ear, the creature moving whichever way his master desired. The lords and kings under the Mogul, and the governors of India, ride on elephants which are decorated as though they were thrones, on which sits the king or nobleman with a slave behind him to keep off the flies. If they are going to war, the king is accompanied by another exactly like him in trappings and costume, so that no one can recognise which one is the king; on each side again there are another two, again on a similar throne, who carry a store of arms for the king, because it is from the sides that the arrows and musket shots are fired at the king. If one of the mock kings is killed, and falls from his mount, the fight continues, until the king himself is killed, whereupon at his death all his soldiers desert to the side of their enemy, the surviving king, and the war comes to an end.

Four elephants together are used to carry cannon with its crew, and others, of particular strength, are equipped with iron chains on their trunk, with which they strike and kill the opposing forces. Yet others are trained to overthrow city defences, so that in India it is customary to equip the city gates with a triple row of caltrops, to prevent them from destruction and ruin by elephants. In the year 1712 the Dutch made a present to the Mogul of six large pieces of cannon, each of them drawn by thirty pair of oxen: when the oxen were found unable to pull the cannon out of the mud caused by a downpour of rain, an elephant was called in, who dragged out the cannon with its trunk and pulled it free of the mud, whereupon the oxen once more hauled it on its way. Some elephants are so tall as to reach a height of twenty-two feet, are as tame as can be imagined, and, as we read so widely in the ancient authorities, their intelligence is very acute, Cicero likening their intellect to that of humans. Although Ludolf and Aristotle among others affirm that the elephant cannot swim, yet in India I personally saw one do so: he entered the water, felt the bottom with his trunk, stepped on till the water covered his feet, at every step trying the bottom again, and if the water is deep enough to cover his trunk he lifts it up and advances until the tip of the trunk is about to be submerged: then he lifts it again and swims like any other animal. I saw in India elephants running loose in the streets who, meeting little babies who could not walk, whom everyone thought they would trample to death, gently lifted them in their trunk, to the bystanders' amazement, and deposited them unharmed in a nearby house. They keep a sharp look-out for their friends, when they meet them, and as a mark of respect salute them by raising their trunk, and by contrast if they could reach their enemies they would deal them a mortal blow. Different authors tell different stories to illustrate that elephants are endowed with reason, but to detail these would be tedious.

The ancient authors make mention of the *Camelopard* or giraffe, which is of such enormous size that a man on horseback can ride upright beneath its belly: its face is like a camel's, though its nature is entirely different, and its forelegs are much taller than its hindlegs: it has very short upright horns about a hand high; it feeds on leaves, which with its long neck held high it plucks from the tops of trees. In the many brooks, rivers and lakes, the hippopotamus flourishes in great numbers, and is a serious predator of the crops. Its body is immense, and its mouth so huge that at full stretch it measures a cubit and a half across. The Ethiopian name for it is cow- or sea-horse, it is chestnut in colour, taller than two oxen, its head is like a horse's but thicker, its eyes and ears are small, its nostrils flared, its feet distinctly fat, and almost round, it has four claws like a crocodile, its tail is small like an elephant's, its skin is almost hairless, and its lower jaw is furnished with four strong teeth six inches long, two of which are curved and as thick as a cow's horn. At night time it leaves the water for the fields to feed, as it lives on green fodder, and unless the farmers keep watch, in one night it wreaks enormous damage on the crops. When in water no beast is more courageous, attacking humans like wild dogs and wantonly destroying whatever they catch. They so dread fire, that one small boy with a lighted torch can put thousands of them to flight. There is a tribe[9] in Ethiopia which hunts this beast with lances and arrows, and feeds on its flesh, which is almost the same as beef.

The country contains the hare, the wild goat, the deer, the wild boar, the camel, the gazelle, the lion, the panther, the tiger, the wolf, the bear, and other creatures of this sort. The rabbit,[10] the camel, the dromedary, an incredible variety of cattle, all in

[9] The Wayto of Lake Tana.
[10] The rabbit is not an Ethiopian animal though the hare is.

size and strength surpass their European counterparts; dwelling in the forests in herds of three or four hundred head, their grazing causes havoc in the cornfields, for which reason they are detested by the farmers, who pursue them with arrows and muskets. Among the forest dwellers is a species black in colour and with branching horns like stags, and another with but one horn on its forehead, scarcely more than a hand long. A great variety of sheep are to be found, some with enormous ears like a French dog and a long neck like a Peruvian cock: others have tails so thick and fat that they weigh fifteen or sixteen pounds: the head and neck of these are black, the rest of them white. Others again are white all over, and have beards like goats, so long that they sweep the ground as they walk, as they do with their tails also. The flesh of all of them is excellent to eat.

All the kinds of draught animals are to be found, pack animals, cart horses, and mill horses, and among them most excellent riding mules. There are a great number and variety of apes which roam through the fields and forests in bands of two or three hundred together: some of them are quite small, others so large that when they stand on their hind legs and lift their forelegs on high, their stature equals that of a man, and many have a muzzle like a pig's, a chest like a lion's, and the rest of the body purely that of an ape: this species is especially fierce and savage, but all alike are marked by an innate cunning and aptitude for deceit.

So much for the animal life of Ethiopia. I now turn to what the modern age regards as important, its gold and silver.

CHAPTER 32

MINERALS AND MONEY

I have already described how Ethiopia could properly be called a land flowing with milk and honey, if the dull and lazy populace did not shirk their daily work, and how its ancient splendour and importance could shine out once again, if they were not too idle to prospect for and dig the necessary gold mines. The whole territory is seamed with veins of metal and of metallic-based medicines, but they permit it all to remain in the bowels of the earth, and content themselves with such of the iron ore as they find on the surface without the labour of digging. Gold is so plentiful that, if they had the inclination, they could find it in quantity, not just in the earth, but in the rivers especially the Niger,[1] and even, to a small extent, on the surface of the edges of the water runnels dug out by the rain. It is in the province of *Damute*[2] that the gold mines are most abundant, and the gold there of the greatest value, so that it is from there most especially, rather than from elsewhere, that the Emperor's treasury could be filled most abundantly: and yet it all remains in the bowels of the earth. In the province of Godgiam,[3] where the Nile's source is located, much gold was once extracted, but today very little, though Helena Augusta is said to have owned gold mines there, dug at her own expense.

The water of Ethiopia is always good, fresh, and healthy: flowing as it does through hills and rocks, and washing the golden

[1] Probably Prutky meant to refer to the Nile.

[2] Damot, a district in southern-central Gojjam, referred to in chapter 19, which, Bermudez and Ludolf had earlier reported, contained large deposits of gold. Whiteway, *op. cit.*, pp. 235, 239; Ludolf, *Commentarius*, p. 105.

[3] Alvarez, who had witnessed the arrival of tribute from Gojjam, stated that 'much gold' was found in Damot where it was washed up after every rainy season. Beckingham and Huntingford, *Prester John*, ii, 426, 457. See also Ludolf, *New history*, p. 31.

mountains and golden river sand, it is ever health-giving and ever palatable. When I entered Ethiopia, at a time of fasting, I drank copiously of the water to relieve both my hunger and my thirst; my health improved daily and I never suffered the least disorder to my stomach or my general health, indeed the more I drank the stronger I became, and thanks be to God I stayed ever healthy, hearty, and active; I attributed this especially to the gold which I absorbed in tiny particles in the sand of the drinking water. The veins of the earth produce gold in abundance, notably as the ancient writers tell us in the province of *Enaria*,[4] where so much gold exists that the whole of Ethiopia could be filled from it, despite the idleness of the inhabitants, the ore there lying closer to the surface than in other provinces. This is confirmed in the report to the Sacred Congregation by Ven. Martyr Fr Prefect Liberatus dated 29 May 1715 N.7. 'His sacred Majesty is desirous of employing skilled workmen and mining engineers with experience of the mining of gold and other metals, which are present in great quantity in the neighbourhood (s.c. of Gondar): since none such can be found, any one possessing these skills ... etc.' Further confirmation comes from Antonio Ferdinandez (*sic*) (quoted by Godinho[5] Bk 1 chap. xi). 'The whole empire is seamed with veins of metal and of metallic-based medicines'. But all is left by the natives to remain hidden in the earth, partly from laziness but partly also from the fear that, if these fomentors of discord be known and recognised, the Turks may be tempted to invade the empire. Their laziness, feeble negligence, and ignorance is the more blameworthy in that they could gather from the Nile great quantities of gold-bearing sand, seeing that towards the cataracts, beyond Sennar, the Mahometan Arabs, using spoons or wooden pans, not only drink water containing gold, but also by washing the gold sand collect a large amount of the metal.

Of silver no mention is made in Ethiopia, no do they prospect for it, seeing that no use is there made of coined money:[6] they

[4] Enarya, a province S.W. of the Gibé river. On the supply of gold from this area, see Pankhurst, *Introduction to the economic history of Ethiopia*, pp. 225–6.

[5] Nicolao Godinho, *De Abassinorum etc.*

[6] This contrasts strongly with Aksumite times, when coins were struck by the rulers Ezana to Kaleb, AD 330–550, in gold, silver and bronze, with a sophisticated system of lettering, stylized regal attributes, and a remarkable uniformity of gold content. See S. F. Munro-Hay, 'The al-Madhāriba hoard of gold Aksumite and late Roman Coins', *Numismatic chronicle*, 1989.

strike ingots of gold, like pieces of Spanish wax, of five or ten ounces' weight, and those who wish to trade cut them into pieces of half drams or ounces as necessary, using their own scales and cutting the gold with a sharp-pointed iron tool and a hammer into the necessary weight: contrary to imperial regulations each trader calculates the weight according to his own judgement, more or less, and many thousands of opportunities are provided for double dealing. It has long been the custom, in place of money, to use rock salt,[7] the valued, principal, and most common medium of exchange, which is quarried in pieces in only one province, once called Balgada.[8] Individual pieces are one hand and a half long, two fingers broad, and three deep, and the nearer or further each province is to the source of supply, the less or the greater is the value of the piece. With the passage of time and in the course of trading with Europeans, they learned to make salt from sea water; but this skill having been forgotten they pay a considerable price for salt, which is a monopoly of the Emperor, who sells salt through official channels and brings in a considerable revenue for his treasury: it is forbidden for individuals to supply salt, and everyone depends on the imperial favour.

The pieces of salt sell at forty to an ounce of gold, or five for a dram: the natives break them into tiny pieces for their daily purchases, and are more willing to accept salt than gold, and even, if given the choice, will take salt and reject gold. In royal Gondar and the neighbouring provinces salt circulates in place of money, while the inhabitants of Godgiam positively prefer salt because of their distance from the salt mines: as far as the province of Syre[9] (exclusively) salt is dearer than gold, and this is true of all the provinces that adjoin the Nile. In Syre however neither salt nor gold is acceptable, but only pieces of cotton or of Abyssinian cotton cloth,[10] or in default of this Spanish silver, each piece of which is worth two florins. Going from Syre to

---

[7] On these bars of salt, locally known as amolé, see Pankhurst, Introduction, pp. 261–5.

[8] Balagada, or ba'algada, or 'Keeper of the tribute', was a title given to the ruler of the Endarta district of Tegré – to which Prutky is here referring. Beckingham and Huntingford, Prester John, i, 79, ii, 553.

[9] Siré, or Širé, a district of south-western Tegré mentioned in chapter 19.

[10] On the use of cloth as a 'primitive money' see Pankhurst, op. cit., p. 266.

Serai,[11] Dobarua and Messaua, all one's daily needs are better purchased by pieces of cloth: indeed if one were supplied wholly with gold one would in that region encounter difficulties, and, rather than take gold, they are in extreme cases willing to accept Spanish silver. It follows that no commodity has an exact price, but every vendor fixes his own.

This then is the Ethiopian currency,[12] ingots of gold of five or ten ounces' weight, broken in pieces to fit the individual transaction, or cotton cloth, of thicker or thinner weave, or pieces of rock salt: salt being preferred to the others, and varying in value from province to province.

[11] Sarayé, also known as Sarawé, a district north of the Marab river, mentioned in chapter 13.

[12] The limited use of foreign coins had long been reported in Ethiopia. Pankhurst, *op. cit.*, pp. 266–7. The principal Spanish coin was the Castilian *pataca*, which was referred to by Bruce, *op. cit.*, (3rd ed.) vii, 78.

CHAPTER 33

TRUE DESCRIPTION OF
THE SOURCE OF THE NILE

Before I pass on to describe the especial characteristics of
Ethiopian behaviour, I wish to discuss a matter which in times
past much exercised the minds of the ancient authors, and which
today causes dissension among many enquirers. Each writer
describes the source of the Nile in the way his fancy chooses.
Others may rely for their facts on what they have read in books,
though they have never ventured into the enormous kingdom
of Ethiopia, may declare as certain what is contrary to the truth,
may buttress their affirmations with the authority of other men's
opinions, may excuse inconsistencies rather than condemn them,
may hold opinions about what they have not seen and yet declare
those opinions to be true: I, who have not only dwelt in Ethiopia
but travelled within its borders in due obedience to my calling,
was determined from the first day I entered the country to
investigate the springs of the Nile and the source of that river:
however, not presuming to walk or ride anywhere without the
Emperor's permission, and not hopeful of obtaining it to view
the Nile, I decided to put into effect my long-cherished ambition
by leaving the palace one day in the early morning, on the pretext
of gathering medicines and of visiting the sick.

I had asked but one reliable servant to load and lead my mule,
and quietly, while the rest were still asleep, I hastened towards
Abbo,[1] where in the neighbouring Turkish town I engaged a
further five Mahometan servants for my protection, offering in
exchange a supply of bread and coffee. Pressing onwards in the
direction of the Nile, I crossed two small torrents through a

---

[1] I.e. the suburb of Abbo at Gondar and the nearby Muslim settlement, both
of which were earlier mentioned in chapter 30.

delightful plain of green meadows, and though the month was December I looked on green corn amid smiling fields, many of them through the laziness of the husbandmen bearing only grass and herbage. So long a journey however along one path proved difficult for five servants on foot, and we halted to light a fire while I refreshed them with good coffee: proceeding on our way across an easy plain where the cornfields delighted the eyes, we came in sight of the Nile about two o'clock in the afternoon. For half an hour before this the ground had been sodden with water and trembling beneath our feet, so that we could scarcely walk, much less ride, our feet were being sucked ever deeper into the mire, and we became extremely fatigued. Despite our fears that we might sink even deeper, I was lucky enough on mule-back to reach the Nile water, where our weariness caused us to rest a while on the green grass. Around were a number of small houses, belonging to various owners, among whom some were dependants of my good friend the queen mother's Minister called *Krijacus*,[2] who lived there in the interest of Ethiopian trade in his capacity as the appointed governor of this region; on learning of my presence he immediately sent his servant to bid me welcome and to refresh me with different delicacies. I meanwhile recruited my strength on the grass, and quenched my thirst with Nile water, when in a short time I was visited by the Minister Krijacus and a large retinue, who treated me with all kindness, provided me with shelter for the night, and regaled me with delicious Nile fish,[3] since as the day was Friday I refused to eat meat.

To make good use of this chance of enjoying the Nile, and to improve and safeguard my own health, I entered the stream, with four servants holding canvas around me in a square as though in a room, to protect me from view; here I washed myself and observed the peculiarities of the Nile. Thousands of men from the province of Godgiam were then in the district, come to trade, and teff and other grains were for sale for pieces of salt, seeing that all goods from Godgiam are transported here along the Nile by small boat, and are bought by the people of Amhara, near the city of Gondar and the neighbourhood. I gazed

[2] Kirakos, a minor courtier who served as governor of Ebenat and died in 1761. Guidi, *Annales regum Iyasu II et Iyo'as*, pp. 155, 206.

[3] For a later account of the fish available in the Gondar area, see Pearce, *op. cit.*, i, 237–8.

in amazement at the boats, about fifty feet long and scarcely six or seven feet wide, which were each drawn up to dry on logs of wood along the banks of the river.[4] Made of thick reeds intricately interwoven, they appeared to me to be disproportionately narrow for safe voyaging, to be sure to overturn at any moment or to be swamped by the water penetrating the reeds, and to be totally unmanageable. But experience has taught me that they return safely to their home, even though the Nile towards Godgiam is broader, wider, and deeper: nonetheless they make the voyage successfully in their tiny boats, or rather cockle-shells, provided that they take care to maintain their balance by keeping still. Just two men make up the crew, who sit motionless at the stern of the boat lest they overturn it, as frequently happens.

I was amazed to see the multitude of wild birds on the Nile, geese, ducks, eagles and a wonderful variety of birds of coloured plumage: it was surprising that they showed no fear of the crowd of men who were present, and with a stone or stick I could have killed any number, but feared the anger of the Ethiopians, who account this a crime. Moreover, they had not forgotten my recent predecessor a French doctor, whose memory aroused their wrath against me, and who in European fashion offered physical opposition to the insults of the people, whereupon his clothes were torn, his person injured, and himself surrounded, so that but for the help of some of the Emperor's servants he would have lost his life. Even though a subsequent complaint to the Emperor resulted in beatings or fines on those responsible, yet his distresses were considerable. Mindful of this I exercised great caution lest worse should befall, and took care to cause no offence, seeing that white men, under the name *Frangi*, excite the hatred of the Ethiopians: but my friend Krijacus was at hand with armed servants to protect me from popular insult, and nothing amiss befell me.

I mean not to imply that this location was the source of the Nile: at noon on a fine day I rode on muleback higher up the slopes of a huge mountain, whose lower slopes were almost precipitous, and from here the Nile water streams forth. It was impossible to go nearer, or to observe the mouth of the spring,

---

[4] Amharic *tankwa*, or reed-boat, earlier described by Almeida. Beckingham and Huntingford, *Some records*, p. 36.

which soaked and made soft and miry the land surrounding it, so that no one dares to tread it for fear of foundering; thus a circle is made around the spring by people traversing the precipitous rocks of the mountain, and this is regarded as the source. Neither in great volume, nor from a great height, but with a tremendous noise does the water leap out from the depths of the mountain, in a quantity by no means adequate to water the countless fields and gardens of Egypt, if ever the plentiful rainfall failed, which as I said continues for five whole months. Scarcely anywhere in the world can it be equalled, a deluge of water rather than rain, and with it terrible thunderclaps and lightning flashes, which begin at the dinner hour and last through the afternoon and all night long; the rain falls, and the skies are ablaze, threatening ruin and destruction to each created thing. Let not the timid approach that country, nor those who hate storms dare to enter it, let them stay quietly in their own homeland lest fear inflict on them illnesses that are incurable. Nowhere else in the world are such raging storms to be found, and the weather is such that my wretched pen cannot describe it.

Various authorities have made various assertions about the source of the Nile, and in default of a personal visit have not scrupled to be swayed by the opinions of others or to make their description fit their prejudice. I myself dwelt for some time in the Empire and took some personal trouble to investigate the truth: I found the source in the western part of the province of Godgiam in a big valley or open space, encircled on all sides by mountains, where there are two fountains in the shape of a circle:[5] an exact description of them was provided on 12 April 1618 by missionaries of my sacred order, and again in 1716 by Fr Pr. Liberatus Veis the Venerable Martyr who was stoned to death: in addition a Catholic called Elias, who lived for many years beside these fountains or sources of the Nile, gave an account which agrees with what I actually saw; two fountains about two fathoms each in diameter, called by the natives Ain[6] which in Hebrew, Arabic and Ethiopian denotes *eye*, with the meaning here of fountain. The two fountains are a stone's throw apart,

[5] The existence of 'two circular pools or wells of water' at the source of the Nile had earlier been noted by Lobo (Lockhart, *op. cit.*, pp. 227–30) and was soon to be confirmed by Bruce, *op. cit.*, iii, 636–8.

[6] Amharic '*ayn*, literally eye. Guidi, *Vocabolario*, p. 490.

the whole surrounding area being miry, so that it is impossible
to get closer than sixty or more paces to the actual fountains,
which well up strongly from the ground to form a small stream,
though no water falls from the mountains. Below the peak, about
one mile from the fountain towards the west, is an inhabited
village called *Guist*,[7] while on the other side below the mountain,
an hour's journey distant, in a valley which leads out from a cleft
in the hills, emerges another small stream, which gradually broad-
ens its channel and flows into the Nile: the natives affirm that
they have often seen streams flowing down the mountains and
seeping through the underground channels, whence the water
bursts forth.

The stream that flows from the source breaks up from the
ground below it, turns eastward two stones' throw further on,
and bends northward: a quarter of a league later a new streamlet
presents itself, bursting forth from the rocky crags, and a short
while later another two flow into it, coming in from the east:
other streams join and others yet again, and the Nile grows
remarkably quickly. One day's journey later it is fed by a great
river called *Jama*[8] and bends westward, until, at three days'
journey from its source, it makes a turn towards the east and
flows through a huge lake, after which the Nile water is markedly
different in appearance from the streams of the neighbourhood.
Next it irrigates the territory called *Aleta*,[9] five leagues on from
the lake, and then bursts through a rocky gorge fourteen fathoms
deep: two huge cliffs almost hide it from sight, so that it nearly
disappears. On its way towards Egypt it now makes a number of
bends, and is fed by another river the *Niger*,[10] almost the bigger
stream: coming from the south, from the black area *Burneo*,[11] it

[7] This locality had earlier been referred to by Lobo (Lockhart, *op. cit.*, p. 228),
who wrote of a 'hill called Guix', and was later described by Bruce, *op. cit.*, iii,
581, as 'the small village of Geesh'.
[8] The Jemma river, a tributary of the Blue Nile, also mentioned by Lobo
(Lockhart, *op. cit.*, 230, 232) and Bruce, *op. cit.*, iii, 537, 579, 582, who likewise
described it as 'large' and 'equal to the Nile'.
[9] Alata, the name variously given to a district, village and stream. Beckingham
and Huntingford, *Some records*, pp. 26, 227; Lockhart, *op. cit.*, p. 232; Bruce, *op.
cit.*, iii, 418, 535.
[10] By Niger the author means in fact the White Nile.
[11] Bornu, which is far from either the White Nile or the Niger. However, these
two rivers were often confused, and the Niger was sometimes believed to flow
through Lake Chad, on which Bornu borders.

thus derives its name Niger or black, and, a swirling and turbulent stream, it joins the Nile south of Upper Egypt: the joint river traverses the whole of Egypt, and flows into the Mediterranean sea at Rosetta and Damietta. It is beyond all doubt that the reason why every year the Nile is swollen by flooding is the rain that falls in Ethiopia and Burneo, beyond which no reason, I think, need be sought, and other ancient authorities have concurred. Strabo attributes it to this, in words given to Aristobulus 'The flooding of the Nile is caused by the southerly rains', Bk xv. p. 692 and Bk xvii. p. 789. The ancients theoretically, and more modern writers by personal inspection, have satisfied themselves that the Nile floods because Ethiopia is drenched in rain in the summer throughout all its area. During the rainy season travel in the Empire is impossible, all the rivers overflow their bridges, there are no ferry boats, few are able to swim, and when in time of need they have to cross rivers they tie ropes to trees on either side, or stretch two beams across, and are thereon conveyed at great risk of their lives.[12]

Caligula was amazed at the yearly inundation of Egypt and could not understand it. Many emperors and rulers believed that the inundation proceeded from the actual source, and sent out exploring parties as though to view a miracle. Thus Julius Caesar sent an expedition, according to Lucan: 'There is nothing about which I would rather be informed than the cause of the flood, which has for so many centuries remained hidden'. Later he adds 'If I but entertained the certain hope of seeing the source of the Nile, I would relinquish the Civil War'. Similarly Nero, according to Tacitus Bk vi. chapter 8, 'sent two centurions to investigate the source of the Nile' of whom Seneca heard the report: 'their journey, they said, was long, and was directed and aided by the king of Ethiopia: with the assistance of the neighbouring kings we reached the far interior, a place of boundless swamps, the exit of which was neither known to the inhabitants nor discoverable by any means'. All these expeditions were useless and illusory, and it is unbelievable that the old kings of Ethiopia, who undoubtedly knew the exact source, should have sent those centurions off to a land of swamps, unless indeed they were afraid

---

[12] On the difficulties of river-crossings see Pankhurst, *Introduction to the economic history of Ethiopia*, pp. 273–5.

of what the expedition might bring about, or perhaps the members of the expedition were tired of the journey and dismayed by its dangers, and fabricated this story.[13] Fruitless is the curiosity of princes, and fruitless the inconveniences it causes, and one of the proverbial examples of wasted labour is this quest for the source of the Nile, as says the poet: 'Nature has revealed this secret spring to no one, nor is it permitted to man to view thee, Nile, in thine infancy'. So too says Claudian: 'Flowing from a secret source which ever conceals itself from the probe of vain reason, the Nile is brought to birth, they say, with none to witness it, nor has it befallen any man to see its fountain head'. But in truth it is a futile task to assign exact sources to any one great river. There are as many sources as there are streams, indeed to every drop of rain you may attribute the river's origin, for, as I said, of the whole of the Nile's flooding, the greater part is due to the tremendous rainfall, and the source as described by valued authorities I myself too have personally seen, and regard as fully established.

Now let us turn to these matters which above all else it is necessary for the Christian to understand, and I will begin with the first foundations of our regained salvation.

---

[13] Ethiopia here probably means Nubia. The centurions may have reached the Sudd, the great swamp in S. Sudan.

CHAPTER 34

THE FAITH OF THE ETHIOPIANS

The Queen of Sheba, who came from the south and from the ends of the earth to speak with Solomon, is thought by some to have reigned in the island of Meroe, and these believe, without a shadow of doubt, that on her return to her own land there began in Ethiopia that recognition of the one true God that Solomon had taught her; the worship of idols was abandoned, she adopted the Mosaic law, and imparted it to her people. There is however disagreement among the learned as to the location of the country known throughout the world as Saba: one theory places it in that part of Arabia known as Felix, not far from the Red Sea, the source of the incense of Saba of which the poets speak; indeed many are attracted to the belief that the three kings, the wise men at the stable in Bethlehem, were called Sabaean: the other theory, referring more precisely to Ethiopia, places it in an area far removed from the first, both in distance and in the Hebrew word for it, in the country later called Meroe after the mother or sister of Cambyses, it is not known which. It does not escape my notice that there are serious authorities who maintain that the Queen of Sheba came from Arabia Felix rather than from Ethiopia, while I know of others who have it that her dominions extended to include not only Arabia Felix but also Ethiopia and the southern part of Egypt, a wide-spreading empire indeed: with this view I would not quarrel, though I do not myself hold it. What I firmly hold to, as propounded by the more learned and proved in this present age, is that the Queen maintained her imperial throne in Ethiopian Saba, and that it was from there that she set out to visit Solomon. I find her called by a variety of names, *Nicanta* by some, *Nictocris* by others,

Nicaula by many, *Macheda*[1] by not a few; indeed this last name
is freely used by the later writers who believe that it was by this
that the Ethiopians called her. She is said to have been endowed
with such wisdom and knowledge of the future as to be regarded
as a Sibyl. There are those who would have her to be the woman
who is spoken of as *the Jewess,* for the reason that she was a visitor
to Judaea, nor are these far from the truth who call her *Sambeta,*
a corruption of Sabaea. Some identify her with the heathen
woman called the *Babylonian,* or the *Egyptian,* or the *Persian.* She
is said to have written twenty-four books, and in them to have
included much relating to the mysteries of Jesus Christ, in
which field she yielded pride of place to no one. However, all
this is unproven. Vincent Ferrer, a man distinguished for his
sanctity and the soundness of his doctrine, left in a written
sermon a description of how, when the Queen was returning
home from Solomon's palace, she found a torrent barring her
road and a tree-trunk set across it instead of a bridge: divine
inspiration caused her to recognize that this was the wood destined to form the cross on which Christ was to be crucified for
mankind's sake, whereupon she dismounted from her mule, and
on bended knees adored the wood in a flood of tears, nor would
she permit any of her retinue to set foot upon it. She then sent
a letter to Solomon to tell him what had been divinely revealed
to her on her journey, on receipt of which Solomon gave orders
that the trunk should be removed from its position and buried
in the earth, and spot chosen was the place where in later times
was built the sheep pool referred to by St John the Evangelist
(chapter v. 2). These stories he piously recounted in the sermon
I refer to, and others also about the same tree-trunk, in glori-
fication of the most holy cross of Christ.

I have touched enough on the Queen of Sheba, who received
from Solomon the knowledge and faith of the eternal Deity,
together with the many rites and rituals of the old law, and passed
them on to her Ethiopian people, as indeed is likely to be true
and constantly attested in the writing of many. For how long

[1] Makeda, the name by which the Queen of Sheba was known in the Ethiopian
legend, the *Kebra Nagast,* or Glory of Kings. See Budge, *The Queen of Sheba and
her only son Menyelek. passim,* London, 1922.

however after her death the true faith persisted among her people can certainly not be established. Without any doubt there still remain, as I shall later show, many of the rites of Judaism. In many sources I find that the son of *Mehilech*,[2] and the grandson of the Queen, *Joshua* by name, immediately on his father's death renounced the religion of the One God and changed to the worship of vain images, forcing his people to do the same by the infliction of penalties upon them. It so came about that from that time onwards the Ethiopian people, who reverted to the worship of idols while retaining some of the forms of Judaism in which they had been instructed, have been at one and the same time Hebrew in formalities but heathen in practice.

But of events that happened so long ago it is difficult to make any pronouncement that reconciles the many contradictions; I now turn to the Christian religion, of which no one denies that its happy and timely introduction to Ethiopia was due to the preaching of the holy apostle, and that, after God, two men have the credit for initiating and preaching it. The forerunner was *Indica*, said to be the name of Queen Candace's eunuch, and he was shortly followed by the Apostle Matthew. The former was baptized in holy water by Philip the deacon on his way back from Jerusalem, and began to impart to his friends the religion which he had then accepted: the latter won by lot Ethiopia, when the Apostles divided the world between them, whither he betook himself and, where the eunuch's work had sown the seed of faith, he applied to the soil a heavier plough, and spread the seed far and wide throughout the whole nation, a mighty labour indeed but rewarded by a no less mighty harvest: indeed most authorities are agreed that of all the lands of the gentiles this Ethiopia of the Abyssinians was either the first, or among the first, to embrace the faith of Christ, and for many years maintained it unimpaired and unsullied, though mingled through ignorance with some Sabaean rites brought in from Judaea at the time of the Queen of Sheba.

These persist to the present day, so that the Christian faith is full of impurities, professed in the mouth rather than felt in the heart, by words rather than deeds, founded on appearance rather

---

[2] For the traditional Ethiopian story of Menilek, son of the Queen of Sheba and King Solomon, see Budge, *op. cit.*

than on the truth of the matter. I can exclaim with Isaiah vi. 5:
*I am a man of unclean lips, and I dwell in the midst of a people of
unclean lips.* Seeing that the Vessel of Election, the holy Paul
Apostle to the Gentiles, has said (Hebrews xi. 6) *But without faith
it is impossible to please Him,* how can I say that this barbarous
nation of Ethiopia is pleasing to God? who boast only of the name
of Christian, and are totally lacking in Christian works. As the
holy Apostles wrote of old (Matthew xv. 8, Mark vii. 6) *This people
honoureth me with their lips, but their heart is far from me.* At the
time when the holy Apostle was sowing the divine seed in
Ethiopia, feeding them on heavenly food and giving them to
drink of sweet nectar, he reproved their determined resistance
Ye do always resist the Holy Ghost (Acts vii. 51): so too found I,
who wished to water the young plants with the dew of divine
sustenance, and to transplant and establish their root in the
garden of Heaven. O nation of Ethiopia, O barren land *Let that
which ye have done suffice* (1 Maccabees ii. 33). I may say that I
made exhaustive enquiries through the households, of old men
and young, of great and small, of grown men in full vigour, of
women, of maidens, and of the young: questioned on their beliefs,
they were in ignorance that the Christian faith is one, and were
divided among themselves by multitudes of errors, each believing
his own creed, professing one way with his lips and another with
his life, one thing in private and another in public. Knowing
nothing of the sign which marks out the Christian from the
heathen, idolator, Jew, or Mahometan, they point when questioned to the cord which they tie around their necks as a badge
of their faith,[3] and, instead of making the sign of the cross in
proper Christian fashion, they obstinately maintain, and defend
the position, that it is the cord they wear that distinguishes them
from other nations. In fact the cord with which they bind themselves is a snare of the devil, and in all vehemence they maintain
that only those who wear it are to be held to be Christian, and,
because we missionaries refused to conform to their foolishness,
they declared that clearly we were not Christians. Ministers and
important officials of the empire, and other rich men, are none
of them content with a small cord, but wear a bigger version

[3] The *matab*, or neck-cord which was traditionally worn by Ethiopian Christians.
Walker, *op. cit.*, pp. 18, 112.

made of multi-coloured silk, three fingers' thick, which hangs from neck to chest, nor does any dare to leave home without it, in the belief that in it resides the whole virtue of the Christian faith; they flatter themselves that in case of sudden death the protection of this badge will ensure their sin-free passage to Heaven, and that without it their salvation is in danger.

In the course of time, in order to secure the accuracy of my report to the Sacred Congregation, I made enquiries as to whether their faith was one, as taught by our master Christ and by the apostles. Lo and behold, in royal Gondar alone I found over thirty-three distinct varieties of beliefs, as the queen mother to the Emperor herself confirmed, and what number should I then find throughout other parts of the empire? Among the townspeople of Gondar are found many who believe in the unity of God and the three-fold nature of his Person, but who regard him as corporeal, having three distinct bodies, that is three persons with three heads, three faces, six eyes, as many hands and feet, and the rest likewise.[4] Lord Christ our Redeemer suffered in his one nature, and died, as God, for our salvation. Yet the men of note and the Emperor's ministers believe that Christ received a material anointing from his Heavenly Father, or according to others from the Holy Spirit; relying for this on the Davidic text, *He anointed him with the oil of gladness.* Others declare Him a priest ordained after the manner of men, embroidering to taste their many ridiculous fictions, and even call him *Schum,* or official, appointed by the Heavenly Father: while they maintain that He was anointed with oil, they have no answer when questioned as to the method by which the unction was performed. Furthermore in the case of all their fictions, although they be vanquished by truly reasoned arguments, yet they obstinately persist in them, placing more emphasis on Christ's divine than on His human nature, and on the mixture of them.

They are ignorant of the number of the sacraments, while of their effect, and of their ordaining by our Lord Christ, they do not even dream. The rite of baptism they observe as the gateway to Heaven, and it alone they celebrate in its proper formula, in

---

[4] Bruce, *op. cit.,* iii, 321, likewise argued that the doctrine of the 'two natures in Christ' was 'all wrapt in tenfold darkness, and inextricable from amidst the thick clouds of heresy and ignorance of language', so that nature was often mistaken for person and person for nature.

Amharic or Ethiopian *Ene eteckmaluck besme Ab u Old u Menfas gaddus Mahadu amlack amin*[5] 'I baptize you, (or immerse you,) in the name of the Father and of the Son and of the Holy Ghost, one God, amen.' They believe moreover that in every birth, at that point of time when the embryo takes shape in the womb, the soul is not implanted by God but formed out of matter, though tainted as the theologians say by original sin, and that it is this that the baptism of water is administered to extirpate: their own most ancient custom is that baptism is administered on the fortieth day after the birth of a boy, and on the eightieth day for a girl,[6] nor are they concerned at the danger of death occurring before the day fixed for baptism, and of the infant dying unbaptized.[7] They compound this error with a further twice-yearly ceremony: on January 12, the feast of the Holy Epiphany,[8] in commemoration and reverence of the baptized Christ, they all in the middle of the night immerse their bodies in the lakes and rivers, men and women, young men and maidens, monks and priests, all partake of the ceremony of washing their naked bodies in the presence of the priests, who say prayers meanwhile, after which they mark the occasion with a number of celebrations, sports, dances, song, rejoicings, and expressions of joy. Various locations beside the streams are set aside for similar baptismal celebrations, whither they all repair to wash their bodies while the priest pronounces the baptismal rite: the whole night long this immoral custom is maintained, until they go home: then at 9 a.m., since the night has passed, they perform the same ceremony a second time; this they call the *baptism of John.* On September 2, dedicated in the Abyssinian calendar to St John

[5] *Ana atamqakak basema Ab wawald wamanfes geddus ahadu amlak, amén.*

[6] Prutky's statements as to the day of baptism for male and female children are confirmed by later observers, including Parkyns, *op. cit.*, ii, 38, and Walker, *op. cit.*, p. 4. Alvarez, it is interesting to note, had incorrectly stated that the baptism of girls took place sixty days after birth. Beckingham and Huntingford, *Prester John*, i, 109.

[7] Alvarez had earlier noted that the Ethiopians were not concerned about the souls of infants who died before their baptism. When he declared that in this way they 'committed a great error' he was often told that 'the faith of their mother sufficed for the newly born'. Beckingham and Huntingford, *Prester John*, i, 109.

[8] For an earlier account of the *temqat* celebrations, as described by Alvarez, see Beckingham and Huntingford, *Prester John*, ii, 344–5. See also Parkyns, *op. cit.*, ii, 78–80, Walker, *op. cit.*, p. 82.

the Baptist, this ceremony is repeated.[9] The Emperor gives gifts
to each of the churches, gold, frankincense, myrrh, and candles,
and is required personally to attend the ceremony, unless prevented by a serious calamity, or by illness. At the time of my own
sojourn the Emperor was gravely ill, and as a substitute for the
royal splendour sent his Treasurer, with a large following of
nobles and a great crowd of people. With shouts of joy, clamour
indescribable, and a mixed musical accompaniment, they washed
themselves in every lake or stream that they passed, their wild
dances caused all manner of confusion to the ministers, all shame
at their nakedness was put aside, and this they called baptism;
indeed all the places that they passed at that time were held in
great honour as being baptistries.

It is a very ancient imperial ordinance in this nation, that every
young boy that is baptized should have his forehead branded
with certain marks, and this is so strictly observed that anyone
taken up without the proper mark loses his liberty, as penalty
for violating the custom, and becomes slave to the Emperor, or
suffers some worse fate. The meaning of the brand on the
forehead is far from clear to those who are responsible for it,
but the three best-known explanations are: the mark of the fire
is a sign that the Ethiopians believe that they are undergoing
that baptism which the Forerunner seems to mean that Christ
would be administering, when he said, as in Matthew, *He will
baptize you with the Holy Ghost, and with fire.* Others hold that the
first emperors of Ethiopia, who professed the faith of Christ,
were in need of some external sign for Christians, so that they
could be distinguished at a glance from the others, the heathen
among whom they lived. Other respondents have other views,
and the true reason for the branded mark I cannot discover.[10]

When infant baptism is administered in the churches after the
elapse of the due days, they baptize without the use of holy oils,
which they do not possess, and the Abuna their Coptic Archbishop, when his old stock was used up, took no heed to bless a

[9] Parkyns, *op. cit.*, ii, 78, later noted that on St. John's day 'the whole population,
male and female, old and young', went down to the neighbouring stream to bathe.

[10] Alvarez had earlier noted that the scars made at the time of baptism were
not produced 'by fire nor for anything of Christianity, but with cold iron, for
ornament, and because they say that it is pleasant to see.' Beckingham and
Huntingford, *Prester John*, i, 110.

further supply, or indeed to possess himself of more oil: even if in times past sacred oil has been used, they ignore it, and the usual practice is for the working priests, or parish clergy, to buy oil from the Mahometans, bless it themselves, and use this instead of holy oil. When in the sixteenth century the Fathers of the Society came to Ethiopia, they discovered an error in the baptismal formula, and that many priests, in ignorance of the usual formula previously recounted and now in use, were saying *I baptize you in the water of Jordan*. At once it happened that many were rebaptized, which became the occasion of serious dissension, until the Emperor Basilides[11] expelled the Fathers from his country; later in a letter to Patriarch Alfonso Mendez he is said to have complained: 'This above all else was hurtful and hateful to our people, that your followers reproved their manner of baptism, and as though they were heathen or publicans drove out their first baptism with a second: especially as in this matter there is little discrepancy between us and Rome.' The Ethiopians to this day, as I have just said, abide by the text of Matthew iii *He will baptize you with the Holy Ghost and with fire*, and in many provinces a red-hot iron is applied to the forehead, nose and eyebrows of the baptized.

According to the rite of the Eastern Church confirmation must be administered by the same priest that administered baptism, and the whole person of the candidate must be marked by the sacred oils in the form of countless crosses; although the Ethiopians follow the Eastern rite, and the practices of the Coptic Patriarch, yet they ignore the rite of confirmation, or ignore its effects although like the Copts celebrating it as a mere ceremony. The archbishop, an ignorant man, takes no thought for the souls in his charge and neglects his duty, and when on occasion some olive oil is brought in from Egypt by the Turks, it is seldom bought by him because it is expensive: it is sanctified by the simple blessing of a working priest and distributed through the provinces by the priests of the church and by the monks of the Abbey of St Anthony, of which the number is countless; it is then sold for money indiscriminately to Mahometans and heathen alike, under the name of Kava Kadus,[12] and such transactions cause no small

[11] Or Fasiladas, who ruled from 1632 to 1667.
[12] Ge'ez *qeb'a qeddus*, or holy oil. D'Abbadie, *Dictionnaire*, p. 283.

scandal and offence, and proclaim the faith of the Ethiopian Christians as stupid, and a profanation of things sacred.

On the divine mystery of the Eucharist[13] I have several observations. The Abyssinians celebrate it only twice in the week, on Saturdays, surprisingly, and on Sundays, once in each place of worship. Everyone stands round in his proper place, alike those initiated into the mystery and those uninitiated, and, chanting, takes communion in each kind, but their procedure for celebrating the holy mystery is far removed from our own, with different vestments for the officiating priest, different rites, and different ceremonies. Their sacred garment, that we call chasuble, in which the Abyssinian priests officiate, much resembles an oblong shirt, while their stole has a hole in the centre, which passes over the head, so that the stole hangs from breast and back; they wear neither amice, nor maniple, nor girdle. During the service the heads of the monks are not covered by their cowl. The priests offer the sacrifice within the sanctuary, and do not show the host to the congregation when they elevate it on high. No one can take part in the service who at its end does not receive communion. The divine ordinance concerning last rites is neither observed nor recognized. The only entrants to the sanctuary are those who are to assist the celebrant, who is not even visible to the rest of the congregation. The chalice and paten are of bronze, the vestments and cloths of cotton, all of them unsuited to so holy a mystery. If any chalice have a hole in it, the hole is stopped with wax, so that the wine be not spilled. At least five assistants attend the celebrant, most of whom through poverty are half naked, and who are usually unable to read but make the responses from memory, with no understanding of their meaning. They use for the eucharist leavened bread made on the same day, and for wine raisins that have been soaked in water and then pressed; the more experienced priests soak them in very little water, but the others in too much, so that the liquid is very unlike real wine.[14] All receive the eucharist in both kinds. The chalice is

---

[13] For later accounts of the administration of the Sacrament see Pearce, *op. cit.*, i, 326–7; H. M. Hyatt, *The church of Abyssinia* (London, 1928), pp. 92–3 and Aymro Wondmagegnehu and Joachim Motovu, *The Ethiopian Orthodox Church* (Addis Ababa, 1970), pp. 34–6.

[14] The making of communion wine from raisins had earlier been noted by Alvarez. Beckingham and Huntingford, *Prester John*, ii, 518. Later, in the early nineteenth century, Parkyns, *op. cit.*, ii, 96, was to observe that this wine was 'merely an infusion of dried raisins.'

similar to the paten in shape and capacity, and a spoon is used
to spoon out the Blood and extend it to the communicant. In
the more important festivals some of the congregation applaud
with their hands, in obedience to the command of David *Clap
your hands together all ye people,* and others beat time with sistra
and drums, like bacchanals, and are so delighted with the noise
that no music would seem sweeter.

The priests fail to use the words of Christ at the consecration,
when He said *Take and eat, this is my body,* but following the Coptic
practice say *This is the body of Christ.* I pass over the consecration
of the chalice, which they perform in an unlawful and invalid
manner, quite contrary to the decrees sanctioned by the supreme
pontiffs. On some more solemn festivals a silver spoon is used to
place the eucharist in the mouths of great and humble alike,
while they drink from the chalice – but this does not occur at
Easter. Indeed the Ethiopian ceremony of consecration matches
the Ethiopian sense of veneration, the sacrament being administered with no previous confession or expiation of sin. The
common practice is that someone who has been living in concubinage for five or six years, totally sunk in depravity, is at length
troubled by a prick of conscience after so much sin, and conceives
the intention of entering into matrimony: the first or next time
that he meets the priest in the street he calls ‘*Abba,* Father, this
woman of mine I have loved for many years, living with her out
of wedlock, and I now intend to contract myself to her. *Abba
eutachem,*[15] Father absolve me’; whereupon the priest, after the
custom of the country as I shall explain in my remarks on
penitence, publicly absolves him, without any confession of
individual sins. After this, the engaged man, at a time to suit
himself, appears with his concubine in church for seven days
running, where both receive the eucharist, and so continue for
the appointed days: whereupon their marriage has been solemn-
ized. Public wedding services, and public divorces, are not part
of their custom, everyone contracts himself at will and divorces
at will.

In externals relating to the eucharist, which they call *Korban,*[16]
for instance in choosing the better samples of grain for purchase
by the church, or in the alms of the faithful, they show a deeper

[15] *Abba yeftun.*
[16] *Qʷerban,* or Holy Communion. D’Abbadie, *Dictionnaire,* p. 269; Aymro
Wondmagegnehu and Joachim Motovu, *op. cit.,* p. 145.

sense of reverence. The sacristan is generally a deacon, who prepares a dough from which to fashion the Host, reciting penitential psalms meanwhile, mixes in flour, and fashions little cakes marked with a cross, which he bakes in an oven within the confines of the church, or otherwise the bread would be considered profane. The celebrants of the mass perform their office within the holy of holies, which is always covered by curtains and where no layman can enter or look in, the whole presbytery being veiled in hangings. There the priests and monks conduct their laughable ceremonies, while the surrounding congregation is separated from them by two not very high walls, in such a way that the outside of the wall reaches to breast height, on the church side. In the midst of the church the women alone take their places and look out: they see nothing of the celebrant, and listen to the Mass as though they were blind, in ignorance of what is happening and of how. Outside the presbytery curtains stands just one monk, in his hand a stick marked at its point with a tiny cross: the monk as precentor makes different gestures, moves his head up and down and from side to side, stamps with his feet and lifts them gradually higher until he is in full swing: ever higher he leaps and dances while his voice rises shriller through all the time of the mass, while the other monks do likewise and the whole congregation follows and imitates his every movement. The shouting and rapid motion exhausts each one of them until they seem delirious or half dead, the sweat pours from their body, and they can scarcely breathe; at last the precentor monk puts his fingers to his mouth, utters a wordless babble, strikes himself on the lips, and behaves like a play actor, the congregation still doing the same. Others again with bells and rattles, and with little drums with bells attached to them, keep time to the dance and clap their hands, while Hallelujah is sung in celebration and various gestures performed, a sight that to the European observer is an object of ridicule. When Mass is over, the women first sing their own concert, raise their voices on high, and clearly and swiftly sing the wordless phrase *la, la, la,* beating time meanwhile with their hands, accompanied by the men; then after kissing the church door they return home. This wonderful singing prolongs the mass to at least two hours' duration, and on fast days and in Lent, when they touch no food until sunset, the priests order the service of the mass for a little before that time, because they believe that the fast would be broken by the bread and wine of the Eucharist. Out of twenty or thirty priests only one celebrates, the others clapping, singing and dancing, and never entering the church without bringing some item of produce, incense, wax, myrrh, wheat or something similar.

Their attitude to penitence conforms to their attitude to the eucharist. In confession they give details neither of the kind nor of the number of their sins, but generally, after a ten or twenty year period, when the conscience of their sinful life stirs them to a desire to reform themselves into a better state, they confess in very general terms, saying to the priest 'We are sinful, unjust, vengeful etc.' They confess anything that suits them, whereupon without any attempt by the confessor to examine, or urge restitution, absolution is given, *Egzier efftach*[17] or God forgives you, and the sinner is absolved without undergoing any penance. In very rare cases is a fast or act of charity imposed upon a penitent, after which he takes the eucharist in both kinds, returns home, relapses into his former sins, ignores the acts required of the penitent, and makes no effort to recall to memory his determination to amend: the confessor leaves him both unquestioned and uninstructed, and the sinner's future life does not reflect his promise of reform. Of attrition or contrition no mention is made, and they pay no heed to the condition necessary to repentance. The new life is usually on a par with the absolution.

The reader should not be surprised at this, because the people lack a master, the flock a shepherd, the sons their father, the vagabonds and castaways their mother. Many people in this country show a natural inclination to good, and to the Christian virtues, but what leader or master is there to develop it? Priests and monks alike are evil and depraved in life and manners, give no instruction or admonishment to good, provide no spiritual food, show not the way to Heaven, are themselves worse than their people, are without learning, and lead both men and women astray. If incommoded by the request of a would-be penitent, they refuse absolution and even terrify with threats of excommunication, which the people fear above all else: they extort any favour they desire, and, once the sin is committed, wickedly promise God's blessing on the sinner, whom they flatter with

---

[17] *Egzi'hér yeftah.*

233

praises while pretending that their own holy office sanctifies the wicked deed. During my time in Abyssinia I encountered many disgraceful incidents, which I omit as injurious to the ear of modesty: one only I will relate, of a young woman who approached a monk for the purpose of confession; attracted by her beauty he insisted 'Lie with me first, and I will absolve you.' The girl was reluctant, but in terror of excommunication assented to his lecherous desires. How wondrous is Ethiopian penitence, and how excellent are these shepherds who like wolves devour the sheep of their Lord. When the girl returned home she told the story of what had happened to her, and made public this pig-like method of confession, but no punishment was visited on the monk, whose sin was regarded as a joke, and a fact of ordinary life. Now let us turn to the last sacraments.

CHAPTER 35

EXTREME UNCTION,
HOLY ORDERS, AND MATRIMONY

Extreme unction, the solace of the dying, has in my opinion never yet reached the ears of the Ethiopians, and is unknown to their hearts. From the time of St Matthew the Apostle they have retained not the slightest recollection of it, and they scorn a sacrament of the church, however much they are reminded of the words of St James v. 14 *Is any sick among you? Let him call for the elders of the church; and let them pray over him, anointing him with oil in the name of the Lord.* This text silences them so that they can produce no reason either for or against it. In the year 1607, Luiz de Azevedo priest of the Society of Jesus, a man of wisdom and piety who with some colleagues was industriously preaching the gospel in Ethiopia, wrote on July 20 to the Fathers in Europe and stated clearly that the sacraments of confirmation and extreme unction were unknown in Abyssinia. Only the rich are visited in sickness by the priests, in the hope of a present; no spiritual consolation is administered, the sacred texts of holy scripture are read aloud in the sick man's presence, and there is frequent repetition of the customary formula of absolution *Egzier Efftach* May God absolve you. The ignorant poor are deceived and deluded with assurances that they are in a state of grace and will win the prize of salvation, while they are allowed to pass from this life without the sacrament of penitence, or the viaticum, or the comfort of the bread of life. On the other hand, how is extreme unction to be effected? If with oil, they are without olives, as I have already said, and therefore without the holy oils. The Abyssinian version of extreme unction is for the friends and relatives to bring large quantities of food and drink to the death-bed, and there to devote themselves to good eating and drinking,

235

while the sick and the dying are neglected, and despatched to Hell in quick time. Often there have been tears in my eyes when I contemplated the wretched Ethiopian poor who lived in such blindness, while they refused the consolation which I tried to give them: so many souls to perish in misery, surrounded by the women with whom they had sinfully cohabited, as they hastened in false security to their eternal retribution.

Apart from the Abuna the Coptic Archbishop there are no bishops in Abyssinia, nor have the ancient rites of the church of Alexandria ever been regarded as interchangeable with those of Rome; indeed in this sacrament they are so far removed from the Roman usage and rite that the Patriarch Oviedo, during the whole period of his life in Ethiopia, always expressed vehement and deserved doubts as to whether the Abyssinian priests were duly and validly ordained, seeing that the form of consecration used by the Abuna was so variable as to appear corrupt. It was for this reason that, in those activities which are proper to those in orders, and which demand a man truly ordained as minister, he could never bring himself to make use of their services in case the sacraments were thereby nullified. Thus it came about that when in the year 1593 a monk of St Anthony, Theclamaria,[1] a priest in Abyssinia, came from Ethiopia to Rome to transact some church business there, he was ordained for the second time in the private chapel of his Eminence Cardinal St Severina by the bishop of Sidon after the full Roman rite: this was done because the Patriarch's doubt had been conveyed to the Pope, and he after previous consultation with the cardinals and other learned men had so ordered it. The fact is further attested by two members of the Society of Jesus then at Rome, men whose integrity of faith is outstanding among that order, Fr Joannes Alvanus and Fr Sebastianus Rodericus; and I myself am extremely doubtful whether the sacrifice of the Mass is validly celebrated, since even today I observed that they conducted the service in a manner very different from our own.

Applicants for ordination and the assumption of orders present themselves many days in advance at the house of the Abuna or

---

[1] Takla Maryam, an Ethiopian ecclesiastic, had served as Arabic interpreter to Emperor Sarsa Dengel who sent him on a mission to Rome in 1591. Beccari, *op. cit.*, x, 21, 358, 361, 392, 401–5, 408, 476.

Archbishop,[2] where standing before the door they earnestly and mournfully repeat again and again 'Lord have mercy upon us.' When this has been done often enough they are admitted to orders without any previous examination or instruction. Ordination takes place twice in the year, on the first occasion all orders being conferred at the same time except the priesthood, while on the second occasion the priesthood alone is conferred.[3] From undertaking the minor orders no one is debarred by age, and not only are those ordained who have reached the age of reason and can walk on their own legs, but also infants, who are entirely ignorant of affairs and who have to be carried in arms. The four minor orders are open to everyone, whatever their physical defect, to the blind, the cross-eyed, the stutterers, the deaf, the flap-eared, the maimed, the lame, and the sufferers of this sort. The usual order of service is as follows: the Abuna sits either in a tent pitched in an open space, like a church, or in a church itself, and reads from a missal, whereupon the postulants arrange themselves in due order and approach him, with their heads bent towards him: he clips from each a portion of hair, allows them all to withdraw, and taking up his book reads a little longer. They meanwhile, in the same order, touch with their hands a set of keys, and repair to the church doors which they proceed to unlock and to lock. Then covering their heads with a linen cloth they return to the Abuna, touch an earthenware jar and pass onwards for a little distance: they then return to him and he lays his hands on the head of each and celebrates the sacred office, filling them to satiety with the eucharistic bread, which the young boys being unable otherwise to stomach wash down with repeated draughts of water. It is extraordinary to see this indiscriminate ordination, which he is compelled to confer on all who desire it lest they rebel against him and expel him from the empire. It is empty fear, not the zeal for good and the love of God, that moves him to confer orders at the bidding of men, he teaches no doctrine because he cannot speak the Ethiopian language, he never

[2] Abuna Yohannes, who had arrived in Ethiopia in 1746, after considerable difficulties with the Turks at Massawa. Guidi, *Arrales regum Iyāsu II et Iyo'as*, pp. 127–30.

[3] Alvarez, a century earlier, had described a mass ceremony at which the then Abun, Marqos, was said to have ordained 'quite 5,000 or 6,000 people'. Beckingham and Huntingford, *Prester John*, ii, 350.

appears in public, he performs no priestly function, and behind the walls of his own house he passes his time in eating and drinking. He cares nothing for feeding his flock with spiritual food, or imparting a desire for holiness, all pleasures are permissible, all actions, all beliefs: this outstanding pastor is thoroughly despised by his flock. Sometimes for the ordination of sub-deacons and deacons he reads the gospel in Arabic which the ordinands do not understand, whereupon they take it in their hands and kiss it, and thus their ordination is accomplished. When the ordination of priests takes place, all lay their hand upon the gospel and he breathes on them, whereupon they are then regarded as ordained; but before they go home they each present to the archbishop a piece of salt as payment for his work, salt in this area being used for money.

Of matrimony and the eucharist I remember that I have already mentioned that anyone can enter into matrimony of his own desire, without applying for permission to the Emperor or to any higher authority, and that individual men may marry as many wives as they choose, and may put them away for the most trifling reasons: the divorced woman may enter into marriage with another, without the least disgrace.[4] In Ethiopia polygamy is forbidden by no civil law, but only by law ecclesiastical, which is not obeyed, an infringement which ought to be punished by excommunication. So Jasu the Emperor, at whose court I acted as doctor, had five wives, full sisters of each other, and seven concubines, and, though insisting that it was contrary to God's ordinance, the Ethiopians I found regarded it of no importance; nowhere among them is to be found a true marriage bond, they take wives for but a short space of time, and only occasionally does marriage last until death. Even the important ministers and officials of state, my own friends, told me that their present wife was their third or fourth, and that they had divorced the others; if on rare occasions it sometimes happens that a man is satisfied with but one wife, it is seldom the first, but generally the second or third, with whom he lives. Thus the whole empire lives in concubinage, bigamy, adultery, and other vices, and with no

---

[4] Bruce, who noted the easy dissolubility of marriage in Ethiopia, claims, *op. cit.*, iii, 306, that he on one occasion at court saw 'a woman of great quality' with 'seven men who had all been her husbands'.

pricks of conscience are sunk in the depths of sin; yet even in this so-called matrimonial bond the tie of fidelity is little observed, and either party feels itself free as occasion arises to enter into lascivious relations with others, and, although pretending faithfulness to their spouse, nonetheless carry on intrigues of illicit love, and search out the opportunity of sinning on every possible occasion. To describe this more explicitly would distress the ears of modesty, and I therefore pass on in silence to other matters.

CHAPTER 36

THE TEN COMMANDMENTS

I will now deal in passing with the Ethiopian observance of the ten commandments, and will put before the reader my personal comments upon it.

The first commandment is regularly broken by the whole population, who are entangled in a net of superstitions, trust more to their own written spells than to God's holy scripture, and live their lives in vain dependence on talismans worn on hand, foot, and body, which render them immune to evil or to chance accidents. Of their written spells, some are of value in securing the favour of a superior, some in acquiring gifts, some for the favour of the nobles, some for gaining office, while yet others serve to avert the malice of man or the power of demons. Many believe that a demon will enter the food they eat, to do them harm, if they put uncovered plates upon the table, so that whatever food they set before another, or eat themselves, they always keep covered lest the power of the devil enter into it. If they suffer loss of blood from an arm or leg they dig a hole in the ground and bury the blood in it, lest in a similar way the powers of evil be enabled to injure them. When empty fear seizes hold of them, they turn not to God but to their contrived spells, which they renew each year, some being written down for them by the monks of St Anthony, and some by the Mahometans. They are commonly threatened by three illnesses in particular, and tend to reduce all others to these three: *micz*, as they call it, attacks a man who after eating soup goes out into the fresh air, whereupon the demon lays hold of him and his whole body is afflicted with pain; seldom therefore do the Ethiopians eat soup, and if ever they do they are careful about going outdoors, preferring to remain at home until they think that the soup has been

240

digested. *Metat*[1] is the second illness, which afflicts those who drink and then sit, eat, walk about, and perform the necessary bodily functions, whereupon the devil enters into the urine, the sweat, or the other bowel motions. They are therefore struck with fear as they relieve the wants of nature, and whatever disease they catch they ascribe to a demon and call metat. The third illness is *medad*:[2] the belief is that in the month of August a demon stalks the provinces of the empire, and causes pain to the head, every ache of which is called *medad* or *ras filtet*: pain to the eye is called *ain metamem*,[3] to the other parts of the body *tecus saat*.[4] To counter these and other illnesses they turn to their written spells.

The second commandment is never transgressed, their custom being to swear not by God and His holy names, but only by the Emperor, or by their ruler, or patron, or by themselves. Their formula is *Hate*, or, *Jasu gemut*,[5] May the king, or, Jasu die, and indeed in oaths they use the phrase *amut* may I die, or my king, or my patron, if what I say is not true: this is said in the sense not that they wish the death of the king, the patron, or themself, but that, just as I do not wish the death of myself or of my king, so I wish what I say to be regarded as true. It is the practice, when paying visits to friends after the custom of the country, to stand up as a mark of respect to the visitor, to which the reply is *be egzier, be ezketna mariam*,[6] by God, by Holy Mary, thus deprecating the honour done to them by the friend who stands up in greeting. This is the worst extent to which the Ethiopians take the name of the Lord their God in vain, and of the other blasphemies, curses and empty prayers and invocations of God and His saints, as practised by the Christians of Europe, they are altogether blameless.

Of the third commandment, *remember that thou keep holy the Sabbath day*, their observance is exemplary. The churches are

[1] Amharic *matat*, or fever. D'Abbadie, *Dictionnaire*, p. 87. Poncet states that during his stay in Gondar he 'often' heard people speak of this illness. Foster, *op. cit.*, p. 143.

[2] Amharic *nedad*, or malarial fever. Guidi, *Vocabolario*, p. 395.

[3] '*Ayn matamam*.

[4] *Tekusat*.

[5] I.e. *Até* or *Iyasu yemut*, the long-enduring practice of swearing by the death of the ruler, which was earlier discussed by Prutky in chapter 24, where he spells the word *jemut*.

[6] *ba-Egzi'hér ba-Egze'etena Maryam*.

circular in shape, surrounded by a double colonnade, and greatly respected by the Abyssinians after their fashion. All those who enter remove like Moses the shoes or sandals from off their feet, those who wear them, though most people go barefoot.[7] No one either strolls in church, or laughs, or converses with another, it is said to be a sin to spit[8] there, and it is furthermore necessary to go to church on an empty stomach, on pain of being debarred from it. Dogs and the other animals that are kept in a city are forbidden to enter not only the church but also the church-yard, and those on mule- or horse-back, who have occasion to pass by the church door, dismount before they reach it, and proceed for a short distance on foot until they are at a reasonable distance from it; it is then permitted to remount and continue the journey.[9] It is forbidden to sit down in church, and at the door, to assist the weary, there are positioned a number of props or crutches with which to support the steps of those who are injured in the leg or are unable through weakness to stand without help, and which act as a rest for the aged and infirm. The plan of the churches[10] is that the main altar is sited in the middle of the church, and divides the choir from the remaining space, which extends to the door. Between altar and door two curtains are stretched from one side of the church to the other;[11] between the first of these and the altar only those are admitted of the initiated priesthood, while the space between the curtains is reserved for those in minor orders: the rest of the church between the second curtain and the door may be occupied by the laity. The churches of old, some of which were reserved for men and some for women, are now common to either sex, but each has its own station assigned to it, arranged in such a way that the men and the women cannot look on each other. They keep holy not only Saturdays with the Jews, but also Sundays with the

[7] This practice had earlier been noted by Poncet who claims that it was for this reason that churches were often 'cover'd with carpets'. Foster, *op. cit.*, p. 138.

[8] Alvarez had earlier reported that the Ethiopians did 'not expectorate or spit' in church. Beckingham and Huntingford, *Prester John*, ii, 511.

[9] The practice of dismounting before a church, as mentioned by Alvarez, was long established in Ethiopia. Beckingham and Huntingford, *op. cit.*, ii, 324, 518.

[10] The interior of the typical Ethiopian round church consisted of three concentric areas, described by Hyatt, *op. cit.*, pp. 117–21, as corresponding to the nave, choir and sanctuary of the Western Church.

[11] 'Every church,' Alvarez notes, had two curtains, one beside the altar and the other 'in the middle of the church'. Beckingham and Huntingford, *op. cit.*, ii, 510.

Christians, and do no manner of work on those days except in emergency at the Emperor's command.[12] The Abyssinians have no better way of celebrating a joyful occasion than by eating and drinking, nor without food and liquor can rejoicing take place. It is therefore not difficult on Sundays and feast days to attract them to church, which is surrounded by numbers of shade-bearing trees, and where great numbers of jars of tacz are collected, which serves them instead of wine. The service once over they swallow down such quantities of liquor that they pass from sobriety first to tipsiness and drunkenness, then to the usual accompaniments of drunkenness, unchastity and quarrelling, and finally when they are truly drunk to armed conflict. Their celebration of Mass is of considerable length, as I said above, and then they honour the Sundays and holy days by the eating of cattle and the drinking of tacz.

The fourth commandment, to *honour thy father and mother*, they have totally cast aside, and again and again the son, provided he is able, will if not murder his father at least deprive him of all his possessions, or, acquiring them by stealth, raise himself to the status of patron, and live in the security of possession while his father is driven into exile: or they will plot to surprise and kill their parents, who on the contrary never put any trust in their sons when they are grown, but commonly send them to live elsewhere, and display to them neither love nor confidence. And how just is the judgement of God, when the illegitimate offspring of a doubtful concubinage, or of adultery, who has been deprived of all education and upbringing in Christian doctrine, who has received no teaching of the divine commandments to save him from punishment, should in his turn be made the hateful and hurtful persecutor of his father. It rarely happens that the son succeeds by inheritance to his father's estate, and it is more usual for someone closer to the father, a relative or a concubine, to lay hands on every detail of it, while the sons and daughters are often left to die in misery, poverty, and starvation.

The sixth, seventh and eighth commandments are openly flouted throughout the empire, with wilful murder even of kindred going unpunished, while fraud, adultery, open concubinage, prostitution, and carnal offences of all sorts, though

---

[12] On Sabbath observance see Ullendorff, *Ethiopia and the Bible*, pp. 109–15.

not sodomy, carry no penalty and are commonly indulged in. If a married woman lives in sin with one of the nobles, she regards this as an honour, and basks among her friends in rays of false glory to which she declares she is especially entitled. Prostitutes who give birth and display the infant in public are richly rewarded when they publish the name of their partner, but the sterile are looked on with hatred and reduced to starvation. Between bondsmen and freemen, monks and priests, unlicensed crimes and sins of the flesh are as common as daily bread, and the iniquities which they commit, as often as they drink water, it would be tedious to enumerate.

Theft, the sin forbidden by the seventh commandment, is a daily occurrence committed in private and in public by whoever is offered the chance. Citizens who sell goods and food in the public streets are robbed, by force often times and often by unfair prices, without any further recourse to obtain justice. The wrongful appropriation of the goods of another is practised even by those appointed to the offices of the state, who all take to themselves what they want, administer affairs to their own liking, and in similar manner appropriate each item that they desire.

False witness against one's neighbour, quarrels, enmities, everlasting disagreements, lawsuits, one and all are a matter of daily news, most officials governing according to influence rather than to justice, and giving unjust judgements in legal cases. They openly confess 'We are liars, sinners, vindictive, doers of evil' – on which I am unwilling to judge whether they be innocent or guilty, of which God Himself must be the arbiter: but where there are so many sins and so many sinners, who can be adjudged to be innocent?

The ninth commandment enjoins '*Thou shalt not covet*'. The whole kingdom is aflame with the fire of lust, and scarcely one in a hundred, nay one rather in a thousand, is there who lives with his first wife rather than with the divorced wife of another: nor are they confined to just one, but marriage at will to a number, and divorce at will, and further marriage, is a matter of daily occurrence.

How scrupulous is the observation of the tenth commandment relating to the possessions of one's neighbour! By ancient custom all things held in common are seized by individuals, what takes the eye of a lord whether in field, meadow, or garden, is snatched from the poor man and conveyed to the lord's house by main force; while the injured party has no possible recourse against the powerful, and no means of obtaining justice.

Many have lived in Abyssinnia before me who have told the same true story. In the year 1551 Andre Oviedo[13] entered Abyssinia with colleagues from the Society of Jesus, and although he strove until the third year of the next century, 1603, that others of the Society should join him there, there was scarcely one who reached him: for immediately after Oviedo's arrival all the ports of the Red Sea, which are in Ethiopia, and which used to be under the rule of the emperor of Abyssinia, were seized by the Turks, who for forty-six years ensured that no Portuguese who tried to enter those parts of Abyssinia was not either captured or killed by them.[14] In the year 1560 Fulgentius Frerius,[15] a priest of the Society of Jesus, was sent there from India to investigate and report on the progress of Oviedo and his colleagues, but was captured and wounded by the Turks in the Arabian gulf, and taken to Cairo. Similarly, thirty years later, Antonio Monserrat[16] and Pero Paez,[17] with priests of the Society, betook themselves to Ethiopia to help the others in their pastoral work, but were captured by the Saracens and spent seven years in harsh imprisonment. More fortunate was Abraham, a priest of the Maronite group of the Society of George, who, when in the year 1595 he came to these shores, was recognised and arrested in the island of Messaua by its Mahometan inhabitants, and cruelly martyred because he refused to renounce Christ: he went early to Heaven. It seems after all that nothing would be more helpful to the work of the missionaries than if at Diu, at which city many ships call each year for the purpose of trade, they established a base in which they could live, and then cross to Ethiopia in shorter time

[13] Andre de Oviedo reached Ethiopia in 1557 as coadjutor to the Patriarch João Nunez Barreto who remained in Goa where he died. Oviedo became Patriarch in 1562 and died at Fremona in 1577. Beccari, op. cit., xv, 260–2; Rey, op. cit., 205 et passim.

[14] The Ottoman Turks occupied the port of Massawa in 1557.

[15] Fulgencio Freire, a Portuguese Jesuit missionary who travelled to Ethiopia in 1555. Beccari, op. cit., x, 48, xv, 139–40.

[16] Antonio de Monserrate, a Jesuit who worked in both India and Ethiopia. Beccari, op. cit., xv, 241–2; Rey, op. cit., pp. 223, 228.

[17] Pero Paez, a Portuguese Jesuit who served in Ethiopia from 1604 to 1622, and was responsible for church and palace building for Emperor Susenyos. Beccari, op. cit., x, 264–8; Rey, op. cit., 223, 240, 254–5 et passim.

and greater safety. Although the Enemy of man's salvation used his instruments to hinder the plan, yet that great man Arias Saldagna,[18] governor of India, erected on firm foundations a house for the Society which was most useful for these and for similar purposes. From this the missionaries journeyed in the very ships of the heathen, with little danger, and landed at length in Ethiopia, where, labouring hard and equally rewarded, they bent their energies to ministering to Catholics and converting heretics. Yet Christ's easy yoke has now been cast off by the Ethiopians, who have backslid into their old ways.

[18] Ayres de Saldanha, viceroy of Portuguese India from 1600 to 1605.

CHAPTER 37

THE ERRORS OF THE ABYSSINIANS FROM TIMES PAST, IN WHICH THEY STILL PERSIST

The Abyssinians have taken from the Jews a number of ceremonies condemned by the Church, and from the Greeks and other heretics a quantity of false doctrines: of their multiplicity of errors, they cleave at the present time particularly to the following: from the Jews they take the practice of circumcision[1] of each sex and the purification, and they keep the Sabbath. At time of fast they take no food until the evening, and they abstain from the flesh of pigs, of hares and of things strangled, from blood, and from fish without scales. They have several wives at the same time, with divorce at will, they deny the existence of Purgatory, and they believe that the Holy Ghost proceeds only from the Father. They affirm that Christ's human nature was equal to His divinity, and recognize that in Christ there was one will, and with it one operation. The service of baptism is held repeatedly: the souls of the righteous which are free of all taint and punishment for sin will not be received into the sight of God, they hold, until the end of the world. They do not obey Christ's command about the viaticum, they confess neither the number nor the kinds of their sins, nor do they think it necessary to do so: they will have it that human souls are formed out of matter rather than created. Many of them have the impudence to claim that those who follow the doctrine of Rome are not simply heretics but worse than the Mahometans. They reject the Council of

[1] An Ethiopian position on circumcision was stated in the Confession of Faith of Emperor Galawdéwos, which declared that his compatriots, knowing the doctrine of St Paul, did 'not circumcise after the manner of the Jews', but because it was the 'custom of the country'. Budge, *History of Ethiopia*, ii, 354–5.

Chalcedon for its condemnation of Dioscorus, believe that only the heathen and the Mahometans are destined for the eternal fire, and declare that each sect has its own peculiar errors, being of the belief that we assert that in the Divine nature there are four persons, because we confess the two natures and two wills of Christ, whereas they recognize only one nature and one will. They assert that the Holy Ghost proceeds only from the Father, and they keep up a number of Judaic rituals. Often I was in company privately, at home, with the especially learned among them, and occasionally with the chief rulers of the churches, and when driven into a corner they admitted their errors, but said that they would not dare openly to acknowledge the primacy of the church of Rome.

They marry several wives, whom they divorce at will, nor do they offer the comfort of the sacrament of unction, nor anoint with holy oil those near to death, nor finally do they fortify the dying with the bread of life; instead of the viaticum the dying man calls to his bedside a crowd of women, who at the top of their voice fill his ear with *voge, voge*[2] in the Amharic tongue, which means nothing but an expression of wonder; with great leaps from the ground they dance high in the air, and are utterly fatigued when the dead man's soul departs. At that moment all the men and women in the company proceed to tear with their nails at their face, forehead, and temples, until the blood runs, to demonstrate their love for the dead man, a practice unalterably observed by all the kindred. During the interment of the body their wounds are re-opened, they lacerate their breasts down to the groin, their appearance is like a spectre, horrible to look upon: for eighty days they bewail the dead in church, with loud and frequent lamentations, songs and dances. Later on the fortieth day they renew the ceremonial laceration of the face, breast and forehead, thus preserving the scars of their wounding for about eighty days.[3]

The monks, being the especial beguilers of a beguiled people, practise a clever trick on the severely ill, blessing a small white head-band and putting it on the sick man's head in place of the viaticum: the patient in this way is enrolled among the order of

[2] *wayo, wayo.*

[3] Mourners in Tegré would, according to Mansfield Parkyns, *op. cit.*, ii 65–6, 'rub themselves so severely on the forehead and temples as to abrade the skin completely, and produce a sore which takes a long time to cure'.

monks, and is thus persuaded to become a religious, and enjoy the spiritual graces reserved to the religious, including the remission of sins; nor do they fail to assure them of recovery from their illness, and of a long life thereafter. Those thus promoted to holy orders, if they die go at once to heaven: if however they recover from their illness, men and women alike continue to wear their head-band for all time, consider themselves as monks and religious, are marked out as separate from the laity, and are addressed by the name *Abba* Father, like ordained priests of a higher rank, the women being treated as female monks, or nuns. What exemplary religious are these, who attribute to their head-band the whole power of religion in their lives, who live the more licentiously and the more wickedly because their head-band gives them a sure hope of salvation, who are ensnared in perishable earthly vanities, who put things temporal before things eternal, who in their heart of hearts believe that the good in life is to live forever, to die never, to enjoy to the full the glittering shadows of this world. I happened to be in conversation with the Queen Mother, and praised to her the heavenly mansions, and the sweetness, above all the joys of this world, of rejoicing in Christ; she replied that it was better to live one's life, and to rule after the manner of a king, or in default of that to govern provinces, and never to die: she scorned that object of desire the utter end of creation, and God the centre of our souls, and she put behind her the glory of the beatific vision: hard it was to raise to the heights a spirit engrossed in feeding on things of this fallen world. Almost all Ethiopians are bereft of such reflections, provided they can fill their throats and their bellies, they make no efforts to acquire the gifts of the spirit or salvation-bearing doctrine, and the life they lead knows nothing of the necessity of a mediator.

The commandments of the church are remembered by no one, the commandments of the decalogue by scarce one in a hundred, while Christ's vicar on earth, the supreme pontiff of the church, they do not recognise as him who occupies the chair of Peter at Rome, but point to their Coptic Archbishop in Abyssinia. Of the Lord's Prayer, or of the angelic salutation or Hail Mary, or of the Apostles' Creed, scarce one knows in a thousand, many are ignorant of the persons of the Trinity, while most are unable to make the sign of the cross although they believe that they do:

but one single finger moved this way and that across the forehead is not the proper way to make it. Denying the existence of purgatory, they exempt their emperor from the pains of Hell, however guilty of it, there being another place reserved for him beneath the earth, where he will suffer none of the pains of hell, though denied the vision of God, preserving the privileges of this life and the services and respect of his subjects. The monks too predict for the Emperor a definite number of years of life, declaring it infallible that he will live so long, and that he cannot possibly die before the stated time.

Seeing that the Christian Ethiopians live in a community which is mixed with Turks, heathen, Jews, and idolaters, with a universal depravity of morals, manner of dress, and iniquity of conduct, it is impossible to know who is Christian, Jew, Turk, or heathen, and when asked of what faith he is the Christian at once points to the cord at his neck, professing himself Christian because the other sects do not have it. The ministers and officials of the empire, of either sex, wear a thicker cord, made of silk in a variety of colours, which hangs down to the waist. On Saturday mornings they go out to visit the churches, where they kiss the door and without further devotion or prayer return home. Mass is attended only occasionally and by very few, since they are bored at seeing neither the priest nor the service; if ever a small number of them decide to attend, they carry on their customary singing, dancing, applause, clamour, and laughter. In such unrestrained licence do they live and so little are they checked by the fear of punishment, that betaking themselves elsewhere they perform the sacred offices exactly as though they were not legally prohibited from so doing: from such loose living it comes about that many of the laity pretend to the priesthood, and in places where they are not known perform the sacred priestly offices.

Monks are distinguished from priests by the cowl, while priests are distinguished from the rest of the people by a cross of wood or metal borne in the hand. Of the other religious orders there are none to profess the enclosed way of life, apart from those whom I discovered to profess the laws and institutes of St Anthony the Great, St Macarius, and St Basil, but of no one of later date; these, entangled in a web of error, are opposed to the Catholic faith above all other, and live a life of total sin. There are also those monks who live in open communities of the de Plurimanis (called locally Pilibanis) and de Hallelujah variety: these in present times are totally without cloisters or restrictions of any kind, each monk having as dwelling place his own cave rather than house, seeing for himself to his own affairs and tasks, and forbidden by no rule from giving or receiving donations. There are many places where monks live alongside professed nuns, the women being indeed kept apart from the communities of the men, but having their dwelling place alongside, which the monks visit at will, and call the places of the world. Many monks have maidservants with them, with whom they live in conjugal relations, while there are even some among them who openly and publicly take wives to themselves, so beclouded is their wretched vision: not even the name of obedience is known to them. Whether by day or by night they go where they will, observing no daily routine, they wander through the towns, attend fairs, transact business as though they are pedlars, and have no restrictions as to clothing. Those who profess a more ascetic way of life bind rough cords about their waist, wear leather clothing, and let their hair grow down to the shoulder; a good number live only on vegetables, and believe the essence of sanctity to lie in fasting,[4] but seeing how often they are taken in crime it is clear this is done not from love of virtue but from a vain seeking after fame. Indeed it is this motive that has led a number of them into solitude, where a reputation gained for sanctity will enhance their worth and lead to a summons to the royal court, where they plunge to the depths of iniquity.

All monks wear the cowl, as though the whole manner of the religious life were to reside in that alone. The same moral licence as in the lives of monks is found in the professed nuns. This is the manner in which each sex is subjected to the discipline of religion; the applicant goes to the monastery, receives baptism, and has certain prayers read over him, whereupon a cowl is put upon him and, the ceremony complete, he departs a member of the order; nor is there in Abyssinia any truth in our rusty proverb that the monk is made not by the cowl but by the manner of life. In the province of Tigré there is a monastery *Abbaquarima*,[5] in

[4] The asceticism of many Ethiopian monks had greatly impressed Alvarez who tells of one existing only on vegetables. Beckingham and Huntingford, *Prester John*, ii, 390–7.
[5] Abba Garima, four miles east of Adwa.

251

which is the tomb of a very holy man who came thither from
Rome, it is said, together with eight colleagues: in times past the
Fathers of the Society were closely connected with two places in
Tigré, the village called *Fremona* where they dwelt, and a town
called *Gorgorra*.[6]

The religious errors of the nation are manifold. On Pope Leo
the Great,[7] who with the Council condemned Dioscorus,[8] whom
they regard as a saint, they heap curses without number, and
circulate wicked lies about his views on the natures and operations
of Christ: further, apart from the preservation of matter, and
miracles, if there be any, they declare that God brings nothing
to pass, from which they conclude that the human foetus is not
created by God but induced out of matter by the actions of the
parents; in addition, they observe many of the religious rites of
the Mosaic sect. Deserters from the Christian religion to the law
either of Moses or of Mahomet, if they return to the faith, are
again baptized in holy water. The same ceremony is performed
over those who have committed a grave crime, or dissolved their
marriage, or joined some heretical sect: where each man freely
believes what he wishes, every day abounds in new heresies, in
which they wander without correction, the Abyssinians being of
a most volatile disposition and not much caring how far they
ought to keep their promises. Plenty of them are brought to
testify that they acknowledge their sins, but to leave their sins
behind them is where they find the difficulty. May the most
merciful God shine His bright light upon them, that in the hour
of death they close not their miserable eyes without the light of
Faith, or die as they live.

The existence of the Empire is almost at an end, such is the
fruit which heresy bears, and out of twenty parts of it almost
seventeen have been lost to the Emperor: a stable and long lasting
kingship and realm argues a true religion, while wherever the
foot of heresy is placed terrible conflict ever accompanies it with
equal tread, and to this day there scarcely exists one prince,

---

[6] Gorgora, a sometime capital of Emperor Susenyos on the northern shore of
Lake Tana. The settlement was the site of a palace and church erected under
the supervision of Pero Paez. Pankhurst, *History of Ethiopian towns*, i, 102–7.

[7] Pope Leo I who held office from 440 to 461.

[8] Dioscorus, Patriarch of Alexandria, who was banished by the Council of
Chalcedon in 451.

whether heretical or sundered from the fountain head of Rome, who has not met a sad and unhappy end. This fact is known to these familiar with the memorials of the past, nor are they few in number whose example proves its truth. Who could bring himself to believe that the empire of Abyssinia, surrounded on all sides by the arms of the heathen and the Saracens, could survive in such a way as not only to resist further diminishment but also to extend its boundaries, unless that true faith in Christ, which protects and extends Empires, be for ever retained, conserved, and extended? All kingdoms which have cast off the yoke of the Roman pontiff, however they may seem likely to live through the centuries, have in a short time perished and lie overwhelmed in their own ruins. Examples are more than memory can recall, and experience is such that faith is unnecessary.

The Abyssinians have no remembrance of the theological virtues, the source of all that is favourable and good, and in practice trust in Faith to an excessive degree, regarding their own as infallibly true, and better than all others. While living the life of beasts they cherish the firmest confidence that they will attain to the joys of eternity, they exercise charity towards themselves with no thought of their neighbour, they scarcely remember the divine Creator of the world, their love is reserved for those who benefit them. As I said before, and now repeat, the Abyssinians hold the worst possible views on the august mystery of the Holy Trinity, on Christ, on the sacraments, on the reward of everlasting felicity, on the eternal punishment of sinners, on purgatory, on the nature of the human spirit, and on the other decrees of the church; they assert that the Holy Spirit does not proceed from the Son, that in Christ there is only one nature, and that equal to the divine, and only one operation; furthermore they call us heretics, as though we said that Christ has two persons because we confess him in two natures and two operations. The soul passing from this life to the next is strengthened by no celestial food, they detail to their confessor neither the number nor the kind of their sins, they each marry several wives, and divorce them at pleasure. Furthermore, they declare that after this life there is no place of purgatory, but that Christians who are sinners are not subject to the eternal pains of hell; that until the day of judgement the entrance into blessedness is denied to the souls of the righteous, though they are admittedly pure and subject to no liability to punishment; and that our souls are of their own nature corruptible, seeing that, like those of the other animals, they are induced out of matter by the action of the parents.

Even today they persist in Judaic superstitions, although they often have heard the word of the apostle: *Behold I Paul say to you, if you be circumcised Christ shall profit you nothing*: Galatians v. 2: let them rightly know that the rituals of Moses were abrogated by Christ. Although occasionally, from ignorance or some other cause, they so observe the law as to provide them with an excuse for some action, yet these many years past they have known very well that their practices are contrary to the teachings of Rome and forbidden by Christ's divine command. Little they care: they are not to be moved from their own opinions, they are half Judaists and half Christians, and they so confuse the Mosaic rituals with Christian worship that it is truly a matter of doubt whether they follow more the old law of Moses or the new law of Christ. They abstain from the flesh of pig, hare, and of things strangled, from blood, and from birds, they eat neither frogs nor crabs, as being forbidden them, beef that has been slaughtered by a Mahometan or heathen they do not eat, while in return Mahometans and heathen take nothing from a Christian. They believe that a Christian whom they see eating forbidden food is not only not Christian but the very worst of men who despises God's laws, worse than the very idolators or heathen; to other sins they pay too little heed, but adjudge as good only these who conform to their own perverse customs, all others being expelled from the empire.

One can therefore say that in one respect or another they resemble every other religious sect: with the Christians they practice baptism and keep some holy days, with the Jews they observe the Sabbath, refrain from pork, and practise circumcision, with the Mahometans they share a number of stupid customs, with the Copts they believe in the single nature of Christ and in various superstitions and errors, with the Greek heretics they deny the supremacy of the Pope as head of the church, the procession of the Holy Ghost, and purgatory, with the heathen they believe in a corporeal deity, and so on with their other false doctrines and beliefs so far briefly outlined. At last after so long a passage of time a true account of the falsities of Abyssinian belief has reached the holy apostolic seat, my various predecessors having given various accounts which suffer either from exaggeration or from suppression, until the year 1607 when a few succeeded in reaching this vast and most distant land, so beset with dangers and difficulties on the journey: at which point however they listened to the accounts of others and described many things which they had not themselves experienced. But what I write now I set before the reader as the fruit of personal conversation, inspection, and experience, nor does it disagree with the true accounts given in times past to a grateful posterity by the priests of the Society of Jesus, Luiz de Azevedo,[9] Andreas Oviedo, Petrus Ribadaneta, Ludovicus Gusman, and other learned apostolic workers.

---

[9] Luis de Azevedo, a Jesuit missionary in early 17th century Ethiopia whose writings were published in the Jesuit work *Lettere annue d'Etiopia* (Roma, 1627). Petrus Ribadeneira (1527–1611), Jesuit hagiolist and author of a famous life of St Ignatius Loyola, the *Vida del P. Igracio de Loyola* (Madrid, 1594). Prutky has misspelt his name. Luis de Guzman, another Jesuit missionary, and author of a well known history of Jesuit missionary activity in India, China and Japan, the *Historia de las Missiones que han hecto los religiosos de la Compagnia de Jesus, para predicar el Sancto Evangelio en la India Oriental, y en los Regnos de la China y Japon* (Alcala, 1601). For Oviedo, see p. 245, note 13, and P. Caraman, *The lost empire, the story of the Jesuits in Ethiopia, 1555–1634* (London, 1985).

CHAPTER 38

FESTIVALS AND THE
WORSHIP OF THE SAINTS

In Abyssinia are celebrated both the fixed and the movable feasts, the Lenten fast-days, Easter, the day sacred to our Lord Christ and the day sacred to His most holy Mother. From the earliest times it has been the custom to celebrate, on appointed days, the feasts of the Apostles, the Evangelists, St Athanasius, St Basil, St Anthony Archimandrite, the Eunuch of Queen Candace, the Queen herself, and other Abyssinian saints, especial honour being paid, with great rejoicing, to Theclaymanoth,[1] whose sanctity is widely known throughout the land (he performed many miracles and raised three from the dead: while still in life he was refreshed by the presence of the Holy Trinity, and translated to Heaven under the protection of Their wings, where to this day he dwells in glory). Michael the commander of the heavenly host and the other Angelic powers are celebrated on the first[2] day of the month in some parts, on the fifteenth in others, while the Holy Virgin the Mother of God, as well as on her thirty-two annual days, is reverenced on the twenty-first[3] day of every month; whoever is suspected of having said the slightest thing to detract from her honour is stoned to death without judicial sentence. Many days

[1] St Takla Haymanot, a holy man of Šawa (c. 1215–1313), and one of the principal saints of the Ethiopian church. Taddesse Tamrat, *Church and state in Ethiopia* (Oxford, 1972), pp. 160–74; G. W. B. Huntingford, 'Saints of mediaeval Ethiopia', *Abba Salama* (1979), x, 271–3, 292, 295–6, 314–5, 336.
[2] The festival of Mikaél was in fact celebrated on the twelfth of the month. E. A. Wallis Budge, *The book of the saints of the Ethiopian church*, (Cambridge, 1928), i, 44, 139, 231, ii, 365, 483, 618, iii, 688, 804, 879, iv, 986, 1110, 1206.
[3] The Ethiopian synaxarium confirms that 'on this day' i.e. the twenty-first day of the month, 'is celebrated the festival of the commemoration of Our Lady the pure and holy Virgin, the God-bearer.' Budge, *Book of the saints*, iv, 1020.

are kept holy in Abyssinia which are not so kept in Europe, and just as one day in each month is dedicated to the Holy Virgin the Mother of God, so the feast is kept of the aforesaid holy man, servant of Christ, who is called Work of the Holy Ghost (this seems to be Theclaymanoth). Greater emphasis is given to the death of John the Baptist than to his birth, and to the Exaltation of the Cross than to the Invention. The worship of saints and of images I found to be more demonstrative here than in Europe, so that wherever they see a holy image they prostrate themselves on the ground, kiss it, touch it reverently with their hands, and then again touch its face, forehead, and eyes.

Many other false festivals are devised for them by the monks, who although for the most part professing the rule of St Basil the Great, yet live many of them within enclosed monasteries and others in unenclosed freedom in the houses of the laity. There is great disagreement between them, some professing the faith of Father Theclaymanoth, others that of Father Eustachianus,[4] and the two parties are at odds, and oppose and oppress each other; hence comes the custom to call some monasteries Theclaymanothian, others Eustachian, though both are almost useless, perform no work or organized study, mislead the people, direct them to the everlasting pit, and live a life at once wretched and scandalous. Despite its serious inconvenience they adhere to the canon of the Nicene Council never to choose a patriarch from among their own people, and, holding rigidly to this ancient ordinance, only recognise as patriarch a Coptic monk despatched to them by the heretical church of Alexandria.[5] When one patriarch dies delegates are at once sent to Cairo for his successor. The Coptic monks dislike the post, for the reason that the journey is inconvenient, the place is far off, the Ethiopian language is unknown, they will have to stay there permanently, and they will be exiled from their own country. No one is eager

---

[4] Ewostatéwos (c. 1273–1352), a holy man of Sarayé in northern Ethiopia, who travelled to Armenia, where he died. He is one of the principal saints of the Ethiopian church. Taddesse Tamrat, *op. cit.*, pp. 197–8, 206–8; Huntingford, *op. cit.*, pp. 270–1, 329.

[5] The rule that the Ethiopian Patriarch should not be chosen from among the people of the country, but should come from Egypt, was not established by the Council of Nicaea. Bruce, *op. cit.*, i, 534, as noted earlier, offered an entirely different explanation, namely that it was part of the agreement governing the establishment of the Šawan dynasty after the Zagwé usurpation.

to accept the offered preferment, until by some trick of the Coptic Patriarch the Turkish power lays hold on one or other, whom the Patriarch orders to be brought in chains before his council, where he is decorated with a more venerable and more beautiful beard, and appointed primate of Abyssinia; the same Turkish power transports him to Ethiopia, but he is quite without zeal or ardour to save souls. In truth the punishment of God is justly imposed upon this people, who are unworthy to dwell in the land of so many sainted hermits: for more than 1,270 years they have lived in schism, heresy, and countless errors (except for one century under the protection of the king of Portugal), they have lingered in an almost continuous state of slavery, and now they justly pay the price; surrounded on all sides by pagans, idolaters, heathen, and Mahometans, it would be surprising if they had not reached this degree of blindness, disaster, and ignorance of the true faith.

I was surprised that the Abyssinians have for so long retained remembrance of the major festivals, Sabaoth,[6] the Nativity of our Lord Jesus Christ, Easter, and Pentecost. When celebrating Easter, a number of priests at about noon dress themselves in ornate pontifical robes, almost all with tiaras on their heads, or episcopal mitres, or the gilded triangular caps customary for patriarchs, set with precious stones: into the market place of the city or inhabited place they lead the people out in procession, not well-ordered as it would be in Europe but wandering hither and thither like sheep, with no devotional prayer but shouting, laughing, and joking by the way. One of the senior monks carries from the church under a baldachin the piece of wood called *Tavot*,[7] covered in a silken cloth, with which instead of a travelling altar the Ethiopians are accustomed to sanctify objects. Carrying a number of torches instead of lamps, they consider that greater reverence is displayed at the festival by dressing up in priests'

---

[6] From the sense of the passage this would seem to mean the observance of Sunday, which however Prutky usually calls Domenica (*sc* dies), or, less likely, of the Sabbath, which he usually calls Sabbata. Sabaoth in Hebrew is unconnected with Sabbath, being an appellation of the Lord as Ruler over all.

[7] The *tabot*, or altar slab, kept in every church as a representation of the Ark of the Covenant, for a detailed account of which see Beckingham and Huntingford, *Prester John*, ii, 543–8.

robes a number of pretty girls as deacons,[8] with a sort of crown on their heads; challenged that this practice is unworthy of the church, and that it is contrary to canon law to admit women to the service of the altar, they reply that the use of boys renders the procession less decorative, and that good-looking girls enhance its solemnity. Whenever the Tavot is delayed and the procession is forced to halt, the monks exhibit no delicacy about sitting on the ground in their priestly robes, chatting familiarly and joking with the little deaconesses until the Tavot is carried from the church, when they stand up, still talking, and proceed in a disorderly troop to the market-place: returning in the same order they hasten to the consumption of their raw beef. The feast of Pentecost is celebrated in similar fashion, but with less parade and less noise.

A principal festival is called *Baal Egzier*,[9] that is the festival of God, the apostles Peter and Paul, the Archangels Raphael and Gabriel, Saint George, and three hundred Holy Fathers, who form, they believe, a Holy Council as a reward for their lives in the Faith: this day is celebrated on July 11, an annual festival carefully observed with all possible ceremony, and in the fear that, as has happened to many others, evil will befall them if they fail to celebrate it. Although the feast of the Holy Cross is held each month, their pride is such in possessing a large part of the True Cross, brought from Jerusalem by earlier emperors, that every year on September 25 they keep the Feast with especial ceremony:[10] the Emperor himself appears in public on his throne for the whole of the afternoon and the night following, the

---

[8] Though Prutky may well have seen girls participating in religious festivals it would seem most unlikely that any would in fact have been deacons. The Ethiopian legal code, the *Fetha Nagast*, or Laws of the Kings, specifies that only men could be deacons. Abba Paulos Tzadua and P. L. Strauss, *The Fetha Nagast. The law of the kings* (Addis Ababa, 1968), p. 48. No other observer ever reported the existence of 'deaconesses'.

[9] *Ba'ala egzér.*

[10] The feast of *Masqal* commemorated the supposed discovery by Empress Helena of the True Cross. Budge, *Book of the saints*, i, 55–6, Hyatt, *op. cit.*, p. 165. A piece of the Cross was said to have been brought to Ethiopia from Jerusalem during the reign of Emperor Dawit I (1382–1411). This relic or another like it was in Gondar during the reign of Iyasu II when it was captured, and later restored, by the soldiers of Sennar. Guidi, *Annales regum Iyasu II et Iyo'as*, pp. 124, 126; Bruce, *op. cit.*, ii, 640–2; Budge, *History of Ethiopia*, i, 300, ii, 455.

portion of the cross being displayed to the people in the market place, and the Emperor with his weapons around him, in company with his watchful populace, demonstrates the care with which he protects the cross from being stolen. During my own sojourn in the country the Emperor was prevented from attending, and sent as his substitute his Treasurer, who robed himself similarly as for the feast of St John Baptist and visited the churches with gifts of gold, frankincense, myrrh, and candles: the people shouted their approval and applause, as he was accompanied by the principal officials and ministers, each with at least thirty or forty servants armed with shields, lances, swords, and muskets: these, mounted on beautifully-caparisoned mules, followed the royal Treasurer, many thousands of men raised an enormous clamour, people without number rushed about in disorder, inspired not by devotion but by curiosity, disorder and confusion reigned, and the Treasurer's patience was very sorely tried. When the presents were lodged in the churches each person kissed the door as a mark of devotion, and immediately, without further prayer, hastened from the last church to the next: the Treasurer, returning through scenes of even worse disorder, hastened about 4 p.m. to the square where the wood of the Holy Cross had been prominently displayed, and sat himself under the royal canopy spread on a rather higher spot as on a throne, where for the whole night he was compelled to keep watch, assisted by his armed guard, while an unlicensed mob of many thousands, all restraints cast aside, feasted off raw oxen, which on that night the Emperor is compelled to present to them: barely had they been killed when they were swallowed down raw, as though by dogs, while bread made of teff was blissfully consumed and tacz drunk to satiety until intoxication followed. The viciousness, buffoonery, clamour and confusion is beyond the power of the pen to describe: many were trampled to death, many killed in viciousness or sport, while on the same night occurred all sorts of obscene behaviour, the Ethiopians' habits of eating being shown up as like those of dogs or other animals. The market square stank so that a man could hardly bear it, and all modesty was forgotten as like a herd of pigs they performed their bodily functions in the open square without regard for decorum or privacy.

260

The Treasurer indeed was to be pitied, who for the whole night had to view this loathsome scene, and stayed wakeful because if he had slept the mob would have been free to despoil and rob him of everything, to strip him naked of his clothing, and finally to carry off the cross: to avoid this he renounced sleep to preserve his own life, such envy and hatred reigning among the Ethiopians, who commit murder on the slightest provocation. Such is their genuine adoration of the Cross and their usual devotion to it, consisting in eating, drinking, and obscene behaviour: the monthly celebrations are of this manner, while the yearly festival is marked by more earnest ceremonies, that is by worse buffoonery, uproar, drunken orgies, murder and obscenity. Each of the important officials on feast days orders the slaughter for his followers of numerous cattle, and feeds numbers of the poor beside, who rush in in crowds from all quarters and increase the uproar, as importunate and starving they gnaw the raw flesh and the surrounding bones like dogs in a charnel house. The great men's servants beat them off with their spears, heedless of the damage they cause to limb or even life, and crowds of people suffer from broken legs or other injuries: ever do the Ethiopian festivals end in such damnation of souls.

Especial reverence is paid to the day of a supposed St *Abbo*,[11] of whom it is related that he neither ate nor drank nor sucked his mother's milk, but was martyred when as an infant he was killed by his mother in a fit of madness. His annual feast day falls on June 29, during the feast of St Peter and St Paul, and from this so-called saint and martyr is taken the modern name of Mount Abbo, where the three venerable martyrs of our seraphic order were once stoned and now enjoy their martyr's crown. *Kuskuam*[12] is another holy day, of which the Arabic name is *Mahruck*,[13] that is Burnt, the Blessed Virgin Mary, they say, being accustomed to walk on a certain mountain so designated

[11] Abbo, a name given to St Gabra Manfas. The feast of Peter and Paul took place on Hamlé fifth which Ludolf equates with June 29 of the Julian calendar. Ludolf *Commentarius*, p. 420.

[12] *Qʷesqʷam*, a festival celebrating the Flight into Egypt. Aymro Wondmagegnehu and Joachim Motovu, *The Ethiopian Orthodox church*, pp. 60, 64, 145. It was held on Hedar sixth. Ludolf, *Commentarius*, p. 397.

[13] Arabic *maḥrūq*.

261

which is situated in Egypt. In her honour they keep holy this day on a high mountain where the present Queen Mother of the reigning Emperor has built her residence, called Kuskuam,[14] the worship terminating finally in the eating of raw beef and the assiduous drinking of tacz.

The cult of holy images is a most ancient custom of theirs, and sincere worship is paid to them. Pictures are displayed of Christ, of Christ's Mother, of the blessed spirits, patriarchs, prophets, apostles and of all the others whom we believe to be enjoying the blessedness of God's presence. There is scarcely a church in which an image of St George the martyr is not visible. The Abyssinians are particularly careful in this, that wherever they paint the likeness of Christ, of the Virgin Mother of God and of other saints, they depict them as black in colour, while on the contrary they use white to show either the wickedest sinners or the powers of evil.[15] For example, in the last supper Christ and the Apostles appear as black, Judas the traitor as white, while Christ in agony is black while Annas, Caiaphas, Pilate, Herod and the rest of the crowd of criminals and Jews are white. Similarly Michael Prince of the heavenly host is black, while the devil beneath his feet is white.

They do not use bas relief,[16] whether in ignorance of the art of engraving or sculpting, or for other causes which I know not. In scarcely a single house is the image of a saint to be seen, lest its frequent worship in the home should detract from the reverence paid in public. For this reason, wherever one is found in a house, it is kept apart in a clean and fitting spot, always covered

[14] The palace at Qʷesqʷam was visited by Bruce who claims, *op. cit.*, iii, 206–15, 221, to have there treated the royal children, then suffering from smallpox. He describes the building, iv, 271, as consisting of three main buildings, the largest 'a square tower of three storeys, with a flat parapet roof, or terrace, and battlements around it'. For other references to this building, which was decorated with red tuff and bas-reliefs depicting animals, see Pankhurst, *History of Ethiopian towns*, i, 158–9.

[15] Prutky's statement that Ethiopian artists depicted Christ, the Virgin Mary and the Saints as black persons and the Devil and sinners as white ones is erroneous. See for example Chojnacki, *Major themes*.

[16] Statues had been produced during the early Aksumite Kingdom, which also witnessed the minting of engraved coins in both pre-Christian and Christian times. Bas-reliefs were virtually unknown in mediaeval Ethiopia, a few interesting exceptions being representations of Lalibala and of an equestrian horseman, possibly St. George, at the church of St. Mary at Lalibala, and some sculpted *mambera tabots*, or boxes containing altar-slabs. G. Simon, *L'Ethiopie* (Paris, 1885), plate 1.

with a veil. Because the common practice is for all priests to carry a cross, it is therefore forbidden to anyone to keep at home an image of the crucifix, it being considered wicked that so august and sacred an object should dwell beneath the roof of a sinful man. Only in church is it to be found depicted, where it is always covered with a curtain.

CHAPTER 39

FASTS

It is engrained in the Abyssinians that the whole perfection of the Christian religion consists in strict fasting, and everyone of them without distinction, great and humble, old men and young, the healthy and the sick, keep the fast days of Lent, when they await the going down of the sun before they will take food, and think it a sin to do so before the stars have arisen; nor at other times is food eaten before 3 p.m. by those on whom fasting has been enjoined; even then they taste nothing save bread of an almost ashen consistency, water, green vegetables or a piece or two of fruit.[1] If to this be added fish, and there are few who do so, they abstain from those that have blood in them and content themselves with lobster, cuttlefish, oyster, polypus, cockles, and such like, which are of little value either to recruit one's strength or to excite one's appetite. They begin Lent on the Monday after Septuagesima so that it lasts for fifty-five days,[2] whereas we Catholics begin it on Ash Wednesday and reckon it to last for forty-six days until Easter, thus, omitting the intervening Sundays, when the only abstinence is from meat, making a total of forty days: the Ethiopians in comparison, who do not fast on Easter Eve, when the Fathers fasted of old, ignore the seven intervening Saturdays and Sundays, on which they abstain only from meat, and reach the same total of forty days.

Through the year they fast every Wednesday and Friday,[3] except during the season from the Resurrection of our Lord at

---

[1] The strictness of fasting and the extent of abstinence had earlier been described by Alvarez (Beckingham and Huntingford, *Prester John*, ii, 389–90, 394–5, 508–9) and Lobo (Lockhart, *op. cit.*, p. 178).

[2] Actually 56 days. Aymro Wondmagegnehu and Motovu, *op. cit.*, p. 63.

[3] On Wednesday and Friday fasts as described by Alvarez and Lobo see Beckingham and Huntingford, *Prester John*, ii, 509, and Lockhart, *op. cit.*, p. 178.

Easter to Pentecost, when in honour of the Resurrection and to celebrate the time of great joy when Christ was mysteriously present on earth they are at perfect liberty to eat meat at frequent intervals every day. In Lent, until sunset, they eat nothing, and the priests celebrate mass a little before sunset and not earlier, in the belief that the fast would be broken by the bread and wine of the Eucharist. On Wednesdays they believe it lawful to eat when the setting sun casts a shadow five feet long, while on Fridays the length must be seven feet. The time between Easter and Pentecost is *Chamsin,* which is their word for fifty. They also fast for twenty days before our Lord's nativity,[4] and for fourteen days, with great strictness, before the feast of the Assumption of the Virgin,[5] nor do they hold any one to be Christian who fails to keep this fast. Before the feast of Saints Peter and Paul the fast is of twenty days. While fasting they eat with their bread some pieces of fruit, and greens cooked without oil or butter, and refusal of these additions is the mark of a particularly severe sacrifice of abstinence.[6] At many times in the year, during the weekdays of Advent, for the six first days of January when the Magi came to adore the new-born Christ, for the nine days which precede Lent, and for the fourteen first days of August before the Assumption of the Virgin, they abstain from the eating of meat, while, in memory of the penitence which the men of Nineveh underwent of old when Jonah preached to them, they fast so strictly for the first three days[7] after the Purification that not even nursing infants are admitted to the breast more often than once in the day.

Our vigils and Ember days are in no way respected, though a strict fast is kept in honour of the holy apostles from the second day before Pentecost up to the feast itself; perhaps thus considering that they are satisfying the requirements of our vigils and Ember days. They follow the Roman rule, or rather the rule of their own church, in Friday abstinence for the death of Jesus Christ, but not in Saturday abstinence for His burial, although

---

[4] This fast actually lasts for forty days. Hyatt, *op. cit.,* p. 158; Aymro Wondmagegnehu and Motovu, *op. cit.,* p. 63.

[5] This fast lasts for fifteen or sixteen days. Hyatt, *op. cit.,* p. 157; Aymro Wondmagegenehu and Motovu, *op. cit.,* p. 63.

[6] This account is confirmed by Alvarez. Beckingham and Huntingford, *Prester John,* ii, 390–1.

[7] This fast is sometimes called after Jonah. Hyatt, *op. cit.,* p. 158.

this custom was instituted in the time of the Apostles: being converts from Judaism they keep Saturdays as a day of rejoicing, and begrudge a Saturday fast, for which reason all Orientals in the church of God commute the fast of Easter Eve to the Wednesday before Easter. Others will have it that that was the day on which the Council was held and the resolution passed to kill Christ, but this is false reasoning because by that argument the fast should be held on the day when our Blessed Saviour was arrested, that is on the Thursday when the Council was held to arrest Him.

All these and some other fasts are kept within the homes of the people, who until sunset neither eat, nor drink, nor smoke tobacco, a practice that at other times they follow in Oriental fashion, until the going down of the sun: a great drain on their health, seeing that they content themselves with greens and with vegetables, and with fish, if they eat them, that are without scales or blood; these they skin, dip three times into lemon juice, bring once to the boil, and eat. They have a number of other foolish and valueless observances, not worth describing, and their superstition is such that they believe it a great sin to take food or drink even for worn out old men, or for those who have finished a march through the heat, or for those on their death bed: indeed they strain the gnat and swallow the camel.

What sort of life is the result of so ill-directed a faith, I set forth for those who wish to read it in the next chapter.

CHAPTER 40

RELIGIOUS LIFE AND MORALS

The life that they lead is very similar to their faith, without which, on the authority of the Holy Apostle (Hebrews xi. 6), *it is impossible to please God*; the Abyssinians not possessing a true faith pleasing to God, how can they lead a life that is pleasing to Him? In fact it is totally at odds with God's precepts and holy laws, and the word of the holy St James can well be held against it (James ii. 26) *As the body without the spirit is dead, so faith without works is dead also.*

Knowing little about good works and caring less, they seldom think of God, but are ever bound up in the things of this world that will pass away, the poor ever seeking to acquire wealth or office, the rich ever anxious to gain more goods and to exalt themselves. Such are the considerations that engross them, and their whole time is spent in obsequious attendance on royal ministers and officials in attempts to curry favour with them: when in the fullness of time they have lost hope of gaining anything, they resort at last to their written spells, which dangle from hand, foot and body, and when divine providence permits them to gain their desire, they attribute this happy outcome, to general admiration, to the effect of the spells, even though up to now they have paid little heed to such superstition. What they avidly desire they obtain by these means, and repose the greatest faith in these empty spells, so that it is impossible to convince them to the contrary, that these are the wicked and unlawful deceptions of the devil. From a tender age these superstitions are engrained in the minds of the children, so that I was greatly surprised to see charms worn by infants at the breast, while I found both old men and young to be scrupulous in preserving them: often in familiar conversation with my good friends I tried to persuade them that spells such as these could do nothing but harm to our immortal souls, according to the decalogue: some I persuaded to throw away their spells, and when I burned them on the fire there arose an unpleasant smell and a loud noise.[1] I particularly noted a number of spells that were secretly worn by young men to bring them success in love, and when I gave them as food to the fire my nose was filled with a great and unusual stink: nevertheless, within a short time many renewed their stock of spells, some to acquire wealth, some luck, some preferment, some love, and some against their enemies, these last especially being inscribed by the neighbouring Mahometans, the friends of the devil: all are regarded with great respect. So steeped are they in this superstition that whether for fear of being slain by their enemies, or poisoned, or done to death by other mischance, they put no trust in their own kindred, or even in their own sons, but are ever afraid of the harmful effects of their ill will: they live like Cain, fugitives and vagabonds.

Their religious life is of the worst: they entirely omit to mark themselves with the symbol of Christianity the mark of the cross, or to salute our Heavenly Father, or to pay respect to Divinity with a Hail Mary, or to say private prayers on arising or retiring, or to offer thanks for mercies granted: they make no effort to raise their hearts to heaven. In the morning they protract until breakfast time their useless conversations, and then continue their usual jokes, songs, games, dances, gesticulations and hand-claps: when the lunch hour comes they gorge themselves on raw meat and toast each other in gulps of their usual tacz, until they fall asleep on full stomachs; if still unsatisfied they visit the house of another to eat and drink some more, where in idle conversation they fill in the time until dinner: the rest of the day is wasted in different trifles at the hands of their servants or serving maids to keep them from slumber: they are as idle as sheep in the field. Thus life in Ethiopia slips by from day to day, with neither prayer, nor celestial meditation for the soul's salvation, nor work of any kind; idleness fills the day, and if occasionally one more devout recites in the morning some of the psalms of David, that is the whole of his day's devotion, and he dreams of nothing beyond. In all the time I spent in Ethiopia I never saw a servant or serving

[1] On Ethiopian charms see D. Lifszyc, 'Amulettes éthiopiens', *Minotaure* (1933), ii, 71–4; J. Mercier, *Ethiopian magic scrolls* (New York, 1979).

maid to pray, or to perform any other act of piety: in idleness, laziness and sleep they steal from the Almighty the time He has allotted them. Common to all is a free licence for every kind of sin, no one walks God's path of righteousness, no one is appointed to teach that holy and just way, no one is fitted to instruct in the doctrines of salvation. The monks of the Abbey of St Anthony, and the many priests, who ought to set to others a shining example of virtue and moral piety, are spread in great numbers throughout the Empire but are uneducated and simple men, ignorant of God's way, of execrable life and morals, who make no pretence of spreading the teaching of our Lord Christ or of instructing the people, live themselves the most scandalous lives, are corrupters of good morals, insist that all conduct is lawful, feed their flocks not with heavenly food but with the poison of snakes, and know not the holy gospel nor the law of God. In place of good salt to savour the food of the spirit they are become savourless and of no avail except *to be cast out and to be trodden under the foot of men* (Matthew v. 13).

Though most Ethiopians have been sprinkled with holy water, and on that account call themselves Christians and profess the Chrstian religion, yet the abominable deeds of their daily life are painful to Christ our Lord, and they are Christians only in name. Justice is in exile from their land, they care nothing for the rights of the individual, each man will injure the next by the theft or robbery of his property, while the judges, if any have recourse to them, will give the appearance indeed of hearing the injured party, but will give judgement in favour of their own friends, and will invent a web of excuses why the injured party should lose his case. The principal officials and ministers of the empire, seeing in meadow, corn-field, or garden something that pleases them, such as a crop of corn, ask 'Who owns that?' and, if they find out that the proprietor is junior, and less powerful, they promptly send their servants with orders to gather and carry in the crop of fruit or corn into their own barns as though it were their own. Let the injured party betake himself even to the Emperor on appeal, he returns with nothing but empty words, and will never recover what has been taken from him, for against the greater ministers and officials there is no ground for taking action. In case of murder, if the guilty man be taken before the judges he is rarely punished, but comes off almost scot free, provided that he flees to a neighbouring place and stays there for a little time: none of the judges will make enquiries after the criminal, the crime is easily forgotten, and when the guilty party shortly returns there is no further record or question against him. I was grieved to see a poor woman murdered in Gondar for three measures of flour, and thought that when such a terrible crime were taken before the Emperor it would be severely punished, but, gracious heaven, the Emperor's reply was 'My father, less consistent than I, ordered many to be executed for their crimes, but then himself died,' with this answer expressing the hope that he himself would live for ever, and that, one person being killed, what use was it to kill a second? – and so the murder went unpunished. His subjects take full measure of their Emperor's culpable mercy, and in their affairs show themselves presumptuous, evil-natured, and murderous.

If in the market place a purchaser is pleased with an article for sale, but not with the price demanded, he takes it by force, and the evil treatment of the sellers causes them often enough to raise their voice in anguish. Where is their refuge, where is justice for them, or satisfaction? Nowhere. Thus it happens that sellers and buyers alike appear in the market-place equipped with spears, swords, and shields, those who offer force are repulsed by equal force, and many are killed. All virtue is scorned, piety, devotion, religious fervour, are alike unknown, pity and charity are trampled down, and in scarcely any other part of the world are so many destitute to be found: in the public squares, in the common streets, lie prostrate the naked, the starving, the weak and the ill, as in a lazar-house: in the last stages of exhaustion, skin scarcely stretching over bone through hunger, they continually assail the ears of the passers-by with *raven raven,*[2] hunger hunger; at the doors of death they redouble their groans, we are dying, dying, they cry; seldom are their cries heard. My own eyes witnessed in royal Gondar how many died of hunger day by day, and scarcely one of the nobles took pity on them. Generally the wretches were unable from weakness to retire at night to a safe place, and the prowling wolves[3] and lions devouring them removed them from the sorrows of the world – yet

---

[2] *Raben*, 'we are hungry', or *rabeñ*, 'I am hungry'.
[3] Probably a reference to hyenas.

even this moved few to pity. Often was I amazed to hear of poor people who lay for two or three days in the streets: I saw them lying dead by the roadside *and there was no man to bury them* (Psalms lxxix. 3). The passers-by put stones on their face, to mark their death, and let them lie for a long time until they stink, and become *meat unto the fowls of the heaven* (ib. 2). Sometimes someone takes pity on them, and with the gift of four or five pieces of salt they are buried in a corner of some nearby church, without any help from the priest or religious ceremony of interment. Like cattle they die and like cattle they are buried, horrible to relate but yet more horrible to witness. So far I have travelled in three continents of the globe, Asia, Africa and Europe, and nowhere else did I find Christian charity so trampled under foot, only the Ethiopians I know to be barbarous and pitiless. Blind and miserable people, luckless in this world, even more unfortunate in the world to come: here like dogs they suffer famine and countless miseries, in the next world even greater ones that they will not be able to avoid, where they will listen to lamentation throughout eternity, and where *there will be wailing and gnashing of teeth* (Matthew xiii. 42, 50). Against their will a life of future evil is prepared for them, they ever throw off Christ's easy yoke, they refuse instruction in the true faith, *For this people's heart is waxed gross, and their ears are dull of hearing, and their eyes they have closed* (Matthew xiii. 15).

All the virtues are held by them in hatred. Innocence appears scarce once in seven years, prostitutes[4] solicit in public, women are violated; one woman was indecently molested by two or three youths in the street, while the onlookers laughed and joked at it, and when I passing by rebuked them for flouting Christian morals and for conduct hateful to God, they laughed and replied that they were doing nothing wrong. If this and other behaviour, not worth recounting, are regarded by the Ethiopians as good, what would they regard as evil, or as sinful? Wherever and whenever a man desires intercourse, he insinuates himself into the good will of the first and nearest woman to him, and works

---

[4] The existence of a *galamota*, or prostitute, at Gondar had earlier been mentioned in the chronicle of the Emperor Iyasu I. Guidi, *Annales Iohannis I, Iyāsu I et Bakāffā*, p. 160. For subsequent accounts of prostitutes see R. Pankhurst, 'The history of prostitution in Ethiopia', *Journal of Ethiopian studies* (1974), xii, No. 2, pp. 160–1.

his will on her: vices of the flesh are thought of as nothing, and are not accounted a sin, when even the young people, in the first flower of their youth, can be seen in places of ill repute, and the servants at the bidding of their masters bring in whatever young woman they meet to satisfy their unbridled passions, with no thought of God. Nor is this remarkable when men and women alike go more than half naked, are without occupation, or shame, or personal modesty: their clothing generally a piece of skin or leather, or thick rough cotton cloth with no other finish than it bore when it came from the weaver's hands. The upper part of the breast is naked, and the buttocks likewise, their nakedness excites the lust each of the other, and when they show respect to someone they pull down their clothes as far as the navel and display themselves half naked. If two people have not met for some time, they exchange warm kisses in public and openly demonstrate their mutual familiarity, this treatment being extended to almost all kinsmen, who greeting each other on this pretext are enabled to satisfy their desires. Wherever a place is allotted for prostitutes to forgather, thither they promptly repair by day or night without restraint: shamelessly they glory in their wickedness, they bear their children openly and proudly in the presence of the people, they are despised if they are sterile but rewarded if they bear offspring, and they name in public the name of their partner and publish their evil deed far and wide, especially if that partner be one of the ministers.

Nor do the young men suffer any punishment who are infected with venereal disease,[5] but are provided by the emperor and ministers, during the process of their cure, with a daily allowance of food and drink: a great crowd of them clamour daily in the hills before the palace for help and sustenance while their cure takes place, and no one is refused. The poorer women offer themselves in exchange for a crust of bread, and this swarming nation is poverty-stricken, lazy, without employment, workshy, ignorant of any craft, and dedicated to licentiousness: every vice possesses them, this even more than their laziness brings down

---

[5] The Ethiopians traditionally attached little or no stigma to this disease, which, according to Charles Johnston, was 'admitted and spoken of without reluctance or shame'. C. Johnston, *Travels in southern Ethiopia* (London, 1844), ii, 267. See also P. Mérab, *Médecins et médecine en Éthiopie* (Paris, 1912), pp. 70, 78–9.

every sort of evil upon the State, and their idleness is rewarded by misery: *Like unto whited sepulchres, which indeed appear beautiful outward, but are within full of dead men's bones, and of all uncleanness* (Matthew xxiii. 27). That a people untaught should lead a life of evil is not surprising, but more to be wondered at are the monks and the priests, who sacrilegiously live with women as their husband,[6] naming their offspring as their children and the women as their wives, and conducting themselves as though they were of the laity: what is good and lawful they depreciate, and confirm their flock in their evil living by their own bad example both in word and in deed. *Neither do they light a candle and put it on a candlestick, but under a bushel* (Matthew v. 15.) lest it giveth light unto all that are in the house, nor do they think of the words of our Saviour *Let your light so shine before men, that they may see your good works, and glorify your Father which is in heaven.* (*ib.* 16). That their actions are totally to the contrary some everday examples used to demonstrate to me. I learned from the imperial treasurer's brother, Lord Joanne of Draco the Queen's minister, of what befell him when he visited a senior monk to sup with him. Serving at table were two women, one young and one old, and, on his enquiring who they were, the monk replied, without a trace of shame, 'the older one is the young one's mother: she was my wife at one time, but now that she is old I have taken to myself the young one, who is better.' The situation of the laity becomes clearer when monks so wicked and so scandalous present the people with such an example of evil.

The religious are not men of wealth, and those appointed by the ministers and the wealthy to watch over their wives and concubines set a bad example to the people, in that while serving at the tables of the rich they do not consider the religious to be worthy to eat with them, except sometimes, on a special occasion, when to gratify the nobles the religious intone an absolution for their continual sins *Egzier efftach* May God forgive you. To procure loose women for the laity on their slightest hint, like common pimps, to wheedle single girls from the strict life of matrimony, to lead the light-minded into evil courses for the sake of the joke, and to abuse them within or without the matrimonial bond, they regard as of no moment, and when the royal Treasurer

[6] It was of course entirely customary, and lawful, for Ethiopian priests to be married, provided that they contracted their marriage prior to their ordination.

responded to one of them 'Abba, Father is not this, if outside marriage, forbidden by the laws of God and highly displeasing to His Divine Majesty?' the monk replied 'There is nothing Lord to prevent it if you wish me to procure the girl for you, it is good (as the Mahometans say) to beget sons' – but when he encountered a second rebuff he had to retire in disgrace, instead of with the present he had hoped for.

To such depths of iniquity has human behaviour sunk in Ethiopia that great and humble, rulers and subjects, are living in all respects a life of open sin: the chief governors of the Empire are rapacious of wealth and oppressors of the poor, and although the annual tribute set by the Emperor is little enough, yet by a number of excuses, and without compunction, they avoid paying even that little, and reduce the amount to scarcely one tenth. They pretend that they have spent the money on various necessities of the state, with no thought of remorse that justice demands they render to each his own, or of the divine command in the words of St Augustine, *the sin will not be forgiven until restitution has been made.* Their consciences are asleep, so that their minds are not on heavenly but on earthly things, and they ever seek that which is their own, not that which is Jesus Christ's.

Like master, like man, servants sent to buy goods forget not their own profit and defraud their masters, ever eager to gain some appointment which will fill their pockets: if they steal from him but two or three loaves of bread a day, even dividing this with his concubines, the theft increases their wealth. The masters know this full well, and, if they want to avoid loss, entrust little to their servants. Nor is this unjust, for *the occasion of sin is the means of punishment.* Evil and in all ways wicked is the life led by the Ethiopians, licentious and contrary to the laws of God, and lust is their pastime. The women flaunt and display themselves to assist their alms-begging, and bring home the reward of their iniquity, while the offspring of their incest and their adulteries they carry around the neighbouring houses to obtain the wherewithal to nourish them: only for a short time do they nurture them before exposing them in the public places, without affection and without upbringing, for others to rear, and if for four or five years they keep them at home in misery, they thrust them out of doors as little girls to seek their bread from door to door: without maternal care they run here and there in lamentation, poor naked starving castaways, many of them dying of hunger save some who out of kindness are taken into the service of the nobles.

The danger above all others is that one may do injury to another, within marriage or outside it, because the Ethiopians are extremely passionate, and long store up their anger within them, until they find a cause of avenging themselves; as is proved by the case of the Emperor's sister, who, unable to avenge herself on her husband in any other way, seized the feet of his dearly-loved child, smashed its head against the wall, and cruelly dashed out its brains, so getting her revenge upon her husband: no crime could be more cruel or more abominable than thus to treat her own child: the brute beasts would be less savage. Care must be taken that no-one suffers an unexpected mischance to life or fortune, since most are poor, stupid, and ignorant, arrogant and contemptuous of all other natures, though they know them not, certain that none can be found like to themselves, scornful of all peoples, holding all others of no account but preferring themselves, certain that the whole world is to be found in Ethiopia: often when asked whether any other part of the universe could equal Ethiopia I smiled in reply, and passed over the question, to avoid envious quarrels: I knew too well for how long they stored up a grievance in their heart.

Their anger is particularly aroused when they see others rewarded, and they are always plotting and contriving to gain possession for themselves of the fortune and advantages of others. These and the many other evils common in Ethiopia it would be tedious to relate in detail, for the enormities of their way of life will become clearer elsewhere, partly from what I have already said, and partly from what I have still to describe.

CHAPTER 41

MANNERS AND CUSTOMS

The manners of the Ethiopians are no manners at all. No trace is to be seen either of upbringing or of nobility of disposition, great men and nobles are distinguishable only by the appointments they hold, their behaviour is regulated by no other politeness than is inborn in them, natural inclination is their only guide, and their passions rage without restraint; desire reigns unchecked, instinct rules reason, the customs of their ancestors are their pattern, and they cleave continually to a barbarian tradition. Inferiors kiss hands on meeting those appointed to the major offices, and if encountering them on the public street strip off their clothes down to the waist; on other occasions they cover their heads with a white cloth and repeat continuously *Endet nau? Boku nau?*[1] how does your excellency fare? is your excellency in good health? to all which questions the usual reply is *Egzier gemascken,*[2] Thanks be to God. Because of the sun's heat the country people have the custom of going naked, with a loin cloth of rough leather or sometimes of cotton, and when meeting each other on the road have different forms of greeting. If the Emperor passes by they pull down their clothes and falling to the ground kiss it three times in homage to him, while other superior officers they greet half naked, their clothes down to their waist: for equals they simply bare the breast and head, with one hand on the breast.

Each of the lords maintains a large train of servants, three or four hundred in number, who in wartime all serve as soldiers: to maintain their dignity the lords seldom or never go on foot, but are always mounted on fine mules, of which they maintain

[1] *Endét naw? Bago naw?*
[2] *Egzi'abhér yemasgan.*

a large number, whose speed and easy gait will carry a man quickly and comfortably and which sell for three or four ounces of gold each. With their master mounted on a finely-equipped mule the servants dispose themselves in front and on each side of it and form his retinue: armed with shields and lances, swords and guns, they sustain the credit of their chief and guard him carefully to keep him from danger. When one minister meets another, each on horseback, he halts for a time and greets the other with bared breast, the servants meanwhile all displaying their nakedness in the manner described above. If a noble is desirous of visiting the house of a neighbouring official, he approaches the door where his servants present themselves naked: their master, unaccompanied, removes his shoes before the chamber door and enters barefoot as a mark of respect, seating himself on the ground where it has been spread with a carpet and cushions near to the couch: meanwhile the master of the house, who generally sits on the couch, covers himself with a white cloth from which his head projects, his hands being hidden in the folds: this is the usual manner of dress throughout the whole of Ethiopia, and is retained even when they are visited by the principal ministers and officials of the Empire. There is also a long-established custom whereby, if friends are not able to visit each other personally, they send servants to them daily to enquire after their state of health, great emphasis being placed on this ceremony.

Anyone not wearing a white cloth, though he wears three other garments, is regarded as naked rather than clothed. This is the only cloth made in Abyssinia, of cotton, and within the house the cloth is so long and broad that it could be wrapped round the body twice over; leaving the house the nobles wear beneath it long leg bands, which hang to the ground and trail behind for the length of at least half an ell: although their magnificence is thus attested, they find it difficult in walking to raise their feet high enough to advance, and they all go everywhere on muleback to avoid this inconvenience. If the weather is wet and the ground muddy, whether on muleback or on foot the mud splashes cover them with dirt, which they account as a mark of their magnificence. To the ministers and nobles of the Empire their leg-bands are like gold: made of very fine Indian cloth or other valuable material, they are embroidered with gold and silver thread, and are worth several ounces of gold. Simple ones generally cost one ounce, but are an embarrassment to the unwary, who have to lift their feet high when trailing the length of their leg-bands on the ground, and fall over as they walk, to present a spectacle to the onlookers. In the more important festivals the leg-bands are even finer and coloured red or blue, and when worn through the mud are spattered and ruined, thus proving their wearers to be true Ethiopians.

The ministers and major officials wear as well a very fine vest made of Indian baft, and above it, in Arab fashion, a small skirt reaching to the knee, or a caftan of fine material, a golden belt[3] round the waist, and on the head a white Turkish sash or cincture at least thirty ells long, which is wound like a turban in a complicated knot and makes a considerable mass on the top of the head. In addition to such costly and luxurious clothing, the whole is covered with the aforesaid white cloth or mantle, which hangs down to the ground and covers the whole body and head. We missionaries when we arrived in the Empire wore Egyptian-style clothing, and were regarded as naked until we followed the custom of the country and assumed the white cloth.

Servants and serving women when out of doors among the populace are clothed simply with a white cloth, but wear short leg bands, six or seven fingers long, to denote their status: so that in the course of their duty they can bare their bodies at the blink of an eye, their heads and feet are always bare. These cloths are of two sorts, a light and a heavier one, each being of the same value, one real or five pieces of salt: extra thin cloths, as thin almost as a spider's web, sell for seven or eight pieces. Yet another sort of cloth is worn, of heavier material again, which is used for a bed coverlet, and sells for three drams of gold, that is, for three reals, and it is is this which the great nobles or major officials generally wear within the domestic circle. When they go abroad they dress in something finer as their personal dignity demands, to the accompaniment of their retinue on foot, one of whom, the master's favourite, wears leg bands of red, which is prized by the servants above gold and all other precious materials; so arrayed they swagger as though they believed that no one could equal them, so highly do the Abyssinians value red, blue, and

[3] These belts were often extremely long, varying, according to Mansfield Parkyns, *op. cit.*, ii, 7, from fifteen to sixty yards, and were about a yard in width.

white, and prefer them to all other colours. Even more proudly do they swagger when they wear the long knife called schotel which hangs down the hip and which they display with the utmost pride; without it they go nowhere, for their evil disposition stirs them up to brawls, and for the most trivial cause one will wound another, stab him, and often murder him, in his wild anger taking no heed into which part of the body be plunges his weapon.

The Ethiopian nation particularly prides itself on its naturally curling hair, which is carefully tended and serves as a hat or covering for the outside of the head. To enhance their appearance, as I said earlier, they arrange their tresses in intricate plaits and anoint them with butter, so that when they take the rays of the sun they glisten like grass in the dew of the morning. So as not to disturb their coiffure or their curls, when they go to bed they each fix, a foot into the ground, a supporting fork, putting their neck between the prongs, and in this manner they sleep the night through with their head hanging from the fork. Some let their hair grow even longer and comb each lock so that it stands apart from the next; since most of them are of great height and elegance, jet black and large-eyed, their combed-out hair gives them a terrifying appearance as of a frightful apparition. So carefully do they tend their long oiled tresses that for most nights they sleep on their face, their neck supported on the forks I have mentioned or on the horns of a hollow piece of wood shaped like a half moon. Many dress their hair while it is black without the use of grease, but many grease it so thickly that they give the appearance of having powdered their hair like Europeans. The coiffure is regarded as more striking if the locks are tied into little plaits like tails, and let hang down separately in the shape of horns. This is the style adopted by the Queen Mother and the principals and nobles of the Empire, who walk abroad entirely covered, head and all, by their cloth, with only half their face projecting.

Since in Ethiopia neither grown men nor youths wear beards, and the sexes are dressed in the same outer garment, it is difficult to distinguish men from women, except when they are bared to the waist. This is a puzzle only with the rich; with the poor it is easy to make the distinction, because all go naked and unclothed except for a loin-cloth of skin or leather or tattered cloth, with no sense of shame. However, to perform their bodily functions out of doors they withdraw into a decent privacy, despite their shamelessness at appearing naked in public. Young men and maidens are less easily told apart, being forbidden to wear their hair long, and compelled to shave the head until their twentieth year; they go bareheaded and barefooted. Indeed the nobles themselves go barefoot at home, and only when they go outside do they take their shoes from the hand of a servant; on horse- or mule-back they ride barefooted, with just the big toe inserted into a small stirrup. Mules are almost always used during the passage of the mountains and hills, the use of horses being restricted by the riders' inability to guide them over the mountain tops, and by the stony nature of the terrain.

In the whole of Ethiopia there are no butchers shops[4] except in Gondar the imperial capital, all animals being slaughtered at home as need arises; at home also is their bread baked. Goods are displayed for sale in the market place on stated days of the week. There are no inns, all travellers through the Empire and provinces being compelled to carry with them their means of subsistence. It is their custom to burn branding marks on the whole body, especially on the chest and the face; the nails on their little fingers are allowed to grow as long as possible, in imitation of the spurs of domestic cocks; indeed they sometimes cut the spurs from off the bird, and fit them to their own fingers. To add to the ferocity and awe of their appearance they stain their hands and their naked feet with the juice of a particular bark which turns from white to red: this is squeezed from the bark into jars in which they soak their hands and feet for several days until they take on the unusual red colour which is so prized.

All the nobles lay great emphasis on a large retinue of servants,[5] and appear in public in the midst of a crowd of people, such that

[4] Three-quarters of a century later the French Saint Simonians Combes and Tamisier likewise noticed that Gondar was the only place in Ethiopia where butchers were to be found. E. Combes and M. Tamisier, *Voyage en Abyssinie* (Paris, 1838), iv, 85–6.

[5] Pearce, writing little more than half a century later, observed, *op. cit.*, ii, 193–4, that there was 'no country' he had seen where people were 'so fond of displaying their dignity, as in Abyssinia'. Elaborating on this statement he added, 'When a chief goes either to court or to church, he has a whole body of armed men to attend him; on a visit he has the same, and indeed men of the lower class, who have only one servant or soldier, are followed by him with his spear or shield wherever they go, should it be only on necessary business within their premises. Every person who owns a little landed property, that may bring him in at most to the amount in cloth or salt of one hundred dollars per year, is always seen with five or six shieldsmen close behind him, and perhaps a matchlock or two in front of him'.

a European would think that an immense expense was being incurred: it is in fact very small, each servant being provided with never more than a double garment costing a dram of gold, or imperial, along with surri[6] or cloth leg-bands one span long; if deserving cases are given an extra garment, for annual salary, this is a special reward and only for the most part paid to the servants of the greater nobles. The rest for their clothing and annual salary have to be satisfied with two garments, and, as the custom is for each lord to employ three or four hundred servants, one thousand garments are enough, at the cost of one thousand drams of gold or one thousand reals. Even this comes not from the nobleman's own resources, but from the imperial treasury, the nobleman being in possession of part of the imperial territory from which he yearly draws the equivalent of at least three thousand garments. Each minister therefore and each official and nobleman maintains countless servants as his train during public appearances, of a quality conforming to the territory allotted to him, all of whom when war is declared are bound to serve as the soldiers of the Emperor and to defend the Empire. The whole territory of Abyssinia is allotted to ministers and officials on the basis that at a time of hostile invasion they shall defend the Emperor and march to war under arms: the nobles are obliged to provide the soldiers with their food, at an allowance of two loaves of bread a day.

With few exceptions the common people through inborn laziness cover their bodies like beasts with undressed hide, each wearing only one, a ram's fleece, attached at its extremities to their arm or leg. They sleep on ox hide without pillows or blankets. Instead of tables they use large slabs of wood, hollowed out with no attempt at polishing, on which without cloth or napkin they sit on the ground to eat their meals. The poor use crockery of black earthenware,[7] the rich plain glass.[8] Apart from the Saracens among them there are few traders, and in few centres, the greater part of the people being engaged in agriculture. The nobles and their servants are much at war, and usually dwell at

---

[6] *Surri*, which Prutky also mentions in chapter 21, was Amharic for trousers.

[7] The use of such pottery was noted by such earlier observers as Alvarez (Beckingham and Huntingford, *Prester John*, ii, 364, 438), Almeida (*Some records*, p. 63), and Lobo (Lockhart, *op. cit.*, p. 170).

[8] Glassware was in fact scarcely used, except as bottles and goblets for drinking *taj*, or mead, which was customarily drunk in a *berellé*, or glass bottle. Lockhart, *op. cit.*, p. 171; Bruce, *op. cit.*, ii, 678; Guidi, *Vocabolario*, p. 320.

the court of the Emperor, rarely though they see him. There are no large cities, and their villages are spread far and wide, protected by no walls and quite unfortified. The biggest of their towns contains scarcely one thousand six hundred houses, and is without castles, citadels, or fortifications. The houses are small and unfloored, and are lacking in elegance, dignity, and almost in craftmanship: their shape is generally round and they are roofed with straw and clay. Letters are unknown among them, and they have no habit of reducing to writing either the decisions of public law-courts or anything else. There are no books, apart from holy writ and those containing the order of services, though the officials in charge of the treasury keep books of receipts and payments.[9]

Now for other facts about Ethiopia.

---

[9] Reference to this tradition of keeping accounts is provided by Pearce, i, 138, who, describing the presentation of dues at Antalo, the early nineteenth century capital of Tegré, notes that the local ruler, Ras Walda Sellasé, was 'always seated on these occasions upon a high gallery to receive the income, and at some distance from him are seated his secretaries, who write an account of the cattle, clothes, etc., that are brought into the court'.

CHAPTER 42

THEIR FOOD, DRINK,
AND OTHER PRACTICES

Wretched as are the wages of the servants, the food provided for them is more wretched still, and is of the simplest, at minimal cost to the master, a daily allowance of two loaves of bread and water from the stream, with an additional portion, to some daily and to some four times a week, of a thickish porridge called schiro,[1] made of a certain sort of grain; this the Ethiopians prize above all other foodstuff, and sprinkled with pepper eat it with relish, though to European tastes it is inedible. Sometimes as a treat a dish of lentils is provided, or of schombera,[2] a kind of Ethiopian pea. At the greater festivals three or four oxen are butchered for them, eaten raw in front of the entrance to the house. Apart from this they receive no other renumeration, but live as contentedly as though they enjoyed all the comforts in the world, since they would be dead of hunger if deprived of their employment, and neither know nor wish to work at anything else, only to walk abroad in company with their master, and to carry shield and lance in his service. Similarly the masters and nobles live in idleness and indolence, and are burdened with few kitchen expenses, seeing that all meat is eaten raw, and they seldom taste anything that is cooked, however hard it be. For a more formal occasion the meat is held to the fire and lightly roasted on each side until the blood runs out, when it is eaten with appetite. As even more of a treat, the raw meat is sprinkled

[1] *Šero*, earlier referred to in chapter 13, was a stew made from chick-peas, lentils, peas, etc.

[2] Amharic *šembera*, or chick-pea, a food which, as earlier observers note, was widely eaten. Guidi, *Vocabolario*, p. 205; Beckingham and Huntingford, *Prester John*, i, 100, 230, 233; idem, *Some records*, pp. 46, 53.

with the bile of an ox or cow, and the food considered even more appetizing;[3] when a guest is being honoured by the slaughter of an ox the host removes the bile while still hot and places it in the mouth of his guest, who swallows it with enjoyment and thanks his host for the favour he has done him.

I described previously how serving men and maids were given two loaves of bread a day: these are not made of wheat or other corn, but of a certain small seed called teff,[4] which is of two sorts, white and black, like mustard or poppy seed, and which grows most abundantly throughout the Empire. The Ethiopians prefer it above all else, the masters eating the white kind and the servants the black: it is prepared by grinding the grain into flour, adding a little cold water, and shaping the dough into thin rounds of about two spans in size, like cakes: this is placed on an iron circular pan on the fire or hot coals, and when one side is done it is turned over to the other and cooked quickly: it is sourish in taste, soft, about half cooked, and insipid: but it is big enough, and doughy, and the Ethiopians swallow it twice a day. Very often curdled milk appears on the table; this they eat freely, with an admixture of pepper, together with their bread, after which they turn to drinking. They have the custom each morning, about 9 o'clock, of paying each other visits, when they are regaled with raw meat and tacz, and not content with one visit they go on to pay three or four more, until they return home well filled with food and in a state of drunkenness; when the lunch hour comes around they again fill their stomachs. To an outsider it seems extraordinary to eat so much raw and bloody meat, seasoned always with quantities of pepper and bile, which is believed to assist ingestion.

Tacz, the usual drink in Abyssinia, is excellent and extremely healthy: it is made of water, honey, and a certain root called *taddo*.[5] Six parts of water, one of honey, and one of this root make a most strong and enjoyable drink; left for five or six days

[3] Almeida observed that 'the most important people' had gall added to their meat, and claimed that it gave it 'a great relish'. Beckingham and Huntingford, *Some records*, p. 63. See also Lockhart, *op. cit.*, p. 171; Parkyns, *op. cit.*, i, 376–7.

[4] *Teff*, *Eragrostis Tef*, referred to in chapters 13 and 29. The pancake-like bread is cooked only on *one* side, not on *two* as Prutky asserts.

[5] Amharic *saddo* or *taddo*, the shrub *Rhamnus tsaddo*, Guidi *Vocabolario*, p. 863. For other recipes see Beckingham and Huntingford, *Some records*, p. 64; Parkyns, *op. cit.*, i, 383.

to ferment in the sun, the scum rising from the honey is skimmed off, and the wine tacz is sealed with clay in an earthenware jar; as it is already well fermented, the jar is opened after six more days, and the result is excellent, like muscatel wine, so warm and strong that the Ethiopians after three or four glasses become extremely drunk. The strength comes from the root taddo, and the pleasant taste from the excellence of the flowers from which the honey is made. Throughout the whole empire it is widely appreciated, and the more gladly consumed for the pleasantness of its taste: it is preferred above all other wine made from grapes. To such stupor of drunkenness do men and women attain that they lose all sense of decency and modesty of social intercourse, and if their potations are prolonged they are not ashamed openly to relieve their bodily necessities into the same vessel from which they drank;[6] the glass is then emptied, but not washed, and refilled with tacz, whereupon they continue to drink themselves into unconsciousness. They make a sort of beer,[7] which they do not know how to brew, and which is very muddy and tasteless and has a purgative effect; they will toss off three or four glasses at great speed and come to no harm, but a European tasting it would suffer from colic or other impairment of health.

Servants seldom drink while they are eating, but are given to drink when the meal is over. Officials and ministers drink as they will, both between and during meals, for which the table is set near the couch of the master of the house. As they seat themselves on the ground, there is set around them, instead of plates, piles of at least thirty loaves of teff, with raw meat in the centre of the table, of which they eat vigorously: yet the lords touch no food with their own hands, a naked slave or slave girl charged with this task being placed in their midst, who feeds each of the guests in turn. She kneads the bread in her hands to make it flexible and soft with a sauce of fat, curdled milk,[8] and ground pepper,

---

[6] Though Bruce, op. cit., iii, 242, 301–5, and others describe 'bacchanalian' banqueting scenes at length this practice is not mentioned by any other observer, and would seem improbable.

[7] Beer, known in Amharic as talla (Guidi, Vocabolario, p. 791), is described inter alia by Lobo (Lockhart, op. cit., pp. 171–2).

[8] Probably a reference to yoghurt, which, though well known in recent times, does not seem to be mentioned by travellers prior to Prutky. The use of 'clotted milk' flavoured with either pepper or honey was later reported by Parkyns, op. cit., i, 381.

while the drops of fat fall from her fingers, a sight nauseating to European eyes. She then with her hands shapes long gobbets of about a quarter of a pound in weight, and with her dirty fingers places them in the mouth of each guest in order of importance,[9] until she has used up all her gobbets in repeated turns: satisfied so far after at least four gobbets, the guests grab at the raw meat, one holding it for his neighbour, and with their knives called schotel cut it into pieces: they hold in their mouth as much as they intend to swallow, cut it off from the joint, and swallow it down one piece after another until they are replete: the meat being raw is impossible for them to chew.

If the guests are people of real importance they sit like graven images and eat nothing with their own hands. The half-naked slave girl presides over the feast, shapes her dumplings or gobbets from the materials mentioned above, a finger in length and about half a hand in width, and puts them in the mouths of the nobles, who swallow them down in concert until their mouths are so full that they can hardly draw breath. Often, when their gullet is so full that they can hardly swallow, the girl strokes their neck with her hands as they sit there motionless, and assists them to do so: this therefore is their notion of the height of luxury, when their mouths have been stuffed so full that it is difficult or impossible for them to swallow, to have a slave to assist them to move the food from gullet to stomach: the meanest peasant in Europe would condemn such behaviour, and blush to take his food in this manner. Often when I sat at the tables of the chief ministers of the Empire I was disgusted to see them sitting round like swollen pigeons, waiting their turn for their mouth to be filled. Sometimes the pieces of food are too large for them, whereupon the girl cuts them up into smaller pieces so that they can be swallowed down more easily. To pay a particular compliment or show especial respect to someone, an ox's foot, for example, is put to a hot fire and roasted a little on each side: this as it were roasted meat is eaten with great relish, and is called *teps*.[10] If they are still not replete they again draw their schotel and cut off on

---

[9] The practice of being fed by servants had earlier been noted by Lobo, who states that the nobles never touched their food, for each had a page, 'who could properly be called a 'gentleman of the mouth', for he put mouthfuls of food in it, the greater quantity at a time the better'. Lockhart, *op. cit.*, p. 170.

[10] *Tebs*, or roasted or fried meat, described in chapter 24.

the table great lumps of raw meat, called *brundo*:[11] one end of
the meat they hold in the mouth, the other in the hand, and
cutting it into pieces eat it up with greater appetite than ever:
satisfied at last, they rise from the table and sit at the edge of the
room, leaning against the wall while they thirstily drink draughts
of their beloved tacz. As more and more friends arrive, so they
sit down to table and eat up in the manner just described the
pieces of bread all stained with blood from the meat, until all
have had enough and move on to another house. Friends and
companions too pay each other the compliment of personal
feeding with such delicate morsels.

At the time of some festival, for which guests have been invited,
both men and women consume enormous quantities of drink,
the men being almost outdone by the women, who spend most
of their time within their own houses without knowledge of
housecraft, their whole day spent in idleness and the company
of visiting men; they keep their throats continually wet with the
drink which they find sweet and delightfully to their taste, and
their feasting is so prolonged that they end up mistresses of the
drinking art. Whether at home or invited elsewhere, they are
adepts at emptying their glass, and any European would gladly
give them best, even if they have not openly befouled, as I earlier
recounted, the vessels from which they have drunk. Sometimes
the more modest women call for a servant or serving maid when
they need to relieve themselves, and are afforded some degree
of privacy by the cloak that covers them, but the noise and the
smell are by no means excluded and are enough to sicken a
modest disposition. In the same way when one friend visits
another and stays with him for a long time, the custom is to lie
on cushions on a couch, and then, when they need to relieve
themselves, to sit naked with their white cloak over them and,
no excuse offered, make use of a disgusting chamber-pot: this
happened to me myself many a time when I was visiting both
the sick and the healthy, and the smell was such that often I was
on the point of swooning. Let not the reader be surprised, or
think it an invented tale, when I recount of the very aunt of the
Emperor, with whom I was a favourite, and who often honoured
me with her presence, together with her different attendants,

[11] Amharic *brendo*, or raw meat. Guidi, *Vocabolario*, p. 324.

that it happened once that she was in the room with me and ordered to have brought to her a wash basin given to me by the Emperor and decorated with mosaic: I had supposed that she wished to see the basin, but quite against my expectation she put it on the ground and sat on it, and thought no shame to use it to relieve herself: when I went to withdraw myself, to avoid watching her, she took me by the hand and said 'Let be, doctor, do not withdraw, this is common to all of us.' If this brought no blush to the cheek of a royal personage, what are we to think of the rest? In Abyssinia there is no sense of shame, the customs are worse than animal, they are a set of peasants, far removed from true human reason. It is fair to say that so far I have travelled by land and sea in three parts of the world, in Europe, Asia, and Africa, and I avow that I have never found men so barbarous, inhuman, uncultivated and sinful as the Ethiopians, who eat raw flesh and are for that the more barbarous and the more like to beasts than to men. From the raw flesh come different bodily ailments, worms, foul breath, and indigestion.

CHAPTER 43

WORMS AND THEIR MEDICINE

The raw flesh so beloved of the Ethiopians, and so much to their taste that they never touch cooked or roast meat, is the cause of severe stomach disorders and of large intestinal worms, two inches long and half a finger in thickness: once each month the Ethiopians suffer great distress from these worms, and when the time arrives for dosing against them they make their presence known by appearing either through the mouth or in the privy. Warned by this sign the natives reduce to powder the flowers, called *cosso*,[1] of a particular tree which grows freely in the woods of the Empire, and mix eight drams of powder with a glass of tacz: eating and drinking nothing at lunch time they take this draught in the evening, and for the whole night until 5 or 6 a.m. they purge themselves vigorously, with constriction of the bowel until the blood runs, and lie exhausted and almost dead from the huge quantity of worms which they have evacuated. After a short rest they arise and take a dish of their usual food, a porridge made of schiro with a good sprinkling of pepper, the flour of the schiro being yellow like pea flour and very beneficial against worms; despite their previous weakness caused by their purgation, they immediately revive when stuffed with this food, whereupon they strengthen themselves with a drink of tacz and again eat of raw flesh to complete the cure. It is furthermore the custom for each servant to be presented by his master at the time of this major purgation with two cups of tacz, because they suffer severely from thirst at that time, and drink deeply when visiting

---

[1] *Kosso*, or *Hagenia abyssinica*, was the most popular taenicide in Ethiopia. Pankhurst, 'The traditional taenicides of Ethiopia,' *Journal of the history of medicine and allied sciences* (1969), xxiv, pp. 323–30; *idem*, 'Europe's discovery of the Ethiopian taenicide Kosso', *Medical history* (1979), xxiii, 297–313.

their friends: then once again they strengthen themselves with raw meat, and convalesce even faster if they can obtain some hot ox bile for seasoning. This is the monthly cure for worms in Abyssinia, and the traveller through the provinces on business or for other purposes provides himself with a supply of cosso powder, lest he be unfortunate enough to die (as has happened) or at least to suffer severe pain. As well as cosso there is another medicine available, a round seed called *encoco*[2] which being swallowed eliminates the worms by vomiting but without acting as a laxative. Similarly the bark of some trees, whose names I do not know, is boiled in water, and the juice drunk, to cure by vomiting both intestinal worms and other illnesses.[3]

They have no knowledge of venesection or of reducing the flow of blood, and are without lancets: under pressure of necessity they sharpen the blades of iron knives and two of them raise the vein in their fingers while the third makes a cross cut through it with no margin for error, as though he were cutting the neck of a chicken: the veins are then sprinkled with a particular sort of dust, and bound up.[4] Sufferers from venereal disease, which is very common in each sex, are cured by medicinal waters; morning and evening the patients go down to the running streams to wash in the cold water, and both men and women are cured by repeated baths; especially famous is a stream two days' journey from Gondar which flows down through the gold mountains, and in which a bath for eight continuous days will generally restore sufferers to their former health:[5] they return home attributing the whole of the good effect to the gold content of the medicinal water.

Other infectious diseases, apart from these and the ones already noted, are not found in Ethiopia: cases of plague are not

---

[2] *Enqoqo*, or *Embelia schimperi* also known as *Combretum acuelatum*, a drug traditionally often used in the treatment of taenia. Pankhurst, 'Traditional taenicides', pp. 331–2.

[3] Two Ethiopian medicinal trees the bark of which was used in the treatment of tapeworm were the *musena* (*Albizzia anthelmintica*) and the *basanna* (*Croton macrostachys*). Pankhurst, 'Traditional taenicides,' xxiv, 330–1, 333.

[4] Bleeding and cupping, according to later observers, were both frequently practised in Ethiopia. Pankhurst, 'Historical examination of traditional Ethiopian medicine and surgery', *Ethiopian medical journal* (1965), iii, 185.

[5] Perhaps the thermal baths at May Čilot by the Angerab river north-west of Gondar. M. Rava, *Al Lago Tsana* (*il mar profondo d'Etiopia*) (Rome, 1913), pp. 38–9. L. Usoni, *Risorse minerarie dell'Africa orientale* (Rome), pp. 477, 479.

recorded, and other poisonous illnesses are not known. The Ethiopians declare that the evil actions of demons are often encountered, who proceed in the night-time through different streets, and kill whomever they meet by blowing in his face, or at least do him an injury. For this reason no one will go out of doors at night on his own at any price, and, if the urgent command of the Emperor insists, a number band themselves together and advance like troops against the enemy. The further superstition is that this demon stalks through the houses, and whomever he finds sleeping alone he severely wounds, or murders, and therefore no one dares to sleep alone but always with someone else, if not with a friend then with an animal, a cat, dog, sheep, etc. They sleep with someone else because if the demon comes he kills the animal and not the man. I learned from my own experience how firmly the Ethiopians cling to this superstition, when I sent one of my servants to take care of some lambs that I had been given at a house some distance away: in the night a lamb had chanced to bleat, and next morning my servant arrived and said to me: 'Well, master, if I had not spent last night in the company of that lamb, I should now have been dead and done for.' I impressed on him how ridiculous and unbelievable this was, but could by no means persuade him out of his opinions. Their indoctrination with this false belief enables the Devil to tempt them into much sin, for three or four sleep together unclothed, putting one of the cloaks which they wear by day on the ground beneath them, covering themselves with the others, and lying asleep joined together two by two like frogs: often in the absence of one of the company they make a sinful excuse of it to bring in girls instead, with whom in the same way they warm their naked bodies under the covering, and commit sins without number: this way of sleeping is practised by all servants, the young men joined together with the women: the masters sleep quietly on their couches, which in Arabian fashion are spread with a coverlet and decorated cushions.

In the morning when they arise they never mark the forehead with the sign of the holy cross, since they have not the custom of prayer, nor of washing the face, nor of forming the sign of the cross. They make out that the demon would get into the water if they washed their face in it, and would do them various sorts of harm, and blow in their face as they washed. The same belief is mostly strictly observed by monks, ecclesiastics, and individuals of the laity, men and women, who keep their faces ever stained by dirt and sweat marks and their foreheads plastered with mud and dust, never wiping off the filth or washing themselves, treating dirt as though it were a badge of honour and as though it added to their reputation. Their hands by contrast they wash most scrupulously before and after eating and often during the day, and they frequently wash their feet seeing that they go barefoot. Their heads are seldom combed, only when they dress their hair, which then remains untouched for six or seven weeks, until the coiffure is somewhat disarranged and the curls tangled, when to renew their elegance they twist their hair variously into bunches, and appear for one or two days as though they were wearing horns, until they again dress their head and treat it with a comb. That is the reason why they never touch their hair with their hands, but dress the hair over the forehead with long thin pronged combs, with which in case of necessity they can scratch their heads.

These facts and others related in different chapters reveal the customs of the Ethiopians. Now I turn to their various plagues.

CHAPTER 44

THE SWARMING
LOCUSTS OF ABYSSINIA

During the time that I was making myself well enough known among the Ethiopians, and engaging the governors and provincial rulers in friendship, I was particularly assisted by divine favour in that the Empire, they declared, was notably free of any plague of locusts, so that our own arrival at Gondar was regarded as a fortunate omen.[1] For seven years previously most of the provinces had been troubled by a severe plague of these creatures, who ate up the crops of fruit and grain, reduced the trees to nothing, cast a shadow over the brightness of the sun, and in a space of two or three hours appeared in dense clouds which raised no small noise and struck horror and perturbation into the country. When with my two colleagues I began to implant the true faith in Christ and to lead the people to the knowledge of God, in the very first month the locusts began visibly to diminish, falling noisily from the sky and emitting a most horrible stench: at this the people declared that the Deity was appeased,[2] and just as for seven years the locusts had brought untold loss and destruction, so at this time God was seen to have shown pity and to have turned away his anger, blessing abundantly the increase of the field, the fruit-trees, the crops, and other necessities of life: each of them gave praise to Almighty God, and rendered thanks a thousand-fold for his manifest goodness

[1] A major invasion of locusts had taken place in the spring of 1749 as mentioned in the royal chronicle which states that a great famine resulted. Guidi, *Annales regum Iyāsu II et Iyo'as*, p. 154.
[2] Alvarez and Lobo had both earlier reported circumstances in which the coming or disappearance of locusts had been popularly associated with the pious or evil character of foreign priests and missionaries. Beckingham and Huntingford, *Prester John*, i, 132–7; Lockhart, *op. cit.*, pp. 191–5.

that for many months they had been free of this noxious insect. This gave us missionaries a wider field for sowing the word of God, and for eight continuous months we were left in peace, our hopes high, to water God's vineyard into greenness, to assist the first flowering of the springing shoots and plants of the holy faith, and to await a good crop and fruitful harvest for God of souls who for so many years had laboured under the yoke of the ruler of Hell, and were now to be plucked from the jaws of tyranny.

Little at that time did we reflect on the wiles of the cunning Enemy, who is ever greedy to devour precious souls and drag them down with him into the pit: little did we think, I repeat, of experiencing delay in propagating the Gospel, but, alas and alack, the machinations of that cunning Foe, fearful that a rich prize would be snatched from him, stirred up a faction against us to bring about our death, or at least our expulsion from the Empire, and stimulated the Ethiopians once again to shake off the easy yoke of Christ, which they had again assumed. A spark beneath the ashes soon burst into a great flame, which flared up everywhere against us, and they were intent on driving us from the Empire or, in their usual way, on stoning us. Buffeted by this great storm we begged God for help, to calm the tossing waves and return peace to the spirits of the natives: but all was in vain, their desire to encompass our ruin only increased, until God heard our sighs, and, perhaps to reduce the rebels to obedience, unleashed on them unexpectedly so great a quantity of locusts that royal Gondar, the whole city of which is built to cover two large mountains, was covered with flying locusts in size resembling small crabs, which darkened the sky, and the noise of whose passage struck all men with horror.

Noonday being my time to visit the sick, I was walking through the countryside and crossing the fields, when the locusts turned day into the darkness of night, and in perturbation of soul I pondered on the punishment of God. Horror seized me and my limbs trembled as I heard the lamentations, cries, and groans of men, and saw the locusts falling on the crops and the fruit, as they flew at a height of about half an ell and raised a great noise and an offensive smell. In a moment everything was eaten up, the land, crops, plants, trees, all were left empty, and the cries and lamentations of the people struck such grief to my heart that a swoon overcame me and from the bottom of my soul I felt pity for them. This feeling was the more sincere in that many well recognised the wrath of God, and that it had been aroused by their rebellion against us, while they openly confessed that the Divinity was angry with them. They declared for their part that the cause of the evil was the prosecution of those who sowed the seed of the divine Word, that while the missionaries were left in peace the people soon felt that God was pleased with them, and that now they were about to feel the wrath of the vengeance He was exacting on behalf of the missionaries. Many of them had already been instructed in the true faith and realised the danger of lingering in their old ways, and that the plague was a sign of God's unappeasable wrath against a nation that had so often proved itself treacherous and resistant to the Holy Spirit. Although they refused to hear the voice of the Almighty preached by us, the groans and lamentations of the people stirred the heart within me, and I marked each happening in turn and recommended the people to Him, Who for man's salvation had sent us into the empire of Abyssinia, while all the while I noted God's punishment made manifest.

It was then that I saw the people catching locusts and eating them raw like crabs, and in answer to my expression of surprise was told that they were good and delicious:[3] no longer therefore did I remain in doubt about the literal interpretation of Matthew iii. 4 about St John the Baptist, seeing that to this day the Ethiopians and the people of Schanckalle regard the locust as a delicacy, and that it was to be a food to the Jews, as promised in Leviticus xi. 22. Not only the poor but also the rich in Ethiopia regard it as a treat, and Father Josephus de St Angelo of Toulouse in his *Gazophilatium Persicum* recounts exactly what I saw, that in Arabia one and all eat locusts with great enjoyment, and keep them for months cooked in a little water with salt and vinegar. To assure myself of this I myself tasted them, cooked in vinegar,

---

[3] Locust-eating in Ethiopia was far from general, and was carried out only by peripheral groups or at times of the most acute hunger. The Muslims of Tegré for example were later reported by Samuel Gobat to have been 'fond' of eating these insects, which they collected in 'great quantities'. The Christians on the other hand ate them only in times of scarcity, and when they did so the priests imposed a 'terrible penance'. S. Gobat, *Journal of three years residence in Abyssinia* (Ashfield, Mass., 1850), p. 393.

and found that they tasted like crabs; and but for an understandable feeling of nausea I would not have refused to eat more of them. Many of the ignorant used to say, and even to write, that St John's locusts were not in fact locusts, but plants, or leaves, or roots, which in the desert were called locusts: they wished to correct St Matthew, and went so far as to say that they were crayfish which St John fished out of the Jordan; but the truly learned refute these suggestions, and take the word locust in its true sense and literal meaning, and if so holy a man as St John the Baptist really ate such creatures, why should we be surprised at the Ethiopians and Arabs eating them?

Father Franciscus Alvarez[4] chapters 32 and 33 wrote the truth when he described how the locusts swarmed in such quantity as almost to cast the sun into eclipse with their thousands of bodies, and how they covered the earth and ate up all things, so that neither grain nor bark nor shrub remained. The swarms in Ethiopia are usually called clouds, their flight is like a rushing wind, they bring noise and disturbance to the woodland trees, and, if of a bluish or ashen colour, the largest of them are as big as the European sparrow. The fathers of the Society of Jesus, in the appendix to their account of Ethiopia in the year 1607 and 1608, p. 324, described how the locusts swarmed into the trees, so that the branches broke under their weight, and how, if in flight they hit a traveller on the head, the man would fall down as though hit by a stone, a proof of their great size.

When God sent a similar plague to Abyssinia on account of the enormity of their sins, its terrible destruction was plain to see, whatever plant, grain, fruit, or crop was visible was eaten up by the locusts, not the slightest plant, leaf, or bark was left, and only naked trunks were to be seen. Nothing remained but wails and lamentations of men, women, boys, infants, the lowing of oxen and draught animals and the bleating of sheep struck desolately upon the ear, and in the whole land of Abyssinia such misery was to be seen, as would have softened even the heart of Pharaoh. You should see, dear reader, what I have experienced, all the roads filled with men going as it were into exile, men and beasts together dying wretchedly of hunger, though the land is rich and can be sown with seed every month, but because the

---

[4] Alvarez, see Beckingham and Huntingford, *Prester John*, i, 132–7.

locusts fly from one place to another, the corn has all been devoured: no other way have they of sustaining life but to collect up these same devouring locusts, strip off the legs and wings and cook the body, or else dry them in the sun and keep them until later, when in time of need they will be thankfully eaten. In Sennar and the neighbourhood they roast them in the fire, and eat them like birds as a delicacy. The eating of this insect was unknown in earlier ages to the less learned, I might almost say to the ignorant, who found nothing on this subject in other writers, and therefore wanted to amend the passages in Matthew iii. 4 and Mark i. 6 or to supply an alternative reading, and to understand, in place of locusts, plants or roots of the desert, or I know not what, or the tips of leaves, or other plants, or even crayfish which St John ate in the wilderness. All these suggestions are now rejected by men of learning, and the meaning of locust is taken in its literal sense. Nor should there be any question as to whether they are safe to eat: I have read in so many learned authorities, and I have myself proved by experiment, that the eating of them did no harm either to me or to any healthy person, nor among the sick have I found any cases where they did harm. There are indeed authors who explain the passage of Numbers xi. 31 by substituting locusts for the quails found in the text.

CHAPTER 45

OTHER BEASTS

In addition to the misery inflicted on the Ethiopians by the plagues of locusts devouring their substance, they are also frequently devoured themselves by wild beasts, which are present throughout the Empire in large number. Every day great destruction is caused by lions, who beside depredations on sheep, oxen, and cows, often prey on humans themselves: nowhere throughout the province does anyone dare to walk alone without a lance, and it is always in united parties and with a loud clamour that men roam the woods and valleys, and yet experience difficulties in driving off the lions, who themselves unite in groups of twenty or more, and in search of food attack the cattle and smaller wild animals.

Abyssinia abounds in oxen and cows of two species, one to cultivate and till the land, the other for the transport of goods throughout the Empire: this species has no horns apart from soft tissue which hangs down from the forehead as though broken. There is yet another species kept for human food which is extremely fat, as big as two European oxen, and is reared always on the milk of two or three cows: this variety has horns of very great length, of a volume sufficient to contain twenty German pints or at least twelve Italian measures of liquid.[1] As there are some provincial governors who own two or even three thousand such oxen and as many cows,[2] the Emperor gains a considerable

---

[1] Lobo had noted that some horns were 'remarkable because each one carries as much as fifteen *canadas*, and the Abyssinians use them as flagons in which to carry wine when they travel'. Lockhart, *op. cit.*, pp. 167–8. For an engraving of an animal with such horns see H. Salt, *A voyage to Abyssinia* (London, 1814), plate op. p. 259; Pankhurst and Ingrams, *Ethiopia engraved*, p. 106.

[2] Lobo had earlier reported that some Ethiopians owned 'many thousands' of cattle. Lockhart, *op. cit.*, p. 167.

revenue from them, seeing that a tenth part[3] of the herd accrues to the imperial treasury, the royal mark called *Tuccus*[4] being branded on the hoof.

Just as in Egypt there are many camels, so in Abyssinia they are infinite in number, and finer and larger: they are of great value in the Empire, but because their favourite terrain is the sand and soft earth, they are of more value in Egypt than in Abyssinia, which is rocky and mountainous; often when climbing mountains they fall under their load, and, unable to arise, groan miserably: they are therefore little suited to Ethiopian conditions.

Crocodiles are everywhere, and prey on humans who are off their guard. Eighteen ells in length and with short feet, they run fast enough, but their onrush can easily be evaded by running obliquely, first one way and then another. They are dark in colour, have a double row of teeth, small but very noticing eyes, and an armour of hard scales which are impervious to shot or to spear, and can only be pierced by a skilful lance blow below the belly. On the sandy shores of the Nile they lay their eggs, eighty at a time, from which the young are hatched by the heat of the sun: the eggs are coloured blue and speckled, and are of the size of small goose-eggs. Just as the crocodile is the foe of man, so in the same river Nile there lives a particular sort of tortoise, two feet long, which is the sworn foe of the crocodile, and whose instinct it is to leave the river, scrape the sand from off the crocodile eggs, and eat them, while tramping underfoot what they are unable to consume. If the crocodile appears at that moment, the tortoise retreats into its shell and pretends innocence: the crocodile, unable to kill the tortoise for its shell, throws it angrily into the Nile, and the tortoise escapes in safety.

Huge serpents are not uncommon, of horrific size, of which Deodatus (*sic*) Siculus[5] Bk. iii. p. 169 wrote long ago that he had seen one thirty cubits long which had been brought alive, at great risk and some expenditure of skill, to king Ptolemy in Egypt: 'seeing that a serpent of such size has come to be seen by so many, it is not reasonable to deny credence to the Ethiopians,

---

[3] This tax of one-tenth of each herd had earlier been mentioned by both Lobo and Almeida. Lockhart, *op. cit.*, p. 167; Beckingham and Huntingford, *Some records*, p. 88.

[4] Amharic *tukus*, or 'burnt in'. Guidi, *Vocabolario*, p. 369.

[5] Diodorus Siculus is the name intended.

or to regard as fables what they so frequently assert'. He also recounts that in his part of the world there are serpents so large that not only do they devour oxen, bulls, and other animals of that size, but even provoke elephants to combat. Dapperus in his description of Africa heading *Quagga* p. 394 says: 'The serpents, or *minia*, are so thick, long, and strong that besides other animals they can kill even a stag, and swallow him whole'. He repeats this under the heading *Angola*, where he says that the people of Angola call this serpent the *embamma*, that it swallows whole pigs, goats, and even stags, and that it is in the habit of lying in the road pretending to be a dead branch and attacking men and cattle who pass by: it is of such thickness that it can scarcely be encompassed by both arms, and travellers often suppose it to be a dead tree and take their rest by it, to their own serious harm. Other smaller snakes lurk in hollow trees, spring suddenly down to attack passing men and animals, lap their coils around them, and strangle them. The natives of Abyssinia for their part wear long knives[6] along the thigh, and when they find themselves or an animal in the coils of the snake they deal it a sudden slash towards the tail and free the prey from death. Wounded, the snake falls off the prey, but if left alone with it, it constricts the prey until the bones are broken, and swallows it up. Wherever it crawls over the earth or sand it always leaves its mark, a circle of three or four feet: because I personally have seen neither the one nor the other, I recount, without commitment, what other writers have described and the Ethiopians have told me. It is said that similar snakes are to be found in America and in Guinea, twenty feet in length, and that when the natives see them they drag logs of wood around them and very skilfully destroy them by burning.

It is wonderful in this country to see the number of wolves and the quantities of bears, while the apes, as big as bears, band themselves together in great herds and with their noise strike horror into the hearts of the travellers. The *Mammetelit* is a very fierce beast that I have already described, and there are others

---

[6] Bruce, *op. cit.*, iv, 148, writing of the Guragés in Bagémder, recalls that they tied to their elbows 'a long, straight, two-edged, sharp-pointed knife, the handle reaching into the palm of their hand'. The whole blade was 'safe and inoffensive' when the arm was extended, but when it was bent, about four inches projected, and was 'bare beyond the elbow joint'.

OTHER BEASTS

that I have noted here and there: there are many other wonderful
things in Abyssinia which would be worth recounting, but because
I was only in the Empire for such a short time and was fully
engaged in the saving of souls, it was impossible for me to pay
more attention to the various wonders, nor was I able to travel
the great distances of that huge Empire, partly because of human
bandits, partly because of the wild beasts, but partly because I
had to win over the hearts of the people; in that mission of
shifting fortunes, and among a treacherous people, I set my face
firmly towards labouring in works of charity to my neighbours,
both within doors and without, and when I was called to more
distant parts my efforts were directed to curing the sick in order
to reap a future harvest of good will. In the little time remaining
to me I will set this out in the next chapter.

CHAPTER 46

HEALING THE SICK

For a long time my converse was solely with the Emperor, so that I was unable as I wished to be of service to the people, but when permission was at last given and the news of our presence made known to the whole nation, sufferers from different diseases came in to me from all parts, clamouring before my door for help, and raising their voices to heaven to beg for my assistance. That my attention to the unfortunate invalids should be the readier, we all three celebrated the Mass secretly at dawn, to leave ourselves freer to tend the sick, and as I had noticed that almost all the Ethiopians suffered from inflammation of the blood from the great quantity of pepper that they daily consumed, and were full of worms caused by their diet of raw meat,[1] I performed operations for phlebotomy in preference to all other treatment, and from 4 a.m. until noon I laboured in nothing else but the cutting of veins and the application of cupping glasses: within three days I counted three hundred and fifty people, who had been some of them cured and some of them relieved of different complaints, in most cases aggravated by too hectic a flow of blood. In the treatment of bruises and countless wounds, in the daily application of plasters, in the care of those suffering from cancerous palsy or unusual forms of venereal disease, by the grace of God's mercy I restored to my patients their former health.

These included three recommended to me by the Emperor as friends of his, and I quickly restored them to their hoped-for state of health: one of them, mere skin and bones, had been unable to leave his house for the last three years, and suffered

---

[1] Almeida had earlier noted that the prevalence of tapeworm was due to the widespread custom of eating raw meat. Beckingham and Huntingford, *Some records*, p. 98.

from gangrene to the whole of one leg and half the genitals: the flesh eaten to the bone and crawling with worms, the stink of his illness was nauseating from afar off, but because the Emperor had introduced him as a friend I made every effort to cure him. I swooned at the sight of him, and the stench coming from his palsy was so odious that my bowels moved within me, but the Emperor's order was so imperative that I put my hand to the task despite my repugnance, and began to cleanse his bruises, wash out his gangrene, and apply active treatments to the diseased areas: after a few days I lost all hope of curing his condition, and besought help of the Almighty, whereupon, by the work of the celestial Doctor, within the space of two months I healed his gangrenous leg, to the general amazement, so that he joyfully approached the Emperor and declared that the cure effected by the doctor had been more divine than human. Another of the Emperor's ministers, who for more than a year had been unable to lift arm or leg, implored my help for his paralysis and ulcers, and was restored to health within four weeks. Another patient was a monk, the whole of the rear part of whose flesh, beginning with the ribs, was gangrenous and full of worms which had eaten to the bone, and whose blood was scorbutic: surprisingly the stench from the former condition was more severe than from the latter. From this condition he had already suffered for several years, but since the monks had it in their power to be of great help, and of great hindrance, to us, it was essential for me to give all possible attention to his case, and for the good name of the Mission I called on God for His assistance and applied plasters, despite my natural repugnance. But behold the mercy of God, Who ever hearkens to true prayer, within the course of but three weeks I observed new flesh to grow, before which the gangrene receded, the patient moved his limb and raised his foot, and within the space of two months I had achieved my object. Who was it but God Who aided me with invisible hand? I also effected another cure, that of a woman of the royal family, for two years past put away by her husband because of her wretched state of health, who with tears besought my help with confidence in its effect. When I saw how serious was her malady, for decency's sake I held my peace about it, and politely excused myself as being unable to be of use to her, as I had no wish to stir up trouble or ill-will for myself among the royal family, and tried to avoid the necessity of treating her. But when shortly I was summoned by the Queen Mother[2] and strongly recommended to take the patient, willy-nilly I undertook the case, and, thanks to God's omnipotence, without Whose help I embarked on no treatment but to Whom I ever heartily prayed, I produced medicines for the royal personage to take, and a few days thereafter never dreamed that the condition was beginning to improve: but messengers now called on me with the joyful news, declaring that I, the least of doctors, had cured the lady of her sickness, and, while it seemed to me scarcely credible, the sick lady herself appeared to render me her thanks. As I had told her to continue with her medicines for a little time longer, it was not I but the mercy of God that had cured her, Who in this way was strengthening the foundations of our mission.

I omit details of many other cases of patients restored to their former health, as a result of which we made many friends among a host of people and were presented with a broad field in which to discourse on the elements of the faith, until the hope of an even richer harvest gleamed brightly before us. But alas, within and without the palace we were well esteemed, we enjoyed the thanks and favour of the Emperor, we could enter the palace at will, we were on terms of friendship not only with the monks but also with the nobles, and were continually honoured by their attendance on us: we began cautiously to preach the Catholic faith, and, finding many of them desirous of embracing it, we deemed the harvest ripe enough and on the point of bringing forth fruits worthy of Christ's sufferings, so that many souls would be reunited within the bosom of the holy Roman church. Weighing matters carefully, we decided to postpone our pious intentions, and bring them into effect only when our own standing within the Empire was more firmly established, considering the recent cases of rebellion there; but little did we suspect the evil outcome of our hopes, and how the Enemy of mankind had not ceased to sow his tares among our crop, and, seeing and foreseeing the great prize that was about to be snatched from him, was spreading untrue slanders about us among the people and wrongly imputing falsity to the Catholic faith. His special instrument was the heretical Coptic archbishop, vice-gerent in Abyssinia

[2] I.e. Empress Mentewwab.

of the Patriarch of Alexandria, and our particular enemy, who willingly joined himself to the conspiracy against us, especially as he saw us entertained within the imperial palace and loaded with gratitude, while he by contrast was hated for his ignorance and was little regarded at court. He left no stone unturned to provoke the people against us, and with falsehood and injustice aroused and embittered them, until the whole Empire was of his faction.

CHAPTER 47

THE PERSECUTION
OF THE MISSIONARIES

As I said previously, the empire of Abyssinia is under the despotic rule of the Emperor, who allots all his lands and provinces to his ministers at his own discretion, a redistribution being made every year at the feast of the Exaltation of the Cross,[1] when he confirms or removes from office and changes one minister for another. Since the youthful emperor Jasu had only reached the age of eight when he ascended the throne, his mother the Queen divided out the provinces among the chief ministers in such a way that, at the time of my sojourn there, the Emperor, now over thirty years of age, saw his treasury diminished and scarcely enough for his ordinary expenses,[2] and began to rule more prudently. He took the provinces out of the hands of his mother and her ministers, had their tribute paid to himself, and resolved to put down certain evil practices of long standing and bad habits that had crept into government. Starting with his own sister, who ruled the heathen province of Godgiam and retained its revenue in her own control, he ordered to be paid into the imperial treasury both her tribute, and that of the Queen Mother and of the other ministers, whereupon the injured parties became disaffected and were driven to action: his sister, with snake-like deceit, took the leading part, and began to arouse the people with the old slander usually attributed to the Catholics, that our eucharist is composed of pork fat and dogs' brains, and that her

[1] *Masqal*, as noted in chapter 27, was also the time when taxes were paid.

[2] On Iyasu's death in June 1755, only three years after Prutky's departure, the treasury was almost empty. The chronicle states that, when Empress Mentewwab ordered gold to be brought to give to the churches and monasteries to pay for her son's funeral commemorations, no more than 80, or in another version of the text 20 dinars, could be found, for the emperor had 'wasted his riches'. Guidi, *Annales regum Iyāsu II et Iyo'as*, p. 182.

brother the Emperor had turned Frank and Catholic, had par-
taken of this with us, and was now the same as we. This odious
statement aroused the whole people to anger, urged thereto by
the Coptic archbishop, who had other good reasons to hate us.

This prelate should properly be called not a shepherd but a
wolf who devours the sheep. As I have already said, he was
trapped by a trick of the Turkish power in Cairo and sent to
Abyssinia against his will by the Patriarch. Uninterested in sound
doctrine, he was chosen or rather appointed to his post despite
himself, and refusing to obey was put into chains below his robes
and force-marched into the interior of Ethiopia by way of Gidda.
He spends his whole life in useless fretting and is totally lacking
in spiritual gifts or pastoral ambitions, his time is devoted to
amassing wealth and to drinking and eating, he possesses no
store out of which to dispense gifts of charity, and none of his
revenue can be conveyed outside the Empire, or even sent to his
brothers in Egypt, because of the intervention of the Turks and
Arabs, who would steal all he tried to send. Having been installed
by force at the Empire's expense, he performs no function but
the conferment of holy orders and the ordination of priests,[3]
which he carries out willy-nilly on whoever presents himself to
him, with no enquiry or further investigation of morals and
suitability, as canon law requires. And alas, the style of ordination
is only too suited to the character of the participants in the rite:
in the case of the minor orders and the subdiaconate the appointment is made without further preparation, simply by reading
them the Epistle for the day, while for the ordination of deacons
and priests the candidates touch the missal, the archbishop reads
to them out of the gospel and breathes on them, they each kiss
the gospel, and depart home to perform the offices of the church.
In confession all are accepted, and absolution is granted without
previous confession, contrition, promise of amendment, or imposition of penance, and when on occasion a sinner is grieved by

[3] Bruce, *op. cit.*, ii, 317, notes that the Abun's 'greatest employment' was
ordination. Describing the ordination of deacons he observes that 'a number of
men and children' presented themselves at a distance, and stood, 'from humility,
not daring to approach him'. He then asked who they were, and they replied
that they wanted to be deacons. On hearing this, after making two or three signs
with a small iron cross in his hand, he blew with his mouth twice or thrice upon
them, saying, 'Let them be deacons'. For an earlier account, by Alvarez, of mass
ordination, see Beckingham and Huntingford, *Prester John*, ii, 349–52.

the remorse of his own conscience, he himself imposes his own penance, generally the giving of alms or other works of charity, or burying a roadside corpse, or having one buried at his expense, or taking into his entourage some youth cast out by his own parents. In the belief that such is sufficient atonement for their sins, and in ignorance of the elements essential to penitence, the flock receives no priestly instruction and lives in blind ignorance, to bewail at once their own unhappiness and that of their negligent shepherd. Apart from such pastoral work as ordination entails, the reverend Archbishop performs no other function, since it is solely to that end that he has been impressed into Abyssinia, and he bows to the will of his barbarous flock: his life is devoted to the sensuous gratification of temporal vanities, he makes no effort, himself a sinner, to win over to himself the affections of his erring people, he rarely or never reads Mass, he leaves his home for public appearances even less, and the Abyssinians show him little or no respect,[4] seeing that this was now the seventh year of his office and not once had he offered his people any spiritual food or exhortation, or learned the Ethiopian language: no course of study interrupted his leisure, he lived to fill his purse and tend his belly, and he was pronounced to be useless by his people, whose greedy slave he was. It follows from this that, on his death, all that remains of the wealth he has amassed becomes the hereditary property of the Emperor.

This then was the exemplary guardian of the flock, as the wolf is called, who, envying us our favour with the Emperor, leagued himself with the Emperor's disaffected sister and with the populace, and frequently sought audience, under the cloak of religion, with the Queen Mother, who was zealous in support of her sect, and was much respected by the Ethiopians. She gave some encouragement to his murmurings, but ever referred their remedy to her son the Emperor, to such effect that for six continual months we foiled all the plots of our enemies and enjoyed the toleration we so needed: we gained the Emperor's permission, the more easily to do our work in his lands, to have four cells constructed in his palace, monastic style, wherein to perform our own religious offices, which up to now we had duly

---

[4] Bruce, *op. cit.*, iii, 317, took a similar view, declaring that the Abun was 'much fallen in esteem from what he was formerly, chiefly from his own little intrigues, his ignorance, avarice, and want of firmness'.

celebrated, but always in secret, at about two or three o'clock in the morning, where we besought divine aid in the conversion of this barbarous people. So great a concourse of each sex frequented our abode, seeking not only to be cured from various bodily ailments but also to be instructed in the teachings of the faith, that we were listened to with earnest attention as though we were apostles and men sent from God. But the harvest was not yet ripe, nor our position in the Empire placed on a firm footing, and it was necessary to proceed with caution and to keep secret our converse with the people, our especial care being directed towards engaging the interest of the Emperor. The Almighty in his mercy so blessed our medical efforts, and so many were freed of the burden of such different ailments, that we secured the affection not only of the people but abundantly of the Emperor.

Summoning me to a private audience the Emperor revealed to me his inmost desires: to secure the spreading of the faith he wished to send me as his ambassador to the Chief Pontiff, then Benedict XIV,[5] to request the help of soldiers from Europe against his unruly people, so that when these had been returned to their proper obedience he could with more assurance declare himself the obedient son of the Roman church, and he gave me such reason to hope for the future conversions of himself and of his whole empire that he filled our hearts with the great spiritual consolation, that within a short time so vast an area as the Abyssinian empire would be united to the holy Roman church, and subject to the rule of the supreme Pastor Jesus Christ. Although in retrospect the complications of the journey, the distances covered, the dangers of the sea and the depredations of the infidel gave us cause for anxiety, yet all was set fair for the saving of souls, and the task must be carried out in a spirit of joyfulness. When the heavy rains had ended, at the end of September 1752, I had to journey afresh through the deserts, mountains, hills and whole country of Abyssinia, through Arabia Felix, the Red Sea, Arabia Petrosa and Deserta, across Egypt, Cairo, and the Nile, take ship again at Alexandria through the archipelago to Leghorn, until finally I arrived in Rome.

But the judgments of God are manifold and like the bottomless pit. As high as the hopes my heart had previously nourished, so

---

[5] Benedict XIV was Pope from 1740 to 1758.

low did I plunge into desolation, and life was a burden to me. Quite unexpectedly, on October 2 of that year 1752, in the morning, I was summoned to audience with the Emperor and received the sad news that we must leave the Empire with all speed. The Emperor's own words were: 'My dear doctor, I am grieved to my heart, but must urge on you all a speedy departure, because my disaffected subjects are in revolt, and, unless I send you away immediately, intend to murder me and you together. For a long time now there have been murmurings against you among the people, though always so far happily stifled. The whole Empire cries out that you are uncircumcised, and that your beliefs are in conflict with ours since you assert the two natures of Christ. No longer can I contain the rebellion that has arisen, especially since the archbishop has received from his patriarch letters of grave importance, which urge him to demand your expulsion, and threaten me with excommunication unless I banish you from my dominions with all speed.' The Ethiopians fear excommunication more than all else in the whole world, and it was the threat of this which caused the emperor to ask us to depart.[6] 'If I am excommunicated' he said 'all my people, my ministers, and other most faithful friends will desert me to display the purity of their faith, and I shall be left alone: when my enemies come, if I had three heads they would murder me.' The poor Emperor was in consternation, and complained that he had never thus far experienced the like, that as soon as the rains had ended the province of Godgiam would rise against him, and would murder him and us together. 'Go, go quickly away, and save your own head and mine with it.' At these unexpected tidings I was so struck with dismay that I could hardly utter a word, but gradually calming and recollecting myself I replied 'Your Majesty's words are hard, and I am unable to make an immediate reply to sad news to which I have not yet reconciled myself: I will consult with my colleagues about this weighty matter,' with which I withdrew.

Scarcely had I reached our quarters when the royal Treasurer appeared, at the Emperor's bidding, to urge our departure from the palace within eight days at the most, and to encourage us

[6] This echoes a statement by Lobo, that the Ethiopians had 'a great fear of excommunication' since their monks and clergy were 'very free with it'. Lockhart, *op. cit.*, p. 178.

with a present of gold: I replied that our journey to the Empire had been undertaken not for the love of gold but to win precious souls for Christ, and that not for gifts, nor for treasure, would we depart from it; that next day at Mass we would commit this difficult problem into God's hands, and then give to the Emperor our considered reply. Before dawn we offered to the Almighty the bloodless sacrifice of our doubts in this new crisis, and the sun had barely risen when the Treasurer appeared for our answer, whereupon we were one and all inspired by the divine light to reply bravely that we would rather die a thousand deaths than depart without the knowledge or command of the Supreme Pontiff of Rome. When our feelings had been relayed to the Emperor we received no further warning to leave, but continued to till the Lord's vineyard with no interruption to our peace, to conversation with the Emperor, or to the visits of the people: just as before I attended his presence at least twice a week to comfort him, and basked in his thanks and prime regard, with never a mention made of our departure, so that a whole month went by in peace, and we rejoiced exceedingly that the anger of the people had been appeased; this being confirmed by the royal Treasurer, we were firmly convinced that there was nothing more to be feared from this rumour. We were then nearly approaching the solemn Ethiopian festival of November 12 called Kuskuam,[7] which I mentioned previously, out of regard for which the Emperor is accustomed to make no controversial move, but, alas, when this was over and we returned to Gondar, we were for a second time warned to depart, by another minister. Our hearts were filled with even more grief and desolation than before, when we were informed that we must abandon all further hope of the Emperor's favour or of bringing souls to salvation, and that all further entry to the imperial court was forbidden us: yet on this occasion also I stood firm, and replied that, despite his formal order to quit the apartments in the palace which had been in the beginning so kindly granted to us for our dwelling, our obedience was impossible, because this was the season of fasting prescribed by the rule of our seraphic order, and because the celebration of the Nativity was at hand; for these reasons I refused

---

[7] The festival of Qʷesqʷam was actually held on Hedar 6, or November 2 of the Julian calendar. Ludolf, *Commentarius*, p. 397.

to depart, but undertook, when the feast was over and the grace of the Holy Spirit invoked, that we would quickly put into effect what our hearts had decided.

We now fortified ourselves against the coming trials by zealous prayers and daily masses, and earnestly begged God's help, often paying secret visits, early and late, to the graves of the three venerable martyrs on Mt Abbo,[8] where we prayed that the popular tumult might be stilled and the rebellion have a favourable outcome. We were well aware that our stay in Ethiopia would be of not much longer duration, and that either we should be forcibly expelled from the Empire or stoned to death after the custom of the country, which gave us a surer hope of winning the precious crown of martyrdom that we had lost in Egypt. After a number of trials and tribulations, at last for the third time on December 1 we were ordered to leave the imperial palace and then to depart the country, and this not at the word of a minister, but insultingly through a message borne by a slave: him I told to his face that I refused to go, but that I wished on the next day, December 2, to present myself personally before His Majesty, and although I received no reply from the Emperor I betook myself to his residence at Kaha, a half hour's distance from Gondar: audience was at first denied to me, but I obtained it eventually, approached his presence undismayed, and after the usual homage addressed him thus: 'Most august Emperor, despite this our third warning, we are neither able nor willing to depart without the agreement and permission of the Supreme Pontiff of Rome to recall us: whatever it pleases you to do with us we care not, and we will endure all evils rather than depart at the command of the Emperor or in the face of popular revolt. The festival of Christmas should be kept within the home, as the assent of the Emperor must confirm and as our Saviour teaches in Matthew x. 40. *He that receiveth you receiveth me.*'

At that time I said no more, but being given leave to depart I returned to our quarters, and found no words to praise enough the divine Omnipotence Who had endowed us with strength against such turmoil and distress within the Empire: for three months now we had withstood the Emperor's expressed wishes,

---

[8] Abbo, one of the principal churches of Gondar: see map in Bruce, *op. cit.*, iv, op. pp. 138–9, and Pankhurst, *History of Ethiopian towns*, pp. 146, 169.

had held our ground within our own dwelling despite so many orders to the contrary, and had shown ourselves ready to endure want, hardship, and the hatred of the whole nation rather than besmirch ourselves by disobedience to the Supreme Pontiff, so contrary to the rules of our seraphic order. Well did we know that through the ages there is no known instance of missionaries penetrating any part of the world who then retreated therefrom of their own volition; we knew too of how the holy apostles were driven, nay flogged, out of one city gate, only to re-enter it by another, and of how the first sainted martyrs of our seraphic order, flogged out of Morocco and expelled into Christian territory, had returned once more and freely preached the gospel of Jesus Christ, without fear of torture or of the fury of tyrants, and intoned to themselves the words of our Saviour (Matthew x. 28.) *Fear not them which kill the body, but are not able to kill the soul: but rather fear him which is able to destroy both soul and body in hell.* With such thoughts in our minds, there was no hope for it but to prepare ourselves for a hard trial, and to consecrate ourselves as instruments of divine law, so that our souls should remain unspotted before their just Judge, and in the eyes of the pastor of the universal Catholic faith.

Our minds were further set on the martyrdom of the three glorious members of our sacred order, who were martyred in Abyssinia, in the city of Gondar, on Mt Abbo, on February 21 (old style) or March 3 (new style) of the year 1716.[9] Three in number, just as we were, despatched as we by the Sacred Congregation, the superior was Venerable Father Liberatus Veis of St Laurentius an Austrian, and the others Venerable Father Michael Pius of Zerbo an Italian of the province of St Didacus, and Venerable Father Samuel of Juno (*sic*) of the province of Milan. Seized at a time of persecution by the rebellious people, their hands tied behind their backs and their clothes torn contemptuously off them, they themselves were taken to Mt Abbo, a journey of two Italian miles from their dwelling, where with a brotherly embrace and on bended knee they fortified their courage by the words of the apostles and commended their souls to their Creator. Then one of the Abyssinian monks, appointed

---

[9] The execution of the three missionaries had earlier been referred to by Prutky, in chapter 15.

to the task, seized a stone, and cried with a loud voice: 'Cursed be he, and excommunicate, and the enemy of our religion and of the Blessed Virgin Mary, who throws not five stones against these condemned enemies of our faith and of the Blessed Virgin Mary.' With these words, amid a congregation of many thousands, the monk was the first to cast a stone against the three dauntless friars, whereupon the entire remainder of the mob covered them with as it were a flood of stones, until at the third hour of the evening they were crowned on Mt. Abbo with the crown that does not fade. The dwelling place of the venerable martyrs was in a place called after the Holy Trinity,[10] on a beautiful and large mountain called *Mida Bolos*:[11] there on a pleasant site they built a suitable house of which the ruins are still visible, and when I was led thither by the parish priest I saw another house built in the Ethiopian style: the situation was delightful, the air sweet, and the position ideal for men of religion, with good water, a variety of trees, and sweet-scented medicinal herbs. Surveying these relics of our predecessors, we hoped to be rewarded with a similar crown.

On December 9 we received our fourth, and strictest, injunction to depart, to which I replied that it was the duty of princes to hold fast to their word and not to break their promises, and that because the Emperor had assented to our celebrating in Gondar the feast of the Nativity of our Lord, I refused to go. On the next day, December 10, I besought an audience, which was refused, along with the prospect of any further, but I replied to the youth who acted as messenger that I was unable to depart until I had laid before the Emperor what he ought to hear. After a further delay I was at last admitted into the imperial presence, and after the usual marks of homage addressed him as follows:

'Your Majesty yesterday again gave us strict orders to depart, orders which I can in no way obey, believing as I do that the word of a king is unchangeable, and the more so that it is that most sacred festival of the Nativity of our Lord that we earlier obtained from you permission to celebrate here, as Christians and as priests. It is not the custom for Christian princes to pronounce a boon at one time and revoke it at another, but the

---

[10] Probably the famous church of Dabra Berhan Sellasé which stands on a hill east of the imperial city. Bruce, *op. cit.*, iv, map opp. pp. 138–9.

[11] Possibly Méda Sellasé, or Field of the Trinity.

voice of a king in the ears of his people should be as the voice of God, true, just, and serious – or so it is in our own country. Your order is the more remarkable, in that, not only in Cairo but also in the island of Messaua beside the Red Sea, we received from Your Majesty letters full of good will, which invited us to your Empire and promised us every sort of imperial favour, help, and grace, and that for all our life long we should dwell in safety in your Empire, under your firm protection, and should be the beneficiary of all sorts of imperial privilege. Relying on the truth of this promise, we recked nothing of all the perils of the journey through deserts and seas, or of the trials and persecutions of men, and we held of no account the hunger, thirst and other bodily discomforts which we had to endure, but came promptly and obediently to join your service, and embraced your Majesty as our lord and right worthy king. In this very place, where your Majesty now sits, you many times promised me to my face my absolute safety, and equally, up to the present time, you have loaded us with favours, which God in His riches will reward. How comes it then,' said I, 'that now Your Majesty withdraws your sacred promise so that my two colleagues and I must now say that we *obey not the king, but obey the law*? On this day I call Heaven and Earth to witness, as I hold my hands on high, I call to witness this place where sits Your Majesty, I call on the mountains around us and on all the elements, that, just as before our faces the Ethiopian people can show no excuse for their conduct nor you avoid our condemnation, so shall it be before the just judgement of the Divine Majesty. Let Your Majesty know, since this perhaps is the last time that I shall be permitted to address your presence, that before God I have no wish to incur blame for negligence, and that I protest that you have not trodden that earnest and true road to eternal salvation, that in these times can be found nowhere but in the Roman Catholic faith, outside which there is no salvation. I fear greatly that you Ethiopians may hear with sorrow the words of our angry Lord in Matthew xxiii. 37. *How often would I have gathered thy children together, even as a hen gathereth her chickens under her wing, and ye would not.*'

So I spoke to the Emperor as though for the last time, as he sat on his couch instead of on a throne; I cared nothing for what I said, speaking what the zeal of the Lord dictated, Who declared, *I also will laugh at your calamity*. I told the Emperor to his face:

'One day, O Ethiopians, you will groan to yourselves, with grief in your hearts, *When I could I would not, and when I would I could not.* Now is the acceptable time, now with our appearance the day of salvation has dawned, it is wrong to fear the rebellion of one's people more than the wrath of God: if a just king is threatened, he is not overthrown.' On his expulsion of us from his kingdom I plied the Emperor with the story of how the Adversary had to be expelled from the kingdom of Heaven by our Champion Jesus Christ: 'Though you call yourselves Christians, you do injury in Christ's name. Your Majesty has received from God the power of ruling your Empire with justice, and will have to render a strict account of your rule, seeing that neither Justice nor Faith is maintained, that all crimes and evil doings go tolerated and unpunished, all men freely turn their hand to what they will, and it is Your Majesty alone who will answer for all men before God's throne. There are many in the Empire who have an active hope of conversion, and who will weep at our departure; who will answer for so many thousands souls who could be converted and returned to the bosom of the holy Catholic church? Your Majesty alone will have to render a strict account. Now for the fourth time are we being pressed to go, and pressed to leave the precious souls of your subjects entoiled in the net of the Devil, and once more I solemnly declare *The earth is the Lord's* (Psalm xxiv) and not yours. I undertake that we will depart, but not from the Empire, only from your imperial dwelling place, lest, as you put it, you incur on our behalf the anger of your barbarous people leading to your death at their hands. But from the earth of the Lord's we will never depart, but will put our firm trust in His mercy, that we shall be preserved even among your wild beasts and animals of the forest: to the heathen shall we turn ourselves and to the wild beasts, preferring them to those that profess and call themselves Christian. But before we depart from you, we will in accordance with the sacred text shake off the dust from our feet against you, as a perpetual testimony of your coming damnation: you are like the Jews, who in times past resisted the holy Ghost, when St Stephen rebuked them *Ye stiff necked . . . ye do always resist the Holy Ghost,* Acts vii. 51: you are *like unto whited sepulchres, which indeed appear beautiful outside, but are within full of dead men's bones, and of all uncleanness.* Matthew xxiii. 27.'

316

Growing warm against him I now dragged the shoes off my feet and shook off the dust before his face, saying 'Are you not now sated with the blood of our brothers, stoned to death on Mt Abbo? Here before Your Majesty I bend down and submit my neck to you, ready, along with my colleagues, to die a thousand deaths in witness of the Catholic faith, the only road to salvation, which, if in the past my words were too feeble to implant by preaching, yet now am I ready to spill my blood upon the ground to nurture to harvest. Here stand I before Your Majesty, who has the power to murder me, fearless of the raging of the angry people, and pondering the grace of our merciful God, Who sent out the Apostles into all parts of the world. *Their sound went into all the earth, and their words unto the ends of the world*, Romans x. 18: and although we missionaries are but their feeble successors, yet were we sent out by the successor of Peter, Jesus Christ's vicar Benedict XIV, to publish throughout the whole world the gospel of truth, which we preach to Turks, heathen, idolaters, pagans, and others who receive us into their lands, and who gradually learn of us to accept the easy yoke of Christ. Only you, O wretched Ethiopians, justly cast aside by God for your continual sins, expel the missionaries, the sowers of the word of God, and trample the heavenly message beneath your feet: for you were written the words of the holy Matthew x. 14. *Whosoever shall not receive you, nor hear your words, when ye depart out of that house or city, shake off the dust of your feet.*'

To these words, harsh indeed, was I inspired by the Holy Spirit, and I spoke them out without respect to man, and in a flame of inner indignation. I hoped and expected nothing but the anger of the Emperor and the attainment in Abyssinia of that crown of martyrdom which had been denied me in Egypt: or confinement in the most wretched of prisons. But contrary to my expectation the Emperor sat still as a stone and heard out in all patience my railing upon him, replying gently. 'Depart, depart, I can help you no more.' In a further reply I declared that we would depart from his palace, but not from the country, which was the Lord's, and repeated the text of Matthew x. 18, 19. *When ye shall be brought before kings and governors for my sake, take no thought how or what ye shall speak: for it shall be given you in that same hour what ye shall speak.* Continuing our discussion I said 'Your Majesty has seen that we have no fear of death, and are

317

ready to die rather than leave your Empire until we have received letters of recall from the Supreme Pontiff.' Weighing up all factors, the Emperor, naturally inclined to mercy and kindness, showed his private goodwill towards us but was powerless to help us in face of the groundless fears that beset him. His affection for us was demonstrated over a long enough time, in view of our four months' refusal to leave his palace, and, uncertain what to decide, he took frequent counsel of his Treasurer, and would gladly have kept us within his Empire if he had not feared the pressures of his barbarous subjects. At length his formal conclusion was that we should be expelled only from royal Gondar and not from the Empire, and he fixed on the province of Tigré as our place of banishment, until the rebellion died down and the reply from Rome was received about our recall: in Tigré we should enjoy the imperial grace and favour in the manner to which we had been accustomed.

This conclusion was brought joyfully to us by our friend the Treasurer, in the expectation that we should quickly assent to such a mark of favour, but we were cautiously inclined to reject it, in case it concealed some private piece of trickery, suspecting that from that province, so close to Messaua, we could be treacherously seized and handed over to the Arabs as slaves. But thinking over the other side of the question, and the likelihood of exposing to further peril from his treacherous and barbarous subjects the merciful Emperor who was truly our sympathizer, we agreed forthwith to withdraw from Gondar to that province for a short time, under definite conditions, and to avoid any possibility of personal deception I humbly prevailed upon the emperor to have summoned to him, in my presence, the governor of the province concerned, the Bahr Nagasch.[12] Him the Emperor ordered to protect us, to supply us with the food we needed, to care for us assiduously in place of the Emperor, and to shield us from any danger to life. All this was done, and we were further gratified by an imperial letter of confirmation sealed with the official seal,[13] so that our anxieties were relieved and we were sent away with quiet minds to our usual dwelling; on December

[12] Bahr Nagaš, the ruler, as noted earlier, of the province between the Marab river and the Red Sea.

[13] For the history of this seal and of Arabic inscriptions on Ethiopian seals, see Pankhurst, 'Ethiopian royal seals', pp. 406–12.

12 I received the promised letter to the following effect, written in the Ethiopian or Amharic language, bearing the ancient seal of a lion holding a cross, and stamped with the words *The lion of the tribe of Judah is the victor*:[14] at the Emperor's wish this had been newly engraved in Arabic characters, and denoted the praise and honour due to God.

In order to justify the results of our stewardship, I have set down the meaning of that letter not only in the Abyssinian language but also translated into Latin.

[14] On the use of the Lion of Judah on seals see *ibid.*, pp. 397–401.

CHAPTER 48

THE EMPEROR'S LETTER
OF EXPULSION IN THE
ETHIOPIAN LANGUAGE

[1] *Mczaf Malecketh Zenegus Iasu, tebdech habe Abba Remedius, ua Abba Martinus:* [2] *Ana Negus Cristian, ua Eslam, baent hackack hazb azez behailea, Kama Tehuru, u sta hagaria Dobarua, heja tehaderu escka Jemedcza maczhaf malacket em habe Leicka, ua rasa Papasat Romani, kama tetmajatu usta hagargemu:* [3] *asme i kabarckemu eckuja habkemu bahr Nagasch mablea, ua masti. Czanta quulu Ena Negus Cristian, ua Eslam Jasu esame backelaja, u bamachtameja.* The translated meaning of this is as follows:-

'The letter of King Jasu, addressed to Father Remedius and Father Martinus. I king of the Christians and Turks, because of the insurrection of my people, enjoin on you most strictly that you go to the province of Dobarua, and there remain until the arrival from the Roman pontiff, the chief and head of the bishops, of his letter recalling you to your province: but since you have not been guilty of any wrong actions, the Bahr Nagasch, the governor of that province, will supply you with food and drink.

---

[1] *Mashafa mal'ekat za-negus Iyasu tasaddat haba Abba Ramédiwas wa-Abba Martinus ana negusa krestiyan wa-eslam ba-enta hakaka hezeb azzez ba-hayleya kama tehuru westa hagarya Debarwa heya tahaseru eska yemasa'e mashafa mal'eket em-habaliq wa-re'es papasat romawi kama tetmayatu westa hagarkemmu esma. i-gabarkemmu ekuya yehabkemmu baher nagaš mabel'a wa-masti zenta k*ʷ*ello ana negusa krestiyan wo-eslam Iyasu esme'e baqalya we-ba-mahtamya.* For the Ge'ez text see O. Raineri, 'La relazione fra chiesa etiopica e chiesa romana (Lettera di Remedio Prutky missionario in Etiopia nel 1752–1753)' *Nicolaus* (1980) viii, 360.

[2] Martin Lang (d. 1759) was a Czech Franciscan who accompanied Prutky on the latter's visit to Gondar and produced a brief report on their travels. Z. Maly, 'The visit of Martin Lang, Czech Franciscan, in Gondar in 1752' *Journal of Ethiopian studies* (1972), x, No. 2, pp. 17–25.

[3] In Ge'ez *hagar*, or 'country'.

All these things I Jasu, king of the Christians and Turks, confirm with my word and seal'.

We received this letter of safe custody, but as there were still fifteen days to run before the Nativity of our Lord this seemed to the Emperor a long time to await our departure, so that on Christmas Eve he sent us yet another message to depart; on my disregarding this I received a second, and then a third, severe injunction to go. When with my colleagues I still refused to budge, we were summoned to the Treasurer's house and duly appeared there, together with the imperial messenger, who pressed for our departure, but I still remitted to the Emperor a negative reply, that we would not quit his palace until, according to his promise repeatedly made to us in the past, we had completed our Christmas celebrations. However, after we had kept Christmas peacefully we were again ordered by the Treasurer to depart, whereupon we recommended to God the whole outcome of our exile, took with us a few prime necessities leaving all the rest in store with the Treasurer, and, having celebrated Mass, departed after noon on the feast of St Stephen Protomartyr, with grief in our hearts at the trials awaiting us outside the royal abode. Like sheep lost among wolves, like children who have lost their father, we tearfully declaimed Psalm 122 *I was glad when they said unto me* as we trusted in the Lord, and firmly believed Psalm 126 *they that sow in tears shall reap in joy*. The people flocked to watch us go, many of them cursing us but many sharing our suffering, so that it could truly be said *He that goeth forth and weepeth, bearing precious seed* (Psalm cxxvi).

As we crossed Mt Abbo, stained with the blood of our three venerable martyrs, we saluted them in the silence of our hearts and prayed for constancy in the hard struggle ahead, wanting nothing more than to be united with them. We now had further cause to wonder at God's providence, since we found secret refuge against our exile by false Christians in a small town, below Mt Abbo, that was inhabited by Mahometans. Here we were taken in and remained for a whole month, unknown to the insurgent populace, in an existence of misery both of body and soul, and ever under the threat of death at the hands of the rebels. Sustaining ourselves on a little food provided by the Mahometans in exchange for medical attention, we never left our house, in case our presence was discovered and we deprived of our lives, for

we were only three leagues from royal Gondar on the banks of
the Kaha, on that side of the city of Gondar that is towards the
stream Angareb: we feared nothing so much as that our lives
might be taken from us with no gain to the Faith and no conversion of souls.

Our sojourn among the Mahometans was known only to the
Emperor, who still in our exile maintained his good will towards
us, to a few of his trustworthy ministers, and to some of our
friends, who used at times to visit us in secret, and relieved the
worst of our pangs of hunger: they showed their true friendship
in exposing themselves to great danger for love of us, often
supplied us with food, and, though they were the Emperor's
principal ministers, were ready to work against his will in supporting and visiting us. Lords Selaffi[4] Schettii,[5] Hate[6] Ailu,[7] Krijacus[8]
and many others of our friends cared nothing for the Emperor's
anger, and so intervened on our behalf that they were on the
point of incurring the punishment of exile; during all this critical
time of our exile they were being instructed in the faith that
leads to salvation, and were eager for the enlightenment of all
manner of religious instruction, becoming so enthusiastic as
repeatedly to dare to demand of the Emperor our permanent
residence in the Empire. But all was in vain, by day and by night
the people gathered in crowds in the hills, and in front of the

[4] Amharic *Assallafi*, a military attendant. Guidi, *Vocabolario*, p. 148.
[5] Assallafi Ešaté, a close relative of Empress Mentewwab, was a prominent
courtier and sometime governor of Damot who later successively held the rank
of *Balambaras, Baša, Dajazmač* and *Blatténge'ta*. He died in 1768. Bruce, who was
confused about the nobleman's relationship to the Empress, describes him
variously as her brother and as the husband of her sister, but he seems in fact
to have been no more than a close kinsman. Bruce, *op. cit.*, ii, 662, 671–2, iii,
202, 214, 533, 549, iv, 230, 694; *idem* (1813 ed.), iv, 98–9. Guidi, *Annales
regum' Iyāsu et Iyo'as*, pp. 11, 161, 165, 172, 175–80, 184, 188–91, 194, 203, 206–7,
237–8.
[6] Amharic *Ato*, short for *Abéto*, a title then given to members of the royal family.
Guidi, *Vocabolario*, p. 457.
[7] Probably Assalefi Ešaté's son Haylu Ešaté, or Ayto Aylo as Bruce called him.
He had been converted, according to the Scotsman, by Prutky's companion
Brother Antony of Aleppo, and (for a time) 'would accept no places or posts' in
the administration. Bruce states that Haylu was 'the richest private man in
Abyssinia', and together with his brother owned half Gondar. He was 'the constant
patron of the Greeks' as well as of 'all the Catholics who had ventured into the
country'. Bruce, *op. cit.*, ii, 694, iii, 199, 240, 533, iv, 68, 230, *idem* 3rd. ed. iv,
98–9, vii, 65, 67. See also Guidi, *Annales regum Iyāsu II et Iyo'as*, p. 11.
[8] The courtier Kirakos referred to in chapter 33.

Emperor's palace chanted against us *Justice, justice against the Franks*; their clamour caused us the greatest anxiety, for, if they had come to know the house where we were living, they would have overwhelmed us under a pile of stones, as is their custom.

Our worries had now lasted for more than four months, and we were awaiting a safe caravan towards the Red Sea, to which we wished to attach ourselves. As we called daily on God for help, at last two Ethiopians appeared unexpectedly, who had returned from Jerusalem by way of Cairo, and who carried letters from the Father Prefect of Egypt. These informed us of the intention of the Holy Congregation, that if our existence in the Empire was insecure, and if our lives were in peril without the opportunity to preach or to exercise our religion, it was in no way the desire of the ruling Pontiff the blessed Benedict XIV that we should throw our lives away with no benefit of evangelization, but that rather as obedient sons we should return and give him news of this ever treacherous nation, and an accurate account of its heresy, superstitions, and errors, which the Sacred Congregation has lacked for so many years; for more than a hundred years the missionaries had mostly been killed and made martyrs, and had brought back no true account of the changes in Abyssinian affairs, for which reason our return would be welcome. In obedience to the earnest wish of His Holiness, and of the Sacred Congregation for the Propagation of the Faith, we were no longer reluctant to return, and quickly made ourselves ready for the journey to Europe: but we kept it secret, lest we should fall into the hands of the rebels.

CHAPTER 49

RETURN FROM ABYSSINIA

A caravan had been collected of more than three hundred men, mainly Turks with some Christians and some heathen, and was about to set off soon to the island of Messaua, towards the Red Sea: since we were thus offered a good chance of joining it and prosecuting our journey in greater safety, we cautiously made our humble supplications to the Emperor for safe conduct, and asked his pardon for all the harm we had caused him in resisting his orders: he generously agreed to assist us, and sent a letter of recommendation in our favour to his governor in Arckicko, who was in authority over the port of Messaua. He further detailed to us two royal servants for our own safety, with strict orders to keep to the mountain paths and avoid the wrath of his rebellious subjects, lest we should fall into their hands and be stoned to death: in addition to these orders for our safe conduct he generously presented us with two mules to assist our journey, and thirty ounces of gold, equivalent to two hundred and forty gold pieces.

So on January 26 of the year 1753, amid a huge crowd of people, most of them weeping at our departure, we sorrowfully quitted our beloved friends and our sheep now left without a shepherd, and, at least in our minds, fixed our tearful eyes and grief-stricken hearts on Mt. Abbo for the last time, in farewell to the venerable martyrs our brothers, whom we besought, although we had not been found worthy to be associated with them, nor strong enough to implant in this land the seed of the holy gospel, that by their merits we might more worthily be enabled to bring forth fruits in another country, and that they would intercede with God for a ripe harvest to be stored in the barn of celestial treasures. Only He knows what trials we had had to bear in our exile for over four months, what terrors for

our safety, what want and poverty, which with all other mischances we offered to Him, Who deigns to rule, comfort and
preserve the hearts of all men, and consoles us for our weakness
with the comfort of His grace. On this day at 2 p.m. we were
handed two further letters of recommendation from the
Emperor, stamped with his ancient seal, to the following effect:
'The letter of the imperial will and command to the people of
Serai:[1] you people of Serai, send forward in peace these doctors
(that is, us missionaries) through your country, and give them
the food they need, because they are sent by us to their own
land.' The meaning of the second letter was : 'This is my letter
of command to the people of my province of Tigré, and also to
my other subjects on the way thither. You people of Tigré, send
onwards in peace and quiet these doctors to their own country,
and provide them with all the usual requirements of food and
drink, because they are sent by us.'

Encouraged by these letters, and by the thought of the many
trials we had overcome, we placed all our hope in God and
proceeded in better heart, halting on this day below the high
mountain where royal Gondar stands, beside the stream Angareb.
Here on either side of the mountain top we saw the site of the
town called *Zelancke*,[2] and between the two mountains a pair of
rivers which here flowed together, the Kaha and the Angareb,
from the first of which the imperial residence of Kaha[3] takes its
name. Here in the open we stayed the night, and sadly bade
farewell to our third colleague Fr Antony of Aleppo, whom the
Emperor was forcibly detaining so that he should transcribe an
Arabic[4] version of the holy scriptures: we two were opposed to
his being left alone in the Empire, and at first were by no means

---

[1] Sarayé or Sarawé, the highland province of the far north, referred to in
chapter 19.
[2] Salamgé, probably Eslamgé, i.e. a settlement of Muslims, 35 miles north-east
of Gondar, and indicated on the C.T.I. map.
[3] This place was mentioned by Prutky in chapter 14.
[4] The influence of the Arabic language was particularly strong in the first half
of the eighteenth century. This was a time when Ethiopian rulers used Arabic
in their correspondence with foreign powers and on royal seals, and when that
language was used in the captions of a number of church paintings. Pankhurst,
'Ethiopian royal seals', pp. 406–15; W. Wright, *Catalogue of the Ethiopic manuscripts in the British Museum* (London, 1877), p. 54; S. Chojnacki, 'A hitherto
unknown foreign painter in 18th. century Ethiopia: the master of Arabic script
and his portraits of royal donors', *Africa* (1985), xl, 577–610.

willing to obey the Emperor's wish, but alas, a short time later we received a sterner message that we should not presume to take the Father with us, as otherwise he would give orders that we should be followed on our journey and put to death, or at least that the Father should be forcibly removed from our company: our grief was the greater that we could not meet force with force, and we parted from him in sorrow.

On January 27 there appeared two princes of the royal family, Hatu Ailu and Hatu Job, who accompanied us on foot for the whole day, and who had had prepared for us an excellent mid-day meal. We then took our supper, with a good appetite, at a place called *Glickaja*,[5] when we had laboriously crossed the first of the large mountains which stretched out so far before us, while all the time they sadly bemoaned our expulsion. 'How are we now to be saved, and receive instruction in the essentials of the faith? Woe to us, with you so unexpectedly sent away who will guide our blind and miserable steps along the way of truth?' With these and similar sentiments they hung around our necks and kissed us with heartfelt sighs of grief, until at the approach of night they bade us a last and sorrowful farewell and returned to Gondar. After their departure our hearts were stricken with a grief more bitter than death, as we reflected on the lamentable loss of the conversion of so many million souls, and that, the corn now being ripe, we should have reaped a most plentiful harvest not only among the common people but also among the nobles, while especially should we have led back into Christ's fold no small number of the priests and of the men of religion, who by now were indeed well disposed towards the Catholic faith.

Deprived by a turn of chance of this new flock, we moved onwards in sorrow with the caravan towards the Red Sea, when looking backwards we beheld from afar off a horseman riding fast towards us; we took heart as we thought that perhaps we were to be recalled to Gondar, or hear something encouraging, but our desires were vain and our hopes deluded, and it was but the confidential servant of our friend and benefactor Prince Hatu Ailu, despatched for our assistance with orders to stay with us for three days, and protect us against the attacks of the natives. He brought with him some lambs and bread-flour, and provided

[5] An unidentified locality.

secure protection against any danger we might meet or any popular uprising. We spent the night in the open, and in the early morning hastened towards a beautiful stone bridge,[6] built in time past by European hands, similar to the bridge at Prague; here we refreshed ourselves in the good water of the passing stream, and started to climb a range of high mountains, dangerous for men and even more heart-breaking for mules. We halted at a place called *Argev*[7] on a little hill, where the wind blew cold enough to cut the skin off one's face, and further on in a nearby village found a bigger caravan, in which when we joined it we saw for the last time our Abyssinian Catholic Gregory Preri.[8] As he was returning to Gondar we commended to his care our beloved colleague Antony of Aleppo, and enjoined him to make every effort to encourage the spread of the Faith, and to let us know immediately if in the future there might be a gleam of hope of our return. We left in sorrow, but in the forest I shot some wild pigeon to keep up our strength, and we secretly ate some fowls.[9]

On January 29 we passed some small hills and the intervening plain, until at a place called *Tammani*, underneath the mountain, the river *Mesaal*, of sweet-tasting water, rendered our night's rest the pleasanter. On the next day we came by way of a plain to a hill with a few houses and a church dedicated to the Virgin Mary ever chaste, called *Laidera*;[10] below this were two tracts of flat land abounding with corn and watered by streams, which we crossed on this day's march and reached another hill called *Dara*,[11] beneath which is another church to the Blessed Virgin, to Whom we prayed for a fortunate journey onward. At length on 31 we crossed a plain set by enormous mountains, and spent the night at a place called *Schombera Zeckem*, where we had to be

[6] One of a number of bridges believed to have been built in the early seventeenth century during the reign of Emperor Fasiladas, the founder of Gondar. A. A. Monti della Corte, *I castelli di Gondar* (Rome, 1938), pp. 57–8.

[7] Angev, shown in the C.T.I. map as Angiva, 18 miles north-east of Gondar.

[8] Michael Georgius Preri, an Ethiopian who had studied in Rome. Beccari, *op. cit.*, 64, 220.

[9] Prutky's journey, which passed by way of several villages which cannot be located, coincided roughly with the modern road from Gondar via Lamalmo to the Takkazé river. After this he travelled more or less straight to Debarwa and Asmara, whereas the road now takes a much longer route via Aksum and Adwa.

[10] Conceivably Ledata, or Ledata Mayam, i.e. Birth of Mary.

[11] Dara, indicated on the C.T.I. map as Daro, 30 miles north-east of Gondar.

satisfied with a few raw peas, because in this area schombera is grown in great quantities, a sort of pointed pea, from which the place takes its name. On February 1 there came in sight a small mountain, but one extremely difficult for travellers who reach it late in the day's march, so that we passed the night not far beyond it, in *Gira Onz*.[12] I would not have it be understood that our night was spent as it would be in Europe, in an inn or convenient lodging, but simply in the forest or desert, in the open air exposed to the wind and the rain. There followed another plain, with a church beside it called *Arbaa Tensai*,[13] or Church of the Four Resurrections, where I saw a great number of wild geese, but was unable to shoot them for fear of the people, and had to be satisfied with the sight of them. After crossing a few more mountains we reached a place with a church called *Mackaru Jesu*,[14] or Pains of Jesus, where there were some small copses and only a moderate amount of water, scarcely enough for the travellers, since the rains last for five months and then cease, and during the other seven months the water is used up by the thousands of men and animals that pass through.

[12] Presumably called after a nearby *wanz*, or river.
[13] Presumably *Arba'e ensesa*, or Four Animals (not *Tensa'é* or Resurrection).
[14] *Makaru Iyasus*, or Suffering of Jesus.

CHAPTER 50

MT MALMO, AND THE AREA BEYOND

Of the mountains of Abyssinia the one most taxing to travellers is Mt Malmo,[1] which we reached on February 3. Though its approach is by way of a wide plain of two hours' travel, the descent of it is terrifying to contemplate and at first sight imposs-ible, since the ordinary manner of walking must be abandoned and the descent made by crawling on hands and feet and maint-aining oneself by a grasp of the rocks. Animals frequently fall off the face to a miserable death, while men have to exercise the greatest caution not to fall and break their limbs, and only by strict attention place their feet on the rocks that lie scattered about. Although the path is stony, the frequent passage of the caravans makes it dusty and sandy, and so more difficult to walk, with the result that the descent takes three hours, and leaves the travellers so weary that they can go no further but spend the night at the mountain foot, though, with the many inconveniences and extortions practised on them by a barbarous people and even more by the official in charge, they would never stay there unless they were exhausted. We missionaries, if we had not been protect-ed by the Emperor's servant, would have had to suffer even greater exactions, the wicked officials of the provinces meting out barbarous treatment to foreigners behind the Emperor's back, and although we had left all our gear in Gondar, books, medicines, copes and vestments, and carried only some cooking pots, a little flour to make unleavened bread, and a humble blanket for sleeping under, yet even on these there would have been taxes to pay. Seeing that we were feeding six servants, the Emperor's minister, and his two foot servants who acted as our

[1] Lamalmo, the difficulties of which Prutky had earlier mentioned in chapter 14.

guard, the provincial minister had no choice, when he saw how we were daily charged with the feeding of nine servants and eight mules: for the traveller across Abyssinia who is empty-handed and without possessions must needs still take mules with him to carry flour and the equipment necessary for bread-making, since no victuals are to be found by the way, and, with the forests and deserts to be crossed, the necessaries of life have to accompany the traveller. There are no inns or taverns available as there are in Europe, nor does one pass through inhabited areas, except those where the caravan is compelled to halt, in the cities of Syre and Serai, where the resident governors, or Dadaczmacz, are stringent in collecting taxes from those who pass that way, and arbitrary in their extortions. They were at that time equally anxious to exact taxes from us on our return from the country, notwithstanding the Emperor's letters that we showed them, and we were harshly treated and subjected to many trials, although we carried with us no merchandize. But they knew that we were returning from the capital and so were unable to lay any accusation against them, and instead of their obeying the Emperor's order to support us and provide us with food and drink, our bellies were left empty enough.

We were however strongly supported by our imperial escort, assisted by the aforementioned letters, and after many complications we departed thence on February 7, and proceeded further into Mt Malmo. In the first part of the day we achieved the top or summit of the mountain, and on that day descended some terrifying precipices, or, more accurately, crawled down them on all fours, for four hours continuously. At last amid the surrounding mountains we reached a small level space, and as we climbed down more and lower mountains there appeared here and there houses resembling hermitages, where we had spent a night on our way to Gondar, the whole area being called *Debbe Bahr*. In a lather of sweat we descended the side of one single mountain, which was followed by a pleasant level area, but this lasted for all too short a distance and was succeeded by the toil of another mountain, down which we had to climb. In extreme fatigue we here spent the night, this whole area of land, with its mountains, being called *Daquusit*.

Proceeding on our way, we came on the morning of February 8 to some exhausting hills down which we must climb, and although they were not high yet were they rocky and full of boulders and thorns, which tore our clothes, feet and hands. Not only did the spines and thorns tear to pieces the cloth that we, like the Ethiopians, wore as a hanging mantle in place of a cloak, called the outer caftan, but our hands, feet, body, and face were lacerated, and only our eyes preserved because we took good care that they should not be hurt. In the whole world no more wretched road can be found than this one, because although it is frequently used by caravans the Ethiopians are so idle that it is never repaired, nor the spines and thorns cut back, and the natives never learn from their own trials, and pay for their negligence in the bodily sufferings of the passers-by. At length, almost in tatters, we descended by a stream of water or torrent which flooded down the mountain and which we had to cross four and forty times: the way led down various slopes, as we crossed the stream so often, and at the last bend of the stream the caravan is in the habit of halting, even if the time is only noon. This area is called by the Abyssinians *Zazema*, where on every Friday a sort of market is held for the neighbourhood and the natives forgather with various articles for sale. While we were halted there a monk appeared of the Abbey of St Anthony, who hawked around the caravan a quantity of holy oil, called by the Abyssinians Kava Kadus[2] and by us Oil of the Sick: 'Come buy Kava Kadus', he cried, and aroused much laughter among the many Mahometans present, who said that we were selling Kava Kadus to the Christians, and that as we had brought olive oil from Gidda and sold it to the monks, there was no need for us to buy it back again.

On February 10 we moved on from there, and made a long ascent of a mountain of many hours' duration, after which we descended and were again pressed to ascend a precipice, to our extreme fatigue; descending yet again we arrived at a long reach of river, beside which we halted for the night; the whole area is called *Unzo*. Continuing on our way in the early morning of February 11, we were reluctantly faced with a huge mountain to climb, on the top of which a small piece of level ground gave us a rest before little by little we had to descend again, in anxiety lest some accident befall, and halted for the night lower down

[2] *Qeb'at qeddus*, or Holy Unction.

by a running stream, the name of the place being in Abyssinian *Ansia*;[3] on each side are high mountains, with a few small huts, while on the summit, as occurred on the day before, a number of dwellings are prominently visible, the abode generally of outlaws or robbers, who build their houses on the high ground so that they can view each of the passers by, and if they are few in number despoil or kill them, or at any rate get something from them by theft. Although our party was so numerous we were yet struck with fear when in the evening we saw a great crowd of people gathered in the upper part of the mountain, armed with swords and lances and supported by twenty-seven mules, who made as if to descend on us from above. It had been reported to them that among the caravan was the Emperor's doctor, that is myself, who was on the way to Messaua loaded with gold and musk, because they remembered a doctor of French nationality, who together with a layman had passed by here two years before myself, and believed that I was in the same situation as he. We were in considerable fear that they would murder us, although all our possessions had been lost in Abyssinia and our necessities left behind us, and we had been expelled and forced to make this long journey in great poverty, as poor as Christ Himself. However, Almighty God struck the robbers with terror and turned them back from us, and when they heard a number of musket shots fired from among the caravan and believed us to be well supplied with arms, they were deterred from attacking us.

In the early morning of February 12 we hastened up the next mountain, each one anxious to be first in case by lingering in the rear he might fall prey to the robbers. With God's help we reached the top in safety, after which a stretch of level ground was followed by a further troublesome descent, to a stream of water called *Darack-Unz*:[4] we then climbed another high hill and down again, and had as it were to repeat the process and go again up and down, until we halted at a place called *Mente-Secla*, where we gazed upon a delightful expanse of level ground covered with fine crops of corn and containing flocks of doves, of which I

---

[3] The C.T.I. map indicates a river called Inzo almost equi-distant between Lamalmo and the Takkazé river.

[4] Literally *daraq*, or dry, *wanz*, or river.

secretly shot three as a treat for our supper. In these parts we had been warned to maintain an alert and careful watch lest we be attacked and killed by the bands of robbers in the neighbourhood, it being their custom to pursue a caravan right to the furthest parts of the Empire. But God protected us on that night also and prevented any ambush, and on the morning of 13 we proceeded on our way down the side of an equally big mountain and across a stretch of level ground to reach a stream of convenient breadth: then again across a short piece of plain and up and down hill, and then across a second torrent, of barely three hands' depth, crystal-clear and with a deposit of gold in its sand; I took a draught of this water for its quality as a purifier of the stomach, and all of us were refreshed and revived for another long ascent. At the top we come to a delightful level area called *Adeckerma*[5] where we spent the night, and although on the hill-top a large village had been built, with a church, yet we avoided it because of a number of unjust exactions that the inhabitants were likely to demand, and passed the night in the open.

On February 14 we made a difficult departure, at dawn, across an easy enough level area but again through thickets of thorny scrub and spiny bushes, as I mentioned earlier, which reopened the unhealed wounds on our limbs and forced us to protect our eyes: hands, feet, bodies, and garments were torn to ribbons, the worse that our departure was in darkness for fear of the robbers, and it was difficult to see. When full light came we saw how torn and wounded we all were, and how covered with blood, but when this painful march was over we halted for the night on a hill called *Medaacia* among the shrubs of a small wood to rest and repair the damages to our persons. Scarcely had we reached the place when we heard a woman weeping and wailing for her husband, who had been mauled and eaten by lions, and of whom she showed us the feet as she dragged them along the ground. Since that area is infested with large numbers of wild beasts, it behoves the caravans to keep very careful watch, with always half of the total awake, to maintain large fires and a continual clamour. On the arrival of a caravan from nearby areas the natives give warning of the dangers of lions, tigers, and other beasts, and tell

[5] Possibly Addi Emer four miles south of the Takkazé river, as indicated on the C.T.I. map.

how within the last few days fifteen people were mauled by lions and devoured, so that everyone lives in terror; the quantity of lions, tigers, and wolves in the empire is a considerable danger to travellers. Similarly the natives told us how a few days previously two travellers were sitting under a tree warming themselves by a fire, when as darkness fell one slept while the other kept watch and lit a pipe of tobacco: while the watchman suspected nothing and remained unconscious of any animal noise, a lion crept silently up from behind, unexpectedly seized the sleeper in his ravening jaws, and leapt down the precipitous hillside to devour him, beyond the possibility of rescue. By good fortune the watchman, who was well armed, put up a stout defence against the approach of the other lion and avoided becoming his prey. Sometimes a number of lions or tigers together will attack two or three men, and maul them dreadfully to appease their hunger, for which reason it is the custom, throughout the whole empire of Abyssinia, through all the provinces and for all journeys short or long, for travellers to band together and for none to dare to walk by himself for even the shortest distance. All the travellers that I saw were furnished with lances, shields, long pointed sticks tipped with iron, and other sorts of arms, for the reason that there are even fiercer animals to be met, more especially a beast called by the Ethiopians *Mammetelit*, which has a human head but in its belly and lower parts is like a dog, and which is more dangerous to travellers than the lion.

It was February 15 when we climbed down a small mountain, and then up a similar one, with shouts from our party and much rattling of lances and swords to frighten and drive off any lions, tigers and mammetelit that might be lurking in the hollows; the way led over a mountain plateau, across two rivers, and down a great mountain, until we reached the river *Teckezy*, the principal river of Abyssinia. This is bigger than all the other torrents and rivers of the whole of Ethiopia, and in the rainy season its excessive flooding and tearing current make it uncrossable; the indolence and laziness of the Ethiopians prevent them from building bridges, and they rashly attempt the crossing at the risk of death and the drowning of many; in the month of September, when the flood is at its height, they even more rashly entrust themselves to leather bags filled with straw, which they place under the belly and attempt to swim to the other side;[6] unable to withstand the fierce current many are drowned each year, and even though strangers see this happening they flinch not from the attempt, but perish through their heedlessness of the danger that others have run; besides which, the woods thereabouts being thick and choked with thorn bushes, a number of thieves lurk there, and if the travellers are few do not scruple to rob them. The custom therefore is for several men to band themselves into groups, partly because of the evil-doers but also because of the many crocodiles and sea-horses, that is beasts with the face of a large hippopotamus, which come out of the river in the evening and injure and devour the unwary; for this reason any servant, who at night time takes animals down to drink and does not carry arms and lances, falls victim to the jaws of the crocodiles and other fierce wild beasts. For greater security it is usual for the caravan which crosses the Teckezy not to halt there for the night, but to withdraw further off to another nearby river uphill on the mountainside, where there is water and wood, and where plenty of armed servants stay on sentry duty throughout the night, throwing stones in all directions and shouting to frighten off the wild beasts, until morning comes and they prepare themselves for the onward journey.

In extreme weariness we continued to climb the mountain, huge, extensive, and apparently unending, up which we toiled panting for five hours, and reached at last a place called *Maii-Temcket*,[7] that is, Baptism of Maii; here we refreshed ourselves on a little bread and sweet water, and made good progress to *Dackaschaha* where we spent the night in utter fatigue. In the morning of February 17 we parted from the caravan, journeyed across a plateau with our servants and our escort, and climbed a pleasant hill where were a few huts, called by the natives *Degasgede*, once the abode of robbers but now cleared of them by the governor of Syre, who had executed them: although it

---

[6] The use of such leather bags to assist in a river crossing had earlier been mentioned by B. Tellez, *The travels of the Jesuits in Ethiopia*, (London, 1710), p. 196. See also Bruce, *op. cit.*, iii, 646–7.

[7] May Temqat, i.e. *May*, or water, used for the *Temqat*, or Epiphany, celebrations, indicated on the C.T.I. map as Mai Timchet. Prutky is in error in thinking that the place commemorated the 'Baptism of Maii'.

was a little out of the way it offered rest and convenience, and for the first time we slept in the society of humans, though not in a house but in our tent. The reason for this was that in inhabited areas there are unjust exactions enforced on the caravans, so that these are shunned, and it is only in the mountains and deserts that the traveller feels at all secure against these unjust impositions, of which the Emperor knows nothing.

CHAPTER 51

ARRIVAL AT SYRE,
AND OTHER PLACES

After such mountains, woods, and impenetrable thickets of thorns and spines, we reached on February 18 the city of Syre, anciently named *Confito*, which is unlike any European city. It is built without plan, it lacks walls and fortifications, it is scarcely one Italian mile in circumference, and is more like a village than a city. The present reigning Emperor Jasu dwelt here for seven years as a boy, and was secretly brought up by his mother after his father's death, as I have already described: at length he was raised to the throne by feminine sleight of hand, as told elsewhere. Not far off can be seen the old city, where once were imprisoned a number of rebels against the Emperor; now that these have been removed the old city is in ruins, and it is in the new city where now dwells the governor or Dadaczmacz, though a few still remain in the old town because of the church, which is of some size and often filled with worshippers. In this city we suffered considerably at the hands of the arbitrary governor called *Zenzelet*, who was greedy for other men's possessions and engaged in warfare with his neighbouring governor *Jeremia*, whose emissaries, sent to arrange peace terms, he had unjustly murdered. Zenzelet would hear nothing of peace but set out boldly to battle next day, to the great consternation of the people; the women fled to the mountains as Jeremia advanced at speed to punish the crime inflicted on his emissaries, and drew near the city: as these critical chances enveloped ourselves and the caravan, it can easily be judged with what terror and horror we were afflicted, since if Zenzelet were thrown back in defeat Jeremia would certainly order the city of Syre to be looted and burned, and its whole population put to death, ourselves

337

included; there was no possibility of our leaving until we had paid the imperial tribute. Popular rumour had it for certain that Zenzelet had been killed and that the victorious Jeremia was approaching with his army; though this was shortly contradicted we were greatly alarmed and were at a loss as to our course of action; our only recourse was a prayer to God, who had preserved us this far from so many dangers by land and sea, that He would of His mercy protect us in the present extreme emergency. At last in the evening in the midst of these anxieties Zenzelet returned victorious, to the applause of the crowd and the sound of trumpets and war cries, and for all that night his soldiers filled their bellies on raw beef and tacz. We ourselves after a detention of four days were given the tyrant's permission, and departed on 22 to our great relief.

Our road led across a plain,[1] beset however by some small copses of thorns and spines, which lasted for several hours, until we reached a small hill with a double village called *Sammama*[2] where we halted for the night. On the next day we had to penetrate similar thickets of thorns and spines, where our clothing, hands, and legs were torn to shreds and all our attention had to be paid to our eyes, and, when a little later we found water under a great leafy tree, we remained there for that night. Again we suffered from the natives nearby, who enforced upon us unlawful exactions, beat us about the body with their swords and spears, and threatened us with chastisement and death despite the Emperor's letters which we carried: for a whole day we suffered this, enduring cares known only to God and not here to be disclosed, so that the name of the place, *Majcka*, is engraved upon our memory. At length the intervention of our imperial escort brought us some relief, but we were despoiled of all our remaining provisions and of our flour, leaving us to seek our sustenance in what we could find in the forest. The forest however Almighty God had filled full of pheasants, for our support, and across a pleasant stream I shot a good number, though with care

---

[1] Prutky's journey continues in a north-easterly direction.
[2] This village, which was one of several which Prutky had visited on his journey from the coast as mentioned in chapter 13, was probably the Semana of the C.T.I. map.

and all due precaution lest we be observed by the intervening houses or by the caravan as we ate them. This place *Adagali*[3] is full of a variety of game, because it is forbidden to the Ethiopians to eat what they have shot, or indeed to shoot at all. A beautiful stretch of level ground, thick trees on all sides, and a supply of water, make the area attractive to game.

We meanwhile were gradually climbing into the hills, and for the second time were arrested by the barbarous and truly unjust inhabitants who wanted to levy tribute on us, but because the thieves and robbers were weaker than we, they made off. For the third time we climbed up, and then for two hours down a larger mountain, picking our way through various summits with a plateau intervening, until with great fatigue we had to descend a mountain even greater than Mt Malmo down to a stream, where we rested for an hour, and then climbed two lofty mountains to a large torrent *Gatinair*.[4] Here for the second time we encountered the refreshment of golden sand and crystalline water, sparkling with tiny particles of gold, and an excellent purgative of the stomach: a draught of this after so many worries imparted comfort to our spirits and hearts. This sand would bring enormous wealth to the Empire if the Ethiopians were less idle and ignorant, and were possessed of any skills: as it is in their heedlessness they will not take the trouble to separate the gold from the sand, and because they want to pick up lumps of gold from the ground like stones they despise that which has to be laboriously collected in small particles.

Beside this golden river we walked for the whole day, and likewise passed the night on its banks. On either side we gazed on huge mountains, of which one called *Mt Thabor*[5] is the loftiest, where once was the royal palace, of European construction, well stored with armaments to provide a sufficient defence. Here lived the father of the present Emperor Jasu, Backaffa Saggad,[6] who

[3] Probably Addi Ghella of the C.T.I. map, 30 miles north-west of Aksum.
[4] Probably the Catina river, immediately north of Addi Ghella, of the C.T.I. map.
[5] This locality, earlier referred to in chapter 13, was probably the Medebai Tabor of the C.T.I. map.
[6] Bakaffa, also known as Adbar Sagad and Masih Sagad.

however at last found the mountains irksome, and chose[7] for his capital a more spacious site, which today is called Gondar city and which was built by him before his death: and yet Mt Thabor is much the pleasanter and more delightful area, and is much better suited for the royal pastime of hunting, as well as being well planted with trees and with the fruits of the lemon, the orange or golden apple, the peach, the fig, the pomegranate, the citron, and other produce of the earth: the idleness of the natives has made of it almost a desert, and it is inhabited only by some monks of the Abbey of St Anthony, who partake of the fruits of the soil, obtained with such little labour, and the lavish produce of the gardens and plantations.

On February 25 we descended from this river through a plain, where we penetrated with difficulty its thickets of thorns and spines, which tore our clothing, legs, and arms so that we barely succeeded in protecting our eyes; it is impossible to travellers to pass this way without injury to some part of the body, and all one's attention has to be directed to preserving the eyes, the Ethiopians in their indolence entirely neglecting to clear the road of thorns or to uproot the bushes. To add to their difficulties travellers are now faced with the ascent of a huge mountain, after which is a plateau and the dry watercourse of *Majameni*, and higher up on the mountainside the monastery of the monks of the Abbey of St Anthony, where we spent an unpleasant night on our journey to Gondar, and on our return preferred to remain by the dry watercourse. Finding no grass for our animals we sent off our servants to buy food in the neighbouring village of *Schacko*, but when the inhabitants seized our servants' best lance and ill-treated and struck them, I was forced to ride there with our escort and the other servants, and had I not been well armed and clothed in a red habit, the sure indication that I was in the Emperor's service, they would have killed us all. They were however impressed by my appearance, and by the arms I carried, which struck them with terror that they might be brought as criminals before the Emperor, and they bowed down at my feet and kissed the earth, begging my pardon and offering restitution of the lance. For a long time they remained before me, praying

[7] Prutky is here in error. Gondar was founded not by Bakaffa, whose chronicle does not tell of his having any such capital, but almost a century earlier by Fasiladas. Guidi, *Annales Iohannes I, 'Iyāsu I et Bakāffa*, pp. 289–344.

me to pardon their fault and remit the punishment they had incurred, and when I had sufficiently shamed them I permitted them to retire.

Returning to the caravan we remained all day in that place, on account of the various wounds of our servants, and then on 27 we climbed a wretched mountainside that was so strewn with stones that it was difficult to find a secure foothold. Here appeared unexpectedly a messenger from a certain governor, *Michail*,[8] that I should betake myself off the road to a house in the mountain called *Adickevelet*,[9] or Ring, to give medical attention to a sick person. Willy-nilly I accepted the governor's suggestion, fearing an evil outcome and the tyranny of this uncivilized people, but was politely enough welcomed with barbarian kindliness, let blood from the patient and aided him with a little medicine, and, on his declaring that he felt an improvement, as a mark of his gratitude obtained alms from him both for myself and for the servants, left him a dose of medicine to take, and was gratefully sent on my way.

On the morning of February 28 I set out after the caravan, and with difficulty accomplished the ascent and descent of a rocky mountain to reach a stream after an hour's journey. Refreshed by a drink from it I was minded to proceed, to be met by a refusal from my impudent and barbarous servants, under the false pretext that in that day's march there was no more water to be found. I persuaded them not to persist in their incivility, and we resumed our ascent and descent of the mountains, of one of which the descent was so deep and so horrible that it was necessary with trembling limbs to crawl on all fours, and the slightest error of foothold would ensure a broken neck: each of us carefully avoided this fate, and at last by God's grace reached the foot in safety. Halting in the valley by a stream we refreshed ourselves with water and unleavened bread, and crossed other hills and villages and a muddy stream: we then came upon another stream, equally muddy and also fetid, called by the Ethiopians *Adennala*, which we rejected, and pressed on up and down further hills, including another lofty and dangerous mountain, until we came to a river better than the earlier one, called *Marackus*. Watered

---

[8] Probably an early reference to Mika'él Sehul, the governor of Tegré, and later master of Gondar.

[9] Probably Adi Q\u02B7ala.

by the river the area was thick with grass and flowers and green all the year round, and its pleasant situation persuaded us to halt there for the night.

On February 29, at first light, we proceeded to climb a higher and more exacting mountain, not without some expenditure of bodily sweat, after which succeeded a beautiful though rocky plateau, with boulders on both the way up and the way down, while on all sides loomed the tops of the mountains, an awesome sight to look on for a whole day: but we were cheered to find water, houses, and fodder for the animals, and although we were extremely tired, in pain from the spikes of the thorn bushes, and footsore from the sharp stones, yet we entered in the evening a delightful level tract, full of corn, and came to Serai, the principal city of this province.

CHAPTER 52

THE CITIES OF
SERAI AND DOBARUA

The city of Serai[1] is extremely small, its houses wretched, and its extent barely one Italian mile: it is built in Ethiopian fashion, unplanned and unformed, and though constructed of stone is roofed with straw against the five months of continuous rain. It scarcely stands comparison with a town of Europe, and contains nothing particularly worth mentioning except only the residence of the one governor, who at that time was a youth whose father had been held in prison in Gondar for a whole year, for sedition; for the first time therefore during this exacting journey the production of the Emperor's letters afforded us a good reception, and we were consigned a house for sleeping as well as food and drink. The young man seemed of an excellent disposition, and had he not had a harsh associate called *Kaber Amlack*,[2] he would have lodged us even better: the associate, being in the habit of robbing the caravans and seizing the goods for himself, was minded to treat us no better, but in the presence of our friend the Greek official Boggiarand,[3] or judge of the infidels and Jews, he dared attempt nothing, and we escaped scot free; the associate being strictly enjoined in the name of the Emperor to exercise every care and courtesy towards us or incur the Emperor's displeasure. Otherwise only God knows how he would have proceeded against us and seized our mules and what remained of our equipment, and although he dared practice nothing against us, yet he made a pretence of buying at least one, the finest of

---

[1] Prutky, who had visited this place earlier, as noted in chapter 13, was probably referring to the village of Addi Baro.

[2] Kebra Amlak.

[3] Presumably one of the two *bajeronds* mentioned in chapter 15.

our mules, which I at last handed over to him for two drams of gold.

For all the rest of our stay I lived under canvas with the Lord Boggiarand until March 7, while the whole caravan, Greek merchants and Turks from Alexandria, rested themselves after two months of a most exhausting journey, with nothing to eat but short rations of unleavened bread and water.

To give the adviser no excuse for imposing on us I persuaded the Lord Boggiarand to send forward the whole caravan with my colleague Fr Martin Lang, while I with the more reliable servant stayed for a further day and night, since my friend the judge was a little indisposed. I eased his condition with bloodletting and medicines, and when he was recovered bade him a last sad farewell with grieving heart, and begged him to make one last earnest prayer to the Emperor to remember us when the time came for our recall. I felt my separation from him as keenly as ever a David from a Jonathan, although he was a Greek and a schismatic, for he had been my friend during the whole of my stay in the country, and in the time of persecution, and we embraced each other in tears when we grievingly parted for the last time. Casting the whole burden on the will of God, I accompanied the judge for a little of his way, and returned towards the caravan, which I found halted for the night at a river beyond Serai.

Next day we set off across a plateau and down one mountain and up another, until we reached a deep valley and halted for the night by a stream. At dawn on March 9 we hastened forwards to reach before noon another city, Dobarua,[4] situated on the mountainside, as wretched a city as Serai, partly because it had been ruined in times of old, and partly through the civil wars within the Empire. An open city without walls or ditch, it was small and unprotected by any military garrison, and at the foot of its mountain was a fine view of a great church to the Blessed Virgin Mary, where every caravan has to halt to pay to the governor or Bahr Nagasch the royal tribute, based on its slaves and merchandize. At that time the governor was about half an hour's distance from Dobarua in the village of *Tadazecka*,[5] where

---

[4] Prutky had earlier visited Debarwa as noted in chapter 13.

[5] This village, which Prutky had also earlier mentioned, was probably Sa'azzaga.

was his usual residence: but in his place he had appointed in Dobarua a Vezir or vicegerent, with other petty under-robbers to cause trouble enough to travellers: not far away was Mt *Tesamni*[6] and a cloister of resident monks, who are regarded by the Ethiopians as holy men because their public reputation is blameless and their private life free from women, whom they do not permit to ascend their mountain – contrary to the usual practice of the Ethiopian monks. In Dobarua in the governor's absence there resided seven substitute governors, differing from the devil only in bodily appearance, such injustice, inequity, and arbitrariness did they display in the exaction of taxes of unimaginable complication. Each item that they saw they took to themselves, not a tax on the merchandize but the whole merchandize itself, and it is thus that the richest merchant passes from out of their hands in a state of destitution, as they take the very skin from his back and practise their extortions with impunity: secure in the knowledge that there is nowhere where they can be accused or punished. Although we missionaries were furnished with the Emperor's mandate that we should be provided with all that we needed, we not only received nothing at their hands but were persecuted by them almost to bloodshed: despite our lack of merchandize and the poverty of our gear we paid four drams of gold to buy them off, nor were we benefited by the production of the imperial letters of authority. 'We are a long way' they said 'from Gondar, and cannot hear the Emperor's voice: in this town it is we who are the kings.' They tried their utmost to separate us from the caravan, so as to be able to despoil us of everything, as some years previously they had despoiled the French doctor as he returned from Gondar with a quantity of gold and musk.

When they had caused enough trouble and distress to ourselves and to the caravan, we at last, after a delay of seventeen days, departed on March 26, setting off through some thorn-bushes and up a mountain of great boulders where we found water, and then continuing across a plain of scrub among flowering trees to our night's halt at a place called *Kembela*.[7] The next day we climbed among trees up a mountain higher than the previous

---

[6] Teramni, 25 miles south of Debarwa.
[7] Probably Addi Gambollo 12 miles south-east of Asmara, indicated in the map in R. Perini, *Di qua dal Mareb (Mareb-mellasc')* (Florence, 1905).

one, after which we walked for two days across a plain beside a river through sweet-scented bushes of sage and rosemary, to a place called *Adaschera Jesu*.[8] Here, to protect them from the greed of the arbitrary local rulers, particularly in Messaua, we sold our mules, and hired oxen to carry our baggage as far as Messaua, at a price of two drams of gold each, or the cloth of Bombay current in the province. Seeing too that we were now far enough from Gondar, near the Red Sea, and believed ourselves safe from exaction, we sent back our imperial escort in the expectation that our troubles were over. Alas, scarcely had we parted from him when all manner of harsh treatment was unleashed against us, extortion was practised on us as though we were a caravan, and we were compelled to make a daily allowance of four loaves and of schiro to those who presented themselves as our guides to the route. We were threatened that, unless they were there to guide us, we should be ambushed and killed by robbers, but that, if they were with us, all the robbers knew them and no harm would befall us. Willy-nilly we consented to all their wicked blackmail, and proceeded further across that delightful plain with its bushes of large green sage, when there arose great cries of excitement at the approach of a party of caravan robbers. Alarmed and confused we were at a loss what to do, because we could not increase the pace of our loaded oxen, and although I on my mule could have escaped by myself, I should have had to lose all my baggage, modest though it was, and of what good was that? We commended ourselves to God and awaited the outcome that pleased Him, but after a period of noise and alarm the robbers took pity and freed us, and we escaped from danger. A little later we reached the village of *Asmera*,[9] where there is a fine church[10] to the Blessed Virgin Mary, which was built of old in the European style by the fathers of the Society of Jesus, has avoided destruction to the present day, and has been preserved in excellent condition together with its interior stone columns: it is much attended by the local people.

[8] A church in honour of Iyasus, or Jesus, possibly at the village indicated in the Perini map as Adi Hauiscia, 7 miles south-west of Asmara.

[9] Prutky had also passed through Asmara earlier.

[10] A picture of an early church at Asmara which Prutky must have seen is reproduced by J. T. Bent, *The sacred city of the Ethiopians* (London, 1846), p. 38. The structure is reminiscent of Aksumite buildings.

On March 30 we entered upon another plateau, and then descended a very lofty but pleasing and gentle mountain, through a wood where we rested on the green grass while a stream meandered here and there with a pleasant rippling sound: the name of the place is *Mejhinzy*. On the next day we climbed a small hill, of which the descent however was long and most fatiguing and consumed a full half day: the place is called *Arve*[11] and *Chedami*, that is, belonging to Mercury and Venus.[12] Below *Mt. Madet* a stream runs through the plain, and at our night's halt we drank of it and found it good: it flows gently between two huge mountains, and on the next day we felt its refreshing power and enjoyed the beautiful green meadows, the different shrubs, the thick grass, the other fruits of the forest, and the smiling woods: that night we lay to rest in long clean grass as on a bed of down. At this time in this part of Ethiopia the small rains begin, and daily spread wider and wider until by the month of May they reach Gondar and the whole extent of the country, when for five continuous months the rain falls day and night, except from sunrise to midday, and Ethiopia is bathed in an abundance of rain.

Near here we could see the monastery of *Bezin*,[13] where dwell many monks of St Anthony, who are scattered also among the nearby mountains to the number of five hundred. All this beautiful terrain and all its fruits is in their possession, who once lived lives of great sanctity, but now, corrupt of morals and imbued with heresy, pass their days in utter depravity. One especial feature of the church of this monastery, as attested by Christians, heathen and Mahometans alike, is a stout stick, plated with gold, which hangs in the arch of the church, and which was placed there in ancient times, when they were in union with the Roman faith, by a monk of upright life. No one knows today for what reason this was done, but the most common story is that if any

---

[11] Arwé, or animal?

[12] This attribution to Mercury and Venus is inexplicable.

[13] The great monastery of Dabra Bizan referred to in chapter 28. The wondrous gold object referred to by Prutky had earlier been seen by Poncet who reports that it was 'four foot in length and of the thickness of a stick', and claims that he passed a cane 'over it and under it and on all sides', and found that it 'did truly hang of itself in the air'. This 'raised an astonishment in me which continues to this very day, finding no natural cause of so wonderful an effect'. Foster, *op. cit.*, p. 153.

monk or layman wanted, as has often happened, to abstract the stick or take it down from the arch, it would always be impossible for him to betake himself from one place to another with the stick in his hand: thieves have often at night time made the attempt, but have always had to depart without their prize. Where lies the truth of this? Although I saw the stick while passing through the church, the brevity of my visit did not enable me to make my own experiment, and without lending credence to a false statement I am not in a position to deny or to confirm the story. If it were true, I should not believe that it could be ascribed to the merits of the monks of the present day, unless perhaps the Divine Majesty were honouring the merits of the holy fathers of old, or else used this merciful way to bring these heretics back to their former acknowledgement of His Catholic faith. One thing I can assert: while we rested for the night beneath this mountain, we saw a mule that a robber had stolen from the monastery: the robber was weeping and wailing and displaying to us a deformity of his hand, and on his own admission declared that through the prayers of the monks he was being punished by God for the theft he had committed: in his anxiety to be cured of his infirmity he in penance voluntarily returned the stolen mule to the monastery. Scarcely had he made restitution when he was immediately restored to health and normality, and when he recounted his experience he impressed belief in it on the whole caravan, since I had seen the whole chain of events and their outcome. All the passers by, whether natives or foreigners, Christian, heathen or Mahometan, regarded the place as holy and showed deference to all the monks, with a liberal donation of alms, nor do they ever dare to act in an evil, prejudicial, or harmful way towards them for fear of the consequences; not that Almighty God would inflict His punishments for the sake of the deserts of the present-day monks who live in heresy, but rather for the sake of the sainted fathers of old, that thus their successors should gradually be brought back to the Roman Catholic religion which they professed of old; or perhaps they are engaged on good works and are receiving their reward in this world, since they will never win to eternal life, or have their reward in heaven.

At that time we were enveloped in a tremendous rain-storm, and passed the whole night in the open air; in the evening we saw seventeen large elephants coming down from the mountain tops, one behind the other, to drink from the stream, their trunks hanging down to the ground. When they had drunk enough they went back up the mountain in the same order, while we with the caravan lay in the grass in silence, lest harm befall us; we saw many other wild animals even fiercer than these, tigers, lions, wolves etc. Seeing that the rain persisted and that there was no hope of better weather, we resumed our journey next day up a long rocky mountain of four hour's ascent, green with woodland and bushes, after which we crossed another wood, albeit on the flat, to reach a place called *Dembick*,[14] where there were at least a hundred small buildings, round in shape and built of brushwood, and surrounded with a hedge of thornbushes. These were designed in the middle of the plain to shelter bulls, cows, sheep and other animals, because in the rainy season, when the grass is at its most plentiful, the beasts are pastured in very large numbers, and when in one part of the Empire or in one province the rain ceases or reduces and the grass begins to fail, the rains increase in another part of the Empire, and the animals are herded thither for their better pasturage; in all areas they are encircled by a strong hedge of thorns, to protect both men and domestic animals at night from the jaws of the numerous lions and other wild beasts. Every night the howls of the wolves and the roars of lions, tigers, and other beasts strike terror to the heart of every stranger who hears them.

This territory is part of the province assigned by the Emperor of Abyssinia to the Najeb or governor of Messaua[15] together with all the buildings on it, and for that reason the leaders of every caravan are bound to pay court and do homage to him, and to make him a present, to avoid the unjust vexations that are the custom of the country: we missionaries presented him with the imperial letters of recommendation with all proper submission, in fear of the harshness to which we were accustomed, and implored his protection. The whole neighbourhood is almost pure desert, called by the Ethiopians *Semhar*,[16] is infested with lions, wolves, and tigers, and generally is the common abode of all sorts of wild beasts. In ignorance of this I took a stroll of

[14] Possibly Dembe four miles south of Aylet on the Ginda'e-Massawa road.

[15] Prutky, as noted in chapter 12, had met this chief earlier in his journey.

[16] Samhar, described by Bruce, *op. cit.*, iii, 251, as a 'small stripe of barren, dry country between the Red Sea coast and the highlands of Hamasén.

barely sixty paces from the caravan, when of a sudden a lion lept out of one ditch and a wolf from another growled and bared his teeth at me, and if they had not been driven off by my good sword and a shout from the caravan, I should have fallen victim to them: thereafter I never separated myself from the caravan. The water there being bad, brackish and foul to drink, we departed on April 4, since even this stinking water was used up by the quantities of animals which are kept there, and which graze between the waterholes and foul them until they are totally destroyed; but because there is no better water available, travellers have to drink of it for at least two days. At last on April 6, after the many discomforts we had borne, of hunger, thirst, fasting, dangers from men and robbers, dangers from beasts and wild animals, inclement weather and many other trials, all offered to God, we reached the island of Messaua.

CHAPTER 53

RETURN FROM GONDAR
TO THE ISLAND OF MESSAUA

Before entering the island of Messaua from the desert of Semhar, I made a detour together with some of the leaders of the caravan to the town of Arckicko, to pay my respects to the governor, entitled Najeb. I handed to him the Emperor's letter of recommendation, which enjoined him that, as in the previous year he had sent us safely on our way to Gondar, so now, as we returned in extreme poverty, he should permit us to depart in peace whatever our destination, and render us prompt assistance, and that for the time of our residence in Messaua he should protect us from harm at the hands of his subjects: as the Emperor's letter expressed it, 'They are poor men who carry no trade goods with them, they refused to take money for their journey, and all of their own goods that they brought with them they have left in Gondar: they are men who care nothing for the things of this world or for their own wealth, and they have left Gondar empty-handed. In sending them onwards in safety, without bodily harm, you will be executing our assured will and making us the more grateful to you, since for the whole of their stay in Gondar we have found these men to be just and good, and we wish them every good fortune on their return to their own country: thus you will engage our imperial favour towards yourself.'

Although I had been much afraid of receiving at his hands the persecution usually meted out to Christians, he welcomed me with unexpected kindness when I handed over the recommendation, and addressed me in Arabic: 'I rejoice at your arrival after so long and tiring a journey, and I observe your downcast appearance and your emaciation. When you arrived in Ethiopia your aspect was more joyful and more vigorous: did I not warn you that the Ethiopians are rough, uncivilized, and barbarous, and not well disposed to learned foreigners? What happened to you, have you not experienced great tribulation and affliction?' To this I made no reply and maintained silence, confining my assent to gestures only, as I knew not whether he spoke thus to try me, and to lead me on into more trouble. But when he invited me to his own table, promising me complete safety and freedom from further alarm, and refreshed me with good food and sweet water, I perceived that his expressions of pity were sincere, and, to facilitate our departure from Messaua, made him a present of a beautiful mule with all its trappings and adornments, which had been the gift to me of the crowned queen, the Emperor's mother, as well as of a decorated cotton tent which had been fitted up for our journey, and of other royal gifts which we had brought thus far out of Ethiopia: gifts to the value of about ten ounces of gold, that is eighty gold pieces.

At last in the evening I came to Messaua and met my colleague Fr Martin Lang; we deposited all our gear in the customs house, and on the next day I found a great crowd of the local Mahometans for me to visit, who were desirous of seeing us and embraced us as friends, in compassion for the misfortune of our expulsion. They showed themselves to us faithful rather than infidel, because when I dwelt among them in the previous year for almost eighty days I cured many by my medical skills and by blood-letting, and performed other works of charity without reward: on my return they received me with great affection, and the support afforded to me by the infidels gave me some consolation for the many afflictions that I had suffered at the hands of the Christians: more than this, on the following day many of them invited me as their friend to dine with them, and regaled me with a variety of dishes, so that I drank of the cup of consolation and gave thanks to the divine Providence.

I met in the island at that time one Lord George Panezzii, a Catholic from Venice, a so-called doctor who was returning from the East Indies; hearing that in the previous year some missionaries had entered Ethiopia, he put in at Gidda, wishing to seek in Ethiopia the fortune that he had lost elsewhere; but when to his regret he heard that a rebellion had broken out in the Ethiopian empire, and that we had been expelled by that barbarous people, he was greatly disturbed and perplexed as to whether it would be right for him to enter the empire without the missionaries, or rather to return to Europe with us. Although for a long time he had been sending letters to the Emperor asking for permission to enter that vast empire, I scarcely believed that he would get one, because I hardly thought it possible that Divine Justice would encourage in his perverse design so wicked a man, who was living in sin with a young slave girl whom he had brought with him from India, an idolatress and a Banian, and conducting himself scandalously for a long period of time. He besought me to baptize the slave girl and then to unite them in legitimate wedlock, but I refused to accede to this, partly because I lacked knowledge of the Indian language, and so was unable to enquire of the young idolatress whether of her own will she wished to assume the Catholic faith, and even less whether she believed in Jesus Christ our Redeemer, and the other requirements of the faith. Even if she had reached years of discretion, I was about to depart in the space of but a few hours, and with the best will in the world was unable to give her proper instruction without making a nullity of the sacrament. I was further distressed by my observation of the many vices that ensnared this Venetian, who refused to abandon his evil habits and was so steeped in vice. His desire to enter Abyssinia, where there was no Roman priest and he would be exposed to many temptations, and his rejection of my serious warning as to his spiritual state, caused me to reject him as one of the Church's unsound members: I was besides ignorant as to whether he would obtain permission to enter, seeing that the wound was still fresh of our expulsion in deference to popular feeling. He himself was a Venetian nobleman, a colonel of hussars in the Spanish army, who had been recalled in 1740 by the Venetian republic when Spain declared war against her August Empress the Apostolic Queen. The Venetian refusing to comply was unable to return to his own country for his disobedience, and sought his fortune in India, where he was reduced to penury and forced to take service under the great Mogul: here he fared well enough for some time, but becoming a prey to his usual restlessness he was unable to remain, and became desirous of seeing Ethiopia and there seeking a further fortune; but he was little likely to secure permission to enter in view of our recent expulsion and the unhealed wound of the popular insurrection.

At the same time on the island were an heretical Greek archbishop with a priest and two deacons, a young merchant, brother
to the lord judge whom I mentioned previously by the name of
his office Boggiarand, and with them a ship's captain, a Greek
called Bajanotti, and three schismatic Greek servants. All these
were most anxious to enter together the vastness of the Ethiopian
empire, but had been put to doubt and confusion by the fact
that, though fifty days had already passed, in which time messages
may be expected to return with the Emperor's reply, they had
received no favourable news.

I myself was happy to remain a few days longer in Messaua to
hear the Emperor's decision, but since a ship was ready to sail I
stowed all our gear upon it, and on April 22, which that year fell
within the Easter festival, we boarded ship, nothing having
arrived from Gondar. Here arose a further vexation: when we
applied for our licence to depart from the Najeb, or governor,
who on our arrival had been so sympathetic and well-disposed,
on our departure he proved himself a veritable tyrant, and though
he knew quite well how poor we were, a payment of five ounces
of gold was demanded of us. I besought various friends of mine
among the infidels to intercede for me, and to confirm the
impossibility of making such a payment: 'These poor doctors
brought seven chests of goods into Ethiopia with them, and now
they have returned empty handed.' However, when money matters are in question among the avaricious Mahometans their heart
is like a stone, so that the Najeb replied: 'I know that you are
poor men, and for that reason ask nothing for myself, but I
require that you make fair provision for my servants: when you
entered Ethiopia you paid them nothing for the many services
they rendered to you, and now on your departure you must pay
them a fair price.' This I discussed with him in all humility and
with repeated arguments, and agreed on an ounce and a half of
gold, leaving us on our departure with a further four and a half
ounces. We then gave thanks to God that he had set us free from
this island, which is small enough in size, scarcely half an Italian
mile long and as much wide, but large indeed in the trouble it
causes to travellers. Barely one third of it is inhabited, the houses
being of wood and straw, with only a few of stone, while the rest
of the island is empty for walking: it is very subject to earthquakes,
which almost every week strike terror into the hearts of the

people. There is no castle to protect it, or cannon, or any sort of
fortification, but only a few soldiers to provide a garrison: soldiers
arrive every year with the *Kaimackan*[1] from the city of Gidda to
exact a tax on all goods imported into Ethiopia and exported
from it; all individuals arriving or returning, even if they carry
no merchandize, must pay a money tax, this extortion being
practised under the pretext of the protection of the Great Sultan
in Constantinople, although in other times the island was under
the sway of the Emperor of Abyssinia. But now the Mahometans
are in power there, partly through the indolence and corruption
of the Ethiopian government, and partly through the ignorance
of the subjects of how to defend their territory, so that one district
after another has been wrested from the Ethiopian empire, which
is hemmed in on all sides by idolaters, heathen and Mahometans,
who are nowadays in the habit everywhere of referring to the
Ethiopians as their slaves.

The island's harbour is of medium size, affording always a
secure anchorage, and is capable of holding at least ten large
ships, and of smaller ones as many as may be, and all can approach
to within sixty paces of the harbour. In the year 1738 a French
ship to India put in at Messaua with several missions from the
Holy See in Rome; the missionaries entered Ethiopia while the
ship returned meanwhile to Mocha to transact some business,
but, though the Fathers had obtained replies from the Abyssinian
Emperor, when the ship returned for them they went back with
it to Europe.

The usual way into Ethiopia with a caravan starts from Messaua,
through the places I have just described, and is the route which
I with my two colleagues twice successfully completed, with the
aid of the divine Grace, though after many dangers, sufferings,
and trials. If another route be preferred, it is possible as part of
a caravan to cross a place called *Dixa*,[2] not far removed from my
own route and the one more usually used by the natives. Yet
another route, safer than the rest, is through *Abu-Alef*, and
another, less practicable, lies through *El-Ed*; this starts directly
by ship from Mocha, without the necessity to put in at Messaua,

[1] Qa'im-maqam: see chapter 12.

[2] Degsa, 30 miles south-east of Asmara, was, according to Bruce, a 'well populated' settlement which played a not insignificant role in the slave trade, Bruce,
op. cit., iii, 84–8. See also Pankhurst, *History of Ethiopian towns*, i, 74.

the ship making for the port of *Beilul*, not far from the port of *Babel Mandel* which the Arabs are well able to locate as it is extremely big and excellently endowed by nature, affords a safe anchorage, and is under Ethiopian rule. The indolence however of the inhabitants, and their lack of interest in trade, means that the harbour is little used, and is garrisoned by a few Arabs; this was the port of entry in past years of Alfonso Mendez when he led the army[3] from Portugal, and came to Ethiopia in a fortunate hour. For almost one hundred years[4] thereafter the Ethiopian empire was obedient to the Roman pontiff, under the protection against rebellion for all that time of the munificence of the king of Portugal, the ever faithful, until the hapless time of the revolts, when the Jesuit Patriarch Alfonso Mendez was expelled the country, together with many missionaries and all the European Catholics, and the Ethiopians shook off the easy yoke of Christ.

In the year 1715 the Ethiopian emperor *Inerus*,[5] to forestall coming troubles, besought the help of the Emperor Leopold, asking him to send a fleet to the port of Beilul, whence an army could easily be led into the interior of the empire; the route is however more arduous than that from Massaua, and several travellers in the past have taken it to their great difficulty. Indeed the French tried the port in the year 1735, the story goes, when they were sailing the Red Sea from the direction of *Cosseir*,[6] and being in need of wood and water set ashore some of their sailors, with no expectation of trouble: however a sudden charge of Arabs from the forest captured them and pierced them with their lances, and their corpses were avidly devoured. When the shipmaster had awaited the return of the party until his patience was exhausted, he landed with a large force to look for his men, but

[3] The Patriarch Mendez did not lead an army.

[4] This is a very odd statement. The Emperor Susenyos professed the Catholic faith in 1622; Mendez arrived in 1625; the Coptic faith was restored in 1632 and the Jesuits were expelled.

[5] This reference is puzzling, for the Ethiopian ruler of this time was not Inerus but Yostos (or Justus), also known as Tahay Sagad who reigned from 1711 to 1716. Emperor Leopold on the other hand reigned from 1658 to 1705.

[6] Quṣayr, a port handling 'coarse India goods' for shipment to Upper Egypt, was described by Bruce as a 'small mud-walled village' built by the seashore 'among hillocks of floating sand'. The settlement had 'several wells of brackish water', and was 'defended by a square fort of hewn stone, with square towers in the angles' and 'three small cannon of iron, and one of brass, all in very bad condition'. Bruce, *op. cit.*, i, 189.

found of them nothing but the bones, and if they had not all been well armed they would have met the same fate; as it was they satisfied themselves with but a little wood and water, and continued on their voyage.

The people of these parts are barbarians, more worthy of the name of wild beasts than of rational beings. During my journey to Ethiopia I made myself popular with them by prescribing medicines and by blood-letting, assisted partly by my musical ability on the harp, which they found truly miraculous, and partly by the services I rendered to the sick, which I administered not only humbly and extremely patiently but also readily. I thus gained the affection of the natives, but I was always careful not to offend anyone or give them cause to revenge themselves on me, because they are extremely vindictive. Those who dwell on the edge of the Red Sea are all of the same disposition, as I know from experience who spent eighty days in Messaua on my first arrival and fourteen on my return; little food is to be found there except what is brought from Ethiopia, wherefore with my two colleagues I suffered no small degree of want, alleviated, thanks to my many charitable medical services, by the birds I shot, by permission of the governor, by which we were daily nourished. The tides of the Red Sea ebb always at about 10 a.m., the ebb and flow affording a thousand paces of walking space, the surface alive with worms and little fishes: here comes a great variety of birds to feed, which as though they were tame do not fly in the presence of man, the natives not being in the habit of shooting them. They easily became my prey, and I daily shot sufficient to supply our needs in abundance, so that the birds made up for the other deficiencies in our diet.

357

CHAPTER 54

DEPARTURE FROM THE ISLAND OF MESSAUA

At last our prayers to God were answered, and when April 29 came we set sail across the Red Sea in the middle of the night, with a fair wind, and at 9 a.m. on the next day put in at the island of Dahlack, which generally can scarcely be reached in two days and nights, and where we remained for three days to purchase a supply of food, water, and wood. While there I noted that it is comprised of eight[1] separate places of habitation:[2] 1, *Dezcko,* 2, *Diballa,*[3] 3, *Sellagit,* 4, *Dahlack village,* 5, *Dorbeschit,* 6, *Dzimhebet,* 7, *Kimliba,* 8, *Nochra.*[4] The island is accessible from every side and is of some size, but is dangerous for shipping from the considerable reefs of rock and coral that surround it: the Arabs are poor seamen and find it difficult of access, with frequent shipwrecks. The natives live a wretched life, since the aridity of the soil, the dryness, and the heat of the sun mean that few or no crops can be grown, and the sower reaps but little harvest. At one time the island prospered exceedingly, with quantities of

[1] Bruce, *op. cit.,* i, 352, states that there were 'twelve villages, or towns', each of about eighty houses with a plantation of dum trees around them.

[2] Six of the first seven of these villages are described by a modern Italian scholar, G. Puglisi, who refers to them as 1. Dass-hò, 2. Dubllu, 3. Salhet, 4. Dahlac Chebir, 5. Derbuset, and 6. Gim'hile. G. Puglisi, 'Alcuni vestigi dell' isola di Dahlac Chebir e la leggenda dei Furs', *Proceedings of the 3rd. international conference of Ethiopian studies* (Addis Ababa, 1969), i, 35–47). 7. could perhaps be a distortion of Jumilah.

[3] Dubéllo, which lay on the eastern side of the island, was its 'old cultural centre'. *Guida dell' Africa orientale italiana* (Milan, 1938), p. 183. Bruce, *op. cit.,* i, 349, who referred to it as Dobelew, stated that it consisted of 'about eighty houses, built of stone drawn from the sea, and covered with bent grass'. See also Valentia, *op. cit.,* ii, 42.

[4] On Nokra see also Valentia, *op. cit.,* i, 32, 39; *Guida dell'Africa Orientale Italiana,* p. 184.

ship-borne trade and the skill which they then possessed to fish for pearl and coral; but this skill is now forgotten, though the supply remains plentiful, and to avoid death by starvation they feed themselves on a single diet of fish. Because of the navigational dangers Turkish ships only seldom call with corn from Egypt, for which reason the islanders suffer much hardship: that this was true in ancient times is strikingly attested by two alabaster statues[5] set up in the town centre featuring a man and a woman, and most probably carved by the Romans when they were in power here; the woman holds in her hands a tray on which are depicted corals and pearls large and small, while the man bears grains of the tam from which they make their bread, and underneath is carved in Syriac characters, to indicate the wretchedness of their condition in those days: 'If in exchange for this tray of gems and coral we had obtained such a supply of corn or other grain, we should not thus wretchedly have died of hunger.' Thus do the Arabs of today remember their ancient wealth, and that their ancestors, as God willed it, perished of hunger on account of their iniquities, crimes, and sins of the flesh, in which sins they too persist to the bitter end, as they lead the life of beasts in the sweat of their face and daily bewail their misery, some with but a rag for clothing and most going naked, while one and all are accustomed to robbing the stranger.

Continuing our voyage on May 4 we reached an open stretch of the Red Sea, almost a part of the high sea, and veering slightly off our course we reached the fine port of the island of *Kameran*,[6] a regular oval in shape and affording a safe anchorage, at least six Italian miles away from the mainland. The mainland, where stands the town or rather village of *Salin*,[7] is part of the kingdom of Jemen, and the island serves as a prison for the king's enemies who are held in a fort surrounded by high walls. The inhabitants of the island act as guards under licence from the king of Jemen, and apply themselves to the making of baskets from the leaves

[5] The funerary stelae on the island have been exhaustively described and the inscriptions transcribed and translated in the masterly work of Madeleine Schneider, *Stèles funéraires mussilmanes de Îles Dahlak*, Institut français d'archéologie orientale du Caire, 1983. There is no reference to Prutky's alabaster statues.

[6] Kamaran Island, which, according to Niebuhr, *Description*, p. 201, was a good and well populated port visited by both European and Indian vessels.

[7] Şalīj.

359

of trees, maintaining themselves by selling the baskets as best they can: the men are wretched and black in colour, and for the most part unclothed. We met with nothing more delightful there than the water held in cisterns which were dug in the rocks, like wells: the water had an excellent taste, free from taint and from the worms we had been thus far accustomed to, and was as plentiful as human nature could want, so that we took of it as if we drank manna from heaven and thanked God for His gift, that in almost a desert He had deigned to refresh us with sweet water. Our Arab sailors danced naked for joy and sang in their jubilation, as they washed their bodies and refreshed their spirits, they too in their way proclaiming their gratitude to the divine creator. Since these wells were about two Italian miles from Kameran, many of the travellers left the ship and hastened towards the city of Mocha by land, to avoid further discomforts by sea; we missionaries returned to the ship, where we found good water and an abundance of fish for sale at a very low price. The fortress is clearly of great antiquity, and was probably built in times past by Europeans, but is now almost a ruin as Mahometans never repair anything; similarly there are various houses built of stone, the governor's palace especially being more commodiously built, but the remaining dwellings are of wood and of wretched appearance.

In the afternoon of May 5 we continued our voyage on the same course, but the wind failed and we made but little headway: but after sunset a better and stronger wind blew up and we made better speed throughout the night: in the following days we often cast anchor, and early on May 12 we reached the city of *Hodide*,[8] a great and fine place mostly built of stone, with a very convenient port which even European vessels are permitted to enter, the city being a trade centre and very flourishing, and full of numbers of idolaters called Banians[9] who trade thither from all parts: next to the port is an island called *Elluhaja*,[10] which is indeed a place of business. For the whole of eight days we remained on board ship, as in a prison, from fear of disembarking and coming to harm of some sort at the hands of this barbarous people, who seldom or never see a Christian and from whom we could have

[8] Ḥudaydah.
[9] Hindu traders, most of whom came from Gujerat.
[10] Al-luḥayyah.

easily suffered some injury or monetary exaction. When the cargo had been loaded we weighed anchor on May 20, the period of our waiting having been somewhat alleviated by the stock we had laid on of some excellent coffee, since in Dahlack is the delightful sight of plantations of trees, like woods, all laden with the coffee fruits. These while still red are sweet and may be eaten like cherries, but inside them, in a white membrane, may be seen two, three, or sometimes four beans, which are roasted to release the odour and so drunk, and six or even eight cups are sold for a crossed thaler. From there the coffee beans are conveyed to Arabia Petrosa, to Gidda and the neighbourhood, and to Cairo, Alexandria, Constantinople, and other parts of Europe.

So we held on our way towards Arabia Felix and the city of Mocha, but on the fourth day, as we lay becalmed and had consumed all our supply of water and wood and abandoned all hope of reaching Mocha on that day, we decided perforce to return once more to the city of Hodide, where we reached port on May 24 to recoup our strength, so impaired by want of food. We decided to enter the city, come what might, as it was absolutely necessary to refresh ourselves, and so we disembarked. However, by God's help we came to no harm at their barbarous hands, but were fortified on good mutton and excellent fruit at a very favourable price.

Amba[11] is a fruit oval in shape, similar in size to a goose egg, sweet to taste and pleasantly scented with juniper, yellow in colour and full of juice, which is health-giving and a febrifuge. Mus is a fruit which I have already described, with an almost divine taste. Dates both fresh and dried, the latter of the sweetest, exquisite grapes, melons of two sorts as well as water-melons, all were on sale in great abundance, and during our three days' stay we were fully refreshed, and forgot the miseries we had previously endured.

Embarking on May 28 and sailing towards Mocha, we encountered a small English vessel of eight guns which was taking soundings to find a channel for a larger ship which intended later to convey her cargo to the city of Hodide, so well adapted to trade and so populous. At one practice I marvelled, which is contrary to Arabic custom: the headdresses of the married women

[11] Mango, Hindi *amb*.

are different from those of maidens, the women wearing as it were horns of coloured or gilded paper, while their faces, hands, feet and whole body are painted in various colours: this is regarded as the height of fashion, and, contrary to oriental custom, the women go unveiled, which the men find most attractive. The wind continuing favourable we made a speedier passage, and on June 2 put in, in a good hour, at the city of Mocha. We had passed through so many dangers from the time of our exile from Ethiopia, such hunger, thirst, and barbarous persecution, that it was with great satisfaction that we set foot on dry land.

CHAPTER 55

THE CITY OF MOCHA

Although ordinarily the route from Gidda to Mocha takes fourteen days, yet the Mahometans, whose ships are laden with a variety of goods, delay their progress by putting in to port after port, and so prolong their journey that the voyage from Gidda to Mocha, which is about one hundred miles and by the direct route on the high seas takes six days with a moderate wind, can take up to six weeks if they put in at the adjoining islands. This is accounted the best part of Arabia Felix, being bounded by the Red Sea and the Ocean: it is generally considered to be subject to the king of Jemen, whose capital is called *Moab*,[1] a city of medium size, surrounded by ramparts of earth, with a number of fine country houses outside them. The city of Mocha,[2] an unwalled port, lies in latitude $13\frac{1}{2}$, longitude 68, and is a place of some size and thriving commerce, not far from the strait of Babel Mandel, at the junction of the Red Sea and the route to Mecca with the Indian Sea. Arabia Felix adjoins Arabia Deserta, and includes the kingdom of *Muscat*[3] as well as that of Jemen.

At disembarkation my colleague and I were fearful that we should have to undergo the usual persecution from customs officials over our modest belongings, but surprisingly the scrutiny they applied to us was kindly, and we were soon installed in the lodging-house of the Prophet Mahomet, so-called, which was like a huge tenement block laid out in many hundred separate cells

---

[1] Al-Mawāhib, about 3 miles E of Dhamār. It had been the favourite residence of the Imam Al-Mahdī Muḥammad b. Aḥmad (1687–1718). The Imam ruling at the time of Prutky's visit resided in San'a (San'ā').

[2] Mukhā. 13° 19′ N, 43° 15É.

[3] Oman ('Umān), then ruled by the Imam Aḥmad b. Sa'īd, founder of the Āl Bū Sa'īd dynasty.

where accommodation was rented to all strangers without discrimination of race or religion. At the moment of our arrival we were cheered at the sight of so many European ships which had put in from India, three French, four English, two Dutch, and one Portuguese, and when on the following day we paid our respects to them all, we found the English to be the most friendly, who many times regaled us with a good dinner and relieved our hunger in every possible way; no less did the Portuguese lavish on us all imaginable marks of kindness, their captain paying us frequent visits and loading us with favour after favour. Only the Dutch proved themselves worse than the Mahometans and cast hard looks upon us: when, thinking to gain their favour, we declared that we were the subjects of Her Imperial Majesty, no good came of it and they remained harsher than the heathen. The French, the English and the Portuguese gave us generous succour, and we wandered freely through the city and the harbour, which has the capacity to accept large vessels, of which each year at least eight put in, laden with the finest Indian merchandize, on which they make a fourfold profit and expend the whole on the purchase of Arabian coffee. Since the port of Mocha is the largest and best in the whole of Arabia, hundreds of ships throng to it from all parts, to load with coffee.

The chief ruler lives not in Mocha but in *Sanaa*,[4] a larger town some twelve days distant, and is generally entitled Imam by the local population, the governor of Mocha being subordinate to him, under the title of *Amir Soliman*. The king or Imam rules the whole territory of Jemen, or *Jamal*,[5] together with all the adjoining towns, villages and islands, as well as Hodide;[6] the Arabs have a tradition that it was from this province that one of the kings came to the crib at Bethlehem. Sanaa, the most magnificent, beautiful and populous city of the whole province, is situated on a high mountain and provided with a fine port on

[4] San'a (San'ā') was the usual capital of the Imam, the leader of the Zaydī sect, which dominated the highlands of the Yemen and at this time also controlled the coastal plain. Amir Soliman means Governor Sulaymān, the second word being a personal name, not a title. For the history of the Yemen in this period see 'The post-medieval and modern history of San'ā' and the Yemen, c. 953–1382/1515–1962', by R. B. Serjeant, in Serjeant, R. B., and Lewcock, Ronald (ed.), *San'ā', an Arabian islamic city*, World of Islam Festival Trust, London, 1983.

[5] There is no justification for the spelling Jamal.

[6] Ḥudaydah.

364

the Red Sea, and could truly be entitled a state, seeing that it bears sway over the large city of *Beit Facky*,[7] itself built on a beautiful plain and including twelve Elamir[8] or chieftains subordinate to the great ruler the Imam. On another mountain some days' journey away dwells another ruler, also entitled Imam, whose people are more numerous though his wealth is less, and who wages continual war against the great Imam of Sanaa, causing the death and destruction of many and much loss to the people and the state: to avert this evil and loss of life the Imam of Sanaa has in effect accepted the position of tributary, and pays an annual toll of thirty thousand scudi to keep the peace. He is regarded as subordinate to his persecutor although his kingdom of Sanaa is the principal lordship of the whole of Arabia Felix and is governed by the Imam as an independent king, whence the whole territory gets its name of Jemen: all its inhabitants are of the Mahometan persuasion.[9]

Usually in time of war the king or Imam rules from his royal city of Moab or *Mohab*, situated on a great rocky mountain at ten days' march from Mocha. At Moab at the time of my visit the king there was a nonagenarian, the greater part of whose kingdom had been seized, because of his age and weakness, by his own two sons who were ambitious of the throne. As these two waged war on each other, a popular military commander prevailed against them and set up another king in place of the old man, who in revulsion at their ingratitude betook himself to a secret hiding-place in the mountains where he lived the private life of a hermit. Whereupon the commander, who at first had pretended that he was but the joint ruler of the kingdom, finally in the confidence of victory took over the kingdom himself, and now unjustly rules in his city of Sanaa.[10]

These petty chieftains practise a curious mode of warfare, attacking each other daily from afar, but in such a way that the bullets of one side fail to reach the encampment of the other;

[7] Bayt al-Faqīh, thirty miles south-east of Hudayda, was described by Niebuhr, *Description*, pp. 198, as 'a sizeable town and the residence of the Dola.'

[8] *Al-amīr*, 'the governor'. The word is singular.

[9] This is incorrect. There were long-established Jewish communities in San'a and other places.

[10] This account is very confused. The ruling Imam at the time was Al-Mahdī 'Abbās b. al-Husayn (1748–75). Though there were rebellions during his reign his authority was not successfully challenged.

the musket is aimed and fired not from the shoulder but from the hip. Everyone is a soldier, and goes almost naked into battle with only a rag for bodily covering, while they throng into the mosques to show their religious fervour and observe their Fridays with great devotion: indeed the governor of Mocha, *Dola* by name,[11] reverently visits the mosque on that day in the company of scores of soldiers, officials and the principal nobles of the place: visiting and returning from the mosque they brandish and fire off their muskets as though about to go to war against an enemy, so that everyone withdraws from doorways and windows to avoid being killed by a random bullet.

The kingdom owes a great debt to the empire of Ethiopia for the coffee crop, which, transferred and transplanted hither from that country, brings in today large sums of money, millions of scudi from the Europeans alone in their shipping from India, with which the inhabitants satisfy their wants.[12] Apart from their valuable coffee they grow nothing but a little wheat and the grain called durra,[13] from which the poor make their bread. Since nothing useful to humans is to be found there, the whole abundance of their wealth is expended on Indian merchandize, the finest of cloth, whole silk, different sorts of valuable stuffs for clothing, grain and other necessities, so that the whole of their wealth is exported back again to India. However, although in Europe we speak of Mochan coffee, no coffee grows in Mocha itself, but within the kingdom nearby, where at times the rains are abundant, especially in a place called Beit Facky, four days' journey away. Here grows the best of the coffee, on a gentle hillside where the trees, two or three fathoms high and planted in copses, are exposed all day to the heat of the sun. Their fruit is plentiful and red in colour, like cherries, and if eaten they have a taste of the cherry about them; otherwise within a white membrane the grains of coffee, two and sometimes three or four, can be discerned. Although the natives of this part grow a small quantity of wheat, yet the bread they prefer is made not of wheat but of durra, the grain of which, in default of mills, the women pound in stone mortars, pour in water to make a dough, and

---

[11] Ar. *dawla*, meaning power, state, government.

[12] Coffee, which grows wild in Kaffa, in SW Ethiopia, had been introduced to Arabia, traditionally early in the fifteenth century.

[13] Ar. *dhura*, sorghum, 'white millet', characteristically a highland plant.

then shape into flat cakes; heated over hot coals they are eaten at once while still warm, because they become tasteless if cold. Some wheaten bread is to be found in Mocha, but is usually eaten only by Europeans, seldom by the natives.

Other crops include millet, granturco,[14] a few garden crops such as radish, wild lettuce and various sweet-scented herbs, *meluchia*[15] a plant much favoured by the women, and sweet corn called in Italian *meliga*.[16] Tree fruits include large and beautiful peaches, plums, and a type of small pear called *bruna*,[17] different from the European pear both in variety and taste, which the Arabs pick before it is ripe, and thus rob it of its value. Excellent grapes are to be found over a season of three and sometimes four months, *golden cream*,[18] and an abundance of citrons, thin-skinned and full of juice, in such plenty that three *camassi* will purchase one hundred;[19] as there are seventy camassi to one Roman scudo, one scudo will buy 2,333 citrons. These are brought in from a particular locality two days' distant from Mocha, where between two steep mountains a pleasant valley is watered by a welling stream, which renders so fruitful the citron trees and the tamarinds, whose mass of trees delight the eye of the beholder, though the tamarinds are not as good and delicious as elsewhere; much better than these are the Indian figs, which I have described already under the name of mus.

The kingdom is more famous for a certain stone called by the natives *Solimanni*, or *Solomon's*, and also by the name of *Gemini* because they originate in the kingdom of Jemen.[20] Various colours are found, dark and bright red, clear white, and transparent: they are called corals by the Arabs, who are unable to distinguish the agate from the stone of Solomon, which is more transparent and brighter, and better for sculpting any sort of

[14] Maize.

[15] Arabic *mulūkhiya*, Jew's mallow, *Corchorus olitorius*.

[16] Italian *melica, sorghum vulgare. Pennisetum*, 'bulrush millet', characteristically growing below 2,000 ft., is probably meant.

[17] Not identified.

[18] Latin *panna aurea*, unidentified.

[19] Ar. *khumsiyya*, Eng. commassie, cammassie, a small coin, at this time of poor silver, later of copper. Its value fluctuated. See R. B. Serjeant, *The Portuguese off the South Arabian coast*, Oxford, 1963, p. 152.

[20] Probably some variety of chalcedony is meant. According to Dozy, *Supplément aux dictionnaires arabes*, *ḥajar Sulaymānī*, Solomon's stone, is calamine, and *ḥajar Yamānī*, Yemeni stone, is agate, or jacinth.

figurine, while the agate is more resistant to the sculptor's chisel. No less plentiful in this kingdom is the supply of incense, which grows freely towards Aden, that is, between Jemen on the one side and Muscat on the other, whence it is exported to all parts of Europe.[21] Arabia Felix breeds hens, ducks, pigeons, quantities of doves, and large wild birds of species unknown in Europe, of which one especially, which I had already seen on the island of Kameran, is called the *Garat*,[22] or by Europeans the flamingo, of beautiful red plumage both above and below the wing, with other colours intermingled; it is a splendid sight, with legs about five feet long and red in colour. The neck is thin and six feet in length, the head rather small, the beak curved, aquiline, and white in colour, while the wings are of three colours, black below and red and white above; the rest of the body is of black and white mixed, and this beautiful bird frequents the seaports and lives on fish. There is a great abundance of snipe, called by the Italians *beccaccini*,[23] and partridge beyond counting, especially during the flooding of a place called *Mura*[24] at six hours' distance, where for shortage of rainfall an artificial lake irrigates the fields, and various crops bring considerable profit to the inhabitants: as well as partridge there are a number of birds, great and small, whose names I omit to mention seeing that the local people profess ignorance of them. Similarly the Dutch who live in Mocha, having an appetite for lettuce, have it brought in from a place called *Tais*[25] some three days' journey away, and enjoy it the more as being a great rarity in these parts.

To make mention of the four-legged animals, of which there are great numbers, their horses are much admired and much valued on all hands for their great strength: there are also asses for sale, larger and stronger than those of Cairo, at one hundred gold pieces each, many and varied mules, beef-cattle of excellent flavour, and goats of unusual and remarkable colours, which are bought by the foreigners and Indians on shipboard and taken by them as a rarity to other parts of the world, especially England

[21] Prutky is of course referring to Ḥaḍramaut, famous from antiquity for producing incense.
[22] The flamingo is found in Yemen but we cannot trace this name.
[23] Italian *beccaccino*, snipe.
[24] Mauza', Later called by Prutky *Mora* and *Musa*.
[25] Ta'izz.

and France. There are wild animals called *Viadi* which are like
small hornless deer,[26] and countless large apes, about the size of
wolves, which are red in their posterior parts: in bands of one
hundred they race towards the traveller shouting and roaring,
when they rear up on their hind legs and strike terror into the
passers-by.[27] Often they are joined by ordinary wolves, named
monkey cats,[28] besides which there are others of fine striped mark-
ing called Hyaenas. There are quantities of large mice, almost
like baby piglets, which dig below the foundations of the buildings
and cause damage,[29] and there are lambs and wethers, similar
to the Alpine variety but with a smaller tail, which are excellent
to eat.

The Red Sea abounds in fish, of which a variety of species go
to feed the natives, of particular excellence being the sea-pike,
and another sort called by the Dutch *Spiring*,[30] by the Italians
Cafali and by the locals *Arabi*. Other sorts are the *Raii* or *Rata*,
equally delicious, while of the sea-crabs the large are of three or
four pounds weight, the smaller are oblong in shape, and the
little ones can be eaten shell and all.[31]

So we missionaries had more than our fill of converse with the
heathen for two whole months, while the incredible heat of the
sun, giving a climate as of a hot bath, made us long for the time
of our departure; though in my life I have journeyed to many
parts of the world I have nowhere encountered such heat, a fact
confirmed by the other European traders out of their experience.

[26] There are no deer in Arabia. Gazelles must be meant, but we cannot explain
the name.
[27] Baboons.
[28] *Gatti magmoni*, Italian *gattomammoni*, baboons. The reference to wolves
suggests confusion with the Caracal lynx: the lynx was sometimes known as the
wolf cat, e.g. French *loup chat*.
[29] Dr David L. Harrison writes: 'It is not possible to be specific about these
large mice . . . In an urban context it is, I suppose, most likely that they were a
local form of the Black Rat, *Rattus rattus*, though I cannot say for certain that
these animals were already present in Southern Arabia in 1753. It could well
have been, however. Certain wild living species of gerbil could possibly have
made their burrows beneath buildings where gardens and cultivation were in the
neighbourhood. Possibly Sand Rats of the genus *Meriones* would be the most
likely or the African Rock Rat *Praomys fumatus*.'
[30] Dr P. H. Greenwood informs us that the smelt is now called *spierling* in
Dutch, but does not occur in the Red Sea. *Arabi* is the local name for the Bluespot
grey mullet, *Valamugil sehele*. *Cefalo* is Italian for the grey mullet. *Raii* are rays.
[31] Bruce, sailing along this route, records that his party caught 'a prodigious
quantity' of the 'finest fish' he had ever seen.

The city of Mocha, the island of Kameran,[32] the neighbouring areas of Arabia Felix, and Persia, exceed all other parts of the world in the strength of the sun and in excessive heat. So the noblemen clothe themselves in nothing but a long shift, while the commoners go for the most part unclothed, or with a small cloth to cover their nakedness. Around noon a deathly silence reigns, neither man nor beast nor bird is to be seen, and in such heat an egg placed on the sand is in a few minutes cooked so as to set, and water gives off steam as though heated over a fire, so that tea can conveniently be prepared. Once when I walked out with the Dutch at about four o'clock in the afternoon, the dog accompanying us began to howl and we ascertained the reason: the skin of his paws was scorched and as it were scalded with boiling water because the sand was like a stove under the rays of the sun. Thus the natives choose only the night-time to make a journey, and, if for some reason they have to walk or ride in the daytime, whenever the sun shines their hands, feet and faces blister in the heat, and, if cold water is thrown over them, the skin peels off a few days later, a fact scarcely believable except to him who has tried it. When the wind blows hot the heat grows greater, and if at such times the traveller fails to fall flat on the ground and somehow take his breath from the air released from the soil, he is bound to die. Even the inhabitants, who are more accustomed to the heat, are similarly tormented, while strangers, especially Europeans, choke to death and die in numbers.

Generally from the month of October the prevailing wind is easterly, from the east or south-east, and blows strongly until February, when it tears up houses and overturns rocks: for this reason all the small houses are made of straw, and when the hot season starts, as some relief to the body, the strong wind whirls them into the air unless they have been removed in good time. While these winds last great care must be taken not to go outdoors while sweating, for fear of an attack of the usual hot fever, followed in eight or ten days by certain death: indeed for Europeans it is even quicker. Unless compelled by necessity all take care when they leave the house, and walk more warmly clad than is comfortable. From February to September the wind stays in the north and north-west, though it is variable and fitful. As

---

[32] Kamaran Is.

the heat grows care is equally necessary, and it is best to go out of doors around the third hour of the afternoon, to accustom oneself to the heat by degrees. For Europeans only September is suitable for holidays, when almost all depart to a place called *Mora*[33] some six hours distant, where they amuse themselves by hunting and rent sleeping accommodation from the Arabs at great expense: they make the most of this time because the rest of the year brings only the heat of the sun and the danger to health from the scorching winds. As in Gidda, in the months of December and January rain falls but three or four times, thereby depriving the people of many food crops necessary to life, which more abundant rainfall would have enabled to grow.

[33] Previously called Mura by Prutky. Mauza'.

CHAPTER 56

DETAILS WORTH
NOTING OF MOCHA

From such a description of the intense heat one would expect that the population would be black of skin, but as colouring is due to natural causes and not to the sun's heat, as I explained of the Abyssinians, the people of Mocha, and of Arabia Felix, Deserta, and the neighbouring area, are neither black nor white but dark-complexioned from the sunshine. They are usually seen in public with a covering round their loins and private parts, though the noblemen wear long shifts, as in Gidda, except in the time of high winds. They are more honest than other Mahometans and better disposed to Christians, and when the European traders entrust to the camel-drivers their bags full of money, unsealed, with which to buy coffee, the journey of four days to Beit Facky passes in complete security, and no case is ever known of any loss, even from highwaymen. On the other hand the dwellers in the Red Sea port are frauds and deceivers, and dishonest in business transactions. The Mochan merchants generally take possession of the merchandize brought by the Europeans without making any payment, but with the obligation to pay within two or three months, when they honestly discharge their debt in money or coffee. Sometimes the Dola or governor pilfers merchandize in his own or the king's name, and then makes difficulties over payment, denying knowledge of the goods when asked to pay and refusing payment. During my visit it happened to the English that a just debt on the king's part of 30,000 patacas was repudiated, and the more wary Dutch seldom or never give delivery of goods except against payment in cash.

The cities and towns of this kingdom seem to be well enough built after the Turkish fashion, though they fail by some way to

372

reach the European standard of order: the principal ones are Mohab,[1] Sanaa, Mocha, Beit Facky, Hodide,[2] Alzevit.[3] Of these Mocha is the chief trade centre on the shore of the Red Sea, with a good harbour which is safe only while the great heat lasts, as already recounted, and unsafe when the winds get up, whereupon all ships must set sail or face the risk of shipwreck. It boasts two forts, poorly provided with cannon, which guard the two horns of the city like the horns of the moon.[4] Except during the windy season, countless trading vessels are to be seen at anchor, which have put in from all parts of the world to buy coffee. With few exceptions the houses are built of stone, three or at least two stories high, but all of them gloomy within from lack of glass in the windows, in default of which the squared apertures are protected by bars; these however have to be treated with caution by many householders on account of the fires that often break out, because many houses being partly built of straw are out of spite set on fire by the soldiery, thus exposing the city to the risk of fire and to damage from thieves and robbers. Only houses built of stone, with high walls, are safe from fire, apart from the combustible nature of the window bars, which are often made of wood. It is on account of this and other dangers that stone houses fetch a high price, a small enough building selling for 2,000 patacas: European strangers, who all for greater safety choose stone dwelling houses, have to pay exorbitant prices for them. My colleague and I, while awaiting our passage to India, lodged in the house of a Mahometan holy man named Prevdo, and for a miserable dark cell with no window paid each week one Roman scudo, because while the European ships from India are in port lodging houses fetch a high price, this season being called in Arabic *musa*,[5] or market time. Each European trader is compelled to contract for his lodging for a whole year, and even when only one month of the year remains he still has to pay for the whole year; nor do they permit another merchant to live with him in the same house without his paying the same price again,

---

[1] Al-Mawāhib.

[2] Ḥudaydah.

[3] Zabīd, fifty miles south-east of Hudayda. Niebuhr, *Description*, p. 197.

[4] Bruce, *op. cit.*, i, 310, notes that the port was flanked by two promontories which formed a semi-circle. Each was guarded by a fort.

[5] Ar. *mausim*, 'season', especially the season of winds favourable for navigation.

and indeed if the merchant departs after only one month, and his associate wishes to continue the tenancy, a further rental payment in advance is again extorted.

The season of musa or market begins in January, when the Dutch ships come from Batavia, the English from Madras and Bombay, the French from *Ponticheri*[6] and Bengal, the Portuguese from Goa, and numbers of other ships from Europe, including Flanders: many Indian ships put in as well, of heathen ownership, and though in times past they employed navigators or captains from Europe, they have now become instructed in this lore and sail their ships on their own, to the Christian traders' great loss. From Surat, from Diu and from other ports do they come, all intent to buy coffee for the more valuable silver currency of Spanish patacas, which the Arabs value above all other coins, or of imperial dollars, since gold coins, of whatever currency, rapidly depreciate from their intrinsic value when subject to the arbitrary caprices of Arab taxation. The patacas and dollars are divided up into pieces, and small change is struck from them, this process bringing much profit to the ruler, who strikes a coin known as the comassi, equivalent in value to the German kreutzer, just as in Cairo the para or medinus is coined. One pataca is exchanged for seventy or sometimes eighty comassi, and with Arab dishonesty the authorities arbitrarily increase or decrease the number of comassi, and defraud the European traders thereby: at one time the pataca is exchanged only for fifteen or twenty comassi, while at other times the governor orders a depreciation of the currency. This is done at the prompting of the idolaters, commonly called Bagniani,[7] who form a substantial part of the population, and who when the pataca is at its highest value in terms of comassi bribe the governor to grant them authority to strike new comassi coins, call in the old at almost no expense, and so fill their own purses while defrauding the Christians. There is another dishonest trick practised among the merchant community, in the shape of an imaginary coin called *kersch*,[8] plural *korusch*, which at about 122 to the 100 patacas is of less value than the pataca: when to the innocent Europeans the

---

[6] Pondicherry.

[7] Hindu traders, Anglo-Indian *banyans*.

[8] Ar. *qirsh*, pl. *qurūsh*. It was not money of account and was 'approximately equivalent to a piece of eight' (R. B. Serjeant, *The Portuguese off the South Arabian coast*, p. 146).

Mochans have to pay for their goods, the contract is in kersch, but when it is their turn to be paid, then patacas alone are acceptable.

Only the Dutch, more astute than the others, trade in spices, cinnamon, carroway, nutmeg, flower of mace, pepper, benzoin a transparent scented gum found in the forests of the Indies, sugar, steel, iron, camphor, thick cloth, ebony, ivory, beautiful Chinese porcelain, Spanish sticks,[9] the so-called reed of India, and excellent aromatic oils: for each of these the Arabs are eager buyers and cluster round them like flies, paying the Dutch whatever they like to ask. The heathen and idolaters from India, and indeed the English traders, bring in fine cloths, sashes or waistbands that can be wound into turbans, the cloth called baft,[10] a fine stuff much used by Europeans for gloves, muslin, Indian silks and bombazine of excellent weave, cotton, rice, corn, arrack, a very potent spirit, distilled at least three times, which burns like fire, as well as Indian pepper; along with a variety of European goods these are much to the Arabs' liking, so that the traders, after loading their ships with coffee, myrrh, Socotran aloes and a number of small trifles, depart with the balance of their receipts in the form of cash.

Now that the Arabs realise the truth about their coffee, that no better is available anywhere else, they have vastly increased its price. On the other hand no Arab is able to enter into contracts to buy or sell, all trade being carried on by middlemen, called by the Dutch *mackelar*,[11] who are idolatrous Bagnians stemming from Diu, and who, as so often happens to the Jews in Europe, live separated from their wives and assist each other in all brotherliness: keen men of business and extremely hard working, they sell and resell goods to the Europeans and the Turks, and, plying their trade of mackelar they deceive and defraud those not of their own caste, growing rich without difficulty, whereupon with a full purse they return to their own land.

Everyone who brings goods in for sale is taxed, the natives at five per cent and the Europeans at five and a half,[12] while

[9] Not identified.
[10] Persian *bāfteh*, 'woven', the name given to a fine calico made especially at Baroch.
[11] *Makelaar*, 'broker'.
[12] The Latin is: *Europei vero semitertium scudum* (*solvunt*), which, relying on Du Cange *s.v.* Tertius, I take to mean 'one half of the ninth part of the scudo', that is one eighteenth, or five and a half per cent.

if the stranger is an Indian by birth the Mahometans skin him to the bone, taxing his merchandize as the fancy takes them, but mostly at ten per cent. Europeans are treated most courteously, and when a ship's captain puts in to the harbour his national flag is flown, he is accorded a military escort with a military band, and conducted on horseback to the palace of the Dola or governor, throwing alms to the populace on the way; the Dola presents him with a caftan or robe of honour, sometimes even with a fine horse, although under the system of restitution and reciprocity the Dola receives back in gifts three times what he gives. Similar honours are paid to the Indian captains, their escort of janissaries continuously discharging their firearms, and on entering the governor's house saluting them with three cheers, a practice which on returning they punctiliously repeat. Although Mahometans elsewhere regard Christians as their enemies, the Mochans are better disposed towards them; the population includes a few Jews, and countless Bagnians who are idolaters.

The English and Dutch traders maintain a permanent factory, and though their expenses are great their profit is even greater. Over a three-year period three officers of the company are stationed at Mocha, guarded night and day by eight soldiers: for food alone their monthly expenses are at least five hundred patacas, for water ten patacas, the Mochan water being fetid and wormy and necessitating its importation from ten leagues off at a place called *Musa*:[13] for a few green vegetables or lettuce, which have to be brought in from a mile off, they pay a pataca, and every small delicacy involves them in great expense, so that the maintenance of these three Europeans costs 700 patacas per month. Notwithstanding these costs, in their three-year tour of duty they turn a profit of at least 80,000 patacas for themselves, quite apart from the profits earned for the trading company; not that this is their own salary paid to them by the East India company, but the return from their own private trading, especially in coffee, by which they enrich themselves. If the price charged to the company for every pound of coffee be raised by one kreutzer, enormous sums of money accrue, which they appropriate to themselves as the just reward of their labour. If

---

[13] Niebuhr refers to the excellence of the water at Mauza, which is at the edge of the mountain zone.

this be the product of Dutch and English theology, yet they are assured of the unspoken support of their superiors, who in times past as the servants of this great company walked the same road and acquired riches for themselves. When subordinates are posted to such places as Mocha, they are charged to be accurate and industrious in the performance of their duties; secondly to maintain the honour, credit and glory of the company; and thirdly not to neglect their own interests. They live therefore in great splendour, with an escort of soldiers when one of the three leaves the building, a number of attendant slaves, and a servant to hold an umbrella over his head: when the principal of the three walks abroad he is accompanied by six armed soldiers and a corporal, and whenever he enters or leaves any house all six soldiers discharge their weapons thrice, to emphasize his importance by this truly regal respect.

Europeans here indulge heavily in *punch* made of arrack or very strong spirit of Pataira.[14] The fermented juice of the cocoa-palm, mixed with rice and sugar, is distilled at least three times to produce a very potent spirit, to which the English are particularly addicted. Their recipe is as follows: to one measure of heated arrack put an equal measure of water, add lemon juice, sugar and nutmeg, and mix thoroughly, throwing in a piece of toasted bread to counteract the flavour of the water. This they drink by day and by night, their drunken slumbers are elegant to behold, and many perish miserably from the burning heat of the climate.

For the whole period of my stay there was no shortage of work for me, whether curing the bodily ailments of the English and the Dutch, or assisting with spiritual medicines the souls of the other Catholics, the French and the Portuguese, many of whom had for many years been deprived of the rite of Holy Communion, because they had been continually engaged in voyaging through Asia and Africa, and there was a great scarcity of priests in these parts. More especially did the many sailors long resident in Mocha look upon us as angels sent from God, and, though so far in our journey through Abyssinia we had been exhausted by hunger, thirst, and misery upon misery, here all the European

---

[14] Perhaps the Portuguese word *piteira*, the agave plant, introduced by the Portuguese into the East from Brazil, and the source of the modern tequila.

nations united to entertain us, and particularly by the English were we loaded with favours redoubled daily; it was but in justice that we the more zealously attended the beds of the dying, though secretly for fear of being sentenced to be burned alive: we rejoiced indeed that so many souls, who would have departed this life without the holy sacraments, were by our presence reconciled to God. The sacrifice of the Mass we performed daily, with due precaution, both in the city where dwelt many Catholics both European and Oriental, and in the Portuguese vessel, where always some spiritual prize was to be won. I was particularly rejoiced at finding a young Fleming of excellent character, who having completed his theological studies was being forced by his parents into holy orders: having no vocation for this he had decided to enter into matrimony with a young woman, but, cast out from his father's house, he ran away to sea in a Dutch ship and after five years fetched up at Mocha. Afflicted with a severe illness he had for a long time delayed making his confession, but, as his condition worsened and he was in his death throes, I had him carried on his friends' shoulders to our own house and prayed that the divine mercy might bring him succour. Lo and behold, his power of speech returned to him beyond all expectation, he made a proper confession, I strengthened him with the viaticum and with extreme unction, and returned him to the Dutch vessel. Here on the return of his death agony I comforted him until his final breath, thanking His Creator of His infinite mercy, and he entered into eternal life.

Not to overweigh the present chapter, I here divide it from the next one.

CHAPTER 57

OTHER EVENTS IN MOCHA

Since the ships from India were due to remain in harbour and no sailings were taking place, we missionaries likewise were forced to be patient a little longer until their departure for India: anxious not to let my time drift idly by I made a detailed scrutiny of the character, deeds and different practices of the Mahometan religion, and just as among the Catholic orders the men of religion vary in their degree of sanctity and righteousness, so among the Mahometans the populace attribute holiness to a class of men dignified by the title of *Schiech*,[1] who are called in by all sorts of people in case of illness, weakness, and various catastrophes, to render an assistance which the people believe infallible. Quite close to our lodging I encountered the rare case of a Mahometan girl who was said to be possessed of a devil, for the cure of which a Schiech of high reputation in the expulsion of devils was summoned: on his arrival the holy man conjured the devil all day until sunset, when on entering the house he raised a loud clamour, and evacuated vomit that was worse than the devil itself. Then lifting his mouth higher and ever higher and bringing it close to the girl's face, he repeated in a terrible voice '*Echrog echrog*'[2] that is 'Come out, devil, come out': whereupon the evil spirit spat in his face, cursing and swearing, so that for the time the Schiech retreated, with various gestures which raised much laughter among the onlookers and which were most curious to behold; meanwhile the poor girl at length died, after two months of wailing, sighing and crying out. Many of the locals hereupon declared that there were living in Mocha various evil men who

[1] Ar. *shaykh*, a term of respect of very varied application.
[2] Ar. *ukhruj*, 'go out'. Prutky's spelling approximates to the colloquial pronunciation.

when they were refused unlawful intercourse with a young woman sent a devil into her by diabolic arts, to revenge themselves upon her by the operation of the devil. If there be any truth in this I leave to the judgement of the reader.

A rarer case was that of a Polish sailor on a Dutch ship, a devout Catholic, who, summoned on board his ship but uncertain of whether she was about to sail, humbly begged me for absolution for the last time, and was sent back to his ship after proper repentance and the comfort of the Holy Communion. During the night somehow he arose half asleep from his bed, perhaps at a call of nature, fell by mischance into the sea while his shipmates slept, and unfortunately drowned. On hearing this I grieved for the man's misfortune; but rejoiced the more that in death he was assured by God's grace of eternal salvation.

A European practice which I found remarkable was to steep in aqua vitae the plucked carcasses of hens, pigeons, goats and lambs, and then to repeat the process; in this way a spirit is produced which is mild and appetizing, the whole virtue of the meat being absorbed into the liquid leaving the flesh like white chalk, without taste or flavour and almost rotten: all the nutriment of the meat is absorbed into the spirit, well-flavoured but expensive, which the European visitors drink in quantity as an accompaniment of their excellent coffee.

In contrast the local Arabs, who for the sake of gain are eager to sell all the coffee they can, content themselves with the toasted husks, and skilfully grind them into a drink which is a substitute for coffee though weaker, this less acceptable version being drunk by the common people: the nobility and wealthier classes gather other husks of the ripe coffee which still retain their red colour, like cherries. This makes a valuable present for the king or chief nobles, the husks being roasted along with their sap and then cleverly ground and cooked like coffee to make a drink whose taste the Arabs greatly prize. For myself, although it was of superior quality, I used to prefer the ordinary coffee made from the grains or beans rather than that made from the husks. This use of the husk is particularly noticeable when in the month of August, or sometimes July, the traders betake themselves for the purchase of coffee to Beit Elfacky four days from Mocha. On the first night they reach a place called *Murez*,[3] and on the second

---

[3] Maushij.

day the anciently famous but now ruinous Alzevit in a fine flat situation. On the third and fourth days there is little to be seen but wretched huts here and there, and then Beit Elfacky is reached.

At that time of harvest the natives make merry, and throughout the Turkish lands roam the *Daruisch,* whom I have described elsewhere, and who are all servants of the devil and turn the heads of the people with a variety of incantations. One that I saw carried a stick covered with ornaments carved into knots and rings, set with spiked nails, and with a sharp iron point at its tip. He paraded up and down while he shook his stick and shouted and cried, and then struck himself with great force and fixed the iron spike in his eye, leaving it there for a considerable time, a frightening sight. More than this, say the natives, Daruisch such as these are compelled to serve for a full year at the shrine of one of the holy men as a kind of novitiate, by which means the virtue of this Schiech or holy man is transmitted to teach them these and similar tricks. According to Arab tradition the Alcoran tells of one Schiech who was highly respected as the great friend and supporter of the false prophet Mahomet.[4] The battle in which Mahomet lost a tooth caused consternation in Heaven, and God immediately sent the Archangel Gabriel to comfort Mahomet and find the tooth and the blood which he had lost, lest a drop of it should fall to earth and destroy the whole world. This Schiech was held in honour while still in the land of the living because in an unusual tribute to Mahomet's tooth he knocked out his own one after another, not knowing exactly which one it was that Mahomet had lost. For this great mark of respect for the false prophet, Mahomet rewarded him with the adornment and investiture of a costly robe called *Caftan,* and desirous of emphasizing even further his goodwill to his supporter, he prayed to God to create for his merits the tree of the fig of Adam, on which in future he could feed and so sustain life, despite his lack of teeth. Throughout the whole of Egypt are to be found these trees of the fig of Adam, distinguished from other types of fig and bearing oblong leaves six or seven feet in length: they produce on each branch a quantity of oblong figs of delicious scent and taste, such as grow in India and Abyssinia in great profusion; I have

---

[4] The story that follows is not in the Qur'ān, but the earliest biography of Muhammad records that at the Battle of Uḥud he was struck by a stone which knocked him down and smashed one of his teeth.

described them elsewhere under the name of mus.[5] The robe up until recent times was kept under guard by the kings of Jemen in a holy sanctuary, but in the last war against the Sultan in Constantinople Mocha was defeated and the robe sent to Constantinople, they say, as war indemnity: whenever the Sultan sets out to battle, this holy robe, bedecked with jewels and precious stones and enclosed within a golden casket, is carried before him as a protective talisman.[6]

These and other empty stories, with a number of examples of Arab stupidity, we began to find tedious as we wasted our time in waiting for a ship. We begged to be admitted on board the Portuguese vessel, partly because of the good Christianity characteristic of this nation, and partly for the particular acts of charity done to us by the captain of the ship; nor should we have been averse to visiting the tomb of Francis Xavier:[7] but though the captain would have taken us to Europe without a second thought, his voyage having to include four other Indian ports was too long to enable us to reach Goa by the month of October, the latest time for a voyage to Europe, and we should have been compelled to spend a whole year at Goa. We therefore made a request for a passage on a French ship, but the captains were resistant and put many difficulties in our way. Our only hope lay in the third French ship, at that time detained in Gidda, but meantime we hovered between hope and fear and were reluctant to reveal the French refusal, and denial of our common Catholic religion, to the English captains, who unasked were often offering us out of their charity a free passage to London and food and clothing beside. It was a great grief to us that we could wring little or no help or kindness from the friends of our religion, but experienced from the English such unasked-for goodwill, and that the Catholics had forgotten about deeds of charity while we were overwhelmed by the open-handedness of the Protestants. In the meanwhile we whispered our prayers to God while watching for the return of the third French ship, whose captain we humbly

---

[5] Ar. *mauz*, 'banana'.

[6] The *khirqa-yi-sharīf*, the supposed cloak of Muhammad, was taken from Mecca, not from Yemen, to Constantinople after the Ottoman conquest of Egypt in 1517, when the Ottoman Sultan replaced the Egyptian as Guardian of the Holy Places, that is, Mecca and Medina.

[7] In Goa.

besought for assistance: we explained to him our wretched condition after our many persecutions in Abyssinia and dangers at
sea, and our disinclination to effect our return through Arabia
Petraea and Arabia Deserta: apart from the obvious danger of
death, which we had only just escaped after sufferings and tribulations, we were poor, almost naked and ill-nourished, and if we
were to return by way of Arabia the natives would be certain that
we were possessed of much gold, which to extract from us they
would not refrain from torture; to give was impossible, and this
would arouse them against our fellow Catholics. We were beset
on all sides, we complained, and we were disappointed that the
French nation was denying us a passage by way of India, while
to accept the English offer would be unsuitable, and would not
afford us a ready passage to Rome. So effective were our pleas
that they won the agreement of the captain of the third ship,
Jean d'Oman, a man of blameless conduct and Christian charity.
He welcomed us in gladness of spirit, not just as missionaries but
as God's very angels, and sent us back happy to our lodgings:
indeed from that moment onward he supplied our every need
for daily sustenance, and generously discharged our weekly
requirement of money, meanwhile giving orders for a suitable
berth to be made ready for our passage to India. Hearing this
the other French captains took shame, quickly retracted their
words, and offered us the same facility, but we in cheerfulness
of heart embraced the opportunity which had been freely offered
rather than extorted unwillingly, and to prepare ourselves for
our journey praised God our Benefactor and daily Preserver.

Our relief however was but of short duration, and another
anxiety ensued to depress us: at the moment of our departure
the Mahometans conspired to prevent us, on the pretext that
because we had put in on a Turkish ship, on a Turkish ship we
must sail, and although we had loaded all our essential gear and
modest luggage on to a lighter to embark on the ship to India,
we were forced back and made to return to Mocha in despair:
the prospect of persecution, extortion of money and other evils
that we had so often experienced struck fear to our hearts, and
in anxiety of spirit we explained our predicament to his excellency
Captain d'Oman. How wonderful is the heroic virtue of a true
Christian! Without flinching, 'Here am I, Fathers,' he replied,
'and whatever happens, and whatever you have to pay to ensure

your departure, I will discharge it immediately.' Such outstanding Christian charity, love of one's neighbour, and respect for the priestly office struck wonder to the hearts of the Mahometans, one of whom I had made my friend by medical treatment and other personal services, and who in return for my kindness spoke up in friendship, 'Good master, come with me and I will obtain from the authorities a licence to sail for you and your colleague.' Leading me before the city magistrate he pleaded for us, 'This good master is no merchant but a doctor, he has bought nothing and sold nothing, far less contracted any debts nor brought harm to any citizen, but on the contrary has brought good health to me and to many other sick folk: why then should he be detained here and prevented from departure? I myself take responsibility on behalf of him and his colleague for any eventuality that may arise.' At this the magistrate granted the licence and free permission to depart, and we again thanked God and marvelled at such kindness on the part of the heathen, where so many Christians are deficient. We betook ourselves to his excellency the ship's captain, who had himself explained our difficulty to the Dola or governor, and on the order being given we were dismissed without further trouble, and boarded our ship with joyful hearts, escaped once again from the cruelties of the infidel.

CHAPTER 58

DEPARTURE FROM MOCHA FOR INDIA

Thus it was that two manifestations of the divine grace were at work over the dangers of our departure, the generous intervention of my Turkish friend, and our freedom from pecuniary extortion. Giving thanks to God we prepared ourselves to set sail and weigh anchor, and on July 29 found ourselves safe in the company of Christians and Catholics, and free of the countless trials and tribulations alike of terrain, man and beast, of Turk, heathen and idolater. On the following evening of Sunday 30 we departed from Mocha, and on the day after that, the 31, reached the so-called gate of the Red Sea, Babel Mandel, where between two parts of the mountains of the Red Sea there protrude two as it were apertures to form the entrance to the Indian Ocean, an arm of the sea running between the two mountains whereby all shipping is compelled to sail. There is a double entrance, a greater and a lesser, and the name of *gate* is given to them not as though they were gates in the sea, but because the entrance between the mountains is more extensive and far-reaching. This forms the greater gate, which however is more dangerous to shipping, whereas the lesser gate, though narrower, has a current that is gentler and offers greater security to passing traffic from its relative freedom from rocky reefs, with which the Red Sea is everywhere obstructed and therefore dangerous at all times.[1] Once past the gate we crossed the dangerous rocks, the Red Sea continuing for at least a hundred miles further until it becomes the Indian Ocean; but our passage was free from danger, and

---

[1] The Strait of Bāb al-Mandab (The Gate of Lamentation) is divided by the island of Perim. The channel on the African side is some twelve miles wide but is dangerous because of shoals and rocks; the channel on the Arabian side is deeper and is about a mile and a half wide.

at about 3 p.m. we reached the mountain of Cape St Antony,[2] the wind being favourable, until on the following day, at 11 a.m. on August 1, we passed another mountain called Aden on our port side between Asia and Africa. Here we had Asia on our left hand and Africa on our right, until on August 2, the feast of Holy Mary and the Angels, the main land of Africa came into view, called by seafarers the last gate of Africa. Here lies the island of Socotra, once the seat of a mission of the Reformed Order of the Friars Minor, where despite our close proximity we did not disembark, although many of the crew were anxious to do so to purchase Socotran aloes for resale in Europe,[3] and we missionaries would gladly have put in to search out the disposition of this people who once were Christian.[4] Fathers of the Egyptian mission were frequent visitors to the inhabitants, labouring in all conscientiousness to turn their hearts to Christ, and in the year 1705 the Sacred Congregation for the Propagation of the Faith once more sent thither missionaries of the Reformed Order, Fr James of Oleggio, Fr John of San Marco, and Fr Samuel of Biumo. They were successful in reaching Mocha under the name of doctors, and Fr James became physician to the king of Jemen, thus availing himself as prefect of an excellent chance to send the other two fathers to Socotra to gather herbs to heal the king's ailments, or rather to win for Christ the souls left in the island and return them to the way of salvation. Armed with letters from the king the two fathers sailed to Socotra on a ship that calls there each year from Mocha for the aloes, landed in high hopes, and traversed all parts of the island, which they found to be arid and very unhealthy on account of the brackish water, which was inferior even to that of Mocha, and the use of which by the islanders was the cause of a great deal of disease: from culpable negligence and laziness the inhabitants refused to search out in the mountains the springs of sweet water, on account of the distances to be traversed, and preferred rather to live lives of misery, though there is an abundance of oxen, cows, goats, sheep, asses, and camels, a scarcity of birds, dates, and garden produce,

[2] Ras al-'Āra, so called because of the loss there in March 1520 of a Portuguese ship, the *São Antonio*.
[3] Socotran aloes were in demand as a purgative.
[4] The Socotrans were converted to Nestorian Christianity at an unknown date, but only vestiges of their faith survived when the Portuguese established a fort there in 1507. It is uncertain when Christianity finally became extinct in Socotra, but it was almost certainly before Prutky's time.

and a lack of corn, rice, and the other necessaries of life. In the main the inhabitants are Mahometan, ruled by a prince called *Gheschen*, the absolute sovereign of the island, in the interior of which dwell a sect of people who are neither Mahometan, heathen, idolaters, nor Christian, but who keep to some of the forms of Christianity, baptizing their offspring in water and pronouncing a few words of worship of God, though in ignorance of the proper ceremony. They baptize their children in praise of the Supreme Lord of heaven and earth, and the traces of Christianity can still be seen in the form of ruined churches and the images and statues of the Blessed Virgin and the saints: indeed the fathers were informed by some of the older among the idolaters that twenty years previously they had sent a message to Goa, begging for priests to be sent to the island, but that, nothing further having been heard after so long a stretch of time, they had lived out their lives without pastors and forgotten the name of Christian. Certainly at that time it would have been easy to obtain from the king of Jemen permission to establish a mission on the island, nor would the prince, the Gheschen, have been unfavourable, but when the missionary fathers surveyed the whole population, which apart from the few just described were all devout Mahometans beyond hope of conversion, they returned to Mocha, especially in view of the decision a little later of the Sacred Congregation to abandon the mission to Mocha along with its hospice.[5]

[5] The ruler of Yemen did not control Socotra which had been subject to the Mahrī Sultan of Qishn (Prutky's Gheschen) on the south coast of Arabia since about 1480. Prutky may have confused three attempted missions to the island. Golubovich, *Biblioteca bio-bibliografica della Terra Santa*, N.S. vol. XIII, Quaracchi, 1930, p. 239, records under the year 1703 that John of San Marco, James of Oleggio, Samuel of Biumo and a lay brother were sent there but could do nothing for the faith because the 'king' would not let them stay.

A document in the archives of the Congregation for the Propagation of the Faith (*Acta*, anno 1719, ff. 280v., 281r.) records that John of San Marco arrived there in 1706, having obtained permission from the 'king' of Qishn on the pretext of searching for medicinal plants. However, the 'king' of Socotra did not allow him to remain or to look for Christians fearing that this might result in a rebellion.

Lastly in 1715–6 three missionaries, among whom was John of San Marco, were detained in Jiddah for several months when trying to reach Ethiopia. While there they were called upon for medical attention to the 'viceroy of Mecca' and his household. They then went to Mocha where they met James of Oleggio. They abandoned their attempt to reach Ethiopia when they learnt of the martyrdom of Pr. Weiss at Gondar and James of Oleggio returned to Rome via Persia. Golubovich says that they seem to have undertaken a mission to Socotra, *op. cit.*, XIII, pp. 257–8.

Our ship drew close to the island at the feast of the Transfigur-
ation, but was prevented from anchoring by a storm of wind,
which at 9 o'clock at night developed into a raging tempest and
imperilled our very lives with the danger of shipwreck at any
moment. Contrary winds sprang up from the four points of the
compass, the rudder was shattered, the sea raged, the night was
pitch black, the tossing of the waves left nowhere to sit or stand
or lie down in safety, while a heavy downpour of rain increased
our peril. Each man held on by his hands where he could to ward
off the chance of ruin, and the strength of the wind rendered it
impossible to furl the spread of sail which was wet with the rain.
The shattered rudder was replaced by two strong steersmen at
the wheel, while amid the raging and foaming of the waves a
rope of at least two hands thickness was broken by the force of
the gale, and the ship was turning hither and thither where the
waves drove it. The sailors and officers were powerless, and all
went down to the shelter of the lower deck, labouring with might
and main to lash the rudder and restore the ship to its proper
course. Our fears were aroused partly by our closeness to land
with its threat of shipwreck, partly by the wild surges of the
storm-driven sea, partly by the rain and the contrary winds; our
spirits were troubled, our hearts were beating, we watched for
the ship's masts to be torn from the keel, as at the mast's foot I
knelt with my colleague and besought aid from on high: our
prayers came from the bottom of our hearts as we commended
our souls to our Creator. Of the three hundred sailors toiling
below not one was to be seen, and we two missionaries were left
alone, wet to the skin from the storm of rain and raging wind,
as we made our prayers to God and fixed our purposes on holy
matters: there was no saint or angel in heaven, so to speak, whose
aid we failed to invoke, as for two hours we endured this critical
state of danger, our faces wet with tears, every vein throbbing,
our agony increased by the terrors of the dying. How much did
our forebodings increase when the ship's navigator asked to be
shriven, and once given absolution commended himself to God:
no hope of safety was left, and the Lord God was our only goal.
A long time later, by favour of His pity, the rudder was secured,
the ship was set on her true course, the storm abated, we were
blessed with a softer breeze, for which manifest grace and favour
we gave praise to God, and I firmly resolved that never in the

whole course of my life could I allow myself to forget it. But the sea remained angry and denied us rest by day or by night, and we ensconced ourselves in corners without possibility of cooking and with only a piece of bread to stay our hunger. As we lay awake for the third night without sleep we experienced the presence of the fabled Sirens, at whose song sailors are lulled to sleep and become the prey of the sea as slumber overcomes them in their time of danger; sweet is the song of the Sirens, and must be counteracted by constant toiling, lest the sailors fall into their deadly embraces.

Scarcely by God's grace had we escaped this danger when on August 8 another arose to threaten us, as a fresh tempest struck, the waves again grew violent, and the ship was lifted up on mountainous surges only to be apparently cast down into a bottomless valley: the disturbance on board was unimaginable, chests and other furniture not securely fastened fell noisily from one part of the ship to another, and even the oxen, cows, pigs and sheep, and the other animals shipped for provender, rolled hither and thither to bruise themselves severely: similarly the human complement, as the rain lasted for six days, could find nowhere to keep their footing in safety, could neither sit nor stand nor lie, and were so enfeebled that we seemed to be drunk. Always we had sight of Socotra beside us, but when at last the wind stilled we crossed its whole extent, so frightening and threatening every year to passing seamen that but few vessels pass close to the island; so it was that in times past the Catholic church found it difficult to provide for its missionaries, until the deserted inhabitants gradually relapsed into heathendom and idolatry.

At last the skies cleared, and daily the navigators began to measure the depth of the water, since if the bottom is struck this is a sign that the Malabar coast has been safely reached. After many measurements and much calculation bottom was found on August 15, at fifty-two fathoms, giving assurance that we had reached the coast, whereupon with a more favourable wind we made sail until on August 22 we sighted the island of *Ceilan*, which is now in the possession of the Dutch and was conquered by them from the Portuguese: the latter, distracted by the war in Europe with Spain, had been unable to reinforce their possessions in the Indies, and being pressed on all sides by their enemies, including the crafty Dutch, had been unable to resist so many foes, and forced to yield to the Dutch that very island of Ceilan, the best of their possessions and a rich source of spices, to their present bitter regret.[6] The landmark of Mt Aden in Ceilan is higher than the Mt Adam of Germany, and it is commonly held to be the death- and burial-place of our first father Adam and of Eve, in whose honour there stands to this day a small chapel built by the heathen with a stone carved in their image, with two or three lamps kept ever alight and a number of small cells very well maintained. So beneath this sculpted stone our first parents are held to lie at rest, and for this reason there are said, in addition to the heathen, to be many Adamites here, a sect of evil-livers where fathers lie with their own daughters.[7] Because the Dutch care less about religion than about trade, looking only to things temporal and too seldom to things eternal, the inhabitants enjoy complete freedom as to the life they lead. There are still many Catholics left here from the time of the Portuguese, some in the service of the Dutch, others making their living by tilling the soil, to all being granted freedom of religion, fruitless though it be, and all being ministered to twice yearly by priests from Goa or from the kingdom of *Gandia*, whose king, who regards himself as king of the sun, moon and stars,[8] is influenced by the piety of his nature to send them: each time the

[6] The Portuguese were expelled from Sri Lanka by the Dutch in 1658.

[7] Prutky is confused. Mt Aden (*sic*) is Adam's Peak. A depression in the rock on the summit is regarded by Muslims as the footprint of Adam, by Hindus of the god Śiva, by Buddhists of the Buddha, and by some Christians as of St Thomas the Apostle. Sir John Mandeville, chapter xxi, records that Adam and Eve bewailed their expulsion from Paradise in this place for 100 years, their tears forming a big lake, which in fact does not exist. Marco Polo states that Adam was buried here, but says nothing about the grave of Eve; Muslim traditions assign various sites to their tombs, notably Jidda as Eve's. The Sinhalese practice of two brothers sharing a wife may have helped to give credence to what Prutky writes of the Adamites. There were two sects of this name, an antinomian sect of the second century which aspired to the innocence of Adam before the Fall, and regarded all acts as morally indifferent once this had been attained, and secondly a Bohemian and Moravian movement originating in the fifteenth century, whose founder, one Ricard, is alleged to have styled himself Adam son of God, to have rejected the sacrament of the Lord's Supper and the priesthood and to have advocated community of women. 'The Mt Adam of Germany' is Adamova Hora in Moravia, 49° 02′ N, 13° 29′ E.

[8] The King of Kandy. Mr C. H. B. Reynolds of the School of Oriental and African Studies, London University, informs us that he claimed descent from the sun and moon, but not to be their ruler.

Dutch protest at the arrival of the missionaries, but cannot forbid it for fear of a revolt by the many Catholics, and, especially as they know of the consent of the king of Gandia, they dare not refuse it.

From *Columbo* it is thirty miles to Mt Aden, where is the above-mentioned round church, constructed of stone throughout, with cells built into it in the heathen manner, and a stone to our first parents, sculpted in the European way, with an inscription in Greek, Latin and Hebrew *Here lie Adam and Eve our first parents.*[9] So suspicious in this island are the Dutch that even in time of peace they will allow no other nation to approach by ship or to land there, but maintain garrisons of soldiers with cannon to drive off any ship which in ignorance of the ban makes to approach the harbour; they are ever in fear of treachery, lest they lose the island in the very way in which they acquired it. Nor is it without good reason that they take such care and trouble to defend it, seeing the quantities of cinnamon out of it that they sell at a high price, and take their profit, so that the provinces of India, of Europe, nay of almost the whole world, are supplied by the Dutch. In such profusion does it grow that not only do they use it for seasoning, but they cook and roast meat with it and burn the surplus, lest with too great a supply they be forced to take a lower price. They own enormous plantations of cinnamon, the trees growing to no great height but very thick and broad, and bearing numbers of fruits of pleasant appearance, wrapped round with rind in complicated layers, but in the centre containing the cinnamon,[10] beautiful to see, pleasant to the taste, fortifying to the heart; the trees are like our walnut trees, bearing fruits not dissimilar to peaches.

Since most of the island is subject to the native king of Gandia, the Dutch are tributary to him, and are every year compelled to bring him quantities of royal gifts of European precious stuffs, cloth of silver and of gold and fine fabrics; further, they must abase themselves before the tyrant, not walking to meet him but almost on their knees, their arms laid aside, their feet bare as they are conducted into the king's presence; before audience is granted they sometimes have to wait a whole month or more,

---

[9] This is nonsense. The shrine on the summit is Buddhist.
[10] In fact the spice is obtained, not from the nut, but from the bark of the tree.

and to endure the arbitrary treatment of a despot to his slaves, all this tyrannical behaviour being supportable provided they come to temporal possessions and heap up wealth for themselves. Certainly no Christian nation would endure such tyrannical humiliation and insult, though the island produces quantities of diamonds under the rule of the king of Gandia, who every year not only gives numbers to the Dutch, but licences them to prospect in a given area, where also quantities of sapphires and rubies are to be found, topazes can be picked up from the rivers, and pearls or margarites are fished from the adjoining sea-coast. Ceilan also produces coffee, poppy, pepper and other herbs and garden crops, and to ensure that the native king leaves them in peaceful possession the Dutch pay an annual tribute, bearing as well as gifts an official letter from the Republic entitled *To the king of the stars, the moon and the sun.* When they are known to be drawing near to an outpost of Gandia called *Hanckavel,*[11] where salt is made, seven major officials from the chief city of Columbo, with thirty soldiers, meet them on the way, and next day lead them to a small place called *Schvidevach*[12] garrisoned with eight soldiers, the beginning of the territory of the king of Gandia; from here other soldiers conduct them onwards, one of the Dutchmen acting as envoy from the Republic and being seated under a baldachin with the gifts, carried by four people bearing four lighted torches and dressed in garments similar to those of our deacons; the envoy being distinguished by costly white gloves and bearing before him a gold paten containing the letter. To keep them from knowledge of the route to the kingdom the native escort takes them through byways, and often they have to wait a very long time for their audience of the king; then when the gifts have been handed over to the royal minister some slight acknowledgement is made to the envoy, a sword or dagger, and to his servants gold- or silver-bedecked caps or some small pieces of money, as though they were of no great matter. They then receive permission to depart, but have to wait for at least two months to be escorted back by a guard, lest they learn the route: they are forced to leave the important city of Columbo, from which comes the customary name of the country Ceilan, or in other words

[11] Hanwella, where there was a Dutch fort.
[12] Sitawaka.

Columbo.[13] That the Dutch are held in no great respect nor much regarded by the king is made clear by the events of the year 1751, when the French nation was courteously invited to visit Ceilan with the promise of perfect freedom and respect: but the French, not being accustomed to such humiliations before a petty king, refused the invitation, and all the more because they would have had to wage a fresh war with the Dutch, who would never have given the island up without a fight, but would rather have allied themselves with the English to force the French to submit: they therefore rejected the favour the king had offered them.

So we sailed onward quite close to the island with a good view of its situation, until in a few hours there came in sight the port of *Galli*, so called from the fact that when the Portuguese came to this part of the island they found nothing but a cock, so they called it the harbour of Galli, and so is it called today.[14] Continuing our voyage we had sight on August 24, at 9 a.m., of Mt *Cappucii*, in the shape of a cowl,[15] and then followed the *Cuccari* mountains, more than thirty in number, a remarkable sight like caps of sugar made from the living rock:[16] shortly afterwards there came in view the feature called by seafarers the Bridge of *Peter*, but without knowing the reason for the name.[17] Then on August 28, at 5 a.m. we reached the end of the island, having completed 150

---

[13] This account is misleading. The route taken by Dutch ambassadors from Colombo to Kandy may have been circuitous in places and it rarely coincided with the modern road, but it varied very little. Delays were sometimes imposed by the Sinhalese purely for astrological reasons. The envoys always had two audiences and began the return journey the day after the second. The King's gifts to them were more generous than Prutky implies: 'Ambassadors usually received silver swords, gold chains and gold rings set with stones, while the secretary got a gold chain and rings and the interpreter only a chain', T. B. H. Abeysinghe, 'Embassies as instruments of diplomacy: a case-study from Sri Lanka in the first half of the eighteenth century', *Journal of the Royal Asiatic Society, Sri Lanka Branch*, N.S. vol. XXX, 1985/86, pp. 17, 18. The same article includes lists of the presents sent by the Dutch to the King in 1717, 1724 and 1730. The name Ceylon has nothing to do with Colombo.

[14] Galle. The name is derived from the Sinhala word for a rock.

[15] The mountain known as Friar's Hood.

[16] The Knuckles.

[17] Point Pedro, the northern extremity of the island. The name is adapted from the Portuguese Ponta das Pedras, Cape of Stones. It has nothing to do with a bridge. The chain of seven islands, known as Adam's Bridge, on the west side of the island, would not have been visible from a vessel off the eastern coast.

leagues, after which follows the coast of *Cor Mandel,* inhabitated solely by the heathen under their own rulers, who have however trading relations with the European nations both in various sorts of merchandize and in slaves. Because we were sailing so close to land the shipmaster continually measured the depth of water to save us from striking and shipwreck, and when the depth was fifty fathoms there appeared a view as of nine towers in the distance, like so many ships in harbour: but it was neither of these, we learned, but the heathen temples called *Pagoti* for the worship of idols, each Pagotum or idol standing displayed upon a stone cube of twenty paces each way, and causing the beholder to marvel how a work of such mass could be transported and lifted thither.[18]

Meanwhile the wind was favourable as we sailed toward the French city of Ponticheri,[19] which we had sight of by the grace of God on August 30, at 2 p.m., and fired off two guns to give notice of our arrival. But the wind changed, our hopes were dashed, and we were driven off course, being unable to find a wind more favourable, to arrive at the English harbour of *Bombai,*[20] where there is a governor with a garrison of soldiers, and which is not far from Ponticheri. With a fair wind the journey takes but half a day, and we cast anchor to stay the night there, but shortly after midnight a better wind blew up, we weighed anchor, one of which was lost overboard from the carelessness of one of the crew, and continuing our voyage we reached the port of Ponticheri at about 10 a.m. on Saturday August 31, having completed since leaving Mocha on July 30 998 French leagues or 3,992 Italian miles.

The careful reader, who perhaps has never been to sea nor is likely to do so, may wish to know how many miles may be journeyed within twenty-four hours if the wind be fair, or middling, or plain contrary, and I therefore append the following schedule to show the distance travelled in each hour, and then in summary how much will be covered in the twenty-four hours.

---

[18] The Anglo-Indian word pagoda, in what was probably its original sense of a pagan temple, quite different from the Chinese buildings to which the name is also given.

[19] The English Pondicherry, French Pondichéry, Tamil Putucceri.

[20] Presumably Fort St David, just south of Pondicherry, is meant.

Beginning after midday on the first day of our voyage, July 30

Hour	Mileage	Hour	Mileage
1	6	7	7
2	6	8	7
3	6	9	$6\frac{1}{2}$
4	6	10	6
5	6	11	4
6	7	12	$3\frac{1}{2}$

After midnight

Hour	Mileage	Hour	Mileage
1	$3\frac{1}{2}$	7	5
2	3	8	5
3	3	9	4
4	3	10	2
5	$1\frac{1}{2}$	11	6
6	3	12	4

In twenty-four hours therefore, with but a light wind, 114 miles were covered, but on the day following, when the wind was stronger, the mileage achieved in twenty-four hours was 160. To give a clearer picture of the whole voyage from Mocha to Ponticheri, I append the schedule for each separate day.

Date	Mileage	Date	Mileage
July 30 (after midday)	10	August 16	31
31	38	17	29
August 1	43	18	25
2	36	19	34
3	17	20	34
4	14	21	21
5	42	22	20
6	48	23	35
7	52	24	40
8	54	25	14
9	52	26	14
10	48	27	34
11	36	28	29
12	30	29	29
13	29	30 (at anchor)	0
14	30	31 (to Ponticheri)	5
15	25		

This sets out the daily run of a ship to India with a good, a middling, and a light wind.

CHAPTER 59

ARRIVAL IN INDIA

It was with indescribable joy that we viewed our landfall at the fort of the city of Ponticheri, and after the boiling surges of the sea reached dry land and the security of a harbour, where ships cast anchor at least half a German mile from the shore because of the high tides and the shallowness of the water. All who wish to disembark are lowered on to small craft in the midst of the breakers; the alternative method is for two naked native porters to link arms, to save themselves from falling when the rough waves break in their faces, and for the visitors to sit one on the neck of each porter and to be carried through the surf, though care must be taken to hold fast the feet of the traveller, lest the surges of the sea, whipped up by the shelving beach, throw water into the eyes of the porter and overturn him together with his load. Whenever they carry European women on their shoulders they treat them with much incivility, jerking and dragging at the legs of their burdens and ensuring them a wetting in the waves, while at the same time confounding them with shouts and exhortations to each other; this is because porterage of European women is an obligation that they have to perform for no remuneration, though their services are in general generously recognized by an annual payment from the governor. We missionaries were carried to land by this method, and cared little when the waves poured over us, provided that we came safe out of the many dangers of the sea: we were like men re-born.

A great crowd of natives appeared on the shore to congratulate the visitors on their safe arrival and to raise a considerable noise in native fashion by handclapping, singing and dancing: among them were numbers who addressed each other in Bohemian and German and loudly complained 'How wretched are we, who have lived so long in this place with no priest who can speak our

396

language, and who can see no sign of the German missionaries whose arrival was expected; where are they? We see them not.' Bitter was their complaint, as they failed to recognize us in our Levantine turbans and semi-Ethiopian dress. Gladly would I have replied to them in German that we were indeed the German missionaries, but after so many years without speaking German we were unable to say a word in it though we understood them perfectly: the only words that came to our tongue were Chaldean[1] or Arabic as though we had never learned the German language, and it was only when the natives led us to his excellency the Governor that we were recognized as missionaries. Beyond description and beyond explanation was the joy of this group of about three hundred Germans who rushed upon us as one man and, falling one after another at our feet, displayed to us such tenderness of spirit as would have turned a heart of stone: 'Oh Father, for so long now are we unshriven and unrefreshed by the Holy Communion, how many sins are there which oppress our souls.' The cries of one matched the cries of another, and we walked among this crowd of people almost as though we were uplifted on high. But we put off until the following day their visiting us and our further care of their souls, being fatigued by our sea voyage, and told them to depart. Meanwhile we were bidden by His Excellency the Marquis Duplex the Governor General of India[2] to relate to him the whole tale of our long journey by sea and by land, and the discomforts and trials we had endured, imploring his favour and support; we were received with all kindness and with promises that he would relieve our every necessity. As a first example of his benevolence he sent with us one of his twenty-four slaves, an idolater from Malabar[3] who held in his hand a long silver stick, like a European equerry; this person conducted us to the hospice of the Capuchin missionary fathers, asking them to supply us with all the necessities of life at their expense, but since these fathers seemed to receive us in a grudging spirit we hinted to his excellency the desirability of betaking ourselves to the missionary fathers of the Society of

[1] Usually means Syriac, but here presumably Amharic.
[2] Joseph François Dupleix, the famous Governor of the French possessions in India, 1742–54. He was made a Marquis in 1752.
[3] Perhaps used here as a term for southern India generally, not merely the future Malabar District, now part of the state of Kerala.

Jesus; at which the Capuchins, fearing the Governor's displeasure, received us thereafter in a more friendly manner.

In the absence of shipping to Europe there intervened a long period of rest, but yet of the consolation of a spiritual harvest, as daily at daybreak we received visits from the Germans and Bohemians, in conversation with whom we gradually gained practice in speaking their languages. Until noon we laboured to catechize children, men and women, and resumed our task until sunset, hearing confessions, remitting sins, and solemnizing marriages which had been delayed for a long period of time through lack of a knowledge of both French and the native language. In some cases we regularized a concubinage into legitimate matrimony, in others we restored to their original state of harmony couples who had nourished grievances against each other, and so great was the work involved that only the midday dinner hour remained free to us; and along with these men and women were the many Bohemians, Moravians and even citizens of Prague who had been captured in the French wars or had deserted from the Imperial army, and who later had been unexpectedly shipped willy-nilly to India among the many European soldiers who are sent abroad every year to maintain the garrisons. In this short interval of time we performed what under Providence I would call a mission to India, laborious indeed but full of satisfaction, as we restored to the Germans there resident their former quietness of conscience, and praised God the Thrice Blest and Greatest for all the gifts of his grace; we heeded carefully the words of St Paul the teacher of the Gentiles that the works of man are of no avail and that, whoever waters and whoever plants, it is God Who gives the increase. Gladly would I have remained to cultivate and to plant in this vineyard of the Lord, seeing that I know of nothing more precious than that a man lay down his life for his friends, but my obedience called me to the Sacred Seat and to the knees of the reigning pontiff Benedict XIV, to render an account of my stewardship in Abyssinia. Although I was lovingly pressed to remain not only by the population but even by his excellency the Governor, I was unable to accept without reference to the Sacred Congregation, and, obedience being the better sacrifice, persisted in my determination to journey to Rome.

Since my stay was to be of long duration I turned my attention to the city of Ponticheri and its more important features, finding it a pleasant place, ceded in times past by the Great Mogul to the French nation,[4] and of considerable size, protected by a strong fort and encircled with thick walls and bastions; apart from native troops the European garrison numbers at least 2,000,[5] well able to repel any hostile attack, and I would reckon the city's circumference to be equal to that of Olmütz the capital of Moravia:[6] there is a circumvallation provided with seven entrance gates.[7] At the time of its cession it was not built in its present fashion, nor were its inhabitants nor its merchants as numerous, whether Indian, European or Mahometan: the wares in which they trade are exquisite, fine cloths of bombazine and silk, the thinnest muslin, beautiful Chinese porcelain, and many other valuable objects interwoven with gold and silver thread are sold at a very low price; the finest of scarves, as fine as gossamer, which in Europe would sell for more than two florins, cost here four or five German groschen.

The French population, which does not exceed a hundred families, site their houses on the side toward the sea, close to the fort, and build them without roofs in the Egyptian fashion, their upper floors being equipped with arbours or rather booths so that at sunset they can stroll therein and enjoy the fresher air, taking their supper there and diverting themselves until midnight: even an occasional fire does no damage to a house with walls but no roof. The rest of the city comprises many thousands of heathen, idolaters and Turks, who dwell in houses some of stone, some, of the poorer classes, of wood, while many live in mud huts like the poor of Europe: but all are the subjects of his excellency the French Governor and are severely punished if

[4] The French were first established at Pondichéry in 1673 at the invitation of the ruler of Kadalur (Caddalore). It was then unimportant.

[5] 'Il y avait environ de 1200 à 1800 soldats blancs à Pondichéry; de 1750 à 1754 il arriva des renforts de près de 2,500', M. V. Labernadie, *Le vieux Pondichéry, 1673–1815*, Pondichéry, 1936, p. 185.

[6] Olomouc, Olmütz in German. It ceased to be the capital of Moravia during the Thirty Years' War. At this time it was being converted into an important fortress, so that it is not possible to say what Prutky meant by the circumference.

[7] Robert Orme, *A history of the military transactions of the British nation in Indostan*, 4th edn., vol. I, London, 1803, p. 101, gives the dimensions of the town enclosed by the fortifications as about one mile from N to S and about 1,100 yards from E to W. The fortifications were destroyed by the British in 1761. Orme says that at the time of the siege five roads led from the town into the country. A plan published by Labernadie, dating from about the time of Prutky's visit, shows six gates.

they break the legal code, with the result that they pay great respect to his prudent direction of affairs, and that not only the city dwellers but a part of the hinterland offers obedience to His Most Christian Majesty, together with some small buildings and villages and several Catholic churches built by the missionary fathers of the Society of Jesus: indeed at more than fifty leagues distance from Ponticheri there are two strong places, built by the Governor, which are designed to resist any attack by natives.[8] Not but what it is the natives who are the rulers of India, and not the Europeans, despite the common belief in Europe that India is in the possession of the European French, English, and Dutch. These can only be said to rule one palm's breadth of India, nor is it true as is said in Europe that the Indians are almost all Catholic, the contrary to which I have proved by an examination of how many Indians are Catholic. That very few heathen and idolaters come forward for conversion is proved by the situation at Ponticheri, where each year scarcely twenty embrace our holy faith, although the heathen population numbers more than 40,000. Indeed it would be truer to say that the Christians of India are either European, or those blacks who in times past were converted under the rule of Portugal and are now born into the faith by the process of descent from Catholic parents, though there are in addition a very few converts made from the Coasts and from the territories of the heathen. If I could report in good faith that one hundredth part of the Indians were Catholic I should be a happy man, but since I dare not affirm this I will only say that India is a long way from Europe and it is but seldom that a missionary returns from thence; when he does so he makes a number of boasts which are far from the truth, and I have personal experience to the contrary.

The missionary fathers in India are to be regarded more as lords than as missionaries, and in the possession of much fertile land live better than many churchmen in Europe; the Capuchin fathers are the parish priests of the city of Ponticheri and collect in fees a fatter revenue than any parish priest in Europe, as well as receiving from their congregation the whole support of their daily nourishment, living like abbots in a cloister. When my

---

[8] Presumably Masulipatam and Karikal, though the latter is less than 50 leagues from Pondichéry.

colleague and I lived with them for some weeks, they dwelt in a good stone living-house with twelve cells and a refectory, but not content with this were building another bigger one from the foundations upward, with arches below and a fine church of great size, like a cathedral. This had been completed to the top of the arches when they were unexpectedly arraigned in Paris and forbidden by the Council of the Most Christian King from any further building, from finishing the arches, and from bringing to completion the cupola which they were planning to build even higher; the fear was that in a hostile attack the church being higher than the fort might overlook it and bring injury to the city: so many thousand scudi had already been spent, and the fathers were exposed to the risk of destroying their building or leaving it thus unfinished.[9] Yet this extravagant building cost the fathers nothing: the whole expense was paid for by their parishioners, as they collected their ample stole fees[10] for baptisms and funerals, and their other sources of revenue can be calculated proportionately from the contribution of M. Duplex, who when as sponsor he visited the church four or five times a year would pay over each time the sum of fifty pagodas, equivalent to fifty gold pieces.

The coinage current in India is the *Poggod*, the *Rupia*, the *Fonam* and the *Duddi*. The poggod is a small round gold coin worth four rupias, the rupia a silver coin worth about one German florin, while the fonam is also a silver coin but of two sorts, of which the larger are worth six to the rupee, the smaller twelve to make the same value. The duddi likewise is a small siver coin, eight of which make one smaller fonam.[11] In the church of the Capuchins money such as this, whether of gold or simply of silver, forms the offertory of the faithful, all parishioners of theirs and

[9] The Capuchin church of Nôtre Dame des Anges was begun in 1739. The work was discontinued by order of the Conseil d'Etat, probably because of the proposed height of the nave. It was subsequently completed.

[10] Stole fee is the fee paid to a priest for sacred services, as baptisms, marriages and funerals, at which the stole is worn.

[11] The pagoda was usually a gold, sometimes a silver, coin, the rupee was silver, the fanam originally gold but later silver, and the doody copper. All these coins varied in value from time to time and from place to place. When the rupee became the standard coin of British India in 1818 the pagoda was reckoned as three and a half rupees. In Prutky's time, on the Coromandel coast, the silver pagoda was equal to thirty-six fanams, the fanam to eight doodies. See *Hobson-Jobson*, s.vv. Cash, Fanam, Pagoda, Rupee.

401

living near the castle at about a thousand yards from the church. Here also is the Governor's Residency, which was once a hovel but has now been turned into a veritable royal palace, surrounded with water and strongly fortified. Indeed, in the last Anglo-French war of about 1750[12] the English bombarded it with more than 7,000 cannon balls of twenty pounds weight in their heated and violent efforts to reduce it, but were not only unsuccessful but failed to cause it any damage, the harbour with its fort being at some distance from the ships, scarcely in fact within range, and offering by no means a safe anchorage: so that on about October 20,[13] the fleet was compelled to sail away, lest it suffer shipwreck in the high winds that arose, and to depart either for Europe or for the high seas or for another haven which offered more security. This victory so ingratiated his excellency the Governor with His Most Christian Majesty that from being a commoner the Governor was raised to a marquisate, and not only was the first of the governors of India to be decorated with the order of St Louis, but contrary to custom, which requires the governor to be changed every three years, he was four times confirmed in his office by the king's express command.[14]

Nor was this undeserved. As well as his outstanding achievements in warfare, in ruling the country, and in general administration, he maintained his palace in such splendour as to excite the admiration of all nations, and in such elegance of style as Europe can scarcely match. I viewed with wonder the richness of the interior, inlaid with gold and silver, and the elegant craftsmanship of the statues on the walls: a double row of niches with ample walking space in their midst is the setting in which all the governors of India, from the first to the present M. Duplex, are magnificently depicted in life size, the cornices being gilded on each side and the niches being twelve in number. The pavement is decorated with the finest Chinese porcelain, and each niche exceeds the last in richness of decoration, until the eye reaches two larger cabinets adorned with windows of glass, their

[12] The siege of Pondichéry by Admiral Boscawen in 1748.
[13] The siege lasted from September 6 to October 16; the fleet sailed away on October 19.
[14] The governors' length of tenure of office had been irregular. When Prutky arrived in India Duplex was already losing the confidence of both the French government and the directors of the Compagnie des Indes. In the autumn of 1753 it was decided to supersede him.

casing set with precious rarities of Red Sea shells and pearls, with red and white corals large and small, with diamonds, emeralds, sapphires and other stones of great value. All this I viewed and greatly admired, especially as for the livelong day every stranger was permitted freely to view and to ponder over the succession of objects of value in each niche. All expressed the greatest wonder at the deeds depicted on the pavement and the fables of China with their beautiful design and exquisite workmanship, some of which here and there were carved from terebinth wood, while others consisted of gems and diamonds of the size of hazel nuts; the whole of this amazing treasure was said generally to be fifty millions in value.[15]

This is scarcely surprising, seeing that a few years previously the Governor was engaged in a war with a native king, defeated him, and acquired so much gold and so many chests of diamonds and other jewels as made him a rich man and enabled him to live in a state of splendour and magnificence equal to any king:[16] in this role he maintained eight elephants, who were paraded before the palace morning and evening and fed with such a quantity of hay or green fodder as each year amounted to four hundred florins.[17] Tamed despite their size, the animals were fed by their attendants, who when they wish to mount signal to the beast by touching its ears with a small-pointed iron tool, whereupon the elephant bows its head and kneels down, and permits the attendant to mount either over its head or over its rump; whichever way the attendant wishes to go he touches the beast with the iron tool, and the elephant directs his steps accordingly. So highly do the Indians value their intelligence that they record how towards his master or his attendant that feeds him the elephant ever remembers with a wave of his trunk his gratitude to his benefactor, while those who have injured or hurt him he ever remembers to injure in return whenever he can. It happened in Ponticheri that some small children were playing in a street when an elephant, injured by his chain, charged upon

[15] The building of the Governor's palace, begun in 1738, had been completed only in 1752. Its splendour was famous. It was destroyed by the British in 1761.
[16] This refers to the victory of the French over Nasir Jang, Nizam al-Mulk, Viceroy of the Deccan, in 1750.
[17] According to the diary of Ananda Rangapillai (Rangapoullé), Dupleix's Indian broker, the Governor had twelve elephants. The most famous, named Venkatachalam, died about the time that Prutky left India.

them: except for the smallest who was too little to run all fled away for fear of being trampled, but the elephant, approaching the baby and carefully wrapping his trunk around him, put him down before the door of his house with such gentleness that he took not the least harm and was restored to his parental home. A similar case involved a drunken soldier who failed to report to barracks at sunset, and was found by the guard sleeping under an elephant's belly. When the guard tried to arrest him and approached the elephant, the latter defended himself with his trunk and shook his head, and the guard were compelled to leave their comrade asleep. When on his return next day he was asked how he had gained the elephant's goodwill, he replied that he was in the habit of giving him some figs each day, and that the grateful animal had protected him while he was asleep. There are a number of other instances of powers almost of reason of which the Indians tell, and which excite the admiration of the audience.

An added attraction of the Governor's palace is its beautiful garden, which contains a variety of wild birds shut up in handsome cages, as well as wild beasts, lions, tigers, bears and the like. Hither resort not only Catholic laymen but also the Jesuit and Capuchin missionaries, between whom there is a coolness, nor do they live in amity with each other. The Capuchin fathers have the cure of the souls of the city, of the French population, and of one district of India nearby. The Jesuits by contrast are stationed outside the city more than a hundred leagues away, tilling the vineyard of the Lord, and are empowered as priests to catechize and convert the idolatrous Indians, whose souls are entrusted to their care; their life is spent almost wholly among the idolaters, to whom alone, and not to Europeans, their life of service is rendered. There are usually five priests and two or three tertiaries[18] to teach the rudiments to European children and to a good number of young Indians, the Jesuits having been assigned to various areas among the heathen, whom they have the task of converting to the bosom of Holy Church. For many years however the Enemy of mankind has been sowing the seeds of discord between these two missionary orders, as appears more clearly in the writings of Fr Norbert, Capuchin missionary to

[18] Lay assistants.

404

India, published and dedicated to His Holiness Father Benedict
XIV, and little spiritual fruit have they brought forth, as they
forever quarrel among themselves.[19] The Capuchins complain
against the Jesuits that they are guilty of idolatrous behaviour,
that they approve the superstitions of the heathen, and that they
adjust their own behaviour to accord with heathen practices.
Because the idolaters believe in the transmigration of souls, the
Jesuits abstain from the meat of cows and oxen; the heathen
practice of wearing a medal round the neck, though the design
is changed into images of piety, such as two human natures united
into one, they continue to tolerate, although most of the populace
believe rather in the old heathen significance; many other decrees
and prohibitions of the Sacred Congregation are flouted, and to
illicit behaviour involving the heathen deity of carnal love they
turn a blind eye or openly permit. Especially are they reproved
that in the case of the poorest people of the lowest condition, to
whom is given the name *Pareas* or slaves,[20] they refuse to visit or
administer the Sacrament, even at the point of death: if they
come near them, the Holy Sacrament is extended to them at the
end of an instrument, and on their deathbed they are carried by
force to the house of the priest and their confession heard at a
noticeable distance from the confessor; after absolution they are
given extreme unction with the use of a similar instrument.[21]
These are but some of the complaints of the Capuchin fathers,
as set down and elaborated in the many volumes of Fr Norbert
of the Capuchins; they have been emended and made an article
of belief by a commission of enquiry of legates sent by papal
authority, and in the year 1704 His Eminence Cardinal Thomas
Maillard of Tournon, apostolic inspector general and Patriarch
of Antioch, brought out the bull of Clement XI against these
abuses and errors: he died full of merit in Macao in 1710, though

[19] Père Norbert de Bar-le-Duc (1703–69), Pierre Curel in secular life, also
known as the Abbé Platel, was the author of voluminous and violent attacks on
the Jesuits. He was in Pondichéry from 1737 to 1740.
[20] I.e. Pariah, properly the name of a numerous and low, though not the lowest,
caste in south India, but loosely applied to all low castes and outcastes.
[21] Prutky refers to the so-called Malabar rites, Hindu practices which the Jesuits
permitted converts to observe. For instance Labernadie says that in the Jesuit
church in Pondichéry 'A l'intérieur on avait élevé, à l'indignation de beaucoup,
une barrière pour séparer les chrétiens des autres castes des parias'. *op. cit.*, p. 204.
These rites were condemned by Benedict XIV in the bull *Omnium sollicitudinum*.

I decline to describe the cause of his death, lest it be believed to prejudice any sacred institution.[22] But after the death of His Eminence there succeeded another apostolic legate the Patriarch of Alexandria, who in 1720 was more successful in composing this dispute.[23] I confess that in India I was present when a number of versions were recounted, and made my observations from personal experience, but it would be tedious to relate the whole affair and, not being appointed judge in these matters, I pass on in silence to further details of my travels.

[22] Charles Thomas Maillard de Tournon (1668–1710), Patriarch of Antioch. He was sent as Legatus a latere to India and China, and was in Pondichéry in 1703–4. In the latter year he issued a decree condemning the Malabar rites. In China he was imprisoned by the Emperor and eventually handed over to the Portuguese.
[23] Carlo Ambrogio Mezzabarba (1685–1741), Patriarch of Alexandria in 1719, sent as Legatus a latere to compose the disputes over the Chinese and Malabar rites.

CHAPTER 60

THE CLOTHING AND
CUSTOMS OF THE INDIANS

In India the men and women alike are olive of skin, and dress
themselves in white robes of the finest weave in the same fashion
as in Ethiopia or Egypt, with the difference that whereas the
Ethiopians wear no clothes except when they leave the home
when they put on a white cloth, the Indians dress after the
Arabian fashion, those that is who are merchants or of some
consequence, the others going about naked with a loin cloth three
or four fingers broad: the garment of the women is rather longer
and of red cloth, emphasizing the breast and hips, and most of
the population go barefoot, apart from a few of the well-to-do
and the noblewomen, who wear slippers which taper to a long
horn-shaped point. The women are most respectful of the
religious susceptibilities of the missionaries or other priests when
they encounter them, not only the converts but even the heathen
and idolaters, and make an attempt to cover their bosoms with
their garment, having been instructed by the Catholics that it is
unfitting to appear before the priesthood in such indecent
apparel. After the fashion of the women of Egypt five or six
earrings are commonly worn, the ears being pierced accordingly,
the hands are covered in rings, necklaces are worn on the neck,
and even the noses are pierced and ornamented with a ring, the
whole of what their husbands give them being spent on personal
finery. Not only the fingers of the hand but the toes of the foot
are beringed, their whole wealth of silver or gold being displayed
on their persons. Even the women who are Catholic dress in the
same way, with long flowing hair secured by red ribbons and the
head uncovered, except occasionally when they cover it with a
red scarf. A praiseworthy custom of the Indian converts when

they encounter a missionary is to come to a halt, clasp the hands
before the eyes and bend the head respectfully, with the greeting
sarue stotiram, Praise, or glory, be to God:[1] this they repeat at all
times of day, morning noon and evening, instead of wishing one
good-day; the priest's proper response is to make the sign of the
cross and reply *aczirvadam, God bless you*:[2] when they are in need
of a favour or benefit they fall to the ground and kiss the earth,
humbly beseeching for the favour without intermission. Even the
children who can scarcely walk or talk correctly have been instructed to run behind the priest and cry *Suami Suami sarue stotiram,
Father Father praise be to God*,[3] to which the proper response to
silence them is *aczirvadam Tambi*,[4] or *Dandaczi*,[5] *God bless you little
brother* or *little sister*: on hearing this they depart comforted and
happy.

Among the customs of the East three provoke particular wonder, that the houses are built of sugar, that churchgoers are
carried sleeping to church, and that congregations eat in church:
the reader may regard these as miraculous, or just plain lies, but
I will show that they are true. The intense heat of the Indian
sun does considerable damage to the buildings, whose walls tend
to crumble and split down the middle unless the mortar be
properly prepared; nor has any better method been found for
the repair of fallen masonry than to slake the mortar in a solution
of sugar and water and leave it to work for several days,
whereupon when the house is built with the sugared mortar the
stones bond into each other as though glued together, and the
walls become as it were vitrified. The sun's heat is repelled, all
danger of collapse or falling masonry is avoided, and thus all
Indian houses can be said to be built of sugar. The scorching
climate is a sore burden to those Christians who live at some
distance from the church and who are unable to make the journey
thither on foot for fear of sunstroke, with the result that all the

---

[1] Sanskrit *sarve stotram*, 'all praise'; the Tamil form of the second word is
stot(t)iram. For this information and for the identification of Indian words and
plants in this and the next two chapters we are indebted to Dr J. R. Marr of the
School of Oriental and African Studies, University of London.

[2] Sanskrit *āśīrvāda*, a blessing from an older to a younger person.

[3] Sanskrit *Svāmi, svāmi, sarve stotram*, 'Lord, Lord, all praise'. *Svāmi* is used in
Tamil as well as in Sanskrit.

[4] Tamil *ācīrvātam tampi*, 'Blessing, little brother'.

[5] Tamil *taṅkācci*, 'little sister'.

merchants and richer folk are carried by black servants in a litter called a *Palengin*,[6] which is furnished with cushions and their personal belongings, covered above with a baldachin, and screened on each side by curtains; the occupants doze off inside while four to six idolaters carry the litter, which is fitted before and behind with round wooden handles covered in black or red leather and protruding about half an ell. These the blacks place on their shoulders and run at speed, while as a further precaution against the sun's heat one of the slaves holds an open umbrella on one side or the other; however far they be from the church they doze peacefully as they are carried thither, and when they draw near the church door their servants arouse them and they enter the porch of the church of God. To prove the third point, it must be realized that the great heat drains and exhausts the body of a continual sweat, so that it needs the refreshment of a red or white preparation of quick lime, called *Cionambu*,[7] with the addition of the green leaves of a certain tree of the country-side, leaves not unlike those of the peach,[8] and with the further addition of a very hard root or globule similar to a nutmeg. These three ingredients including the lime each person carries round with him in a special box, and at all times and in all places they chew the leaf and the fragment of nut, and although it has no taste nor do they extract any juice from it, they spit out the residue with their own saliva and firmly believe and declare that it provides moisture for the body and purifies and cools the blood. This triple mixture, of which the Indian name is *Strocka*,[9] stains the teeth red as though the chewer were spitting blood, and the houses of the nobility are furnished with spittooons held in readiness to preserve the floor from being stained with its spots. Their continual chewing in church is mistaken for eating by foreigners who know not the custom, and their spitting stains

[6] I.e. palanquin, a word of Sanskrit derivation.
[7] Tamil *cunnāmpu*, lime.
[8] The betel-vine, *piper betel* L.
[9] No word at all like this is possible in Sanskrit or Tamil; it seems to be Czech, which he may have partially forgotten, as he had German. Mr M. J. Pollock Librarian of the Royal Asiatic Society has made enquiries on our behalf which suggest that it may be a phrase incorporating the word *troška*, meaning a little piece or morsel, perhaps preceded by the preposition *so*, 'with'. Prutky is referring to the delicacy well-known as *pān* in northern India, consisting of a piece of areca-nut, wrapped in betel leaf and flavoured with lime, &c.

the floor as though with blood; though the missionaries have often tried to persuade them that the practice shows lack of reverence to the Godhead, they have never been able to relinquish it, and maintain that the custom is second nature to them.

These then are the three remarkable customs of India, which along with others I closely observed while I dwelt for two months in Ponticheri, freed from the fear of the persecution of the Infidel and with my mind at rest. I made my petition to various friends that we were restored enough to sail to Europe immediately, our strength recruited and our constitution refreshed with delightful fruits, some of whose names I will mention in the next chapter.

CHAPTER 61

INDIAN FRUITS

Seeing that it would be tedious to mention all the fruits of India, I have decided to include only those whose taste pleased me. The *Attas* is oval in shape, coming to a point like a pointed pear; the flesh has a knobbly appearance within the skin, which is separated by hand rather than with a knife; it is soft enough to be eaten out of the skin with a spoon, like butter, is full of small seeds, and is of a taste which at least to my palate excels that of all the fruits of Europe: the appetite for it grows with eating.[1] Another fruit is the *Kojavas*, similar to a pear and not very large, which contains within it hundreds of small very hard seeds, and which is white until ripe and then turns red; though pleasing enough to the palate, it is not very highly regarded because of the countless seeds which have to be removed.[2] The *Azar* or *Urackay manok* is the same as that called in Dahlack of Arabia Felix the amba, but tastes better and sweeter: in the months of November and December it is eaten in even greater quantity than in Arabia and is the size of a goose egg, yellow in colour, beautifully scented, not unlike the Juniper.[3] Muz the most delicate of fruits, to which I have referred in my descriptions of Ethiopia and Arabia, is properly called the Indian fig, and is of three sorts, the green, the yellow and the red, of which the red is the sweetest and best of the three, and with a more delicate taste, and could be called the fruit of the earthly paradise: there is in fact a fourth species, squarer in shape, not so good nor so sweet as the others and of rather harder consistency, which the Indians generally soften by

[1] The custard apple, *anona reticulata*.
[2] Tamil *kovāppalam/koyāppilam*, guava.
[3] Tamil *ūrkāy māṅkāy*, 'pickled mango'. We cannot explain *azar*. *Amb* or *amba* is the usual name for the mango in north India. Dahlack refers to the Dahlak islands in the Red Sea.

411

toasting over the fire, thereby improving its flavour: *Banian* is its name.[4]

I tasted another fruit called *Cili*, whose flower is red like a garden tulip and whose fruit is small and red and shaped like a small date; steeped in vinegar or spirit it is so strong that it seems to burn the tongue, and for a long period of time; wishing to taste it I paid for my curiosity with a burned tongue, though the Indians who are accustomed to it consume it in vast quantities, just as they eat ginger and fresh pepper like bread with great appetite, and claim that they purify the blood.[5] The tamarind grows better and more perfectly in India, and in greater quantity, than in Arabia or Egypt, and is excellent to give coolness in the heat of the East: it is freely eaten as part of the daily diet, and is beneficial to health. The peaches of India are larger and sweeter than in Italy, and, after those of Ethiopia, are the largest and best tasting, full of juice and the delight of all who eat them: but first of all, the queen of fruits, renowned even as far as Europe, is the pineapple, which grows in the greatest plenty in the fields which are full of its low plants, scarcely one cubit in height; the fruit is the size of a man's head and is indeed a pleasure to eat, of the sweetest of flavours surpassing that of all other fruits. The pointed top is covered with hard pointed prickly leaves, and the skin is hard like the pine of Europe: it is so sought after in India, particularly by the black slaves, that they would rather be deprived of life than of the pineapple, and the fields have to be protected by the landowners and harsh penalties laid down to stop unauthorized picking, although the slaves would rather incur the punishment than refrain from the pineapple. To the European this fruit is injurious, causing diarrhoea in those who eat too much in the heat, and the more experienced of the settlers steep the pineapple in red wine, boil it up once on the stove, and then eat what they please without ill-effects.

India also produces the coconut which grows on very tall trees, loftier than the European pine or oak, among the leaves of which the nuts grow in clusters to a weight of five or six pounds each, like balls covered with a hard skin two fingers thick. Within the skin, once opened up, a white fleshy substance is found, which

[4] Arabic *mauz*, 'banana'. The reference to frying is correct, but Prutky seems to have appropriated the name of *Ficus bengalensis* L., the banyan tree.

[5] Chilli, red pepper.

can be removed with a spoon and which refreshes the eater with a watery taste not unlike cooked greens, while within this fleshy material is contained a quantity of the sweetest water, excellent to quench the thirst and to purify the blood. The coconut tree is of the utmost utility to the Indians, providing food, drink, clothing, housing and fuel; on the appetizing flesh they stay their hunger, with the water they quench their thirst, from the pounded rind they spin a thread from which they make various clothing materials, the wood provides material for whole houses, the leaves, so broad and thick, provide thatch for the roofs, and for every need of the inhabitants this tree has a service to offer. Not unlike the coconut is another tree rather smaller called *Lataagnie*, whose fruit is inedible but whose leaves are long and broad and like palm leaves can be made into roofs which last for thirty years.[6] I tasted yet another fruit shaped like the amba of Arabia, which is steeped in vinegar and eaten with great enjoyment as an accompaniment to meat and rice: its name is the greater *aczar*.[7] The plant called *battath* with its very long roots is grown throughout the fields of India, and when roasted on hot coals is better than Italian chestnuts: it is eaten especially by the poor,[8] who also plant another root commonly called *Pistaschi*,[9] which grow in great abundance and are roasted in the ashes together with the rind until they turn red, whereupon the edible part can be removed, three or four kernels from each rind, of a nutty flavour. There are also apples in India, soft and reddish in colour, which when skinned and flavoured with sugar are pleasant to eat and beneficial to health in the hot weather.

Such are the more exotic of the fruits of India, the fare of the nobility and the merchants, and, though there are many others of slight value which are the food of the commoners, I think it useless to mention them as they are of no importance. All kinds of garden produce are grown, lettuce, green vegetables, broccoli, much better than those of Europe because of the sun's greater heat, and more delicate to eat. They are quite without bread

[6] Not identified.
[7] Not identified.
[8] Sweet potatoes or yams. The word used is derived from the Portuguese name for the potato, *batata*, which came to be used in several Asian languages for various root crops.
[9] Pistachio nuts.

413

made of wheat or of any other grain, nor do they plant corn, which is imported from Europe at great expense solely to make bread for the Europeans. The rest of the population, all the Indians and the poorer Europeans, eat rice boiled in water instead of bread, and being used to this from youth up they live in great contentment and grow big and strong on it. An even greater expense is paper imported from Europe, with the result that the Indians write all their documents or letters to each other with a pointed metal tool on leaves plucked from the sugar cane of three fingers width: all their correspondence, including business contracts and agreements on other matters, are so transcribed, and they exchange similar leaves with each other instead of letters. But the next chapter will better describe the customs of the heathen.

CHAPTER 62

HEATHEN CUSTOMS
AND BURIAL CEREMONIES

The customs of the heathen and idolaters are so contrary to true reason that the Christian spirit rejects them, and the stranger is struck with amazement when he meets them for the first time; for myself I had but arrived in Ponticheri when I was amazed to see a bridal pair being carried solemnly around in a palanquin, the bridegroom at the head and the bride at the foot, while an escort conducted them through the streets singing, dancing and playing musical instruments until evening, when perforated iron pots on long poles were set alight instead of lamps, and added the illumination of fire to the celebrations: when tiredness overcame them the bridal pair were taken home, to put the finishing touch to the ceremony. The same system prevails in the case of death, when the corpse is immediately washed carefully, all hair shaved from the body, and then wrapped in a white robe and laid in a palanquin; it is then conducted through the town with song, dance and clamour, with various games being played in the streets; the mourners cast mud and dust on their heads and even throw dust in the air, wailing like beasts without reason, and at last bury the corpse outside the city in a special place after the Ethiopian custom. In the lands under heathen rule the custom flourished until recent times that on her husband's death the wife to attest the truth of her love leaped upon his funeral pyre and threw herself alive into the flames, unless she wished to get the reputation among her relations and neighbours generally of wickedness, immorality and dishonesty: this was the way in which she proved the sincerity of her wifely love. However, in the present age, after living beside Christians and associating so long with them, they have realized that this is unlawful and contrary to the will of God, so that this stupid custom is less prevalent, not only in Catholic but also in heathen districts.

Even at the present day they believe firmly in the transmigration of souls into oxen and cows, with the result that they will eat no beef nor other meat in case they are devouring the soul of their father or mother or other relation. Indeed so great a respect do they bear these beasts that their excrement is burned to ashes, mixed with a reddening agent and some water, and daily smeared morning and evening upon the forehead and breast; for even greater religious purification they use the excrement raw, with red or white colouring matter, for their anointment. There are in fact men of religion appointed for this very purpose, who carry cow dung round the houses in a box and mark everyone on forehead and breast with a pencil. So blind to reason are they that they believe that this preserves them from all kinds of sickness, and a dying man is happy indeed who can grasp the tail of a urinating cow and wash himself in cow urine, thus assuring himself of eternal salvation: despite these and other follies a miserable death overtakes them.

Very few converts are made to the true faith, although daily they talk with Catholics on terms of friendship and are well informed on the faith and on Christian morality; but they cleave firmly to the unbending formalities of their idolatrous so-called devotions. A leading missionary told me sadly of an idolater, a woman, with whom he had been friendly for many years and firmly hoped would turn Catholic; when he plied her with a host of good reasons why the Roman Catholic faith was the only road to salvation, she replied shortly 'Father, why weary yourself to make me a Christian? We idolaters and heathen lead a more devout and more moral life than many Christians: you drink wine and get scandalously drunk: you live lives of shame, you eat meat, every sensual vice is common with you, and equally the tenets that you preach as divine commands you do not yourselves observe; you are for every sinning, and live for pleasure. We on the contrary, we idolaters and heathen, abstain from all these, we take neither wine nor flesh nor fowl, we eat nothing that has life, far less do we commit those sins that you Christians commit each day, nor do we steal other men's wives but rest content with our own; our state of idolatry that you rebuke I firmly believe to be the better. Press me no further Father I beg of you. I

416

maintain my resolve to continue as I live and as I am.' At these unwelcome words the missionary blushed and was silent, knowing well what scandals, what terrible sins, are committed in India by the Europeans; excessive drinking, scandalous and immoderate sexual behaviour with the natives, have prevented the conversion of thousands and are the cause of spiritual ruin, for which the Almighty will exact a strict account. How often do the missionaries sorrowfully listen to these taunts and realise that a hundred are turned away sooner than one converted to the Catholic faith.

This too is the reason for the covert hatred of Christians which lurks in the hearts of most of the heathen, who lose no opportunity of doing an injury to the enemies of honourable behaviour and to the sinners against the teachings of their own religion. Indeed the very heathen of Ponticheri bear so great a grudge against Europeans, at least against those who trade with them, that they murder them whenever possible, often boarding their ships in gangs under the pretext of buying goods from them, and then while the merchants and sailors are thinking no harm plunging their knives into their breasts and seeking safety in flight: they rejoice at the honour of putting an end to such scandalous Christian lives. The result is that at the present time the ships that approach this coast or district permit no heathen to come aboard until he has been inspected and asked if he carries a weapon; then however he is permitted on board because the merchants make enormous profits and sell at an exorbitant rate the opium which is so eagerly sought after and eaten by the heathen, and of which fifty pounds sell for 1,000 dollars or more; and the western traders have to be on their guard against dishonesty and loss lest they be paid out in their own coin.

After so many battles and such continual disagreements and conflicts, each European nation has established its own territory in India, the French in the important city of Ponticheri with its neighbouring districts under its own governor, the Portuguese in *Goa*, with some neighbouring islands and districts, the English in *Bombay*, a tiny island among the other lands of the Europeans, though they are also in possession of a small place called *Forsendevi*[1] with a useful fort close to Ponticheri, and also *Mottraz* or *Modras* is under their control.[2] The Dutch are sovereign in the

[1] Fort St David, just south of Pondichéry.
[2] Madras.

finest territory, that of *Patavia*, and of the very productive island of *Ambon*,[3] where on small shrubs, like bushes of one year's growth, grow the cloves, which eaten green with rice are quite delicious, with a sweet and refined taste, a wonderful fragrance, soothing to the stomach and leaving a pleasant odour behind them which persists for the whole day. But they must be taken only in moderation because of their heating tendency, though the Indians are more accustomed to them and the richer classes eat them daily mixed with rice. This island of cloves is about sixty Italian miles from Patavia, the produce of which brings in huge sums of money, especially the nutmegs, which grow in great profusion near Patavia in the neighbouring island of *Bauda*[4] whose nutmegs make it a vision of delight: they grow like large Italian nuts, with the shell enwrapped by the flowers of the nutmeg: while the shell is still green it has a soft and delicate taste, and the nuts cooked with sugar together with the shell and the flowers produce an especially strengthening dish, a specific for the heart. In my travels I have experimented in the eating of it, and it is well known among the nobility of Europe, to whom the Dutch sell it. Such are the particular territories ruled today in India by the nations of Europe, as far as the short duration of my sojourn enabled me to view them. The coast of *Malabar* is under the sovereignty of the heathen, among whom in perfect peace live a large number of missionaries, mostly Franciscans who settled there when the first Portuguese colonies were established, and built their hospices there: they minister to more Catholics than in other parts of India because they have led many idolaters into the bosom of the Roman church.[5] The coast of *Coromandel*, as also *Comorin*, is in heathen hands though they maintain good trading relations with the Europeans. *Bengal* the biggest state with the largest neighbouring territory is in heathen control with its own native governor an idolater,[6] who is well disposed to trading with all the European nations; it contains missionaries who are Capuchins for the Propagation of the Faith, as well as Jesuits who have charge of the souls of the Europeans.

---

[3] More generally known as Amboina.
[4] Banda.
[5] The converts were not so much 'idolaters', i.e. Hindus, as the so-called Christians of St Thomas.
[6] In fact a Muslim.

All the other areas known to geographers are under the sway of heathen and idolaters, and are governed under the supreme authority of the Great Mogul.[7]

When I had sufficiently examined these and other matters, the principal concern in my mind was to continue as soon as possible with my predetermined journey to Rome. I pressed his excellency Governor Duplex to let me depart with the first ships, partly so that I could the quicker discharge my obligation to the Sacred Congregation, and partly because the voyages of the first ships were less at risk from the weather and not exposed to so many storms: but many Parisians and other Frenchmen, gentlemen of the first rank, were already in occupation of the berths in the first ships, leaving no more proper accommodation for us, and we began to encounter the greatest difficulty in departing, being offered a place in the second ships sailing in December and January. So late a departure was a serious setback to my apostolic mission, with the risk that in the meantime further missionaries might be despatched by Rome to no avail and the Sacred Congregation involved in no small expense, and with this fear in mind I was more eager to press the Governor through the mediation of a number of friends. My argument however rational met with a negative, but our good friends, who knew the Governor's habit of mind, gave us some hope of success, and knowing that I had brought with me a harp of David and that the Governor was a lover of music, advised me when I was invited to dinner to produce and offer to play my harp to the music-loving Governor.[8] So it came about that, having sought permission to bring my instrument, which had never before been seen or heard in India, I began at the end of dinner to play and sing the hymn to Mary, so much to the admiration and pleasure of the Governor and his guests that I was required to play the same piece a second time, whereupon I realised that the Governor was of a mind to reward me, as he kindly and spontaneously enquired what favour I wished for in return for this delightful musical treat so much to his taste. I modestly replied that I desired nothing so ardently as permission to board one of the first ships that I might the sooner fulfil the duties of my obedience, which was so precious

---

[7] By this time the real authority of the Mogul emperors was very limited.

[8] Dupleix's love of music was celebrated.

to me. Lo and behold! Having been asked to give but one more performance I soon afterwards received a most kind assent to my request, his excellency remarking that the music of so sweet a harp must be marred by no note of sorrow, so that my harp secured for me my passage among the first ships, and where my prayers and the intervention of friends had failed my instrument succeeded. Nor was this unreasonable, seeing that David played before Saul and Satan departed from him, as holy scripture says, and I too played on my harp and every difficulty departed, and in addition to the many benefits conferred on me I received at last the boon of my departure. Thanks be to God, for almost two months I busied myself in soliciting my passage, and in little more than one moment I finally obtained it, not to speak of further unexpected and considerable kindnesses, such as the generous payment to the ship's captain of two hundred Roman scudi or one hundred pagodas or one hundred gold pieces to convey my colleague and myself to the port of L'Orient in France. In addition to paying for our food, drink and clothing, he gave each of us thirty shirts and numbers of Indian scarves, as well as various items necessary for such a long voyage, candied fruits to strengthen the stomach, crystallized pineapples, peaches and other confectionery, and all out of his unparalleled generosity. To put in a word his truly royal liberality, he expended on our behalf more than 700 rupees or German florins, and in addition to this at the moment of our departure he presented each of us as well as his many favours with twenty-five rupees of gold and his beloved consort sixty of silver, to the admiration of all who saw it, asking nothing more of us in return than that in celebrating Mass we make of them the usual remembrance, which truth to say was only their just due. He also entrusted to me his four year old niece who was being sent to school in France, because she had been well acquainted with me in Ponticheri and was fond of me: I was to comfort her if perhaps the long sea voyage distressed her, and take care of her as occasion demanded. Throughout the subsequent voyage I associated with no one else and plied her with continual attentions, in memory of my benefactor.

CHAPTER 63

DEPARTURE FROM INDIA FOR EUROPE

After rendering our respectful thanks for his goodness to our most generous of benefactors, we embarked on October 19, the feast of St Peter of Alcantara, on the French ship *Lis* under the command of Captain Bear, and calling on the name of the Almighty weighed anchor and set sail at 2 o'clock in the morning.[1] At about midday we drew near to the small island of *Roderici*[2] which is garrisoned by a French officer and twelve soldiers, who, wretchedly housed, are stationed there to protect it from invasion or other eventualities, and gather for their own consumption the plentiful produce of the island and its excellent sea-fish and turtles, of fifty or sixty pounds weight: there is an abundance of everything save human society and they live a hermit-like existence, since shipping only puts in there in cases of real necessity or of tempest, and our own ship likewise continued on its voyage to another island subject to the king of France, *Mauritz*.[3] Arriving on December 1, we anchored and remained at moorings there until January 27 to tranship cargo and take in further victuals. The island is large and fertile, of great value to the French who have settled it for about thirty years and whose farmers are spread throughout its whole area: the housing is commodious, a mixture of fine dwellings or small palaces in the European style, and the colonists reap a plentiful harvest since they hold their fields and property free of all royal taxes. The houses of the Europeans are built beside the harbour in a straight double row, each settler possessing in addition his own farm on

[1] Ananda Ranga Pillai, vol. VIII, Madras, 1922, pp. 341, 344, mentions the arrival of the *Lys* from Europe in May 1753.

[2] Rodrigues Island, to the east of Mauritius. In spite of what Prutky seems to imply he obviously cannot have reached Rodrigues on the day he left Pondichéry.

[3] Mauritius.

the island; the Governor, a man of merit, rules from a strong double-walled fort sufficiently garrisoned to resist any hostile attack, and because a large part of the island remains uncultivated new settlers are constantly arriving for whom new stone houses are constantly being built, with good hopes for future advantage.

A most unpleasant feature is that all the field work for lack of oxen or horses is performed by poverty-stricken slaves, who are used like brutes or cattle to plough or harrow the soil without respect to the Christian name to which they have been converted: it is harsh treatment to good Catholics to force them to plough, to dig, to turn the soil and to labour in the sweat of their face. Nor is bread provided for their sustenance: a certain sort of wood called *majeck*[4] is ground with its roots and given to the labourers in place of bread, just as in Germany Indian cress is ground and sieved for cattle food; after the Ethiopian fashion it is rolled out into thin cakes and cooked on a large round grid-iron for their daily nourishment. The proprietors maintain for this sole purpose a great stock of these roots, which when heated on the iron plate take on the white colour of curds, but which provide no nourishment or sustenance to the wretched slaves who taste meat but three or four times in the year. This miserable so-called bread is their sole sustenance, while from sunrise to sunset they labour without rest on a diet of excessive water because of the heat of the sun: barefoot, shoeless, clad only in a long shift of blue cloth, they excite the greatest sympathy in the observer, especially as the landowners, not satisfied with the value of their labour, trade in them like cattle without regard to their profession of Catholicism. It is not surprising that they are ripe for rebellion and the French compelled to be on their guard against an unexpected uprising and murder, since for every European there are at least fifty blacks, upstanding strong men who would easily overwhelm all the Europeans if they could but get arms. Thus the congregation at every holy day or Sunday is protected by a guard posted outside the doors of the church, and the settlers live in a justifiable state of insecurity, seeing that a few years ago at divine service all the slaves suddenly united and would have slaughtered them to a man had not the plot been betrayed before it was fully hatched: indeed they have cause to fear the just anger of God,

[4] French *mâche*, corn salad or lamb's lettuce, *Valerianella locusta* L.

knowing well as they do that all Christians are redeemed by Christ's blood from the service of the Devil, but not carrying this precept into practice. Grieving at these and other sins I arraigned the Catholic settlers as being harsher and more tyrannical than the very Mahometans, knowing personally that Christians in Turkish hands are better clothed, fed with more nourishing food, fortified daily with good bread and meat, and loved by their masters as their own sons: in this island by contrast the behaviour of the Christian French was not that of humans but of worse than barbarians. Much more could be said on this subject, but I pass on in silence as my custom is.

One more thing must be said. Many French nationals are found in the island who behave worse than the heathen and idolaters and who without reproof live lives of the greatest shame; I recount but one incident out of a long series. In the year 1752 shortly before our arrival here it befell that in her husband's absence a young woman was brought to bed first of a son, and then on the third day, as she rested after the labours of birth, of five puppies. What a sin was here! In course of time the truth of the matter came to the ears of His Most Christian Majesty, and one puppy, embalmed, was sent back to France with the guilty woman for judgement and punishment at the University of Law; the other puppies were on the same day put to the fire, the proper desert of the guilty woman also had not the shameful circumstance, never before heard of in France, excited the pity of His Most Christian Majesty, whose innate goodness and compassion imprisoned the woman in a house of religion for the rest of her life, while the dog was claimed for scientific examination. As I spent some weeks on the island I heard from devout persons many stories which I omit to mention in detail for modesty's sake, because they would bring offence to the ears of the honourable. The spiritual shepherds of this island and its inhabitants are the Lazarist missionary fathers of the New Congregation of St Vincent de Paul, who have three hospices here which contain, one three priests, one two, and one one priest only with a layman. Like other seculars they own slaves to till the land, but treat them rather better, giving them better clothes and better food. As for agricultural produce, there is a sufficiency of rice, no great abundance of wheat, and plentiful supplies of maize, but the deficiency of wine and some other articles has to be made up by imports from Europe. At the present time pits have been sunk for the extraction of iron ore, of which it is said that the whole island is composed: in the course of time it is hoped to discover other more valuable minerals. There are no watermills but only wind-mills, as apart from the sea the island is without running water or rivers.

The missionaries of the island welcomed us in most charitably, and for the whole of our stay entertained us hospitably and refreshed us after the fatigues of our voyage. We noted their enthusiasm for the daily task and the zeal and cheerful patience with which they gave instruction to the people and knowledge to the ignorant; every evening after sunset the blacks congregated in the hospice forecourt, where in their midst the nonagenarian superior of the mission, full of zeal for the Lord, fervently preached to them the way of salvation and the kingdom of God, catechized them, and to conclude their period of instruction declaimed the Lord's Prayer and many others, the people repeat-ing the words after him. His zealous enthusiasm was truly apos-tolic as the love of his flock surrounded him, and as he blessed their departure with a father's affection he appeared like an angel sent from God, and converted many to the Faith that leads to salvation.

Our ship meanwhile had taken on board a mixed cargo for Europe, and with five others was preparing to set sail, delighted at our approaching departure, when quite unexpectedly a quarrel arose between the ships' captains, of which the cause was a Parisian girl who had been secretly smuggled aboard a ship at L'Orient and taken to the city of *Macao* in China, despite the very strict regulation of His Most Christian Majesty that no one should be allowed a woman on board the royal ships. Alas, in secret dis-obedience the French captain of one ship had crossed as far as Ponticheri and was sailing towards Macao with the girl, when the ship was tossed from side to side and could make no further headway in the face of a dangerous storm: the cause of this being held to be the girl and the deadly sins committed with her by the captain during the whole voyage from Europe, the captain at length was seized by remorse and implored God's aid with a firm promise of amendment: if for the rest of the voyage the winds were favourable he would disembark the girl at the next port of call. Lo and behold, God in His mercy, at the moment the sinner returned to his obedience and promised repentance, outpoured His grace, and the ship from then on proceeded fairly to the coast of China, where the girl was put off on shore despite her cries and tearful entreaties. Here an English ship took pity on her and carried her to Macao, from which at that same time another French ship was returning to Europe; neither knowing nor caring about the earlier difficulties this ship took the girl aboard, and put her conduct and behaviour under the watchful scrutiny of the chaplain until she was disembarked at Mauritz for onward shipment to Europe. So just at the moment when we were eager to set sail, no captain was willing to take the girl with him to brave the dangers of the deep, and each protested loudly at the imposition, until the Governor took up her case and recommended the girl to my care. When we left port on 27 January 1753 (*sic*) the Governor's friendly persuasion had had its influence on our ship's captain and true Christian Captain Bear. 'Two missionaries and the ship's chaplain will ensure complete propriety throughout the ship.' The difficult task entrusted to the captain and myself gave us all cause for apprehension lest we were shipping another Jonah against God's will, and that the girl was an enemy of God who would bring us all to disaster. Before our departure I interviewed and prepared her, heard her confession and administered the Sacrament, and filled her heart with the fear of God: she was then taken on board and well guarded in the powder room[5] where we never allowed her to appear in public nor to speak with anyone, save on the many occasions when she made her confession to me. The Holy Communion changed her from an erring Magdalen to a truly penitent and devout woman, and at the port of L'Orient she was released from custody and set safely ashore, and restored to her mother who was still living.

---

[5] At that date the powder-room on board ship was habitually used as a place of detention.

CHAPTER 64

THE ISLAND OF BOURBON

Having expressed to the missionary fathers our lively sense of thanks for their generous forebearance with us over so long a stay and for the many kindnesses we had received, we finally bade our last farewell to them and to our French friends among the laity on January 27 of the year 1753 (*sic*), and, our ship being stocked with all available necessities of life, we spread our sails to a favourable wind and made such a fair run that on the third day we were so fortunate as to reach the French island of *Bourbon*, otherwise known as *Mascarein*.[1] Here for various reasons we again anchored and indeed were fortunate to do so, because on that very night while we lay at anchor we were struck by a violent storm which would have inflicted severe damage on us in the harbour, or even complete destruction, if the ship had not been made fast with five cables. Sky and land dissolved into each other and all elements of nature were like to be destroyed, so that we each of us gave thanks to God that we were fairly fixed on dry land. Three days were spent in buying a further store of poultry, fowls both common and Indian, ducks, geese, chickens and sheep, found in more abundance in this island than in any other, as also of rice, dates, and many other sorts of fruit, though the dates are smaller than those of Egypt. Their coffee is good, second in quality only to that of Mocha, whence in times past it was exported and transplanted out of Arabia Felix; the bean remains green, because there is not the same degree of heat here as in Arabia, but the coffee is excellent with plenty of taste, and its small granules contain such goodness as to surpass any grown in the

---

[1] Its name was changed to Réunion at the French Revolution, to Bonaparte in 1809, back to Bourbon in 1814, and to Réunion again in 1848. The Mascarene Islands also include Mauritius and Rodrigues.

West. To gain more exact information I climbed on the day after our arrival the mountains which contain the coffee plantations, which at that season were full of ripe red fruit like cherries, of a truly delicious taste. The plantations of coffee bushes are very widely spread among the mountains and are planted with great regularity; they are of no great height, the leaves being as broad as those of a peach, and I was delighted to be able to make a true examination of them; I spent several pleasant hours in the plantations. I then paid a visit to the missionary fathers, who received me more as though I were an angel from heaven than a mere mortal, and overwhelmed me with all sorts of kindnesses.

The island is of similar size to the island of Mauritz, and grows in great plenty every kind of agricultural and garden produce, as well as an abundance of every sort of beast: since our captain had for his journey onward to the port of L'Orient to make provision of food and drink for thirty-four persons at his own table, he had bought three hundred fowls, hens, ducks, geese and many Indian fowl, as well as having already taken on shipboard thirty oxen, about one hundred sheep, seventy large pigs and many small ones, and four milking cows, that the guests of his table should lack for nothing. A similar provision, greater or less, was made by each captain according to the quality of the ship and the rank of the passengers. Few slaves are to be found in Bourbon island, nor do they labour at the plough or harrow, because the land is heavily peopled with Europeans, who own beasts of burden to work the fields, either oxen or cows, and who feed their slaves better and keep them for domestic service. The garrison consists of a few soldiers, among whom I discovered two Germans, one of whom was in absolute despair because he was being detained there beyond the period set down in his terms of surrender: had I not approached his excellency the Governor and besought him that the man be allowed to depart with us, he would have thrown himself into the sea and met a miserable end. The island's Governor is a personage of importance and wealth, well provided like the whole population with the necessaries of life, and is open-handed and generous to all comers; he presented us with one hundred pounds of coffee for our own use, and although its export from the island is strictly forbidden by royal command, yet as a mark of special favour he gave us a written licence to take it into France with us.

All stores having been taken aboard we set sail on February 3, and the wind continuing fair we passed on February 17 the island of *Malacascar,*[2] which is under the rule of the heathen, who permit but few Europeans to trade with them though there is a very flourishing slave market there. The French obtained from the present chief permission to construct a stronghold on a small island near the mainland, and built it to a good standard of security; a few years later they seized possession of another strong point on the mainland beside the sea, but before it was fully fortified their negligence and rashness led them to keep no proper watch, with the result that an unexpected night attack by the idolaters overturned the entire construction and massacred the French. They are now aware of their danger, and having obtained the chief's permission have built a strong fort which they protect by a guard post, and prosecute their trade in slaves with a greater sense of security.[3]

At length around the time of St Matthias's day the weather began to change, the sea grew rough and the waves surged up, although elsewhere throughout the Indian Ocean the months of February and March are favourable to the mariner: a storm of terrible danger came upon us, the seas raged, and death stared us in the face, from which it was to be understood that we had entered the vicinity of the *Cape of Good Hope,* so feared of all seamen. On February 26, and even more on the day following, the fury of the sea filled us full of fear for seven days in succession, while we meantime held out more and more into the high seas, lest we be caught close to land and shipwrecked, so that we made many hundreds of miles of seaway without in any way advancing our true course; nor was it possible to sit and eat at table, each man clinging to some corner to save himself from falling and breaking a limb. So horrible and dangerous was it as to be scarcely credible to the reader or hearer who has not personally experienced it. If it had been possible, the fury of the raging sea would have drained the veins of a bloody sweat: what pious wishes, what

[2] Madagascar.

[3] Again, Prutky's history is confused. The French occupied Fort Dauphin on the mainland of SE Madagascar from 1643 to 1674, when it was abandoned. The island of Ste Marie to the south of Antongil Bay was ceded to them in 1750, but the French agent and his companions were soon massacred. It was reoccupied in 1753 but abandoned again four years later.

good resolutions are directed to God by all seafarers! To Him
alone are they known. However, we found again that after the
clouds comes the sun, and on March 8 we began to breathe again
from our fears as the wind abated and the sea grew calmer, and
we rested ourselves a little. Up to now the violent winds and
streaming rain were enough to overturn a house, and the terrible
tempest which had raged around our ship had so filled our
nostrils with the roar and rush of the waves that we could each
scarcely hear the other speak, and the sailors were forced into
indescribable exertions: until on the aforesaid March 8, the feast
of St Rosa, the waves diminished, our anxieties were eased, and
we thereby deduced that we had now passed the Cape of Good
Hope. The winds had driven us off course by many degrees into
a great detour, and we had spent fourteen days in this terrible
passage of the Cape and been forced many hundreds of miles
into deep water, off our proper course. But praise be to God we
came safe off, and as is customary at sea we gave thanks to the
Almighty by solemnly singing on March 10 the Ambrosian hymn,
and, as it was the second Sunday in Lent, by offering to Him a
sung Mass. The captain ordered for all hands a special repast of
better food and drink, and entertained us and all who dined at
his table to a splendid meal and excellent wine; especially to our
taste was a white wine of the Cape of Good Hope, which for
goodness and delicacy of taste surpassed almost all other wines;
like heavenly nectar it delighted all our table, and seemed even
better than the wine of Tuscany: every spirit was refreshed after
the dangers of the deep.

Scarcely were we a little restored when another mishap occurred, when on March 12 a sailor who was taking in sail at the top
of the mast chanced to fall into the sea: the alarm was raised, the
sails at once shifted and the ship hove to as though stationary on
the waves, whereupon with all speed a small boat was lowered
with eight men to seek the sailor who was tossing hither and yon
amid the waves; a lookout at the masthead, who could see him,
indicated to the crew with a white scarf whither to direct their
course, and within the space of half an hour he was found afloat,
and rescued to the general admiration, though if he had been
unable to swim he would long before have been food for fishes;
but thanks to Him Who rules the waves of the sea he was preserved
and brought back on board half dead, where he was restored to

health by medical attention. A few days later we passed the island of St Helena, a possession of the English who maintain there a governor and a stronghold with a garrison of soldiers, but since we did not disembark there I am unable to relate any particulars of it. Shortly afterwards we approached another desert island which belongs to no nation and which affords little wood or water: discovered in times past by the Portuguese on the feast of Our Lord's Ascension, it was honoured by them with this name.

CHAPTER 65

ASCENSION ISLAND

During the time when the Portuguese were sailing the oceans in their voyages of discovery of islands and continents, they spied land from afar and approached this island on the day of the Feast of the Ascension of Our Lord Jesus Christ; not knowing the name of this newly discovered locality they honoured it with the title of Ascension as a mark of respect to Our Saviour and to the day of its discovery: to this day it is known to mariners as Ascension Island. Approaching it on Passion Sunday March 31 at about 5 p.m., we lay at anchor there, as is the custom of all passing ships, to recuperate our strength after the dangers undergone off the Cape of Good Hope. For this purpose the island is well suited, being abundantly stocked with fish of all sorts and shapes, of such beauty and variety of colour as to call forth our wonder at the bounty of God; as it was almost possible to catch them in the hand, the sailors were every minute taking on the hook many pounds weight of fish, whose flesh, firm, excellent and full of flavour, tasted better than meat itself.

Being located in latitude 7° 57′ the island has an indescribably hot climate, and being almost wholly volcanic is uninhabited and deserted: there are likewise in many places dangerous invisible holes, as it were chasms covered with sand, which draw the unwary walker into their depths, as many of the rash and curious have already proved at the cost of their life. It is however possible to pick one's way carefully, though the earth trembles and moves beneath the feet, and it is thought that quite soon the whole island will sink into the sea, despite its rocky composition; the force of the sun and the volcanic activity heat the stones almost to dust, and they display a variety of colours, glassy, iron-like, white and red. A remarkable feature in an almost wholly volcanic terrain is a tall high peak which rears up in the centre, as it were

431

part of terra firma, its six leagues' extent providing in the higher parts a reliable source of food and pasture to a great number of roaming wild deer and goats brought here previously by Europeans and multiplied by breeding, watered also by permanent lakes and pools which are fed by the frequent rain storms: the provider of all this, the green mountain, stands in sole superiority, the other lower peaks being dry and coloured black, white or red.

Ascension Island is particularly famous for its numbers of turtles, of four hundred and even five hundred pounds' weight each, enough to feed the whole of our ship's complement of three hundred sailors, and the captain's table, and the rest of those returning to France, a total of about four hundred people;[1] one turtle provided dinner for all these with a variety of meat, the flesh having the appearance of beef but making a soup which tasted better than chicken soup and had anti-scorbutic properties. The turtle provides three different sorts of meat, one like venison, one, from a higher part of the carcase, like veal, and the third like beef; if properly cooked and seasoned it is indistinguishable from them. Eaten roasted in its own fat with its shell we found it a more delicate dish than any veal or pork, and equally we tasted a variety of cakes made with its eggs than which nothing better can be imagined: a thousand eggs are laid by each turtle[2] over a period of thirty days, large, round, bigger than a hen's egg and covered with a very fine skin, but to be eaten sparingly because in the great heat they are conducive to bile. There are but two months, March and April,[3] when it is possible to take the turtle, which land at night from the sea on the shore of the island, lay their eggs in the sand and carefully conceal them, the sun's heat hatching out the eggs in the space of three weeks:[4] it is then that the mariners take them, the sailors forming themselves into three or four different parties down the beach and silently keeping watch until the turtle digs up the sand with her feet to lay her eggs, when the hunters fall cautiously on her and turn her over; they then return to their watch as before, until by these

[1] The Green Turtle, *Chelonia mydas* L.
[2] Prutky exaggerates: 100 to 250.
[3] From Christmas to midsummer, Isobel Gill, *Six months in Ascension*, London, 1875, p. 75.
[4] Two months, *ibid.*

means in one night they have taken twenty or more: the legs are bound with a rope, great care being taken to avoid the bite, for which wound there is no cure,[5] and in the morning the haul is taken on board ship: next night the procedure is repeated, until each ship has provided herself with at least eighty for her victualling. We ourselves captured seventy in two nights, setting sail on the third day, and every morning a bowl of turtle soup took for us the place of any other food or drink to refresh the constitution and purge the blood, and from then onward different members of our company were cured of different complaints. Only the female is eaten, never the male, who escorts his mate to the shore for her to lay her eggs but remains in the sea to await her and never touches land: if after a long time she fails to return, the male returns to the open sea and thus can never be captured. At one time it was believed by many that the eggs only remain in the sand for nine days; the young then hatch out and on that very day or the one following make their way into the sea as tiny chicks only if they escape a bird which is their enemy: this species of crow is found here in great numbers, having a long tail divided into two forks, and being endowed with night vision though blind in the daylight:[6] it preys not only on the eggs but even more on the young of the turtle. These birds too are of value to mankind, a remarkable general medicine being made from their fat and from the grease which is found in holes within their bones when the sinew has been removed. To obtain this grease the mariners go to the trouble of sitting by day in holes in the ground to capture the birds in quantity, after which the fat is extracted and taken to Europe; in the same way some baby turtles are brought to France to see if there they will grow to the same size.

Strengthened by our meals of such excellent fish we were preparing to set sail, when alas another misfortune overtook us, one of the sailors being noted missing after a hunt for birds: not knowing whether he had had the misfortune to fall into a hole, or had lost his way and thus failed to return, the captain left on

[5] Doubtless because it was believed it could crush the bones. The strength of its jaws was legendary. Pliny, bk IX chapter 10, states that it can crush stones. Ulisse Aldrovandi, *De quadrupedib' digitatis oviparis*, Bonon., 1637, p. 713, says that one which was brought to him in Bologna broke a thick stick with one bite.

[6] Skuas, but they have diurnal vision.

the shore, to cover all possibilities, a supply of bread, salt, meat, stockfish, water and other necessities, so that if by chance he were still alive and found his way back, he could be brought safe home on one of the six other ships that were due to put in here. With sails set we proceeded on our course before a wretched wind, due to our proximity to the Line that we were about to cross, while the shifts of the inconstant breeze brought great quantities of rain by night and day to vex the crew in their labours, as they had to toil ceaselessly without sleep and in wet clothes. Little or no headway was made, the wind was contrary if it blew at all, and we remained becalmed, while every hour the rain fell six, seven or more times until the sun shone, and we stayed in one spot. As all seafarers know, for about six leagues before and after the Line the same light airs prevail, though there is no danger to fear, and often every wind was stilled and it was as though we stood on dry land, the ship being as steady as though at anchor. Many observers recount descriptions of natural changes, bodily tiredness, pains to the stomach or head, or changes in temperature, but thanks be to God none of these happened to me nor did I observe any one of them, as though I had not crossed the Line; nor indeed did I notice anything special in my comrades. Despite the fictions of the different writers in their accounts I experienced nothing similar, and am compelled to assert that writers such as these are speaking of occurrences that are unusual, or miraculous, or invented. It is the custom on board ship to indulge in a number of pranks when crossing the Line, exchanging blows, falling on to the deck, soaking one another with water, which they call baptism, and indeed the only ones to be soused are those who are crossing the Line for the first time. For this reason, though they wished to honour us missionaries with such a baptism, we refused it, saying that when a priest was present it was unlawful for a layman to confer baptism, and so we were left in peace to disport ourselves with the others. Meanwhile we were advancing slowly onwards away from the Line, and when we had made six or seven leagues the breeze freshened behind us, and as we made better speed we thanked God for such a successful crossing: it is only in these two months, when the daily rainstorms are more frequent and the winds blow up suddenly from all quarters, that the crossing is somewhat easier and some progress at least can be made towards the shortening of the

434

journey: in the other months of the year even more time is taken in making the transit.

Pursuing our course until April 8 a new mischance occurred, and we watched one of the soldiers fall in feigned madness into the sea: a good draught of sea water dispelled his madness, and he hastened to tear the clothes from his body and swim naked in our sight lest the weight of his clothes should impede his swimming and he lose his life. For more than half an hour he floundered in the waves until by the same crew of sailors in their cockboat he was plucked out from danger, whereupon he ceased from his delirium and returned to his senses, well purged in sea water. On April 14 we celebrated the Easter festival with all the ceremony that we could muster, and offered to the Almighty the sacrifice of the Mass: this was the first time amid all our hardships that my colleague and I fortified ourselves with a morsel of meat, because before we reached Ascension Island and its beautiful fish we fed ourselves throughout Lent on horse beans or ship's biscuit or some form of vegetable. By a papal dispensation those who journey through the Indies by sea are permitted to eat meat at any time, but we two, in gratitude for the many blessings bestowed on us by God by sea and land, and especially for the perils from which He had delivered us, had from the time of our expulsion from Ethiopia foregone this privilege of eating meat and contented ourselves with a low diet. This practice kept us healthy and active even in the fasts enjoined by our Sacred Seraphic Rule and the other fasts of Holy Church, and our health was as good as if we had fared sumptuously every day; others, who ate meat, were assailed by various illnesses, and we watched many of them die and become food for fishes. The ship's sole chaplain, an Augustinian with a broad sleeve, together with a Portuguese Jesuit returning from China, continued to eat meat and protested enviously at our fasting, hating us as eccentrics and setting the Captain against us to deny us our small starvation rations: their envy at our deed of virtue made them regard us as their enemies. But shortly afterwards the Blessed Lord struck down this grumbling chaplain with a severe illness, which caused him to return to his senses and repent of his illwill, humbly apologizing for the harm he had done me; whereupon I administered to him the sacraments of Penitence and Eucharist, and in thirty days he was restored to health: for ever after he refused to eat meat during fast times in thanks for the recovery of his health. The French were amazed that in place of his previous condemnation of us he joined us in fasting right to the end of the voyage.

The turtles lasted for all of this time, being soaked in sea water morning and evening, and retaining their substance without further feeding as they lay upside down for the whole day; any that becomes too weak is thrown out into the sea to preserve its life. To us the turtles were of the greatest value, as we fed on them for sixty days, and as well as our morning soup we were served at the Captain's table with the intestines and liver, which, specially cooked in its own fat, was not unlike bacon: this had an excellent effect on the health of the company, and cured all sufferers from scurvy, scab, and inflammation caused by internal heat, especially those whose first or second voyage it was on these Indian seas. These, to speak with all respect, were purged of a black, almost coalblack excrement, which raises no small alarm among the ignorant lest they have ruptured some vein in the body: I myself was alarmed at the possibility of a rupture and sought medical advice, but the doctor smiled and assured me that it was beneficial to the constitution, but does not appear in those who are making the voyage for the third or fourth time. All sailors are indeed glad to hail the harbour of Ascension Island to be cured of various illnesses which the doctors are often unable to treat.

We passed meanwhile a number of islands which apart from the harbour at St Helena we had no wish to approach, but desired above all to reach the end of this long voyage. At last by God's grace, after many prayers felt deeply from the heart, we were overjoyed to reach on 26 May 1754 the French port of L'Orient in lower Brittany.[7] Since our departure from Ethiopia we had spent eleven months simply in sailing the Red Sea and Indian Ocean, quite apart from the delays in the harbours and islands, which occupied as much time as the voyages. Wishing to append a daily schedule of our voyage I obtained from the navigator himself a daily note of our degree of latitude and of our daily run during the whole period of it. Before reaching the port of

[7] L'Orient owes its origin to the French East India company which in 1666 made an establishment there for its eastern trade.

L'Orient, passing shipping has to halt by the fort or harbour of the royal city of *Port Luis*,[8] and the captain is compelled to salute the king's admiral with a broadside of cannon and to inform him by trumpet of all his cargo and of the port from which he hails: only then do they betake themselves to L'Orient, at half an hour's distance. This royal city, though small and not very populous, is protected by a numerous garrison: there is a parish church and a monastery of the Recollet Order of the Friars Minor, while at half an hour's distance is another, dedicated to St. Catherine Virgin and Martyr, of some size but boasting only five brothers owing to lack of postulants. But before describing the port, I set out the schedule of our voyage.

[8] Port Louis, formerly Blavet, opposite L'Orient on the south side of the Blavet river. It was the original port for French trade with India.

CHAPTER 66

DAILY LOG OF OUR VOYAGE
THROUGH THE INDIAN OCEAN

This schedule sets out plainly the distances covered during the voyage in the years 1753–4 of the French ship *Lis*, commander Captain Bear, of the royal city of Port St Louis, which sailed from the French port of Ponticheri in India on the morning of October 20, bound for the island of Roderici.

Month of October					
Day	Latitude North	French leagues	Day	Latitude North	French leagues
21	10° 39′	36	23	8° 40′	$14\frac{1}{2}$
because the angle of the Pole			24	8° 55′	14
is observed through the			25	9° 14′	$11\frac{1}{3}$
sextant at noon, it is always at			26	8° 30′	$18\frac{1}{2}$
noon that the distance			27	8° 28′	2
travelled in the previous			28	7° 33′	20
twenty-four hours is calculated.			29	6° 12′	29
Thus on			30	5° 19′	$19\frac{2}{3}$
22	9° 22′	$19\frac{2}{3}$	31	4° 36′	18
				Total leagues	$202\frac{2}{3}$

Month of November					
Day	Latitude North	French leagues	Day	Latitude South	French leagues
1	3° 51′	$27\frac{1}{3}$	6	0° 18′	$16\frac{2}{3}$
2	3° 40′	$55\frac{1}{3}$	7	1° 21′	$12\frac{2}{3}$
3	2° 57′	$18\frac{1}{3}$	8	1° 54′	11
4	1° 58′	$20\frac{1}{3}$	9	4° 24′	56
5	0° 30′	$33\frac{1}{2}$	10	6° 8′	35
Here we crossed the Line for			11	7° 20′	$24\frac{1}{3}$
the first time			12	8° 21′	$20\frac{2}{3}$

438

Day	Latitude South	French leagues			
13	9° 12′	17	23	19° 54′	$53\frac{1}{3}$
14	14° 10′	18	24	19° 41′	$38\frac{1}{2}$
15	10° 38′	24	25	19° 53′	28
16	12° 18′	$57\frac{2}{3}$	26	19° 54′	30
17	13° 43′	$52\frac{1}{3}$	27	19° 54′	$38\frac{1}{2}$
18	15° 7′	$52\frac{1}{2}$		At about 5 o'clock we passed	
19	15° 51′	49		the island of Rodrique (sic).	
20	16° 50′	50	28	20° 6′	$37\frac{2}{3}$
21	18° 28′	56	29	19° 56′	$34\frac{1}{3}$
22	19° 31′	$58\frac{1}{3}$	30	19° 46′	$32\frac{1}{2}$

Total leagues for November 1,059

Month of December

Day	Latitude South	French leagues
1	20° 0′	$14\frac{1}{3}$

At about 6 a.m. we were sailing close to the island of Maurice, but being blown about eleven leagues from the harbour by contrary winds we first cast anchor at around noon, a distance from Ponticheri of $1,261\frac{2}{3}$ leagues. After taking in water and an adequate stock of other necessities we sailed for the island of Bourbon, to which I referred earlier, on the night of January 27.

Day	Latitude South	French leagues
28	20° 27′	32
29	—	14

In the afternoon of that day we cast anchor in a place called St Paul,[1] and took in further stores of poultry and other items already described, as well as of Bourbon coffee which after Mochan coffee is superior to all others, whose grains or beans are a bright green in colour, and which deceives Europeans into buying it as coffee from the Levant. We stayed about three days in the island, and on the day following, February 3, made no

[1] The second town of the island, about 18 miles west of the capital St Denis.

headway on our journey. Therefore

Month of February

Day	Latitude South	French leagues	Day	Latitude South	French leagues
4	23° 0'	42⅔	16	33° 26'	18⅓
5	24° 48'	40⅔	17	34° 15'	29⅓
6	26° 48'	52⅓	18	35° 13'	19
7	28° 14'	50⅓	19	35° 6'	11
8	29° 17'	49⅔	20	35° 36'	9
9	29° 31'	29⅔	21	35° 9'	21
10	30° 4'	39	22	34° 52'	7
11	30° 42'	24	23	35° 30'	13⅔
12	31° 31'	28	24	35° 33'	24⅓
13	32° 26'	37⅓	25	35° 21'	42
14	33° 7'	44	26	35° 3'	22
15	33° 2'	21⅓	27	35° 36'	11
			28	35° 48'	40

Total leagues for February   726⅔

Month of March

Day	Latitude South	French leagues	Day	Latitude South	French leagues
1	37° 5'	34	were overjoyed to cross the		
2	35° 35'	30½	tropic of Capricorn.		
3	38° 30'	60⅓	Encouraged by this we		
4	38° 21'	33⅓	proceeded:		
5	38° 33'	24⅔	16	22° 7'	34⅓
6	39° 25'	9¼	17	21° 11'	26
7	37° 51'	35⅔	18	20° 32'	19
8	36° 1'	55⅔	19	19° 35'	26
9	34° 45'	48	20	18° 10'	23
Today after much anxiety we passed			21	17° 6'	30⅔
the Cape of Good Hope successfully			22	15° 53'	35⅓
10	32° 4'	62	23	14° 20'	37⅔
11	29° 58'	52⅔	24	12° 45'	37⅓
12	28° 5'	47⅓	25	11° 32'	32
13	26° 16'	44⅔	26	10° 34'	26
14	14° 31'	43	27	9° 40'	24½
15	23° 19'	36	28	8° 51'	23⅓
Today while experiencing			29	8° 3'	27⅔
certain physical changes we			30	7° 55'	42⅓
			31		39½

Total leagues for March	1,101½
Total leagues for February	726⅔

So from the islands of Bourbon to Ascension the reckoning of French leagues is 1,828.

We reached Ascension Island at about 4.30 p.m. on March 31, and cast anchor there, it being common practice for shipping to put in there to recruit their strength on the excellent fish of all kinds shapes and colours, and of delicious taste as, together with the turtles, I have already described at length. When we had sufficiently fortified ourselves and taken in a store of fish and turtles, we weighed anchor on the night of April 2 and resumed our journey with the success that can be observed from the schedule.

Month of April

Day	Latitude South	French leagues	Day	Latitude North	French league
3	7° 11′	20	17	6° 33′	35
4	6° 23′	$35\frac{2}{3}$	18	8° 3′	42
5	5° 12′	$36\frac{1}{3}$	19	9° 30′	40
6	3° 39′	42	20	11° 2′	44
7	2° 32′	29	21	12° 47′	$47\frac{2}{3}$
8	1° 34′	$25\frac{1}{2}$	22	14° 25′	41
9	1° 17′	$8\frac{1}{3}$	23	16° 20′	46
10	0° 29′	$18\frac{2}{3}$	24	18° 10′	$38\frac{1}{3}$
Today by good fortune we crossed			25	19° 15′	$37\frac{1}{3}$
the Line for the second time			26	21° 34′	$33\frac{1}{3}$
11	0° 42′ North	$25\frac{1}{3}$	27	23° 6′	$29\frac{1}{3}$
12	1° 50′	29	Here we crossed the		
13	2° 32′	$14\frac{2}{3}$	tropic of Cancer		
14	2° 55′	$8\frac{1}{3}$	28	25° 2′	$38\frac{2}{3}$
15	4° 24′	32	29	26° 5′	$36\frac{1}{3}$
16	5° 21′	$30\frac{1}{3}$	30	28° 40′	$36\frac{2}{3}$
			Total leagues for April		901

Month of May

Day	Latitude North	French leagues	Day	Latitude North	French leagues
1	30° 43′	$41\frac{1}{2}$	9	40° 34′	$38\frac{2}{3}$
2	32° 26′	$34\frac{1}{3}$	10	41° 37′	$37\frac{2}{3}$
3	33° 56′	30	11	42° 46′	$39\frac{1}{3}$
4	34° 21′	$8\frac{1}{3}$	12	43° 56′	$55\frac{1}{3}$
5	34° 48′	$9\frac{1}{3}$	13	45° 21′	64
6	36° 0′	$24\frac{1}{3}$	14	46° 19′	$53\frac{1}{3}$
7	37° 32′	$31\frac{1}{3}$	15	46° 25′	$17\frac{2}{3}$
8	39° 8′	$39\frac{1}{3}$	16	46° 44′	$29\frac{1}{3}$

Day	Latitude North	French leagues	Day	Latitude North	French leagues
17	47° 7′	36	22	47° 12′	19
18	47° 46′	40⅓	23	47° 44′	24⅓
19	47° 44′	27	24	—	15
20	46° 51′	18	25	—	—
21	47° 0′	13	26	—	—
				Total leagues for May	746

Since many of the sailors and travellers bring Indian merchandize into the country with them, contrary to the ban imposed by the Company of the Indies, the ship hove to by a small rocky islet covered with bushes, where all the prohibited merchandize was landed. Then, on the second or third day following, their especial friends collected the goods secretly by night in small boats to take them into their own homes, thus evading the inspectorate; it was not therefore until May 26 that we finally reached the haven which had been the subject of such longing.

For a better appreciation of our voyage I append a brief summary of the miles, or French leagues, travelled from place to place, together with the number of days taken, viz:

	Days	Leagues
From the port of the city of Ponticheri to the Isle de France, or Mauritz, took	42	1,261
From the island of Mauritz to Bourbon took	3	46
From Bourbon to Ascension Island took	56	1,828
From Ascension Island to France took	51	1,642
Total	152	4,777

which is equivalent to 19,108 Italian miles.

Because the whole of this schedule presents only details of latitude, from which on its own it is impossible to determine the location of a place, I have decided to set out in the following schedule our longitude on at least some dates, for the better recognition of our angle to the Pole. The standard degree of longitude is ordinarily determined from the Green Height,[2]

---

[2] Latin is *promontorium viride*. Perhaps an echo of Greenwich, which by that date was in general use by British and Dutch mariners, though not, as Prutky says, by the French. The meridian of Greenwich was universally adopted in 1885.

which the French locate in Paris and the English in London. By noting more closely the longitude of definite places on definite days, I set out the facts for consideration.

October	20	98° 22' East	February	25	22° 40'
November	5	86° 52'		26	21° 4'
	6	87° 4'		27	21° 0'
				28	18° 34'
December	11	56° 31'	March	1	18° 29'
January	29	55° 5'		2	18° 36'
February	15	32° 16'		3	18° 50'
	16	31° 16'		4	18° 44'
	17	29° 46'		5	18° 17'
	18	28° 59'		6	18° 10'
	19	29° 5'		7	17° 7'
	20	28° 29'		8	14° 31'
	21	27° 24'		9	12° 4'
	22	27° 30'		10	10° 16'
	23	26° 42'		15	3° 0'
	24	25° 13'		31	15° 18' West

With this glimpse of the daily journal of our voyage, and observations of the height of the Pole in degrees and minutes of latitude, and as far as possible of the longitude, I proceed to an account of my further journey through France.

CHAPTER 67

THE PORT OF
L'ORIENT IN FRANCE

Although we put in also at the American island of *St Dominico*,[1] a French possession, I can give little information about it because we remained there for but a few days for ship's stores. I therefore pass it by to relate that after halting at the royal city and port of *Ludovici*,[2] and the captain's communication to the royal governor of all the information needed, we reached the second port and city of L'Orient and cast anchor there. Our arrival was greeted with joyful celebrations and the cheers of the onlookers, whereupon there appeared a number of inspectors to protect against fraud the Company of the Indies and His Most Christian Majesty. Although they enquired into every item, even of the belongings of foreign arrivals, in their efforts to prevent the import into the kingdom of goods prejudicial to the Company's interests, yet they were easily deceived and found nothing, seeing that, as I related a little earlier, every ship before reaching the harbour casts anchor by a certain islet five or six hours away and there conceals all private merchandize, of many thousands of value, lest it fall into the clutches of the royal treasury. Then at sunset there appear a number of small boats, whose crews have been previously well instructed in their task and well paid by the travellers, to take and hide away the boxes full of merchandize, so that in the morning when the inspectors appear they find nothing further. I myself saw how, when more valuable goods

[1] St. Dominico is modern Hispaniola, divided then between the French colony, now the Republic of Haiti, and the Spanish colony, now the Dominican Republic. This is the only occasion when Prutky mentions a visit to America, despite his claims in chapters 28, 40 and 42.
[2] See note 8 to chapter 65.

were in question whose owners were unwilling to let them be hidden on the islet for fear of theft, the inspectors were met with a valuable present and all the goods permitted to be carried off to the owners' own houses, despite the strictest regulations.

We two missionaries being without merchandize were unaffected by these difficulties, and gladly disembarked at L'Orient; as we looked for lodgings we were unexpectedly welcomed charitably in by one Joanne Hollenburg, a Swedish Catholic and the local surgeon, who with his French wife were so good as to meet our needs for food and drink, and lodged us as though we were their dearest friends. Viewing the city attentively I found it, though small, yet fine and built to an excellent plan, well defended, populous, and very fortunate, I could truly say famous, in its inhabitants, both for the many millions worth of goods and precious things brought from India, and for the very kind treatment by its citizens of visiting foreigners, who lived in true peacefulness alongside them: and this kindness led them the more bravely to resist their enemies, such as the English who in 1746 failed in their attempt to storm the city,[3] which had already in 1720 been rebuilt and fortified, and honoured with its own bishop.

To him as was but fitting I paid my humble respects, and, that I might reap the spiritual benefit of my voyage, besought his permission to give public absolution to four Lutherans who by the Holy Spirit had been led back into the bosom of the Holy Catholic Church. These and two more besides I conducted into the cathedral church with the utmost ceremony and to a full congregation, and with the assistance of six clergy performed the office of Profession of the Holy Faith to the great satisfaction of the crowd, who had never or seldom seen a similar ceremony in the city of L'Orient; even more did they admire the vocal facility exhibited in the absolution of a Pole, and of his recitation of his Profession of Faith. The conclusion of these ceremonies brought us the esteem of the Lord Bishop and of all the clergy, and a host of kindnesses from the citizens, but as another ship was already about to sail we departed amid the love of our friends, saying farewell to all and presenting our kind host and benefactor, as a mark of our gratitude, with half an ounce of Ethiopian gold.

[3] Under Admiral Lestock and General Sinclair.

445

Boarding a French ship we began our voyage on June 8, and sailing sixty leagues with good success through a bay of tossing waves we entered the fast-flowing river *Iccaron*,[4] whose rushing current added speed to our course, though the entrance to its mouth is not without danger because, just as in the neighbourhood of Alexandria the Nile fights with the Mediterranean Sea, so also here the salt water beats against the sweet and throws its waves on high, with the frequent threat of danger. Meantime with God for our guide we felt some fear as we overcame the river, and after a surther thirty-five leagues reached on June 10 the city of *Bourdeaux* (*sic*). This city no less I found on inspection to be beautiful, large, well fortified, populous, and a very active trading mart, adorned with the magnificent metropolitan cathedral of St. Andrew the Apostle, the seat of an archbishopric, with a Benedictine and especially with a Carthusian abbey, and with a fine large seminary under the direction of the Lazarist missionaries. There are also a number of convents for either sex, and for the Recollets, but the principal monastery is that of the Observants of the very flourishing province of *Aquileia*,[5] containing sixty brethren. Though yet other orders, the Theresian conventuals, the Jesuits and many monasteries own wide cloisters there, yet the pride of place both for buildings and for church belongs to the Dominicans.

The harbour is in the shape of a half moon, and can accommodate ships both large and small up to three hundred at once; all nations call there for the great abundance of excellent wine, fine muscat of excellent taste and by no means expensive, a two pint flagon selling for three soldi, whose like I have tasted nowhere else in the world. A particularly good feature of the city is that on each side of the river it is guarded by a well built fortress, capable of strongly resisting any attacking force, which in an assault on the city would be compelled to pass between the fortresses, and instead of victory would undergo complete destruction by gun fire. The city and adjacent territory is a delightful area, appropriately named in French *La Guyenne*.[6]

---

[4] Iccaron: presumably the Garonne.

[5] Aquileia: a mistake for Aquitania. In a later passage Aquileia is altered in the ms to Aquitania (Aquitaine).

[6] The name Guyenne is a corruption of the Latin Aquitania. Prutky tries to connect it with the Latin *gaudens* 'happy' or 'smiling'.

As we pondered these and other matters throughout the city, we aroused considerable wonder among the citizens by our manner of dress, which was that of African missionaries, and even more by four young Chinese of our company, together with a missionary just returned from China, who had been sent to study in Naples at the College for the Propagation of the Faith. Crowds ran up on all sides of us to view those returned from such far-off lands, and especially to gaze at the young Chinese, with their small eyes, brown colouring, and short snub noses; this aroused no small degree of wonderment, and such a host of questions and satisfactions of curiosity were demanded of us that we could scarcely cross one street without molestation. When the city Governor heard of this, being no less eager to see us, he invited us into his palace and, listening carefully to the answers to his various questions, treated us with great respect; with even greater kindness he was so good as to facilitate our further free and unmolested passage through French territory. As we entered the palace amid a great crowd of people, the captains of two Prussian ships gazed fixedly upon us and besought a private interview; opening their heart to us they offered their services if perchance we were in need of any pecuniary assistance, and when with thanks we replied in the negative responded more confidentially: 'Dear friends, do not endure any want of necessities, but come to us and our other brothers, and you will be amply provided for.' When I replied 'Who are these brothers?' the answer was, 'They are the Freemasons, are you not of their number?' Seeing that these captains in their simplicity knew not that they were speaking to papal missionaries, we turned them away with a jest, saying that they must go in peace and that we were in no need of such charity of iniquity.

When the feast of Corpus Christi came round on June 13 we made the sacrifice of the Holy Mass to the Almighty, and left the city of Bourdeaux by river, putting up in the evening at a place called Appellit;[7] proceeding on our way we reached at about midday of June 14 the town of *Semackero*,[8] hoping that, arriving just at dinner time, we might comfort ourselves with a hot dish at the monastery of the Observant Fathers of St Francis. But God bless us, though the bell sounded they refused to open the door, and we in hunger dedicated ourselves to the Holy Spirit and

[7] Paillet.
[8] St Macaire.

447

repented bitterly that for love of our brothers in religion we had left the left bank of the river and the small city of *L'Angon*,[9] renowned for its wine which is celebrated and praised throughout Europe, where all the hospitality we were offered we humbly rejected, and then from our own brothers received nothing: indeed although the city contains a college of the Society of Jesus, we refrained from approaching it, so as not to slight our brethren. That night, though, we hoped for better fortune in the city, on the right bank, of *La Réole*, which is small but beautiful in itself, and where is a famous monastery of the Benedictine Fathers, which looks like a very castle. On 15 we stayed our hunger somewhat at the village of *Guturas*[10] which is a small parish with an adequate church, and then in passing viewed the city and parish of *Marmando*,[11] with monasteries of the Observants and the Capuchin monks, though we did not disembark for fear that we should knock on the monastery door and again be driven off without a hearing.

The next day, June 16, falling on a Sunday, we arrived starving at the village of *Tallibourg*,[12] where I humbly begged the parish priest to be allowed to celebrate Mass for the crew of my vessel, to facilitate our journey. The priest declared that he was not able to give such a licence as it was forbidden by the order of his bishop, but when I desired to see the said order I read that it concerned vagabond priests and those absent from their church without orders from their superior: thinking to persuade him by the decree of the Sacred Congregation I moved him not, and, even though I assailed him with the Council of Trent and a number of theological arguments, he uttered scarcely one word in reply, and knowing no Latin barked at me in his silly French. Little enough learning did I see in him as he knew not how to rebut the arguments I put to him, and I fairly washed his head without water. When finally he said that we could hear Mass said by himself I refused from suspicion of Jansenism,[13] and I

[9] Langon.

[10] Couthures-sur-Garonne.

[11] Marmande.

[12] Taillebourg.

[13] Jansenism, declared heretical by Innocent X in 1653 and again by Alexander VII in 1656, was rigorously repressed in France by Louis XIV, more favourably regarded by the Regent Duke of Orleans, but again repressed under Louis XV. It nevertheless retained a number of sympathizers, particularly among those French clergy of nationalist (Gallican) sentiment. On several occasions in France Prutky will be seen to be in conflict with the local clergy.

departed in distress of soul, reflecting that by Catholics I was prevented from saying Mass even on a Sunday, whereas I used to celebrate it daily among idolaters, heathen, and barbarous nations where I was exposed to continual danger. However, this distress too it was but fitting to offer to God, as I reflected that on one side of the river we were passing the French province of Aquileia the greater, and on the other the province of *Casconia*,[14] the next small city being *Omust da Genest*,[15] the site of a monastery and of the Chapter of the Vicariate.[16] Not far from this was a town called *Tumens*,[17] small but full of Lutherans and Calvinists, with a monastery of Observants and a parish priest, and then in due course the village of *Monheur*[18] with another pastor, zealous for the souls of his flock, who at night visited our boat and sorrowfully complained that he was the unfortunate parish priest of at least 660 souls, of whom scarcely one hundred were Catholic: all were tainted by the disease of Calvinism, so that in the whole neighbourhood there were meetings by night, under their minister and seducer, to which almost 6,000 others adhered, with grievous loss to the Catholic religion: although all this was strictly forbidden of old by the zealous piety of the kings of France, yet in these times it is covered up throughout the kingdom by the lukewarm churchmanship of the Ministers of State, and although the Lord Bishop is full of divine fervour yet the secular arm will not assist him, and he is forced to weep at the damnation of so many souls. Next morning we left this place and viewed the very ancient town of *Le port Sainte Marie* where there are Capuchins, Carmelites and the monks of their order and a large parish, while on the other side of the river is another convent of Benedictine nuns, followed by the village of *Saint Elero*[19] and a solitary parish with its church.

---

[14] Gascony.

[15] Le Mas d'Agenais.

[16] The headquarters of the vicar-apostolic.

[17] Tonneins.

[18] Monheurt. This part of France was the centre not only of the Albigensians of the eleventh and twelth century but also of the protestant Camisards of the eighteenth century. These were not put down until 1706, by the Duke of Berwick.

[19] St Hilaire de Lusignan.

CHAPTER 68

OTHER CITIES ON OUR
JOURNEY THROUGH FRANCE

Although the fatigues of the journey, continued over so long a period, had gravely weakened us, we were none the less delighted at the variety of our views of so many objects, cities, towns and nations, which sustained us through these same difficulties, and on June 18 we reached a new city, one of the chiefest and most famous, called *Agen*, the seat of a bishopric, and containing a renowned chapter house named from times past for St Caprasius. The city, one of the most ancient in France, is well built and adorned with many religious houses, of the Observants, the Capuchins, the Augustinians, two convents of Carmelite nuns and six monastic houses: of special interest were the nuns of St Joanna, who were clothed for procession in a black scapular with a red girdle and a white mantle of pure silk which swept the ground, while on the neck they wore a figure of St Joan as a pendant on a red ribbon of three fingers' breadth: their magnificent dress and grave deportment gave them a truly queenly presence. Never elsewhere had I yet seen this justly celebrated order, and I greatly admired their religious sensibility, praising God for the wonders of His creatures. The Franciscan Observants of this city are listed as belonging to the senior province of Aquitaine, the lesser province being less flourishing and smaller, so that while in the senior province there are nineteen monasteries as well as convents of Religious, in the lesser there are no monasteries, the friars remaining under the charge of the bishops.

The city contains as part of a magnificent Observant monastery the farfamed and large royal library full of fine books, which is free for study to any clerical or lay student and is under the wise sole guardianship of the Observants to ensure that none of the books is removed. The librarian, one of eighty brethren, is well paid by His Most Christian Majesty and has the duty of invigilating in the library, the monastery being known as that of the Great Observance. Here I found in the crypt the uncorrupted bodies of the dead brothers, a great company: their incorruption is believed to be natural and due to the dryness of the sandy soil, but to me it seems by no means marvellous to see the uncorrupt bodies of so many venerable Friars Minor, who have kept to the letter our Sole Seraphic Rule, when the lively proclamations of Supreme Pontiffs have declared them living martyrs, and that Friars Minor in their pure rule can ever be canonized. I was the more confirmed in the religious perfection of these my brothers by the many days during which my colleague and I were received with not merely fraternal but rather I should say angelic charity by the then Father Principal, named Defur, a man of virtue and merit who loaded us with kindnesses, while we were heaped with favours far beyond our deserts by the chief noblemen, many Religious, and monks; though often invited to their tables we humbly declined, on account of the fatigues of our journey, and we seldom went outside the monastery. Our main diversion was simply the library, enriched as it was by antiquities and royal rights and favours, but when we had sufficiently read and wondered at the books of a number of authors we prepared ourselves for departure, and on June 20 set off cheerfully with heartfelt expressions of friendship.

We passed the town of *Le Billar*[1] where the Dominicans and the parish priest care for the souls of the Christian people to their great edification, and then followed the village of *Egnia*[2] whose parish priest was a man of exemplary conduct; on 22 of the same month we reached the small town of *Labadio*,[3] nearby which on a hill is a fine Benedictine monastery thirty-six leagues from *Tulosa*.[4] Anxious to celebrate Mass my colleague and I climbed the hill, and were told to wait for the issue of permission while the abbot himself was celebrating; when we humbly sought his assent he asked us whether we had the written permission of the diocesan bishop, to which I replied that such was impossible

[1] Auvillar.
[2] Vignes-sur-Garonne.
[3] Probably Boudon.
[4] Toulouse, which Prutky spells in different ways.

for those coming from such distant lands, and countered with the decree of the Sacred Congregation, which was a more than sufficient licence as coming from the Pope himself. Quite against our expectations the abbot unjustly replied that 'We here acknowledge our own bishop as Pope' – at which I so flared up that I hailed him as a heretic and as one disobedient to the Holy See, him and his company of monks alike; adding also 'While you are all of you astray from the road of Roman truth, and recognize another as Pope, my colleague and I glory in our Roman Catholicism and even more in our calling as apostolic missionaries, and I no longer have any wish to offer the Holy Sacrifice in this your church, the abode of heretics.' At this the abbot and the many bystanders were not a little shaken, and, excusing himself that in denying me permission his motives were not all that evil, he invited me to the meal now being prepared in the refectory; I however despised him as the enemy of the Holy Roman Church and the Chief Pontiff, and departed in bitterness of heart, reflecting that in my extended journey from Ethiopia, among infidels, idolaters and barbarous nations, when I suffered sore trials and dangers of thirst and hunger, I had never undergone such injuries as here among these what I must call nominal Catholics:[5] with bitter tears we commended our every hurt to God the Vindicator.

Nor was this cup of sorrow sufficient: at around eventide we reached on Saturday the city of *Dardon*,[6] and were even more chagrined to enter the monastery of the Recollets and make humble supplication, since the next day was Sunday, that we might have lodging for the night and permission to celebrate the Holy Mass: both these requests were refused us by the Father Principal, who similarly required the diocesan bishop's written permission, a thing impossible for travellers from Abyssinia and India. I demonstrated to him that he was the subject not of the bishop but of the very reverend Father General of the whole order, to whom and to whose decree he alike owed obedience, but I was unable to convince one who ignored or knew not the rule of his own order, and departed from him in contempt. Scarcely had we left the monastery when we found in the market

[5] Compare note 13 to chapter 67.
[6] Not identified.

place a number of ecclesiastics and civilians and were disturbed that they seemed hostile to us: but after they had asked us who we were they refreshed with good food and drink our constitutions which had been undermined by so long a journey, and willingly admitted us to the altar of the Lord; and, so that on the next day Sunday June 23 we could facilitate our journey by saying Mass for our crew, they gave us the host and chalice out of a nearby hermitage whose hermit had been killed by robbers a few weeks previously. We duly performed the sacred ceremony, and I then left my colleague in the boat and directed my steps to a place called *Spinas*,[7] whither I hastened to celebrate Mass on the following day and obtain a plenary indulgence at the solemn feast to be held there. Again I was unfortunate, gaining permission neither to lodge that night in the cloister nor to celebrate Mass the next day, and I was forced at a late hour to enter for my night's lodging an inn full of drunken men; here I endured such rudeness as to rob me of all repose, and at 3 a.m. I resumed my journey to Tolosa and hastened to meet my colleague, disturbed in spirit at my many mischances in France, but making offering of them to the Almighty.

[7] Lespinasse.

CHAPTER 69

THE CITIES OF TOLOSA, BEZIERS, AGDE AND CETTE

Praise be to God for all His gifts and favours lavished upon us throughout our journey. Making my humble supplication for the many trials I had already borne that strength would be furnished me to bear with a thankful heart the hardships of the road ahead, I was so fortunate as to keep the rendezvous with my colleague in the city of Tolosa, which lies in a pretty valley beside the rivers *Araxe*[1] and *Orio*,[2] is well fortified and well garrisoned, and is of ample size, distinguished by a Chapter house and many convents of either sex. After a journey of thirty-six leagues I approached at the city's entrance the convent of the Paulane fathers,[3] and had I not found an excellent knowledge of the Sacred Congregation in the Father Sacristan, who had once lived in Rome for many years, I should have most probably once again found difficulty in celebrating Mass. But in fact after a modest repast I entered the city and inspected its churches and other sights, and then leaving the centre encountered my colleague on the river bank at the home of a glass maker from Bohemia. Here for four days we remained in his small cottage built on the river like a boat, while we collected together our needs for the journey, and then set off by the canal, which had been dug at great expense to the royal treasury.[4] At first sight it seems a miracle: the water, confined by locks and gates, appears from the height of it to be unnavigable for the approaching boat, but the lock-gate has been

---

[1] Ariège.
[2] Hers.
[3] More usually called Barnabites.
[4] The canal was built in 1666–81 largely at the expense of Paul Riquet of Beziers. In Prutky's time the Garonne from Bordeaux to Toulouse was not yet canalized.

scarcely opened when the boat slowly descends, the higher water flowing into the lower produces an even channel when the gate has been raised, and navigation is as uninterrupted as though the water had always been on the same level. This method of boat travel I had never before seen, nor in the rest of my travels did I meet a similar artificial waterway: the whole of this part of France, which is furnished with every convenience for its people and its traders, produces a considerable revenue, although the dues paid by the traveller are but small, and we two, despite enjoying every convenience, paid only one real thirty grosschen while crossing the several regions of France, Brittany the greater and lesser, or as some have it upper and lower, Aquileia, Casconia and the various cities and places along this canal, *Nigra*[5] and *Villa Schorie*[6] otherwise known as *Castell Naudarie.*[7]

It was well towards evening when we entered the small town of *Treves,*[8] the abode of Capuchin fathers, but despite our earnest prayers to be allowed to lodge the night in the cloister they refused us even their doorway, and although the day was sacred to the two Chiefs of the Apostles[9] our humbleness was of no avail and we were forced to go to a common inn. However on the following day we were able to offer the sacrifice of the Mass, and proceeded to the town of *Samal,*[10] similarly the residence of two Capuchins, who again refused our request for the kindness of a night's lodging; but among the houses of the laity we found an Irish army captain who had once met with much kindness and many favours in the kingdom of Bohemia and repaid them to us, saying that in no part of the world had he met a people so faithful, genuine and friendly as in Bohemia; we praised God that in the midst of our evil chances there was always some comfort to cheer us.

We continued our usual canal journey to the city of *Beziers,* the seat in his Chapter house of the Lord Bishop and the location of many religious orders, a place of great antiquity and beauty, well built and blessed with a good climate, a fertile and delightful

[5] Négra.
[6] Not identified.
[7] Castelnaudary.
[8] Trèbes.
[9] SS. Peter and Paul, June 29.
[10] Le Somail.

region; indeed the ancient saying still holds *If God wished a dwelling-place on earth He would choose Baeterrae.*[11] Here the canal terminates, and all baggage is transported overland at a trifling cost to another canal, by which in the space of five hours one reaches the city of *Agde* or *Agatha*, handsome, well built, very populous, and sited at the mouth of the Gulf of Lions, a short distance from the Languedoc canal. Languedoc is a most thriving province, ninety leagues in extent from east to west and about eighty leagues from north-east to south, usually divided into an upper and a lower Languedoc, of which the latter is the more fertile with all sorts of produce, all kinds of grain, livestock whether beasts or birds, the olive, the fig, all other varieties of fruit, and fish beyond counting, since the province includes besides the Rhone a number of rivers of which the more considerable are the *Tarn* which passes *Montauban* to join the *Garonne*, the *Ariege* which flows into it by Toulouse, and the *Aude* which passes *Carcassone* to receive the waters of the *Fresquel*, which the French have joined by means of a canal or small river called the *Lers* to connect again with the Garonne. This it is which is commonly called the Canal du Languedoc. Upper Languedoc contains eight dioceses and lower Languedoc eleven, but as the French geographers provide ample information on them I think it vain to enlarge further.

We meanwhile continued on our way in the mouth of the Agde canal, where we found a number of foreign ships, on which we had the opportunity of a prompt departure, but, because the supply of ships sometimes fails, travellers anxious not to waste time uselessly press on to the lake-side city called *Cette*,[12] otherwise known as the port of St Louis.[13] Two large rivers called *Cete* and *Rue* are named after the city, whence one soon reaches the Mediterranean Sea, the starting point of the canal of Languedoc and four leagues from Agde; the commodious harbour faces towards the city of *Marseille* or *Massilia*. At Agde we paid a visit to the Lord Bishop, an upright man of exemplary virtue and a most zealous shepherd of his flock, who every year visits every single part of his diocese to feed his sheep on God's holy food, preaching, examining, remitting sins, in fact performing the

[11] Its Latin name.
[12] Sète.
[13] Prutky is here confusing Sète with Aigues Mortes a little to the east.

missionary function: not content with offering us services which we humbly begged leave to refuse, he decided to pay our sea passage as far as Massilia, and sent us forward in true kindness. For the time of our stay we lived for some days at the establishment of the Conventual Fathers, scanty in number and bitter poor, who despite their own want yet welcomed us in with all charity. On July 2 we embarked on a Genoese ship and sailed across the Gulf of Lions, very rough and dangerous, indeed often the cause of shipwreck, into which flows another river,[14] and in which every year, especially in winter and at night, many ships are wrecked by a very strong wind which blows off the land; although the crossing usually takes less than four hours, the wind is very dangerous and those on shipboard are often hard put to it for many hours. We, thanks be to God, crossed successfully on the day on which we started, and around evening reached the city of Massilia, handsome, very ancient, of no great size,[15] and situated between two headlands of mountainous appearance, guarded by fortresses. Displaying every sort of fine merchandize and thronged with countless traders including foreigners, it was originally built by colonists from the Greek people of Phocaea who dwelt in part of Asia Minor, and once gloried in the name of Republic; now it is the seat of the bishop suffragan of Arles, with a famous university and a port which is completely safe in all weathers even for the bigger ships which trade from the Levant, and which is used alike by merchantmen and ships of war, many of His Most Christian Majesty's naval vessels being stationed there; if however the larger ships from the Indies put in they are unable to enter the harbour and lie at anchor off the island of *Iff* (*sic*), at a quarter of an hour's distance, beneath the castle of the same name. The city is reckoned to be of great antiquity, having been founded six hundred years before the birth of Christ, and is now distinguished by the famous Abbey of St Victor, secularized a few years ago, though there remain the ecclesiastical chapter with seventeen parish priests as well as many schools for young people, a very ancient college of the Priests of the Oratory, and various religious houses for both sexes.

[14] Presumably the Rhône.
[15] The growth of Marseilles to the second city of France began in the nineteenth century with the French North African empire and the opening of the Suez canal.

We on disembarking entered the great convent of the Observants, with a newly-built church finely, indeed magnificently, decorated, and seeing that there was also there a monastery of the Recollets, I went to greet Reverend Father Benedict, lately returned from Jerusalem, an acquaintance of mine who was once French chaplain at Alexandria. When he saw me he was dumbfounded, believing me to be still tarrying in the kingdom of Abyssinia, while at that moment the Count de Desnevall was awaiting admission, who passed himself off everywhere as supreme commander of the navy of the king of Denmark,[16] and persuaded many Alexandrian merchants by his deceitful tongue into selling all their goods and retaining only the money necessary for their journey; in this way he brought them to total ruin, including a worthy French merchant M. Curet. Having rejected our advice none of them achieved their intended goal, but each one by one bewailed in penury his miserable fate.

Many marvellous details of the antiquities here could be related, but for them I refer the careful reader to the French authorities; even if we had visited other parts of France, Lutetia the capital,[17] Augusta Suessonum,[18] Laudunum,[19] Noviodunum,[20] Nîmes or Nemausus and many other towns, these the French writers have praised up well enough, and I pass each one by. As we drew near to the holy city of Rome I wanted to make mention of just one other city, and on July 11 on an ordinary French tartan crossed Brabantia[21] and arrived safely at the next port.

[16] Bruce, bk V ch. 13, gives an amusing account of 'Peter Joseph le Roux, count de Desneval', a German who had been a Rear Admiral in the Danish navy, had resigned his commission in 1739, and was proposing to reach Ethiopia by sailing up the Nile in an armed barge.
[17] Paris.
[18] Soissons.
[19] Lyons.
[20] Nevers.
[21] Not identified.

CHAPTER 70

THE CITY OF TOULON OR
TELO MARTIUS OR PORT TELO

Toulon or *Telo Martius* is a fine city, the seat of a bishop subject to the Metropolitan of Arles, not very populous but an important trading mart for the good French wine. It is also equipped with shipbuilding yards as befits the best harbour in the Mediterranean, and is very well fortified to provide a naval base in time of war. It is a pleasant city, containing monasteries of different religious orders of either sex, and is plentifully supplied with food. There had at that time been issued a strict edict by His Most Christian Majesty, contrary to his usual practice, that all Turkish pirates must be denied access to French territory because they had broken the terms of their agreement with him and boarded two Genoese ships when they were close to French soil. After weighing up every consideration we continued on our voyage, passing the mountains of Piedmont and the island of *Corsica* with its lofty peaks, while everywhere beside the sea shore we noticed fortifications raised against hostile attack. We had excellent views of towns, villages and a chapel dedicated to the Holy Mary, until there came into sight the enormous Monte Cristo upreared in the middle of the sea, on the other side of which could be discerned the smiling land of Tuscany and the port of Leghorn. With a fair wind we reached on July 16 the papal port of Centum Cellae, as the Romans named it of old, its modern name being *Civita Vecchia*.

Although small the city is very well built and fortified, and to mount attacks on the Turkish pirates of the Mediterranean is garrisoned with its own papal soldiers and galleys, among whose crews are great numbers of prisoners enslaved in chains for their crimes, not only Christian but also Mahometan, who without

459

intermission sweat and labour at the oar, and among whom I noted both priests and laymen who were being schooled in proper behaviour. Since the harbour is of adequate capacity great numbers of ships are to be seen, both Italian and foreign, with merchandize of all kinds, nor is any annoyance done to any stranger, of whatever religion or nationality, thanks to the impartial affection extended to each one by the Sacred Pontiff the common father of all; indeed the city has been distinguished not only by a number of religious orders but also by being made the seat of a bishop, whose care for his sheep is exemplary so that I found the whole population most zealous for our holy faith. However, we had no desire to stay longer, and, being pressed by time to put an end to so long a journey, we resumed our way, by land rather than by sea. Now the people of the place maintain that the poisonous and harmful air makes it impossible for the night-time traveller to sleep without his body swelling up and death intervening without remedy of any sort; we therefore completed twenty-four Italian miles before breaking our fast at an inn and refreshing our horses, and then after a further twenty-four miles we arrived at around 10 a.m. at the holy city of Rome. Joy reigned in our hearts as we passed through the people's gate and entered a church to render to the All Highest our profound thanks for the many dangers that we had overcome by land and sea, and for the many tribulations from idolaters, heathen and other infidels.

A little later we directed our steps towards Montorio[1] of St Peter, the missionary college, where our unexpected arrival from such far-off realms aroused the greatest wonder, each vying with the other in their eagerness to hear of the new wonders from the provinces of Africa: at that very time the Sacred Congregation was on the point of sending out a group of several missionaries, and much expense would have been caused if we two missionaries had not appeared. But we had no wish to let time slide idly by in Rome, and on the following day presented ourselves before the Sacred Congregation and the then prefect of missions His

---

[1] Montorio on the Janiculum, the headquarters of the missionary activity of the Franciscans. Montorio was then believed to be the site of the martyrdom of St Peter.

Eminence Cardinal Spinelli,[2] who declared it impossible to hear by word of mouth the outcome of our mission, and ordered us to present him with a written and succinct report,[3] for eventual transmission to Pope Benedict XIV. In due obedience to this command I delayed not to collect a stock of necessities, the quicker to effect my departure from Rome, and for the second time returned to Egypt, making my third successful voyage to Alexandria from Leghorn in the year 1754 (sic). At that time various changes in relationship with the Copts had made necessary the presence in Rome of Father Paul d'Agnona[4] prefect of the mission, and, his absence having lasted a long time, we all in Egypt were anxious for his return, the more that a number of disturbances and legal disputes had crept into our relations with the Coptic people, and the presence of our superior became urgently desired.[5] Since we had no hope of his imminent arrival, it was agreed by all the missionaries and by the vice-prefect that it was necessary that I should present myself at Rome to explain more effectively there the causes of such disorders in the mission, and to recall the Father Prefect. When all my business had been successfully completed, and I myself ordered to betake myself to the land of Egypt for the third time, I was under the necessity of placing once again before the Sacred Congregation the affairs of the Ethiopian mission, and in order not to transcribe here the same document for the second time, I set out the final concise account of 30 November 1756, which is similar to the earlier one.

[2] Giuseppe, Cardinal Spinelli, Archbishop of Naples 1734–54, Cardinal in 1735, Bishop of Ostia 1761, died in 1763. He was considered to be an enemy of the Jesuits.

[3] See Introduction.

[4] Paolo d'Agnona had been imprisoned and threatened with impalement along with Prutky and Martin Lang at Girga in Egypt in 1751. He became Prefect of Missions in Egypt and Ethiopia in the same year.

[5] A vicariate for the Catholic Copts had been established in 1741, but Athanasius, Coptic Bishop of Jerusalem the first Vicar-General, proved to be of doubtful orthodoxy and was replaced in 1744. Numerous difficulties persisted in the relations between the Vicariate, the Prefect of Missions, the local Latin community, the Muslim authorities and the Vatican.

CHAPTER 71

SHORT REPORT ON THE MISSION TO ETHIOPIA, AS PRESENTED TO THE SACRED CONGREGATION FOR THE PROPAGATION OF THE FAITH

In times past many vain attempts have been made to enter the Empire of Ethiopia, but, on March 19 in the year 1752, I, Friar Father Remedius Prutky of Prague in Bohemia, missionary in Egypt and vice-prefect of Ethiopia, of the Reformed Order of the Friars Minor of St Francis, ascribed to the Province of Bohemia, succeeded in reaching the royal city of Gondar, capital of the Empire of Ethiopia, in company with my two reverend colleagues, Fr Martin Lang of Bohemia and Fr Antony of Aleppo, both ascribed to that same province. Many were the trials and woes that we experienced in our journey through the Red Sea, the deserts of Egypt, and the three Arabias, and our weariness was great, but our health was good and our spirits unimpaired when we were conducted into the palace with all customary ceremony and due honour by the chief Imperial minister called Nagadras, the title of the Treasurer.

Well refreshed with food and drink we took a night's rest, and on the following day were conducted to audience with the Emperor, who at that time was in his residence at Kaha, at half a league's distance from the capital. Bowing to the ground in his presence and kissing it in Ethiopian fashion, we were received in kindly manner and questioned about various aspects of behaviour in Europe. Here in the same residence we remained, respected by individual lords and excellently entertained, while we enjoyed almost daily converse with the Emperor and, with due precaution, with his august mother, with the principal

462

courtiers, with all sorts and conditions of persons, and even with many of the monks of St Anthony, whose power throughout the Empire is great and who, along with the whole populace, are of remarkable moral habits. We carefully sifted and scrutinized their inborn evil conduct, their natural inclinations and changeable and inconstant motivations, while we pondered upon their outstanding abilities and the wide-ranging powers of their intellect, which however are still-born through lack of instructors; on the one hand they can well distinguish good from evil, while on the other they are unbridled in their moral behaviour, they put no curb to loose living, and as a nation are given over to every sort of vice, perverse in morals, manner of life, conversation, and faith. Nevertheless their greatest glory is the name of Christian which they bear, and they mark themselves off from the neighbouring heathen, idolaters, Turks and Jews by the collars of different colours which they tie around their necks. Nominal Christians, in word and not in heart, in profession and not in deed, in appearance and not in the truth of the matter, it can well be said of them *This people honoureth me with their lips, but their heart is far from me.* All the more carefully then did I enquire, in my conversations with great and humble, grown men and youths, monks and laymen, since they gloried in the name of Christian, what was the distinctive mark of the Christian faith; all of them immediately pointed to their neck, round which as round a dog's neck was fastened their collar, making out that, though worse in morals, by this they were distinguished from those same Turks, heathen, and all the rest.

Out of a hundred individuals I would say that scarcely one, nay none did I find who knew how to make the sign of the holy cross; the Christian faith is fragmented among them, each believing according to his own judgement, and for lack of teachers and instructors of sound doctrine they fall ever into the darkness of different heresies. Simply in the royal city of Gondar, as I heard from the mouth of the Queen Mother herself, I found the tenets of the Faith divided into three and thirty different classes, and what then must be the varieties of belief in the other parts of so many provinces? If they could but acquire true instructors who could persevere in the task, their minds would be malleable, provided they were not perverted from the truth and confirmed in their wicked customs and evil dogma by the disgraceful moral standards of the monks and priests of the church who abound throughout the Empire, and who for the sake of petty gains of daily food and clothing commit the worst of sins against the commands of God, presuming to instruct the people while concealing their own every sin.

The present Emperor who occupies the throne is thirty-three years of age, is kindly, merciful, and naturally inclined to gentleness and flexibility, and provided that he were helped by the power and military assistance of one of the kings of Europe, he would speedily bring the whole Empire of Ethiopia under the easy yoke of Christ, because he is naturally inclined to the Catholic faith; but being up to now shrouded in the darkness of heresy he is prevented from recognizing the light of the true faith. Although he is well provided with soldiers and with the wealth of the provinces of his vast Empire, retaining beneath his sway twenty-two domains, part kingdoms and part provinces, some larger and others smaller, yet his people are so stiff-necked and prone to rebellion, so ensnared in a net of iniquity, that with his own forces he is barely able to stand against them, much less subdue them, and the political affairs of Ethiopia are in turmoil.

Thus there are divisions of creed among the Ethiopian people according to individual choice, but most people profess belief in One God, Triune in three Persons: this Deity is however corporeal, with three distinct bodies in three divine Persons, with three heads, three mouths, six eyes, six ears, and so on. They declare that our Lord Christ was our Redeemer but that it was under one Nature, as Deity, that He suffered, was crucified, and died for our salvation, since He could not have endured such pains in His human nature. The lords and imperial ministers believe that Christ was materially anointed by the Heavenly Father, while others have it that He was appointed by the Holy Ghost as Schum,[1] or official of the heavenly host, relying on the Davidic text *He anointed him with the oil of gladness.* Others hold that Christ was ordained priest by God the Father after the manner of men, and others again profess a number of other beliefs as their spirits move them.

---

[1] Amharic *šum,* literally an 'appointed' person, or chief. Guidi, *Vocabolario,* p. 226.

Of the number, effect, and name of the sacraments they are wholly ignorant, nor does it occur to them to consider either what they mean, or who instituted them.

Baptism they believe to be necessary to salvation, and they enunciate the proper formula when they apply the water, saying in the Amharic language during three immersions '*Ene eteck-maluck besm ellab, u old, u menfas Kadus, ahadu Amlack, amin.*[2] I immerse you in the name of the Father and of the Son and of the Holy Ghost.' In the Coptic tradition they baptize boys on the fortieth and girls on the eightieth day after birth, and if on that day the baby is ailing baptism is not permitted; when as often happens the child fails to complete the aforementioned span of days, they scruple not to permit it to depart this world without the rite of baptism. The possibility arises that baptism may be conferred before the days of purification have been completed, seeing that an unpurified woman may not enter the sanctuary and the mother herself carries the infant to baptism. In case therefore of a mistake that needs rectifying, each individual renews his baptism twice yearly in running streams designated for this purpose, on the festival of the Three Kings and on that of St John the Baptist: then everyone without distinction, men and women, young men and maidens, religious and lay, bathe naked in the appointed rivers, while groups of priests, similarly naked, offer the sacred formula and cleanse the people by this so-called rite of baptism. Since this ceremony is performed in the middle of the night many acts of lewdness and stupidity take place, and the whole is repeated after dawn on the following morning. The rivers are regarded as baptistries, and treated with reverence and respect by all who cross them.

Confirmation, though sometimes in the Oriental tradition administered at the time of baptism by any parish priest, they basically ignore, being so unsophisticated that not only do they know nothing of the sacrament, but are even lacking in holy oil: this is because olive oil is seldom if ever imported into Ethiopia, and if ever the Mahometans bring any in from Egypt, it is hallowed only by the blessing of a parish priest. And yet it is for this end that the Ethiopians employ the Coptic Archbishop, who is extremely ignorant, has no knowledge of the Ethiopian

[2] *Ené atamqehalahu basema ab bawald bamanfes qeddus ahadu amlak, amén.*

language, pays little heed to the priests and none to the people, allows all matters to be carried on as the people themselves desire it, corrects or contradicts no one, indeed knowingly consents in their sins, conceals their faults, and even winks when the priests sell the holy oil at a profit, a grave scandal to our Faith in the eyes of the Mahometans, who call the holy oil Kava Kadus.

The Eucharist is administered by the Ethiopians after the Coptic formula *This is the body of God*, apart from a few who dispute this form of consecration.

Penitence is a sacrament not in use, and anyone who feels the pricks of conscience will hail from afar a priest walking abroad '*Abba efftachen*,[3] Father absolve me,' to which the priest replies '*Egzier efftach*,[4] May God absolve you' with no confession of individual sins and no imposition of penance. The sacrament is unknown, and the prerequisites for the sacrament, confession, contrition, attrition, determination to amend, are all omitted, and the priests themselves being without instruction are unable to instruct the people.

Extreme unction, or the viaticum, is entirely unknown, no priest fortifies the dying with that comfort, they are let to die like cattle, and instead of the sacrament there appear the monks of the Abbey of St Anthony, who put a white cap on the heads of the dying and receive them into their own confraternity, thus assuring them, they say, of life eternal. Poor blinded souls, simple and ignorant, they are more properly to be pitied as they are seduced by their wicked pastors and enmeshed in the toils of the devil, while the words of their priests corrupt the true teachings of Christ. The very dying are strengthened by no help from their priests, but lie like cattle amid the wailing of six or seven women, who leap into the air and cry at the tops of their voices *Voge voge*,[5] always the same phrase, which in Ethiopian has no meaning apart from wonderment at what is happening; they strike and tear with their hands at face, breast, and forehead, until the wretched sufferer gives up the ghost. At length they wash the corpse, shave the hairs from the body, sew it into a white cloth, and bear it away for burial amid a host of meaningless ceremonies.

[3] See chapter 34 note 15.
[4] See chapter 34 note 17.
[5] See chapter 37 note 2.

Ordination, as with the Copts of Egypt, is administered to anyone however ignorant, even if they are unable to read, provided that a present is made to the servants of the Archbishop for admission into the dwelling of that prelate, who, without any enquiry into suitability or age or any examination of morals or date of birth, is compelled to comply with the wish of everyone who presents himself, unless he wishes to bring down upon himself rebellion, misfortune, or even death itself; so arrogant in spirit are the Ethiopians, so highly do they regard themselves, so contemptuous are they of all others, so firmly do they regard the Abuna as bound in servitude to them: whatever they desire it is his task to provide, because it was to this end that he was called into Ethiopia by the Emperor at the expense of the Empire. Thus it is that he provides them with no spiritual teaching, and is ignorant of the Ethiopian language and makes no effort to learn it: for seven years before our arrival had he been in Ethiopia, yet he had learned not a word of the language, rarely or never appears before the people, and celebrates mass even less frequently; he remains for ever shut behind the walls of his house, where he eats, drinks, and cares nothing for feeding the flock entrusted to him: he believes and performs whatever his people decide, so that in works and in deeds no one follows the example of this remarkable variety of shepherd.

Matrimony as a sacrament is non-existent, and all practise as it were polygamy in Turkish fashion with three or four concubines, whom they put away at will in favour of others more to their liking. Circumcision is practised both of men and of women, as well as the ancient rite of the churching of women, the keeping holy of the Saturday Sabbath, fasting from natural food until sunset, and abstinence from the flesh of pigs, of hares, of things strangled, and from fish without scales. They deny the existence of Purgatory, and that the souls of the righteous will enjoy the eternal glory before the end of the world, and believe that their Emperor will not taste of the pains of Hell, but that if he deserves them will be imprisoned in underground confinement, without being subjected to any torment. They reject the Council of Chalcedon while regarding Dioscorus as a saint, in whose errors and Nestorian heresies they are steeped: they remember nothing, and know less, of the primacy of the church of Rome, and regard the church of Peter as being located in Abyssinia. Of the ten commandments, the theological virtues, and the other things necessary to salvation they know nothing, they disregard the laws of nature, and, in a word, they observe nothing of the true doctrine of Christ. They share with every nation some belief or other, with the Christians baptism, with the Jews the Saturday Sabbath, with the Turks plurality of wives, divorce, and circumcision, with the heathen superstition; since the same can be said of the many other examples of Ethiopian blindness, what sort of life, equity, or piety is likely to arise therefrom? Bloody are the tears that should be shed for them.

Scarcely one in a thousand is able to say the Lord's prayer or the Hail Mary, and yet despite this they regard their own faith as infallible and better than any other, and themselves more perfect than anyone else. So they are persuaded by the many monks of the Abbey of St Anthony and by their ignorant parish priests, who themselves have no one to teach them, and make time for no form of study, but live a life of evil and corrupt courses that befoul God's way. Thus the priests, instead of teaching Christ's people, lead them astry, themselves living lives of more open scandal than the laity; the good among them are totally corrupted in morals, all things are permitted and approved, even that which is naturally evil, and instead of the bread of heaven they feed their flock with the poison of serpents; the holy gospel and the divine laws are a plaything, and instead of good salt they serve that which is good for nothing but to be cast out and trodden under the foot of men. Thus it comes about that, even if the whole empire of Ethiopia could boast itself the subjects of a Christian emperor, and that the Christian religion was flourishing, yet the corrupt morals of the Ethiopians would do harm to our lord Christ, seeing that they are Christians only in name.

The Blessed Virgin Mary, the holy apostles and the other saints they honour in their accustomed fashion, not just with an annual festival but with one every month, when one day is kept holy to the Virgin, one to the holy apostles Peter and Paul, and others to many other saints. On these days they rest from labour, but they omit to mark the day by prayer, and celebrate it only by feasting, drinking, singing, dancing and various jollifications.

There is no administration of justice, innocence is violated, piety is not observed, and all the other virtues are disregarded;

theft, robbery and murder are committed with impunity, the laws of God, of the church, and of nature are flouted, and no wonder, seeing that they live in licence without fear of being brought to punishment. There is a total lack of instructors in the truth of the Faith, or of any barrier against sin, there is none to arouse them to the practice of virtue, they are forgotten of God and have no apostle to preach to them. It is indeed remarkable that still, in the midst of Turks, heathen, and idolaters, they have persisted for so long a time in the name of Christian: poor Ethiopians, cast off from the church of Rome, they are more to be pitied than censured in their outer darkness, and unless speedy help comes to them in the form of preachers of the Gospel, I fear that all of them by degrees will embrace Mahometanism or one of the heathen faiths.

On our departure from the Empire at the time of our expulsion, I found very many, both monks and laymen, who were well disposed towards embracing the Catholic faith, and for the whole of my stay in Ethiopia I found souls eager to hear the Catholic teachings, this desire burning with a bright flame even among the principal monks; often in secret did they prostrate themselves at my feet, and promised their obedience to the Supreme Vicar of Christ, for as long as we missionaries remained firm and steadfast within the Empire. When the unfortunate rebellion arose, and we were forcibly expelled, they parted from us with many lamentations, as is shown in the letter of the Emperor, and in that of our recall by the Sacred Congregation.

CHAPTER 72

HOW FOR THE FUTURE
A MISSION COULD BE
MAINTAINED IN ABYSSINIA

Our hearts when we departed were troubled and sad, our hopes
having been dashed of reaping a ripe harvest and storing it
securely into the granary of God, instead of which we were cast
forth with no spiritual consolation to cheer us. The Sacred Congregation bids me advise them, if a new mission were to be sent
on the always arduous and dangerous road to the Empire, in
what manner the mission should be conducted that the missionaries, so many times now expelled and even martyred, might not
be robbed of their just reward in souls for salvation: my reply is
that the missionaries must be steadfast and courageous to stand
firm against every calamity that meets them, even a cruel death,
and that they should be skilled in some of the practical arts, or
take with them artisans with such skills,[1] for lack of which the
missionaries themselves will suffer: let them be doctors skilled in
physic and surgery, who will smooth the mission's lengthy journey and save them much expense. To ensure the mission's stability
within Abyssinia, it will be of the greatest advantage if one of the
missionaries be of episcopal rank and dignity, because whenever
feeling is aroused against the missionaries the people are terrified
of excommunication at the hands of the local archbishop. Since

---

[1] Ethiopia's need for craftsmen had earlier been propounded by Ludolf, who
recalled Lebna Dengel's appeal to the King of Portugal in the early sixteenth
century for 'Printers, Armourers, Cutlers, Physicians, Chirurgeons, Architects,
Carpenters, Goldsmiths, Miners, Bricklayers, and Jewellers'. That this national
desire had in no way abated was evident, he argued, from the fact that when
Ernest, Duke of Saxony, asked his friend Abba Gorgoreyos what his country
most needed from Europe the latter replied, ' *Tebebat, Arts and Handicraft Trades;*'
well understanding, that neither Merchandize nor any other Calling could well
be follow'd without the help of the Workman's Tool'. (p. 392).

this race of barbarians fears nothing worse than excommunication from the church, so it is ready to submit to no authority more easily than to that of a bishop, which at time of rebellion is the only way to sustain the mission and to counter the fulminations of excommunication against all who oppose the expulsion of the missionaries. The bishop of the mission will by his authority reassure the terrified people, all the more so as the Ethiopians are drawn towards the priesthood and other orders by the solemnity of the ordination ceremonies; thus the missionaries, converting the more able and ordaining as priests those who have received proper instruction, will thereby gain a valuable tool in the preaching of the Faith, a tool which will be especially useful in time of rebellion through all the provinces of this widely-scattered Empire.

One must further bear in mind the negligence and idleness in performing their ecclesiastical functions of the heretical bishops, who seldom or never exercise them properly in public, while the only archbishop in Ethiopia has never so far officiated in public, nor exercised any pontifical function in the presence of his flock; the whole nation, thus far deprived, would rejoice to see the episcopal ceremonies of the Roman rite, so much more beautiful and more solemn, which they have not experienced for almost 150 years. Certainly when they see our ecclesiastical hierarchy, with all things arranged properly in due order, the spirits of all men will be drawn towards the missionaries, even of the monks who so far are even more the rulers of the people than is the Emperor himself. In addition, the monks and ecclesiastics will be the better disposed to us when they experience the better, quicker, and more careful service that the missionaries will afford them in Christian doctrine, charity, divine offices, and ecclesiastical ceremonies, than they have received from their own superior the archbishop, whom they regard as no better than their slave, bought into their service by their own money. Further strength will be added by the Catholic bishop's blessing of the holy oil, of which in Ethiopia there is ever a shortage and which the Ethiopians are said to be ever anxious to possess, and when they observe its ceremonial they will recognize the splendour of the holy Roman church as the sole true teacher which gives light to the whole world, far removed from the dingy drabness of their own heretical church. This tendency of theirs I can confirm from

471

my own personal experience: during the more than three months of our persecution, when we lay in hiding here and there in sore trouble, I was often asked by my friends, not only by the imperial ministers but also by the monks and priests of the church, whether any of us had been raised to the rank of bishop: even in defiance of the will of the Emperor and of the rebellious people would they have protected us in their own provinces, but it was neither right nor fitting for us to tell a lie, and thus our last possible defence against exile was unobtainable, and we were forced to quit the Empire with the consequent great loss of souls converted to salvation.

This is my reply, which I make without personal bias, and to whose truth I am ready to swear if the Sacred Congregation desire me, and with a reverent kiss of the sacred purple I once and for ever attest this as the truth.

After explaining by word of mouth a number of related matters, I was granted on 22 August 1754 an open audience of his Holiness Pope Benedict XIV;[2] entering the courtyard I found the supreme pontiff seated in his chair by the table bearing many books and a crucifix, and after three genuflexions I bowed myself at his feet, after implanting a kiss upon his sacred cheek. I was most kindly received by his Holiness, who bade me draw closer and placed his sacred hand upon my head, while he discoursed familiarly with me on the outcome of the mission to Ethiopia, and for three quarters of an hour paid careful attention, with fatherly eagerness, to each item of my story. He bade me take back to the Sacred Congregation that he was minded once again to reassume the apostolic role, and was profuse in spiritual thanks to me; I received his blessing, kissed the holy cross at his feet, and after three reverent genuflexions made my departure, in wonder that the Vicar of Christ had received with such kindness the least of worms on this earth.

Although I was advised to rest in Rome after the fatigues of such a journey, I decided without delay to return to the Egyptian mission, but having first obtained permission from the Sacred Congregation to visit my relatives in the kingdom of Bohemia, I duly betook myself thither.

[2] Prospero Lambertini, born 1675, succeeded Clement XII 1740, died 3 May 1758.

CHAPTER 73

DEPARTURE FROM
ROME FOR GERMANY

The Chief Pontiff's enthusiastic encouragement of my resumption of the Egyptian mission left me with no dearer wish than to cut short my journey and resume my apostolic labours as soon as possible: on August 22 therefore I left Rome at 2 a.m., with the benefit of travelling by post, safely crossed the Papal States, and then in the course of five days and four and forty posts I passed through the famous cities of Siena, Florence, Bologna, Modena, Mirandola and Mantua, and on August 29 had completed a further two imperial and three Venetian stages, the second of which brought to my view a fortress cut from the living rock called *Occlusa*,[1] with a river running below, its bridge and gate being built between rocky cliffs, and forming an impregnable stronghold against those wishing to ascend: in this area there is no other crossing into the Veneto apart from a rough path cut in the rock right beside the river below, scarcely wide enough for one vehicle, which takes one into the Empire.

After the three Venetian stages followed one imperial post to the city of *Rovereto*, and a further double post to *Tridentum*,[2] a small but handsome town which roused my admiration, and famous for the Council of Trent. Here after a modest repast I took four posts to *Bolgianum*[3] commonly called *Pautzen*, a city of the Tyrol, and then on September 1 reached the city of *Aenipontum*,[4] the famous foundation of the Emperor Frederick II[5] and

---

[1] Chiusa di Verona, on the modern main road between Verona and Rovereto, described in Baedeker 1899 ed. p. 20 as 'a rocky defile commanding the pass.'

[2] Trent. Prutky prefers to use the Latin name if possible.

[3] Bolzano, German Bozen.

[4] Innsbrück.

[5] Not the famous Emperor Frederick II, but Archduke Frederick of a junior branch of the Hapsburgs.

the recipient of the favour of many other emperors. Having reached here from Rome in the space of eight days I was somewhat fatigued, but had no wish to miss the chance of viewing the monastery of the Reformati, so finely built and so adorned by the many gifts of the Roman emperors.[6] It is embellished by a beautiful church and by bronze statues of the king-emperors of either sex, displayed life-size in excellent array, while in the middle of the church appears the famous tomb of Maximilian,[7] father of the Emperor Frederick. Many other noteworthy items I have been unable to describe with accuracy, being pressed for time, but one monument that I think worthy of mention is the chapel within one side of the church called the silver chapel, which is constructed of Indian ebony, a material more precious than silver, and whose altar, made also of ebony and inlaid with silver, is accounted to be of very great value; where also appears before the altar to the Blessed Virgin a bronze statue of the Emperor Frederick[8] with his knees bent, and wearing the very stockings which he wore upon the road, of black whole silk, still today unblemished after 200 years. While the emperor was absent at the chase his wife Philippina, some merchant's very beautiful daughter, was put to death by his subjects for envy's sake, as the mother of so great a royal line; her veins were cut in the bath and her body totally drained of blood. The returning emperor, suspecting nothing, was overwhelmed with grief to find his consort dead, and as a perpetual token of his love ordered her corpse to be buried in the same chapel, and her effigy carved in stone stands yet at the chapel entrance. There are besides many other monuments of antiquity to be seen there, but as they can be found in the works of other writers, to them I refer the kind reader.

On September 3 I left Anipontum (*sic*) for *Salisburgum*,[9] travelling seven posts on the same day, and soon reached the royal city of *Lintium*,[10] so that in the space of five days and nights I

---

[6] *Holy* Roman emperors.
[7] Maximilian I (1459–1519) was the son and not the father of the Holy Roman Emperor Frederick III.
[8] Archduke Ferdinand II (not Frederick), son of Emperor Ferdinand I, morganatically married Philippina Welser in 1557. But the story that she was murdered in her bath is now considered a fable.
[9] Salzburg.
[10] Linz.

had reached thus far from Mantua, with very little pause for refreshment. In my haste to reach *Bohemian Budejovice* I was completely exhausted by the fatigue of travel, having completed the whole of this journey from Rome in fifteen days. Here at least I had one day's rest: then I sped through the cities and towns of Bohemia, my own dear country, visiting my friends and relations, until I reached the capital *Prague* on the day sacred to my Seraphic Father St Francis. Here in adoration of the holy relics of the Bohemian miracle-worker St John of Nepomuk[11] I twice offered at his tomb the sacrifice of the Mass, that he might bless the further journeys of my apostolic mission, now to be resumed in Egypt. For but a few days did I dally in Prague, despite the honours and comforts heaped on me by my friends, lest I should be too long delayed from my fixed purpose by the imminent bad weather of winter. From Prague to *Bruna*,[12] capital of the march of Moravia, and then in the month of October to *Znoyma*[13] did I journey, where I delayed a few days before hastening to Vienna, capital of Austria, and seat of their Highnesses the Emperor and Empress.

[11] The patron saint of Bohemia.
[12] Brno.
[13] Znojmo.

CHAPTER 74

ARRIVAL IN
VIENNA IN AUSTRIA

For many years I had wished to see Vienna, and my wishes were fulfilled at midnight on 25 October 1754 when I entered that imperial city, being lodged at the house of the illustrious and distinguished knight Ignatius de Rollersburg canon of Olmütz, then serving his three-year term of office. Because the imperial court was at that time residing outside the city at Bellofonte or Schönbrünn, I was introduced to their Imperial Majesties[1] by the favour of his most excellent lordship the Count de Klevenmüller, and kindly received in a private audience on October 27, which fell on a Sunday. With indescribable goodness on the part of their Majesties I was asked who I was, from whence did I come, my nationality, what I sought in Vienna, to which in all humility and the respect due to such majesty I replied that I was a missionary of the Propagation of the Faith, that I had just returned from the empire of Abyssinia, that by nationality I was Bohemian, the lowest of their subjects, and that I had been ordered to return once more to the Egyptian mission; recounting briefly the tale of my journeys in Asia, Africa, Egypt and the Arabian deserts as far as the Red Sea. At his Caesarean Majesty's request for a description of these Arabian deserts, I replied that they are those very ones, full of solitude and without human cultivation, through which of old the people of Israel journeyed at God's command from the harsh slavery of Egypt to the land

[1] Maria Theresa (1717–80), Archduchess of Austria and Queen of Hungary and Bohemia, and her consort Francis Stephen (1708–65), Grand Duke of Tuscany and, from 1745, Holy Roman Emperor. Prutky seems to refer to him as the Caesarian Majesty and to Maria Theresa as the Royal Majesty. It seems that Francis rather than Maria Theresa became Prutky's patron.

476

of promise or Palestine, which they reached after forty years, having crossed the Red Sea dry-shod as Holy Scripture testifies. I carefully explained every aspect of these regions as far as the first Red Sea port of Suez, speaking at some length until the time came for the celebration of the sacrifice of the Mass, when I obtained of his Caesarian Majesty with a gracious kiss of the hand his favour and permission to withdraw; with great gladness of heart did I then complete the sacrifice before the holy crucifix of Frederick in the imperial chapel. On my next day in Vienna I again entered their Majesties' palace and was admitted to audience, thanks to the inborn goodness of so great a ruler, when I recounted the further vicissitudes of my wanderings and the unusual sights I had seen in the wondrous east, such as the Red Sea, the bath of Pharaoh, Mount Sinai, the burning bush of Moses, the place where the children of Israel worshipped the calf, the resting place of the body of St. Catherine Virgin and Martyr, and the manners, customs and antiquities of those parts, my description lasting for about two hours. How I admired the patience with which their Highnesses accorded me a hearing; and as I prolonged my stay in Vienna I was several times honoured, however unworthy, with the happiness of attendance on their Majesties.

Meanwhile I had the pleasure of viewing the Caesarian collections, the display of coins of both gold and silver, and many other objects in the imperial cabinets, and was then conducted through the whole gallery and shown all the items of interest and value from first to last, in the viewing of which I spent many hours as I wondered at the different beasts and birds of Asia and America. I derived particular pleasure from the garden plants, when I saw those which I had seen in Asia and America, with which Vienna would well stand comparison, especially in view of the excellent planting and protection of each specimen at the hands of a Dutch gardener returned from America. The garden of Vienna could not unjustly be called the garden of delights, and I marvelled to behold in every rare variety there all the profusion and fruitfulness of either Indies.

Although I protracted my stay in Vienna for a second month, honoured with audiences and with generous favours from both their Caesarian and their Royal Majesties and plied with kindnesses by many lords and ministers, yet my mind ever burned to return to the Egyptian mission, and to live for seventy days in Vienna was enough and more; although the winter weather was an argument to the contrary, yet it prevailed not against the ardour inspired in me by the souls of the castaways. Their Sacred Majesties supplying me with letters of recommendation I was planning to effect my return through Constantinople, but hearing that the Sultan of Turkey[2] had yielded to fate in the year 1754–5 I mistrusted the feasibility of that route, knowing too well the Mahometan character which in the absence of a ruler gives way to an excess of violence and tyranny. I therefore petitioned anew the Caesarian Majesty and found favour in his sight, viz. a passport to pursue my journey as far as Egypt through the countries and dominions under Austrian sway, Tuscany and the port of Leghorn. And lo! despite the many benefits already granted, not only did both their Majesties provide me with letters of recommendation, but gave orders in their kindness that the whole expenses of my journey should be paid for by land and sea right as far as Alexandria, adding the sum of one hundred gold pieces for my own personal expenses. At the last imperial audience that I was granted I repeatedly offered my thanks for such great kindnesses heaped on my unworthy head, but was told that no trace of obligation would attach to me if I would but pray the All-Highest for the continued safety and prosperity of each Highness, the Caesarian and the Royal. I was none the less put under obligations to many ministers for the favours and good offices lavished upon me, and on 18 January 1755 left my dear motherland, and the city of Vienna, for the tribes of the infidel.

[2] Mahmud I reigned 1730–54.

CHAPTER 75

DEPARTURE FROM VIENNA
AND JOURNEY THROUGH ITALY

I can never adequately commend the Imperial generosity for the favours that in their goodness they lavished on me, when I recall that thanks to the great favour of his Caesarian Majesty I was not only permitted free passage by land, but provided with everything necessary to sustain life, so that by God's grace I was able to make a happy start and completion to my journey from Vienna to Venice. Here, recommended by the imperial court to the imperial minister the Count de Rosenberg, who was also commercial consul, I was received in most kindly fashion and spent three days in the city. I could have taken the shorter route to Leghorn via Florence, being provided with imperial letters of recommendation to the lord governor the Count de Riscecourt, had I not nourished a desire to visit other parts of Italy. I therefore chose a more roundabout route, and directed my course through Lombardy, Piedmont, Sardinia and Modena to the state of Genoa, wishing to view the recent ravages caused there by the Austrian army. I therefore ascended a range of lofty mountains, called locally the *Bochetta*,[1] which were at that season covered with ice and snow and most difficult, indeed almost impossible to climb: but attempting their crossing circumspectly, I made my way successfully if dangerously across a barrier which had been declared impassable.

Around the city of Genoa I was grieved to behold the sad damage caused by the Austrian army, the beautiful buildings

---

[1] Not identified. Perhaps Rochetta Ligure, north of Genoa. The route from Venice to Genoa could be said to lie through Modena, Lombardy, Piedmont and Sardinia, which in 1720 was united with Savoy to form the Kingdom of Sardinia and Savoy.

lying in ruins, the gardens, vineyards etc. destroyed, because the Serene Republic[2] either would not or could not assist her subjects out of her own strength. But the grief I felt for the destruction and ruin thus caused was balanced by the pleasure I experienced in viewing the famous *Genoa*, nicknamed *The Proud*, one of the finest and largest of European cities, which lies in the shape of an amphitheatre or half-moon built on the sea, and which after the Venetian republic is of the first consequence: it is populous, counting its inhabitants at about 80,000 souls, and its commerce is of the most prosperous. The cathedral church of St Laurence is truly magnificent, and the palace of the Duke, commonly known as Doge, is beautiful indeed, together with its Arsenal, which contains many sorts of antique armour. The seaport is large and spacious and offers a most safe anchorage.

In the year 1684 the Republic was under attack from France, and in 1747–8[3] from Austria, to whose arms she at length made submission. Refusing however to bear the Austrian yoke, especially when they saw cannon being removed from the Arsenal or armoury and they themselves forced by the Austrian soldiery into the toil of rendering assistance, the citizens began a movement of revolt. During the removal of pieces of cannon from the armoury it happened that a large piece fell to the ground, and the citizens refused under threat of force to raise it up again; from this sprang the rebellion. At that time there was but a small detachment of Austrian troops stationed in the city, a consideration which caused the citizens to rush to arms and by superiority of strength to overwhelm the Austrians by their own might and expel them from the city, thus restoring their old liberty, to their own great credit and to the disgrace of their enemy. From that time onward they have nourished the greatest resentment against the Germans, and as an everlasting memorial have heaped over with stones the cannon that fell to the ground, and have left quite unaltered both it and the place where it fell: this they show to all strangers as the beginning of the revolt against the house of

---

[2] The Serene Republic is the title of Venice. But Genoa was independent of Venice, and was part of the anti-Austrian coalition, of which the heads by 1746 were France and Spain.

[3] The Austrian capture of Genoa and their expulsion by the Genoese is in fact dated to 1746: the incident was part of the War of the Austrian Succession 1741–48.

Austria. For my part, I viewed the sights of Genoa as a missionary in Arabian costume, having been warned by a good friend not to betray myself as a German and perhaps suffer some hurt from the hatred for Germans of the Genoese populace; I wandered through the streets of the city until I reached the spot where the cannon had fallen, when lo, a crowd soon gathered, and with great animation recounted the tale that here was the beginning of the German disaster.

After eight days when I had seen all the sights of Genoa, I resumed my journey by sea to the *Portus Liburnensis*,[4] which I reached safely after eight hours. Here I was received in a most friendly fashion by Don Ginori the city governor, a gentleman of the greatest distinction and the imperial commander of the harbour installation, and overwhelmed with numerous kindnesses from many of the nobility of Leghorn and the Levantine merchants. Meanwhile I received from Rome an order from the Sacred Congregation for the Propagation of the Faith that I should wait for another missionary who was coming to Egypt. I was therefore obliged after so much effort to tarry for eighty days in Leghorn until the arrival of a junior missionary enabled me to prepare my departure.

[4] Leghorn, the port of the Grand Duchy of Tuscany.

CHAPTER 76

DEPARTURE FROM LEGHORN
FOR EGYPT FOR THE SECOND TIME

By the good offices and assistance of the Governor of Leghorn and Commander of the imperial harbour installation I was provided with all my needs, and on May 26 boarded a French ship, Captain Joanne Michelon, a most competent officer, my every requirement for food and drink as far as Alexandria having been secured for me by the grace of the august Emperor. God blessed us with favourable winds, we were able to steer a direct course, and undisturbed by fears of shipwreck we safely reached the port of Alexandria on the eve of St John Baptist, that is on June 23, and in company with six other fathers bound for the Holy Land we joyfully entered our hospice, which is that of the Observant Friars Minor, where we remained for several days in torment from the extreme heat. Soon however I bestirred myself towards my old mission, safely reached the mouth of the Nile by way of the Mediterranean sea, and on the same day put in at Rosetta. Early the following morning we resumed our voyage, exposed daily and nightly to the heat of the sun; once again were we beset by the many and great difficulties of the journey and the dangers of both land and water, until at length I was thankful to enter Cairo on July 14, the feast of St Bonaventure; having rendered thanks to God I entered, unexpected, the hospice of the Propagation of the Faith, and was received with heartfelt joy by the Prefect[1] of the mission and other fathers, and by the whole Catholic people.

Soon resuming my old work of apostolic missionary, I laboured in the vineyard of the Lord and yearned to gather in a hundred-

---

[1] The prefect was no longer James of Kromeriz but Paul of Agnona; compare chapter 70 note 4.

fold harvest of souls, rejoicing meanwhile in my heart that I was found worthy to aid these poor dear Christians with spiritual services; and I repeatedly recalled the many previous tribulations which I had endured in Abyssinia, the everlasting journeyings and the danger to life itself, beside which my many tasks in Egypt seemed all easy and in comparison delightful, although in themselves they were hard enough as my body ran with sweat from the rays of the sun and the heat by day and by night brought on by its fierceness. While so employed in peacefully tending the souls in the little vineyard of Cairo, I was ever minded to go back to Upper Egypt and indeed to the city of Girge,[2] as being the scene of my first lost martyrdom. Fr Paul of Agnona however, the prefect of the mission, was preparing to depart to Rome to the Sacred Congregation for the Propagation of the Faith, to discuss a number of important pieces of business relating to the mission, and was anxious to leave around the middle of August 1755; he therefore dissuaded me from going to Upper Egypt, and required of me on my hope of salvation and on my obedience that I should continue in the Cairene vineyard, where indeed I found much at which to toil and sweat, in the instruction and conversion of the heretical Copts and numerous Greeks, as well as enduring at times the insults of impertinent Mahometan youths. Nevertheless for the whole of this year nothing noteworthy happened in Cairo, and we fed the Lord's flock in peace enough without any of the uprush of persecution, whether from Mahometans or from Greek heretics, that had marked other years.

On 13 February 1765[3] however we experienced the anger of the earth against us, and at around 10 o'clock at night, as I was engrossed in the reading of Arabic, the earth began to quake with unexpected and horrible tremors such as to unloose the foundations of the buildings and split the most solid walls, which seemed on the point of falling into the depths of the abyss. We had earlier been conscious of a terrible underground rumbling, as of the arrival of four-horse chariots, the earth heaving into the air and threatening universal ruin; since in addition there arose the shouts of men, the lamentations of women, the wails

[2] Modern Girga, between Asyût and Qena, the scene in 1751 of the persecution of the missionaries, of whom Prutky was one.

[3] *Sic*, a mistake for 1756.

483

of children and the roars and bleats of animals, the Day of Judgment seemed at hand. Together with the Vice-Prefect I went down to pray for help in the domestic chapel before the Holy Sacrament, when I felt the marble stairs moving under my feet despite their massive weight, and the veins and limbs of my body began to shake when I saw on the altar that the massive marble statue of the Blessed Virgin Mary, which was large indeed, was rocking and bending from side to side: I expected at any moment to be overwhelmed beneath a pile of stones. Amid these straits and bloody sweats we did not forget to commend our souls to God, nor to absolve each other from our sins, as we awaited the pity or the punishment of God the Avenger. For about eight minutes and three repetitions of the tremor did these anxieties last, until they ceased when God's pity stilled the commotion, and nothing was left for us but to sing praises to God's mercy that we had not been destroyed, and that His compassion had not deserted us in this manifest danger to our very lives. During this night many of the Mahometans and Christians alike met their deaths from terror and from shock, while many were overcome by madness and their different diseases exacerbated, as they sought help throughout the streets. On the following day all we missionaries went out and about busily visiting the houses of the sick, especially the Catholics, and did our best to relieve both men and women from the terrible convulsions and other ills from which they suffered, offering medicine to their bodies and ghostly consolation to their souls. However, there were not enough of us in the whole of this day to help each individual, and with my own hands before noon I had let the blood of more than one hundred people of either sex; it was consequently necessary to beg the assistance of lay surgeons, French and Italian, to help the missionaries in this work of charity, although this was contrary to the usual custom in Egypt. In the space of eight days the needs of the sick were still far from satisfied.

But as the cases of illness eased, I eased not my labours in tilling the vineyard of souls entrusted to my care, unheeding of the heat of the day or night but seeking to bring back straying sheep to the sheep-fold of the Lord. It happened one day, as I hastened about noon to pass to our hospice through a narrow street, that I came face to face with three infidel janissaries, armed as is their custom with swords, long knives and muskets, whom

I could in no way avoid. These ruffians assaulted my furiously: 'Stop' they cried, 'curse you, and come here.' In obedience and humility I complied, when they seized me by the collar, drew a long knife and held it my breast as they heaped blows and blasphemies upon me for an infidel, cruelly pushing me from side to side, pricking me and threatening me with death. I meanwhile trembled and made no reply, not knowing the cause of their attack but not daring to ask, as I patiently awaited whatever might be the outcome of their cruelty, but even while I was as certain as could be that from their hatred of the Catholic faith I should be run through and fall victim before them, God's invisible hand plucked me at the price of a few blows from all too visible barbarity, and I offered the whole misadventure to God, Who suffered and died for me before ever I was born.

CHAPTER 77

FRESH DEPARTURE
FROM CAIRO FOR ROME

There had arisen at that time between the Venetian consul living in Cairo and the Coptic community a number of points of conflict, for the resolution of which Fr Paul of Agnona, Prefect of the mission, had for the past year been engaged in Rome, though without obtaining any decision from the Pope; this caused much disturbance within the mission, losing us many souls for salvation and greatly hindering our dearest wish, the conversion of the Copts. I was therefore requested by Fr Vice-Prefect Joseph of Sassello[1] to depart again for Rome, seeing that I was known in the Roman Curia, but because after traversing so many provinces my health had scarcely yet recovered from the journey, this request came as a considerable burden to me. Nevertheless the common good had to take precedence over individual convenience, the salvation of souls was a prime consideration, and the arguments were so weighty for both preserving the missions and making them more effective that I at length consented, in the sure knowledge that obedience is the better sacrifice. For the greater glory of God therefore and for the salvation of souls I for the third time undertook all the fresh dangers involved in a journey by land and sea from the Levant to Europe, and, provided with written instructions from my superior the Vice-Prefect, I girded myself for the voyage. It was thus on 2 July 1756 that I set off down the Nile from New Cairo to the place in Old Cairo called Bolack,[2] provided with but few items of luggage and those of the most necessary; relying only on God's providence I joined

---

[1] Giuseppe Francesco di Sassello was sent to Egypt in 1740 and became Prefect of Missions in 1760.

[2] Modern Būlāq, which at that date was the port of Cairo on the Nile.

a company of Mahometan infidels in a tiny ship's cabin, which I had to share with twelve Turks and where I could scarcely stand erect, much less sit down. Assailed by their blows, insults and blasphemies I suffered in silence and patience for five days and nights for the sake of the divine blessing in the life to come. At last on July 8 I put in at Rosetta, and lodged at the hospice of our Brothers of the Holy Land, staying there until July 11 when in the early morning I set off through the desert for Alexandria, not wanting the disturbance of a further voyage down the Nile and through the Mediterranean sea. In the midst of this journey I suffered yet another annoyance, when for a short rest I entered a hut erected for the convenience of travellers, and found it full of Mahometans, Arabs and janissaries, so that at nightfall I had to take my rest in a crowd, like a dog in an underground cave, and to endure a host of injuries from the impudence of these robbers, unable to sleep for fear lest I lose my life at their hands; at the second hour of the night while the rest were asleep I departed in absolute silence in company with four Christians and three Cairene Turks, and approached Alexandria at sunrise. Entering our hospice here I was kindly received by the brothers, and although I was anxious to be off was compelled to delay from July 12 to 31 for lack of shipping.

Finding at last a ship of Ragusa, Captain Don George Philippaci, a most competent officer, we weighed anchor at dawn, but meeting contrary winds on the following day made very little headway, so that it took us eight days of sailing before we got sight of the *Land of the Seven Capes*,[3] so called from its seven lofty and pointed mountains, or vulgarly *Caramania*. Caramania is thirty miles from the island of *Rhodes*, which was once the possession of the Knights of Malta, but is now under Mahometan rule; very strong contrary winds were ever driving us into the Archipelago and away from the island, and we were not far from shipwreck when we called upon the Holy Virgin, the star of the sea, on the day of Her Assumption into Heaven, that is August 15, and safely entered the harbour of Rhodes. The island is not especially fertile of wheat, but abounds in other grain, in garden produce, in melons, citrons, olives, wine, honey, wax, excellent soap etc. The

[3] Yedi Burun, on the Turkish coast S. of Fethiya. Modern Karamania is further to the east, being due north of Cyprus.

inhabitants are mostly schismatic Greeks, who with no reproach of conscience mingle their blood with that of the Turks and hand their young daughters over in marriage to Mahometans. It is certainly true that the Rhodian Mahometans are not so opposed to Christianity as those of Cairo, Alexandria or elsewhere, but because of their opposition to the Christian faith no small loss of souls results therefrom. Beautiful cloth is woven in the island, both tablecloths and chair covers, as well as several sorts of stuff from camel hair etc.; the climate is extremely healthy and the sky always unclouded, such that no single day passes without sunshine. The capital city of Rhodes takes its name from the island, and offers an excellent anchorage, naturally strong and extremely resistant to hostile assault, since an attacking force would have in the first place to cross between two huge crags or mountains which are each heavily fortified and turreted, and which are very adequately garrisoned by the Mahometans. In times past there stood on these two crags a huge brazen Colossus,[4] representing Apollo, whose right foot rested on the support of one crag and the left on the other, while a ship with all sail set could pass beneath. This Colossus was once reckoned one of the seven wonders of the world, but when in A.D. 655 the Saracens seized the island from the Christians they thought that treasure was to be found beneath such structures and destroyed almost all of them, as was their practice throughout Egypt and elsewhere, together with many of the rarities of antiquity. According to another account the Colossus was overturned in an earthquake, and then fifty-five years later re-erected by the Romans, until the barbarians seized Rhodes from the Christians, cut up the Colossus into pieces, and transported it to Egypt on 900 mules, applying the bronze to various purposes.

At the end of the Holy War, when the Knights of St John had been driven from the Holy Land, they again seized the island out of Saracen hands and in the year 1309 settled it as their stronghold and the seat of an archbishop, which they enjoyed together with the whole island for 213 years. But in 1522 Solimann II, Sultan of Turkey, again made head against it, so that it ceased to be a Catholic archbishopric, though the Greek

---

[4] The Colossus did not bestride the harbour. It was prostrated by an earthquake in 224 B.C.; the fragments were removed after the Arab conquest.

schismatics so maintain it to this day. The Knights of St John stoutly defended the city of Rhodes for a full half year, without securing any help from Christendom, but at last were compelled to surrender on terms, after ninety thousand Saracens had perished in the siege. It was the very chancellor of the order, named Andreas Amara or Amarat, a Portuguese, who is said to have been the hidden enemy who surrendered this strong and well fortified city, because the Sultan of Turkey had promised him his daughter in marriage; but when the city had been handed over the Sultan rejoined on him: 'If you wish to be united in wedlock with my daughter you must first put off your Christian skin,' and ordered the skin to be cruelly flayed from his living body, which was then placed in a bed sprinkled with salt and pepper.[5]

While I was making these observations in Rhodes a more favourable wind spring up, which wafted us across to the port of *Cavalieri*,[6] now deserted of any human contact but inhabited in times past and the possession of a noble Genoese cavalier, along with the island of that name, and because the harbour is believed to have been built by him it bears this name to the present day. This same nobleman was also at one time, up to 1355, lord of the island of *Meteline* or *Mitylene*,[7] anciently called *Lesbos*, but the envy of other Christian nations brought it about that after 1442 the Republic of Genoa lost possession of this and other islands which had been seized from the Saracens: notwithstanding the fact that the Genoese were compelled to pay the Sultan an annual tribute of 18,000 German thalers. The circumference of Meteline is forty-five French leagues, and it is more important than all the other islands of the Archipelago, producing an abundance of fine wine and fruit, especially figs,

[5] Andre Amaral, 1450–1523, was High Chancellor of Rhodes. He was beheaded on a charge of treasonable correspondence with the Ottoman Sultan Suleyman during the siege in 1522. Prutky's story is fanciful. It has been claimed that Amaral was falsely accused by partisans of the Grand Master Phillippe de Villiers, whose election he had opposed.

[6] Kastellorizon or Megistē, also known as Castelrosso, occupied by the Knights of St John in 1306. Their garrison was massacred and their tower demolished in October 1443 by the forces of the Sultan of Egypt.

[7] Mitylene (Lesbos) is very far to the north of Prutky's course through the Greek islands: it was in the possession of the Genoese noble family of the Gateluzi from the thirteenth to the fifteenth century. Presumably Prutky's comment on Cavalieri is an echo of this.

and containing also a supply of beautiful marble; its principal city is of the same name, *Meteline*, but is not as flourishing as of old and lies partially in ruins; it maintains however for its defence a strong fort. During our voyage in the Archipelago we passed on August 16 the port called *Simia*,[8] which is inhabited by a few Turks who however all live at some distance from the port, at least seven Italian miles away, because nothing grows beside the sea and they thus make no attempt to cultivate the soil. The reason why the harbour and inhabitants are called Simia is because like apes they are in the habit of imitating other nations, and labour at nothing save tasks that they have observed others doing. They are well skilled in swimming in the sea like fishes, and let themselves down to the very bottom, so that if a vessel has lost something overboard the islanders are well able to restore it from under the water, provided that they are well paid. Fishing in the sea is their general method of sustaining life, and they pay no tribute to the Sultan. The common story is that no father allows his daughter to wed until she has been properly taught to swim, like the men.

[8] Modern island of Simi.

CHAPTER 78

THE ARCHIPELAGO
AND SOME OF ITS ISLANDS

Although the Red Sea and Indian Ocean are full of dangers to shipping, the Archipelago[1] causes no less anxiety to its navigators because of the many rocks and reefs which project into the sea from all sides for a distance of two hundred and fifty Italian miles; if the winds be contrary, the result is often shipwreck. Our own course being beset by contrary winds and taking us close to a rock, we should have incurred a not dissimilar fate on August 17, and as we crossed the channel in the sea that leads to *Stanchio*,[2] tossed hither and thither by the tempest, we were exposed afresh to the danger of shipwreck on the rock known as *Episcopi*.[3] To avoid disaster we changed course to the island of *Nios*[4] or *Nia* to provision our ship there, our stores having been almost used up after so many days of exposure to contrary winds; yet despite our anxiety to make harbour in Nios, it was only after toil and sweat that we reached it on August 24.

This island though small is fertile, producing corn, figs, citrons, apples, grapes and other fruit; the inhabitants are mostly Greek schismatics, with among them a few Catholics and one clerical missionary from the Propagation of the Faith, who for twenty years has been planting and tending his vineyard here, unproductive though it be; the Catholic families number but five or six, and endure harsh treatment from the Greek heretics. At the time of my arrival on the island the Missionary Father was in a serious

---

[1] Prutky is quite correct in referring to the Greek islands of the Aegean by this name. Only by extension was the name applied to *any* group of islands.

[2] Cos. Stanchio corresponds to Turkish Istankay.

[3] Modern Tilos.

[4] Modern Ios.

decline, and it fell to me to treat the sick among the Catholics, administering the Sacrament, letting blood and prescribing medicine, and I brought much comfort to this miserable folk who were otherwise destitute of help. As the neighbours heard this they hastened to me in droves and tearfully besought my help under the stress of their different illnesses: to all of them I administered treatment for a whole day, as far as I could, letting blood and administering medicine, seeing that they were deprived of any assistance whether from a physician or from drugs; and indeed if any of them had been otherwise cured of his illness, it would have been a miracle. In thanksgiving for this their treatment of me was most excellent, as I was plied with good wine and a most plentiful store of fruit for my onward journey, especially at the hands of the kin of Lord George Drago (*sic*) of Nios, Treasurer to the Emperor of Abyssinia, of whom I made mention earlier in chapter 50;[5] in reply to their questions I offered them the consolation that he was still in the land of the living, though they were most anxious to see him once more before he died.

From this island of Nios is visible another, at two Italian miles' distance, called *Santorini*[6] or *St Erini*, in Latin *Thera*; other names for it are *Theresia* or *St Helena*. Apart from a few schismatics or heretics all its inhabitants are Catholic, the Mahometans repairing there only to exact the annual taxes. The priests of the Catholics are Reformed Friars Minor, Jesuits and a number of clerics deputed and maintained by the Sacred Congregation for the Propagation of the Faith. At three Italian leagues from Santorini is a rock or scylla which some years ago for the first time appeared out of the sea, in a place where the depth of water was said to be but sixty-eight paces until as the water level fell and the rock rose up only eight paces' depth of water was left. Fishermen today reckon when they are fishing that a ship that strikes the rock will remain stuck upon it and can only be removed by great exertions, and that when it is removed a huge sulphurous flame is emitted and causes much damage to the villages in the neighbouring islands. This continued for about three years until another rock appeared nearby, when the flame ceased to issue

[5] Last mentioned in chapter 52, not chapter 50.
[6] The name of the island is Santorini, Thera being the name of the island's ancient capital.

out of the first rock. The ashes that remain give ocular proof that the earlier rock has been totally destroyed by volcanic action.

By noon on August 27 we had purchased in Nios the ship's stores that we needed and again embarked on board ship, when favouring winds caused us almost to fly as we passed the last island of the Archipelago *Kimolos,* or in Latin *Cimolis,*[7] which is also called *Argentina* after the silver mines which it contains; here there dwelt one single Franciscan missionary, a Neapolitan, to serve the Catholic population, the island being but small and the Catholic inhabitants few. There followed the last and most dangerous of the rocks called *Milos,* which with God's help we passed in safety, and then the *Cape of St Angelo,*[8] part of the *Morea,* near which is the Venetian island of *Cerigo,* in Latin *Cytherea*[9], a wretched place indeed, where the many schismatic Greek inhabitants are in the habit out of bitter poverty of selling their own sons into slavery. Once past this there followed shortly *Cape Matapan,* in Latin *Promontorium Taenarum* or *Tanara,* which is part of Morea and called *Laconia* or *Braccia di Mania;*[10] its inhabitants bear the name of *Mainothae* and are simply robbers and pirates, whom the very Turks have often repressed but never rooted out or totally subdued. They thus constitute what is as it were an independent republic, which as well as the three cities of *Vitulo, Magni* and *Proasti*[11] consists of three hundred and fifty-six wretched villages, most of which have been burned down by the Mahometans but whose inhabitants, caring nothing for this, increase and multiply like beasts in the local caves or like foxes in holes. They are none the less firm friends with the Maltese, with whom they ally themselves, being Greek schismatics, in courageous and unceasing naval warfare against the Mahometans, although their sway does not extend over more than twelve thousand people.

[7] Kimolos is in fact much smaller than Milos.
[8] Modern Cape Malea.
[9] Modern Kithira.
[10] On modern maps Mani. This peninsula, which projects south from the Peloponnese (the Morea) was part of the ancient Laconia (Sparta), but was more recently famous for its piratical inhabitants, the Mainotes, whose desperate resistance to the Turks is commended by Prutky. They took a prominent part in the wars for Greek independence, but their alliance with the Maltese is an invention of Prutky's.
[11] Magni and Proasti are unidentified. Vitulo may be Itylo, which was a centre of the Mainotes.

On September 5 a continuance of the calm weather caused us to make but little headway, while the captain of the ship was struck down with fever and no doctor was on board; blood-letting being the only suitable remedy I performed the operation myself, and with the medicines I carried with me effected a complete cure on the third to the fourth day. Since there was another ship in company with ours, the other captain transferred to our ship to visit his sick colleague, and brought with him a turtle of thirty pounds' weight which had been recently captured, and with which we were glad to recruit our strength, all discomforts forgotten. On the next day with more favourable winds we progressed to within sight of the mainland of Morea and of its city *Modon*, in Latin *Methone*,[12] the seat of the Sangiak or Governor of the whole of the Morea and of a Greek bishop; the city has a good and well fortified harbour, and is populous, rich, and an important centre for trade, while to its east lies another ancient city, no less strong, possessed equally of a good harbour, by name *Coron* or *Corona*,[13] which lies in the bay of the same name and is the seat of a Greek archbishop; in the area is a small island called *Sapienza*, a nest of pirates. However, whether the winds were contrary or favourable the tedium of the voyage was such that we did not land on the Morea, but decided for our necessary refreshment to press on to the famous island of *Malta* or *Melita*.

[12] Modern Methoni.
[13] Modern Koroni.

CHAPTER 79

MALTA OR MELITA
AND OTHER SMALL ISLANDS

Great was the joy in our hearts when on September 10 we landed
in the harbour of Malta and its capital city[1] of the same name,
Malta or Melita, the outpost of Christendom and the hammer of
the Mahometans, where for some time we stayed to refresh
ourselves with the finest and best of fruit and wine. Some
geographers declare it to be part of Africa and others part of
Europe,[2] since it is not far from Sicily. After the knights of St
John or of Jerusalem were driven out of Rhodes, whence they
took the name of the knights of Rhodes, they were presented by
the Emperor Charles V with this island of Malta, thus gaining
their present name of the Knights of Malta. The number of
inhabitants extends to about sixty thousand, of whom the simple
people speak a corrupt form of Arabic, or ancient African or
Carthaginian, while the nobility speak Italian, French or German.[3] The land is fertile, though little corn is grown since plenty
is imported from Sicily outside the island, and the countryside
is productive of good wine, flax, silk, melons and other garden
stuff; wood however is extremely expensive and in its stead the
poorer classes as in Egypt commonly make use of dried cattle
dung. No poisonous insects are to be found there, and this
according to ancient tradition is ascribed to the sanctity of St Paul
the Apostle, who in his voyage to Rome was bitten here by a
poisonous viper, but took no harm from it, whereupon all
poisonous insects are said to have fled the island.

---

[1] The capital of Malta is Valletta, but see note 4 below.
[2] Part of Europe, and now an independent republic.
[3] Maltese is closely related to Arabic and has sometimes been described as an
Arabic dialect. Its relation to Punic is a matter of controversy.

The capital city also is called Malta[4] and is composed of three distinct cities: the first is called *Valetta* from the name of its founder the Grand Master; otherwise known as the *New City* it embraces the magnificent buildings of the Grand Master's Palace and of the Hospital of the knights of the same order, together with the principal church dedicated to St John Baptist: the second city is called *Victoriosa* or *Borgo San Angelo* because in the year 1565 it was fiercely besieged for four months by Sultan Solimann II of Turkey but defended itself courageously and drove back the Sultan and his army summarily and victoriously; it contains the magnificent palace of the Holy Inquisition, the Arsenal, the prison-house of the slaves and the Greek church, which is the most ancient of all of them: the third part is called the *Old City*, said to be invincible, and is in particular the seat of the bishop of the whole island.

When I had made these brief observations we resumed the further course of our voyage, but were again affected by the tedious calm of the sea which caused us to make but little headway, our passage taking us past the three small islands of *Lampadosa*, *Limosa* and *Pantalaria*,[5] of which the first two belong to Malta and are inhabited by a few Christians, the first supporting one priest though at one time it contained also a hermit who was doing penance there; in the second island, which is but three Italian leagues in extent and correspondingly infertile, even fewer inhabitants are to be found. The third island on the other hand, called Pantalaria, belongs under the protection of the King of Sicily to the Duke *de Requescens*[6] and is not far from that kingdom; it numbers at least eight thousand inhabitants, Sicilian and Spanish, and has an excellent harbour and four fortresses with their own commanding officer. The city is strong, its houses are built in the European style, and it possesses all kinds of

[4] The capital of Malta was founded in 1566 by Grand Master Valette of the Knights of Malta when he had repulsed the Sultan of Turkey after a siege of four months. The city is divided into five quarters, the Citta Nuova or Valletta Proper, Vittoriosa, Floriana, Sanglea, and Barmola. The Old City of which Prutky speaks is the old capital Mdina, situated inland, which is the still the (joint) seat of the bishopric, the church of St John at Valletta having been raised to the status of a co-Cathedral in 1798, after Napoleon had expelled the Knights.

[5] Modern Lampedusa, Limosa, Pantelleria, all now administered as part of the Italian Province of Sicily.

[6] The Spanish Requesens family were princes of Pantelleria from 1311 until 1553, when the chief town of the island was sacked by the Turks.

munitions of war and a garrison sufficient to fend off any Turkish attack, despite its proximity to Tunis. Although small, barely eight Italian miles in size, it abounds in every sort of produce necessary to sustain life, and on September 14 we arrested our course with the intention of tarrying there a while; but quite unexpectedly there arose the wind which we had so long desired and was so favourable to us, called in Italian *Sirocco* and in Latin *Euro-Notus*, which filled our sails and carried us happily forward.

Yet was this short time of happiness soon followed by further mischances: the wind waxed ever stronger, the waves of the sea foamed everywhere about us, a terrible tempest followed, and amid the crashing of thunder, the flashing of lightning and torrents of rain we hastily set our course towards Sardinia. Even more terrible to behold was that at about 4 p.m. the darkness came upon us so thick as to strike us with the horror of the Day of Judgment; so awful was it to see the sailors' confusion, the intensity of the toil demanded by the management of the sails, the tossing of the ship and the heaving of the sea, and a terrible fear came upon us that at any moment we could expect to be shipwrecked. This indescribable tempest lasted continuously for thirty hours, while I meanwhile, alone and single in the hold or keel at the bottom of the ship, on my knees was intent to implore God's aid for the whole of the crew. At length by God's mercy on September 16, at about 6 p.m., the storm ended, and in the calm that followed the waves of the sea reached to the height of the tallest of towers; I could neither stand nor sit nor lie, much less compose myself to sleep. On September 17, the feast of the stigmata of St. Francis, the sky was clear, and to render thanks for the many mercies we had received I offered to the Almighty on shipboard the sacrifice of the Mass: at other times it had been my custom every day to offer this celebration to the Divine Helmsman on behalf of the whole ship's company, and it was only for the three days of tempest that the tossing of the ship prevented me from doing so. We resumed our voyage with feelings of relief, but not for long, and in a short time, to wit on September 19, our spirits were overwhelmed with yet more grief and despair when a terrific storm arose and frightful winds broke the ropes which operated the wheel or helm and we poor wretches were tossed amid the squalls hither and thither, and the danger of shipwreck was manifestly imminent. But fortune, or rather

Divine Providence, rendered assistance to the helmsman; a rope being passed beneath the ship, the wheel or helm which projected out towards the bridge was strongly grasped in the hands of the crew until it had been again secured by more ropes fastened below, and thus were we freed from the clear danger of shipwreck.

On the same day at about 1 p.m., after such heartfelt tribulations and mental anxieties, we arrived safe and sound at the port of Leghorn, so long desired and the object of so many prayers; our thanks were raised to God that He had freed us, and especially myself, from the dangers by sea and land and from the wiles of a barbarous people by which I had been beset, and that He had granted me that I might reach dry land in a Christian and Catholic country. For one and fifty days had I tasted the sea's dangers, and suffered the extreme of hardship in the matter of food and drink, my drink consisting of a little of the wine of Ragusa, of the cheapest sort and watered at that; indeed it was a little water, rotten and brackish, slightly tinged with poor wine. Certainly I had received evil enough treatment and was in a state of total collapse and weakness from such a journey when I touched dry land, which I looked on as paradise on earth. I refreshed myself on good bread and wine and on the finest European fruit, and gladly accepted confinement in a rather distant hospital, although I was to endure it for forty days, to undergo what is called the quarantine: as the Orient at that time was infected with fever, I was forbidden to enter a nearer hospice.

CHAPTER 80

ARRIVAL AT THE HARBOUR
AND CITY OF LEGHORN

My troubles by sea and land behind me, I entered on September 22 the hospital of St James, as I said, to undergo quarantine, and there for some days I lived comfortably enough, when lo, just as I had begun to regain my bodily strength after the voyage, I was struck down with a very severe tertian ague whose bouts lasted for five or six hours continuously, a fresh occasion for me to practise patience, as I was troubled with it throughout three whole weeks. Yet although I was in a state of weakness I nevertheless heard confessions of the Orientals and other nationals who were in quarantine with me, and rejoiced that I was strong enough for eternal glory's sake to effect something of spiritual benefit: at last thanks be to God I was myself cured of the fever.

It was on about November 1 that I left the hospital, and remembering God's mercies towards me decided immediately on the first day of my release to climb the hill of Montenero,[1] the shrine of the Holy Virgin, and to offer to God the bloodless sacrifice of the Mass: when I had put this into effect, and offered my homage to the Virgin Mother of God the source of miracles and the Patroness of sailors, commending myself to Her further maternal protection, I returned downhill to Leghorn, and in the space of eight days had made all necessary arrangements. Determined to perform with all speed the duties of my obedience, I prepared myself for my journey to Rome, and it was on November 9 that I left Leghorn for the inland territory of the Grand Duke of Tuscany, where all was planted with vines, trees and gardens

---

[1] The pilgrimage church there still contains a miraculous picture of the Madonna.

499

like a paradise on earth, and disposed in such excellent order as to delight my soul, which praised the Creator in His creation. I was happy to reach the celebrated city of Siena, the famous birthplace of St Bernardino and St Catherine, whose sacred relics, now at rest among the Dominican Fathers, and holy calvary exposed at a small altar for public worship, I adored with reverence. The chief monument of antiquity in the city is the cathedral, magnificently built after the Gothic style in black and white marble throughout, paved with the same marble, and skilfully adorned with representations in mosaic of the Passion of Our Lord Jesus Christ and of the massacre by Herod of the Holy Innocents for Christ's sake, as well as with many other figures and tapestries; the whole is preserved even today in excellent condition, to the admiration of visitors, and includes the wooden chair of St Bernardino of Siena, from which he used to preach. Many other monuments of antiquity could be here described, but I have thought it right to omit them because they can be found set out in more detail in the writings of others. But one institution I would not wish to pass over in silence, namely the school of equitation which was founded by his highness the Holy Roman Emperor Francis I Grand Duke of Tuscany,[2] and whose fine horses, along with the cost of running and maintaining it, are provided by the nobility at their own charges, in gratitude to the Grand Duke and in token of their love for him. Here it is open to all the nobility, of whatever rank, to learn any style of horsemanship that may be necessary, and for example at the time of my visit two Roman princes were at exercise in the school, as I saw with my own eyes.

But time was pressing since I left Leghorn, and girding myself for the onward journey I set off for *Viterbo* along the royal road, so excellently constructed. Viterbo is a handsome enough city of some size, situated within the *Patrimony of St Peter*,[3] and is itself a bishopric. Its most remarkable spectacle is the body of St Rose of Viterbo, which to this day is untouched by corruption, supple, and of an extremely sweet odour; this I visited to worship the virgins who had dedicated themselves to God, and offered the sacrifice of the Mass.

---

[2] Prutky's patron. See Preface note 1, chapter 74 note 1.
[3] The Papal States.

CHAPTER 81

THIRD ARRIVAL AT
THE HOLY CITY OF ROME

The final goal of my protracted journey, long desired and the object of so many prayers, I finally achieved with gladness on November 17 when I joyfully entered the holy city of Rome, the capital of the whole world, and for a third time was to visit the dwelling place of St Peter and St Paul. I immediately went up on Montorio to the missionary college which lies within our monastery of the Reformati and is sacred to St Peter the Apostle, where I chose me a lodging or dwelling place. Here I embraced my dear friend Fr Prefect Paul of Agnona[1] who had spent a whole year in Rome, and in consultation with him compiled a list of each point to be put forward to the Sacred Congregation for the Propagation of the Faith for their careful consideration, with valid arguments to support them. I then approached His Eminence Cardinal Spinelli, supreme Prefect of the missions, who despite a frowning countenance when he received me on our first interview none the less showed favour towards me when he had listened to the reasoned arguments we put forward, and, after a fresh audience with the Supreme Pontiff Benedict XIV and a convocation of the College of Cardinals, matters were drawn to the desired conclusion, though this so far had proved impossible of achievement; all the points in favour of the missionary fathers and the increase of the poor souls of Egypt were resolved in a most favourable manner and confirmed by decrees, to my own great satisfaction.

This being now my third month in Rome I decided to return in joy to my old tasks in Egypt, but the Supreme Pontiff being

[1] Now prefect of the Egyptian mission, Paul of Agnona had withstood, with Prutky and Martin Lang, the cruelties of the 'Persecution of Girga' in May 1751.

at that time in poor health[2] I was ordered to remain for a further month, and visited meanwhile all the more important of the holy places and the seven basilicas within and without the city, imploring the help of the holy apostles for my third return to Egypt. The thought of experiencing yet again such a long journey did not greatly depress my spirits, but I pondered within me in the light of my recent experience how the many dangers by sea and land, the everlasting wanderings through the world, the tribulations and the hard living were depleting my bodily strength to the point of weakness. Nevertheless I plucked up my courage again for the greater glory and honour of God, for the salvation of souls and for the increase of the Catholic faith, trusting besides in the grace and the help of God, and saying with St Paul *I can do all things through Him Which strengtheneth me.* On March 16 therefore I left the holy city on my return journey, with many an internal prayer to God and many an invocation of the bodies and relics of all the saints, as I made my humble supplication to Almighty God and His saints for the help and strength necessary to resume my sacred mission.

[2] Pope Benedict XIV died in the May of the following year, 1758.

CHAPTER 82

THIRD RETURN FROM THE HOLY CITY TO THE MISSION, AND THE ACCEPTANCE IN ITS STEAD OF A FIELD CHAPLAINCY IN THE ARMY OF TUSCANY

It was March 20 when I once more reached the city of Leghorn and made enquiries about the next ship to sail for Egypt, but during the delay thus caused a new order reached me from the Sacred Congregation for the Propagation of the Faith in Rome to arrest my journey at Leghorn until a decree arrived concerning the despatch of further missions to Egypt; truly the Pontiff's continued illness was delaying everything concerning the eastern missions that I was to convey thither. Overcome by boredom and the length of time that I had already tarried idly in Leghorn with no souls to save, I was urged to go to Florence to undertake there a pastoral office with the Imperial military forces: as I subjected this matter to full consideration, and weighed up at the same time the importance of the salvation of souls, my mind was swayed by a variety of arguments both for and against it, and being prevented by my missionary vows from making such a decision on my own authority, I deferred to the Divine Will my fate and His plan for me. The matter was referred to Vienna and his sacred Caesarian Majesty, who had already become acquainted with me on a former occasion, and, the Sacred Congregation also assenting, I was unable[1] to deny my poor services to such a task however arduous, and reminded myself that my mission would be equally fruitful among Christian soldiers; thus on receiving a

[1] But compare Kleinhaus, who states, p. 350, that Prutky was unwilling to accept the military chaplaincy, and was prepared to return once again to Egypt. A. Kleinhaus, *Historia studii linguae Arabicae*, Quaracchi, 1930, pps. 349–352.

posting as senior field chaplain I was in hopes that I was obeying the Divine Will, which was thus disposing of me without regard to my own deserts, despite the fact that for many years I had been conscious of internal urgings and anxieties that my prime vocation from God was to the barbarian peoples.

Despite these feelings I undertook on 5 December 1757, for the reasons already given, the spiritual care of 1st Imperial-Florentine Regiment, with the eager desire that I might store into the celestial barn a harvest equal or greater than that which I might perhaps have reaped among the barbarian peoples, and that being found a worthy shepherd I might receive my eternal reward in another place. I therefore composed my spirits from their considerable anxieties, and hoped for the future that after my wanderings through so many kingdoms and provinces I would at last pitch my tent firmly in Florence and peacefully give service to God and my neighbour; and my soul sickened at the thought of embarking again upon those perilous travels. Yet not even this goal did I achieve: the tumult of war having broken out in Germany, the Florentine reserve troops also were called up by the Court of Vienna against the mighty army of the king of Borussia,[2] who was at that time laying waste almost all the hereditary lands of Austria. This unlooked-for lot fell also upon me, who for my knowledge of Bohemian, German, Italian and French, nationalities with which the Florentine reserve troops were brigaded, was compelled despite my reluctance to march to Germany in their company, where for five whole years it was my fate to experience the calamities of war in many a bloody battle and skirmish, such as at Glatz, Schweidnitz, Landshut,[3] etc.; it was my fate to be present, but it was far from my pleasure, since I lost too many of the sheep entrusted to me, some by violence in battle, some from natural causes in the shape of contagious diseases: indeed in the first year more than a thousand perished from the high fever, by which I myself was three times infected but thanks to the protection of God's grace, though near to death, escaped safe and sound. At the end of five years there

---

[2] Frederick II of Prussia, or Frederick the Great. Borussia is the Latin for Prussia.

[3] Three famous battles of the Seven Years War of 1756–1763, when Maria Theresa of Austria tried and failed to regain from Frederick of Prussia the Austrian territory which he had annexed in 1741.

followed the long-desired peace between the King of Borussia and the Queen of Bohemia and Austria, on the conclusion of which I with the scanty remains of my flock returned to Tuscany, accompanying until we came to Florence more than four hundred sick, to whom by day and night I administered both physic and the Sacrament, though most of them died on the way.

Here in Florence was I intent on repose and on making it my last resting-place, but the 1st battalion of my regiment being stationed in the Mediterranean at Portoferraio or in the island[4] of that name, I was compelled to follow them at Easter to administer the food of the spirit, after which I directed my steps back across the sea to Siena, that famous Italian city, where I enjoyed two years of happy quiet and as their shepherd rendered spiritual services to the Florentine garrison. In Florence the capital of Tuscany, whither in the third year I had been transferred, I had thought to finish the last days of life that were left to me, but not even this object of my desires did I obtain, since there followed the unhappy death[5] of his highness the Emperor Francis I Grand Duke of Tuscany, which at one blow destroyed the harvest that my heart had longed for and my labours attempted to secure, and ruined every hope that I had placed in him. On the succession to the Grand Duchy of his son Peter Leopold all the military forces of Florence were demobilized together with their chaplains, and I determined to write again to the Sacred Congregation for the Propagation of the Faith and put myself under their orders.

———

Thus far the journey of the Reverend Father Remedius Prutky of the Minor Order of Reformed Franciscans, nursling of the Mother Province of Bohemia, written in his own hand apart from the final sheets.[6] Its further continuance was cut short by his untimely death in Florence on 9 February 1770. The course of the rest of his life another hand has set down in the following appendix, compiled partly from his own writings and partly from reliable reports.

[4] Portoferraio is the capital of the island of Elba.
[5] Francis died at Innsbruck in 1765. He was succeeded as Grand Duke of Tuscany by his son Leopold.
[6] The amanuensis takes over from Prutky in chapter 73 and continues to the end of chapter 82. The same hand wrote the Preface and also Appendix I.

APPENDIX I

The author of these journeys Fr Remedius Prutky was finally assigned by the Sacred Congregation for the Propagation of the Faith to the vice-prefecture of missions in Russia or Muscovy in the year 1766, in which office he remained in St Petersburg until 1769.[1] A number of points of dispute arose however between himself and his subordinate missionaries, and the case was brought to the attention of the Court of St Petersburg, who then issued a rescript or arrangement as to how in the future the missionaries should be governed; the aforesaid prefect however, being opposed to this arrangement as prejudicial to the liberties and immunities of the Church, and refusing to accept it without the assent of the Sacred Congregation, was punished by expulsion from Russia, and in the above-mentioned year 1769 returned to Rome, there to plead his cause at the Apostolic Seat before the Sacred Congregation. The arrangement or regulation issued by Her Highness Empress Catherine II[2] is to the following effect, translated out of Ruthenian[3] into Latin.

Regulation issued by Her Imperial Majesty of all Russia, and made known to the whole Catholic community of St Petersburg in the refectory of the hospice of the Reformed Friars Minor on 2 April 1769.

The Catholic community has humbly petitioned Her Majesty: *Firstly.* That the Sacred Congregation should give it the

[1] For a full treatment of Prutky's tenure of office as vice-prefect of the mission in Russia, see Ryšavý, 'Die Reformaten Mission in Rüssland unter dem Missionspräfekten Fr Remedius Prutky,' *Archivum franciscanum historicum* XXVII (1934), 179–223.

[2] Catherine the Great, 1729–96, Empress of Russia, succeeded her husband Peter III in 1762.

[3] Russian. Strictly the name of a branch of the Russian people living in Galicia, the word Ruthenian was used as an alternative for Russian.

freedom, subject to the candidate's ability to care for souls and
to his willingness to act, to choose for itself a suitable superior,
and one who is either fluent in or at least acquainted with the
languages that are necessary here.

Secondly. That on the death of the superior the Catholic community shall be free to elect another from the existing fathers to
be the senior, since the ability of each cleric is better known to
the community than to the Sacred Congregation: but the elected
superior shall be summoned to be confirmed in Rome.

Thirdly. The community shall be free to choose proctors of the
Church, who together with the superior shall have power of
disposition in the material affairs of the Church and its resources;
also in the disposition of stole fees, houses, matters appertaining
to the church and the hospice, and other alms already given or
to be acquired, so that out of them a church can be built and
other necessities provided.

Fourthly. The borrowing of money shall only take place with
the agreement of the community, which is to have the management of it: it shall not be permitted to the superior to enter into
obligations as collateral.

The accusation that they have acted in contrary fashion is
levelled against the superiors or prefects, who have left the
country with or without accounting for their actions, so that in
the event the whole burden has been left on the shoulders of the
community.

Moreover in almost all past years the Sacred Congregation in
the following specific matters has failed to satisfy the community,
but has done it positive harm through the superiors or prefects
that it has sent out: missionary fathers were appointed who knew
only Italian, so that there were as many as three here, too many
for the few Italian residents: while there is a shortage of speakers
of German, French and Polish, especially in the cities of Kronstadt, Reval[4] and Riga, whence it happens that the administration
of the sacraments and the conduct of divine services have shown
grave deficiencies. Further it has often happened that through

[4] Now Tallinn.

false and underhand dealings in Rome other prefects have been substituted, against the wishes of the community, while worthier and more suitable candidates have been passed over.

Finally. The community solemnly contests the view, which all the superiors used to affirm and affirm to this day, that all the resources of the Church of St Petersburg, together with the houses and the church itself, belong to the Church of Rome; and declares that all such resources are at the disposition of the community, as well as everything appertaining thereto and all gifts which were made and given for the community's peaceful and quiet possession, or will in future be given or instituted, seeing that the Church of Rome has never so far given any subsidy towards the cost of building.

For this cause We make the following regulation which must be observed forever.

Section 1. The fathers of the Roman Church

1. Since at St Petersburg there are four nations, German, Polish, French and Italian, the fathers too ought to be fluent in these languages, or at least in more than one.

2. The superior should be called the *senior,* and his colleagues *curates of souls* rather than truly *missionaries,* seeing that by the terms of the privilege granted them on 28 February 1724 it was only conceded that they should conduct the exercise of their own religion, not that they should enlarge the Roman faith.

3. Although by the terms of this mandate there ought to be only four fathers together with their superior, it is none the less conceded that at St Petersburg there may be six fathers and the superior, because with the increase in the number of Catholics throughout the whole empire the fathers have to be despatched to various destinations.

4. Beyond this number of Franciscans there can be no fathers of any other order. The superior is held responsible to despatch fathers to Kronstadt, Hamburg, Riga and Reval whenever necessary.

5. The fathers of the Church cannot remain in Russia for longer than four years: however, if the community is satisfied with them it is granted as a concession that they may remain for

another four years, in order to save the expenses of the community on their inward and return journeys.

Section 2. The superior

6. It shall be permitted to the parishioners to choose one out of the six fathers as superior.

7. This elected superior shall be obliged to ensure the observance of this regulation without the slightest alteration.

8. The superior at St Petersburg must ensure that the six fathers are Franciscans, keeping watch throughout Livonia[5] Ingria[6] etc. that no priests of another order are lingering there, and on becoming aware of any such must immediately report them to the Ministry of Justice: with the exception of those fathers who are in the entourage of a minister or are serving on merchant ships.

9. The superior shall take care, and his colleagues shall obey him, that no action is taken beyond what falls within the jurisdiction of the Catholic Church; the superior shall further forbid his colleagues within the Russian Empire to persuade the Christians of any other sect or convert them to their own faith, in accordance with Our mandate of 28 July 1763.

Section 3. Retirement and installation of fathers

10. If any father retires, the superior and elders of the Church shall inform the Ministry of Justice as the properly constituted court, who will immediately alert the Foreign Ministry to write for another father to be sent, as in Our mandate of 1 November 1766.

11. The newly-arrived father must present himself before the Ministry of Justice with his credentials.

12. Once given permission by the Ministry the superior must introduce the said father to the church, and in the presence of the Secretary of the Ministry must administer according to the rite of the Roman Church the oath of fidelity as laid down in the printed copy, the oath to be countersigned by the Ministry of

---

[5] Now included in Latvia.
[6] The Russian province which stretched south-west from St Petersburg.

Justice; only then shall the superior install the father according to the usages of the Church.

Section 4. The method of choosing and confirming the superior

13. As soon as the post of superior becomes vacant, the remaining fathers and the elders of the Church are obliged to inform the Ministry of Justice.

14. The Ministry of Justice with the consent of the fathers and elders of the Church shall appoint a day for the election of the new superior, who shall be elected by the community of the four nations with the exception of those who happen to be strangers and have only spent a short time in Our service: these are excluded from voting.

15. On the appointed day of election, in the presence of the Secretary of the Ministry, the community, after Mass and an address relevant to the election, shall cast their votes, and those unable to be present shall fulfil their obligations in a written note. The Secretary will read out the terms of their authority to elect a superior.

16. Each nation shall vote separately, one after the other, in the presence of the leaders of the Church. The Secretary will make a documentary note of the votes both written and verbal. If no agreement can be reached, he shall be elected superior who has the most votes.

17. At the end of the election the Secretary will announce to the parishioners their new superior, who will then commence his term of office.

18. The new superior shall be obliged before he leaves the church to produce a written undertaking that he is prepared to abide by this Our regulation in all points exactly, and this undertaking will be held in safe-keeping by the Ministry.

19. The Ministry of Justice will be obliged to inform the Foreign Ministry immediately of the newly-elected superior and seek their confirmation, that the news may be known everywhere.

20. Since the community has set down many criticisms of the present superior, let it be known to all according to this Our regulation that they must proceed to the election of a new superior, and that until that time the present superior is deposed, though we account him too as a candidate. If he has more votes

he too can be confirmed in office, but if he has less let him be deposed and another elected; and let him return to the place whence he came.

Section 5. The syndics and elders of the Church

21. Similarly the Ministry of Justice shall appoint a day for the election of syndics or elders of the Church, who are to be elected by the community.

22. Each nation shall elect two, that if one be prevented from acting the other can come to his assistance.

23. Each nation can elect two as it wishes.

24. When the day of election has been appointed, the superior, under the direction of an officer deputed by the Ministry of Justice, shall give an address and then proceed to the election according to the number of votes cast, these being recorded by the officer and the elections confirmed by the Ministry.

25. These eight elders must faithfully assist the superior in the management of affairs, and should be respected as being as it were delegates of the community.

Section 6. The maintenance of the resources of the Church, and the duty of elders

26. All the resources handled by the superior and elders must be regarded as goods of the Church, belonging to the Roman Church and not to individual clerics.

27. The assets of the Roman Church are as follows: 1. Its buildings and their annual rents. 2. Legacies. 3. Moneys bequeathed and denoted for the support of the Church by benefactors from within the community and from outside sources. 4. Stole fees, as from weddings, baptisms, funerals etc., apart from that which is freely given by many. 5. All moneys which are being or have been sent by rich persons or from other provinces to build the church, such as foundation funds etc.

28. Out of these resources the fathers should be maintained not merely at subsistence level but handsomely.

29. The Church elders when they begin their term of office are obliged to enquire carefully into the present state of the Church at that time, and to make an inventory of all its possessions, such as, in the case of buildings, whether anyone has

introduced into them something that may be harmful: they must also make an inspection of whether the buildings are in a good state, examining for example the foundations, vestments, precious vessels, library, in a word, everything connected with the Church.

30. Included in the inventory must also be a schedule of the Church's moneys, its debts both short- and long-term, and, if there chance to be any such, any deposits by individuals, so that in the course of future administration this inventory can serve as a reliable basis for their successors.

31. The inventory, together with all the Church papers, contracts, obligations and other written material, the Church's money and its daily income, must be lodged in a chest under the seals of the superior and elders, and none must dare to open it without their permission and knowledge.

32. All documents, obligations and contracts must be carefully examined, and if any have to be altered a judicial enquiry must be held, and it is the task and duty of the elders to defend the Church's interests in the proper courts of law, so that the superior is not impeded in his spiritual tasks, because the elders are his fellow-workers.

33. The syndics are required to bring to a conclusion any construction work that has been started, though with the agreement and under the control of the superior, so that debts contracted with the knowledge of the community, under which at the present time many members of the community may be labouring, may be paid out of Church resources.

34. Alms solicited for the benefit of the Church are as it were money under the control of the community, and can be applied to purposes according to their wishes, under the protection of Our laws.

35. The community must take care that its church and the buildings belonging to it are kept in a good state of preservation, and if there be any deterioration that it is repaired.

36. We are graciously pleased to indulge the superior and permit the whole community to found one church school, whose pupils shall be only Roman Catholics.

37. The superior and elders of the Church have the power to accept all incoming moneys and legacies, and are obliged to sign all contracts and obligations: it is especially incumbent on the

syndics that such documents are signed and sealed in due order in the presence either of the cantonal or the state authority.

38. The superior is empowered to accept small incoming sums of money, but he must make careful note of them, and not less than every three months have them countersigned by the syndics, who must carefully examine them and note them in the books.

Section 7. Accountability of syndics and their retirement

39. If after three years the syndics seek to retire, they must first present complete accounts to the community and justify them with quittances or receipts, so that the community can clearly see all expenses and their handling of them.

40. To audit the accounts the community is empowered to appoint professional accountants, able to reveal all receipts and expenses, including those of materials.

41. After the accounts have been audited and approved the syndics have the power to apply to resign, and if they cannot be persuaded to continue in office their application is granted.

42. If the syndics refuse to continue in office, others must be elected and the previous ones released by the superior and the community with a vote of thanks, seeing that they deserve recognition for faithful service.

Section 8. Court of law to which the Roman Catholic Church is subject

43. Wishing for the future to eliminate entirely all disputes and conflicts between the community and the clerics, conflicts that have chiefly arisen from the fact that the Roman Church has no prescribed rule for the conduct of business, so that the parties in dispute have no arbiter to whom they can have recourse to terminate or conciliate their suits, Wherefore,

44. Our gracious will is that for the future all suits between the clerics and the community or syndics shall come before the Ministry of Justice, seeing that all other Christian nations and the internal affairs of their churches come there to judgment. The Ministry of Justice shall be the judge of every dispute in short order, and shall bring it to a conclusion.

45. And since for a long time in Our empire Our predecessors have allowed all Catholics the free exercise of their religion, We too are graciously pleased to allow it: in no way therefore and

on no pretext or cause whatever shall the Ministry of Justice dare to involve itself in giving judgments on matters of administration that concern the tenets of faith of the Catholic Church and its fundamentals.

Section 9. Retirement of fathers

46. It has already been laid down in paragraph 3 that all the fathers are permitted to remain here together with the superior and the elders: in view of this permission, great attention must be exercised to ensure that not only the superior according to his deserts but also the other fathers are provided with all necessities of life, that they may have no cause of complaint.

47. If any father refuses to remain here, another must be sought as laid down in section 3, and when the new father has attested the oath of fidelity, the Ministry of Justice armed with the testimony of the superior and the syndics will in the name of the whole community procure from the Foreign Ministry a passport or letter of safe-conduct for the father in question to go to whatever place he pleases.

Section 10. The Capuchin fathers in the city of Moscow

48. According to the ancient institutions of the Russian Empire the prefect of the Catholic Church in Moscow is of the Capuchin order, together with one colleague as assistant: the Ministry of Justice there has the task of instituting a system for the conduct of business parallel with that of St Petersburg, and of appointing one or two syndics of the Church who will have charge of all resources and other necessary matters, and will place the community's affairs upon a surer footing.

49. The father prefect of Moscow shall be free to associate with himself another colleague of the same order, if necessity arises.

50. For the rest, the Capuchin fathers also shall in all law-suits be subject to the Ministry of Justice, as the Franciscans.

Section 11. Priests in the new territories

51. The priests serving the colonists shall be subject to the protection of the Chancery, and are to be only of the Franciscan order, as they now are: when they arrive they are to present

themselves before the Ministry of Justice, swear the oath of fidelity in the Catholic church, and in all things come to judgment before the Chancery.

This regulation must be lodged in the original at the Ministry of Justice, with a copy to the superior.

St Petersburg
12 February 1769 o.s.

Catherine

The compilation of this regulation is said to have been the work of two priests, Fr Adolph Frankenberg and Fr Marquand, together with a Ruthenian senator named Teplov,[7] president of the Ministry of Justice and a Lutheran, their intermediary being a Catholic confectioner, one Feser by name, who was as it were the fount and head of the rebellion which had now for fifteen years been disturbing the past peace and tranquillity of the Catholic Church in St Petersburg. When Fr Adolph had finished his seven-year term of office and the new prefect had arrived, namely Fr Remedius Prutky, Fr Adolph received from the very reverend Commissary General Fr Joseph Maria of Vedano letters of obedience instructing him to leave, on the receipt of which he queried whether it were permissible for him to come to Rome: because at the time when the assembly of the General Chapter was held at Valentia in Spain, and Fr Adolph had received permission to betake himself to Rome from the very reverend Vicar General, he had refused to set out, giving as a pretext that the letters of obedience were invalid as having been issued by the very reverend Minister General. But this was a false reason. Far different from it was the true reason, that the letters of obedience arrived before the above-quoted regulation had been completely drawn up and published. The excuse prevented his departure, so that in good time he could attain his goal, the office of prefect which he had so long desired and which he eventually obtained by underhand means when he had drawn up the new regulation in his own favour. On 17 July 1768, with the above named confectioner Feser acting as intermediary, all the fathers were summoned before Senator Teplov without the knowledge of the prefect Remedius, and all of them, apart from Fr Donato

---

[7] Dr W. F. Ryan informs us that G. N. Teplov was one of Catherine's ablest and most influential officials, and an unscrupulous fixer.

of the Thuscian[8] province of the Reformati, duly appeared before the senator without the permission of their lawful superior, contrary to Canon Law D1 § 7 n. 165: here they were informed of a direct order in the name of the Empress that none of the fathers could be posted out of the Empire before the publication of the new regulation, which on the advice of Frs Adolph and Marquand had been so drawn up as to restrict or even thwart the exercise of all proper authority by lawful superiors or by the Sacred Congregation for the Propagation of the Faith, as the reader may see for himself.

Meanwhile there arrived for Fr Adolph from the very reverend Minister General a third letter of obedience, in which he was instructed that on its receipt he must return to his own province, viz. Austria, or suffer the penalties inflicted by our Order on the disobedient and contumacious. He refused however to obey, on the grounds basically of the new regulation which had not yet been published. To this end a copy of Canon Law had been smuggled out of the hospice, unknown to the prefect, and brought to the said Senator Teplov, who, putting a sinister interpretation upon it, strictly forbade the prefect from removing any of the fathers from the mission unless he wished to go, adding that it was the Empress's express order that the fathers should be permitted complete liberty of residence here, despite the fact that they were not part of a formal cloister and were not confined to a cloistered observance.

Finally in 1769 there came an order from the Ministry of Justice to Fr Remedius the prefect that on April 2 he should call a meeting of the Catholic community in the hospice or residence: the meeting in the refectory was attended by the Councillor, Secretary and two clerks from the Ministry of Justice, and the Secretary in the presence of the fathers and laymen read out the above quoted regulation in Ruthenian. Confusion now seized the Catholic people and a terrible outcry and clamour arose, since almost all with gnashing teeth rose up against the aforesaid fathers and the five principal Catholics who were the authors of this innovation: 'It is a lie' they cried 'that the community has petitioned for these rules, we know nothing about it. It is false to call on us in the name of the whole community, since it is only

[8] i.e. Tuscan.

five individuals who have made the petition; we are Catholics, and our dependence is on the Church of Rome and the Sacred Congregation, and not on any ministry run by Lutherans.' Some good Catholics were in tears, others were raising the cry *Out of the windows with these authors of iniquity etc.* To soothe the bitterness of their feelings the Fr Prefect led the whole community to the church, and since most of them did not understand Ruthenian he explained the whole regulation in German, and demonstrated how prejudicial it was to the immunity of the ecclesiastical jurisdiction. He then according to the procedure laid down gave formal notice to the Ministry of Justice of the promulgation of this new regulation, and humbly besought them to be graciously pleased to delay the satisfaction of the matters petitioned until he had obtained the decision of Rome, without which he neither could act nor dared to do so; at the same time he asked according to paragraph 47 of the new regulation for letters of safe-conduct for the departure of Fr Adolph, but was unsuccessful on either count.

On April 24, at the end of the feast of Easter according to the Greek rites, there appeared at the hospice refectory the five principal ringleaders, *viz.* Feser the confectioner, Perkin a merchant and notary, the lodger at his house, a theatrical player or actor, and fifthly an architect, all nominally Catholic but disturbers of the public peace and of mutual harmony. Accompanied by the senior clerk of the Ministry of Justice and two subordinates from the department of state, they summoned the Father Prefect and his subordinate clerics to the aforesaid place, the refectory, and had read out to the prefect the urgent order of the Empress whereby Her Majesty commanded that he should betake himself immediately out of the Empire and hand over to Fr Adolph all the keys of the church and hospice. Collecting his religious equipment he was conducted to the gate of the hospice where a carriage was ready, and with an army lieutenant and one escort as companions of his journey he was delivered at the Empress's expense to Mictavia the capital of Kurland.[9]

From here in the company of Fr Donato of the Tuscian province of the Reformati, who bade farewell to Russia for the same

[9] Part of modern Latvia, Courland was at that time part of Poland, and as such outside the Russian empire. The then capital, Mitau (Mictavia), is now called Jelgava.

reason but voluntarily, he crossed Saxony and Bohemia and betook himself to Rome, to give an account of his expulsion and of his stewardship before both the Apostolic Seat and the Sacred Congregation for the Propagation of the Faith. Broken in strength by his labours and long journeys, he decided to return to his mother province, that is Bohemia, but, entering Florence where he wished to complete his business with the Grand Duke of Tuscany, Leopold of Austria, he there ended his life. Turning aside to the hospice of the Reformati he fell victim to a mortal sickness, whether of mind or body I know not, and after a few days rendered up his soul to his Creator, that is on 9 February 1770. It is said that the Grand Duke Leopold I of Tuscany had destined him for a bishopric, but it is uncertain if this is true. He sent before him to Bohemia some of his less important equipment, which consisted partly of his unfinished writings (just as this itinerary is incomplete), partly of books and partly of ecclesiastical vestments. But his property and more precious possessions, his timepieces, silver surgical instruments etc. which were seen to be in his possession during his passage to Rome, were not seen again in Bohemia after his death. Whether it was Florence which swallowed them or the carrier on the road, who arrived in Prague with the chest open and unlocked, is known only in Heaven. This much is certain, that many beautiful, rare and precious objects were seen by many to be in his possession. May God grant that he, who had seen and journeyed to so many and such extensive kingdoms, may for his reward himself see the kingdom of Heaven, whither we doubt not that his journeys have now betaken him.

LETTER OF INVITATION
TO THE MISSIONARIES TO VISIT
THE EMPIRE OF ETHIOPIA

All who wish to visit the Empire of Abyssinia are of necessity compelled not only to exercise the greatest caution, but also to obtain the permission of the Emperor, lest their journey be impeded by the heretical Coptic patriarch, to whose decisions the whole Empire is obedient in every article of the Faith, and who is ever jealous lest the souls that are now his subjects may be rescued from darkness and shown the light of truth. So careful in the past had been his precautions that the missionaries for many years had never been able to enter: however, when the Emperor himself took note of it, he of his own accord despatched letters by a special envoy called Michael, who reached Cairo on 24 May 1751, bearing a letter in Greek addressed to the Superior of the Holy Land. However, because in the course of time the missionary function in Ethiopia had been the field not of the Observant but solely of the Reformed Friars Minor, the envoy decided to hand his letter not to the Observants but to Fr. James of Kromeriz[1] the head of the Egyptian mission. Wrapped in a silken envelope embroidered with gold and fastened with golden pins, and sealed and protected by a paper covering, the letter bore an Arabic superscription to the following effect: 'From his Imperial Majesty, Emperor of Emperors[2] Jasu Addiam

---

[1] Jacobus da Cremisirio, Beccari, *op. cit.*, i, 185, 210, 218–9.

[2] Prutky's rendering of *Negusa Nagast*, literally King of Kings, the title traditionally accorded to Ethiopian monarchs. It was often equated with 'Emperor' by Europeans. This title can be traced back in Ethiopia to ancient Aksumite times. S. Pierre Pétridès, *Le livre d'or de la dynastie salomonienne d'Ethiopie* (Paris, 1964), pp. 187–96.

Saggad,[3] son of Jasu Backaffa Saggad, to the European Lords.'
Inside the envelope was a letter written in Greek on linen paper,
as follows:

'I speak as the rightful ruler by Divine Omnipotence of Upper
Ethiopia[4] and the great realm of Caffatin,[5] Lord and Protector

[3] This designation is somewhat muddled. Iyasu II, also known as Adyam Sagad
II, was the son of Bakaffa, also known as Masih Sagad, the son of Iyasu I, also
known as Adyam Sagad I.

[4] It is unlikely that the ensuing names of provinces were in the Emperor's
original letter. They seem to have been inserted by Prutky who seems to have
taken them from a letter of the 1620's from Emperor Lebna Dengel to the King
of Portugal. In that epistle the Ethiopian ruler, according to Alvarez, had
described himself as 'Emperor of the high and vast Ethiopia, and of great
kingdoms, lordships and lands', and, specifically, of 1. Xoa (Sawa), 2. Cafate
(Gafat), 3. Fatiguar (Fatagar), 4. Angote (Angot), 5. Baruu (Bora) 6. Baliganje
(Bali and Ganz), 7. Adea (Hadya), 8. Vangue (Bugna), 9. Goyamme (Gojjam),
'where the Blue Nile rises,' 10. Amara, (Amhara), 11. Bagamedri (Bagémder),
12. Dambea (Dambeya), 13. Vague (Wag), 14. Tigremahon (Tegré), 15. Sabaim
(Saba) 'where was the Queen of Sheba', and 16. Barnagais (country of the Bahr
Nagaš), 'lord as far as Egypt'. Beckingham and Huntingford, Prester John, ii,
495–6. Prutky's letter from Iyasu is similarly made to claim jurisdiction over
'Upper Ethiopia' – apparently a reformulation of Alvarez's 'high Ethiopia', and
'the great realm of Caffatin' – presumably a rendering of the earlier writer's
'Cafate'. The text, like the letter of Lebna Dengel, then proceeds with a list of
provinces over which the monarch was supposed to hold sway. Prutky's version
omits three of the provinces listed by Alvarez, i.e. Šawa, Fatagar and Angot, after
which it enumerates the rest in exactly Alvarez's order, i.e. 1. Varra (Alvarez 5.
Baruu, i.e. Bora), 2. Valigunasis (Alvarez 6. Baliganje, i.e. Bali and Ganz), 3. Adis
(Alvarez 7. Adea, i.e. Hadya), 4. Gojarisis (Alvarez 9. Gojam, i.e. Gojjam) 'as far
as the Nile', a phrase likewise used by Alvarez, 5. Amaris (Alvarez 10. Amara,
i.e. Amhara), 6. Vagusimetri (Alvarez 11. Bagamidri i.e. Bagémder), 7. Amais
(which by its position in the text was presumably Alvarez's 12. Dambea, i.e.
Dambeya), 8. Vaguzzi (which likewise must be Alvarez's 13. Vague i.e. Wag), 9.
Tygremann (Alvarez 14. Tigrimahon, i.e. Tegré Makonnen or Tegré), 10. Sabaim
(Alvarez 15. Sabaim i.e. Saba), and 11. Varnagassus (Alvarez 16. Barnagas, i.e.
country of the Bahr Nagaš) 'and Lord of Nubia up to the boundary with Egypt'
(which corresponds with Alvarez's 'lord as far as Egypt').
  Prutky was not the first to draw in this way on Alvarez. A generation or so
earlier the Dutch author Valentyn, when publishing a translation of an Arabic
letter from Emperor Yohannes I to the governor of Batavia, had likewise introduced into it Lebna Dengel's references to his royal ancestors, as well as a partial
list of the provinces over which the earlier monarch claimed to rule. Valentyn's
text was however in some places so corrupt that a recent Dutch scholar, Van
Donzel, was unable to identify all the names cited by Valentyn, or indeed to
relate them to Alvarez's text. F. Valentyn, Oud en nieuw Ost Indien (Dordrecht–
Amsterdam, 1724–26), i, 305–6; Van Donzel, Foreign relations, p. 48.

[5] Prutky seems to have assumed that Iyasu claimed to be the ruler of the Cafates,
or negroes (see chapter 26), presumably towards the Sudan. However, given the
fact that this passage was borrowed from Alvarez, it is clear that the word Caffatin,
which should have come later in the text, actually referred to Gafat, a people
who had once lived south of the Blue Nile but had since moved north of it.
Beckingham and Huntingford, Prester John, ii, 576–7.

of Varra[6] Valigunasis[7] Adis[8] and Gojarisis[9] as far as the Nile, of Amaris[10] Vagusimetrii[11] Amais[12] Vaguzzi[13] Tygremann[14] Sabaim,[15] the kingdom of the Queen of Sheba, and Varnagassus:[16] Lord also of Nubia[17] up to its boundary with Egypt. Given in our royal palace of Gondar in Ethiopia on October 18.

'Most Reverend Father who presides over the Holy Land, most excellent master and most reverend protector under divine Providence of the most sacred sepulchre of our Lord Jesus Christ. I am a devout admirer of your Paternity, and I pray God always that He will preserve you in prosperity and holy health. I now wish to draw to your attention how in ancient times past many of your nation often came here, though in these later years they were prevented from coming, according to the will of the Emperor my predecessor, who ruled from my throne. Today however, during the period of my rule, they can come without any danger, and to any skilled craftsmen, possessors of various branches of knowledge, we offer favour, prosperity and success in their undertakings; furthermore, to any merchants who may venture here we offer every privilege, and they will be held in honour without being exposed to difficulty: gunsmiths[18] will meet with our favour, their products will be pleasing and perfect to us, and they themselves will be treated with all honour. To assure you of the truth of our intentions, this letter which I now send to you is the foundation of your future security. Finally I beg

[6] Bora, a province near Angot. Beckingham and Huntingford, *op. cit.*, ii, 495.

[7] Bali wa Ganz, i.e. Bali and Ganz. Of these two provinces, the former lay between Fatagar and Dawaro and the latter between Waj and Bali. Beckingham and Huntingord, *op. cit.*, ii, 495, 579.

[8] Hadya, or Adia as it is likewise written on Ludolf's map, lay between Lake Zway and the Gibé river. Beckingham and Huntingford, *op. cit.*, ii, 572.

[9] Gojjam.

[10] Amhara.

[11] Bagémder.

[12] Presumably, by its position in the text, Dambeya.

[13] Probably Wag.

[14] Tigremahon, i.e. Tegré.

[15] Saba, the country of the Queen of Sheba, i.e. the Aksum area.

[16] *Bahr Nagaš*, i.e. the region ruled by that functionary. The reference to the Queen of Sheba should relate, as in Lebna Dengel's letter, to Sabaim. Beckingham and Huntingford, *op. cit.*, ii, 496.

[17] Prutky's reference to Nubia may have been based on Valentyn's text of the letter of Yohannes I where he is made to claim sovereignty over that country. Van Donzel, *Foreign relations*, pp. 48, 70. See also pp. 72, 98.

[18] The Latin text is *arcularius*, which means 'casket-maker.' The word *arcuarius* means 'maker of bows,' here rendered as 'gunsmith,' which better suits the sense.

you, and all those who owe allegiance to Your Sanctity, that you beseech on my behalf Our Lord Jesus Christ and the Holy Virgin, that He may grant me perfect safety and total victory over the infidel races who are my enemies.'

This letter agrees with that sent in Greek, which was sealed on the exterior with three seals, one of which was engraved with Arabic characters while the other two were in Abyssinian, and bore the impress of a lion carrying a cross with the inscription *The lion of the tribe of Judah is the victor,* as was made clear in the chapter of our expulsion from the Empire.[19]

[19] Chapters 47 and 48.

BIBLIOGRAPHY

d'Abbadie, A., *Dictionnaire de la langue amariñña, Paris, 1881.*

Abeysinghe, T. B. H., 'Embassies as instruments of diplomacy: a case-study from Sri Lanka in the first half of the eighteenth century', *Journal of the Royal Asiatic Society, Sri Lanka branch* NS vol XXX 1985/86, 17, 18.

Aldrovandi, Ulisse, *De quadripedib' digitatis oviparis*, Bonon. 1637, 713.

Aymro Wondmagegnehu and Motovu, J., *The Ethiopian Orthodox church*, Addis Ababa, 1970.

Badger, G. P., *The travels of Ludovico di Varthema*, London, 1863.

Baker, S. W., *The Nile tributaries of Abyssinia*, London, 1867.

Basset, R., 'Etudes sur l'historie d'Ethiopie', *Journal asiatique*, 7 ser. XVII (1881), 315–434, XVIII (1881), 93–183, 285–389.

Beccari, C., *Rerum Aethiopicarum scriptores occidentales*, 15 vols, Rome, 1905–17.

Beckingham, C. F., *The achievements of Prester John*, London, 1966.

Beckingham, C. F., 'The quest for Prester John', *Bulletin of the John Rylands University Library*, LXII (1980), 291–310.

Beckingham, C. F. and Huntingford, G. W. B., *The Prester John of the Indies*, 2 vols, Cambridge, 1961.

Beckingham, C. F. and Huntingford, G. W. B., *Some records of Ethiopia, 1593–1646*, London, 1954.

Béguinot, F., *La cronaca abbreviata d'Abissinia*, Roma, 1901.

Bender, M. L., Bowen, J. D., Cooper, R. L. and Ferguson, C. A., *Language in Ethiopia* (London, 1976), pp. 40–2.

Bent, S. T., *The sacred city of the Ethiopians*, London, 1896.

Budge, E. A. Wallis, *The book of the saints of the Ethiopian church*, 4 vols, Cambridge, 1928.

Budge, E. A. Wallis, *History of Ethiopia, Nubia and Abyssinia*, 2 vols, London, 1928.

Budge, E. A. Wallis, *The Queen of Sheba and her only son Menyelek*, London, 1922.

Burnell, A. C., *Hobson–Jobson*, London, 1903.

Bruce, J., *Travels to discover the source of the Nile*, 5 vols, Edinburgh, 1790.

Burton, R. F., *Personal narrative of a pilgrimage to Al-Madinah and Mecca*, 2 vols, London, 1893.

P. Caraman, *The lost empire, the story of the Jesuits in Ethiopia, 1555–1634* (London, 1985).

Cerulli, E., *Etiopi in Palestina*, 2 vols, Rome, 1943–7.

Cheesman, R. E., *Lake Tana and the Blue Nile*, London, 1936.

Chojnacki, S., 'A hitherto unknown foreign painter in 18th. century Ethiopia: the Master of Arabic Script and his portraits of royal donors', *Africa*, XI, (1985), 577–610.

Chojnacki, S., *Major themes in Ethiopian painting*, Wiesbaden, 1983.

Combes, E. and Tamisier, M., *Voyage en Abyssinie*, 4 vols, Paris, 1838.

Crawford, O. G. S., *Ethiopian itineraries circa 1400–1525*, Cambridge, 1958.

Crawford, O. G. S., *The Fung kingdom of Sennar*, Gloucester, 1951.

Crummey, *Priests and politicians: Protestant and Catholic missions in Orthodox Ethiopia 1830–1868*, Oxford, 1972.

Dillmann, C. F. A., *Lexicon linguae Aethiopicae*, Leipzig, 1865.

Donzel, E. J. van, *Foreign relations of Ethiopia. Documents relating to the journeys of Kodja Murad*, Istanbul, 1979.

Donzel, E. J. van, *A Yemenite embassy to Ethiopia 1647–1649*, Stuttgart, 1986.

Doughty, C. M., *Travels in Arabia Deserta*, 2 vols, London, 1924.

Dozy, *Supplément aux dictionnaires arabes*, Paris, 1881.

Dufton, C., *Narrative of a journey through Abyssinia*, London, 1867.

Forskal, P., *Descriptiones animalium, avium, amphibiorum, piscium, insectorum, vermium, Hafnia*, 1775.

Foster, W., *The Red Sea and adjacent countries at the close of the 17th. century*, London, 1949.

Fouyas, P. G., 'James Bruce of Kinnaird and the Greeks in Ethiopia', *Abba Salama*, II (1971), 161–78.

Freeman-Grenville, G. S. P., *Christian and Muslim calendars*, 2nd. edition, Oxford, 1977.

Freeman-Grenville, G. S. P., 'The late Francesco Carbone's collection of thalers from Yemen.' *Numismatic chronicle*, 1977.

Giamberardini, G., *Lettere dei prefetti apostolici dell' Alto Egitto nel secolo XVII*, Cairo, 1960.

Gill, Isabel, *Six months in Ascension*, London, 1875.

Gobat, S., *Journal of three years' residence in Abyssinia*, Ashfield, Mass., 1850.

Godinho, Nicolao, *De Abassinorum rebus, deque Aethiopiae patriarchis Joanne Nonio Barreto et Andrea Oviedo, libri tres*, Lyons, 1615.

Golubovich, G., *Biblioteca bio-bibliografica della Terra Santa*, NS vol XIII, Quaracchi, 1930, 239.

Guebre Sellasié, *Chronique du règne de Menelik II, roi des rois d'Ethiopie*, 2 vols, Paris, 1930–1.

Guida dell'Africa orientale Italiana, Rome, Consociazione turistica italiana, 1938.

Guidi, I., *Annales Iohannis I, Iyasu I et Bakaffa*, CSCO, Scr. Aeth. ser. alt. v, 2 parts, Paris, 1903, 1905.

Guidi, I., *Annales regum Iyasu II et Iyo'as*, CSCO, Scr. Aeth. ser. alt. vi, Paris 1912.

Guidi, I., *Il 'Fetha Nagast' o 'Legislazione dei rei'*, Rome, 1897.

Guidi, I., 'Le liste dei metropoliti d'Abissinia' *Bessarione*, VI (1899), 1–16.

Guidi, I, *Vocabolario amarico-italiano*, Roma, 1901.

Harris, W. C., *The highlands of Aethiopia*, 3 vols, London, 1844.

Herodotus, *The histories*, II, IV.

Hitti, P. K., *History of the Arabs*, London, 1953.

Hughes, T. P., *A dictionary of Islam*, London, 1885.

Huntingford, G. W. B., *The historical geography of Ethiopia*, Oxford, 1989.

Huntingford, G. W. B., *The land charters of northern Ethiopia*, London, 1965.

Huntingford, G. W. B., 'Saints of mediaeval Ethiopia', *Abba Salama*, X (1979), 257–341.

Hyatt, H. M., *The Church of Abyssinia*, London, 1928.

Johnston, C., *Travels in southern Abyssinia*, 2 vols, London, 1844.

Jones, W., 'A conversation with Abram, an Abyssinian, concerning the city of Gwendor and the sources of the Nile', *Asiatick researches*, I, (1788), 383–8.

Josephus, Flavius, *The works of Flavius Josephus*, London, 1822.

Kirwan, L. P., 'A pre-Islamic settlement from the al-Yaman on the Tanzanian coast', *L'Arabie préislamique et son environment historique et culturel.* Actes du colloque de Strasbourg 24–27 juin 1987, Université des sciences humaines de Strasbourg, *Travaux du centre de recherche sur le Proche-Orient et la Grèce antique*, 10.

Kleinhaus, A., *Historia studii linguae Arabicae et Collegii Missionum ordinis fratrum minorum*, Quaracchi, 1930. 349–52. (Kindly made available to us by Fr. Sabino di Sandoli, OFM, Bibliothecarius Terrae Sanctae.)

Kolmodin, J., *Traditions de Tsazzega et Hazzega*, 3 vols, Rome-Upsala, 1912–15.

Labernadie, M. V., *Le Vieux Pondichéry, 1673–1815,* Pondichéry, 1936, 185.

Le Blanc, Vincent, *The world surveyed and travailes of V. Le Blanc, or White*, London, 1660.

Lefèbvre, T., *Voyage en Abyssinie executé pendant les années 1839, 1840, 1841, 1842, 1843,* 6 vols, Paris, 1845–8.

Lejean, G., *Voyage en Abyssinie*, (Paris, 1872).

Levine, D. N., *Wax and gold. Tradition and innovation in Ethiopian culture*, Chicago, 1965.

Lifszyc, D., 'Amulettes éthiopiens', *Minotaure* (1933), II, 71–4.

Lobo, J., *Voyage historique d'Abyssinie*, Paris and La Haye, 1728.

Lockhart, D. M., *Itinerario of Jeronimo Lobo*, London, 1984.

Ludolf, Hiob, *A new history of Ethiopia*, London, 1684.

Ludolf, Hiob, *Ad suam historiam Aethiopicam ante-hac editam commentarius*, Frankfurt, 1691.

McCann, J., 'The Ethiopian chronicles: an African documentary tradition', *North East African Studies*, (1979). I, 47–61.

Mahtama Sellasé Walda Masqal, 'Portrait retrospectif d'un gentilhomme éthiopien', *Proceedings of the third international conference of Ethiopian studies*, Addis Ababa, 1970, III, 60–8.

Maly, Z., 'The visit of Martin Lang, Czech Franciscan, in Gondar in 1752,', *Journal of Ethiopian studies*, 1972, X, 2, 17–25.

Marcus, H. G., *The life and times of Menelik II, Ethiopia 1844–1913*, Oxford, 1975.

Massaja, G., *Lectiones grammaticales pro missionariis qui addiscere volunt linguam amaricam*, Paris, 1867.

Matthew, A. F., *The teaching of the Abyssinian church*, London, 1936.

Mérab, P., *Impressions d'Ethiopie*, 3 vols, Paris, 1921–9.

Mérab, P., *Médecins et médecine en Ethiopie*, Paris, 1912.

Mercier, J., *Ethiopian magic scrolls*, New York, 1979.

Metodio Carobbio da Nembro, 'La missione etiopica nel secolo XVIII' in J. Metzler, *Sacrae Congregationis de Propaganda Fide memoria edita, 1700–1815*, Rome, Freiburg, Vienna, 1973, II, 478–82.

Monti della Corte, A. A., *I castelli di Gondar*, Rome, 1938.

Mooney, H. F., *Glossary of Ethiopian plant names*, Dublin, 1963.

Munro-Hay, S. C., 'Aksumite chronology: some reconsiderations' *8th. international conference of Ethiopian studies*, Addis Ababa Nov. 1984, *Jahrbüch für Numismatik- und Geldgeschichte*, XXXIV, 1984, 107–28.

Munro-Hay, S. C., 'The al-Madhariba hoard of gold Aksumite and late Roman coins', *Numismatic chronicle*, 1989, 83–108.

Munzinger, W., *Ostafrikänische studien*, Schaffhausen, 1864.

Nersessian, V. and Pankhurst, R., 'The visit to Ethiopia of Yohannes To'vmačean, an Armenian jeweller, in 1764–6', *Journal of Ethiopian studies*, XV, (1982), 79–84.

Niebuhr, C., *Description de l'Arabie*, Amsterdam, 1774.

Niebuhr, C., *Voyage en Arabie*, 2 vols, Utrecht, 1776.

Orme, Robert, *A history of the transactions of the British nation in Indostan*, 4th. edition, vol 1, London, 1803, 101.

Othmer, C., 'P. Liberatus Weiss, OFM, seine Missionstaltigkeit und sein Martyrium (3 Marz 1716), *Archivum franciscanum historicum*, XXX, (1927), 336–55.

Pacelli, M., *Viaggi in Etiopia del P. Michelangelo da Tricarico, Minore Osservante, ne' quali si descrivono le cose più rimarchevoli ed osservabili incontrate in quella regione sulle orme del Ludolf, De La Croix, ed altri celebri scrittori di quei luoghi*, Naples, 1797.

Paez, Pero, *Historia da Etiopia*, Oporto, 1945.

Pakenham, T., *The mountains of Rasselas*, London, 1959.

Pankhurst, R., *Economic history of Ethiopia, 1800–1935*, Addis Ababa, 1968.

Pankhurst, R., 'Ethiopian royal seals of the 17th. and 18th. centuries' in G. Goldenberg, *Ethiopian studies. Proceedings of the 6th. international conference*, Rotterdam, 1986, 397–417.

Pankhurst, R., 'Ethiopian taxation prior to the time of Menilek', *North-east African studies*, V, (1984), 3, 59–81, VII (1985), 1, 23–47.

Pankhurst, R., 'Europe's discovery of the Ethiopian taenicide Kosso', *Medical history*, XXIII, (1979), 3, 297–313.

Pankhurst, R., 'Historical examination of traditional Ethiopian medicine and surgery', *Ethiopian medical journal*, III, (1965), 4, 157–72.

Pankhurst, R., *History of Ethiopian towns*, 2 vols, Wiesbaden, Stuttgart, 1982, 1985.

Pankhurst, R., 'The history of leprosy in Ethiopia to 1935', *Medical history* XXVIII (1984), 1, 57–72.

Pankhurst, R., 'The history of prostitution in Ethiopia', *Journal of Ethiopian studies*, XII, (1974), 2, 159–78.

Pankhurst, R., *Introduction to the economic history of Ethiopia*, London, 1961.

Pankhurst, R., 'Letter writing and the use of royal and imperial seals in Ethiopia prior to the 20th. century', *Journal of Ethiopian studies*, XI, (1973), 1, 179–208.

Pankhurst, R., Misoneism and innovation in Ethiopian history, *Ethiopian Observer.* VII (1964), 3, 287–320.

Pankhurst, R., 'Some notes on the historical and economic geography of the Mesewa area (1520–1885)' *Journal of Ethiopian studies*, xiii (1975), 89–116.

Pankhurst, R., *State and land in Ethiopian history*, Addis Ababa, 1967.

Pankhurst, R., *A social history of Ethiopia*, Addis Ababa, 1990.

Pankhurst, R., 'Status, division of labour and employment in nineteenth and early twentieth century Ethiopia', *University College of Addis Ababa ethnological bulletin*, II, (1961), 1, 7–57.

Pankhurst, R., 'The traditional taenicides of Ethiopia', *Journal of the history of medicine and allied sciences*, XXIV, (1969), 3, 323–34.

Pankhurst, R. and Ingrams, L., *Ethiopia engraved*, 1988.

Pankhurst, R., and Pearson, T., 'Remedius Prutky's 18th. century account of Ethiopian taenicides and other medical treatment', *Ethiopian medical treatment*, X, (1972), 1, 3–6.

Parkyns, M., *Life in Abyssinia*, 2 vols, London, 1853.

Paulos Tzadua and Strauss, P. L., *The Fetha Nagast. The laws of the kings*, Addis Ababa, 1968.

Pearce, N., *Life and adventures of Nathaniel Pearce*, 2 vols, London, 1831.

Penzer, N. M., *The harem*, 1936.

Perini, R., *Di qua dal Mareb (Marèb-mellasc')*, Florence, 1905.

Perruchon, J., *Les chroniques de Zara Ya'eqob et de Ba'eda Maryam*, Paris, 1893.

Petrides, S. P., *Le livre d'or de la dynastie salamonienne*, Paris, 1964.

Philby, H. St. John, *The Queen of Sheba*, London, 1981.

Plowden, W., *Travels in Abyssinia and the Galla country*, London, 1868.

Poladian, T., *The doctrinal position of the monophysite churches*, Addis Ababa, 1963.

Powne, M., *Ethiopian music*, London, 1968.

Prescott, H. F. M., *Once to Sinai*, London, 1957.

Pritchard, J. B., *Solomon and Sheba*, London, 1974.

Puglisi, G., 'Alcuni vestigi dell' isola di Dahlac Chebir e la leggende dei Furs', *Proceedings of the third international conference of Ethiopian studies*, Addis Ababa, 1969, I, 35–47.

Raineri, O., 'Le relazione fra chiesa etiopica e chiesa romana (Lettera di Remedio Prutky missionario in Etiopia nel 1752–1753)' *Nicolaus*, VIII (1980), 2, 351–64.

Rassam, H., *Narrative of the British mission to Theodore, King of Ethiopia*, 2 vols, London, 1869.

Rava, M., *Al lago Tsana (il mar profondo d'Etiopia)*, Rome, 1913.

Rey, C. F., *The romance of the Portuguese in Abyssinia*, London, 1929.

Red Sea and Gulf of Aden pilot, 1955.

Ricci, L., *Contributi alla storia del regno di Iyasu II di Etiopia*, doctoral thesis, Rome, 1937–8.

Robbe, Jacques, *Méthode pour apprendre facilement la géographie*, Paris, 1685.

Rüppell, W. P. E. S., *Reise in Abyssinien*, 2 vols, Frankfurt, 1838–40.

Rutter, E., *The holy cities of Arabia*, London, 1928.

Ryšavý, 'Die Reformaten Mission in Rüssland unter dem Missionspräfekten F. Remedius Prutky', *Archivum franciscanum historicum*, XXVII (1934), 179–223.

Salt, H., *A voyage to Abyssinia*, London, 1814.

Schacht, J., *Introduction to Islamic law*, Oxford, 1982.

Schneider, Madeleine, *Stèles funeraires mussulmanes des Îles Dahlak*, Institut Français d'archéologie orientale du Caire, 1983.

Schnèider, R., 'Les débuts de l'histoire éthiopienne', *Documents pour servir a l'histoire de la civilisation ethiopienne*, VII, 1976, pp. 47–54.

Schoff, W. H., *The periplus of the Erythraean Sea*, London, 1912.

Sergew Hable Sellassie, *Ancient and medieval Ethiopia to 1270*, Addis Ababa, 1972.

Serjeant, R. B., 'The cultivation of cereals in mediaeval Yemen', *Arabian studies*, 1974, I, 25–74.

Serjeant, R. B., *The Portuguese off the South Arabian coast*, Oxford, 1963, 152.

Serjeant, R. B., 'The post-mediaeval and modern history of San'ā' and the Yemen, ca. 953–1382/1515–1962' in Serjeant R. B. and Lewcock Ronald (eds.) *San'ā'*, *an Arabian Islamic city*, World of Islam festival trust, London, 1983.

Simon, G., *L'Ethiopie*, Paris, 1885.

Slessarev, V., *Prester John. The letter and the legend*, Minneapolis, Minnesota, 1959.

Somigli, T., 'La Francescana spedizione in Etiopia del 1751–4 e la sua relazione del P. Remedio Prutky di Boemia OFM.' *Archivum franciscanum historicum*, VI (1913), 129–43.

Somigli, T., 'L'Itinerarium del P. Remedio Prutky, viaggiatore e missionario Francescano (Alto Egitto), e il suo viaggio in Abissinia, 21 febbraio 1752–22 aprile 1753', *Studi francescani*, N.S., XXII (1925), 425–60.

Stella, G. O., 'Il viaggio in Etiopia di Michelangelo Pacelli (1789–90)' *Miscellanea di storia dell' esplorazione (1986)*, XI, 109–32.

Taddesse Tamrat, *Church and state in Ethiopia 1270–1527*, Oxford, 1972.

Tellez, B., *Historia geral de Ethiopia a alta*, Coimbra, 1660.

Thevenot, Jean de, *The travels of Monsieur de Thevenot into the Levant*, 3 vols, London 1687.

Thomas, H., *The discovery of Ethiopia by the Portuguese in 1520*, London, 1938.

Tornillo, A., *Annales sacri et profani*, 2 vols, Frankfurt, 1916.

Trimingham, J. S., *Islam in Ethiopia*, London, 1952.

Ullendorff, E., *Ethiopia and the Bible*, London, 1968.

Ullendorff, E., *The Ethiopians*, Oxford, 1973.

Ullendorff, E., *The Semitic languages of Ethiopia. A comparative phonology*. London, 1955.

Usoni, L., *Risorse minerarie dell'Africa orientale*, Rome, 1952.

Valentia, George, Viscount, *Voyages and travels to India, Ceylon, the Red Sea, Abyssinia and Egypt*, 3 vols, London, 1809.

Valentyn, F., *Oud en niew Ost Indien*, 5 vols, Dordrecht–Amsterdam, 1724–6.

Vittorius, Mario, *Chaldeae seu Aethiopicae linguae institutiones*, Rome, 1552.

Walker, C. H., *The Abyssinian at home*, London, 1933.

Weld Blundell, H., *The Royal Chronicle of Abyssinia 1769–1840*, Cambridge, 1922.

Wellsted, J. R., *Travels in Arabia*, 2 vols, London, 1838.

Whiteway, R. S., *The Portuguese expedition to Abyssinia in 1541–1543*, London, 1902.

Wright, W., *Catalogue of the Ethiopic manuscripts in the British Museum*, London, 1877.

INDEX

Aarafat, Mt, *see* Gebel Elauraffat
Abagamedri, *see* Bagemder
Abases (Abassia, Abatos), 123–4
Abba Garima (Abbaquarima), 251
Abba Salam, *see* Frumentius
Abbay (Abay) r., 125
Abbo Mt, 199, 215, 261, 312–14, 317, 321, 324
Abbo, St (St Gabra Menfas), 261
Abraham, priest and martyr, 245
Abu-Alef, Red Sea port, 355
Abu Bakr (Becker), first Caliph, 42
Abun Yohannes, Head of the Ethiopian Church, 145, 228–9, 236–8, 249, 307–8, 465, 467
  as Prutky's opponent, 304, 310, 519
Abyssinia, Abyssinian, 20, 75–357 *passim*, 467, 470, 519
Adagali, *see* Addi Ghella
Adal (Adel), 123, 126
Adam, 41, 390–1
Adam, Mt (Adamova Hora), 390
Adam's Peak (Aden, Mt), 390–1
Adamites, sect of, 390
Adaschera Jesu, *see* Addi Hauiscia
Addi Baro (Addo Baru, *perh.* Barra), 80, 343
Addi Emer (Adeckerma), 333
Addi Gambollo (Kembela), 345
Addi Ghella (Adagali), 339
Addi Hauiscia (Adaschera Jesu), 346
Addi Mongonti (Addomongolo), 80
Addi Qʷala (Adickevelet), 341
Adea (Adis), *see* Hadya
Adeckerma, *see* Addi Emer
Aden, 132, 368, 386

Aden, Mt, *see* Adam's Peak
Adennala, 341
Adickevelet, *see* Addi Qʷala
Adigo and Aylo, sons of the Emperor, 174
Adwa (Adaua), 130–1, 251, 327
Aenipontum, *see* Innsbruck
Afar, *see* Dankali
Africa, 36, 103–4, 122, 271, 288, 377, 386, 447, 460, 476, 495
Agami (Ajam), 36
Agaw, Agawmeder (Agau), 131, 205
Agde (Agatha), 456
Agen, 450
Agnona, Fr Paul of, xiii–xiv, 323, 482–3, 486, 501
Agordat, 134
Ahmad b. Saʿīd, Imam, 363
Aian, Ain, 'Ayn, 117, 218
Aigues Mortes (St Louis), 456
Akala Guzay (Guray), 125
Aksum (Axum), 91, 104, 130, 140, 176, 327, 521
Alata (Aleta), 219
Aleppo, 190
Aleppo, Fr Antony of, xiii–xv, 322, 325–7, 462
Alexander, Patriarch of Alexandria, 110
Alexandria, 63, 236, 257, 309, 344, 361, 446, 458, 461, 478, 482, 487
Al-Mahdī ʿAbbās b. al-Ḥusayn, 365
Al-Mahdī Muḥammad b. 'Aḥmad, 363
Almeida, 128, 136, 142, 149–50, 153–4, 183, 191, 193, 204, 217, 281, 284, 299, 302

533

Al-Qāḍī al-ḥayy (Elkadi Elhai), 13
Alvanus, Fr Joannes, Jesuit, 236
Alvarez, 91, 97, 136, 142, 191, 193, 211, 227–8, 230, 237, 242, 251, 264–5, 281, 293, 296, 307, 520
Alzevit, see Zabīd
Amais (Bagemder), 520–1
Amaral (Amara), Andreas, High Chancellor of Rhodes, 489
Amba Sel (Ambasel), 130
Amboina (Ambon), 418
America, 179, 190, 203, 300, 477
Amhara (Amara, Amaris), 91, 125, 130–1, 216, 520–1
Amir Soliman, 364
Ananda Ranga Pillai (Rangapoullé), 403, 421
Angerab (Ankareb) r., 90, 290, 322, 325
Angiva (Angev, Argev), 327
Angola, 122, 300
Angot (Angote), 125, 520
animals, domestic, Arabia, 1–3, 28, 368, 386
  Ethiopia, 67, 133–6, 145, 204, 210, 276, 299, 346
  elephants, 206–9, 348–9, 403–4
animals, wild, Arabia, 29–30, 369, 404
  Ethiopia, 82, 84–5, 201, 204–5, 209–10, 298–9, 300–1, 333–5, 339, 349–50
Ankareb r., see Angerab
Ansia r., see Inzo r.
Antalo, 282
Anthony, St, monks of the order of, 81, 229, 236, 240, 250, 256, 269, 331, 340, 347, 386, 463, 466, 468
Antongil Bay, 428
Aoage, see Wag
Appellit, see Paillet
Aquitaine (Aquileia), 446, 450, 455
Ara, see Harar
Arabia, xi, 48, 105, 135, 245, 295, 364, 366, 369, 383, 412–13, 462, 476.
Arabia Deserta, 35, 49, 309, 363, 372, 383
Arabia Felix, 35–6, 49, 63, 104–7, 206, 222, 309, 361, 363, 365, 368, 370, 372, 426
Arabia Petrosa, 48, 201, 206, 309, 361, 383
Arabs, 2, 9–10, 12, 16, 34, 367, 371, 374–5, 380, 382

Arba'e ensesa (Arbaa Tensai), 328
Archipelago, 487, 489, 490–1, 493
Argentina, see Kimolos
Argev, see Angiva
Ariège r. (Araxe), 454
Aristotle, 189, 208
Arium, see Dawaro
Arkiko (Arckiko, Hergigo), 68–9, 324, 351
Arles, 457, 459
Armenia, 36
Arve, 347
Ascension Island, 430–3, 435–6, 441–2
Asia, 36, 103, 179, 271, 288, 377, 386, 476–7
Asma Giyorgis, (Adbar Sagad II, Backaffa Masich Sagad, Masih Sagad), emperor, 72, 94, 102, 114, 129, 134, 172, 339–40, 520
Asmara (Asmera), 78, 327, 345–6, 355
Aspis, 123
Assab (Avalites, perh. Zeila, Zayla'), 123, 126
Assallafi Ešaté, see Selaffi Schettii
Asyût, xiii, 483
Atbara r., 123
Athanasius, Coptic Bishop, 461
Athanasius, St, Patriarch of Alexandria, 109, 256
Aucagerle, see Awsa Gurrale, Awsa
Aude, r., 456
Augustinian Order, 435, 450
Austria, 63, 136, 475–6, 478–81, 504–5, 516
Auvillar (Le Billar), 451
Avalites, see Assab, Zeila
Avia, see Hadya
Awsa Gurrale, Awsa (Aucagerle), 125
Axum, see Aksum
Axumites, 104
Aylet, 349
'Ayn, see Aian
Azevedo, Luiz de, 235, 245, 255
Aznaf Saghed (Zadenghel, Asnaf Sagad II), emperor, 113

Bāb al-Mandab (Babel-Mandel), 132, 356, 385
Babylonia, 36
Backaffa Masich Saghed, see Asma Giyorgis
Ba'eda Maryam I, (Ba'eda Mariami, Cyriacus), emperor, 112

Bagémder (Abagamedri, Bagemdra, Bagameder, Begamder, Begember), 125, 127, 130, 300, 520–1
Baghdad, 36
Bahr Nagaš (Barnagassus, Varnagassus), 79, 129, 139, 191, 318, 320, 344, 520–1
Bajanotti, Greek captain, 354
Balagada, Ba'algada (Balgada), 213
Balaw (Balvus), 134
Bale Gama, 129
Bali and Ganz, (Baliganje, Valigunasis), 520–1
Banda (Bauda), 418
Banians (Bagnians), 66, 353, 360, 374–6
Barmola, suburb of Valletta, 496
Barnagassus, see Bahr Nagaš
Barra, see Addi Baro
Barreto, João Nunez, Patriarch, 245
Bašelo r., 91
Basil, St, 250, 256–7
Basilides, see Fasiladas
Bassera (Basra), 36
Batavia (Patavia), 374, 418
Bauda (Banda), 418
Baylūl (Beilal, Beilul), 132–3, 356
Bayt al-Faqīh (Beit Facky), 365–6, 372–3, 380–1
Beano (Juno), Fr Samuel of, missionary martyr, (perh. identical with Samuel of Biumo), 100, 114, 261, 312–14, 317, 324
Bear, ship's captain, 421, 425, 429, 435, 438
Beglerbey, 134
Beilul, see Baylūl
Beit Facky, see Bayt al-Faqīh
Belessa (Belasa), 130, 171
Bellad Elablis, see Bilād Iblīs
Bellofonte (Schönbrunn), 476
Beltzagadi (perh. Sagadé), 131
Benedict, Fr, 458
Benedict XIV, Pope, 96, 101, 309, 311–13, 317–18, 320, 323, 398, 405, 461, 472–3, 486, 501–3
Benedictine Order, 446, 448
Benedictus of Theano, 191
Bengal, 374, 418
Bercke, see Birkat-al-Ḥajj
Bercke Elpharaun, see Birkah Fir'aun
Bethlehem, 222
Beziers, 454–6

Bezin, see Dabra Bizan
Bilād Iblīs (Bellad Elablis), 44
birds, 28–9, 67, 200–3, 217, 333, 357, 368, 433
Birkah Fir'aun (Bercke Elpharaun, Pool of Pharaoh), 7, 477
Birkat-al-Ḥajj (Bercke), 2
Biumo, Fr Samuel of, missionary in Socotra (perh. identical with Samuel of Beano), 386–7
Blavet, see Port Louis
Boa, see Bur
Bochetta (perh. Rochetta Ligure), 479
Bohemia, Bohemian, xvi, xxvi, 396, 398, 454–5, 462, 472, 475–6, 504–5, 517–8
Bologna, 473
Bolzano (Bolgianum), 473
Bombay, 374, 394, 417
Bora or Baruu (Varra), 520–1
Bordeaux (Bourdeaux), 446, 454
Borgo san Angelo, suburb of Valletta, 496
Borussia (Prussia), King of (Frederick the Great), xxv, 504–5
Boša (perh. Boxa, Roxa), 127
Boscawen, Edward, Admiral, 402
Boudon, see Labadio
Bourbon Island (Réunion), 426–7, 439, 441–2
Boxa, see Boša
Brabantia, 458
Braccia di Mania, see Laconia
Bridge of Adam, 393
Bridge of Peter, see Point Pedro
Brittany, xv, 436, 455
Brno (Bruna), 475
Bruce, James, traveller, xi, xv,
  Arabia, 11, 14, 17, 20, 24, 26, 34, 49–50, 53, 57, 60–1, 358, 369, 373
  Messawa, 66–7, 70
  Ethiopia, customs, 77, 110, 120, 133, 147, 150, 154–7, 160, 164–7, 177–8, 188, 194, 199, 201–2, 205, 207, 226, 238, 281, 285, 307–8
  Ethiopia, geographical, 83, 85, 91–2, 128, 134, 136, 219, 313
  Ethiopia, royal court, 161–2, 170–1, 173–4, 262, 322
Bua, see Bur
Budějovice (in Bohemia), 475
Bugna (Vangue), 520
Buja r., see Buya r.

Būlāq (Bolack), 486
Bur peninsula (Boa, Bua), 125, 134
Burneo (Bornu), 219–20
Buya r. (Buja), 85

Cafate, Caffatin, Caffer, see Gafat
Cairo, 51–2, 55, 57, 63, 178, 315, 374
  as field of mission, xiii–xvi, 482–3,
  486
Caligula (Gaius), Roman emperor, 220
Canal du Midi, xv, 454–6
Cancer, Tropic of, 14, 441
Candace, Queen, 107, 224, 256
Cappuccii, Mt (Friar's Hood), 393
Capricorn, Tropic of, 440
Capuchin Order, 100, 397–8, 400–1,
  404–5, 418, 448–50, 455, 514
Caramania, see Karamania
Carcassone, 456
Carmelite Order, 449–50
Carthusian Order, 154, 446
Casconia, see Gascony
Castelnaudary (Castell Naudarie), 455
Cataracts, 91, 185, 188, 212
Catherine the Great, Empress, xvi, 506,
  515–7
Catina r. (Gatinair), 339
Cavalieri, see Kastellorizon
Celtan Cequed, emperor, see Susenyos
Centum Cellae, see Cività Vecchia
Cerigo, see Kithira
Cète r., 456
Cette, see Sète
Ceylon (Ceilan, Sri Lanka), 389–93
Chad, Lake, 219
Chalcedon, Council of, 248, 252, 467
Charles VI, Holy Roman Emperor, 133
Chedami, 347
Chile, 190
Chinese, 133, 402–3, 406, 424–5, 447
Chiusa di Verona (Occlusa), 473
Cicero, 207–8
Cimolis, see Kimolos
Cività Vecchia (Centum Cellae), 459
Claudian, poet, 221
Claudius (Aznaf Saghed, Galawdéwos,
  Asnaf Sagad I), emperor, 112, 247
coffee, 19, 63, 195, 361, 364, 366, 374–
  5, 380, 426–7
coinage, 5, 6, 11, 18, 20, 51, 70, 75,
  119, 212–14, 367, 374–5, 401, 420
Columbo, 392–3
Comorin, Cape, 418

Compagnie des Indes, 402, 442, 444
Conch, Konta, (Conche), 127
Confede, see Qunfudah
Confito, see Siré
Congo r., 122, 132
Constantinople, 63, 151, 178, 355, 361,
  478
Constantius Zara Jacub, see Za'ra
  Ya'qob
Conventual Fathers, 457
Coptic Church, 1, 6, 229, 258, 305, 307,
  310, 461, 467, 483
Coromandel (Cor Mandel), 394, 401,
  418
Coron, see Koroni
Corsica, 459
Cos (Istanköy, Stanchio), 491
Cosseir, see Quṣayr
costume, Arabia, 14, 32–3, 36, 38, 55,
  362, 370, 377
  Ethiopia, 79, 118–19, 152–6, 159,
  162–3, 230, 250–1, 276–81, 291–2
  India, 397, 407–8
Courland, see Kurland
Couthures-sur-Garonne (Guturas),
  448
crops, cereal, Arabia, 20, 28, 367
  Ethiopia, 67, 78, 87, 89, 192–3, 283–
  4, 328
  elsewhere, 423, 456, 487
crops, other, Arabia, 27–8, 367, 375
  Ethiopia, 67–8, 192, 194–7
  elsewhere, 386, 391, 409, 413–14,
  418, 422, 456, 477, 487, 495
Cuccari Mts (The Knuckles), 393
Curet, Monsieur, French merchant,
  458
Cyprus, 487
Cytherea, see Kithira

Dabra Berhan Sellasé, church, 313
Dabra Bizan (Bezin, Bizen), monastery,
  191, 347
Dacan, see Deccan
Dahali, 126
Dahlak (Dahlack) islands, 36, 134–5,
  358, 361, 411
Dakaschaha, 335
Damascus (Schami, Sham), 35, 55, 190
Dambagwena (Dambabokuna), 84
Dambeya (Dambea), 125, 128, 131,
  520–1
Damietta, 220

Damot (Damote, Damute), 128, 130, 136, 206, 211, 322
Dankali (Dancali, Afar), 125, 132, 190
Dapperus, 300
Daquusit, 330
Darack-Unz, 332
Dardon, 452
Daro (Dara), 327
Daruisch, see Dervish
Dassé, 130
Dass--hò (Dezcko), 358
Daver, 88
David II (Lebna Dengel, Wanag Sagad I), emperor, 112, 520-1
David III (Adbar Sagad I), emperor, 114, 177
Dawaro (Davvaro, Arium), 126
Debarwa (Dobarua), 77, 79-80, 191, 214, 320, 327, 344-5
Debbeb Bahr (Debbebahar), 86, 330
Deccan (Dacan), 191
Defur, Principal, 451
Degasgede, 335
Degsa (Dixa), 355
Dembe (Dembick), 349
Denmark, king of, 458
Derbuset (Dorbeschit), 358
Derokavia, 86
Dervish (Daruisch), 381
Desnevall, Count de, 458
Dezcko, see Dass-hò
Dhamār, 363
Diballa, see Dubllu
Diodorus Siculus, 299
Dioscorus, 248, 252, 467
Diu, 245, 374-5
Dixa, see Degsa
Djezan, see Jīzān
Dobarua, see Debarwa
Dola, 366, 372, 376, 384
Dominican Order, 446, 451, 500
Donato, Fr, missionary in St Petersburg, 515, 517
Dongola, 179, 190-1
Dorbeschit, see Derbuset
Draco, Joanne, Boggiarand, 92, 169, 273, 343-4, 354
Draco of Nios, George or Gregory, Nagadras or Treasurer, 71, 73-4, 90, 92-3, 95, 143-4, 152, 169, 228, 260-1, 273, 310-11, 318, 321, 462, 492
Dubllu, Dubello (Diballa), 358

Dupleix (Duplex), Joseph-François, Marquis, governor, xv, 397-9, 401-3, 419-20
palace of, 402-3
Dutch, Holland, in East Indies, 208, 389-93, 400, 417-8
in Mocha, 364, 368-70, 372, 374-8, 380
Dzimhebet, see Gim'hile

Ebenat (Ebegniat), 131, 216
Edom, Sea of, see Red Sea
Egnia, see Vignes-sur-Garonne
Egypt, Egyptian, 66, 82, 124, 134, 188-9, 192, 218-20, 309, 359
as seat of mission, xi, xiii-xiv, 1, 312, 386, 461, 475, 482-4, 520-1
Elba, see Portoferraio
El-Ed, Red Sea port, 355
Elesbar (Ella Asbeha, Caléb the Holy), emperor, 111, 212
Elias, Ethiopian Catholic, 218
Elkadi Elhai, see al-Qādī al-ḥayy
Elluhaja, Ellochia, see Luḥayyah
Emfraz (Entfaras), 136
Enarya (Ennaria, Neria), 127, 136, 178, 212
Endarta (Enderta), 130, 213
Enebesi (Ennebese), 131
England, English, in Mocha, 361, 364, 374-8, 382-3
elsewhere, 400, 402, 417, 425, 430, 442-3, 445
Ennaria, see Enarya
Enzu r., 85
Episcopi, see Tilos
Equator, (The Line), 126, 178, 434, 438, 441
Eslamgé, (Zelancke), 325
Ethiopia, Ethiopian, xi, xii, xiv, 24, 75-357 passim, 366, 415, 422, 462, 464-71
Europe, European, xi, 271, 288, 374, 417, 422, 428
Eustachianus (Ewostatéwos), holy man, 257
Eve, 23, 41, 390-1

Fasiladas (Basilides, Facilides, Seltan Sagad II, Alam Sagad), emperor, 103, 113, 229, 327, 340
fasts, Ethiopian, 264-6
Fatagar or Fatiguar, 126, 520

Fāṭimah (Fatme), 17
Fazughli (Fasculum, Fascul), 128
Ferrerius, Vincentius, preacher, 223
Feser, confectioner, 515, 517
festivals, Ethiopian, 256–9, 261–2, 268, 311
  Masqal, 141, 182–3, 260–1
Fethiye, southern Turkey, 487
fish, 7, 16, 31, 62, 79, 90, 198–200, 369
Flanders, Fleming, 374, 378
Florence, xvi, xxvi, 473, 479, 503–5, 518
Floriana, suburb of Valletta, 496
Fort Dauphin, Madagascar, 428
Fort St David (Forsendevi), xvi, 394, 417
France, French, in Mocha, 356, 364, 374, 377, 382–3
  India to France, 393, 399–400, 402, 404, 417, 419–20, 422–3, 425–8, 436, 438, 442–3
  in France, 444–61 *passim*
  Louis XV King of, 400–2, 423–4, 444, 451, 459
Francis, Grand Duke, Holy Roman Emperor, xvi, xxv, 136, 475–9, 499–500, 503, 505
Franciscans (Reformed Order of the Friars Minor), 177, 386, 418, 462, 492–3, 501, 506, 509, 518–19
Franciscus of Rivarolo, Fr, missionary in Ethiopia, 114
Frankenburg, Fr Adolph, missionary in St Petersburg, 515–17
Freemasons, 447
Fremona, 176, 245, 252
French doctor, 217, 332, 345
Frerius, Fulgentius (Fulgencio Freire), Jesuit missionary, 245
Fresquel r., 456
Friar's Hood, *see* Cappuccii, Mt
fruit, Arabia, 13, 27–8, 33, 361, 367, 386
  Ethiopia, 62, 90, 194–6
  elsewhere, 411–13, 456, 487, 495
  bananas (Indian fig, *mus*), 28, 62, 195, 361, 367, 381–2, 411–12
Frumentius, St (Abba Salam), 109, 176
Fung, kingdom of, 134

Gabra Menfas, St (St Abbo), 261
Gabriel, João, Portuguese settler in Ethiopia, 124, 206

Gafat (Cafate, Caffatin, Caffer), 140, 179, 520
Galla (Oromo), 127, 129, 134, 152
Galle (Galli), port in Ceylon, 393
Gamarcansa (Gananuara), 131
Gandia, *see* Kandy
Ganz, *see* Bali and Ganz
Gari r., 125
Garonne r. (Iccaron), 446, 454, 456
Gascony (Casconia), 449, 455
Gateluzi family, 489
Gatinair r. (*perh.* Catina r.), 339
Gazophilatium Persicum, 295
Gebel Elauraffat (Jabal 'Arafāt, Mount Aarafat, Mount of Recognition, Mount of Sacrifice), 40, 42, 44
Gebl Ettur (Jabal al-Ṭūr), *see* Sinai
Gebel Firan (Jabal Fīrān, Jibbel Foran, Mountain of Mice), 60
Gebel Giamrat (Jabal Jamrah, Mount of Stones), 42
Gebel Tombol, *see* Tombol, Mount
Gembua, *see* Yanbu'
Genoa, 459, 479–81, 489
Gerar, 76, 185
Germany, German, 186, 189, 390, 396–8, 422, 427, 473, 480–1, 504
Gezan, *see* Jīzān
Gheschen, *see* Qishn
Gibe r., 127, 212, 521
Gidda, *see* Jeddah
Gim'hile (Dzimhebet), 358
Ginda'e, (Kinda), 76, 349
Ginori, Don, governor of Leghorn, 481–2
Gira Onz, 328
Girga (Girge), xiii–xiv, 461, 483, 501
Gish (Geesh, Guist, Guix), 219
Glatz, battlefield, 504
Glickaja, 326
Goa, 245, 374, 382, 387, 390, 417
Godinho, N., 105–7, 126–7, 132, 212
Gojab r., 127
Gojjam (Godgiam, Gojarisis, Goyamme), 130–1, 136, 184, 193, 197, 205–6, 211, 213, 216–8, 520, 521
  as separate province, 174, 306, 310
gold, 117, 127, 133–4, 136–7, 140–1, 143, 211–14
Gomma (Goma), 127
Gondar, xv, 75, 87, 90–1, 101, 133, 156, 161, 169, 173, 178, 186–7, 189,

Gondar—*continued*
194, 199, 212–13, 226, 270–1, 280,
290, 294, 311, 314, 318, 322, 325,
340–1, 347, 462–3
Good Hope, Cape of, 116, 428–9, 431,
440
Gorgora (Gorgorra), 252
Gorgoreyos, Abba, informant of
Ludolf, 139, 186, 470
Goroma, 127
Goyamme, *see* Godgiam
Gragna (Grañ, Ahmād Ibn Ibrāhīm al-
Ghāzī), 126
Graro mountains, 116
Greece, Greek, 5, 6, 9, 18, 66, 493
as Ethiopian royal servants, 73, 156,
169, 343–4, 354, 492
Green Height (*perh.* Greenwich), 442
Guinea, 122, 300
Guist, *see* Gish
Guragés, Ethiopian ethnic group, 300
Gusman, Ludovicus, Jesuit, 255
Guturas, *see* Couthures-sur-Garonne
Guyenne, 446

Habašet, Habesch, 122, 124, 131
Ḥaḍramaut, 368
Hadya (Adea, Adis, Avia), 123, 520–1
Hahau, emperor, *see* Naʻod
de Hallelujah, order of monks, 251
Hamasén (Hanesim), 78, 129, 131, 349
Hamburg, 508
Hanwella (Hanckavel), 392
Harar (Ara), 123, 126
Hassane, 7
Hate Ailu (Haylu Ešaté, Ayto Aylo),
322, 326
Hatu Job, 326
Hawzén, 139
Hayda (Hauza), 85
Helena Sallo Vangela, 112
Hergigo, *see* Arkiko
Hers r. (Orio r.), 454
Himyarites (Homeritae), 103–4
Hollenburg, Joanne, Swedish surgeon,
445
Hsi-an, 133
Ḥudaydah (Hodeida, Hodide), 36, 53,
360–1, 364–5, 373

Iccaron r., *see* Garonne
If (Iff), island, 457

India, Indians, xi, 36, 122, 191, 207–8,
353, 364, 366, 374–6, 379, 382–3,
396–420 *passim*
Indian Ocean, 132, 363, 385, 428
Indica, eunuch, 224, 256
Inerus, emperor, 356
Ingria, Russian province, 509
Innsbruck (Aenipontum), 473–4, 505
insects, 2, 3, 7, 53, 495
Inzo r. (Ansia), 332
Ios, *see* Nios
Iraq, 36
Istanköy, *see* Cos
Italy, 479, 484
Itylo (Vitulo), village in the Morea, 493
ivory, 127, 134, 206–7
Iyasu I (Adam Saghed, Adyam Sagad,
Jasock, Jasu), emperor, 113–14,
157, 177, 520
Iyasu II (Odiam Saghad, Adyam Sagad
II, Berhan Sagad, Jasu), reigning
emperor, xi, xiv–xv, 70–2, 79, 115,
118, 125, 129, 134, 137, 144, 238,
270, 303, 306–7, 519–21
childhood, 170–4, 337
court, 153–7, 159–61, 165–9
imperial attributes, 138, 140–1, 146,
148, 150–1, 182–3, 241, 259
Prutky's dealings with, 93, 96, 98–9,
101, 116, 215, 309–12, 314–22,
324–6
Prutky's report, 462, 464, 467, 469,
472
aunt of, 287–8
sister of, 275, 306, 308

Jacobus (Yaʻqob, Malak Sagad II),
emperor, 112–13
Jama (Jemma), 219
Janjero (Gengero, Zingerum), 126
Jansenism, 448
Jasu, emperor, *see* Iyasu I, II
Jeddah (Gidda), 5, 11, 17, 18–34
passim, 39, 45–6, 48, 50–3, 57, 69,
307, 352, 355, 363, 371, 382, 387
Jelgava (Mitau, Mictavia), 517
Jembo, *see* Yanbuʻ
Jemen, *see* Yemen
Jeremia, local ruler, 337–8
Jerusalem, 37, 128, 224, 323, 458
Jesuits, in Ethiopia, 78, 176, 229, 235,
245–6, 252, 255, 296, 346

Jesuits—continued
  in India etc., 397, 400, 404–5, 418,
    435, 446, 448
Jews, Judaea, 100, 224–5, 242, 247,
    254, 365, 375, 463, 468
Jīzān (Djezan, Gezan, Qīzān), 49, 61
Joannes I (Yohannes I, Af-Saghed,
    Alaf-Sagad), emperor, 113, 520–1
Josephus, Flavius, 106
Josephus de St Angelo, Fr, 295
Julius Caesar, 220
Jumilah, see Kimliba
Justus (Zei Saghed, Tahay Sagad),
    emperor, 114, 356

Kaffa, 366
Kaha r. and palace, see Qaha
Kaher, 81
Kaimackan (Qā'im-maqām), 69, 355
Kamaran (Kameran), 359–60, 368, 370
Kandy (Gandia), king of, 390–3
Karamania, 487
Karikal, Indian fortress, 400
Kastellorizon (Castellrosso, Cavalieri,
    Megistē), 489
Kava Kadus (qeb'a qeddus), 229, 331,
    466
Kebra Amlak (Kaber Amlack), 343
Kembela, see Addi Gambollo
Kerala (Indian state), 397
Kimliba (perh. Jumilah), 358
Kimolos (Cimolis), 493
Kinda, see Ginda'e
Kithira, (Cerigo, Cytherea), 493
Klevenmuller, Count de, 476
Knuckles, The, see Cuccari Mts
Koba, 7
Konfodah, see Qunfudhah
Konta, see Conch
Kopidlno, birthplace of Prutky, xiii
Korhara (perh. Addi Qorqora), 131
Koroni (Coron), 494
Kosair, see Quṣayr
Krijacus (Kirakos), 216–17, 322
Kroměříž (Cremsirium), Fr James
    Ržimarž or Kzimar of, xiii–xv, 93,
    96, 101, 519
Kronstadt, 507–8
Kurland or Courland, 517
Kusckuam, see Qʷesqʷam
Kzimar, see Kroměříž

Labadio (perh. Boudon), 451
Laconia (Braccia di Mania, Mani), 493
Laidera (perh. Ledata), 327
Lalibala, 262
Lamalmo (Malmo), 87, 327, 329–30,
    332, 339
Lampedusa or Lampadosa, 496
Landshut, battlefield, 504
Lang, Fr Martin, xiii–xv, 320, 344, 352,
    453–4, 461–2, 501
Langon (L'Angon), 448
Languedoc, 456
La Réole, 448
Lasta (Laesta), 126, 130–1
Latvia, 509, 517
Lazarist missionaries, 423, 446
Le Billar, see Auvillar
Le Blanc, V., 106
Lebna Dengel, emperor, see David II
Leca, see Walaqa
Ledata, see Laidera
Leghorn, see Livorno
Le Mas d'Agenais, (Omust da Genest),
    449
Lembo, see Yanbu'
Leo I, Pope, 252
Leopold I, Holy Roman Emperor, 133,
    356
Le Port Sainte Marie, 449
Lers, r., 456
Le Somail, (Samal), 455
Lespinasse (Spinas), 453
Lestock, Richard, Admiral, 445
Limosa, Mediterranean island, 496
Linz (Lintium), 474
Lion, Golfe du (Gulf of Lions), 456–7
Livonia, 509
Livorno (Leghorn, Portus Libur-
    nensis), xvi, 309, 461, 478–9, 481–
    2, 498–500, 503
Lobo, J., 107, 131–2, 166, 205, 218–19,
    264, 281, 285–6, 293, 298–9, 310
locusts, 144, 293–8
Lombardy, 479
London, 382, 443
L'Orient, xv, 420, 424–5, 427, 436–7,
    444–5
Lucan, poet, 220
Ludolf, Hiob (Ludolph, Job), 106, 126–
    8, 130–2, 139–40, 186–7, 189–90,
    195, 201–2, 204, 206, 208, 211,
    261, 311, 470
Ludovici, see Port Louis

Luhayyah (Ellochia, Elluhaja), 61, 63, 360
Lyons (Laudunum), 458

Macao, 405, 424–5
Macarius, St, 250
Macheda, see Sheba, Queen of
Madagascar (Malacascar), 428
Madeboy Tabor Hills, see Tabor Hills
Madet, Mt, 347
Madras (Mottraz, Modras), 374, 417
Maghrib (Magreb), 35
Magni, village in the Morea, 493
Magrebini, 97
Mahaola, 127
Mahmud I, Sultan of Turkey, 478
Mahometans, see Muslims
Mahon (Tegremahon), 139
Mailecko r., see Makalako
Maillard of Tournon, Cardinal, 405–6
Mainotes (Mainothae), 493
Majameni, 340
Majcka, 338
Makalako r. (Mailecko r.), 89
Makara Iyasus (Mackara Jesu), 328
Malabar, 179, 191, 389, 397, 405–6, 418
Malay coast, 36
Malea, Cape, 493
Malhovitz, 78
Malindi (Melindi), 124
Malmo, see Lamalmo
Malta (Melita), 494–6
Malta, Knights of, 487, 495–6
Mani, see Laconia
Mantua, 473, 475
Maqalé, 130
Marab, 81
Marab r. (Merev r.), 82, 123, 129–30, 214, 318
Marackus, 341
Maria Theresa, Empress, xvi, 353, 364, 475–8, 504–5
Marmande (Marmando), 448
Maronite Christians, 245
Marquand, Fr, missionary in St Petersburg, 515–16
Marseilles (Massilia), xv, 456–8
Martinique, 187
Mascarene Islands (Mascarein), 426

Massawa (Messaua), xiv–xv, 62–6, 68–70, 74–6, 78, 87, 131–2, 134, 191, 214, 245, 318, 324, 346, 349, 350–2, 354–7
Masulipatam, Indian fortress, 400
Matapan, Cape, (Promontorium Taenarum), 493
Matthew, St, Apostle, 107–8, 224, 235
Matraka, see Mitraha
Mauritius (Mauritz), 421–3, 425, 427, 439, 442
Maushij (Murez), 380
Mauza' (Mora, Mura, Musa), 368, 371, 376
Mawāhib, Al (Moab), 363, 365, 373
May Čilot, 290
May Gwagwa, 176
May Temqat (Maii-Temcket), 335
Mdina (Medina), old Maltese capital, 496
Mecca, 4, 13–14, 22–3, 27, 29, 35–40, 43–4, 46, 48–9, 53, 57–8, 363, 387
Medaacia, 333
medical treatment, in Arabia, 19–20, 53–5, 57–9, 370, 377
in Ethiopia, 67, 160, 180, 188, 289–91, 302–4, 341, 352
elsewhere, 436, 484, 504
Medina, 4, 13, 44, 46–7, 49, 58
Mediterranean Sea, 220, 446, 459, 482, 487
Megistē, see Kastellorizon
Mejhinzy, 347
Melindi, see Malindi
Mendez, Alfonso, Jesuit, 133, 176, 229, 356
Menilek (Mehilech, Menyelik), 224
Mennas, see Minas
Mente-Secla, 332
Mentewwab, Empress, xv, 144–5, 161–4, 172–4, 216, 262, 306, 308, 322
Prutky's dealings with, 94, 101, 249, 304, 462–3
Mérab, Dr P., 188
Merev r., see Marab
Meroe, 123, 222
Mesaal r., 327
Messaua, see Massawa
Methoni (Modon), 494
Mezzabarba, Carlo Ambrogio, Patriarch of Alexandria, 406
Michael, imperial envoy, xiv, 519

Michail (*perh.* Mika'el Sehul, governor of Tigré), 341
Michelon, Joanne, ship's captain, 482
Mida Bolos, 314
Milos, 493
Minā (Munā), 43
Minas, (Adam Saghed, Mennas, Wanag Sagad II), emperor, 113
Mirandola, 473
Mitau (Mictavia), *see* Jelgava
Mitraha (Matraka), 175
Mitylene (Meteline, Lesbos), 489
Moab, *see* Mawāhib, Al
Mocha (Mukhā), xii, xv, 27, 51, 131–2, 190–1, 355, 361–87 *passim*, 394–5
Modena, 473, 479
Modon, *see* Methoni
Mogul, The Great, 191, 208, 353, 419
Mombasa, 126
Monheurt (Monheur), 449
Monomotapa, 127
Monserrat, Antonio, Jesuit, 245
Montauban, 456
Monte Cristo, 459
Montenero, 499
Montorio San Pietro, xiii, 460, 501
Mora, *see* Mauza'
Moravia, xxv, 398–9, 475
Morea, 493–4
Moscow, 514
Mota, 131
Mountains of the Moon, 205
Mozambique, 179
Muna (Mina), 43
Mura, Musa, *see* Mauza'
Murez, *see* Maushij
Muscat, 36, 363, 368
Muscovy, 506
music, 71, 148, 157, 167–8, 419–20
musk, 127, 133–6
Muslims (Mahometans, Saracens), in Arabia, 2–3, 6, 363–5, 372, 376, 379, 383–4, 387
in Ethiopia, 123, 125, 178–9, 183, 199, 215, 240, 245, 268, 281, 321–2, 331, 352, 354–5

Nagadras, *see* Draco, George
Najeb (Na'ib, Governor of Massawa), 67–9, 71, 76, 349, 351, 354
Na'od (Anbasar Bazar), emperor, 112
Na'od (Hahau, Anbasa Seyon, Nahu, Nahum), emperor, 112

Nasir Jang, Nizam, 403
navigation, Muslim, 11–12, 17, 26, 60, 62–3, 358–9
European, 361, 385, 421, 424–5, 444, 454–6
perils at sea, 64, 388–9, 426, 428–9, 435, 487, 491–2, 497–8
ships' logs, 394–6, 438–443
Necos, king of Egypt, 12
Negra (Nigra), 455
Neria, *see* Enarya
Nero, Roman emperor, 220
Nestorianism, 15, 42, 386, 467
Nevers (Noviodunum), 458
Nicaea, Council of, 109, 257
Nicolao, Venetian explorer, 47
Niger, 116, 211, 219–20
Nigritia, 116, 129
Nile r. (Blue Nile), 91, 123, 128, 170–1, 174, 188–9, 199, 212, 299, 446, 482, 486–7, 520–1
its source, xv, 215–21
Nile r. (White Nile), 219
Nîmes (Nemausus), 458
Nios (Ios), 73–74, 491–2
Nokra (Nochra), 358
Norbert, Fr (Pierre Curel), 404–5
Nubia, 134, 221, 521

Obin, 116
Observants, Order of, 446–7, 450–1, 458, 482, 519
Occlusa, *see* Chiusa di Verona
Ockara, *see* Wagara
Oecie (Aoage), *see* Wag
Ogge, *see* Ved
Ohni, Mt, *see* Wahni
Oman, Jean d', ship's captain, 382–4
Omust da Genest, *see* Le Mas d'Agenais
Oleggio, Fr James of, missionary in Socotra, 386–7
Olmutz, 399, 476
Oromo, *see* Galla
Orio r., *see* Hers
Oviedo, Andre, Jesuit, 245, 255

Paez, Pero, Jesuit, 176, 245, 252
Paillet (Appellit), 447
Panezzii, Lord George, Venetian, 352–3
Pantellaria (Pantalaria), 496
Papal States (Patrimony of St Peter), 473, 500

Paris (Lutetia), 443, 458
Patavia, see Batavia
Patrimony of St Peter, see Papal States
Paulane (Barnabite) Order, 454
Perim island, Red Sea, 385
Perkin, merchant, 517
Persia, 36, 63, 370, 387
Peru, 190, 203
Peter Leopold, Grand Duke of Tuscant, xxv, 505, 518
Philip the Deacon, 106, 224
Philippaci, ship's captain, 487
Philosturgius, 104
Piedmont, 459, 479
Pliny, 134, 189
de Plurimanis (Pilibanis), order of monks, 251
Point Pedro (Bridge of Peter), 393
Pole, North, 438, 442
Pondicherry (Pontichéri), xv, 374, 394–6, 398–400, 402–3, 406, 410, 415, 417, 420–1, 438–9, 442
Pope, The, (Papal Office), 236, 249, 452, 460, 469
Port Louis (Blavet, Ludovici, Luis), 437–8, 444
Portoferraio (Elba), 505
Portugal, Portuguese, in Ethiopia, 78, 117, 124, 133, 173, 179, 206, 245–6
    in East Indies etc., 364, 374, 377–8, 382, 386, 389–90, 400, 417–8, 430–1
Portus Liburnensis, see Leghorn
Prague, xxvi, 327, 398, 475, 518
Preri, Gregory (Michael Georgius Preri), 327
Prester John, 115–17, 122
Prevdo, Muslim holy man, 373
Proasti, village in the Morea, 493
Promontorium Taenarum, see Cape Matapan
Protestant, 377, 382
Prutky, Fr Remedius, xi, xiii–xvi, xxiii, 320, 462, 501, 503, 505–6, 515–18, 520–1, et passim
Ptolemais Auxume, 123

Qaha r. and palace (Kaha), xv, 91–3, 101, 154, 156, 169, 312, 322, 325, 462
Qena, 483
Qishn, Sultan of (Gheschen), 387

Qīzān, see Jīzān
Qunfudhah (Confede, Konfodah), 34
Quṣayr (Cosseir, Kosair), 35–6
Qʷesqʷam (Kusckuam), 162, 262

Rābigh (Rabeck, Rabey, Rabac), 14, 22
Ragusa, 487, 498
Raptus, see Rhapta
Rās al-'Āra, see St Anthony, Cape of
Rās al Faras (Ras Elfaras), 60
raw meat, 77–8, 117–8, 164–6, 283–4, 286, 289, 302
Recollet Order, 437, 446, 452, 458
Red Sea, (Sea of Edom), xiv, 4, 7, 8, 10–11, 23, 25–6, 33, 64, 66–7, 104–5, 107, 123–5, 131–2, 190–1, 222, 245, 318, 326, 346, 357, 359, 363, 369, 385, 403
religious ceremonies, Catholic, 65, 101, 302, 308, 424, 445, 447–8, 450–1, 453, 484
    Ethiopian, 81, 97, 109, 242–3, 247–54, 263, 267, 269, 271, 291–2, 347–8, 463–4, 468, 470–1
    sacraments, 69–70, 227–38, 465–7
    Indian, 405, 408–9, 415–17
    Muslim, 2, 12, 14–16, 35–45, 47, 55, 59–60, 379, 381–2
de Requesens, Ducal house, 496
Réunion island, see Bourbon
Reval, see Tallinn
Rhapta (Raptus), 116
Rhodes, 487–9
Rhône r., 456–7
Ribadaneta (Ribadaneira) Petrus, Jesuit, 255
Riga, 507–8
Riman, Jakub, or James of Kroměříž, xv
Riquet, Paul, canal builder, 454
Riscecourt, Count de, 479
Robbe, Jacques, 132
Rochetta Ligure, see Bochetta
Rodericus, Fr Sebastianus, Jesuit, 236
Rodrigues Island (Roderici), 421, 438–9
Rollersburg, Ignatius de, 476
Rome, xv, xxvi, 96, 236, 383, 460, 473, 486, 515, 517
Rosanagum (Rozanegus), 127
Roseires, 128
Rosenburg, Count de, 479
Rosetta, 220, 482, 487

Rovereto, 473
Roxa, see Boša
Rue r., 456
Russia, xvi, xxv, 506, 508, 517
Ržimarž, see Kroměříž

Sa'azzaga (Tadazecka), 78, 80, 344
Saba or Sabaim, 103–5, 140, 222, 520–1
Sacred Congregation for the Propaga-
    tion of the Faith, xii, xvi, xxv, 212,
    323, 398, 405, 448, 452, 454, 460–
    2, 469, 472, 481, 483, 491–2, 501,
    503, 505–6, 516, 518
Sagadé, see Beltzagadi
St Angelo, Cape, see Malea, Cape
St Anthony, Cape of, (Rās al-'Āra), 386
St Denis, capital of Mauritius, 439
St Dominico (Hispaniola), 444
Saint Elero, see St Hilaire de Lusignan
St Erini, see Santorini
St Helena, Atlantic island, 430, 436
St Helena, see Santorini
St Hilaire de Lusignan (Saint Elero),
    449
St John, Knights of, 488–9, 495–6
St Louis (Aigues Mortes), 456
St Macaire (Semackero), 447
Ste Marie island, Mauritius, 428
St Paul, port in Mauritius, 439
St Petersburg, xvi, xxv–xxvi, 506, 508–
    9, 514–15
St Severina, Cardinal, 236
Saldagna, Arias (Ayres de Saldanha),
    viceroy, 246
Salhet (Sellagit), 358
Salīj (Salin), 359
salt, 213–14, 238
Salzburg (Salisburgum), 474
Samal, see Le Somail
Samén (Senin), 90, 131–2
Samhar (Semhar), 349, 351
Sammama, see Semana
Sanaa (San'a), Yemen, 364–5, 373
Sanglea, suburb of Valletta, 496
San Marco, Fr John of, missionary in
    Socotra, 386–7
Šanqella, see Shangalla
Santorini (St Erini, St Helena, Thera),
    492
Sapienza, 494
Saracens, see Muslims
Sarawé (Sarayé, Serai), 77, 80–1, 129,
    147, 214, 257, 325, 330, 342–4

Sarbakusa (Serbraxos), battle of, 147
Sardinia, 479
Sarsa Denghel (Sereza Denghel, Malak
    Sagad), emperor, 113, 236
Sassello, Fr Joseph of, 484, 486
Savoy, 479
Šawa, see Shoa
Saxony, 517
Schacko, 340
Schami, see Damascus
Schankalle, see Shangalla
Schiech (shaykh), 379
Schombera Zeckem, 327
Schönbrunn (Bellofonte), 476
Schvidevach, see Sitawaka
Schweidnitz, 504
Selaffi Schettii (Assallafi Ešaté), 322
Sellagit, see Salhet
Semackero, see St Macaire
Semana (Sammama), 82, 338
Seneca, 220
Senin, see Samén
Sennar, 24, 91, 113, 134, 150–2, 190–1,
    212, 297
Serai, see Sarawé
Sereza Denghel, see Sarsa Denghel
Sergius the Nestorian, 15, 42
Sète (Cette), 456
Shangalla (Šanqella, Schankalle), 133,
    152, 178, 295
Sheba, Queen of, (Macheda), 94, 99,
    104–5, 129, 222–4, 520–1
Shoa (Šawa, Sua, Xoa), 128, 256, 520
Sicily, 495–6
Sidon, Bishop of, 236
Siena, 473, 500, 505
Simi (Simia), Greek island, 490
Sinai, Mt, (Gebl Ettur, Jabal al-Tūr),
    xi, 8–10, 12, 49, 477
Sinclair, James, General, 445
Siré (Seré, Syre, Confito), 77, 82–3,
    130, 147, 172, 213, 330, 335, 337
Sirens, the, 389
Sitawaka (Schvidevach), 392
slaves, 24–5, 178–9, 422–3, 428
Society of George, 245
Socotra, 375, 386–9
Solimann II, Sultan of Turkey, 488–9,
    496
Solomon, King, 99, 105, 129, 172, 222–
    3
Spinas, see Lespinasse
Spinelli, Cardinal, 461, 501

Stanchio, *see* Cos
Strabo, 103
Sua, *see* Shoa
Suakin (Sawakin, Suwakin, Suaquen), 36, 107, 123–4, 133
Sudan, 123, 128, 133–4, 207, 221, 520
Sudd, 221
Suez, xiv, 4–6, 9, 11, 49, 477
Surat, 374
Susenyos (Celtan Cequed, Malak Sagad III, Seltan Sagad I, Susneus), emperor, 100, 113, 245, 252, 356
Syre, *see* Siré

Tabor hills (Madeboy Tabor, Thabor), 82, 339, 340
Tacitus, 220
Tadazecka, *see* Sa 'azzaga
Ta'if, (Taif), in Hijaz, 27, 48
Taillebourg (Tallibourg), 448
Ta'izz (Tais), in Yemen, 368
Takkazé r. (Teckezi), 84, 123, 130, 327, 332–5
Takla Haymanot (Abrak Sagad, Le'ul Sagad, Gerum Sagad, Teckle-haimanut), emperor, 114
Takla Haymanot, St, *see* Theclay-manoth
Takla Maryam, *see* Theclamaria
Tallinn (Reval), 507–8
Tambén, 136
Tammani, 327
Tampsis, 134
Tana, Lake, 125, 131, 136, 175, 189, 195, 209
Tanara, *see* Matapan, Cape
Tarn r., 456
Teckezi r., *see* Takkazé
Tecklehaimanut, *see* Takla Haymanot
Tellez, B., 91, 189–90, 204
Telo Martius, *see* Toulon
Teplov, Russian senator, 515–16
Teramni (Tesamni), Mt, 345
Thabor, *see* Tabor hills
Theclamaria (Takla Maryam), 236
Theclaymanoth (St Takla Haymanot), 256–7
Theophilus (Téwoflos, Asrar Sagad), emperor, 114
Thera, *see* Santorini
Theresian Order, 446
Thilckim, 131

Tigré (Tigris, Tegré), 83, 91, 124–5, 130, 132, 134, 139, 147, 176, 181, 193, 213, 248, 251–2, 282, 295, 318, 325, 341, 520–1
Tigremahon, *see* Tigré, Mahon
Tigrius, 139
Tilos (Episcopi), Greek island, 491
Tombol, Mount (Qadimbal, Kotumbal), 49, 59
Tonneins (Tumens), 449
Torniello, A., 105
Toulon (Telo Martius), 459
Toulouse (Tulosa), 451, 453–4, 456
T'ovmacean, jeweller, 141, 167
Trebat, *see* Yathrib
Trèbes (Treves), 455
trees, 195–6, 412–13
Trent (Tridentum), 473
Trent, Council of, 448, 473
Turkey, Turks, 36, 52, 375, 383, 385, 423, 459, 487–9, 493
  in Ethiopia, 98, 100, 134, 138, 146, 212, 245, 324, 344, 463, 467–8
turtles, 432–3, 436, 494
Tuscany, Tuscan, 429, 478, 505, 515, 517

Uelkait, *see* Walqayt
Uhud, battle of, 381
Unzo, 331

Vague or Vaguzzi, *see* Wag
Vagusimetrii, *perh.* Bagémder, 521
Valigunasis, *see* Bali and Ganz
Valletta, 495, 496
Vangue, *see* Bugna
Varnagassus, *see* Bahr Nagaš
Varra, *see* Bora
Ved (Ogge, Wed), 126
Vedano, Fr Joseph Maria, 515–16
Venice, 352, 479–80, 486
Venkatachalam, elephant, 403
Vienna, 63, 136, 475–9, 503–4
Vignes-sur-Garonne (Egnia), 451
Villa Schorie, 455
Villiers, Phillippe de, Grand Master, 489
Virgil, 105, 189
Vitelleschi, Fr Mutio, 176
Viterbo, 500
Vittoriosa or Victoriosa, suburb of Valletta, 496

Vittorius, Mariano, grammarian, 181
Vitulo, *see* Itylo

Wag (Aoage, Oecie, Vague, Vaguzzi), 126, 131, 520–1
Wagara (Ockara), 90
Wahni, Mt (Wayni, Ohni), 170–4
Waj, 126, 521
Walaqa (Leca), 125
Walda Sellasé, Ras, 282
Walqayt (Uelkait), 131
Wayto, Ethiopian tribe, 209
Webi Šabelli r., 126
Wed, *see* Ved
Wies, Fr Liberato of, missionary martyr, 100, 114, 126–7, 212, 218, 261, 312–4, 317, 324, 387

Xavier, St Francis, 382
Xoa, *see* Shoa

Yanbu' (Gembua, Jembo, Lembo), 13–14
Yathrib (Trebat), 46
Yedi Burun (Land of the Seven Capes), 487

Yemen (Jemen), 46, 49, 103, 359, 363–5, 367–8, 382, 386–7
Yohannes I, *see* Joannes

Zabīd (Alzevit), 373, 381
Zagwé, 257
Zambesi, r., 127
Zambra, 140
Zamzam (Zemzem), 43
Zanzibar (Zanquebar), 116
Zar' a Ya'qob, (Constantius Zara Jacob, Qʷastantinos), emperor, 112
Zaydi sect, 364
Zazema, 331
Zegé, Lake Tana, 195
Zeila (Zayla'), 123, 126
Zelancke, *see* Eslamgé
Zenzelet, local ruler, 337–8
Zerba, Fr Michael Pié of, missionary martyr, 100, 114, 177, 261, 312–14, 317, 324
Zet or Set (Zethe), 127
Zingerum, *see* Janjero
Zinj, 126
Znojmo (Znoyma), Moravia, 475
Zway, Lake, 126, 521